J

SAMS Teach Yourself

Windows® XP

in 21 Days

SAMS

201 West 103rd St., Indianapolis, Indiana, 46290 USA

Trademarks

All terms mentioned in this book that are known to be trademarks or service marks have been appropriately capitalized. Sams cannot attest to the accuracy of this information. Use of a term in this book should not be regarded as affecting the validity of any trademark or service mark.

Warning and Disclaimer

Every effort has been made to make this book as complete and as accurate as possible, but no warranty or fitness is implied. The information provided is on an "as is" basis. The author and the publisher shall have neither liability nor responsibility to any person or entity with respect to any loss or damages arising from the information contained in this book.

ASSOCIATE PUBLISHER
Jeff Koch

EXECUTIVE EDITOR
Terry Neal

DEVELOPMENT EDITOR
Steve Rowe

MANAGING EDITOR
Matt Purcell

BOOK PACKAGING
Justak Literary Services

COPY EDITOR
Carol Light

INDEXER
Sherry Massey

PROOFREADER
Lara SerVaas

TECHNICAL EDITOR
Russ Mullen

INTERIOR DESIGNER
Gary Adair

COVER DESIGNER
Aren Howell

PAGE LAYOUT
Jay Hilgenberg

Contents at a Glance

Appendixes

Table of Contents

About the Author

John Mueller is a freelance author and technical editor. He has writing in his blood, having produced 51 books and over 200 articles to date. The topics of his writing range from networking to artificial intelligence and from database management to heads-down programming. Some of his current books include a SOAP developer guide, a small business and home office networking guide, and a Windows 2000 Performance, Tuning, and Optimization book. His technical editing skills have helped over 25 authors refine the content of their manuscripts. John has provided technical editing services to both Data Based Advisor and Coast Compute magazines. He's also contributed articles to magazines, including SQL Server Professional, Visual C++ Developer, and Visual Basic Developer. He is currently the editor of the .NET electronic newsletter for Pinnacle Publishing.

When John isn't working at the computer, you can find him in his workshop. He's an avid woodworker and candle maker. On any given afternoon, you can find him working at a lathe or putting the finishing touches on a bookcase. One of his newest craft projects is glycerin soap making, which comes in handy for gift baskets.

You can reach John on the Internet at JMueller@mwt.net. John is also setting up a Web site at `http://www.mwt.net/~jmueller/`. He invites you to visit his site and make suggestions on how he can improve it. One of his current projects is creating book FAQ sheets that should help you find the book information you need much faster.

Dedication

This book is dedicated to Skippy, fearless watcher of apple trees in summer and warmer of feet in winter.

Acknowledgments

Thanks to my wife, Rebecca, for working with me to get this book completed. I really don't know what I would have done without her help in proofreading my rough draft. She also helped research, compile, and edit some of the information that appears in this book.

Russ Mullen deserves thanks for his technical edit of this book. Russ greatly added to the accuracy and depth of the material you see here. In addition, he sent some of the URLs you see spread throughout the book and helped research some of the tougher areas of the text.

This book required a lot of discussion with other people. A special thanks goes to Gerry O'Brien. Day 17 wouldn't exist without his help. Many of the development staff at Microsoft assisted with this book by providing answers to my never-ending questions. The members of the various Microsoft newsgroups were also a source of constant aid. Some of the material in Day 18 is the result of aid from members of the Novell support staff.

Matt Wagner, my agent, deserves credit for helping me get the contract in the first place and taking care of all the details that most authors don't really think about. I always appreciate his help. It's good to know that someone wants to help.

Finally, I'd like to thank Terry Neal, Steve Rowe, Marta Justak, Carol Light, and other members of the Sams staff for their assistance in bringing this book to print. Writing this Windows XP book presented many logistical challenges, and I appreciate their willingness to give me the time required to put a good book together. I especially appreciate Terry's help in locating someone with Linux experience to help with Day 17 and his aid in obtaining some of the software required to write the book.

Tell Us What You Think!

As the reader of this book, *you* are our most important critic and commentator. We value your opinion and want to know what we're doing right, what we could do better, what areas you'd like to see us publish in, and any other words of wisdom you're willing to pass our way.

As an Associate Publisher for Sams, I welcome your comments. You can fax, email, or write me directly to let me know what you did or didn't like about this book—as well as what we can do to make our books stronger.

Please note that I cannot help you with technical problems related to the topic of this book, and that due to the high volume of mail I receive, I might not be able to reply to every message.

When you write, please be sure to include this book's title and author as well as your name and phone or fax number. I will carefully review your comments and share them with the author and editors who worked on the book.

Fax: 317-555-4770

Email: feedback@samspublishing.com

Mail: Jeff Koch
          Sams
          201 West 103rd Street
          Indianapolis, IN 46290 USA

Introduction

Windows XP: it's new, it's controversial, and it's on your desktop. Some people are calling Windows XP a minor upgrade with some flash and dazzle added. Other people consider the features of Windows XP new and exciting. Still other people view Windows XP as a major threat to civilization as we know it. No matter where you fit in the spectrum of Windows XP readers, there's something for you inside this book.

Teach Yourself Windows XP in 21 Days will show you that Windows XP contains more in new features than you think it does. The flash and dazzle is real, but so are features such as enhanced multimedia and the capability to burn CDs without a third-party utility.

The biggest benefit of using Windows XP is that it combines the stability of Windows 2000 with the flexibility of Windows 9x. If you found Windows 2000 couldn't run your application but Windows 9x crashed too often, Windows XP has a lot to offer you. This book shows you how to access and use the new compatibility features.

For business users, Windows XP offers some major improvements in help desk support. The use of Remote Desktop has the potential to change the face of enterprise-level computing completely. You'll also love the new accessibility features. Never have you been able to make connections so quickly and so easily.

So, what does Windows XP have to offer the weary network administrator? You'll find that this version of Windows contains many features that will keep you at your desk and not at someone else's desk reinstalling their operating system. Windows XP prevents disastrous changes more often, offers remedies for those it can't prevent, and even fixes for those it can't reverse. Finally, Windows XP helps you track and fix performance problems by offering more counters in an easier-to-use package.

The big question, then, is whether Windows XP will meet everyone's needs. You'll need to read on to discover the answer to that question. Together, we'll uncover places where Windows XP fails to fulfill its promise and others where it succeeds better than Microsoft ever imagined. However, only you can decide if Windows XP meets your needs fully or if it's missing features critical to you. Windows XP might become your dream come true or it might be the dream unfulfilled. Wherever you fit in the spectrum, this book will help you learn, overcome problems, and enjoy using Windows XP.

Intended Audience

It's always a good idea to know who's supposed to use a book. I wrote this book for a solid intermediate to possibly advanced-level readers, but the text is written in such a manner that if you are still a little new to computing, you can still learn a lot about this exciting operating system from Microsoft. I'm targeting someone who wants to perform tasks quickly—who doesn't want to spend a lot of time reading theories. (Of course, some theory will appear in the book for explanation purposes.) The reader could be anyone from a network administrator to a home user interested in getting the latest game working. If you're in the target audience, you'll find the learning materials fast paced and packed with lots of tips and helpful information.

Teach Yourself Windows XP in 21 Days focuses on the kinds of tasks that you commonly perform. Sections like "Unattended Installations" will appeal to network administrators, especially those in small businesses. Likewise, Day 7 will appeal to gamers and multimedia users who demand the best possible performance from their systems. While the book is task oriented, it offers a broad enough range of information to make everyone who uses Windows XP want this book. For example, during Day 21 you'll learn to fix equipment you really don't understand today.

This book assumes that you have some computer experience. While it assumes some knowledge of Windows, it doesn't expect you to know much more than how to use a mouse and issue basic commands. I also presume that you have some experience issuing simple commands, such as running applications. You won't need to know how to perform complex tasks, such as configuring applications. In other words, this book is for someone with intermediate to advanced computing skills.

Conventions Used in this Book

There are several conventions used within this book that will help you get more out of it. The first is the use of special fonts or font styles to emphasize a special kind of text; the second is the use of icons to emphasize special information.

- There are some situations when I'll ask you to type something. This information always appears in bold type like this: Type **Hello World**.
- Code normally appears on separate lines from the rest of the text. However, there are some special situations when small amounts of code appear right in the paragraph for explanation purposes. This code will appear in a special font like this: `Some Special Code`.

- Definitions are always handy to have. I'll use italics to differentiate definitions from the rest of the text like this: A *CPU* is a required part of your machine.

- In some cases, I won't have an exact value to provide, so I'll give you an idea of what you should type by enclosing it in angle brackets like this: Provide a <Machine Name> value for the Name field.

- You'll always be able to recognize menu selections and command sequences because they're implemented like this: Use the File | Open command.

- URLs for Web sites are presented like this: `http://www.microsoft.com`.

 Notes

> *Notes* help you understand some principle or provide amplifying information. In many cases, a note is used to emphasize some piece of critical information that you need.

Tip

> All of us like to know special bits of information that will make our job easier, more fun, or faster to perform. *Tips* help you do the job faster and more safely. In many cases, the information found in a tip is drawn from experience, rather than through experimentation or documentation.

Caution

> Any time you see a *caution*, m ake sure that you take special care to read it. This information is vital. I'll always uses the caution to designate information that will help you avoid damage to your application, data, machine, or self. Never skip the cautions in a chapter and always follow their advice.

WEEK 1

At a Glance

Week 1 tells you about Windows from the user's perspective. You'll learn about new Windows XP features, how to install Windows, and how to use the interface features. This week also tells you how to use Windows efficiently. It doesn't matter if you're surfing the Internet, playing a game, or working with an accessory. The main goal this week is to help you understand Windows usage techniques. Of course, we'll cover many fun areas, and you'll learn many tips, too. The following list tells you more about each day:

- Day 1, "Introduction to Windows XP," investigates three main topics. The first topic explores the question, "What can Windows XP do for me today?" The second topic answers the question, "How has Windows XP changed?" Finally, the third topic talks about real world requirements to install Windows XP.

- Day 2, "Windows XP Installation and Configuration," begins by covering the major requirements for an upgrade. The installation sections examine four procedures: character mode, GUI, network, and unattended. Finally, we'll discuss what you need to do to perform an upgrade of your system.

- Day 3, "Exploring the Interface," covers all of the essentials of navigating Windows. You'll learn how to work with the various Windows objects and how to create new additions to your Taskbar. You'll also learn how to manage the desktop. This includes selecting themes, working with screen savers, and adjusting video settings. A special section provides you with a wealth of productivity tips to help you accomplish tasks faster.

1

2

3

4

5

6

7

- Day 4, "Getting Online," provides details on how to create three different Internet connection types and discusses the need for Internet Connection Sharing (ICS) in a networked environment. You'll also learn the essentials for using Internet Explorer, including how to adjust its operation using the Internet Options applet. The day ends with some tips for searching the Internet.

- Day 5, "Using Outlook Express," shows how to use the free e-mail and news browser that comes with Windows XP. This includes coverage of all Outlook Express configuration options. Of special importance are tips on making the e-mail and newsgroup "surfing" experience safe.

- Day 6, "Accessory Overview," provides an overview of the accessories that you'll commonly use with Windows to perform work. The highlight of this day is the use of accessibility features. They not only help those with special needs, but they can also help when environmental conditions threaten to make computing difficult.

- Day 7, "Playing with Multimedia and Games," discusses new features, such as Windows Movie Maker, that will allow even novices to create interesting presentations without buying additional software. The game sections begin with a short look at the four standard games that come with Windows. We'll then look at problems that include configuring game controllers and getting games to install correctly. Finally, we'll discuss methods for troubleshooting games played over a network.

WEEK 1

DAY 1

Introduction to Windows XP

Windows XP represents a new page in the Windows book. Microsoft has changed the interface yet again. There are new features to encounter, and Windows XP brings a new level of reliability and stability with it. However, Windows XP isn't just an upgrade of the interface that adds some new widgets to play with; it also contains new features within the operating system kernel. While Microsoft based Windows XP on Windows 2000 technology, they've learned a lot since the Windows 2000 release. The one feature of Windows XP that everyone is sure about is that there are no longer two code bases for Windows. (The operating system code for Windows 9x is completely different from the operating system code for Windows NT and Windows 2000.) Everyone will use the same basic operating system, which means that Windows XP should become the easiest version of Windows to manage ever.

Despite all of the good news that comes with Windows XP, not everyone is sure that it's worth the price of an upgrade. In some minds, Windows 2000 represents the best operating system that Microsoft has created to date. This older version of Windows offers all of the features these people want, along with the stability and reliability that they need. It's true that Windows 2000 is a hard act to follow, but Windows XP is up to the task. It allows you to do more, in less time, with fewer hassles.

Many industry pundits are saying that the big winners with Windows XP are those upgrading from Windows 9x. Windows XP offers the security that Windows 9x can't offer, but also enables users to run applications that Windows 2000 would never consider running. For home users, especially gamers, Windows XP represents the best operating system Microsoft has produced to date.

By the time you complete this day, you'll know whether Windows XP is the best choice for your organization. You'll also know how Windows XP will improve the computing environment for your users. We'll discuss the new and updated features that Windows XP provides. You'll spend a little time discovering if your hardware is up to the task of running Windows XP. As with all previous versions of Windows, this one comes with some new hardware requirements. Finally, we'll discuss some of the problem areas when using Windows XP. No, Microsoft still hasn't produced the perfect operating system, but this one is much closer to an ideal operating system for many users.

Note

When writing a book, errors can and do creep in. Please feel free to contact me at JMueller@mwt.net if you find any errors in this book. I'm also available to answer any questions you might have about my book. I'll post updates to my Web site at http://www.mwt.net/~jmueller/.

Why Windows XP Is a Good Choice

Someone out there is already groaning because of the name of this section. If you've already bought Windows XP and don't want another sales talk, move on to the next section. Of course, I'm not here to sell anything to anyone. Most people realize that Microsoft's marketing arm has the ability to sell products; it's something they do quite well. However, I wanted to provide an unbiased view of why Windows XP is a good choice for an operating system upgrade or as an operating system for that shiny new box sitting in your living room. That's the purpose of this section.

I perform many different tasks on my computer system, as many of you do. On some days, I spend the whole day typing at my word processor. The load on my system is light, and I doubt that I'm taxing any operating system that I may have installed. On other days, I write application code, enter data into a database, or figure out my taxes. These tasks require a little more stability and operating system horsepower. Playing games is a pastime when I've completed all my work. Despite the fun aspect of games, you'll find that they're one of the more complex tasks you can perform on your workstation.

No matter what task you're performing, Windows XP is more reliable and stable than Windows 9x. In some ways, it's also more stable than Windows 2000 because Microsoft has had time to work out some of the bugs in the system. So, one of the best reasons to update to Windows XP is to be able to do your work with fewer hassles.

The new interface is another reason to use Windows XP. You can actually choose between three functional interfaces with this product. The first is a simple interface that most novices will like, but it will make power users feel claustrophobic. Figure 1.1 shows what this interface looks like.

FIGURE 1.1

The new Windows XP interface is extremely easy to work with but limited in functionality.

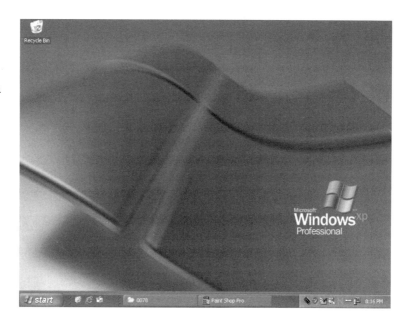

The second interface is a little more powerful and uses the new Windows XP look. I consider it a good choice for the average user. This interface looks like a cross between the simple interface in Figure 1.1 and the Windows 2000 interface shown in Figure 1.2.

Finally, you can choose to go back to the Windows 2000 interface shown in Figure 1.2. (Microsoft implemented changes in the Windows 2000 interface that we'll discuss in Day 3.) Power users who don't like gizmos will probably use this interface most often. This third interface allows you to work quickly, but also offers a bit less in the way of help. We'll look at all three interfaces as the book progresses so that you can make a choice of which one to use.

FIGURE **1.2**

Power users may want to try the Windows 2000 interface for Windows XP to gain maximum flexibility.

Note

Figures 1.1 and 1.2 show the user interface if you install Windows XP and don't perform any customization at all. Normally, you'll want to customize the interface to meet your specific needs. For example, you might not want to see the Taskbar unless you're selecting something from it. Many users change the appearance of the Desktop as well. We'll discuss various customizations during Day 3.

Security is another issue that you should consider when looking at Windows XP. Yes, Windows 2000 already provides good security (and Microsoft keeps fixing new security holes as they appear), but many Windows XP users will upgrade from Windows 9x. No matter which version of Windows XP you use, you'll gain access to better security if you're upgrading from Windows 9x. You'll even find a few improvements, such as a personal firewall, if you're upgrading from Windows 2000. However, there are some flaws in Microsoft's approach to security writing, and I'll pursue them in the "Windows XP Problem Areas" section of the chapter.

The final reason to upgrade to Windows XP is compatibility. I always had problems getting unruly applications to run under Windows 2000 (it did run some applications that Windows NT wouldn't touch, so Microsoft is definitely moving in the right direction). A test of my game applications shows that many of them run fine under Windows XP

1

(we'll explore game issues more during Day 7). Of course, Windows XP still won't let an application trash the system. It simply provides better monitoring so that you can run more applications on your system.

How Can You Use Windows XP?

Obviously, you'll use Windows XP to run applications, which includes everything from productivity applications to games. It's the new features of Windows XP, however, that will make the most difference in how people use it. For example, the new features in the Windows Media Player extend your ability to work with audio and video sources. You'll find that the new Windows Movie Maker allows you to create animations with relative ease. The point is that while you'll use Windows XP for all of the tasks you performed in the past, this product allows you to do a lot of new things as well.

Microsoft had different goals for Windows XP than either Windows 2000 or Windows 9x. Remember that Windows 2000 is an operating system designed for corporate America. As a result, it doesn't run games well, but it provides a stable platform with robust security. Windows 9x is Microsoft's home and small business operating system. While this version of Windows does run games and educational software well, it doesn't provide the security needed by today's user. In addition, Windows 9x often fell short in both reliability and stability. Some users regularly reformatted their hard drives just to get a fresh start with an irksome operating system that failed every few moments. The main design goal for Windows XP is to provide security, reliability, and stability, yet allow a maximum of applications to run.

Someone's going to try to convince you that you're really getting two operating systems with Windows XP—business and home use. The fact is that Windows XP is more of an amalgamation of the two. During testing, I found that Windows XP runs most, but not all, games and educational software. In addition, while Microsoft did improve security greatly, they made configuration choices that leave the security status of Windows XP in doubt. For example, you'll find that they assumed that everyone would want to use automatic login. We'll explore these areas as the book progresses.

This leaves the question of how you'll use Windows XP. The answer depends on how you used your operating system before the upgrade and what you plan to do in the future. Users with a fresh installation of Windows XP and no past Windows experience will want to spend additional time answering this question. In the past, I used to maintain two partitions on my hard drive to meet my computing needs. The Windows 2000 partition allowed me to write applications, maintain my database, and perform other work-related tasks. The Windows 98 partition allowed me to relax while playing a game. I no longer need two partitions when working with Windows XP. It provides enough flexibility to meet all of my computing requirements.

Note

My system does include one additional partition. I maintain a DOS partition for my diagnostic software. Windows is a wonderful operating system for daily tasks. However, as we'll see during Day 21, Windows XP still hides too many hardware details to provide a good platform for diagnosing machine ills. For this reason, I'll probably continue to maintain a DOS partition and use my DOS-based diagnostic software for the near future.

One of the things you should do during this day is figure out how you plan to use Windows XP. This version of Windows includes many new and interesting features, but you need to decide whether these features will allow you to work faster or better. As the day progresses, you'll have opportunities to spend some hands-on time with Windows XP. This is the only way that you'll be able to determine how you can use this product.

What's New in Windows XP?

We've already explored some of the new features in Windows XP in this chapter. For example, we discussed some of the new (for Windows 9x users) or improved (for Windows 2000 users) security features in the "Why Windows XP is a Good Choice" section. In this section we'll discuss additional new features and provide more details about those that I've already introduced.

This book discusses two versions of Windows XP, the Professional Edition and the Home Edition. As their names imply, the Professional Edition meets the needs of those who work in a professional environment, such as an office. It provides features you won't find in the Home Edition, but at a higher cost. Microsoft designed the Home Edition to meet the needs of a family or lightweight applications. In other words, you need to decide which version to obtain based on your needs and the amount of money you're willing to spend.

Windows XP Professional Edition is a true superset of the Windows XP Home Edition. In other words, they both have the full Home Edition feature set. The following sections will tell you what both versions of the operating system provide and then detail the extra features offered in the Professional Edition.

Tip

Microsoft wants you to know what new features you'll find within each version of Windows. You'll find a list of the Home Edition features at http://www.microsoft.com/windowsxp/home/guide/featurecomp.asp and the Professional Edition features at http://www.microsoft.com/windowsxp/pro/guide/featurecomp.asp. Neither list is complete, but they do give you a good idea of how Windows XP compares to its predecessors. It's a good idea to keep these lists in mind as you decide how you'll use Windows XP.

Common Features

Some new features are common to both the Home Edition and the Professional Edition. In some cases, the Home Edition provides a limited version of the Professional Edition feature, but in many situations, the loss of functionality relates to corporate use. The following sections provide details about the most important features.

User Interface Features

Windows XP comes packed with new user interface features. These features will help improve user productivity and dramatically reduce training time. Microsoft's major emphasis on the interface is to hide features that users don't need very often and to make commonly used features instantly available. For example, if you use an application regularly, it will appear in the initial list in the Start menu as shown in Figure 1.3. However, if you use the application only occasionally, you'll need to select it from the More Programs list.

FIGURE 1.3

Many Windows XP User Interface features customize themselves automatically based on usage patterns.

Some of the new user interface features come in the form of conveniences. For example, the new interface will allow user switching with a minimum of problems. One of the problems with these features is that while they make it easier to switch between users, they also keep the account open after the user has made the change. Most organizations (and parents) will view this as a security risk because a novice user could access a power user's account given the current setup. We'll see how to fix this particular problem during Day 16.

In the past, Microsoft has tried various ways to make searching for information easier. My personal preference was the search features found in Windows 98. They were fast and easy-to-use, while the search capabilities in Windows 2000 barely worked in most cases. Search Companion is a new feature with capabilities somewhere between Windows 98 and Windows 2000. It uses the Windows 2000 interface, but search results are more consistent. In addition, Search Companion changes its interface to match your current task. This means that a search on the Internet will look different from a search on your local drive even though you click the same button.

Remote Assistance

One of the most discussed new features of Windows XP is Remote Assistance. This feature allows one user to support another through a remote connection. The two users build a peer relationship that allows one user to take over another user's computer for the sake of demonstrating a new task or fixing a problem.

Unfortunately, any time you allow someone to take control of your system, you're also creating a security risk. More than a few network administrators have already expressed concerns about this feature.

Windows Movie Maker

One of the more interesting features is Windows Movie Maker, shown in Figure 1.4. This product allows you to work with multimedia files to create a movie or at least animation. You can control elements, such as the timing between each graphic. This feature allows you to overlap graphic elements so that you can use the same background for a sequence of images.

The utility also allows you to add annotation. The voice track follows along with the animation track so that you can make adjustments in timing. You can adjust the volume levels as well. Unfortunately, Windows Movie Maker doesn't include a full set of audio modification features.

FIGURE 1.4

Windows Movie Maker will allow you to create your own short movies or animations.

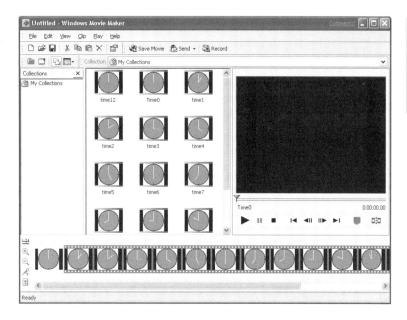

The example in Figure 1.4 shows a series of still images. You can also record live images. In short, Windows Movie Maker provides enough functionality for someone to create a small presentation or home video. It's not a professional quality tool. We'll discuss Windows Movie Maker more on Day 7.

Reduced Need for Reboots

If you've ever installed a complex application, you know that they often require multiple reboots. Each reboot wastes time that you could spend on some other activity. Windows 2000 began a trend where applications required fewer reboots. Windows XP continues this trend. Theoretically, you should see far fewer reboots as you upgrade applications.

Tip

> Your older applications won't know that Windows XP supports fewer reboots, so they'll always ask you to reboot the machine after an installation is complete. In some cases, you'll still need to reboot if the application installs a new driver that it must load during system startup. The new Windows applications will know they can load the driver dynamically, but these older applications will lack the code required to do so. In other cases, you won't need to reboot because Windows has the required support installed. In most cases, I'll try starting a simple application before I reboot the machine. I've been surprised to find that many applications that tell you a reboot is required don't need one with Windows XP.

Easier Installation

We'll cover many of the installation tools during Day 2. It pays to know, however, that Windows XP contains many features designed to make installation easier. For example, you can use the migration tool to move settings from one machine to another. This was originally an unsupported tool in the Windows 2000 Resource Kit. The savings in setup time can be substantial, especially if the machine supports more than one user.

A new feature known as *Dynamic Update* ensures that your Windows XP setup is up-to-date from the outset. The installation routine searches the Web for new drivers and other files to bring your system up to the current standard. Normally, you would have to install Windows, search for the updates yourself, and manually install them after you had Windows working.

Unattended setups are a requirement in any large organization. Previous versions of Windows hampered network administrators' efforts by supporting a subset of the full installation features. With Windows XP, you can control all installation options during an unattended setup, which means you will have less work to do later.

The System Preparation Tool (SysPrep) allows you to create an image of the system installation that you need on several computers. This includes business applications. SysPrep allows you to clone this setup across multiple machines, further reducing installation time.

You can also install Windows XP from a remote location. This feature allows you to control the installation from another site, such as the network administrator's workstation. Windows XP even allows you to use this feature with SysPrep. The only caveat with this feature is that you must have Active Directory installed. This is problematic because many organizations have chosen not to use Active Directory—they may use an alternative, such as Novell's NetWare Directory Services (NDS), or a simple domain setup.

Professional Edition Exclusive Features

The Professional Edition of Windows XP will cost quite a bit more than the Home Edition because it contains more features. As previously mentioned, this is the version of Windows that you'll want to use if you mainly use your machine in a professional setting. For example, most business users will want this edition to gain full access to important security features.

The following sections will discuss unique Professional Edition features. Some of these features already appear in Windows 2000 Professional but they don't appear at all in Windows 9x or in the Home Edition of Windows XP. Each section will tell you when a feature also appears in Windows 2000 Professional.

Enhanced Scalability

Scalability is the capability of an operating system to increase its processing and resource handling abilities. This is an important issue because scalability determines your ability to upgrade a computer system as your needs increase. For example, adding a second processor will increase processing speed only if the operating system can support a second processor. Using a high-speed data connection only helps when the operating system provides support for the hardware and software used to create the connection. Increasing disk size is only useful when the operating system supports the larger disk. Let's see how Windows XP enhances scalability.

Windows 2000 Professional already provides dual processor support. However, dual processor support is relatively new for anyone moving up from Windows 9x. Having two processors do the work enhances performance. You don't necessarily get things done twice as fast, but you'll notice a definite increase in speed. The computer also operates more smoothly—you don't notice pauses as often because there are two processors performing work in unison. Even those who have used the dual processor support under Windows 2000 will notice some differences with Windows XP. For example, Windows 2000 had problems detecting both processors on one of my workstations; Windows XP installs the correct support every time.

Of course, the question is whether you actually need two processors on a workstation. We'll discuss this issue as the book progresses. You'll find that you have to work around dual processor issues to get some applications to run. Games are especially susceptible to problems in a dual processor environment.

Tip

Windows XP supports two compatibility modes to ensure applications will run as anticipated. When an application won't run under Windows XP, you can set it to run in either Windows NT or Windows 9x compatibility mode. Unfortunately, compatibility mode still won't fix some problems, such as those brought on by dual processor incompatibility.

The scalability features of Windows XP Professional also include the capability to use 4GB of RAM. While Windows 2000 Professional also supports this feature, this is a new addition for users upgrading from Windows 9x, which only supports 512MB. The extra memory that Windows XP supports will allow you to run larger applications in the future. Many applications are already bumping up against the 128MB of RAM that hardware vendors supplied as a default in the recent past.

Full NTFS-Based Security

Windows XP supports many of the same file security features that Windows 2000 Professional does. For example, you have full access to the benefits provided by Kerberos. In addition, you can encrypt individual files to protect their content. However, this new version also adds some new benefits.

One change you'll notice is that you can encrypt a file with multiple user accessibility. Windows 2000 Professional only allows single user encryption, which means that you have an option of securing or sharing a file. With Windows XP, you can encrypt the file and still share it with a select group of users.

Tip

> Windows XP also offers smart card support out of the box. This feature allows user identification using a credit card-sized smart card. Windows 2000 Professional didn't offer smart card support out of the box. This feature affects the system as a whole. It allows the use of hard-to-guess passwords, while acknowledging that it's hard for users to remember these kinds of passwords.

Desktop Management

Windows XP supports both local and group policies. A *policy* is a means of defining security in a general way. For example, you could create a policy that says all users have to change their passwords every 10 days. Local policy management allows you to control the users on a single machine. This is your only option in the absence of a domain. If you have a domain setup, however, you can also use group policies. A group policy overrides the local policy and allows the network administrator to control all of the machines on the network by defining a single set of conditions. Another tool, Resultant Set of Policy (RSoP), allows you to monitor the effects of any group policy changes on a single user or computer. We'll discuss policies in more detail during Day 16.

File Management

Some of the new Windows XP file management features will require a little time to get used to if you've worked with other versions of Windows. For example, this version of Windows offers improved handling of file associations. If you download a file from the Internet and don't have an application, such as Word or Corel Draw, that can access that file, Windows XP can often provide an application suggestion for you.

Another useful feature is association repair. Users will often install a graphics or media program to handle certain types of files. When the user uninstalls the program, the file association is broken, leaving the file an orphan even if there are default Windows programs that could open it. Windows XP solves this problem by associating files with default Windows XP applications if there aren't any third-party products installed to handle the file association.

One feature that many users like is the capability to burn CDs without installing a third-party product. This was always problematic with previous versions of Windows because the third-party products often produced conflicts with existing Windows files. The Windows XP CD burner is a very simple application; you'll still want to use third-party products when creating complex setups.

The Web Distributed Authoring and Versioning (WebDAV) protocol allows you to publish files or folders to any Web service that provides the required support. This protocol provides automatic encryption and decryption to keep your data secure, which also makes the data transfer process transparent.

Dual View Monitors

This new feature allows you to send the same desktop information to two monitors. Most people will find this feature helpful for presentations. The audience can look at one monitor while the presenter works with the LCD display on his laptop. This feature also comes in handy for training scenarios where you want a trainee to see precisely what you're seeing.

Note   Don't confuse this feature with multi-monitor support. The multi-monitor support allows you to drive multiple computer desktops from a single computer. In short, it allows you to extend the display area across multiple computers.

XP Networking Support

Windows XP supports all of the features that you'll find in Windows 2000. In addition to standard Windows 2000 features, you'll find a wealth of new features, such as wireless support. Microsoft recognizes that most organizations will have to create hybrid networks that contain a mix of desktop and wireless devices in the near future.

Another new feature is network awareness. This feature allows the operating system to determine when a machine has changed locations. The operating system and some applications may require configuration changes to access another domain controller or to access resources on the network when a location change occurs. In the past, the network administrator would need to make these changes manually. Windows XP tries to make any required changes automatically.

You can also use Windows XP to create a bridge. This feature allows a workstation to act as a connection point between a standard Ethernet connection and a wireless connection. Most companies buy a separate machine for this purpose, and you may find that you still require one. The usefulness of this particular feature depends on how much network traffic the bridge would have to support.

Windows XP may look like a new operating system, but it includes features that you've seen before. Remember that Microsoft based Windows XP on the Windows 2000 kernel. This means that you get the same reliability and stability as you would with Windows 2000, only with more functionality.

Windows XP also needed to borrow some features from Windows 9x in the area of user friendliness. This operating system will replace Windows 9x as the platform that users need to support games as well as home systems. Small companies will also rely on Windows XP as their Windows 9x replacement. The fact is that Windows 2000 wasn't a very friendly environment for running games or for use with some types of educational programs. It enforced the rules so strictly that some of these applications refused to run.

The following sections will discuss the updated features you'll find in Windows XP. These features already exist in some form in either Windows 2000 or Windows 9x (and in some situations, both). We'll discuss why these features are important and how some of them fall short of the ideal.

Enhanced File Management

Windows XP includes several updates to the standard Windows Explorer interface. You can now access a Tiles view. This view provides an extended view of your files. The problem that many people complained about is that the tiles are so large that they make it nearly impossible to see an entire directory of files at the same time. You'll want to use this view when an extended view of your data is required, and you don't mind scrolling a lot to see all of the files.

You'll also find that you can group like files together. The groups look similar to the entries in a glossary. You can group them by name, type, size, and modification date. Look for third parties to add extensions that will allow you to group files in other ways. For example, you might group Word documents by author or music files by musician.

The two default folders, My Music and My Pictures, have changed as well. The My Music folder uses a thumbnail view that allows you to organize your music more easily. The My Pictures folder includes a wealth of new features, including the capability to order pictures in the folder directly from an online site. This means you could take pictures with your digital camera this afternoon and send an order to get them printed without going to the photo store first. Microsoft also enhanced My Pictures with direct links to your camera and scanner; file manipulation features, such as compression and the ability to upload your files to a Web site; and the ability to view your pictures as a slideshow.

Connectivity

Windows XP contains the same networking features as found in Windows Millenium. You can use Home Networking Wizard to create a home network setup. The Web Publishing Wizard allows you to publish documents online. Finally, the Scanner and Camera Wizard allows you to create connections to your favorite device. All three of these features include some minor improvements. For example, you'll find the Scanner and Camera Wizard includes more devices in the list.

Internet Connection Sharing (ICS) has a few changes as well. You can now disconnect an ICS connection from a remote location. This allows you to use the phone for a voice conversation. Another new feature is the addition of a personal firewall. This particular feature is long overdue and a welcome addition in a world where crackers break into systems at an ever increasing rate. Otherwise, ICS works much the same as it did for Windows 9x. You'll also find that a few old features are gone, such as the capability to combine several dial-up connections into one data stream (Multilink Aggregation).

Note

For the purposes of this book, the term *cracker* will always refer to an individual who breaks into a system on an unauthorized basis. This includes any illegal activity on the system. On the other hand, a *hacker* will refer to someone who performs low-level system activities such as testing system security. In some cases, you need to employ the services of a good hacker to test the security measures you have in place, or you risk suffering the consequences of a break-in. This book will use the term *hacker* to refer to someone who performs services that are both legal and authorized.

Help and Support Center

Microsoft continuously improves its online help system. The reason is simple; supporting a user through automated methods is more cost effective than providing trained support staff.

You'll find that the Help and Support Center is a big improvement over previous versions of Windows. Instead of providing help files and HTML-based help, the Help and Support

Center is a one-stop place for Windows information. The consolidation of many sources of help into a single source makes it a lot easier to find the information you need.

The new Help and Support Center draws on more information sources than previous versions of Windows. You'll find that it uses both local and Web resources equally well.

If you can't find the information you need using the Help and Support Center, you can use this utility to get help from a friend or professional. The Help and Support Center provides access to Microsoft Remote Assistant, newsgroups, MSN communities, and Microsoft Assisted Support. In some cases, a Microsoft support representative will ask to take over your machine to help diagnose a problem. There's a separate Microsoft Support account that allows lower-level access to your machine than the normal Remote Assistance account.

Automated System Repair

Windows XP includes the same System Restore feature found in Windows ME. Some changes to the interface make this feature easier to use. In addition, the feature doesn't seem quite as aggressive as in Windows ME, where it would occasionally interfere with application upgrades.

Windows Update has also experienced some changes. You'll find that this feature is extremely aggressive now. Windows Update will automatically nag you to install changes whenever it detects they're available online. This feature does include a few positive changes. For example, any change you download will apply to all users of the computer, not just the person downloading the update. This feature alone should save considerable time for the network administrator. Windows Update automatically searches for driver updates whenever you install a new device on your system. Home Edition users will find Windows Update integrated with the Help and Support Center.

You'll find that Windows XP provides support for two important file-related features. Windows 2000 already supports both of these features, but you'll find that the support is either lacking in Windows 9x or significantly upgraded in Windows XP. The first feature is system file protection. Whenever an older application tries to overwrite a system file, Windows XP will restore the newer version automatically. The second feature is side-by-side DLL support. This allows network administrators to get around the problems of "DLL Hell," which occurs when Application A requires one version of a DLL, while Application B requires a second version. With side-by-side DLL support, an application can access the version of the DLL that it needs to operate correctly.

The Professional Edition also supports two important device driver features. The first is the capability to verify device driver functionality. The Device Driver Verifier runs a stress test on your device driver so that you can check it for failures before you're in the middle of an important task. The Device Driver Rollback feature allows you to remove an errant driver and replace it with one that you know works. This means you can test the compatibility of a new driver and easily get rid of it if you discover that it won't work properly on your system.

User and System Management

Windows XP offers a variety of improvements over existing user and system management features. The first improvement of this nature is borrowed from Windows ME. You can choose to boot the system into a Safe Mode of operating using a variety of startup options. These options allow you to remove parts of the operating system (except core elements) that you suspect cause boot or other failures. For example, you can choose to boot the system without any network support.

Windows 2000 users are already familiar with the Microsoft Management Console (MMC), but this is a new feature for Windows 9x users. For those of you not familiar with this feature, the MMC is a container application that holds modules. For example, you can start MMC and drop in the computer management module (known as a snap-in) if you want to manage your computer. A security snap-in allows you to manage local or group policies, while a performance snap-in allows you to tune your system. The combination of MMC and one or more snap-ins is called a *console*, and Microsoft provides many of these consoles as part of the Administrator's folder. MMC looks the same in Windows XP as it does in Windows 2000. The only major difference is that you have more configuration options in many cases. We discuss this feature in more detail in the "An Overview of Computer Management" section during Day 8.

Another Windows 2000 feature that makes an appearance in Windows XP is the Recovery Console. This command line console allows you to recover your operating system if the graphical user interface (GUI) becomes inaccessible. You can use it to format drives, start and stop services, read and write data from a local drive, and perform other administrative services. Some administrators actually prefer to use the command line at all times because they feel it's faster than using the GUI tools.

Hardware Requirements

It's time to look at the hardware requirements for Windows XP. Some people equate a new operating system with a new system, but that's not necessarily the case. Many existing systems will run Windows XP just fine.

> **Note**
>
> Microsoft provides a list of recommended hardware requirements for both the Home Edition (http://www.microsoft.com/windowsxp/home/guide/sysreq.asp) and the Professional Edition (http://www.microsoft.com/windowsxp/pro/guide/sysreq.asp). These requirements show what you need to use Windows XP, but they don't reflect the realities of the computing environment. You'll want better hardware in most cases.

Of course, you don't want to spend a lot of money on a new system that will be out-of-date in a year, either. The following list reflects a realistic minimum that will allow you to use most business software, educational software, productivity aids, or games. Some applications will require more. For example, action games tend to use a lot more resources than role-playing games. Likewise, graphics applications require more processing horsepower than a typical word processor.

- **450MHz Pentium II/III processor or AMD equivalent**   Windows XP will run on a slower processor, but you'll find that it runs too slowly to perform useful work. After testing Windows XP on several machines, I found that Microsoft's minimum was just too slow for today's business needs.

- **256MB of RAM**   Windows has always run better with more RAM. I tried several RAM and swap file configurations. In most cases, Windows ran processor-intensive tasks better with 256MB of RAM than with lower values. Unlike Windows 9x, there is no 512MB limit on Windows XP. However, the performance benefits seemed to drop after reaching 256MB (even though you will see a slight performance increase).

- **5GB (preferably larger) hard drive**   Hard drive space is cheap today and vendors know it. Every application I get requires yet more disk space. At one time I thought my 9GB drive would never run out of space—I was wrong. This figure comes from combining the disk requirements of Windows XP with Microsoft Office XP and adding additional space for e-mail, data, and a simple graphics application.

- **CD or DVD drive (include recordable media if you won't have any other means of backing up your data)**   You'll need a CD drive as a minimum for your system because many applications, including Windows XP, now come on CDs. You could install Windows XP using a network setup, but a CD is a more convenient method for small networks and home users. DVD drives come in handy if you want to watch movies on your machine or read data from products that come on

DVD. A DVD-RAM drive also makes a good alternative for tape drive backup on small networks. Finally, a CD-RW drive is useful for backups on your machine, if you don't mind swapping CDs as needed. You can also use it for archiving or exchanging data with other people.

- **1024×768 display**   At least some of the dialog boxes for Windows XP won't fit properly in a smaller display. In addition, gamers expect many upcoming games, such as Civilization III, to require higher resolution displays.

- **Keyboard and mouse**   These are basic requirements for any version of Windows.

- **56KB modem (unless you're planning on using cable or some other means to connect to the Internet)**   Connectivity is a big issue for most people today, so it pays to have a modem at your disposal. I usually install a modem in all my machines so that I can connect to the Internet even if a high-speed connection fails. Using a dial-up connection is better than not having a connection at all.

This is a relatively modest system by today's standards, which could explain one reason that many people choose not to upgrade their hardware as often as they did in the past. Your computing needs may require advanced hardware, but most people will find that this setup works just fine for most needs.

Windows XP Problem Areas

Developing software, especially operating systems, is a complex process. It's unlikely that anyone could get everything right the first time. Of course, many people point to the many problems they've experienced with Microsoft products and Microsoft's inability to fix them. It's true that Windows seems to have more problems than just about any other product, but it's also important to consider the environment in which Windows operates. Let's just say that Windows is less than perfect.

You'll experience problems with your Windows XP installation. For example, Microsoft somehow managed to change NTFS just enough so that Windows 2000 can't read a Windows XP partition. If you want both operating systems on your machine (as a developer might), then you'll need to format the drive with Windows 2000 first and then install Windows XP.

As with every other version of Windows that ever existed, you'll run into problems with device driver support. Many users complained during the beta process that their Windows 2000 drivers wouldn't work with Windows XP. For the most part, you'll need to ensure that a driver will work before you install it. In most cases, Windows XP provides a default driver that works, but often the Windows default driver doesn't use all of the advanced features of a piece of hardware. Using this generic driver makes sense until your hardware vendor releases a Windows XP compatible version. Yet, should there be a Windows XP compatible driver available from a hardware vendor, your best choice would be to use the vendor's driver because it is designed to take full advantage of the features present in their hardware.

Security is an area where Microsoft legitimately dropped the ball, and many people have called them on it. The Home Edition of Windows XP has some artificial limits on what you can do to secure your system. Sure, the password protection and personal firewall are both available, but you'll find that you can't access the security features that NTFS provides for your disk drives. This limit is artificial—Microsoft had to add code to enforce the limitation. This is one of those marketing decisions that people will complain about during the entire Windows XP life span. If you need to encrypt your data on disk, you'll either have to buy the Professional Edition or use a third-party product.

Summary

This day provided an overview of Windows XP. You learned why Windows XP is an important upgrade to the Windows line of operating systems. Of course, your personal needs will determine how beneficial Windows XP is to you and your organization. That's why you need to decide how you'll use Windows XP in advance. No matter how good the marketing arm of Microsoft becomes, the decision to purchase and install Windows XP is still a personal one.

Today's lesson also told you a lot about the contents of the Windows XP package. In this lesson, you discovered the following points:

- How Windows XP makes it easier to manage the operating system because it consolidates the code base for the entire Windows line.
- How you can make the best use of Windows XP in your organization.
- The feature differences between the Home Edition and the Professional Edition.
- The features that Windows XP provides beyond those found in older versions of Windows.
- How some features in Windows can actually reduce the cost of running your system.
- The hardware requirements for using Window XP.
- Where Microsoft still has more work to do with this operating system.
- Why in some cases, Windows XP requires more configuration time than older versions of Windows (Microsoft made things more difficult in an attempt to simplify the interface).

Q&A

Q: Which version of Windows XP is right for me?

A: The general answer to this question is that you should use the version that has the feature set you need. A better answer is that businesses should use the Professional Edition because it provides the best security. Home office users might be able to use the Home Edition, but Microsoft designed the Home Edition for people who need an operating system for the family. If cost is a concern, you might consider using the Home Edition, and then beefing up security and other features with third-party product additions.

Q: Where will I find the most peer support for Windows XP?

A: Many people feel more comfortable talking about operating system problems with other users. Of course, the fact that peer support is free often has a lot to do with the question as well. As of this writing, the best peer support is available on the Microsoft public newsgroups for Windows XP. These newsgroups usually come under the heading of microsoft.public.windowsxp. If your ISP doesn't carry any Windows XP specific newsgroups, you can always contact the Microsoft news server (news.microsoft.com) directly.

As Windows XP becomes more popular, you'll see non-Microsoft newsgroups appear on the scene. One such newsgroup is alt.os.windows-xp. The advantage of using a non-Microsoft newsgroup is that you often get better, or at least unbiased, help.

Q: Do I have to have an Internet connection to use Windows XP?

A: Windows XP will work best if you have an Internet connection available. Some features, such as automatic updates, require an Internet connection. You can still use Windows XP with your favorite applications without an Internet connection.

Q: Will Microsoft's new personal firewall protect my network completely?

A: If crackers want to break into your system, they will. A firewall offers a modicum of protection against the casual cracker. Think about it this way. A personal firewall will make it easier for the cracker to decide to attack someone else. The only way to guard against crackers is to have good protection and to constantly monitor your system for problems.

Workshop

It's the end of the first day. Let's see if you were listening! You can find answers to the quiz and exercise questions in Appendix A at the back of the book.

Quiz

1. What's the most noticeable change in Windows XP?

2. What's the main design goal for Windows XP when compared to previous versions, such as Windows 9x or Windows 2000?

3. Will Windows XP run every Windows application ever created?

4. Will the Home Edition allow you to use NTFS security?

5. What's the difference between DualView and multi-monitor support?

Exercises

1. Create a "hit list" of Windows XP features to explore.

2. Determine if your system will run Windows XP.

3. Look for Windows XP problem areas in your system.

DAY 2

Windows XP Installation and Configuration

Microsoft has attempted to make each version of Windows a little easier to install. Users of Windows 3x will remember how painful that installation could become if you had anything other than the hardware that Microsoft anticipated. Giving the old installation routine an incorrect answer out of simple ignorance ensured that you'd perform the installation again. Windows 95 was a little better, and Windows ME/2000 made the process almost automatic, except for a few answers. Installing Windows XP is about the same level of complexity as Windows 2000 in most cases. The reason I say that it's basically the same is that Microsoft has added some of the flexibility that it took out of the previous version back into Windows XP.

While installing Windows XP is relatively easy if you choose a default installation, you still need to plan. In addition, you need to select the installation type that best suits your needs. Most home users will install Windows XP directly from the CD, but business users may want to install it from a network or create an unattended installation scenario. You also have to choose between a character mode or graphical user interface (GUI) installation.

Some users will want to create a *dual boot setup*, which means they can choose to boot one operating system from two installed on the machine. Actually, the technique used for a dual boot installation works equally well for creating triple or even quadruple boot setups. The point is that you can boot more than one operating system by using this technique. I normally install two operating systems on all my workstations, so I normally create a dual boot setup. The first operating system I install is DOS. It allows me to play older games and perform diagnostics on my machine without interference from Windows. The second operating system is Windows XP.

Once you have Windows installed, you'll normally want to install some upgrades. Even though Windows XP goes through the extra effort to ensure that all DLLs are updated during the installation process, there are other features, such as .NET support, that you may want to install. (Microsoft's .NET technology is a new way of developing, installing, and using applications that prevents problems such as DLL conflicts from occurring.) Knowing what you want to install in advance helps make the installation process go faster (another reason to perform some pre-installation planning).

Finally, you'll want to check that everything on your system works before you begin the arduous process of installing application software. Getting a good installation is important if you want Windows to run with few problems. This means checking for errors of various types. You'll want all of your hardware operational and all drivers functional before you install anything else. The system should boot without creating any Event Log entries.

As you can see, we'll cover a lot of ground today. All of this information will help you create a Windows installation that runs well and experiences few problems. A stable platform is worth its weight in gold, and it all begins here.

Planning Your Installation

It's important to plan your installation. This is easy if you're a home user or small business because all you need to do is ask yourself what you need to get your work done. Large organizations have more of a challenge because the person using the computer isn't the one performing the installation. In both cases, you need to ask the same questions. I use the following checklist when planning my installation:

1. List all of your hardware. Get drivers as needed and available. Determine if Windows provides native support if the vendor doesn't supply a driver. Obtain updated hardware as needed.

2. Learn about the operating system feature set. Determine which features will provide the greatest benefit and plan to install them.

3. Determine which installation technique will work best for your organization. For example, larger organizations may want to use a network, a remote, or an unattended install to save administrator time.

4. Set the time aside to perform the installation. Rushed installations are a major cause of problems. Try to schedule installations around user downtime.

5. Determine which updates you want to install and download the appropriate software if necessary. You want to be sure that you have all required update software on hand so that you will spend the minimum time performing the installation.

6. Obtain a list of applications for the target machines. Gather the required software. Ensure that you have enough licenses to cover all of the installations.

7. Perform a complete system backup so that you can recover from a failed installation. You also want to store any local user data so that you can restore it later. Make sure you save any application settings by exporting the required registry settings before making the backup.

We've already performed the first two steps in Day 1. The exercises in that chapter asked you to check your hardware and to list the operating system features you'd like to learn about. All you need to do is take the results from those exercises and apply them to the installation procedure in this chapter. You'll find that many of the exercises in this book will help you with the tasks you'll perform on the days that follow.

The installation procedures that we'll explore today will help you determine which installation technique will work best for you. Read each section to learn the advantages and disadvantages of each method.

Step 4 is actually the hardest part of the process if you're working for a large business. I know of one network administrator who has to jump through a lot of hoops to accomplish anything. She works for a large law office, and the lawyers need access to their machines 24 hours a day, 7 days a week. Needless to say, she has to get quite creative to do anything major, such as an operating system upgrade. It's important that you set and communicate definite times for installs and upgrades when working in a large organization. Of course, you'll want to schedule plenty of time to perform the task because rushed installs seldom work out. Here's how I normally plan my installation time:

- 2 hours for the operating system.
- 15 minutes for each device driver installation.
- 1 hour for each major application.
- 1 hour for data restoration.
- 30 minutes for configuration.

You'll find that your time varies from mine, at least a little, but that these are good time estimates for many applications. Of course, you won't be sitting in front of the machine the whole time. Windows XP performs many steps automatically, so you can simply monitor the system as the installation progresses. You need to monitor the setup if you don't set up an unattended installation because the installation program will ask questions at the beginning and end of the process.

Some network administrators that I know don't plan at all for application installations after an operating system upgrade. It's true that you can usually restore the application and its settings from a backup. However, as a recent installation showed me, this isn't always a certainty. It's better to plan the time required to install the applications from scratch and finish early, than to tell users that their system will be ready in a short time and then delay deliveries due to unanticipated complications.

Of course, it always pays to back up your own system before you replace it. If everything fails and you can't deliver the system with an operating system upgrade, you can at least deliver a working system that has the old operating system intact. Even if you don't want to make a complete backup, you'll want to save the user's local data and application settings. We'll explore the techniques for saving and restoring application settings on Day 12.

Installing from the CD

The most common way to install a few copies of Windows XP is to place the CD directly in the drive. In fact, most home and small business users will use this method. Even some large businesses will use this technique for test setups before large-scale deployment.

Windows XP offers two interfaces for installation. Both interfaces are equally easy to use, but the GUI is nicer looking and many people prefer it for that reason. The GUI also offers mouse support, a nicety that the character mode interface lacks. The following sections will look at the installation routine for both interfaces.

GUI Installation

The graphical user interface (GUI) installation is the one that you'll commonly use for system updates. If the system already has a copy of Windows on it and you want to upgrade to Windows XP, you start the installation process by inserting the Windows XP disk into the CD-ROM drive. The drive should detect the new CD automatically and start the Windows XP installation program. (If the drive doesn't start the installation program automatically, you can double click SETUP.EXE on the Installation CD.)

The following steps lead you through the installation process. I'm assuming you've already placed the CD-ROM in the drive and can see the initial setup screen.

Tip

> Unlike the character mode installation, the GUI method allows you to check your system for compatibility problems before you install Windows XP. To check system compatibility, start the Windows XP installation. Select Check system compatibility, and then select Check my system automatically. You'll see a Performing Dynamic Update dialog box. Windows XP will perform a survey of your system against the Microsoft Web site. Eventually, you'll see a Report System Compatibility dialog box that tells you about any problems with your setup. Fixing these problems will help ensure that your installation completes successfully.

2

1. Click Install Windows XP. Windows XP will ask what type of installation you'd like to perform. If you want the quickest possible installation, choose the Upgrade option. Choosing the New Installation option will reformat your drive, which means installing and configuring all of your applications. However, this method also presents the fewest compatibility problems when you complete the installation. The rest of the procedure assumes you'll perform an upgrade of your current Windows installation.

2. Choose Upgraded (Recommended) and then click Next. You'll see a License Agreement dialog box.

3. Read the agreement, choose I accept the agreement, and then click Next. You'll see a Your Product Key dialog box.

4. Type the product key that appears on your CD-ROM sleeve. Setup will ask if you want to perform an upgrade check of your system.

5. Check for system updates. After Windows XP checks for problems with your system, it will display a Report System Compatibility dialog box. If you perform the compatibility pre-check, this dialog box should be blank.

6. Click Next. Windows XP will copy some files to your hard drive. It will reboot after a few moments. Setup will display an installation dialog after it reboots your system. The Progress indicator will show the status of the file copying process. Setup will complete this second round of file copying with another reboot. More file copying and reboots will occur as you read your favorite magazine. Just be patient and wait for the process to complete. At some point, Windows XP will boot one last time, and you'll see the product activation screen.

7. Activate Windows, if desired. If you don't activate Windows XP now, it will remind you to activate the product every few days. You have a limited time to acti-

vate your product before it stops functioning. Microsoft provides methods for activating Windows XP using an Internet connection or your telephone. Click Next. Windows XP will ask if you want to register your product. You can skip this step and perform it later, just like product activation.

8. Register Windows, if desired. Click Next. You'll see a success screen.

9. Click Finish to the complete the process.

Character Mode Installation

The character mode installation is the one that you'll commonly use for new systems or for systems that experience problems using the GUI installation. It doesn't provide some of the features of the GUI install, such as mouse support or a nice interface, but it does work.

The character mode installation begins in one of two places. First, you can put the CD into your machine and allow the machine to detect Windows XP automatically during the boot process. In this case, you don't have to format the host drive in advance or worry about having any other operating system available.

The second starting point is from the DOS prompt. Some systems still come with CD drives that don't automatically detect an operating system on the CD-ROM. In this case, you'll need to use a copy of DOS. You can start DOS from the floppy drive, or you can format the hard drive and install DOS there. In both situations, you'll need a driver for your CD-ROM drive and MSCDEX (available with DOS). The following steps assume that you've managed to access the Windows XP CD in some way and started SETUP.EXE.

1. After you start Setup, you'll see prompts that allow you to install small computer systems interface (SCSI) support and automated system repair. If you have a system with a special SCSI driver, select the driver installation when prompted by pressing F6. However, most SCSI systems for workstations don't require a special driver. Windows XP will continue to load all of its support files during this time, so don't worry when it doesn't stop immediately after you press F6.

2. Follow the prompts to install SCSI support, if necessary, and allow Windows XP to continue to load. Eventually, you'll see a Welcome to Setup window. This window has three options. Press F3 if you want to exit Setup (you'll see a restart window that automatically restarts your system). Press R if you want to repair your system.

3. Press Enter to continue the installation. Setup will display a licensing screen.

4. Click F8 if you agree with the terms (which will allow you to continue the installation) or Esc if you disagree (which will automatically restart the system). Setup will search your system for drives that can hold the new operating system. Once it

searches all the drives, you'll see a list of them, along with the partitions on each drive. (A partition is an area of a drive that's set aside to hold data and applications for a particular operating system.) You may see a note that the drive contains unpartitioned space. This space is available on the drive but hasn't been set aside for a specific use.

5. Select a partition or unpartitioned space to install Windows XP and click Enter. Be careful about selecting a partition. Setup will erase anything in a partition as part of the installation process if the content of the partition isn't compatible with Windows XP.

6. If you select unpartitioned space, Setup will ask how you want the partition formatted. Using the File Allocation Table (FAT) format will provide better compatibility with existing operating systems. Using the NT File System (NTFS) format will provide you with better security, data compression, and data access.

> Setup provides a quick and a standard formatting method. The quick for-matting method is better if you know the quality of the disk and want to save time. Setup simply creates the partition and adds the required settings without performing a surface check first. The standard formatting technique is better if you don't know the quality of the disk. This formatting technique takes considerably longer (ten or more times longer), but performs a com-plete surface check. Using the standard technique ensures that the drive is completely usable when you complete the Windows XP installation.

7. Select a formatting technique and press Enter. After Setup completes formatting the drive, it will reboot the system. You'll see the first screen of the GUI setup. Click Customize if you want to change the language used as a basis for regional settings within Windows. This dialog controls the way Windows displays time and date, currency, and other regional settings. Click Details to change the keyboard settings for Windows. This includes selecting layout options, such as the Dvorak layout, as well as language options.

8. Perform any required regional and language setup tasks and then click Next. Windows will ask you to enter your name and your company's name.

9. Type your name and company name, and then click Next. Windows will ask you to enter your product key. This key appears on the back of the CD cover.

Caution   It pays to make a copy of this cover product key and place it in a safe location in case the original gets lost. Subsequent installs of XP won't be possible unless you have the product key.

10. Type the key code and then click Next. Windows will ask you to enter a computer name and an administrator password. It's important to give your computer a friendly name, especially when working on a network. The default name provided by Setup is usually hard to remember. Don't leave the administrator password blank. Otherwise, your system will be easy to attack. Using a complex password is your best defense again crackers.

11. Type a computer name and administrator password. Click Next. Setup will ask for modem and telephone information.

12. Type any information required to use the modem and telephone. Make sure that you include any information required to dial out, in addition to the area code for your location. Note that there's additional information you can enter for modem and telephone use later, such as calling care and area code rules. We discuss these additional settings in the "Phone or Modem" section during Day 10. Click Next. Windows will ask about the date and time.

13. Enter any required date and time information. Click Next. Setup will begin installing network components, giving your tired hands a much-needed rest. You'll see a Network Settings window. Generally, you can use the typical network settings to complete the installation. However, if you have a complex or an oddly configured network, you'll want to customize the network settings.

14. Choose Typical or Custom network installation and then click Next. If you choose a custom network installation, add and remove any required components. Be sure to add any custom network drivers at this point. However, it's essential that you only use Windows XP drivers or your system may fail to reboot. Setup will ask if you want to make this computer part of a workgroup or a domain.

Tip   Most home and small office networks use a workgroup for their network setup. Larger networks use a domain. The easy way to determine which option to choose is that a domain requires Windows Server on your network configured as a domain controller. Only the Server (and alternatives such as Advanced Server) can provide domain services. If your network consists of machines that have the Home Edition or the Professional Edition loaded, then you'll always use the workgroup setting.

15. Choose between a workgroup and domain connection. Type a name for the connection (use the same name as every other computer on the network). Click Next. Setup will give you a long break as you read your favorite novel. Eventually, Windows will reboot. You'll see a Welcome to Windows screen.

16. Click Next. Windows XP will check your Internet connectivity. You can choose to configure the Internet now or skip it and configure it later using the Internet Connection Wizard. We'll discuss the Internet Connection Wizard during Day 4. The process is the same no matter when you perform the setup.

17. Set up your Internet Connection, if desired. Click Next. Windows XP will ask if you want to activate Windows now or wait until later.

18. Activate Windows, if desired. Click Next. Windows XP will ask if you want to register your product. You can skip this step and perform it later, just like product activation.

19. Register Windows, if desired. Click Next. Windows XP will ask if you want to set up some user accounts. A default account with your name will appear, but you can add other users to the list. However, it's actually better to set up the users after installation because Windows won't assign security or make other setting changes if you add users at this screen.

20. Add users, if desired. Click Next. You'll see a success screen.

21. Click Finish to complete the process.

Installing from a Network

If you have a network setup, it may be possible to reduce the time required for an installation by using the network installation method. In this method, you install Windows XP from a server to the workstation using a network connection. The workstation doesn't require a CD-ROM drive to perform this kind of installation, but it still comes in handy for installing applications later.

A client must have a floppy drive in some cases. The Remote Installation Services (RIS) client resides on a floppy that you can place in the workstation. This client will boot the workstation and allow it to start installing Windows XP. Failing that, the client will need a boot electronically erasable programmable read-only memory (EEPROM) chip installed on its network interface card (NIC). The EEPROM knows how to create a network connection, contact the server, and download booting instructions. In both cases, the NIC installed in the client must be on the list of RIS recognized products.

The server also requires a special setup. Obviously, it requires a network connection. The faster the connection, the better for RIS purposes. You also have to install both Active

Directory and Remote Installation Services on the server. The RIS tree should appear on a separate partition of your server's hard drive to ensure that the Windows XP installation files aren't corrupted. You can find the complete installation requirements at `http://www.microsoft.com/windows2000/techinfo/planning/management/remotest` `eps.asp`.

At some point, you'll have RIS installed and the client connected to the server. The actual installation process looks the same as the one in the "Character Mode" section of the chapter. The only difference from a user perspective is that the installation information moves over a network connection instead of directly from the CD-ROM.

Unattended Installations

You'll normally create an unattended installation scenario when you have to install Windows XP on many systems. The work required for an unattended installation isn't worth the time for just two or three installations. An unattended installation is one where you answer all the installation questions in advance using a file. Setup reads the file during the setup process and uses those values for configuration purposes.

Organizations will often combine unattended installations with network installation to make the process of updating the operating system close to automatic. Of course, if anything does go wrong, no one will know until the installation is complete because no one will be monitoring the install. Even if someone were monitoring the installation, they'd never see a break in the process so they could stop it.

Many people think the Setup program in the root directory of the Windows XP installation disk is the installation program. Setup is simply a nice front end for running other applications. The actual setup program is WINNT32 for GUI installations and WINNT for character mode installations. You can find these programs in the \I386 directory of the Windows XP setup disk. Both programs access "command line parameters" that modify the way they work. A command line parameter is an additional piece of text that the application reads as it starts. Because a command line parameter modifies application execution, some people also call it a switch.

Both WINNT32 and WINNT allow unattended installations. They both require the use of the /s:<Source Path> switch. The Source Path parameter tells the installation programs where to find files it needs during the installation process. WINNT32 also requires the /unattend:<Answer File> switch, while WINNT uses the /u:<Answer File> switch. So, if you wanted to start an unattended installation program, you'd type one of the following:

```
WINNT32 /s:C:\MyDir /unattend:MyAnsers.txt
WINNT /s:C:\MyDir /u:MyAnswers.txt
```

So, what is an answer file? This file contains the answers to the questions that Setup would ask if you were at the computer. You can find an example of the answer file in the \I386 directory of the Windows XP distribution disk under the name of UNATTEND.TXT. Open this file, and you'll see that the questions and answers follow the same format as the setup process in the "Character Mode" section of the chapter. The answers have a very specific format because Setup will look for these keywords in the file. For example, the user name uses the FullName keyword like this:

```
FullName = "My Name"
```

Notice that an equals sign and the value you want to assign as an answer follow the keyword. All of the answers follow precisely the same format. Of course, you need to know the right keywords and the values to assign them. The UNATTEND.TXT file contains the most common keywords and answers. You should be able to create a standard Windows setup by modifying this file.

You may notice when you look at UNATTEND.TXT file that it doesn't answer every question. For example, it doesn't allow you to install additional networking protocols. Setup uses default values whenever possible if it doesn't find the answer to a question in the answer file. All of the essential questions have answers in UNATTEND.TXT, so this file works just fine for a standard installation. The Windows XP Resource Kit will contain a complete list of answer file keywords, anticipated responses, and default answers. If this resource kit isn't available at the time you read this, you can still use the Windows 2000 Resource Kit (`http://www.microsoft.com/WINDOWS2000/techinfo/reskit/`).

After you create and test the answer file, you can begin an installation and go have coffee until it completes. For that matter, you could start the installation process using a script entry for the user's login script or any other method that your company decides to use. The point is that the installation process is automatic, and users will end up with a new copy of Windows on their machines without any intervention.

Creating a Dual Boot Setup

Windows XP handles multi-boot setups without too many problems. The main difference from a user's perspective is that you'll see an additional menu when you start the machine. The menu will appear for 30 seconds by default and then choose the default operating system if the user doesn't select one.

The best approach to take when creating a multi-boot setup is to create a separate partition for each operating system. In the past, some Windows 9x users would use a single partition for both Windows 9x and Windows NT/2000. This practice leads to problems that you can't easily solve. Of course, you must use a separate partition for advanced operating system setup, such as a Windows XP and Linux combination. Interestingly enough, I actually saw a Windows NT/NetWare combination once, but this is probably unusual today. Normally, I maintain a separate DOS partition for my diagnostic applications, but this isn't a requirement. (We'll discuss diagnostics in detail during Day 21.)

You need to consider a few additional constraints when creating a dual boot setup. The first task to perform is installing all non-Windows XP operating systems that are compatible with the Windows XP boot manager. For the most part, this means you're limited to Microsoft products. You can dual boot DOS or Windows 9x using the Windows XP boot manager, but don't expect to create a dual boot setup consisting of Linux and Windows XP.

If you want to create a dual boot setup with two operating systems that don't get along, you'll need a third-party product, such as PartitionMagic from Power Quest (http://www.powerquest.com/products/desktop.html). You'll install this product first, create partitions to hold the two operating systems, and then install them. The problem here is that these third-party products are reliable until they come across an operating system they don't understand. Never attempt to install a new version of Windows (or any other operating system) on a system that relies on a third-party partitioning product until you have a known good backup of all partitions.

At some point, you'll need to decide which operating system is the default. Third-party products will likely have a configuration utility to help you with this task. When working with Windows XP boot manager, you can change the default by using the Default operating system field of the Startup and Recovery dialog box. You access this dialog box by clicking Settings in the Startup and Recovery section on the Advanced tab of the System Properties dialog box (accessible by right clicking My Computer and selecting Properties).

Installation will consist of multiple operating system install sessions. You select a different partition for each operating system you want to install. This leaves you with a separate environment for each operating system.

Windows XP Upgrades

It would be nice if operating systems came completely ready for use. Windows XP does a better job in this area than any previous version of Windows. However, as with every other operating system, you need to check for patches, updates, new security releases, and new applications. Most vendors provide Internet sites for downloads, and Microsoft is no exception.

The following sections will help you through the process of upgrading your Windows XP installation before you begin application installation. You want to install these updates before the applications to ensure that the operating system is completely stable when you begin using it. While the upgrade tips in these sections don't cover every contingency, they do cover the most common and important upgrades for your system.

Upgrade Tips

When you initially install your operating system, it's a clean environment. The operating system has all of the files that the vendor originally wanted it to have. Yes, your machine is essentially non-functional at this point, but it will never be in a purer state than it is in now.

Unfortunately, even vendors make mistakes. Microsoft detractors tend to think that they make more mistakes than anyone else, but often it's a matter of getting caught more often. Politics aside, your copy of Windows will require updates to make it the best possible platform for your applications. The following tips will help you to perform the required updates with fewer problems and a better result.

- **Always download all of the updates to your hard drive.** In many cases, Microsoft will offer to update your system directly, but this leads to problems if you have to apply the update to more than one machine or need it again later. Keeping an update directory on your server, a backup tape, or another machine ensures that you can return your system to a known good state whenever you need to.

- **Check update file dates.** Microsoft has gotten better about keeping their Web site updated, but they still don't do a perfect job. You may find several versions of the same update file, depending on where you look online. The files provided by Windows Update are usually the newest, the Microsoft download area comes next, and Knowledge Base articles rank third. Downloading an update from a Microsoft product site may be your only choice, but be sure to check other locations first.

- **Verify the need for an update.** Sometimes, Microsoft will issue several overlapping updates. Service packs often consolidate updates that they released as individual files. This is especially true in the security area. So, the best option is to download the service pack first to see which problems it fixes before you download individual files.

- **Read the documentation.** Some people download updates because someone in a magazine told them to do so. If you don't read the documentation that comes with an update, you only have yourself to blame if the update harms your system. Some updates serve special needs, and you won't need them all. Make sure you read the documentation and understand what the update does and how to install it properly.

2

- **After you have the newest files downloaded to another system, create a checklist.** Using a checklist ensures that you apply all of the required updates.
- **Place the entries in the checklist in date order.** Apply the updates in date order. Installing the oldest update first ensures that old updates won't overwrite new versions of system files, even by accident. This technique also ensures that the system contains the latest versions of utilities.
- **Reboot after each update.** Yes, Windows XP is supposed to require fewer updates. However, it pays to take this extra step to ensure that your system will still boot and operate correctly after each update. If you install all of the updates, reboot the machine, and only then find out it doesn't work, you won't know which update to blame for the problem.
- **Validate the effect of each update whenever possible.** It's true that you won't be able to validate at least half of the updates you download. For example, you wouldn't want to hack your system, just to make sure that a security patch took effect (at least not at this stage of the installation process). However, validating that pressing Ctrl-Alt-F9 no longer turns the screen pink with purple spots is easy to do and something you should check.

Using Windows Update

You'll find Windows Update on the Start menu. Windows used to wait for the user to select this entry to find new updates on the Windows Update site. Some users would add Windows Update to the Scheduled Task utility list. Most, however, simply ignored the icon and didn't get any updates done. The "Using Automatic Updates" section tells how this practice has changed under Windows XP.

When you start Windows Update, a copy of Internet Explorer opens and goes to the Windows Update site. You must enable scripting to use Windows Update. If you have scripting set up as a prompt option (as I do), you'll need to say yes to running scripts.

Windows Update will begin by checking the Windows Update control on your system. If your copy of the control is outdated, Windows Update will ask to download a new copy. Once this is complete, Windows Update can begin the process of comparing your system state to the update list online. Normally, you'll need to click an icon to begin the scanning process. The scanning process works better if you close all applications on your system.

Eventually, Windows XP will show you a list of updates for your system. Microsoft groups these updates by criticality. Make sure you install all critical updates, especially those related to security.

You'll also find application and feature updates on Windows Update. It's a good idea to keep applications and features you often use updated. However, it also pays to read how the new version of the application or feature will work. Some people choose not to update their applications because they like the way the old ones work.

To install an update, select it from the list. Microsoft offers you the chance to obtain detailed information about the update, and you'll want to read that information before you make a commitment. After you have a list of updates to install, click Install and follow the directions. The update process does vary from update to update, but normally you'll download the update, watch Windows install it automatically, and then reboot your machine if needed. A few updates may require manual installation or configuration.

I always maintain a directory containing uninstall instructions for all updates that I install. The uninstall instructions appear with detailed information you should read about the update. You never know when Microsoft will remove an update from the list. The directory of uninstall instructions is your assurance that you can remove any changes that an update makes.

Using Automatic Updates

You really don't *use* automatic updates; it's an automated Windows XP feature. Windows XP will check for updates on the Windows Update site at regular intervals. If it finds an update you need, you'll see a dialog box showing the update and a short description of what it does. You can choose to download the update immediately or wait a few days. After the time interval you choose lapses, the automatic update feature will check the Windows Update site again and display the updates you need to perform.

Installing DirectX Support

Microsoft is constantly upgrading DirectX support for Windows. Most Windows games, some educational software, and some graphics applications rely on DirectX for performance reasons. Generally, Microsoft will make the latest version of DirectX available as a Windows Update site download, but this isn't always the case. If you want to ensure that you have the latest version of DirectX installed on your system, you need to check the DirectX site at http://www.microsoft.com/directx/.

Of course, the problem is figuring out which version of DirectX you have installed on your machine. Microsoft doesn't make this information easily accessible. What you need is a utility named DXDIAG.EXE. This utility normally appears in the SYSTEM32 or one of the Program Files directories. You can normally start it by clicking Run in the Start menu, typing **DXDIAG** in the Open field, and clicking OK. Figure 2.1 shows what the System tab of the DirectX Diagnostics Tool looks like. (We'll discuss this application in detail during Day 7.)

FIGURE 2.1

*The DirectX
Diagnostics Tool tells
you which version of
DirectX your machine
has installed.*

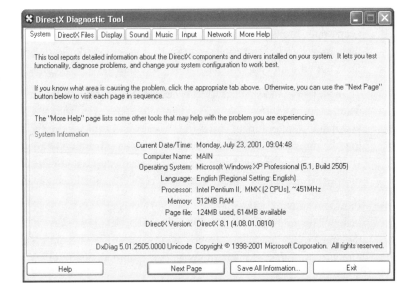

Notice the DirectX Version field near the bottom of the display. In this case, I'm using DirectX 8.1. The numbers in parentheses next to the version number contains the "build" information for DirectX. You'll only need this information if a product support representative asks for it.

If your system needs a new version of DirectX, click the download link on the DirectX Web site. You'll need to provide a directory for the download. I normally maintain an "Updates" folder for operating systems, devices, and applications I own, so I provide the Updates directory as the download path.

After you download the new file, you'll need to install it. This means closing all applications. Go to the download directory and start the setup program. The setup program will tell you what to do next. Generally, you just have to wait for the update to complete and reboot your machine.

Locating Other Important Upgrades

Microsoft doesn't always make updates easy to find. For example, I'll often look through articles in the Knowledge Base site (http://search.support.microsoft.com/kb/c.asp) to see if I need to apply any updates. You can search for Knowledge Base articles by product, but I find searching using the What's new within the last X day(s) option works better. This allows you to see all of the new Knowledge Base articles for complimentary products, as well as the product of interest.

Another good place to look for updates is Microsoft Product Support Services, located at (http://support.microsoft.com/support/downloads/default.asp). Microsoft normally categorizes the top downloads on this site. For example, this is where I look for new versions of Internet Explorer and updates to my games. This site doesn't carry all of the available updates, just the essential news-making updates. At the bottom of this page is a list of additional download sites.

You can find some of the best update information in Microsoft newsletters, such as Microsoft Developer Network (MSDN) Flash. You can subscribe to newsletters at http://www.microsoft.com/info/WhyRegister.htm. Each newsletter contains information about current product status, pointers to Knowledge Base articles, and alerts for training and other product learning opportunities.

Checking the Installation

At this point, you've installed Windows XP and performed all of the required updates. However, you're still not ready to install applications. So far, we haven't checked the validity of the installation. You don't know if the operating system is stable or even if everything is working. It's time to check your installation for flaws before you begin installing applications. The following sections show you how.

Checking the Logs

The Windows XP Setup program might create logs as it installs the operating system. However, it usually creates these logs only if it experiences an error or has a special event to report.

You'll find these logs in the root directory, the Windows directory, the Windows subdirectories, or the Program Files directory. The logs will have a TXT or LOG extension, with LOG being the most common. The Windows directory alone can contain a massive number of LOG files, so it's important to look for logs with the word *error* in the title, such as SETUPERR.LOG.

All of the files are in text format, so you can use any word processor to open them. I'll normally open logs of interest and look for the words *error* and *warning* in them. These entries are most likely to tell me about deficiencies in the installation and provide me with clues on where to look for solutions. Some of the files are huge, so you'll want to use a search to locate important information.

If you look through the list of log files and don't see anything of interest, it's likely that Windows XP didn't make any important log entries. However, it's a good idea to keep the logs in mind as you check your system. Sometimes a log file will provide amplifying information for a problem you find using other techniques.

Using Device Manager

The Device Manager does a lot more than allow you to look at your device setup; it also points out hardware errors. To view the Device Manager, right-click My Computer and select Properties. You'll see a System Properties dialog box. Select the Hardware tab and then click Device Manager. You'll see a Device Manager dialog box like the one shown in Figure 2.2.

FIGURE 2.2

The Device Manager dialog box allows you to quickly find hardware errors.

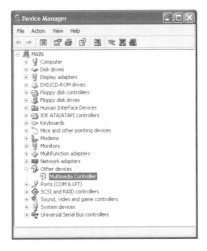

Notice the highlighted device in this list. The device is marked because it isn't functioning correctly. Right-click any marked devices and select Properties. You'll see a Device Properties dialog box. The General tab of this dialog box contains a Device Status field that tells you what's wrong with the device. In many cases, the problem is device driver related. Devices typically fail to install properly under Windows XP for four reasons:

- The device isn't on the hardware compatibility list and therefore isn't supported.
- You attempted to install an old version of a device driver that isn't compatible with Windows XP.
- The device configuration is incorrect.
- The device conflicts with another device in the system.

We discuss configuration issues during Day 10. You'll learn about diagnostics during Day 21. However, these two problems won't appear as often as you think during an initial installation. The main problem is one where Windows doesn't provide a device driver, or it loads an incompatible device driver. The most common fix for this problem is to check with the device vendor for a Windows XP-specific device driver. A good second choice (in some cases) is a Windows 2000 device driver.

Consulting Event Viewer

Event Viewer is one of the last places to look for problems with your installation. You can open Event Viewer by accessing the Administrative Tools folder in the Control Panel or the Start Menu. When you open the Event Viewer, you'll see that it contains three log files: Application, Security, and System. We're most interested in the System log, but you'll also want to view the Application log.

One problem people experience when using Event Viewer is that they don't use it properly. The best way to use Event Viewer to diagnose installation problems is to clear all of the logs, reboot the system, and then check the logs for new entries. This method ensures that you're looking at current problems. Figure 2.3 shows a typical set of System log entries.

FIGURE 2.3

The Event Viewer tells you about current system events.

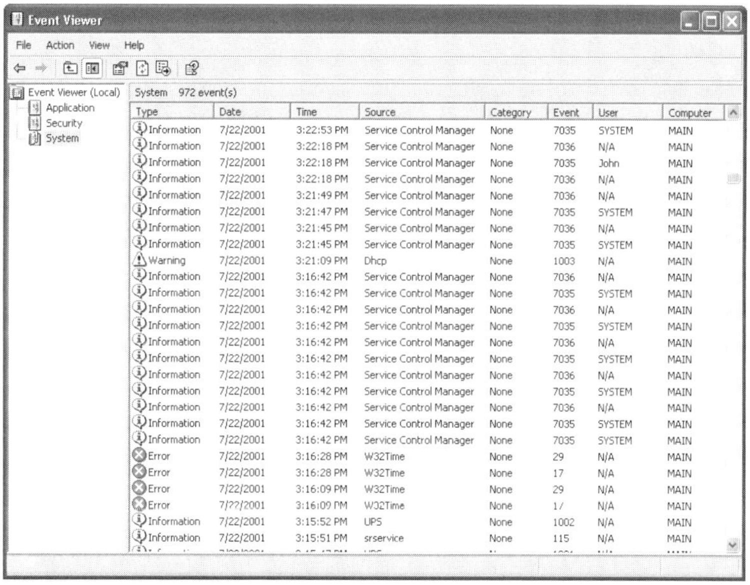

Notice that Figure 2.3 shows three error messages and one warning message. Those are the types of messages that you want to concentrate on when looking for problems with your system. Double-click a message, and you'll see an Event Properties dialog box that contains details about the error. The Description field contains the best information about the problem, the error number, and places to look for additional help.

You'll know you're finished with Event Viewer when you can boot your system without creating any new warning or error messages. At this point, check the non-critical event messages for any other problems. It's unlikely that you'll find any. Most of the messages will say an application started or tell you about some other mundane event.

Summary

Today you learned how to install Windows XP on both new and existing systems. We've also discussed network, unattended, and dual-boot installations. You learned how to update the operating system and check it for problems before installing any applications.

More than a few people view the Windows installation process as overly difficult and time consuming. However, Microsoft has made great strides over the years in reducing both installation time and complexity. Often, the problem resides with the installer. You've learned something more important than installation procedures today; you've learned how to organize the installation process so that it takes the least possible time and always results in a stable system.

Q&A

Q: What happens if I install an update and the system won't function properly?

A: This is where it pays to read the documentation before you install anything. Microsoft normally tells you how to remove an update if it turns out to cause problems for your system. Make sure you follow the removal instructions to the letter. In almost every case, removing an update immediately after you apply it results in a system that functions as it did before the update.

Q: How does Windows Product Activation (WPA) affect my ability to perform an unattended installation?

A: It makes an unattended installation difficult or impossible for the small business that buys individual copies of Windows XP. Microsoft is waving WPA for large accounts that buy site licenses, but many small businesses can't afford such licenses. The only way around this problem is to create a template answer file and then modify the product key value to create a separate answer file for each machine on your network. This will still save time, but it's more work than it should be.

Q: What do I do if I can't find a device driver for my device?

A: Some developers will get so frustrated with the constant upgrade cycle that they'll make a device driver available for a functional device that vendors have decided not to support. This is especially common with graphics adapters because the upgrade cycle for them is exceptionally intense. Unfortunately, there isn't a central area to download these third-party drivers, and you have no way of knowing how well they'll work. The best place to look for answers is on the Windows XP newsgroups. You should also spend some time looking for solutions with a good search engine, such as Google.

Workshop

It's the end of the second day. By now you should have Windows XP installed and configured. The installation should have any required upgrades in place. All you need is some applications, and you'll be ready to go. You can find answers to the quiz and exercise questions in Appendix A at the back of the book.

Quiz

1. When would you normally use the CD-ROM installation technique?
2. Can you place Windows XP and Linux on the same machine?
3. What's the name of the DirectX utility that tells the current DirectX version number?
4. What are the three logs commonly found in the Event Viewer? Which ones should you be concerned about for operating system installation purposes?

Exercises

1. Complete a Windows XP installation on your own machine.
2. Perform all required system updates before you install any applications.
3. Check your system's functionality.

DAY 3

Exploring the Interface

The user interface for an operating system is its spokesperson. The rest of the operating system does the work, but the user interface is what people see. Therefore, it's important that the user interface gives the user the best impression. Windows XP provides more than a few surprises when it comes to the user interface. Not only do you get more interface choices than ever before, but you'll also find that this interface is more flexible. Windows XP allows you to have things your way—at least, to an extent.

We'll begin by looking at the most important tool in the Windows user interface, Windows Explorer. At one time, Windows Explorer and Internet Explorer were two separate tools. Today they're the same tool with two different user interfaces. Therefore, I'll use the term *Explorer* to talk about both applications. We'll use the Windows Explorer version of the interface because we'll discuss Internet Explorer during Day 4. Remember, however, that you can perform the same actions with both tools within the limits of each application's interface.

Our next discussion will also include managing the user interface. I'll show you how to change various interface elements so that you can switch from the simple Windows XP interface to a Windows 2000 look-alike and everything in between. By the time this day is over, you'll know enough about the Windows XP user interface to create a comfortable environment for yourself or anyone you're working with.

An Overview of Windows Explorer

Of all the tools in Windows XP, the most important tool to learn is Windows Explorer. This single tool provides access to resources, both local and remote. You can use it to view Web pages, as well as the content of your disk drives. Using Windows Explorer, you can set security on your drives and use the Address bar as a command line substitute. Context menus allow you to manipulate objects in various ways, and you can even extend Explorer to fulfill other needs. Figure 3.1 shows a typical example of the Windows Explorer interface. However, as we'll see today, this is just one of many ways to view this utility.

FIGURE 3.1

Windows Explorer is the one tool that everyone should learn to use.

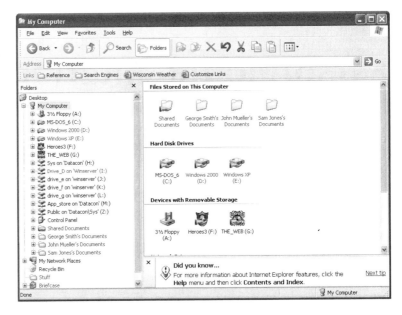

Beginning at the top of the display, you'll see the main menu and three toolbars: Standard Buttons, Address Bar, and Links. (Microsoft might hide the Links toolbar by default, use View | Toolbars | Links to display it.) I'll describe each of these toolbars in the "Toolbars" section that follows. You'll use the View | Toolbars menu options to activate and deactivate each toolbar. The dots on the left of each toolbar allow you to move it. (Microsoft might lock the toolbars by default, use View | Toolbars | Lock the Toolbars to remove the check next to this option.) When you have the toolbars in the desired position, use the View | Toolbars | Lock the Toolbars command to remove the dots and keep the toolbars in place.

Below the toolbars is the data area. As you can see, Windows Explorer as shown in Figure 3.1 contains two vertical panes (you might see other configurations). Changing some of the settings will vary the number of panes between one and two. The right, or detail pane, is always present. Each pane serves a specific purpose as listed below.

- **Explorer Bar**   The Explorer Bar pane normally appears on the left side of Windows Explorer. This pane contains a hierarchical view of your drives (as shown in the figure), a search form, or even a list of contacts. We'll discuss the Explorer Bars in more detail in the "Explorer Bars" section that follows.

- **Details**   You'll normally see a list of objects in this pane. The content of this pane will vary but will generally include details about the object selected in the Explorer Bar pane. For example, if you select the Folders Explorer Bar and choose a folder, the Details pane will contain the files within that folder. Likewise, if you perform a search, the Details pane will contain a list of objects matching the search criteria.

The Tip of the Day is a special pane that appears between the middle and right panes. You'll use the Tip of the Day to learn more about Windows Explorer. Turn this feature on and off using the View | Explorer Bar | Tip of the Day command. The Next Tip link within the Tip of the Day pane allows you to view each tip in the database in rapid succession.

The very bottom of the Windows Explorer display contains a Status Bar. This helpful element provides quick information about a selected object. For example, if you select a file, the Status Bar will show the file size. If you don't have any objects selected, the Status Bar tells you the number of objects within the current container. Finally, when you select multiple objects, the Status Bar contains the number of objects selected and could contain other amplifying information. You turn this feature on and off using the View | Status Bar command.

One of the Explorer Bars that you'll use most often is the Folders Explorer Bar. In fact, Windows Explorer will normally start with this Explorer Bar. You can divide the Folders Explorer Bar into several functional areas. The following sections tell you about each of these areas and detail how you can use them to your benefit.

My Documents

One of the features that has followed users around for several versions of Windows is the My Documents folder. (In some cases, Windows XP might use your name for this folder such as John's Documents.) This folder can appear in a number of places, such as the Desktop. It's also one of the folders that appears within Windows Explorer. Microsoft has set aside a My Documents folder for each user on the machine. It's your private storage area.

Windows XP includes a new feature. You'll only see it when using single pane folders and only if you select the Show Common Tasks in Folders option on the General tab of the Folder Options dialog box. Figure 3.2 shows this view of the My Documents folder when you select this option from the Start menu (in order to obtain the single pane view).

FIGURE **3.2**

The Task pane for several of the My Documents subfolders provides special functionality.

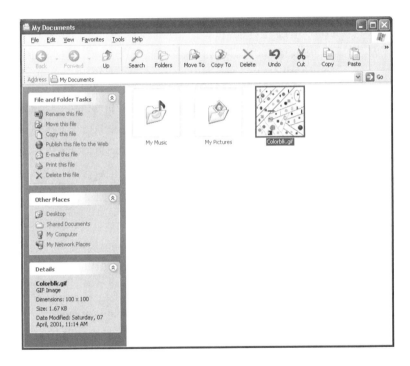

As you can see, the My Documents folder contains two subfolders: My Pictures and My Music. These folders are special because they provide additional capabilities when you continue to use the Task pane on your machine. The Task pane for the My Pictures folder contains a special set of tasks that allow you to view your pictures as a slide show, order prints of your pictures from the Internet, or print copies of your pictures. You can also set a picture as the wallpaper for your Desktop. Figure 3.3 shows an example of these extra commands. Likewise, the Web content for the My Music folder contains special tasks that allow you to play all of the entries in the folder or shop for music online.

FIGURE 3.3

The My Pictures folder contains special commands to manage your pictures.

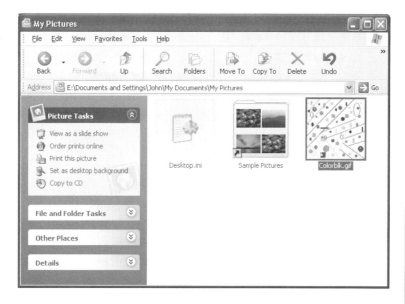

You can also change the appearance of the My Pictures folder. Right-click on any open area in the folder and choose View | Filmstrip from the context menu. The folder now contains a set of picture-viewing tools as shown in Figure 3.4. (Note that you might see a My Videos folder that contains an extended set of these controls.) Selecting an object will allow you to use the controls to size the picture and move from one picture to the next. The tools also include two controls for rotating the picture, a handy feature when working with pictures captured in landscape, rather than portrait orientation. Without it, you'd have to tilt your head sideways to see the picture at the correct orientation.

FIGURE 3.4

You can modify the My Pictures folder to contain special picture viewing controls.

Pocket PC users who have ActiveSync installed on their system may see a My Pocket PC folder here. This folder will contain all of the data files from your Pocket PC. This folder doesn't appear to provide any special functionality other than a link to your PDA.

Some people don't need the My Documents folder. Company policy might dictate that you place all user data on the network so that it's easy to monitor and backup. What this means is that you'll have an empty My Documents folder hanging around on your system. You can get rid of this folder from the Desktop by using the Tools | Folder Options command to display the Folder Options dialog box. Select View and clear the Show My Documents on the Desktop in the Advanced Settings list.

Unfortunately, My Documents will continue to waste space in Windows Explorer and on your hard drive. You can temporarily remove it from Windows Explorer by highlighting the object and pressing Shift+Delete, but the action is temporary. My Documents will grow back even more determined to stay in place. Attempts to delete the folder from your hard drive will fail with an error message. I even tried logging in as another user with administrative privileges to delete the unwanted and unloved folder from my system. The attempt worked, but the folder grew back the next time I started the machine. In short, Microsoft has determined that you'll have a My Documents folder whether you need it or not. Removing it from your Desktop will have to be enough to satisfy you.

My Computer

The My Computer section of Windows Explorer is where you'll find all of the local machine resources. You share these resources with everyone else who uses this machine. Unlike My Documents, you don't personally own these resources and may not even be able to see them all, depending on your rights on the machine. The important thing to remember is that My Computer will show all of the local resources you can access.

My Computer will also contain any mapped network drives. As far as the system is concerned, a mapped network drive is the same as a local drive. The act of mapping a drive creates a pointer from your machine to the network drive. You'll use the Tools | Map Network Drive command to display the Map Network Drive dialog shown in Figure 3.5. Select a local drive from the Drive list box and point to a network drive using the Folder combo box. Notice the Browse button next to the Folder combo box; it allows you to search for a network drive. Check the Reconnect at Login option if you want Windows to reestablish the connection each time you start the machine.

You can perform a number of tasks by right-clicking the local drive and selecting options from the context menu. For example, you can expand and collapse the hierarchical display. You can also rename, share, or format local drives, and disconnect from mapped drives. The Properties command will display a dialog similar to the one shown in Figure 3.6.

FIGURE 3.5

Mapping a network drive is as easy as pointing a local drive to a location on the network.

FIGURE 3.6

The local drive's Properties dialog contains a number of tabs that allow you to monitor and manage disk drives.

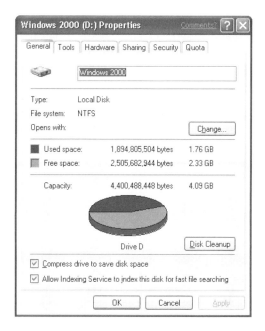

The number and names of the tabs you'll see depend on the type of drive resource you're viewing. Figure 3.6 shows a typical set of tabs for an NT File System (NTFS) drive. The General and Hardware tabs are the points of interest for this section. We'll discuss the Tools tab on Day 21, the Sharing and Security tabs on Day 16, and the Quota tab on Day 8. Depending on your system setup, you may see other specialty tabs. For example, you'll see additional tabs if you install the NetWare client. These tabs include special client features, such as the capability to set network drive security without starting the Network Administrator application.

Let's begin by looking at the General tab. You'll always see the drive name at the top. Changing this entry also changes the name of the drive.

Below the drive name entry, you'll see three pieces of information: Type, File system, and Opens with. The Type entry tells you whether this drive is a local or network drive. The File system entry tells you the drive format. (This entry can vary significantly depending on the clients you have installed.) For example, the Microsoft client simply reports that the drive is NetWare compatible. The NetWare client will report the types of support loaded for the drive, including long filename support. The Opens with field is normally blank because you use Windows Explorer to open the drive. If you see an entry here, it means that another application configured the registry to use something other than Windows Explorer.

The next section of drive information tells you disk space usage. It shows both used and free space. As with everything else, the client you install will determine how many other entries you may see. Network vendors could include entries that show the amount of compressed versus uncompressed disk space. This entry is misleading in some cases. A client may not provide an accurate reading of compressed network drives, leading you to believe there's less space available than the drive can really provide.

The final section of this dialog contains two options. Setting the first option will compress your drive. You have the option of compressing the entire drive or just the root directory. Compressing the entire drive can take time, so make sure that you check this option when you have plenty of time to wait for the process to complete. The second option allows the Indexing Service to index the drive for fast searches. Be aware that checking this option doesn't start the Indexing Service. You need to start it using the Computer Management console found in the Administrator Tools folder. We'll discuss this tool on Day 8.

The Hardware tab appears in Figure 3.7. Notice that this tab displays a complete list of all drives on your system, but not the partitions on the drives. This tab provides a quick look at the physical hardware on your system, rather than the logic drives that you normally work with. Each entry provides a drive manufacturer name (when available), model number (when available), location, and status.

The Troubleshoot button displays the Help and Support Services window shown in Figure 3.8. This series of dialogs will help you diagnose and fix many common drive problems. However, the vast majority of the solutions are Windows specific. You can't depend on Help and Support Services to provide you with hardware-specific support. That information appears in your vendor manuals or at a vendor-specific site online.

FIGURE 3.7

The Hardware tab allows you to see the hardware behind the partitions on your drive.

Help and Support Services also ignores commonsense errors that Microsoft assumes users will catch by themselves. This is a little shortsighted because everyone needs help with those head-slapping errors from time to time. For example, I had one client whose CD-ROM drive suddenly quit working. A quick trip to the office showed that the CD-ROM was upside down in the drive. It was something that I should have considered while talking to the user on the telephone, but the problem didn't become obvious until I actually looked at the drive.

The Properties button displays a dialog similar to the one shown in Figure 3.9. This is actually a quick way to access the drive's entry in Device Manager (discussed on Day 10). The tabs you see will vary by the device and device drivers loaded on your system. Figure 3.9 shows a typical set of tabs.

Essentially, these tabs allow you to monitor and manage the physical device that holds your data. The options you see will vary by device. For example, you might see settings that control the write-ahead, the capability of Windows to use memory to improve the drive's performance.

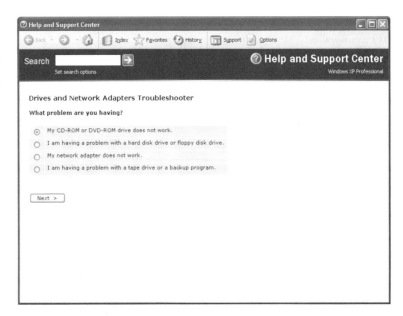

FIGURE 3.8

Help and Support Services will assist you in finding many Windows-specific drive errors.

FIGURE 3.9

The drive device Properties dialog contains detailed information about the selected hardware.

My Network Places

My Network Places contains a list of drives and folders similar to those found in My Computer. However, instead of looking at the local machine, you're now looking at the entire network. In most cases, unless you're the administrator, you won't see all of the resources the network has to offer due to limitations in access. My Network Places presents your view of the network.

There's a special icon within My Network Places called *Entire Network*. This is actually a placeholder icon; it doesn't represent a physical resource. If you attempt to open a Properties dialog for this particular icon, Windows XP will display an error message stating that the properties aren't available. Below this icon is a list of network resources as shown in Figure 3.10.

FIGURE 3.10

The Entire Network icon is the starting point for searching for network resources.

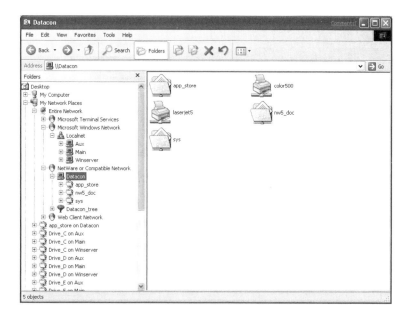

Notice that Figure 3.10 shows two different networks. The first is Microsoft based, while the second is NetWare based. LocalNet, the Microsoft network, contains three machines. If you expanded the machine displays, you'd see a list of drives that you could further expand into folders. The NetWare network consists of a single server.

The hierarchical display in the Explorer Bar doesn't always tell you the full story about network resources. Notice that the NetWare server display on the left shows three drives. The Details pane on the right shows that this server also supports two printers. As you can see, it's important to look at the Details pane when you're searching for a network resource.

After you go past the Entire Network icon and its contents, you'll notice a series of drive icons. These are actually drive shortcuts. Windows XP attempts to locate every drive you can access on the network and automatically provide a shortcut so you don't have to search for the resource. The drive names are the same as the names within the Entire Network hierarchy, making it easy to tell where a resource belongs.

Network shortcuts are an extremely handy feature. They allow you to create a connection with any network resource, local or remote. Creating a new network shortcut is easy. Click My Network Neighborhood in the Folders Explorer Bar. The Details pane will contain an Add Network Place icon. Double-click this icon to start the Add Network Place Wizard. Skip past the Welcome screen, and you'll see a Select Network Place Provider dialog box similar to the one shown in Figure 3.11. Note that you may have other service providers installed on your machine, so your list may not match mine.

FIGURE 3.11

Use the Add Network Place Wizard to add new network shortcuts to your system.

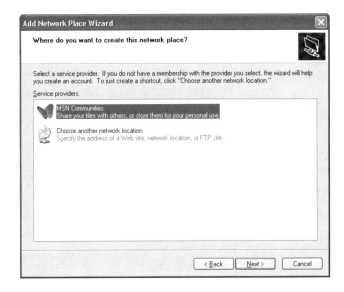

> **Tip**
>
> Windows XP has MSN provider support installed. The MSN provider will allow access to an online storage site. You can use online storage equally well from work or at home. MSN is a handy way to keep your data in one place and still make it accessible from any machine you use that has the proper support installed. The downside to this approach is that it's hard to create a backup of the data. Many enterprise installations will probably use this technique as a last-ditch effort, rather than a preferred method, because of the perceived danger to data.

I'll use the Other Network Location approach for this example, but the procedure for creating a network shortcut is essentially the same no matter which provider you use. After you select a provider, click Next and you'll see some type of source selection dialog. Figure 3.12 shows the selection dialog for Other Network Locations. The final step is to provide a name for your shortcut. I normally use something short but descriptive to ensure I'll remember where the shortcut points are later.

FIGURE **3.12**

You need to select a source for the network shortcuts you create.

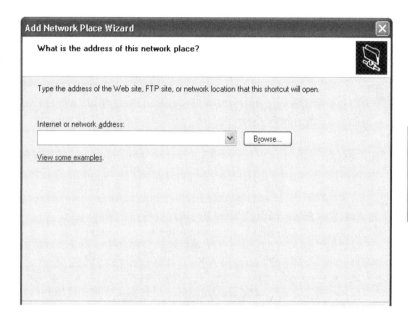

FIGURE **3.12**

You need to select a source for the network shortcuts you create.

It's important to realize that a network shortcut can point to any network resource, including both Web and file transfer protocol (FTP) sites. For example, I created a network shortcut for the FTP site associated with my Web site. This allows me to create files locally and move them directly to the FTP site by using Explorer. Unlike local or even remote drive resources, you can only manipulate files on FTP and Web sites. This means you must create a local copy of the file in order to edit it.

Recycle Bin

The Recycle Bin is a temporary place to store files that you want to delete later. The files are still on the hard drive, but Windows could remove them if it needs more hard drive space. You can also manually empty the Recycle Bin. For example, you'd definitely want to delete the contents of the Recycle Bin before you optimized the hard drive. Figure 3.13 shows a typical view of the Recycle Bin within Windows Explorer. Notice that I used the Details view, in this case, because I want to be sure that the file I'm deleting is the one that I no longer want.

FIGURE 3.13

The Recycle Bin holds files you no longer want to keep.

Using the Recycle Bin is easy. You can right-click the icon on your Desktop or within Explorer to empty the entire Recycle Bin, view its contents, or change its settings. When you open the Recycle Bin, you can delete files individually or as part of a group. This is also the only way to restore files to their original location. Just select the files you want to restore, right-click, and choose Restore from the context menu.

One limitation of the Recycle Bin is that you can't look at files within folders. A folder acts as a single entity within the Recycle bin. This means that you must restore the folder to its original location before you can view its contents.

You can make some changes to the way Recycle Bin operates. Right-click Recycle Bin and choose Properties to display the Recycle Bin Properties dialog shown in Figure 3.14. Notice that there's a Global tab and an individual drive tab for each drive on your system. Most people choose to set the Recycle Bin properties globally, but Windows XP does give you a choice.

The slider near the middle of the Recycle Bin Properties dialog allows you to set the amount of hard drive space that the Recycle Bin can use. This setting is important to performance because you want to keep enough hard drive space open for the swap file and user data. Of course, the larger your Recycle Bin is, the longer files stay intact so you can retrieve them. Still, the default 10% value used by Windows XP seems a tad extreme to me. That means on an 18GB hard drive, you'll use 1.8GB for the Recycle Bin. That's larger than the swap file Microsoft recommends in most cases. Using a value that's close to reality is a good idea. I normally set mine to allow 100MB of storage space for the Recycle Bin, just in case I have an extra large file to delete.

Most users should keep the Display deleted confirmation dialog option checked. This dialog warns you that the files in the Recycle Bin will become unavailable after you choose to empty it. This dialog has saved me from emptying the Recycle Bin by mistake several times.

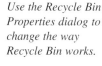

FIGURE 3.14

Use the Recycle Bin Properties dialog to change the way Recycle Bin works.

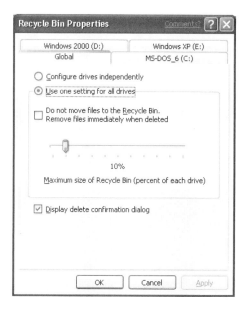

Briefcase

Windows has had Briefcase support for quite some time. It used to be an optional element that you installed after you completed the Windows setup. However, Windows XP comes with Briefcase support built in.

Briefcase is a useful tool for laptop users. It allows you to create a synchronized copy of a file at work, carry it home in your briefcase on the laptop, do some work on the file, and then resynchronize the file at work the next day. You'll find that Briefcase provides an easy method for carrying data around, and it prevents many of the problems that laptop users have with missed edits. We'll discuss the features of Briefcase fully during Day 13.

The problem for at least some users is they'll never know Briefcase exists because the default Windows display lacks a Briefcase. You need to create a Briefcase before you can access one. Right-click the Desktop and choose New | Briefcase from the context menu. The Briefcase will then appear within Windows Explorer as well. Figure 3.15 shows a sample Briefcase with files loaded.

FIGURE 3.15

Briefcase is a convenient tool for carrying files between work and home.

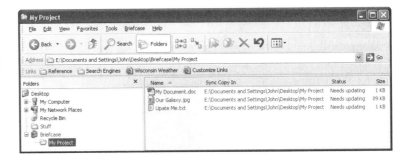

Other Elements

You need to know about other elements of Windows Explorer in order to obtain maximum use from this utility. For example, we haven't yet discussed techniques for configuring Windows Explorer so that you can see things the way you'd like to see them. The following sections will describe some of the more common configuration issues. After you complete this section, you'll know enough about Windows Explorer to work quickly and efficiently.

Explorer Bars

Windows Explorer comes equipped with several Explorer Bars. An Explorer Bar is like a plug-in that changes the personality of Windows Explorer. We've been using the Folders Explorer Bar quite a bit so far, so you should have a good idea of what this Explorer Bar looks like and what it can do for you. However, these features are only the tip of the iceberg.

The Search Explorer Bar shown in Figure 3.16 helps you look for data on your system. This is the standard Search Explorer Bar. Windows XP also provides a Search Companion-style Explorer Bar that adds animated effects and a simpler interface. You can select this alternative search option by checking the Use Search Companion for Searching option on the View tab of the Folder Options dialog box.

Notice that you can provide a filename, text within a file, or both as search criteria. The Look In field contains the location you want to search. It includes an option for searching the entire computer system or My Network Neighborhood. You can also choose locations further down the hierarchy, such as a specific disk drive or folder. The Explorer Bar allows you to limit the scope of your search using criteria such as date and time ranges, file types, file size, and options that include a case-sensitive search (for systems that support it). The Search Explorer Bar also includes a link to the Index Server and current Index Server status information.

FIGURE 3.16

The Search Explorer Bar helps you find files on your system, the network, or even the Internet.

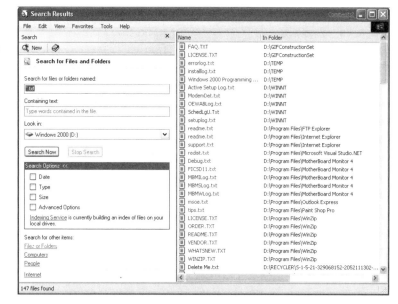

Tip

Because you can create a shortcut to FTP and Web sites, Search will also work for Internet locations. In most cases, you must create a network shortcut for this feature to work. In addition, I found that I often had to make the request twice with secured sites. The search would fail the first time but succeed the second.

There are other forms of Search besides the file or folder search we just discussed. You can search the Internet for a specific Web page, business, or e-mail address. The Search Explorer Bar also includes options for searching for people or computers on your local network. We'll discuss many other forms of searching as the book progresses.

The Favorites Explorer Bar appears in Figure 3.17. At this point, you should recognize the crossover between Windows Explorer and Internet Explorer. What Figure 3.16 shows you is essentially a two-pane view of the Internet. You can make Internet Explorer look precisely the same. In short, the demarcation between the two applications is largely one of initial interface. We'll discuss Internet Explorer and the Internet more during Day 4.

The History Explorer Bar shown in Figure 3.18 is another crossover display. In this case, you'll see a list of links that you recently visited in the Explorer Bar and the content of the selected Web site in the Details pane. We'll discuss how you can set the longevity of Web site history during Day 4.

FIGURE 3.17

Windows Explorer and Internet Explorer begin to look the same when you display the Favorites Explorer Bar.

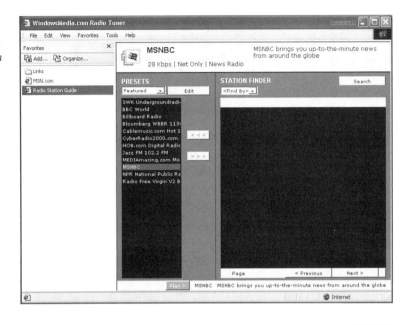

FIGURE 3.18

The History Explorer Bar allows you to revisit a Web site that you've checked recently.

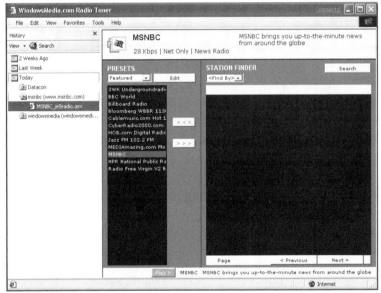

The Media Explorer Bar combines the Windows Media Player with Windows Explorer. You can search both your local drive and the Internet for content to play. When you first start the Explorer Bar, you'll see a media player similar to the one shown in Figure 3.19 in the Explorer Bar pane.

FIGURE **3.19**

The Media Explorer Bar allows you to search for and play media from both the Internet and your local drive.

The VCR-style controls at the bottom are self-explanatory. They work just like the same controls on your system at home. The point of interest on this display is the Media Options drop-down menu.

Media Options offers four choices: More Media, Radio Guide, Settings, and Play. Selecting More Media will take you to the `http://www.windowsmedia.com/mg/home.asp` Web site. You can download a variety of media sources from the Web site, including both music samples and movie trailers. When you select a media source, Explorer loads it into the media player in the Explorer Bar (at least when the scripting works right one the Web page) and plays your selection.

The Radio Guide displays the same radio station site as shown in Figure 3.17. This site allows you to select a source of streamed media to listen to as you work.

You only have three Settings options from which to choose. The Play web media in the bar option is the one that transfers control to the Media Explorer Bar when you select a sound or video source. Clearing this option causes Explorer to start a separate copy of the media player for each selection you make. The Ask for preferred types option tells Explorer that you'd like to keep track of your selections and use them as criteria for making future selections. Finally, Reset preferred types removes your selection preferences. This is a good option if you start noticing your selections become fewer. Sometimes Explorer does more filtering than you'd like it to perform.

The Play menu allows you to play local media files. When you select the Media File option, Explorer displays an Open dialog box you can use to select a source. Windows Media Player accommodates an amazing list of audio and video file formats, so you should be able to play just about any file on your machine.

The Contact Explorer Bar is the least complex of all the Explorer Bars we've discussed so far. This Explorer Bar simply provides a list of the contacts in your Address Book. If you want to send a message to a particular contact, double-click the contact's name, and you'll see an empty e-mail message appear. You can also send e-mail to multiple recipients by Ctrl-clicking each recipient in turn, right-clicking one of the selected items, and choosing Send E-Mail from the context menu. You'll find that the context menu also contains options for dialing a telephone or making contact using Instant Messenger. Finally, you can change the properties for any contact in the list.

Toolbars

Windows Explorer includes three toolbars: Standard Buttons, Address Bar, and Links. You can add or subtract any of these toolbars using the options on the View | Toolbars menu. Figure 3.20 shows all three toolbars in place.

FIGURE 3.20

Windows Explorer provides three toolbars.

As previously mentioned, whenever you see the dots on the left side of the toolbars, you can move them around to suit your needs. Here's a description of each toolbar:

- **Standard Buttons**   You'll use this toolbar to access general Explorer functions. I'll show you how to modify the buttons displayed on this toolbar later in this section. Optimizing this toolbar will help you use Explorer more efficiently while eliminating some of the clutter.

- **Address Bar**   Use this toolbar to access resources directly or perform tasks such as searches. One of the more interesting ways to use the search feature is to type the Microsoft Knowledge Base number for an article you need to read. For example, if you type Q123456, you'll see an article about a bug where MSCDEX may not detect a disk change under certain circumstances.

- **Links**   This is actually a special portion of your Favorites list. If you check Favorites, you'll see a Links folder. Anything you place in this folder will appear on the Links toolbar. This makes the Links toolbar especially useful because you can customize it for the places you visit most often. I normally place two folders in my Links folder. The first contains a list of search engines I like to use, and the second contains a list of reference information, such as an online dictionary.

You customize the Standard Buttons toolbar by using the View | Toolbars | Customize command. Figure 3.21 shows the Customize Toolbar dialog box that you'll use to change the appearance of the Standard Buttons toolbar.

FIGURE 3.21

Use the Customize Toolbar dialog box to change the appearance of the Standard Buttons toolbar.

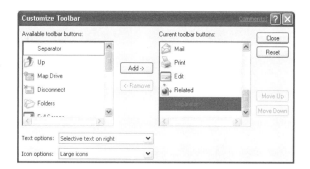

The Available toolbar buttons list box contains all of the commands that you can add to the Standard Buttons toolbar. The Current toolbar buttons list box contains the commands that you can currently issue with the Standard Buttons toolbar. You'll use the Add and Remove buttons to move buttons between the two lists.

The Move Up and Move Down buttons allow you to reorganize the Standard Buttons toolbar and make it easier to use. Of course, there are times when the order of the buttons isn't enough. In these cases, you can move a Separator from the Available toolbar buttons list to the Current toolbar buttons list. If you make a complete mess of the Standard Buttons toolbar, you can always click Reset to return the Standard Buttons toolbar to its default state.

Another important feature is the capability to change the text on the toolbar. The default state is to display text for selected buttons to the right of the button. You can also choose to display text below each button or to have no text at all.

The final optimization is large icons versus small icons. The large icons are easier to see, and many people prefer them for that reason. The small icons consume less space, so you can place more on the Standard Buttons toolbar without seeing the continued (>>) icon. Generally, I find that I prefer the large icons because I don't need to include any text with them. Leaving out the text saves some space, making the use of small icons unnecessary.

Task Pane

The Task pane of Windows Explorer can provide up to four types of data. However, the most common pane configuration contains the three areas of data shown in Figure 3.22: File Tasks, Other Places, and Details. You only see this pane if you use the single pane (folder) view of Windows Explorer. In addition, you must select the Show Common Tasks in Folders option on the General tab of the Folder Options dialog box.

FIGURE 3.22

The Task pane normally includes three areas of data.

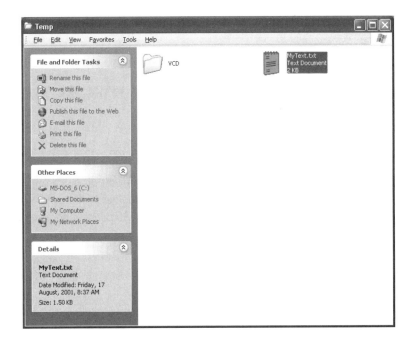

The tasks area changes by type of object. In this case, we're looking at a file, so you see the File Tasks area. This is an alternative to using the context menu. A single click is all you need to perform the task.

Next is the Other Places area. The content of this area varies by context. When you're looking at a disk drive, you'll see options to return to the root directory (when required), My Documents, Shared Documents, My Computer, and My Network Places.

The final area is Details, which contains detailed information about the selected object. The content of this section varies by object type. Interestingly enough, you can't customize the content of this area, at least not with a menu or wizard.

FIGURE 3.23

The Details view is heavy with information but could prove overwhelming for novice users.

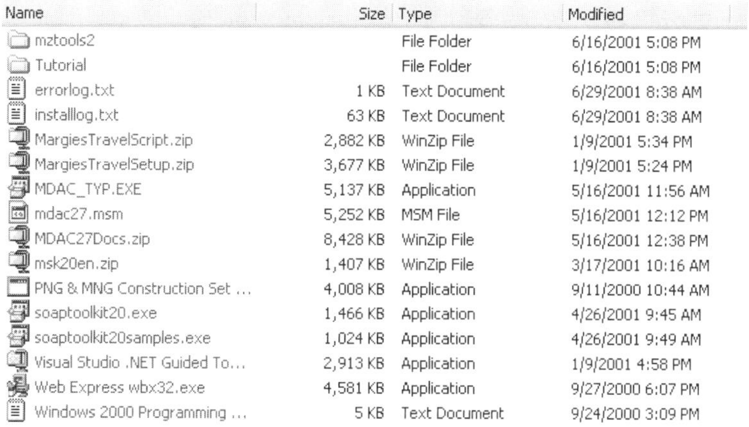

Name	Size	Type	Modified
mztools2		File Folder	6/16/2001 5:08 PM
Tutorial		File Folder	6/16/2001 5:08 PM
errorlog.txt	1 KB	Text Document	6/29/2001 8:38 AM
installlog.txt	63 KB	Text Document	6/29/2001 8:38 AM
MargiesTravelScript.zip	2,882 KB	WinZip File	1/9/2001 5:34 PM
MargiesTravelSetup.zip	3,677 KB	WinZip File	1/9/2001 5:24 PM
MDAC_TYP.EXE	5,137 KB	Application	5/16/2001 11:56 AM
mdac27.msm	5,252 KB	MSM File	5/16/2001 12:12 PM
MDAC27Docs.zip	8,428 KB	WinZip File	5/16/2001 12:38 PM
msk20en.zip	1,407 KB	WinZip File	3/17/2001 10:16 AM
PNG & MNG Construction Set …	4,008 KB	Application	9/11/2000 10:44 AM
soaptoolkit20.exe	1,466 KB	Application	4/26/2001 9:45 AM
soaptoolkit20samples.exe	1,024 KB	Application	4/26/2001 9:49 AM
Visual Studio .NET Guided To…	2,913 KB	Application	1/9/2001 4:58 PM
Web Express wbx32.exe	4,581 KB	Application	9/27/2000 6:07 PM
Windows 2000 Programming …	5 KB	Text Document	9/24/2000 3:09 PM

Details Column Selection

The Details view is one of the most flexible and functional views that Explorer provides. Some power users never use any other view because of the wealth of information this view provides. Figure 3.23 shows the default content of the Details view.

While the default view does contain a lot of information, the Details view has a lot more to offer. There are two easy ways to customize this view. First, you could simply right-click the column headers. You'll see a context menu containing the data the Details view can display. Check marks appear next to each choice that the Details view currently displays. Just select the new data you want to see, and Details view will display it automatically.

Another method for changing the content of the Details view is to use the View | Choose Details command. You'll see a Detail Settings dialog box like the one shown in Figure 3.24. Check the data options you want to see and then click OK. Notice that this dialog allows you to change the size of the fields and rearrange their order. You can do the same thing by directly manipulating the columns, but many people find this method easier and more precise.

FIGURE 3.24

The Detail Settings dialog allows you to configure the Details view.

Changing the View

The working environment you choose determines how productive you are and whether work is fun or a chore. Microsoft sets up Windows XP a certain way, which is the environment you see when you start Windows XP after installing it. Microsoft chooses the simplest and most limited set of features for the interface because they expect advanced users to modify their environment as needed for comfort.

We've already discussed many optimizations you can make to your setup. For example, you know about the various Explorer bars including Search, Favorites, and History. Now we're going to explore the interface further. You'll learn how to reconfigure your Start menu and generally change the appearance of the Windows XP environment.

Selecting and Configuring the Start Menu

Everyone uses the Start menu at some time during the day. No matter how well you organize your data, using a data-centric approach for working with Windows will only go so far. You need access to the Start menu in order to find applications that don't manipulate data (utilities), work with more than one file at a time (spreadsheets and word processors), or create a new data file.

Windows XP actually comes with two completely different Start menus. The first is the simple menu that you see when you initially start using Windows XP. The second is a classic type that looks similar to the one in Windows 2000. The following sections look at both menu types. Because the Start menu is such an important part of your daily Windows experience, you'll always want to perform this particular customization.

Selecting a Start Menu

Choosing a Start menu is relatively easy. Right-click Start and choose Properties from the context menu. You'll see a Taskbar and Start Menu Properties dialog like the one shown in Figure 3.25. Notice that there are two menu selections. If you choose Start menu, you'll see the simple Windows XP menu. Selecting Classic Start menu displays a Start menu that looks similar to the one in Windows 2000.

FIGURE 3.25

Windows XP offers two different Start Menus.

Note that both menus offer a Customize button. You click the Customize button associated with the selected menu to make changes to the appearance of the menu. As we'll see in the following sections, you can do quite a bit to customize both menus, but each offers significantly different customization options.

Aside from the physical appearance differences between the two Start menus, you'll also see differences in the way Windows maintains them. The Classic Start menu relies on the organizational skill of the user. Microsoft provides you with a certain organization, but you're free to move things without too much trouble. The Classic Start menu also presents all of the applications installed on your machine. It's up to you to find the one you need.

The simple, or Windows XP, Start menu presents only the applications you use most often. This means you not only avoid the clutter of the Classic Start menu, but applications can hide as well. You must manually select the More Programs icon to see all of the applications installed on your system. In sum, the simple Start menu is the optimal choice for novice users and those who don't require access to a broad range of applications. It really is the easiest interface to learn.

Simple Start Menu

The simple, or Windows XP, Start menu provides a simplified interface when compared to the Start menu in Windows 2000. You'll find that this theme also applies to the configuration issues for this Start menu. Figure 3.26 shows the General tab of the Customize Start menu dialog box.

As you can see, this tab offers access to features such as large and small icons. You can also choose the number of menu items on the Start menu. The Clear button will clear the list so you can start over. You can also choose to have Internet Explorer and Outlook Express icons on the Start menu.

The Advanced tab shown in Figure 3.27 provides a little more in the way of configuration options. Notice that this tab provides optimizations to the appearance of the Start menu. You can choose to animate the Start menu as it opens. While this feature looks neat, it does waste resources and processing cycles, which is why Microsoft probably turns it off by default. The Open submenus on hover option allows the user to move from item to item without clicking all the time. This is a real time saver. The Highlight newly installed applications option is also a good feature because it makes it easier for new users to find their applications.

The list in the middle of the dialog box is one of the more important configuration options. It allows you to choose the items that appear on the right side of the Start menu. You can't unpin or delete the items on the right side of the list, so this represents the only way to reconfigure that part of the menu. In some cases, you can also choose how items appear on the Start menu. For example, you can display the Control Panel as a menu or a link. If you choose the link option, Windows XP will open the Control Panel in a separate window.

FIGURE 3.27

The Advanced tab allows you to control the appearance, operation, and content of the Start menu.

The last configuration option on this menu is the recently used document list. Selecting this option displays the recently used documents on the Start menu, allowing the user to employ a data-centric approach when working with some types of applications, such as a word processor. The Clear List button allows you to clear the most recently used documents list. For example, you might want to use this option after you complete a project.

Classic Start Menu

The Classic Start menu offers the user little in the way of protection. You get all the clutter that Windows 2000 had, but you also gain complete access to all of your applications with little trouble. For this reason, power users will likely prefer the Classic Start Menu.

The customization process for the Classic Start menu is about the same as it was for Windows 2000. When you click Customize in the Taskbar and Start Menu Properties dialog, you'll see a Customize Classic Start Menu dialog box like the one shown in Figure 3.28.

As you can see, this dialog allows you to change the way the Start menu presents information. For example, you can choose to use a menu for the Control Panel (expanded form) or open the Control Panel in a separate window. One of the options that I always select is Display Administrative Tools. This option places an Administrative Tools folder within the Start menu. I can access the administrative tools I need without digging through the Control Panel to find them.

FIGURE 3.28

The Customize Classic
Start Menu dialog
looks very similar to
its Windows 2000
counterpart.

The Add and Remove buttons control content within the Start menu. You can add an application that normally doesn't appear on the Start menu, such as the Registry Editor (RegEdit.EXE). Just click Add and follow the prompts. I often wonder why Microsoft doesn't include a special option to automatically add these specialty tools to the Start menu.

The Advanced button opens a two-pane copy of Windows Explorer that's right at the Start menu. You don't have to search for the correct entry within \Documents and Settings.

The Sort button sorts all of the menu entries. You can sort individual entries by right-clicking the menu and choosing Sort by Name from the context menu. This button makes sorting considerably faster.

Finally, click Clear to clear the various lists. This button clears the most recently used documents list. The explanatory text is a little misleading, in this case, because it gives you the impression that the Clear button works with the History Explorer Bar as well. It doesn't; all this button clears is the Documents entry in the Start menu.

Folder Options

You may wonder why I didn't cover folder options as part of Windows Explorer. After all, the Tools | Folder Options command appears within that application. The fact is that Folder Options changes more than just the Explorer interface. Everything you do with this customization will affect the general Windows XP display as well. Every folder you work with will change unless you manually set the options for that folder. The following sections will explain each of the Folder Options dialog box features.

General Options

The General Options tab controls how you interact with folders. It contains three options. The first determines if you use Windows classic folder or enable Web content. If you select the Web content option, you'll see the Web Content pane that we discussed earlier. This pane appears in all folders, even the single-pane folders normally used to hold data files.

The second option determines if you open each folder in the same window as the existing folder or in a new window. Using the existing window tends to keep the display less cluttered. You can use the Back and Forward buttons to move between folders. Using multiple windows has the advantage of allowing you to compare the contents of folders with greater ease. It's also easier to move data between folders when you have a separate window for each one.

The third option determines if you use a single- or a double-click to perform a default action on a file or folder. The single-click method is faster, but the double-click method is the one that most people are accustomed to using. I also find that many people have a hard time displaying the context menu when using the single-click method. The technique you use depends on how attached you are to the traditional way of working with files and folders in Windows.

View Options

The View tab provides some important options. Figure 3.29 shows the options on this tab. Notice that this tab contains advanced features, such as the use of multiple colors for displaying compressed or encrypted files and folders. The tab also contains two options that affect your ability to see hidden files. The first are the two Hidden files and folders options. Select the Show hidden files and folders option if you want to see the majority of your files. You'll also need to clear the Hide protected operating system files option if you want to see everything on your drive. Some users are amazed at what Microsoft considers a protected operating system file. I won't go through all of the options in this list, but it's well worth your while to spend some time looking through them.

The View tab also includes the Like Current Folder and Reset All Folders buttons. Both of these buttons reset the folder settings for all folders on your system. If you select Like Current Folder, Windows will use the current folder as a template. The Reset All Folders button will set all folders to the Windows XP default settings.

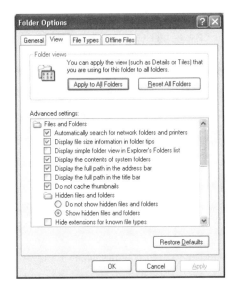

Figure 3.29

Use the View tab to control advanced viewing options.

File Types

The File Types tab contains a list of all of the file types registered on your system. The Details area will tell you about the file extension. For example, you'll learn which application will open the file extension.

The New and Delete buttons on this tab allow you to create new file extensions and to get rid of old ones. When creating a new file extension, all you need to provide is the extension. You can also associate the file extension with an existing file type. It's essential that you delete file extensions with care. Even if you remove the application that normally handles the file, Windows may supply a default application that you could use instead.

The Change button allows you to perform a simple association with the highlighted file extension. All you need to do is select an application to associate with the file. Unfortunately, this won't handle every file association need. In that case, you need to click Advanced. This opens the Edit File Type dialog shown in Figure 3.30.

As you can see, this dialog allows you to create complex file associations. You can use it to create multiple actions for each file extension. Creating a file association includes assigning a name to the action, adding an application to open the file, and deciding whether you want to use a simple filename pass or a complex Dynamic Data Exchange (DDE) opening scenario. We'll look at the process of working with complex file associations during Day 12. You can also use buttons in this dialog to edit existing actions or delete actions you no longer require. The Set Default button will set the highlighted action as default. Windows XP uses this action when a user double-clicks the file.

FIGURE 3.30

The Edit File Type dialog allows you to create complex file associations.

The final three options determine how Windows XP interacts with files retrieved from remote sources. I always check the Confirm Open After Download option to ensure downloaded files always receive a virus check. Showing the file extension can also help reduce the risk of opening a virus-infected file posing as data. Finally, the Browse in Same Window option determines if Windows XP opens a separate window to display this file.

Offline Files

Windows XP allows you to download content from the Internet for offline viewing. This allows you to take your time reviewing a document rather than rush through it in an effort to save money on connection time. However, you need some way to control the use of local hard drive space for offline file viewing, and that's where this tab comes into play. Figure 3.31 shows the Offline Files tab.

As you can see, most of the options are straightforward. You need to enable offline files before you can use them to store Internet content. It's also important to choose a synchronization strategy. Most people prefer to synchronize files after they finish their online session. That way, Internet Explorer synchronizes any new offline files before you log off. In addition, you'll waste less time waiting to access the Internet when you initially log on.

The next three options control how Windows XP interacts with the user. You can tell Windows XP to remind you about the offline status of your data at specific time intervals. Creating an Offline Files shortcut on the Desktop allows you to access the offline data faster. Finally, you'll want to encrypt sensitive offline data to keep it safe.

FIGURE 3.31

Use the Offline Files tab to control how Internet Explorer uses drive space to accommodate offline viewing of Internet content.

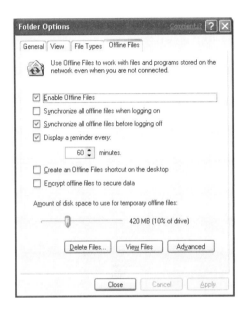

The slider near the bottom of the dialog is especially important because it controls disk space used to store offline data. As with everything else Microsoft does, they assume you want to use a full 10% of the drive to store offline content. In some cases, you may want to set that much space aside. However, in most cases, you'll want to experiment with lesser values first to see if you can use drive space more efficiently for other tasks.

Working with the Taskbar

The Taskbar is the area at the bottom of your display. It holds the Start menu at one end and the clock at the other. In between these two extremes, you see all of your applications. Many of us take this part of Windows for granted. The following sections will discuss the Taskbar in detail. You may find that you have new uses for this feature that you didn't think of in the past.

Toolbars

Everyone is familiar with the Quick Launch toolbar that appears on the Taskbar. However, few people realize that the Taskbar has three additional toolbars that you can use to create a more efficient environment: Address, Links, and Desktop. In addition to the standard toolbars, Windows XP provides the means for adding new toolbars of your own design. By adding just the right toolbars, you can create an environment where everything you need appears right at the bottom of your display. This section shows you how to accomplish this task.

Existing Toolbars

Windows XP comes with four standard toolbars. The Quick Launch toolbar is the only one of the four that most users see. It has a lot of potential that people never use. For example, I place my common applications, the ones I use every day, on this toolbar. I don't include applications that I start using a data file, just those that I start by themselves. Unfortunately, you can't just drag an icon over to the Quick Launch toolbar and expect it to work. You need to manually add the icon to the \Documents and Settings\<User Name>\Application Data\Microsoft\Internet Explorer\Quick Launch directory. It's more than likely that you'll need to restart your system to see the effects of the changes you make.

The Desktop toolbar is another one that I use regularly. If you use a data-oriented approach to managing your work, you can place the folders for your various projects on the Desktop and clear everything else off. Now, when you add the Desktop toolbar to the Taskbar, what you'll see is a list of your projects. Click on a project file, and it'll open. All you need to do is double-click a file, and you're ready to work.

The Address and Links toolbars come in handy for those who spend a lot of time on the Internet. The Address toolbar looks the same as the one you use within Windows Explorer. Just type the location you want to find, click Go, and Internet Explorer will open. Likewise, the Links toolbar looks the same as the Links toolbar in Explorer. Depending on how well you customize this particular feature, you may find that you don't open Internet Explorer for standard needs again.

Adding New Toolbars

As nice as the four toolbars that come with Windows XP are, you may find that you want something of your own design. Windows XP allows you to create toolbars of your own. The first step is to create a directory with the content of your toolbar. Add everything that you'll want to display on the Taskbar.

After you create the directory, you have to add its contents to the Taskbar. All you need to do is right-click the Taskbar and choose Toolbars | New Toolbar from the context menu. You'll see a New Toolbar dialog box. Find the directory you created in the hierarchical list and click OK. Windows XP will add the new toolbar to the Taskbar.

Window Management

Sometimes you create a mess on the Desktop and want to clean it up quickly. The Taskbar context menu contains four options for creating order from the chaos that is your Desktop:

- **Cascade Windows**   Lines the applications one on top of the other at an angle from the upper left corner to the lower right. This arrangement allows you to see all of the open applications and choose the one you want by clicking the title bar.

- **Tile Windows Horizontally**   Places the applications one on top of the other from the top of the display to the bottom. Windows XP resizes each application window to fit as much of it as possible within the allocated space.

- **Tile Windows Vertically**   Places the applications side-by-side from the left side of the screen to the right. Windows XP resizes each application window to fit as much of it as possible within the allocated space.

- **Minimize All Windows**   Clears the Desktop by minimizing all windows. You can select the window you want to view from the Taskbar.

Taskbar Properties

The Taskbar allows you to set certain operational parameters. For example, it allows you to decide if it stays out in the open all the time or hides until you need it. You access the Taskbar properties by right-clicking the Taskbar and selecting Properties from the context menu. You'll see the Taskbar tab of the Taskbar and Start Menu Properties dialog box shown in Figure 3.32.

As you can see, the upper half of this dialog controls how the Taskbar appears to the user. You can tell it to hide itself so that you can gain some additional Desktop space for your applications. Of course, when you do need the Taskbar, you'll want to ensure it sits on top of the other windows so that you can actually see it. Windows XP includes a new feature called grouping. We discussed this idea briefly during Day 1. Essentially, it places like items together so that you can more easily find them. After you arrange your Taskbar to your liking, you'll probably want to lock it so that none of the features are moved out of place by accident.

The bottom half of the display configures the Notification area (Taskbar tray for those upgrading from previous versions of Windows). The first option displays the Clock when checked. The second option determines if Windows XP hides icons in the Notification area when not needed. The idea behind this feature is that you'll free additional Taskbar space for application and other toolbar icons. Clicking Customize will display the Customize Notification dialog box, which allows you to set how Windows XP handles each icon.

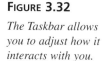

FIGURE 3.32

The Taskbar allows you to adjust how it interacts with you.

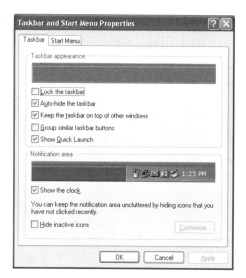

3

Date/Time Adjustment

Nothing much ever changes with the date and time adjustments for Windows. This dialog box has remained essentially unchanged from the very early days of the product. Double-click on the clock, and you'll see the Date and Time Properties dialog.

The Date and Time tab of the Time Properties dialog allows you to set the current calendar date manually. You can also set the time by using either the analog or digital clock.

The Time Zone tab contains a map of the world and a drop-down list of time zones. You select your current time zone so that Windows knows how to change the time as required. There's also an option that tells Windows XP to automatically compensate for daylight saving time.

Windows XP comes with a new feature. You'll find it on the Internet Time tab. This feature allows you to select a universal time coordinator (UTC) site online to synchronize the time on your computer. Every time Windows XP detects a live Internet connection, it will poll the site you select for the current time and date. If either value is incorrect, Windows XP will automatically adjust it for you.

Task Manager

Anyone who's used Task Manager in the past will recognize the Windows XP version. You use Task Manager to track applications on your system, monitor performance to an extent, and even check up on people using your system. The following sections tell you more about Task Manager.

Application Management

The Applications tab of the Windows Task Manager window contains a list of applications currently running on your system. The application information includes status. Most applications will simply say they're running. If you see an application with Not Responding as its status, you'll probably need to highlight it and click End Task. In short, Task Manager provides this method for recovering from an application error.

You can also use Task Manager to start a new application. Just click New Task and provide an application name. Likewise, you can highlight one of the tasks in the list, click Switch To, and Task Manager will give it focus.

One of the features that you won't see immediately will come in handy when we look at games during Day 7. Right-click any running application and look at the context menu. You'll notice a Go to Process entry that allows you to find this application on the Processes tab.

Working with Processes

There are two types of processes on your machine. Applications create the first type. Every application has at least one process associated with it. A process is a thread of execution. Think about it as a single task that you have given the application to do. The system creates the second type of process. Services normally create the processes, which execute in the background.

Monitoring processes on your system can tell you a little about system performance. For example, if you see one application grabbing all of the CPU cycles and memory, then you know that you need to monitor that application. Sometimes you need to end an errant process before it crashes the system.

The default Processes tab display includes the name of the process, the process owner, and the amount of CPU time and memory the process uses. You can add more columns by using the View | Select Columns command. For example, you might want to know how much time the application spends reading from and writing to disk. Task Manager provides columns that contain this information.

Monitoring Performance

Task Manager provides two tabs' worth of performance information. The Performance tab appears in Figure 3.33. It provides about the same information as previous versions of Windows. The Network tab is new. It provides statistics on your network, such as the number of bytes read and the current level of activity.

FIGURE 3.33

You can use Task Manager to perform some high-level performance monitoring.

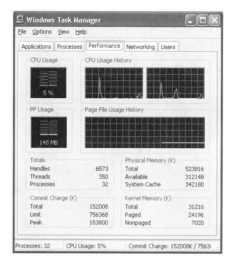

Notice that the Performance tab display in Figure 3.32 shows two windows for CPU Usage History. That's one window for each processor on the test machine. You can also set Task Manager to display just one window with the combined average for both processors using the options on the View | CPU History menu.

The View | Update Speed menu allows you to adjust the interval between performance monitoring checks. A longer interval enables you to see trends with greater ease. A shorter interval allows you to see instantaneous peaks in activity. This feature can tell you if a performance problem applies to a certain application. It also allows you to see the effects of system performance tweaks faster. We'll discuss the whole issue of performance in detail during Day 9.

Managing Users

Have you ever wondered who's lurking on your system looking for information they shouldn't have? Windows XP provides a new Task Manager tab that allows you to monitor user activity on your system with greater ease. The Users tab shows everyone who's logged into your system and their status.

This tab also allows you to disconnect, log off, or send messages to other users. You could use this feature to send all users connected to your machine a message that you'll shut down in a few minutes. After the interval is past, you could use the Disconnect or Log Off buttons to remove the users from your system before you shut it down. Theoretically, this should reduce the amount of information that's lost because someone doesn't get off your system in time.

Managing the Desktop

The last item on the agenda for today is the Desktop. You can completely change the appearance of the Desktop in Windows XP. All of the options you'll need are in the Display Properties dialog box. Just right-click the Desktop and choose Properties from the context menu to display the Display Properties dialog box. The following sections will explain each of the tabs in detail.

Using Themes

Themes have been around for quite some time now. Under previous versions of Windows, they allowed you to change the wallpaper on your system, assign some new sounds, add a new screen saver, and generally make your system more attractive. Windows XP takes the process much further. You can now change the appearance of the system as a whole by switching themes.

Windows XP ships with two themes. The first is the Windows XP theme that you'll see when you first start Windows XP after installation. The second is called Windows Classic. It changes the display to look like Windows 2000. Of course, to obtain the full Windows 2000 effect, you also need to change the Start menu and customize Explorer. Still, by providing two interfaces with one operating system, Microsoft gives everyone an interface they can work with.

Desktop Configuration

The Desktop tab looks much the same as it has in previous versions of Windows. However, Windows XP packs a little more into this tab. Initially, you'll see the wallpaper options. You can place new wallpaper on the Desktop and stretch it to fit, if necessary.

The Customize Desktop button takes you to the Desktop Items dialog box. The General tab contains all of the options required to display and change Desktop icons such as My Computer, Recycle Bin, and My Documents.

The Web tab of this dialog contains all that remains of Active Desktop. This tab allows you to add or remove items from the Active Desktop. You can also add new content. Given the low profile of Active Desktop and the paltry number of settings, Microsoft has probably set this feature aside as a bad idea.

Screen Saver Settings

The Screen Saver tab contains a picture of your monitor at the top. This monitor contains a preview image of the screen saver that Windows XP will use. Click the Settings button, and you can change the characteristics of the screen saver. The Preview button allows you to see what the screen saver will look like in action.

Windows XP adds a new feature to this display. The Return to Welcome Screen option forces the current user to log off when the screen saver starts. You still see the screen saver, but when the screen saver deactivates, you need to log back into the system as normal.

The bottom of the dialog contains a Power button. Click it, and you'll see the Power Options Properties dialog box. We'll discuss this feature during Day 11.

Changing Windows Appearance

The Appearance tab allows you to adjust Windows XP features, such as the color of the toolbars and the test used to display information. However, there's a new twist to this display when working with Windows XP. You'll notice a Windows and Buttons drop-down list box near the middle of the dialog box. This list box contains two entries: Windows XP style and Classic Windows. This setting adjusts Windows XP between a Windows XP and a Windows 2000 appearance.

If you select the Classic Windows option, you can choose a basic color scheme and font size. If you want to change the particulars of the display, you need to click Advanced. This displays the familiar dialog that you've used in the past to adjust individual screen colors and fonts.

The Effects button allows you to add or remove special effects from the system. For example, Windows XP uses the fade effect for menus and tooltips by default. You can also add 3D effects and font smoothing.

Adjusting the Video Settings

The final tab, Settings, determines the hardware settings for your display. This tab allows you to change the number of colors that the monitor will display and the resolution. An odd change from previous versions of Windows is that you can no longer use 256 colors. Windows defaults to using 16-bit color and above. We'll discuss the advanced settings for this dialog box during Day 10.

Summary

This has been one of the longer days in the book so far. Learning how to use every feature of the Windows XP interface can be a daunting experience. However, it's well worth your effort to try every feature. Learning how to perform tasks quickly frees you to concentrate on the things you like to do and reduces the time you spend worrying about problems with your computer system.

Q&A

Q: If Windows Explorer and Internet Explorer are essentially the same tool, why have both?

A: Windows Explorer and Internet Explorer started out as two separate tools. As Microsoft added features to both, their feature sets merged, making it difficult to tell one tool from the other. Today you only need to use the tool that best meets your work style. Some people still use both because they like having the separate interface for local and Internet browsing.

Q: How can I use offline content to make myself more productive?

A: The most obvious way is that you'll spend less money paying for connection time you don't need. However, using offline storage pays dividends in other ways. For example, you can pass the offline data to your laptop and read it on a plane during travel time. Offline data also comes in handy when you want to read a little and don't want to waste time creating a new connection every time you change pages.

Q: How much will I gain if I spend the time customizing my system?

A: You'll become more efficient in several ways by customizing your system. First, there's a gain in system performance. I found that getting rid of the elements that I didn't need sped up my system by about 5%. You'll also find that you can perform tasks quicker if you don't have to worry about the interface getting in the way. Finally, most of us work faster when we're in a familiar work environment. Customizing your system will keep things familiar so that you can work at your best.

Q: Is there any absolute method for configuring the Windows XP interface for best performance?

A: No, everyone's needs are different. Not only do you use different applications than everyone else, but you also see things differently than they do. There's no one right answer to the problem of Windows interface configuration, which is why it's so important to play with the interface to see what it can do.

Workshop

It's the end of the third day. By now, you've learned what Windows XP can do for you and how to install it. Now it's time to see how much you know about interacting with it. You can find answers to the quiz and exercise questions in Appendix A at the back of the book.

Quiz

1. What's an Explorer Bar? What is its purpose?

2. What are the names of the three toolbars, which of them can you modify, and how?

3. Why must you exercise caution when changing settings in the Folder Options dialog?

4. What are the four Taskbar toolbars?

Exercises

1. Play with Windows Explorer to learn how it works.

2. Choose a Start menu and customize it.

3. Experiment using and customizing the default Taskbar toolbars, and then create one of your own.

3

DAY 4

Getting Online

The Internet is playing an increasingly large role in the daily activities of most computer users. Businesses and home users alike get online to research information, talk with friends and associates, make purchases, and download software. Before you can garner the benefits of the Internet, you need a connection. So, one of the first things we'll discuss today is how to create an Internet connection.

Most people use a browser to interact with the Internet. After you establish a connection to the Internet, you'll use the browser to go various places (also known as *surfing*). Using a browser is one of the tasks we'll be discussing. Of course, other applications also allow you to interact with the Internet. We'll discuss NetMeeting today as part of the Internet experience. It's an application you can use to collaborate with other people online. This particular tool also works on an intranet or even a local area network (LAN). Tomorrow, we'll discuss Outlook Express, and you'll learn about Remote Desktop Connection on Day 6.

Internet Explorer provides a lot of flexibility in how you interact with the Internet. Knowing how to make changes to Internet Explorer's settings is important. For example, you can limit your security risks when working with certain Web sites by turning off specific features, such as scripting support. You can also protect your privacy by changing the privacy settings. All of these settings may seem confusing at first, but you'll quickly learn which ones to use for a given situation. Settings that you use often will become second nature after a while.

Our final concern today is learning to look for information online. The Internet is immense. Finding a needle in a haystack is child's play compared to finding the right piece of information on the Internet. Using the right search engines and techniques can save you considerable time and make your surfing experience a pleasure, rather than a chore.

Creating a Connection Using Internet Connection Wizard

You can create new Internet connections in several ways. The standard approach is to use the New Connection Wizard shown in Figure 4.1, which you'll access by using the New Connection Wizard icon in the Network Connections applet of the Control Panel. In most cases, however, you can save time and effort using the Internet Connection Wizard directly. For example, if you decide to create an entirely new connection, it requires four additional steps to use the New Connection Wizard. Part of the reason Microsoft made this change is to ensure that you can access an MSN connection with relative ease. However, the New Connection Wizard also places a needless burden on those who don't want to use MSN. With this in mind, we'll use the Internet Connection Wizard throughout the chapter.

FIGURE 4.1

The New Connection Wizard consolidates connection techniques and provides a new interface to the Internet Connection Wizard.

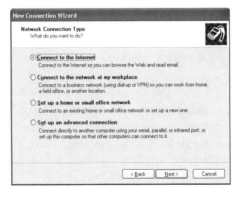

> **Tip**
>
> Using the MSN connection necessitates using Passport, a technology that stores your personal information on Microsoft's server. Many industry specialists consider Passport unsafe for a number of reasons. You can read more in Brian Livingston's column for InfoWorld (`http://www.infoworld.com/articles/op/xml/01/09/10/010910opl ivingston.xml`). Even if Passport keeps your data safe, there are privacy issues to consider. More than a few privacy organizations also feel that Passport is too invasive. In short, use the MSN option with care.

The Internet Connection Wizard, shown in Figure 4.2, is one of the first tools you'll use in creating a connection to the Internet. You access this tool by opening the Run dialog (Start | Run), typing ICWCONN1 in the Open field, and clicking OK. As you can see from the figure, you have three major connection methods from which to choose. When you start Internet Explorer the first time, you'll see the Internet Connection Wizard instead of the browser (unless someone has already created the connection). You can also access the Internet Connection Wizard from the Start menu and from the Connections tab of the Internet Properties dialog box (discussed in the "Setting the Internet Options" section).

FIGURE 4.2

The Internet Connection Wizard allows you to connect to the Internet in three ways.

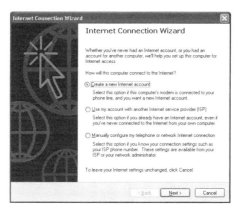

This tool helps you to create several kinds of connections, both direct and LAN-based. You can run the wizard as often as you like, but it's easier to obtain all of the information you need and fill everything out on the first pass. Unless you move regularly, most people use one or two Internet connections over long intervals.

The following sections will introduce you to the Internet Connection Wizard. You probably won't need to read every section, just those that pertain to the type of connection you want to create. For example, anyone creating a direct connection can skip the "Working with LAN Connections" section.

Note

> If the Internet Connection Wizard fails to create a connection at any time during the connection setup process, it will display an error dialog box. The dialog box will include options for checking the number you dialed, your modem properties, and the dialing properties. Check all three properties and try again. However, this tactic doesn't always solve the problem. If you're certain that all of your connection properties are correct, close and restart Internet Connection Wizard. In some situations, the Internet Connection Wizard will experience a problem creating a connection and will continue to fail until you restart the application.

Creating a New Connection

Many of you will begin your first Internet experience using Internet Explorer under Windows XP. This means that you won't have an Internet Service Provider (ISP), someone who provides a connection to the Internet. Therefore, the first step in creating a connection is to find an ISP in your area. This section discusses the Create a New Internet Account option shown in Figure 4.2. You can open the Internet Connection Wizard by opening the Run dialog (Start | Run), typing ICWCONN1 in the Open field, and clicking OK.

One thing I'd encourage you to do is shop around for an ISP. The market seems to keep prices about the same, but sometimes you find a deal on connection or other fees. In other cases, you'll find an ISP that provides more storage space for a personal Web site or other features. If you don't care about any of these special features and only want a connection with a low monthly fee, then using this route will probably produce the same results as calling everyone in town. The following steps show you how to create a new connection by first locating an ISP:

1. Ensure that you select the Create a New Internet Account option. Click Next. You'll see a dialog containing one or more Microsoft ISP referral telephone numbers.

2. Select a telephone number and click Next. Internet Connection Wizard will dial the selected number. If there are any service providers in your area, Internet Connection Wizard will show you a list.

3. Choose one of the ISPs and click Next. At this point, you'll see one of two screens. If you choose one of the vendors that normally appear in the Online Services

folder, you'll see a completion dialog. Otherwise, you'll see a sign-up dialog. This dialog allows you to provide your personal information to the ISP.

4. Fill in the required information and click Next. You'll see a list of billing options that will vary by vendor.

5. Choose a billing option and then click Next. You'll see another personal information dialog that includes credit card information.

6. Fill in the required credit card information and click Next. At this point, the Internet Connection Wizard will dial the ISP and complete your setup. Because this part of the procedure varies by ISP, you'll need to follow the instructions provided by the ISP to complete the process. After you complete this setup process, you'll be ready to configure your Internet mail account. Proceed to the "Creating an E-mail and Newsgroup Account" section of the chapter. Of course, you could always exit the Internet Connection Wizard now and create your e-mail and newsgroup accounts later.

Transferring an Existing Connection

Installing Windows XP when you have an ISP means transferring the current information to the new setup. Many ISPs will require you to set up your connection manually, a process that we discuss in the "Manually Creating a Connection" section. However, some ISPs (especially major carriers) allow you to transfer the information directly from the Internet. Only some of the ISPs that belong to the Microsoft Internet Referral Service support this feature, but it's worth checking. If your ISP doesn't provide this service, Internet Connection Wizard will automatically start the manual configuration process for you. This section shows you how to perform the automated account transfer. You can open the Internet Connection Wizard by opening the Run dialog (Start | Run), typing **ICWCONN1** in the Open field, and clicking OK.

1. Choose the Use My Account with Another Internet Service Provider (ISP) option on the Internet Connection Wizard dialog box shown in Figure 4.2 and then click Next. You'll see a dialog containing one or more Microsoft ISP referral telephone numbers.

2. Select a telephone number and click Next. Internet Connection Wizard will dial the selected number. If there are any service providers in your area, Internet Connection Wizard will show you a list.

Note

You'll see a My Internet Service Provider isn't Listed option at the bottom of the list. Select this option if your ISP doesn't appear on the list. Click Next to start the manual setup.

3. Choose one of the listed vendors and click Next. Internet Connection Wizard will dial an 800 number for the vendor you've selected and then display the vendor's identification dialog. This dialog will ask you for identification information that the ISP will use to find your account and download the required setup information to your computer.

4. Fill in the required information and click Next. The ISP will look up your setup information, download it to your computer, and then end the connection. Proceed to the "Creating an E-mail and Newsgroup Account" section of the chapter. Of course, you could always exit the Internet Connection Wizard now and create your e-mail and newsgroup accounts later.

Manually Creating a Connection

Manually creating a connection to the Internet isn't difficult, but it's more time consuming and you need more information to start the process. The manual installation process actually supports two connection types: *LAN* and *modem*.

When working with a LAN connection, you'll need to ask your network administrator about the particulars of your network. For example, you need to know whether your network uses a proxy server. If so, then you need to know the IP address of the proxy server to create a connection to it in some cases. We'll discuss some of these options in the "Working with LAN Connections" section of the chapter.

When working with a modem connection, you'll need the ISP telephone number and any special connection information. Your ISP should supply all of the required information. We'll discuss the modem connection process first, and then move on to the LAN connection process in the section that follows. You can open the Internet Connection Wizard by opening the Run dialog (Start | Run), typing **ICWCONN1** in the Open field, and clicking OK.

1. Choose the Manually Configure My Telephone or Network Internet Connection option on the initial Internet Connection Wizard dialog box shown in Figure 4.1 and then click Next. The Internet Connection Wizard asks whether you want to create a connection using your LAN or modem.

2. Choose the I Connect through a phone line and a modem option, and then click Next. Internet Connection Wizard will ask you to enter the telephone number used to access your ISP, as shown in Figure 4.3. This dialog also allows you to choose whether to use the area code in dialing the ISP. An area code might be necessary in rural areas where the ISP is outside of your normal dialing area. In addition, you'll need an area code when dialing into the ISP from outside of the area code's service zone.

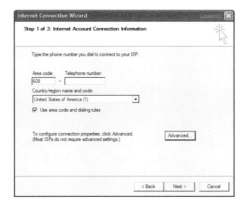

FIGURE 4.3

Internet Connection Wizard will ask you to supply the ISP's phone number as a minimum.

> **Note**
>
> Your ISP may provide you with some special configuration options for your connection. Click Advanced to display the Advanced Connection Properties dialog box. These configuration parameters include the kind of connection the ISP offers: point-to-point protocol (PPP), Serial Line Internet Protocol (SLIP), or Compressed Serial Line Internet Protocol (C-SLIP). You can also change the logon procedure (besides logon name and password) and both the IP and DNS addresses for the connection. In most cases, the default settings for these advanced options will work just fine. The only time you need to adjust them is if the ISP tells you to do so in the instruction sheet that you'll receive when you sign up for service.

3. Fill in the required information, make any required changes to the Advanced settings, and click Next. Internet Connection Wizard will display a dialog that asks for your user name and password.

4. Type the required information, and then click Next. Internet Connection Wizard will ask for a name for your new connection.

5. Type a descriptive name for the connection and then click Next. It's now time to set up your Internet e-mail account.

Working with LAN Connections

LAN connections are becoming common as users create larger networks. Some home networks even use LAN connections now so that everyone using the network can share a single connection to the ISP. This is especially helpful when you have a high-speed connection, such as a cable modem. You can open the Internet Connection Wizard by opening the Run dialog (Start | Run), typing ICWCONN1 in the Open field, and clicking OK. The following steps tell you how to configure a LAN connection:

1. Choose the Manually Configure My Telephone or Network Internet Connection option on the initial Internet Connection Wizard dialog box (shown in Figure 4.2) and then click Next. The Internet Connection Wizard asks whether you want to create a connection using your LAN or modem.

2. Choose the I Connect through a Local Area Network (LAN) option and then click Next. Internet Connection Wizard will ask you to enter your network specifics as shown in Figure 4.4. Notice that the default option is to automatically discover the proxy server and its settings. You can also use a script to access the proxy server or manually connect to it. It's unlikely that you'll need to check more than one of these options, although Internet connection Wizard allows you to do so.

FIGURE 4.4

LAN connections require knowledge of the LAN configuration.

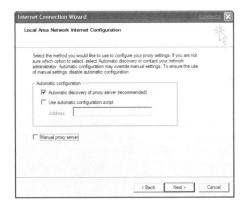

3. Select one of the proxy server configuration settings and then click Next. If you select the Manual proxy server option, proceed to step 4; otherwise, proceed to step 5.

4. You'll see a proxy server configuration dialog box like the one shown in Figure 4.5. Unless you have a large network, you'll normally supply a single address for all network functions. Click Use the same proxy server for all protocols if you want to use a single address. If you do have more than one proxy server, make sure that you fill in only those addresses that your server can handle. Modern servers normally support HyperText Transfer Protocol (HTTP), Secure, and File Transfer Protocol (FTP). Some servers also support Gopher, and a few support Socks. It's also important to provide a port number for each address. For example, HTTP connections normally use a port number of 80, and FTP connections normally use a port number of 21.

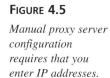

Figure 4.5

Manual proxy server configuration requires that you enter IP addresses.

5. Click Finish. You're ready to connect to the Internet. Proceed to the "Creating an E-mail and Newsgroup Account" section of the chapter. Of course, you could always exit the Internet Connection Wizard now and create your e-mail and newsgroup accounts later.

Creating an E-mail and Newsgroup Account

You'll use this section after you complete one of the four Internet connection sections. After you create a connection to the Internet, the Internet Connection Wizard will automatically start the e-mail and newsgroup account configuration process. It's important to understand that your connection is already operational. You can use Internet Explorer to access the Internet before you configure anything else. This procedure simply makes Outlook Express functional.

If you decide to skip the e-mail and newsgroup configuration process for now, Outlook Express will ask you to perform it the first time you start the application. When you start this procedure from Outlook Express, you'll start at step 3. The following procedure assumes that you're completing the process from the Internet Connection Wizard; the process may vary slightly if you begin by opening Outlook Express after completing the Internet Connection Wizard.

1. You should see the Internet Mail Account dialog box. This dialog allows you to choose between creating an e-mail account immediately and waiting until later. If you choose No at this dialog, you'll see a completion dialog. Just click Finish to complete the process. The completion dialog allows you to dial your new connection immediately, if so desired. The steps that follow assume that you want to set up an e-mail account.

2. Choose Yes and then click Next. If you have one or more existing e-mail accounts, Internet Connection Wizard will ask if you want to use one of the existing accounts

or create a new one. If you choose an existing account, the Internet Connection Wizard will ask you to accept the settings for that account and then show you the completion dialog. The steps that follow assume that you want to create a new account.

3. Select the Create a New Internet Mail Account option and then click Next. The Internet Connection Wizard will ask you for a display name. This is the name that other people will see when you send them e-mail messages.

4. Type the display name that you want to use and then click Next. Internet Connection Wizard will ask for your e-mail address. This is normally your login name, followed by an at (@) sign, followed by your simple mail transfer protocol (SMTP) server name. It looks something like this: jmueller@nowhere.net.

5. Type your e-mail address and click Next. The next dialog will ask you what kind of server you have: HTTP, Internet message access protocol (IMAP), or SMTP. In addition, you'll have to provide both incoming and outgoing server names. In the case of an HTTP connection, both servers will have the same name, so you'll just have to enter this information once.

6. Configure your Internet mail settings as needed and click Next. The next dialog will ask for your username and password. Use the username for your e-mail, not the one used to log onto the Internet.

7. Type your name and password and click Next. You'll see the completion dialog.

8. Click Finish; you're ready to go online.

 Note You now have an e-mail account configured. We still haven't created a newsgroup account for Outlook Express. You'll learn how to create newsgroup accounts and perform other Outlook Express tasks during Day 5.

Internet Connection Sharing Ins and Outs

Internet Connection Sharing (ICS) allows you to share a single connection with more than one person on the network. In most cases, all you need to do is perform a simple configuration task at the host machine. Start by right-clicking the connection in the Network Connections dialog and choosing Properties from the context menu. Select the Advanced tab, and you'll see a dialog like the one shown in Figure 4.6.

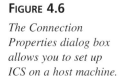

FIGURE 4.6

The Connection Properties dialog box allows you to set up ICS on a host machine.

Check the first option to allow other people to use your connection to the Internet. Microsoft assumes that you also want to connect to the Internet any time someone on the network makes a request. In addition, they assume that you want to allow everyone access to the connection settings.

Normally, it's a good idea to allow automatic connections, unless you want to connect every time someone wants to access the Internet manually. The only time this presents a problem is if you know the connection is down or if the host machine can't spare the resources to provide a connection. In these cases, you'll want to clear the second option on the Connection Properties dialog box.

It's almost never a good idea to allow access to the connection properties. Unless everyone on the network is a network administrator, you'll want to keep the settings private, which means clearing the third check box in the Internet Connection Sharing group.

Click OK and the host machine is ready to go. Windows XP may ask you to reboot the machine, but this isn't required in most cases. The only remaining step is to reconfigure each of the client machines to use a LAN connection, instead of a phone connection. You do this by following the steps in the "Working with LAN Connections" section of the chapter. Note that you'll always set the connection to discover the proxy automatically when using ICS.

Users do experience a few surprises when trying to use ICS. The first rule to observe is that ICS never works in the presence of a domain because a domain requires a Domain Name System (DNS) server. ICS provides DNS by default, one that you never need to configure because it's so simple. The problem occurs when the DNS for the domain and the DNS for ICS don't get along. If you want to create a shared connection for a domain, you'll need to set up Network Address Translation (NAT), a proxy server, and Remote Access.

Windows XP will always change the IP address for the host machine to 192.168.0.1. This means that the host machine address will differ from the client machines. In most cases, you'll need to reboot the clients to obtain a new IP address for them.

If the client machine still fails to use ICS, open a command prompt and type **IP CON-FIG**. Press Enter. You should see three entries. The first is an IP address that should start with 192.168.0. The second is a subnet mask. The third is the Default Gateway, which should have an entry of 192.168.0.1. In a very few cases, you may have to open Network Connections, right-click the LAN connection, and choose Properties. Locate the Internet Protocol entry and click Properties. You'll see the Internet Protocol (TCP/IP) Properties dialog box. Select Use the following DNS server address and type 192.168.0.1 in the Preferred DNS server field. Click OK twice and restart the client.

Some clients are simply stubborn and will refuse to cooperate. You can also try to manually enter an IP address in the Internet Protocol (TCP/IP) Properties dialog box, but this usually won't work. If the client were seeing the host, then it would have obtained an address automatically. However, I've seen this particular trick work in the past because the client didn't renew its IP address.

Another diagnostic is to see if you can reach the server at all from the client. Open a command prompt and type PING 192.168.0.1. Press Enter. Ping will test the server connection four times. If the connection is successful, you'll see entries like this one:

Reply from 192.168.0.1: bytes=32 time<1ms TTL=128

If you don't see the reply entry, it's time to do some diagnostics. We'll discuss diagnostics of various types during Day 21.

Working with Internet Explorer

Internet Explorer is your window to the Internet. It allows you to browse for information, read books, chat with others, shop, and perform other online tasks. Any other browser can perform the same tasks. However, because Internet Explorer comes with Windows XP, we'll discuss it today.

The following sections show you how to perform common tasks with Internet Explorer. You'll learn how the various commands work and what to do to keep your system safe. Internet Explorer is a simple application to use, but it does provide some complex configuration options that may cause problems. For example, just ensuring that your system is secure involves several configuration steps. In short, although you'll eventually find yourself moving around the Internet without much thought, configuration is one of those tasks that's less than straightforward to perform.

Using the Explorer Bars

Internet Explorer comes with all of the same Explorer Bars that we discussed for Windows Explorer in the "Explorer Bars" section of Day 3. It also includes some special Explorer Bars that will make your Internet Explorer better and help you find things faster. The following sections tell you about these special Explorer Bars.

Search versus Search the Web

Internet Explorer comes with two search interfaces. The first is the Search Explorer Bar that we discussed in Day 2. The second is Search Companion. Both interfaces enable you to find information on the Internet, but Search Component does it with an easier to use interface, while the Search Explorer Bar provides greater flexibility. You'll also find a third alternative in the form of Search the Web. You start this engine by typing a search string in the Address field. The easiest way to think about the differences in the two search techniques is that Search will look at more than one Web search engine, while Search the Web always uses MSN Search.

When you first start Internet Explorer, it uses the Search Companion interface shown in Figure 4.7. To search for anything online, type a keyword and click Search. Your Search Companion will begin digging for information.

FIGURE 4.7

Internet Explorer initially provides search services by using Search Companion.

While the Search Companion is cute, some people will tire of it rather quickly. Click Change Preferences, and you'll see a dialog box similar to the one shown in Figure 4.8. This dialog box enables you to get rid of the animated character by selecting Without an animated screen character, yet continue to use the Search Companion interface if desired. For that matter, you can click With a different character to choose a different animation.

FIGURE **4.8**

You can choose to change the Search Companion features.

Some people would prefer to use the classic Internet Search. To set up this option, click Change Internet Search Behavior. Select the With Classic Internet Search option, choose a default search engine, and click OK. Internet Explorer will take you right back to Search Companion in most cases. Close Internet Explorer and open a new copy. At this point, you'll see the classic Internet Explorer Search Explorer Bar.

The classic Internet Explorer version of Search Explorer Bar appears in Figure 4.9. Notice that it looks similar to the one found in Windows Explorer but that the functionality is different. This Search Explorer Bar looks for information on the Internet, so naturally some of the fields are different.

FIGURE **4.9**

Search Explorer Bar in Internet Explorer looks similar to the one found in Windows Explorer.

One of the smallest, yet most important, buttons on this Explorer Bar is Customize. Click Customize, and you'll see a Customize Search Settings dialog box like the one shown in

Figure 4.10. This window allows you to set how the Search Explorer Bar will look for information on the Internet. Notice that you can select from several search engines and even change the order in which Internet Explorer will search them. You can also select Search Companion as your default search dialog.

FIGURE **4.10**

Search allows you to customize the way it looks for data on the Internet.

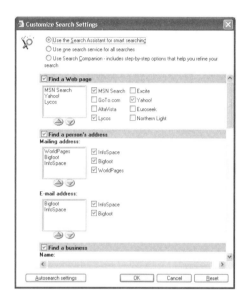

Tip

Google is one of the favorite search engines in use today, yet it doesn't appear on Internet Explorer's list of search engines. One solution to this problem is to use the Google Toolbar (http://toolbar.google.com) in place of the Search Explorer Bar. There's also an option to add the Google Toolbar to your browser (http://www.google.com/options/toolbar.html). You could always go directly to the Google Advanced Search site (http://www.google.com/advanced_search). If you don't mind editing your registry, you can always modify your browser to use Google by default (http://www.google.com/options/defaults.html). Microsoft also provides a Knowledge Base article at http://support.microsoft.com/support/kb/articles/q198/2/79.asp), but the instructions aren't complete for Internet Explorer 6x. It's better to use the instructions found on the Google Web site.

You don't need to open the Search Explorer Bar to use Search the Web. Simply type whatever you want in the Address field and Internet Explorer will open Search the Web

for you. Another way to use this search engine is to access it online at
`http://auto.search.msn.com/advanced.asp`.

Search the Web always brings up a simple Explorer Bar that contains a search field, a Go
button, and a link for Advanced Search. You only have a choice of one search engine,
MSN Search. Enter one or more search terms and click Go, and MSN Search will take
you to a list of topics that fit the search criteria. Click Advanced Search, and you'll see a
form like the one shown in Figure 4.11. The advanced page allows you to perform
searches that rely on region, date, language, domain, and other criteria. You can also
specify a media type, such as images, video, ActiveX controls, Shockwave, and
JavaScript.

FIGURE 4.11

Search allows you to customize the way it finds data on the Internet.

Tip

Search the Web does restrict you to a single search engine. However, you don't have to use MSN Search if you're willing to edit the registry by hand to add a different search engine. Look for the HKEY_CURRENT_USER\Software\Microsoft\Internet Explorer\Bar\Panes\ key. One of the subkeys (normally {3E16A332-0371-45E2-8001-0CCAA64059C5}) will contain the Search the Web entry. Change the URL value to your favorite search engine and the Title value to the engine name. We'll discuss the registry in depth during Day 12.

As you can see, while Search is the choice that offers the most flexibility, Search the
Web has more depth. You can use either search method, but Search is more likely to
produce good results for general topics, while Search the Web is better for in-depth,
focused topics.

Printing Tips

Internet Explorer 6, the version expected to ship with Windows XP, provides more in the way of printing than its predecessors did. For example, if you see a picture that you like, you can hover the mouse over the picture and see the tiny toolbar shown in Figure 4.12. This toolbar contains options to save the picture to any location on your system, print the picture, send it to someone else, or open the Pictures folder (the default location for saves).

FIGURE 4.12

This tiny toolbar appears when you hover the mouse over a picture.

 Note

You must enable scripting to allow the picture toolbar to appear. The script is internal to your Internet Explorer setup and will run even on Web sites that don't have a script associated with them.

The reason I'm discussing pictures by themselves is that they represent the hardest element to print properly. Depending on the capabilities of your printer, the output from a direct print can range from humorous to downright terrifying. If you don't know what I mean, try printing a picture that contains mostly dark colors. It will end up a hideous variant of its old self with most of the details hidden from view. Likewise, pictures that are long or narrow tend to look almost like cartoons when you print them. The secret is to know when to output the picture to your printer directly from Internet Explorer and when you need to send it to a graphics application first. Here are some tips you can try to get pictures to look right:

- Always save the picture to disk instead of outputting it directly if the picture is light, dark, long, or narrow. Use a good graphics application to output the graphic instead, modifying the color palette as needed for a good result.

- Always use the best output setting for Internet graphics. The printer may work slower, but you won't have to reprint the image to get something useable.

- Try the system's image color management (ICM) first and then the printer's ICM. Don't attempt to print graphics without any color management at all. Save problem images to disk and manipulate the color palette as needed to obtain good output.

- Set the ICM Intent setting of the Printer Advanced Options dialog box (accessible through the Advanced button found on the Paper/Quality tab of the Printer

Preferences dialog box) to Pictures first, Graphics second. The Pictures setting results in higher quality output for most images.

- Use the Centered setting for the Printable Area field of the Printer Advanced Options dialog box. This setting reduces aspect ratio problems in the printed output. It also reduces the chance that part of the picture will be cut off.

- Check the Printer Advanced Options dialog box for any hidden picture and graphic settings. For example, Internet Explorer always selects the wrong quality setting for my color printer. Using the picture setting allows me to print graphics that normally look terrible when using the default settings.

- Use a high quality paper. Cheap paper with poor surface qualities always reduces output image quality.

- Printing text or a combination of text and graphics isn't a picnic with any browser. The formatting tags used by the Web site owner often make a difference between a page that prints well and one that doesn't. Many small business and individual user Web sites use simple formatting, which always prints well. However, news sites and those sponsored by large companies often use complex arrangements that won't print on a standard page or print in such a mangled form as to make the output unreadable. Pages that use an abundance of frames and tables are often the most problematic of all. Here are some tips that you can follow when working with text or a combination of text and graphics:

- Always wait for all graphics to download. Refresh the page if any graphics appear fuzzy or partially rendered. The Web site owner designed the page with fully rendered graphics in mind, so printed output may look less than appealing without graphics in place.

- Use a non-frame version of the Web page whenever possible. A page that uses frames is unlikely to print well because of the way the design forces certain elements to appear in specific places.

- Look for a printer-friendly version of the Web page. This is especially common on news sites. The designers realize that their pages won't print well, so they provide the printer-friendly version for your use. Unfortunately, the little graphic or link used to access this version can be small and hard to find, so be prepared to look.

- Download problematic pages. The act of downloading the page often helps by getting rid of elements that won't print well. Some of the elements won't appear on the printed output, but you'll still capture the content.

- Try viewing the page with all scripting turned off. In some cases, the Web site designer tries to create fancy effects using scripts. Unfortunately, these effects don't print well.

- Grab a screenshot of the page and print it as a graphic. Use Alt+Print Screen to place the browser window on the clipboard. Place the graphic within your favorite graphics application using Edit | Paste. Edit as needed to format for the printout.

- Try checking the Print background colors and images option found within the Printing section on the Advanced tab of the Internet Options dialog box (accessed using the Tools | Internet Options command). In some cases, Web designers will include critical display elements as background, rather than foreground, images. Internet Explorer normally prints just the foreground in the interest of clarity.

- Adjust your printer settings. We've already discussed some printer settings in this section of the chapter. The same printer settings that affect graphics will often affect text output as well.

Sending Links

You've just seen the most exciting Web site known to man (or woman, for that matter). How do you tell your friend about it? You could copy the link from the Address field and paste it in the e-mail, but Internet Explorer provides an easier way to perform this task.

Use the options on the File | Send menu to send a copy of the current Web page to your desktop or e-mail. Internet Explorer even supports two methods of sending the information. Use the Page by E-mail command to send the entire page to your friend or the Link by E-mail command to send just the URL.

Sending the entire page takes more time and uses more bandwidth than sending just the URL. Use the URL method for Web pages that are unlikely to change immediately. The page method works best for information that will change quickly. For example, some sites include a thought of the day or other content that changes on a daily basis.

Sometimes you want to send just a graphic on a page, rather than the entire page. We saw in the previous section that hovering the mouse over a graphic displays the tiny toolbar shown in Figure 4.12. Select the Send button, and you'll see a Sending Image dialog like the one shown in Figure 4.13.

FIGURE 4.13

Use this dialog to determine how you'll send a graphic to someone else.

Notice that you can send an original or optimized graphic. Using the optimized settings makes the graphic smaller and reduces the quality of the image. This process also reduces the size of the file and makes it easier to download. Use the Show more options link to change the way Internet Explorer optimizes the graphic. The Settings dialog box allows you to adjust both the size and the quality of the image. Of course, sending a small, low quality image is fast, but sometimes results are less than perfect. Figure 4.14 shows an example of a picture that uses the smallest size and the lowest quality setting. In this case, the picture turned out well, but your results may vary. The original picture is 45KB, while the optimized version uses a mere 16KB.

FIGURE 4.14

Small, low quality images transmit quickly but may not look very good at the other end.

Importing and Exporting Cookies and Favorites

Those of us who use more than one machine know what it's like to have settings on one machine that you don't have on the other. A user relies on the Favorites they store on a machine to find Web sites quickly. In some cases, such as using Passport or shopping online, cookies are also important. Internet Explorer makes it easy to export these settings from one setup and import them into another.

Use the File | Import and Export command to start the Import/Export Wizard. Click Next to get past the initial Welcome dialog box, and you'll see a series of import and export selections as shown in Figure 4.15.

Select the Favorites Export option, and you'll see a copy of your Favorites list. You can choose to export everything (the default) or a single folder. The dialog box doesn't support multiple folder selections, and you can't export a single shortcut. You must export Favorites an entire folder at a time.

FIGURE 4.15

The Import/Export Wizard will present you with a series of import and export options.

No matter which of the four options you select, the next step is to select a directory. Windows XP will suggest your personal folder, but you can browse to any folder on the system. After you click Next, the final screen tells you the Import/Export Wizard is ready to finish. Click Finish to complete the task.

Understanding Web Page Properties

Most of us surf the Web without knowing much about the Web pages we visit. In some cases, this isn't a problem because the information isn't critical—we're visiting just for fun. What happens, though, if you visit the site looking for information that will meet business or other critical needs? How do you know that the information you're seeing isn't ten years old and no longer valid today? While Internet Explorer can't help validate the quality of the data you receive from the Web site, it can tell you a little about the page that you're viewing.

Right-click the Web page and choose Properties from the context menu. You'll see a Properties dialog box similar to the one shown in Figure 4.16.

You already know the contents of several of the lines. For example, you know the URL of the page. The size property tells you how much storage space the page will require. You can also determine if the page uses encryption. The most important feature is the date. This tells you the last time the author modified the Web page. In most cases, the date is a good indicator of the timeliness of the data it contains. If the author hasn't changed the page for a long time, it's almost certain the information it contains is out of date as well.

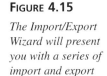

Note

When working with a site that does use encryption, verify that the Connection field of the Properties dialog contains information about the encryption method used. You should look for the highest encryption level possible. Although 40 bits is okay, 128 bits is much better. Also, look for a recent version of secure socket layer (SSL) support. Any version 3.0 or above is usually acceptable.

FIGURE 4.16

Every Web page has a Properties dialog box that will tell you a little about the content.

FIGURE 4.17

Make sure that you check the validity of the certificate and the issuer name when working with secure sites.

Notice the Certificates button near the bottom of the Properties page. Click Certificates on secure pages to discover the identity of the issuer. Figure 4.17 shows a typical certificate. Checking this information helps you determine if you trust the secure connection created by the Web site. You also need to consider other factors, such as the reputation of the vendor and the time he's been in business, but a good certificate is the place to start.

The Details tab of the Certificate dialog box contains information that most of you won't need to worry about unless you're paranoid about the issuer's identify. The Certification Path tab contains a diagram of how this certificate relates to those above it in the path. This tab is the one you should look at if you want to see the hierarchy of certificates used to validate this one. The bottom of this tab also tells you if the certificate is valid.

Working with Related Links

Internet Explorer provides a feature called *Related Links*. This is another way to search for Web sites. However, you're using the content of the current Web site to search for more. In most cases, using this feature will provide you with access to more Web sites with similar content after you find one that you like.

You activate the Related Links feature by finding an initial Web site and then using the Tools | Show Related Links command. A Search Explorer Bar will open, and Internet Explorer will begin the search. If the search engine finds additional sites with similar content, they'll appear in the Search Explorer Bar pane so that you can select them.

Favorite Sites

If you spend any time at all on the Internet, you'll eventually find that some sites require frequent visits. Creating a shortcut to that site means that you won't have to spend time remembering the URL for `http://www.whatchamacallit.com`. Storing these shortcuts in the same place makes them easy to find, and organizing them keeps clutter at bay. Welcome to the world of Favorites. This is a special folder that Internet Explorer uses to store shortcuts to your favorite places online. The following sections will help you understand how to work with your Favorites list.

Browsing Offline

Imagine that you visit the same Web site every day and use it to access a static set of links to other places. The Web site might even be a page on your company's network that you visit while you're on the road. Wouldn't it be nice if you could see the page instantaneously, even when you don't have a connection to the Internet? That's what offline browsing will do for you. It places a copy of the Web page on your hard drive that Internet Explorer will use when a connection is unavailable. Using offline browsing can save time and definitely reduces frustration.

4

Setting up a Web page for offline browsing is easy. Open the Favorites menu in Internet Explorer. Locate the Web site that you want to view offline. Right-click its entry in the menu and select Make available offline from the context menu. You'll see an Offline Favorite Wizard dialog box. Click Next to move past the introduction screen.

The next dialog box you see will ask if you want to download additional pages if this page contains links. The wizard will ask how many levels you want to go beyond the initial page if you do decide to download additional pages. You have to be careful about this setting because going too many levels deep could incur a huge penalty in hard drive space—more than many people realize until their hard drive is suddenly full. After you select some download options, click Next.

The next screen will ask when you want to synchronize the content. You can manually synchronize the content (the default setting) or create a synchronization schedule. The synchronization schedule will download the Web page after the number of days you specify have passed at the time you specify. You could set the synchronize feature to download the content every seven days during your lunch hour for a weekly update that you won't even notice. Select the synchronization options and click Next.

Many Web sites require that you log in. The next screen asks for your user name and password for the Web site. Make sure that you enter the name and password you use for that specific site, rather than the name and password used to log onto the Internet or Windows. This is the last step. Click Finish, and Internet Explorer will download the contents of the Web page. Now, whenever you need to look at the Web page, it will be available.

Adding a Page to Your Favorites

As you browse Internet sites, you'll want to create links to those that you use most often. Adding a Web page consists of locating it onscreen and then using the Favorites | Add to Favorites command to display the Add Favorite dialog box. The first thing you'll want to do is click Create In so that the dialog box looks like the one in Figure 4.18. Otherwise, all of your links will appear in the same place.

Notice the Make available offline option. This allows you to make the site available offline without using the wizard (unless you want to). The offline content will use the default settings, which means that only the Web page you select is downloaded, and it will only synchronize when you manually ask Internet Explorer to do so. Click Customize if you want to change any of these defaults.

Some Web sites have terrible names. They don't describe what the Web site is about, and you're almost certain to forget why you placed the Web site in your Favorites list. Make sure that you give the Web site a name that you can understand before you save it to disk.

FIGURE 4.18

Click Create In so that you can organize your favorites as you create them.

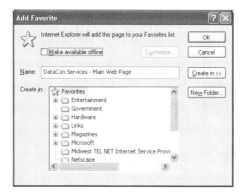

It's also important to keep your Favorites organized. Otherwise, you'll find yourself with a huge list of links and no way to figure out which one you want to use. The hierarchical structure shown at the bottom of the Add Favorite dialog box allows you to choose a location for your new link. You can also add a new folder if this is a unique link and you expect to create several more like it.

Organizing Favorites

Despite your best intentions, the Favorites folder will need occasional reorganization. You'll need to move links around to reflect your current way of working with the Internet, delete old links, and create new folders to hold project-specific links. Consider it a spring-cleaning task, and you'll be ahead of most of us.

Begin organizing your Favorites by using the Favorites | Organize Favorites command. You'll see the Organize Favorites dialog box shown in Figure 4.19.

FIGURE 4.19

The Organize Favorites dialog box allows you to move links around and delete those you don't need.

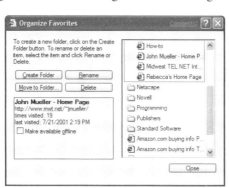

The four buttons in the Organize Favorites dialog box work much as you'd expect. Highlight a location and click Create Folder to add a folder in that location. Likewise, if you don't like the name of a link or folder, click Rename and type a new value for it. The Delete button doesn't permanently delete the highlighted item; you'll find it in the Recycle Bin if you change your mind. The Move to Folder button changes the position of the highlighted item in the Favorites hierarchy. When you click this button, Internet Explorer displays a Browse for Folder dialog box. Find the new location for the item or folder and click OK. Internet Explorer will move it to a new location.

Notice this Make available offline option in Figure 4.19. This is only available for links because you can't download a folder. When you check this option, Internet Explorer adds a Properties button. Click Properties to change the download schedule and other offline properties. This method of setting offline availability actually allows more flexibility than using the Offline Favorite Wizard. You can control the size of the download and even send yourself an e-mail when the content changes as shown in Figure 4.20.

FIGURE 4.20

The Link Properties dialog box allows you to refine offline-viewing features.

Setting the Internet Options

Microsoft tries to make Internet Explorer extremely flexible. You can change many Internet Explorer features by accessing the Internet Options dialog box shown in Figure 4.21 using the Tools | Internet Options command.

FIGURE 4.21

*You configure Internet
Explorer using the
Internet Options dialog
box.*

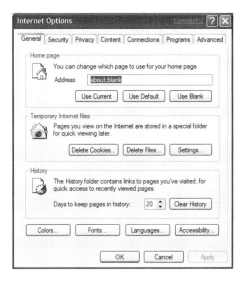

In the following sections, we'll discuss each of the tabs within this dialog box. We won't discuss every option on every tab. However, you'll walk away with enough information to make Internet Explorer a truly flexible environment for your Internet browsing needs.

General

The first option on the General tab shown in Figure 4.21 allows you to change how Internet Explorer starts. You can type any address that you want in the Address field. For example, if your company has an intranet site, you can tell Internet Explorer to start every session by checking that page. Internet Explorer also provides three default destinations. Use Current will change the address to whatever site you're viewing. Use Default will take you to the MSN Web site. Finally, Use Blank starts Internet Explorer but leaves the choice of initial destination up to you. This is the option to use if you start from a different location every day. Otherwise, you have to waste time stopping the default page from downloading.

The General tab allows you to change the way Internet Explorer interacts with Web sites. Every Web site you visit creates temporary files. Eventually, the number of temporary files will increase until you've used up the hard drive space on your system. Of course, this is a less than optimal way to browse the Internet, so you need some method for clearing the old temporary files quickly. Delete Cookies and Delete Files eliminate the majority of the temporary files for you. Click Settings if you want to tell Internet Explorer how to automatically delete the files. Internet Explorer will watch the amount of disk space you set aside and delete the oldest files as needed.

Internet Explorer also tracks the sites you've visited. This feature works with the History Explorer Bar to allow you to find places you looked at but didn't put into Favorites. The problem is that these links also consume space (albeit a small amount of space). Many people don't use the History Explorer Bar, so this space is still wasted. You can clean up the history files by clicking Clear History. Keeping the history files clean is a matter of setting Days to keep pages in history to 0.

The final four buttons—Colors, Fonts, Languages, Accessibility—control the Internet Explorer environment. You can choose how Web pages appear in your browser, at least to a certain extent. The Web page designer may set specific options, so the view you see is the one that the designer wants you to see. You can override the color choices that the designer makes by using the options on the Accessibility dialog. In fact, if you take the extra time to create a style sheet, you'll find that you can control almost every aspect of the Web page appearance.

Security

Internet Explorer uses a zone security setup. For example, when you go online, that's one zone. Working on a local intranet is another zone. You can also add individual URLs to either a Trusted Sites or a Restricted Sites zone. Internet Explorer assumes that any address that doesn't go through the proxy server is an intranet address, but you can also add addresses to the Local Intranet zone.

Adding sites to any of the zones is easy. Select the zone you want to modify and click Sites. You'll then see a properties dialog for that zone. To add sites to the Trusted Sites or Restricted Sites zone, type the URL for the site and click Add. Highlight a site and click Remove to delete it from a particular zone. The Local Intranet zone requires a little more work. Open the Local Intranet dialog box by clicking Sites and then clicking Advanced. The resulting dialog box looks and acts the same as the one for the Trusted Sites and Restricted Sites zones.

Each zone maintains separate security settings, so you need to adjust each one separately if you want to make a general change to all of them. You can use either Custom Level or Default Level security. Click Default Level, and you'll see a slider bar that goes from High to Low. The Low setting is almost the same as not setting security at all.

Using the Custom Level option allows you to adjust each security setting individually.

Click Custom Level, and you'll see a Security Settings dialog box containing entries such as Download signed ActiveX controls and Installation of desktop items. Most of these entries allow three values: enable, disable, and prompt. The prompt setting is the best one to use if you're unsure about the effect of a security setting. Internet Explorer will ask for verification every time it runs into a situation where the security rule will take effect. After you see how the security setting will affect your browsing, you can choose to enable or disable it.

Privacy

Most people who used pre-6.0 versions of Internet Explorer will remember that the privacy settings used to appear in the Security Settings dialog box. Internet Explorer 6.0 attempts to simplify the security settings by placing privacy settings on a separate tab. The Privacy tab contains two controls: a Privacy Preferences slider and an Import button.

The Privacy Preferences slider moves from Low to High, with Medium being the default setting. At a high level, Web sites can't even store cookies on your system. This means you can't do certain activities, such as shop online or use many of the Microsoft Web sites. Most online shopping systems rely on cookies to keep track of your purchases, along with other information.

The medium security level allows more flexibility. For example, Web sites can now store cookies on your system as long as they have an acceptable privacy policy. Both the medium and high security levels report when a site doesn't have an acceptable privacy policy in place. Just look at the status bar, and you'll see an eye with either a yellow or red circle if the policy isn't satisfactory. Double-click the eye, and you'll see a dialog like the one shown in Figure 4.22.

FIGURE 4.22

Internet Explorer tells you when a Web site fails to provide an adequate privacy policy.

Note that in this case, the Web site I'm viewing does have an acceptable security policy, but the banner ads have privacy problems. In fact, since I started using this feature, I've found that many Web sites try to follow the rules. The banner ad sites are the ones that flood me with cookies and try other odd things when I visit the main site. For this reason, I keep my privacy policy set to high until I go to the checkout of a Web site I trust for purchasing goods or to a responsible vendor for technical information.

Content

The Content tab helps you control the information viewed by Internet Explorer users. It controls three main areas of Internet Explorer functionality. The first section is the Content Advisor. Web sites supposedly provide input similar to that used by the movie industry that tells Internet Explorer what type of content the site contains. If the site has content that the Content Advisor settings disallow, the user can't view the information. In reality, the system doesn't work. Pornography sites seldom advertise that they contain "R-rated" material.

The second section controls your certificates. Click Clear SSL State if you want to clear the certificates from Web sites from your local cache, which forces Internet Explorer to download a new copy of the certificate the next time you visit the site. At first, this feature may not seem important, but it's essential if you shop online regularly. By forcing a new download of the certificate, you can flush out crackers posing as the site in question. The Certificates button allows you to check any certificates issued to you for identification to other parties. You use certificates to exchange information with secure Web sites and to encrypt personal e-mail. Finally, click Publishers if you want to view the people, publishers, and certification authorities that your system trusts. Normally, you don't have to worry about this setting unless someone issues a false certificate (as happened with Microsoft recently) or you no longer want to trust an individual.

The third section controls the storing and distribution of personal information. Internet Explorer allows you to create a profile that helps identify you to other people. Consider it a form of electronic business card. You also have access to an AutoComplete feature. This feature allows you to fill in forms without retyping the information. For example, you can use it to add your name and address to a form with a simple click.

Connections

The Connections tab contains information about the connections that you have with the Internet. Click Setup, and you'll start the Internet Connection Wizard, which we discussed in the "Creating a Connection Using Internet Connection Wizard" section of the chapter.

The middle of the Connections tab contains a list of network connections for your machine. Normally, this section contains dial-up connections, but it could contain other connection types depending on how you set up your system. You can add new connections using Add, or remove old connections using Remove. If you have more than one connection, you can use Set Default to decide which connection to use automatically. Click Settings if you want to reconfigure a connection. For example, you may want to change the name and password information or set the connection up to use a proxy.

This part of the Connections tab also contains three options. Select Never dial a connection if you have a LAN connection setup (such as when you're using ICS) and never want to use a dial-up connection. Select Always dial my default connection if you have a single workstation setup or this is the host machine for an ICS setup. Finally, Dial whenever a network connection isn't present tells Internet Explorer to check for a network connection first and then dial if the connection isn't present. In theory, this option should provide you with the best of both the LAN and dial-up connection worlds. In practice, Internet Explorer often makes the wrong choice, which makes creating a connection frustrating at best.

Click LAN Settings to display the Local Area Network (LAN) Settings dialog box. This dialog box contains the same settings that we created in the "Creating a Connection Using Internet Connection Wizard" section of the chapter for a LAN connection. It allows you to change your selections about automatically detecting the server and the address to use for a proxy.

Programs

Like most browsers, Internet Explorer relies on "helper" applications to perform certain tasks. The Programs tab contains entries for tasks such as HTML editor, e-mail, newsgroups, and calendar. These helper applications are important because they allow you to open links and perform other tasks with Internet Explorer. The drop-down list boxes on this tab allow you to change the programs used for helper tasks from the defaults normally associated with Internet Explorer to other applications you may have installed on your system.

Advanced Options

The entries on the Advanced Options tab are a hodgepodge of settings that don't appear within other dialog boxes or that Microsoft considered too dangerous for the average user. You can modify everything from accessibility features to security settings using the options on this tab. In fact, we already discussed one such option in the "Printing Tips" section of the chapter.

The best advice I can offer when using these options is to think twice before checking many of the options. In some cases, it might be a good idea to maintain a log of the changes you make because some settings can have unintended results. For example, you may choose to disable script debugging in the interest of security, only to find later that you have to reboot your machine after visiting some Web pages because you can't break out of errant script code.

You'll want to spend time reviewing all of these options. In some cases, Microsoft made some dubious decisions regarding the default settings. For example, you'll find a Check for publisher's certificate revocation option in the Security section that's cleared by default. This means someone can offer you a revoked certification (one that's bad) and Internet Explorer will never know the difference. I always check this option even though it slows online access when using secure Web pages.

This is also the tab to check when it comes to types of encryption technology that you want to use. For example, Internet Explorer assumes that either SSL 2.0 or SSL 3.0 is an acceptable encryption technology. You may want to ensure that Internet Explorer only uses SSL 3.0 to better protect your system. Likewise, Internet Explorer assumes that you don't want to use Private Communication Technology (PCT) encryption. Although this is a less used technology, it's also simpler and a little more secure than some SSL implementations.

One of the more interesting sections on this tab for laptop users is Multimedia. Internet Explorer assumes that you want to play everything. You can keep these options selected, but you'll find that your battery will last longer and those around you will be less irritated if you turn the multimedia options off. This is especially true in close quarters, such as in an airplane, or areas where electricity may not be available, such as a car.

Using NetMeeting

NetMeeting has appeared in various forms in Windows since Windows 95 (and perhaps before). It's a collaboration tool that works only within the Windows environment. However, you can "call" others over a LAN, wide area network (WAN), metropolitan area network (MAN), or the Internet, making this product extremely versatile. You can use NetMeeting to perform a variety of tasks including the following:

- Offer remote assistance.
- Chat.
- Transfer files.
- Collaborate with others.
- Provide training.
- Hold impromptu meetings.

Normally, you can access NetMeeting using the NetMeeting entry in the Programs\Accessories\Communications folder of the Start Menu. However, Microsoft has recently begun to rethink their collaboration strategy and thinks that you may prefer a Web-based alternative. This new alternative requires an Internet connection, and it won't work if you have an intranet setup using your LAN. This is one reason I think that NetMeeting is an important product to keep. We'll discuss this Web-based alternative in the "A New Way to Collaborate" section during Day 6.

If you find that you can't access NetMeeting using the Start menu, you can always use the Run command to start CONF.EXE, the file that starts NetMeeting. The following sections will help you set up NetMeeting and show you how to use some of the most important features.

Getting Set Up

The first time you start NetMeeting, you'll have to perform some setup. NetMeeting will need to know more about you and your system to create an environment that's helpful for collaboration. The following steps will help you complete the setup process. I'll assume that you're starting at the initial Welcome screen that tells you what you can do with NetMeeting.

1. Click Next to get past the Welcome screen. NetMeeting will ask you to enter your name, e-mail address, location, and any comments. Many companies will use the Comments field to include a title or other descriptive information for the person. The Location field could contain something as simple as your location within the company or could include city and state for larger companies.

2. Type your user information and then click Next. You'll see a dialog that asks about directory server information. Microsoft makes a NetMeeting directory available. This directory allows you to find people with like interests online. However, using the directory means having an Internet connection available. The directory is only useful if you don't know whom you'll contact. Most companies using NetMeeting don't require this support, so you'd clear the first option (which looks up information in the directory) and check the second option (which prevents NetMeeting from publishing your user information online).

3. Select the directory options and click Next. NetMeeting asks what type of connection you'll use. This connection information not only determines how NetMeeting will connect, but how it optimizes communication. For example, NetMeeting understands that sending full video over a slow dial-up connection may not be feasible.

4

4. Select a connection option and click Next. NetMeeting will ask if you want to add shortcuts to your desktop and Quick Launch toolbar. These options are especially important if you can't find NetMeeting in the Start menu.

5. Choose one or more shortcut options and then click Next. At this point, you need to tune your audio settings. NetMeeting allows you to use voice communications instead of typing everything. Of course, you'll have to have a microphone attached to your system to make this feature work.

6. Click Next to get past the first audio tuning screen. You'll see a device selection screen.

7. Select record and playback devices and click Next. You'll see a playback test screen.

8. Test and adjust the playback volume and then click Next. You'll see a record test screen. If you don't see any input, make sure that your microphone connects to the correct input on the back of your machine (most have both a microphone and a line input connection). Verify that the microphone is on.

9. Test and adjust the record volume; then click Next. You'll see a success screen.

10. Click Finish. Figure 4.23 shows the main NetMeeting display (with a call in session).

Figure 4.23

The main NetMeeting display provides access to a variety of communication features.

Making and Receiving Calls

Making calls is easy. Simply click the telephone (Place Call) icon. NetMeeting will display a Place Call dialog box. Type the name of the person or machine you want to contact and choose one of the entries in the Using field. The Automatic setting usually first looks at the network and then searches the directory for the requested entry.

Note   Always use the machine name when making network calls. NetMeeting won't be able to identify contacts by individual name.

Click Call. You'll see a dialog stating that NetMeeting is waiting for the response from the machine you called. The recipient will hear a telephone ring and see a dialog saying that you want to contact them. If they click Accept, NetMeeting will establish contact. On the other hand, clicking Ignore displays a message on the caller's machine saying that you didn't accept the call. If you call but the other party doesn't answer, NetMeeting will display a non-acceptance message.

Using the Whiteboard

The Whiteboard feature is one of the better accessories for NetMeeting. It allows you to draw ideas on a whiteboard that everyone in the meeting will see. This application looks similar to Microsoft Paint but includes some interesting features as show in Figure 4.24.

FIGURE 4.24

The Whiteboard feature of NetMeeting allows you to draw your ideas for everyone to see.

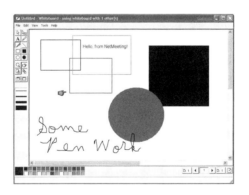

As you can see, the Whiteboard includes the standard drawing features, such as hollow and filled shapes. You can create simple drawings by using a combination of lines, squares, and circles. In addition, you can add text of any shape using the Text tool.

Some added features make the Whiteboard more than a standard drawing tool. For example, any text you create with the Text tool is an object. You can select it by using Selector tool and moving it around. This also applies to all of the shapes and even the items you draw with the pen.

NetMeeting also includes two new tools. The first is the highlighter. It allows you to highlight text or other objects in the same way that you would on paper. The second is the pointer. It shows up as the purple hand in Figure 4.24. If you want to point to something, just move the hand to the right area.

So, what happens when you run out of "virtual paper" due to screen real estate? Whiteboard allows you to add more pages to the current session. You can use the arrows in the lower right corner to move from page to page. Whiteboard also allows you to save your creation to disk to view offline or to resume a conversation later.

Using Chat

There are a number of ways to communicate with other people by using NetMeeting. For example, you can use voice communication by default the second it establishes a connection. However, while using voice communication over a network is quite doable; using it over a dial-up connection may not produce the intended results. That's where Chat comes into play.

You start a chat by clicking Chat at the bottom of the main NetMeeting display. The Chat dialog contains an upper window that holds the contents of the conversation, a Message field you use to type your messages, and a Send To drop-down list box.

To create a new message, type the content in the Message field, select one of the entries in the Send To field, and click Send Message. The message will appear in the upper window with your name attached so that the recipient will know who sent the message. Use the View | Options command to display the Options dialog if you want to change the message presentation. For example, you can add the time and date to the entries or place all of the information on one line. As with all other NetMeeting applications, you can save the Chat session to disk.

Sharing Applications

One of the best features of NetMeeting is the capability to share applications. You can use this feature in a collaborative, training, or assistant mode. Used for collaboration, two people can work on a document together, even if they're miles apart. For example, collaborating on a word-processed document can prove difficult unless you have a feature such as the one found in NetMeeting.

In the training mode, a teacher can perform a task and then watch the student perform the same steps. The advantage is that the teacher doesn't have to watch over the student's shoulder. In addition, training need not occur with both people in the same location.

Finally, the assistant mode allows you to do everything from showing a user the right set of steps to perform a task to modifying the setup of a machine. The assistant mode is handy because it allows you to see what the user sees, making problem resolution more likely. In addition, you can tell if the problem the user sees is due to poor usage techniques.

You begin sharing an application by starting it and loading any files you need. Click Share Program on the main NetMeeting dialog box and you'll see a Sharing-Programs dialog box. Choose the application you want to share and then click Share. Everyone will see the application at this point.

There are a few caveats to remember when sharing applications. First, only one person has control of the application. If you don't allow control of the application within the Sharing-Programs dialog box, no one can request to use it. The application runs slowly compared to its usual pace because NetMeeting redraws the screen on everyone's machine. Finally, remember to keep the size of the application display small enough so that everyone can see it. Determine the maximum size screen for everyone in the session in advance and then reduce the size of the application screen slightly to accommodate everyone's needs.

Summary

Today we spent time learning about Internet Explorer. As you now know, Internet Explorer is a powerful tool for browsing the Internet. It allows you to find new information, track the sites you like, determine if you trust a site, and perform tasks such as downloading files to your hard drive. Internet Explorer also allows you to send information to other people. You can send links or pages using e-mail, download the page to your hard drive, or print the page and send it using regular mail.

We also talked about NetMeeting. This collaboration tool relies on Windows as an operating system. You can start a conversation with anyone who has NetMeeting installed as long as you know where to find them. NetMeeting provides collaboration tools, such as the Whiteboard and a chat mode, and allows you to share applications with other people. You can use it across any network connection, both local and the Internet.

Q&A

Q: What do I do if Internet Connection Wizard fails to provide a list of ISPs in my area?

A: This problem won't happen very often, even in rural areas. However, if Internet Connection Wizard does fail to turn up a list of ISPs, try your local telephone company first. Many local telephone companies also provide Internet service as part of their offerings. If the local telephone company doesn't offer Internet services, try your long distance carrier or talk to someone at a local computer store to see if they have any suggestions. Your local yellow pages will likely have listings as well.

Finally, you can try TheList (http://www.thelist.com) an Internet resource for those searching for an ISP.

Q: What do I do if a Web site asks if I want to install a certificate before I see the Web page?

A: Generally, Webmasters won't ask you to make this decision, so a Web site asking you to install the certificate is already suspect. The dialog that asks if you want to install a certificate should contain a link or button that allows you to view the certificate. When you view the certificate, ensure that you trust the issuer. You may want to contact the issuer and confirm that the certificate is valid before you accept it. Always use a proactive approach to security, especially when it appears that the remote server is doing something out of the ordinary.

Q: How do I view Web pages written in other languages or using other alphabets?

A: Ensure that you download the proper language set from Microsoft's Web site. Normally, Internet Explorer will ask if you want to do this. If it doesn't, you need to enable the Font Download option on the Security Settings dialog box. (Access this dialog box by using the Custom Level button found on the Security tab of the Internet Options dialog box.) You may also need to use the View | Encoding command to select a different encoding method.

Q: What do I do if an entry on the Programs tab of the Internet Options dialog box is blank?

A: A blank entry means that Internet Explorer couldn't find an application to perform this helper task on your system. One of the most common blanks is for the Calendar entry. If an entry is blank, your system will still perform as expected; you just won't be able to perform that task when using Internet Explorer. In short, don't worry about it, but remember to add the application to the list if you install one later.

Workshop

It's the end of the fourth day. Today we've learned about creating Internet connections, working with shared connections, and using Internet Explorer. Now it's time to see how much you know about Internet connectivity. You can find answers to the quiz and exercise questions in Appendix A at the back of the book.

Quiz

1. Are you required to create an e-mail and newsgroup account at the time you create the Internet connection?

2. Is it true that Search the Web limits you to a single search engine using MSN Search?

3. What entries should you look for in the Connection file of the Properties dialog box when working with Internet Explorer?

4. What's the main problem in setting the number of link levels too high when downloading offline content for Internet Explorer?

5. Which levels of SSL support does Internet Explorer use by default?

6. What special features does the NetMeeting Whiteboard offer?

Exercises

1. Create an Internet connection for your machine. Make sure that you configure an e-mail and newsgroup account as well.

2. Decide with search engines are the right ones for your needs.

3. Start creating a Favorites folder and organize it as needed to keep information readily available.

4. Use NetMeeting to create an online communication session with someone else.

4

DAY 5

Using Outlook Express

Yesterday we discussed the intricacies of using Internet Explorer to explore the Internet. The ability to find information you need online is a start in the right direction, but it doesn't fulfill every need. You need Outlook Express (or another) e-mail application to fulfill the need to communicate directly with others who have similar interests. Using an e-mail application frees you from making appointments to talk with other people at a time when they're available. It's more like writing a letter to them; they can read the letter and respond at their leisure.

Today we'll discuss how you can use Outlook Express to fulfill your e-mail needs. We'll talk about both e-mail (private communication) and newsgroups (public communication). Most people would assume this means getting a couple of accounts and starting to write. However, you need to know how to set up those accounts before they become useful. In addition, you'll want to protect your privacy by communicating in the right way.

We'll also discuss an unfortunate trend in online communication, spamming, which is the work of a spam artist. *Spam* is an unwanted communication from an individual who usually wants to sell you something or damage your machine in some way (sometimes both). The problem with spam is so severe that some countries have made it illegal, and many countries are looking for ways to put an end to it. You don't have to be the spam artist's next target. Today, I'll show you how to avoid the spam artist and still participate in discussions with others online.

Getting Started with Outlook Express

We began by creating a connection to the Internet yesterday. This involved finding an ISP and configuring Internet Explorer to use the account the ISP provides. The "Creating an E-mail and Newsgroup Account" section contains the information you need to begin using Outlook Express. Yesterday, I gave you the choice of creating an e-mail account immediately or waiting until later. Today is later. The first step in using Outlook Express is to create an e-mail account.

After you create an e-mail account, Outlook Express will open, and you'll see a display similar to the one shown in Figure 5.1. This display includes a Web page that directs you to various Outlook Express functions. You can bypass this page by using configuration settings we'll discuss later. You can move both the menu and the toolbar around by using the same technique we used for Windows Explorer. However, you can't hide either one of them. The other two windows contain the default set of folders and your list of contacts. We'll see later that you can add folders as needed to organize your messages.

FIGURE 5.1

Outlook Express begins with a simple display for checking your e-mail.

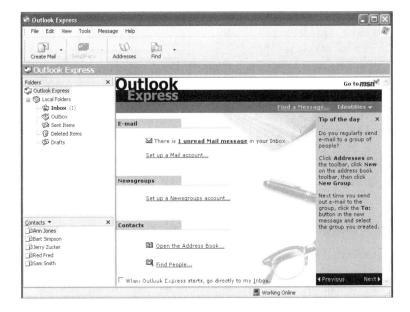

Creating Newsgroup Accounts

Note that the display only shows an e-mail account. If you want to access newsgroups, you'll need to add one or more newsgroup accounts. The following steps show you how to create a newsgroup account:

1. Click Set up a Newsgroups account. The Internet Connection Wizard will appear and ask you to enter your name. This is your display name, the one that everyone will see. If you decide to use "Heavy Dude" as your handle, this is where you'll enter it.

2. Type a name and then click Next. The Internet Connection Wizard will ask you to enter an e-mail address. Everyone from a newsgroup will reply to this address. If you type your real address, every spammer will also know how to contact you and send you unwanted e-mail. Some people enter JoeNoSpam@NoSpam.MyISP.Net. Because the spam artist uses scripts to generate their e-mail lists, this technique can keep them at bay. You can also blank this field when you complete the wizard.

3. Type your e-mail address or something that will thwart spammers. Click Next. The Internet Connection Wizard will ask for your news server address. Your ISP will provide this information when you sign up for an Internet account.

Note

> The Internet News Server Name dialog box also contains a My news server requires me to log on option. Check this option if your ISP provides you with a name and password to log on to the news server. It's unusual that an ISP would go this route. Don't confuse this option with the one that enables you to log on to the connection. Normally, password-protected news servers are run by other companies. For example, some companies use password-protected news servers for product testers. If your ISP requires a name and password for the news server, check this option and click Next. The Internet Connection Wizard will ask you to type your user name and password. You'll notice that Outlook Express also supports Secure Password Authentication (SPA).

5

4. Type your news server address and click Next. You'll see a success message. At this point, you have a newsgroup connection, but no idea which newsgroups that connection supports.

5. Click Finish. Outlook Express will ask if you want to download a list of newsgroups. This is a prerequisite for subscribing and viewing newsgroup content. You only need to perform a complete newsgroup download once.

6. Click Yes. Outlook Express will begin downloading the newsgroup list. This process can take a long time, so you might want to pet your cat or get a cup of coffee. Outlook Express will display a Downloading Newsgroups dialog box during this process. An average news server hosts between 100,000 and 105,000 newsgroups, but the number can vary. Outlook Express will display a Newsgroup Subscriptions dialog box like the one shown in Figure 5.2 when it completes the download process.

FIGURE 5.2

The Newsgroup Subscriptions dialog box allows you to manage your subscriptions.

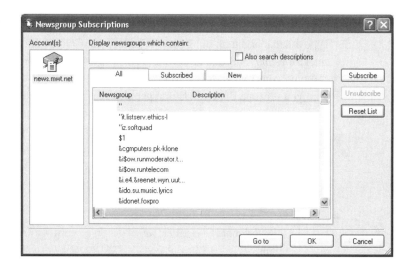

7. Subscribe to one or more newsgroups and then click OK. You're ready to spend some time in public forums. (We'll discuss the issue of subscribing to newsgroups in the next section.)

If the newsgroup list download fails for some reason, click Reset List in the Newsgroup Subscriptions dialog box. This will restart the download process. Unfortunately, Outlook Express always begins downloading the list from the beginning; you can't resume a newsgroup list download.

Subscribing to and Viewing Newsgroups

News servers support tens of thousands of newsgroups. Finding the one that you want would seem like looking for a needle in a haystack. In fact, given the odd names that newsgroups use, finding a needle in a haystack might be easier. At least you'll know what you're looking for when you see it.

Fortunately, Outlook Express provides an easy way to find the newsgroups that you want to view. Click Newsgroups to display the Newsgroup Subscriptions dialog box, which contains a list of available newsgroups and their Descriptions; this is the first place to start. Just type one or more keywords that seem to fit what you need. For example, if you like role-playing games, you might type "rpg" in this field. You don't want to type both "rpg" and "gamer" because that would eliminate all the newsgroups. It's important to type one word, see the effect, and then decide if you need a second word. You'll also want to use lowercase letters, in most cases, because Outlook Express uses a case-sensitive search mechanism.

Note

> The Newsgroup Subscriptions dialog box contains an Also search descriptions option. This option is supposed to provide better search capabilities for Outlook Express. However, this option normally won't produce any discernable results because most news servers don't provide descriptions. If you click this option, Outlook Express will ask to download the newsgroup list again. Make sure that you want to wait for the results before clicking Yes.

After you find a newsgroup that you want to try, highlight it and click Subscribe. You'll see an icon appear next to its entry in the list. The newsgroup will also appear on the Subscribed tab. Click OK after you've subscribed to all of the newsgroups that you want. You'll see the news server and the newsgroups you subscribed to appear in Outlook Express.

FIGURE 5.3

Viewing a newsgroup is as simple as clicking on the entry you want.

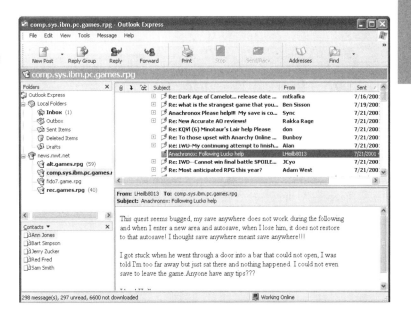

5

Viewing newsgroups after you subscribe is a matter of clicking the newsgroup entry. Outlook Express will download the headers from the newsgroup. A *header* is a subject. It would take too long for Outlook Express to download every message, so it downloads just the subjects so that you can see if you're interested. Figure 5.3 shows a typical example of a newsgroup entry.

Notice that the upper pane contains a list of subjects and that the lower pane contains the message for the currently highlighted subject. All you need to do is highlight a subject that looks interesting in the upper pane and read it in the lower pane. At this point, Outlook Express is completely ready to use. We'll explore newsgroups in more detail later today.

Using Outlook Express Mail

One of the first tasks you'll perform with Outlook Express is reading, creating, and sending e-mail. Personal communication is one of the biggest benefits of having an Internet connection for many people. The following sections will examine the e-mail functions of Outlook Express. We'll discuss the details of how you send and receive messages.

Connecting to a Mail Server

You've already configured Outlook Express for e-mail connections. However, until you establish a connection with a mail server, you won't see any new messages. The easiest way to get your e-mail is to click Send/Recv Outlook Express will establish a connection with the mail server and download all your mail. Notice the down arrow next to the Send/Recv button. Click the down arrow, and you'll see that you can also choose to send or receive messages only. We'll see in the "Outlook Express Options" section that you can also configure Outlook Express to send and receive messages automatically.

Working with Folders

Organizing your messages is an important part of using Outlook Express, especially if you depend on e-mail to conduct business. Figure 5.1 shows the default folder setup for Outlook Express. By the time we add newsgroup support in Figure 5.3, there are more folders. You can add more folders on top of the defaults that Outlook Express provides. For example, you might want to add folders for each of your projects so that you can keep the e-mail sorted, and your project organized.

To add a new folder, right-click anywhere within the Local Folders hierarchy (including Local Folders) and choose New Folder from the context menu. You'll see a Create Folder dialog box. Type the name of the new folder in the Folder name field and choose a location for the new folder. Click OK, and Outlook Express will add the new folder.

If the new folder doesn't appear in the right place or if you want to move the folders around to organize them better, simply click the file and drag it to the new location. You can also delete and rename folders as needed by right clicking the folder and choosing the appropriate option from the context menu.

After you have the folders you need in place, you can move e-mail messages to them. The easiest method is to click the e-mail and drag it to the storage folder. However, you might want to create a copy of the e-mail, rather than move it. In that case, right-click the e-mail and choose Copy to Folder from the context menu. You'll see a Copy dialog box that contains a hierarchical display of the current Local Folders setup. Choose the folder you want to use for the copy or click New Folder to create a new destination for the copy.

Sending an E-mail Message

You can use any of several methods for sending an e-mail to someone else. The first method is to create a new e-mail by clicking Create Mail. You'll see a New Message dialog box like the one shown in Figure 5.4. At the top of this dialog box are fields for listing who will receive the message. The Subject field allows you to enter a subject for the message so that the recipient can tell at a glance what the message contains (at least at basic level). Finally, you'll see the message area.

FIGURE 5.4

The New Message dialog box contains everything you need to send a message.

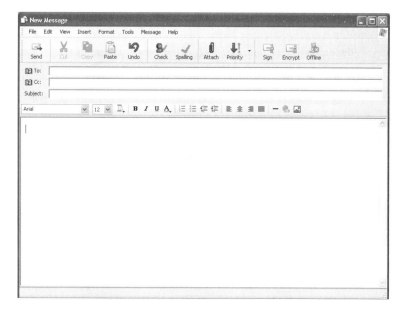

5

The toolbar buttons for the New Message dialog box allow you to perform most common tasks. Generally, I don't use the menu commands unless I need to format the message or perform some other special tasks. The Send button sends the message to the recipients that you've added to the top of the message. You can set up Outlook Express to perform a spelling check before you send the message, or you can click Spelling on the toolbar. The Check button allows you to check all of the recipients' names against those in your address book.

Tip

> You may notice that the spelling checker sometimes fails to work after you install a new version of Outlook Express or another application. In many cases, this is because the new application has deleted, corrupted, or over- written one or more files. An application could also break the spelling checker by changing one registry entry. The fix for this problem is relatively straightforward. Use the information found in the Knowledge Base article at `http://support.microsoft.com/support/kb/articles/Q224/1/76.A SP` to fix the problem. Make sure that you close and then restart Outlook Express to see if the changes work.

Click Attach if you want to send an attachment to someone. You'll see an Insert Attachment dialog box that allows you to locate the attachment on your machine or the LAN. Note that many network administrators set their network up to discourage the use of attachments because of the viruses they can contain. It's normally a good idea to place attachments in an encrypted ZIP file or secure them in some other way.

Outlook Express does include some security features. You can digitally sign messages by clicking Sign. Click Encrypt if you want to encrypt the message. Both of these features require you to get a digital certificate from a third party, such as VeriSign. This organiza- tion verifies your identity and then creates a digital certificate that you can use for verification. Any recipient can then view the digital certificate and verify your identity.

The Offline button allows you to compose long messages offline. When you click Send, Outlook Express will create a new connection and transmit the message. You can also assign messages a priority of low, normal, or high by using the Priority button. Low and high priority messages receive a special icon. You can use the priority levels to help people sort their e-mail by level of importance.

One trick you should know when creating a list of recipients is the way Outlook Express handles recipients. The New Message dialog box shown in Figure 5.4 shows a To: field and a Cc: field. These fields allow you to enter a list of primary recipient names and those who only receive copies of the message. Both sets of e-mail addresses will appear in the message, so everyone knows who received the message. However, a third type of recipient you should use in some situations is the Bcc (blind carbon copy). Click To: in the New Message dialog box and you'll see the dialog shown in Figure 5.5.

FIGURE 5.5

Use the Select Recipients dialog box to create Bcc recipient lists.

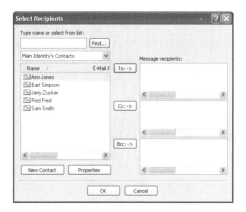

You'll need to select a name from the contact list and then click Bcc:-> to place it in the Bcc: list. A Bcc recipient receives the e-mail, but his or her e-mail address doesn't appear anywhere within the message. This means that you can send a message to a group of Bcc recipients and only you will know their e-mail addresses. This is an important tool as privacy becomes a larger concern. Hiding the e-mail address of friends when you send them a cartoon or inspirational message is important because it keeps their identities private and thwarts the efforts of spammers.

Managing Your Address Book

Outlook Express uses an address book to store information about your online contacts. The address book comes in handy in a number of ways. For example, when you type a name into the recipient list for a message, Outlook Express will look for a matching entry in the address book. Outlook Express will automatically complete the name for you when it finds a matching entry. Of course, you'll want to verify the name is the one you want to use. You can also use the address book as a simple contact manager because it includes address and telephone information. In fact, other users can send you their electronic business card and Outlook Express will add it into the address book at your request.

The first order of business is to add names and e-mail addresses to the address book. You can do this by right-clicking a message and selecting Add Sender to Address Book from the context menu. This only adds the sender's e-mail address and a generic name derived from it. You still have to add other information to the entry manually.

You can also use the Tools | Address Book command to display the Address Book dialog box. This dialog box contains two panes in an Explorer-like configuration. The left pane contains a hierarchical display of contact lists, and the right pane contains the contacts and groups within those lists.

The menu associated with the New button allows you to create three kinds of entries: folders, groups, and contacts. Use folders to organize your contact list. All you need to do is move a contact from the main list to the new folder. Groups allows you to send messages to more than one person using a single recipient entry. Finally, contacts are individual recipients of your messages.

After you create a new contact or highlight an existing contact and click Properties, you'll see a Properties dialog box similar to the one shown in Figure 5.6. Notice that there are tabs for entering complete contact information.

FIGURE 5.6

The Properties dialog box allows you to enter contact information.

The Name tab contains the person's full name and e-mail address. Only the default e-mail address appears on the recipient line for an e-mail message, but you can store other e-mail addresses as needed. The Home and Business tabs contain physical contact information, such as the person's address and company information. These two tabs also contain a field to type the contact's personal and company Web site URLs. The Personal tab allows you to enter the name and birthday of the contact's spouse and children. You can also enter an anniversary date. The Other tab contains notes and a list of the person's group affiliations. Use the NetMeeting tab to hold contact information, which includes the conferencing server and conferencing address. Finally, you can store digital IDs for each contact, making it possible to exchange encrypted mail.

The Address Book dialog box toolbar contains buttons that allow you to delete and print contact information. You can print both individual contacts and entire groups. The print output is flexible. You can print groups as phone lists. Individual contacts can appear in phone list, memo, and business card format. Outlook Express provides options for configuring the preferences for each print format. For example, you can print long entries in landscape versus portrait format. You can also set the printer to perform dual-sided printing (if the printer supports this function).

Click Find People if you need to locate someone online. This feature works the same as the Search for People option of Windows Explorer. In fact, both applications use the same form. You can search for people using a variety of services, including VeriSign and Yahoo.

The final Address Book button is Action. You can perform three actions with most contacts: Send Mail, Dial, or Internet Call. The Dial option uses a phone connection, and the Internet Call relies on entries on the NetMeeting (or other conferencing) tab.

Tips for Safe E-mail Usage

Receiving an e-mail can make or ruin your whole day. While bad news is a part of life and good news is always welcome, you'll want to avoid the third type of e-mail. Messages that appear to contain something interesting but end up giving your machine a virus aren't any fun for anyone. In addition, most virus makers aren't content to ruin just your machine; they want to ruin the machines of all your friends as well. In short, this is one time when sharing isn't caring.

E-mail is essential for most Internet users. You use e-mail to conduct business and keep in contact with both friends and family. However, it's important to maintain a safe environment during your e-mail sessions. That way you enjoy the pleasure of e-mail without the pain. The following tips will help keep your e-mail sessions fun:

- Don't open attachments from people you don't know. A new contact has no reason to send you an attachment. If you receive an interesting-looking e-mail from someone you don't know, delete it. That's the best way to keep your system safe from harm. Yes, your curiosity will surely suffer indignities with this approach, but it's better than getting a virus.

- Enable file extensions by clearing the Hide extensions for known file types option found on the View tab of the Windows Explorer Folder Options dialog box. Many virus writers try to convince you that their file is safe by hiding a harmful extension with a good one. For example, MyVirus.TXT.JS will appear as MyVirus.TXT in Outlook Express, if you hide extensions. This JavaScript file could do just about anything to your system. However, when you open the file, you'll think it's a text file. The strange thing is that the file will actually look like a text file until it's too late to do anything.

- Carefully examine attachments received from friends and family. If you have any doubts, keep the message closed until you confirm that they sent the message. Remember that virus writers depend on the trust relationship you develop with family members to spread their files.

- Save all attachments to disk and perform a virus check. A friend or family member may have sent you a virus-filled file by mistake. You also want to keep your virus checker updated so that it can actually spot any viruses that come your way.

- Keep your system secure. Use a personal firewall to keep crackers at bay. Check your system for unusual activity on a regular basis (I do it once a week). Keep all of your security software updated. Make sure that you use strong passwords, only send non-executable files to other people, and generally watch for security problems as you work online.

Okay, this is fine for security, but you need to consider some other issues when working with e-mail. We discussed one of those issues, privacy, in the previous section. You owe it to those you communicate with on a regular basis to keep their privacy intact. After all, you wouldn't want other people to spread your name and e-mail address all over the Internet. This means using the Bcc entry when sending messages. You should also remove message headers for forwarded content. That way, the only e-mail address that you send with a message is yours.

Working with Multiple Accounts

Outlook Express allows you to create multiple accounts for the same installation. Each account has separate e-mail and newsgroup sections associated with it. This allows you to keep the particulars of each account separate. You should use this setup to keep your work account separate from your home account, or the children's account separate from that of the adults.

Use the File | Identities | Add New Identity command to create a new identity. You'll see the New Identity dialog box. Outlook Express requires a name for the identity as a minimum. You can also check Require a password and type a password if you want to secure the identity. After you configure the new identity, click OK. Outlook Express will ask if you want to switch to the new identity in order to configure it. Click Yes, and you'll see the Internet Connection Wizard appear. You'll follow the same e-mail configuration process we've used in the past. When you finish, you'll have a new identity to use.

Now that you have multiple identities, you can use the File | Switch Identify command to switch between identities. You'll see the Switch Identities dialog box, which contains the identities, a Log Off Identity button, and a Manage Identities button. Select a new identity by highlighting it in the list and clicking OK. Click Log Off Identify if you want to log off and close Outlook Express.

You can access the Manage Identities dialog box shown in Figure 5.7 from several locations. The most direct way is to use the File | Identities | Manage Identities command.

As you can see, this dialog box contains a list of the identities that you've defined. Notice that Outlook Express has grayed out the Remove button. You can only remove secondary identities. Click Properties if you want to change the identity properties, which include the property name and password status. Click New if you want to create another new identity.

Notice the two drop-down list boxes at the bottom of the Manage Identities dialog box. The upper list allows you to choose the identity used to start Outlook Express add-on applications that require an identity. The lower list allows you to choose the default identity used when an application can't ask which identity to use. In most cases, you'll never need to worry about these entries because most applications don't rely on your e-mail identity. However, the entries are available should you have an application that needs them.

FIGURE 5.7

Use the Manage Identities dialog box to keep track of your identities.

5

Using Outlook Express News

Outlook Express provides news services as well as e-mail services. We've already discussed earlier today the methods for creating a connection to the newsgroup server and adding your first newsgroups. This section will provide you with the details you need to have a fun newsgroup session.

Configuring Outlook Express Newsreader for Use

You didn't see all of the news server connection settings when you initially created your connection. To change the news server settings, right-click the news server entry and choose Properties. You'll see a News Server Properties dialog box.

The General tab of this dialog box contains fields for your personal information, including Name, Organization, E-mail Address, and Reply address. The content of these four fields won't affect your ability to use the newsgroups, but they'll affect the ability of others to contact you. Generally, a one-word name is fine, but removing the content of the other three fields will keep spammers at bay. However, this technique also makes it impossible for anyone to contact you. A good alternative is to use a spammer-resistant address, such as the one discussed in the "Creating Newsgroup Accounts" section.

You'll use the Server and Connection tabs as needed to maintain your setup. The Server tab defines your connection to the news server, and the Connection tab defines your connection to the ISP. It's unlikely that you'll use either tab unless you change ISPs or experience a major configuration change.

The Advanced tab appears in Figure 5.8. This tab contains several settings that you may want to try to optimize your server connection. You'll never change the Server Port Number or check the This server requires a secure connection (SSL) option unless your ISP or newsgroup moderator tells you to do so.

The Server Timeouts slider is an important setting. Microsoft assumes that everyone has a fast, error-free connection to the Internet. The truth is that many people have dial-up connections to ISPs with overloaded servers. Setting this slider higher will allow you to send and receive newsgroup messages with fewer errors. Of course, you won't want to set it too high because that will mean waiting a long time for real error messages to appear.

This dialog also contains two posting rules that affect every newsgroup. The first is to break apart long messages. You can select a value that defines the term *long*. This is a good setting if you find yourself writing *War and Peace* every time you connect to the Internet. Some people with dial-up connections may not want to wait to download your tome without knowing if they can use the information it contains. The second setting tells Outlook Express to ignore the newsgroup-sending format and use either HTML or text all the time. Many newsgroup readers don't support HTML, so users consider using HTML on a public newsgroup extremely rude. In fact, one or more users will probably contact you to tell you just how rude it is. Generally, you want to use simple text for posts on public newsgroups. Private newsgroups are another matter, and you'll want to contact your moderator for specifics.

FIGURE 5.8

The Advanced tab allows you to control the connection settings.

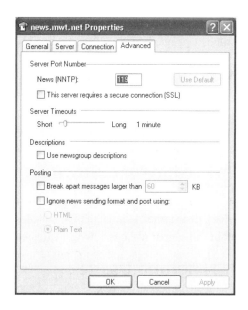

Individual newsgroups also have settings that you need to consider. The most important configuration requirement is the synchronization option. When you select the news server entry in Outlook Express, you'll see a Synchronize Account button at the top. Click this button if you want to download the new content from all newsgroups at one time. This saves a lot of time and allows you to pet your dog while you wait. However, you need to decide what to download because the default setting is to download nothing at all. You can choose to download all messages, just the new messages, or just the new message headers. Downloading the headers (subject lines) is the fastest technique and a good choice for newsgroups where you only read a few messages using a live connection. Select the New Messages Only option when you plan to read most of the newsgroup messages using a live connection. The All Messages option is the safest bet if you plan to read your messages offline, but this is also the most time-consuming method.

You can also save hard drive space by optimizing the compression settings for individual newsgroups. Right-click a newsgroup and select Properties from the context menu.

5

Select the Local File tab, and you'll see a dialog box with four options. Click Compact if you want to get rid of unused space within the newsgroup folder. Outlook Express does not get rid of this space by default, so the newsgroup folders can become bloated. Click Remove Messages if you want to keep the downloaded headers but want to conserve space by getting rid of the message bodies. Delete and Reset will delete both headers and message bodies. However, Reset will also tell Outlook Express to download the headers again. The Reset option is the one to use if your newsgroup account begins to act odd. For example, users often complain that their response to a message didn't post when, in reality, the newsgroup file is corrupted, and they simply can't see the post.

Writing a Newsgroup Message

You'll interact in more ways with newsgroups than you will with e-mail. When you look at a newsgroup message, you can choose to respond to the group (Reply Group) or to the individual by using e-mail (Reply). You can also post a new message by clicking New Post. The message dialog you use for all three actions looks similar to the one shown in Figure 5.4. However, for online messages, you'll see two fewer buttons. You can't encrypt content for a newsgroup. In addition, although you think the message is of the utmost importance, you can't assign it a priority. In every other way, the message dialog works like the one we discussed in the "Sending an E-mail Message" section. You even have a Cc: field for sending an e-mail response along with your newsgroup message.

Tips for Safe Newsgroup Usage

As previously mentioned, newsgroups provide public forums that you can use to discuss ideas with a group of people. The operative word, in this case, is *public*. Some users get the idea that the discussion is limited to those in the conversation, and that's a mistake. Yes, it feels like you have a tight-knit, intimate group sharing ideas, but the reality is still one of worldwide exposure. When you leave a message on a public forum, anyone who can access that forum can see the message.

Of course, everything we discussed in the "Tips for Safe E-mail Usage" section also applies here. Interestingly enough, some virus writers will place their surprise packages on a newsgroup hoping that people will open a package there that they wouldn't in their e-mail reader. The two main issues are to have fun but also to exercise care.

Another policy you'll likely want to adopt is keeping personal information to a minimum. Most people know not to include their address or telephone number in a newsgroup message. However, you also want to exercise care with other personal information. For example, I'm far more likely to use the phrase "my wife" in a newsgroup than my wife's actual name. The less someone can garner from your e-mail message about those around you, the less likely it is that they'll successfully steal your identity or do something more mundane like call and harass you. I try to describe things in general terms and keep my personal information protected. It's up to you to determine how much personal information you want to give up before you feel unsafe.

You should also observe the same courtesy online that you do in person, even when other people don't. In fact, I often extend additional courtesy online because it's so easy to get into an argument over a misunderstood communication. Some people use newsgroups as an opportunity to act hostile toward others. In most cases, it's better to use your best manners in order to obtain the answers you need to your questions.

A final bit of safety comes in the form of protection for children. Almost every public newsgroup I've seen has a problem with pornography or R-rated language. If you allow children to spend time on unmonitored public newsgroups, they'll see the types of messages that you'd never allow them to view anywhere else. Filtering and parental monitoring help, but the safe bet is to use online services that cater to the needs of children.

Outlook Express Options

Like Internet Explorer, Outlook Express allows you to configure just about every aspect of the application. In fact, Outlook Express easily surpasses Internet Explorer when it comes to configuration frenzy. You access the Outlook Express Options dialog box using the Tools | Options command. The following sections describe each of the tabs on this dialog box.

General

The General tab of the Options dialog appears in Figure 5.9. As you can see, this tab controls quite a few automatic Outlook Express features. One of the more interesting features in the General section is the capability to go directly to the Inbox, instead of starting at the Outlook Express level. This saves time for people who don't use the options on the Web page but use the menus or toolbar instead. A new option tells Outlook Express to start Messenger automatically so that you can receive instant messages while you read your e-mail.

The Send/Receive Messages section controls how Outlook Express interacts with your online connection. If you set Outlook Express to automatically download messages every so often, it's also a good idea to tell it to play a sound when you receive new messages. However, you'll likely want to turn sounds off if you're working in a cubicle to avoid bothering other people around you.

5

FIGURE 5.9

The General tab affects many of the automated features.

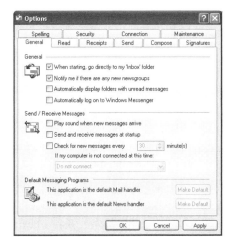

Read

The Read tab appears in Figure 5.10. This dialog box affects both e-mail and newsgroup messages. The Reading Messages section affects how messages appear within the various panes. One of the more interesting features is the capability to mark messages as read after a certain time interval. This feature affects newsgroups more than e-mail because you can set the newsgroups to hide messages that you've already read. Of course, you don't want to set this value too low or you might mark a message as read before you've had a chance to see it. This feature is interesting because you can read part of a newsgroup and then come back later and read the rest without having to wade through the message you've already read.

One of the more important settings is the capability to change the color of watched messages. Again, this feature doesn't affect your e-mail much, but it does affect newsgroups. Marking messages as watched enables you to find messages of interest quickly when you don't have time to read the entire newsgroup. However, using the wrong color can make it hard to see which messages are marked.

Tip

You can mark a message as watched or ignored using the Message | Watch Conversation or Message | Ignore Conversation command. The Watch/Ignore column of Outlook Express also allows you to toggle between the watched and ignored states. After you begin using this feature, use the option on the View | Current View menu to change the way Outlook Express displays messages. The Hide Read or Ignored Messages option allows you to remove any conversation that you don't want to participate in after you've seen it the first time.

The two options in the News section control how Outlook Express handles the news-groups. Generally, it's best to keep both of these options cleared. The first selection limits the number of headers that Outlook Express downloads when you select or syn-chronize the newsgroup. It's more efficient to download all the headers at once than it is to constantly ask Outlook Express to download another set of headers. The second option automatically marks all messages as read before you exit the newsgroup. This means you don't get a second chance to look at unread messages in many cases. If you really want to mark all the messages as read, you can add a Mark All button to the toolbar or use the Edit | Mark All Read command.

Tip You add new buttons to the Outlook Express toolbar the same way you do with Windows Explorer. Right-click the toolbar and choose Customize from the context menu. Select the new buttons you want in the Customize Toolbar dialog box.

FIGURE 5.10

Use the Read tab to change Outlook Express elements, such as the appearance of header text.

The font you use to display messages can make a big difference in how long you can read e-mail and newsgroups. Click Fonts if you want to change the fonts used to display message. The Fonts dialog box allows you to choose between two font types: fixed and proportional. You also choose an encoding method, which determines the use of special characters. Finally, you choose the font size, but in general terms. Instead of using a spe-cific font size in points, you'll use a size from smallest to largest.

Receipts

The Receipts tab allows you to ask for a receipt from the person who receives your message. This feature allows you to determine when someone has read your message, even if they don't respond. You can ask for a receipt for all messages by checking the Request a read receipt for all read messages option. Outlook Express also provides the Tool | Request Read Receipt command in the New Message dialog box if you only want to ask for receipts on certain messages.

You can also set Outlook Express to react to read receipt requests. Normally, Outlook Express will prompt you to respond to a read receipt request. However, you can also set it to ignore all requests or to respond to requests automatically.

Send

The Send tab shown in Figure 5.11 allows you to set the way Outlook Express handles messages that you send to other people. The sending options tell Outlook Express to perform tasks such as sending a copy of all your outgoing e-mail to your Sent folder. This setting can be especially helpful if you have to keep track of message threads. Anyone in business will want to use this feature to maintain a "paper trail" of online conversations.

FIGURE 5.11

The Send tab controls how Outlook Express handles outgoing mail.

These options also control message content to an extent. For example, the Include message in reply option tells Outlook Express to perform a process known as *quoting*. Many e-mail authors use quoting so that they can answer sender questions in line (directly beneath the question). Other people use it to maintain the paper trail of message traffic.

Notice that this dialog also controls the format of your messages. You can use plain text or HTML for either your e-mail or newsgroup messages. As previously mentioned, people often respond well to HTML-formatted e-mail messages, but few newsgroups welcome them.

Compose

The Compose tab affects how your messages appear to other people. You can modify both the font and stationery used for your messages. The tab includes separate controls for e-mail and news, so you could make your e-mail special and keep your news plain.

A business card feature allows you to attach your electronic business card to all of your messages. Again, you have separate controls over your e-mail and newsgroups. Business associates expect you to attach business cards to your e-mail, in some cases, but this practice could be unwelcome in newsgroups where HTML is unwanted.

Signatures

The Signatures tab shown in Figure 5.12 allows you to add a "signature" to the end of your messages. A signature isn't necessarily your name in written form. It could be anything that identifies you or that you want to say as part of every message. A better way of looking at this feature is as a "sign off" message. You can use text, graphics, or a combination of text and graphics for your signature.

FIGURE 5.12

Your sign off message, or signature, appears on the Signatures tab.

5

You can control how your signature is used. For example, you can add a signature just to outgoing messages, or you can add one to everything. There are also separate signatures for e-mail and newsgroup use. In fact, you can assign a different signature to every news server that you use.

To create a signature for a special news server, click New. Give the signature a name. Provide some content in text and/or graphic format. Click Advanced to display the Advanced Signature Settings dialog box and then place a check mark next to each account that will use the signature.

Spelling

The Spelling tab determines how Outlook Express handles spelling checks on your messages. The first two options determine if Outlook Express automatically checks your documents for errors before it sends them and if it makes suggestions for misspelled words.

Four options determine what special conditions Outlook Express observes when it performs a spelling check. For example, you can ask Outlook Express to ignore all words in uppercase. You can also ignore Internet addresses and words with numbers in them.

Finally, you can select the language you want to use for the spelling check and edit the custom dictionary. The custom dictionary stores words that you add to the dictionary as correct words. When you use a lot of jargon in your writing, the custom dictionary is especially helpful.

Security

The Security tab is one of the most important tabs to learn about in Outlook Express because it helps you to maintain a safe working environment (see Figure 5.13). Given the Internet environment today, two of the most important options are Redistricted sites zone (More Secure) and Warn me when other applications try to send mail as me. The first option restricts the amount of leeway you give other sites. The restricted zone setting allows very little to take place without asking you about it first. It also prevents other sites from performing tasks such as placing cookies on your system.

The second option helps prevent viruses from sending e-mail in your name. This is a "must use" setting. It's one thing to pick up a virus and infect your own machine; it's quite another to infect all of your friends' machines as well.

The third option on this tab is handy if you want to restrict the kinds of attachments that you can open. Unfortunately, the list is extremely small, making it tough to conduct business with this setting on, in some cases. You should try this setting to see if it works for you because it does provide much needed security.

The Secure Mail section of this dialog box allows you to obtain and import a digital certificate for your system. Click Tell me more if you want to know the details. Clicking Get Digital ID will take you to a location on the Internet where you can obtain a digital certificate from a trusted authority. Finally, you'll click Digital IDs to view your current IDs and manage them. The Certificates dialog box allows you to import a certificate obtained from a third party.

FIGURE 5.13

Use the Security tab to create a secure environment for your e-mail and newsgroups.

After you have a Digital ID, you can use it to encrypt messages and digitally sign all of your messages. Encrypting messages ensures that the data remains safe and no one can tamper with it. Using a digital signature ensures that everyone will know when they receive a message from you.

Connection

The Connection tab determines how Outlook Express interacts with your Internet connection. The default settings tell Outlook Express to ask you before it switches dial-up connections, but not to hang up after sending and receiving messages. You can change either of these settings.

Normally, Outlook Express shares a connection with Internet Explorer. The Change button displays the Internet Properties dialog box and allows you to assign a separate connection for Outlook Express.

Maintenance

Every part of your system requires some kind of maintenance. I find it helpful when the computer is willing to help me perform the maintenance or does it automatically. That's the purpose of the Maintenance tab shown in Figure 5.14.

5

FIGURE **5.14**

The Maintenance tab ensures that Outlook Express continues to run smoothly.

As you can see, the settings on this tab control when and how Outlook Express maintains your message files. For example, you can tell Outlook Express to clean out your Deleted Items folder automatically when you exit the application. This is one way to ensure that spam you receive goes to the bit bucket in the sky.

Notice the troubleshooting area at the bottom of the dialog box. Check one of these options if you want to track Outlook Express activity in a certain area. For example, you may experience problems with your e-mail. Keeping a log of activity can help you analyze the problem and fix it.

Summary

Today, you've learned about Outlook Express and seen how to use it for both e-mail and newsgroup purposes. Outlook Express is an extremely versatile tool, but it can prove to be complex to use because it provides so many configuration options. Generally, you'll want to spend time ensuring that you configure all of the options for Outlook Express one time rather than attempt to do it piecemeal. Of course, as soon as you can converse with other people online, you'll also have to watch out for those who spread spam. Make sure that you have a good time while online, but keep an eye out for problems, and ensure that you configure your system to discourage unwanted attention.

Q&A

Q: **How can I be removed from a spam list after someone picks up my e-mail address?**

A: Theoretically, you should be able to ask the organization sending the spam to take you off their list. This practice does work with legitimate organizations. However, the reality for most spammers is that you shouldn't contact them at all. Spammers keep lists of known good e-mail addresses and pass them around to other spammers. The second you respond to spam, even to tell the spammer that you don't want their product, they know they have a good address and will never leave you alone. The best way to handle this problem is to ignore the spam and filter it out, if possible. Eventually, spammers will think that your e-mail address is invalid and remove it from their list.

Q: **How do I detect an attachment that's a possible virus attack in disguise?**

A: We've already discussed many of the issues today, but I could probably write an entire book on cracker and virus writer strategies and still not cover the topic. You should spend some time learning the executable file extensions for your system. For example, EXE (executable) and BAT (batch) files have been around forever. Scripting files include both JS (JavaScript) and VBS (Visual Basic Script). One of the stealth script file extensions is the SCR (scrap) file. If you have any doubts about someone's virus message, check it out at one of the many hoax sites, such as http://www.vmyths.com/, http://www.ciac.org/ciac/, and http://www.symantec.com/avcenter/.

Q: **I've seen people use fancy backgrounds on their messages. How can I add backgrounds to my messages?**

A: Look at the Create Mail button on the toolbar. The down arrow next to the button will reveal a menu containing stationery selections. Highlight one of these options to use stationery for your message. You can also highlight Select Stationery. Selecting this option displays the Select Stationery dialog box. You can use any existing HTML file for stationery. If you don't see something you like, click Create New and follow the wizard's instructions to create your own custom stationery.

5

Workshop

It's the end of the fifth day. It's time to see how much you know about using Outlook Express for both e-mail and newsgroup communications. You can find answers to the quiz and exercise questions in Appendix A at the back of the book.

Quiz

1. How do you obtain a listing of newsgroups if the newsgroup download fails?

2. How do you send a message using the Bcc recipient list?

3. What are the font sizes used in Outlook Express?

Exercises

1. Set up Outlook Express to use newsgroups.

2. Send a simple e-mail to a few friends. Use this opportunity to test out some of the features provided with Outlook Express.

3. Go online to a newsgroup and start a new thread about a favorite topic.

4. Try using the watched and ignored messages feature to reduce the time required to view your newsgroups.

5. Use the information in the Outlook Express Options section to configure Outlook Express.

DAY 6

Accessory Overview

Windows XP comes with a lot of what I call "gadgets." They're useful little programs that perform one or two tasks well, but they don't fit into one of the major application categories, such as word processing. Accessories are important parts of the operating system. You need to know that they exist for those times when you need to do some maintenance or perform a special task.

One of the most important accessory categories we'll look at today is the Accessibility features. Some people will immediately think that these features are for those with special needs. I find that they're useful for the average user, too. In fact, you'll find that I've found a lot of special ways to use these features in my own work as you read the "Working with the Accessibility Features" section.

Many of the other Accessibility features augment your work in some way. For example, the Character Map utility doesn't do anything so amazing that you'll tell your friends about it. On the other hand, used correctly, Character Map can tell you a lot about the fonts installed on your system, besides helping you copy special characters to your documents.

We'll also discuss collaboration. You've already learned about NetMeeting during Day 4. Today we'll learn about the new techniques that Microsoft provides in Windows XP. Some of you may find that you prefer these techniques to the older NetMeeting way of doing things.

Working with the Accessibility Features

The Accessibility features provided with Windows XP allow you to enhance the environment to meet specific needs. Some people will fail to see the significance of these improvements, but everyone can use them. For example, at the end of a long day, my eyes are often tired, and I don't want to work too hard to focus on the print on the screen anymore. Using the Accessibility display features can give me an end-of-the-day boost for my tired eyes. Likewise, I've used input enhancements, such as MouseKeys, to add precision to cursor movements. I don't need this help all the time, but it's handy to have when I do need it.

The following sections show you how to use the various Accessibility features. These sections include tips on how you can use these features to make the Windows environment a little friendlier. If you're like me and prefer to keep your eyes from going crazy at the end of the day, then you'll definitely want to check out the display and other features that Accessibility can provide.

Accessibility Wizard

You'll find the Accessibility Wizard on the Start | Programs | Accessories | Accessibility menu. The main purpose for using this wizard is to set up Windows for your accessibility needs. You don't have to use the wizard, but it does make things easier if you have many changes to make. The following steps take you through the configuration process.

 Note   The following steps provide a basic guideline on using the Accessibility Wizard. You may perform some intermediate steps depending on which option combinations you select.

1. Start the Accessibility Wizard. You'll see a Welcome screen.

2. Click Next. You'll see a Text Size screen as shown in Figure 6.1. What you need to do at this screen is select the smallest text that you can comfortably read, that is, without squinting or moving forward in your chair.

3. Select a screen size that you can comfortably see. Make sure that you sit back in your chair and select a font that's clear. Click Next. You'll see a Display Settings dialog box. This dialog box contains four display settings. You can choose a new

font, switch to a lower screen resolution, enable the Microsoft Magnifier, and disable personal menus. The wizard automatically selects some of these options based on your answers on the previous screen.

FIGURE 6.1

The Text Size screen allows you to adjust the display to make it easier to read.

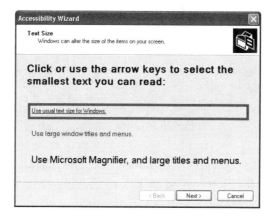

Tip

The easiest way to increase the size of fonts onscreen is to lower the screen resolution. However, while this makes the fonts bigger, it doesn't make them any sharper. To make the fonts sharper and therefore easier on your eyes, use the options on the Advanced Appearance dialog box (accessible by clicking Advanced on the Appearance tab of the Display Properties dialog box) to increase the actual font size. For example, if you select Active Title Bar in the Item list, you'll see that it has a Font and Size value associated with it. Increase the Size value until you can see the display well. Using this technique increases the number of pixels used for each character and ultimately makes the display clearer.

4. Select one or more display settings and click Next. You'll see a Set Wizard Options dialog box that contains four options for various accessibility needs as shown in Figure 6.2. Note that the last option on this list is to set the administrative options. This option allows you to set the time intervals required for some actions to take place.

Note

The following steps assume that you selected all four options on the Set Wizard Options dialog box. If you only selected one or two of the options, you'll find that you can skip some of the steps.

6

FIGURE 6.2

*These four options
control some of the
basic Accessibility
features.*

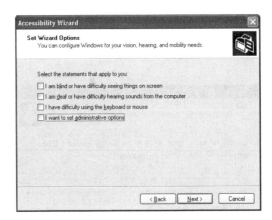

5. The Scroll Bar and Window Border Size dialog box shown in Figure 6.3 allows you to make the scroll bar and window border larger so that they're easier to size, move, and manipulate. Select the smallest size that you can see clearly. Choosing a larger size may consume screen real estate that you need for other purposes. Choose the entry on the far left if you want to use the standard-sized scroll bar and window border. Click Next.

FIGURE 6.3

*Using a larger scroll
bar makes it easier to
scroll through a docu-
ment, while a larger
window border makes
it easier to move and
size windows.*

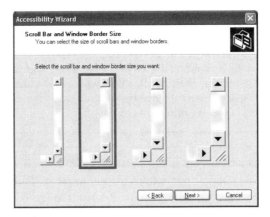

6. The Icon Size dialog box allows you to choose between three icon sizes. The icon on the far left is the default size. Note that icon text size increases with the size icon you use. This is an important consideration because the text may be large enough to read even if the icon isn't clear. Choose an icon size and then click Next.

7. The Display Color Settings dialog box shown in Figure 6.4 allows you to reset the display colors to other options. I usually select a high contrast option when I've had a long day and my eyes need a rest. The High Contrast White is useful for

more than tired eyes; I also find that it works well on my laptop when I'm working outside. Choose a display color setting and then click Next.

FIGURE 6.4

Select a display color setting that matches your viewing needs.

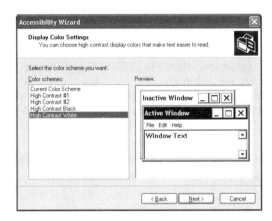

8. The Mouse Cursor dialog box show in Figure 6.5 contains nine settings. You can adjust your mouse cursor size and color settings. These options also come in handy when working with a laptop. The medium-sized cursor is easier to see in direct sunlight. Select a mouse cursor and then click Next.

FIGURE 6.5

Use the options on the Mouse Cursor dialog box to enhance your ability to see the mouse in every situation.

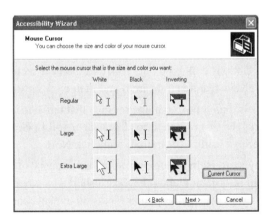

6

9. The Cursor Settings dialog box allows you to choose the blink rate and cursor width. I usually set the blink rate low when working on a laptop to keep the cursor from disappearing. The cursor width feature comes in handy when I'm doing a lot of data entry or working with forms on the Internet. The wider cursor is easier to

see when the developer outlines each field in black. Select a cursor blink rate and width, and then click Next.

10. The SoundSentry dialog box contains settings that tell Windows to display a visual signal such as a flashing title bar each time that the system plays an event sound. For example, SoundSentry reacts to the default beep.

Tip

You can use SoundSentry to alleviate some of the noise problems in tight quarters. For example, people who work in cubicles could turn their sound off and use this feature as a visual signal that the system has made a sound. Select Yes to turn SoundSentry on (if desired) and then click Next.

11. The ShowSounds dialog box contains settings that tell Windows to display a caption each time that the system plays a sound or speech. As with the SoundSentry feature, the ShowSounds feature could keep things quiet in close quarters. Select Yes to turn ShowSounds on (if desired) and then click Next.

12. The StickyKeys dialog box contains settings that tell Windows to use single key presses in combination. For example, instead of pressing Ctrl+Alt+Del all at once, you can press the keys one at a time. You can also use this feature with other key combinations, such as Alt+F (used in most applications to open the File menu). Select Yes to turn on the StickyKeys feature (if desired) and then click Next.

13. The BounceKeys dialog box contains settings that tell Windows to ignore repeated key presses. If you press repeated keys too quickly, Windows will ignore the extra key presses. Interestingly enough, this feature is called FilterKeys in the Accessibility Options dialog box described in the next section. Select Yes to turn on the BounceKeys feature (if desired) and then click Next.

14. The ToggleKeys dialog box contains settings that tell Windows to play a sound when you press the Num Lock, Caps Lock, or Scroll Lock keys. Select Yes to turn on the ToggleKeys feature (if desired) and click Next.

15. The Extra Keyboard Help dialog box contains settings that tell Windows to display additional help information about keyboard shortcuts, when available. This feature can help users who want to keep their hands on the keyboard rather than use a mouse. I'll turn it on sometimes just to see if the application provides poorly documented shortcuts that I need to know about. Select Yes to turn the Extra Keyboard Help feature on (if desired) and click Next.

16. The MouseKeys dialog box contains settings that tell Windows to use the numeric keypad to control the mouse cursor. This feature is handy for anyone who works

with graphics applications. Using MouseKeys allows precise placement of graphic or text elements on a page. You use a series of numeric keypad controls to direct mouse actions, such as clicking (5) and double-clicking (+). Select Yes to turn the MouseKeys feature on (if desired) and then click Next.

17. The Mouse Button Settings dialog box contains settings that tell Windows to switch the mouse buttons as needed. This feature allows left-handed people to place the mouse on the left side of the keyboard and use the mouse naturally. Select Right-handed or Left-handed and then click Next.

18. The Mouse Speed dialog box contains a slider used to control the mouse speed. Slow the mouse down if you have trouble positioning items on screen. You must move a slow mouse further physically to obtain a proportion amount of movement on screen. Place the slider bar somewhere between fast and slow and then click Next.

19. The Set Accessibility Timeouts dialog box adjusts how long the Accessibility features remain active after a period of computer activity. You can also choose to leave the Accessibility features on all the time. The reason for a timeout is to allow more than one person to use the computer. If one person needs an Accessibility feature and another doesn't, the timeout feature makes the computer self-adjusting. Select a timeout value and then click Next.

20. The Default Accessibility Settings dialog box contains settings that apply the current Accessibility feature settings to the local account or to all accounts on a system. Choose between the default and the current user profile setting and then click Next. You'll see a completion dialog box.

21. Click Finish. The Accessibility Wizard will apply all of the settings you made.

Accessibility Options

The Accessibility Options dialog box shown in Figure 6.6 allows you to access each of the Accessibility features directly. You'll find this applet in the Control Panel. Each tab controls one or more features.

You'll find the same settings that we discussed for the Accessibility Wizard. All of the settings allow the same options; you simply check or clear a checkbox instead of choosing Yes or No. Some of the features also include Settings dialog boxes. Each Settings dialog box controls special settings for that feature. For example, you can use the Settings for StickyKeys dialog box to select a hot key for the StickyKeys feature. You can also select a notification mode and options, such as turning StickyKeys off if the user presses two keys at once. The following list tells you which accessibility feature you'll find on each tab and indicates whether those features include special settings:

6

FIGURE 6.6

FIGURE **6.6**

The Accessibility Options dialog box allows you to control the Accessibility features directly.

- **Keyboard:** This tab includes the StickyKeys, FilterKeys (BounceKey), and ToggleKeys features, all of which provide additional settings. You'll also find the extra keyboard help feature on this tab.

- **Sound:** This tab includes the SoundSentry and ShowSounds features. Neither feature includes any special settings.

- **Display:** This tab includes the high contrast feature. The special settings allow you to choose a shortcut key for the feature. In addition, you can select from more schemes than the Accessibility Wizard provides. This tab also includes the cursor options (blink rate and cursor width).

FIGURE **6.7**

The General tab contains the SerialKeys accessibility feature, something you can't set using the Accessibility Wizard.

- **Mouse:**   This tab includes the MouseKeys feature. Some of the special mouse features that you set in the Accessibility Wizard appear on the Settings for MouseKeys dialog box. This dialog box also allows you to select a shortcut key.

- **General:**   This tab appears in Figure 6.7. Notice that it includes all of the administrative settings, such as the amount of time the Accessibility features remain active during a period of computer inactivity. This tab also contains a special accessibility feature that you can't set using the Accessibility Wizard—SerialKeys. The SerialKeys feature allows you to use an alternative input device in place of the keyboard and mouse. Click Settings if you want to change the serial (COM) port settings for this alternative device.

Magnifier

Whenever you start the Magnifier, you'll see a band open at the top of your screen. This band contains a magnified version of the information contained at the mouse cursor. You can change the size of the band by dragging the line separating it from the rest of your display using the mouse, just as you would for the Taskbar.

Tip

> As a developer and someone interested in drawing, I often use Magnifier to see how other people create small screen elements, such as icons. It's hard to obtain just the right color combinations without help at times. Viewing someone else's work can mean the difference between trial and error, and result in getting the drawing right the first time.

The default magnifier setting will magnify items by a factor of 2. You can change this setting by using the Magnifier Settings dialog box shown in Figure 6.8. This dialog box opens whenever you start the Magnifier. When you click Exit, the Magnifier also stops.

Notice that you can change the tracking technique that Magnifier uses to home in on the action. The default setting tells Magnifier to follow any activity on the screen. However, you can clear one or more of these check boxes to reduce the level of activity.

You'll also find three check boxes in the Presentation section. The first tells Magnifier to invert the screen colors. This makes it easier to contrast the normal appearance of your display with the magnified version. You can also start the Magnifier Settings dialog box minimized. Finally, you can clear Show Magnifier to get rid of the band at the top. This is a handy feature if you need more screen real estate for a short time and don't want to disable Magnifier in the interim.

6

FIGURE **6.8**

The Magnifier Settings dialog box allows you to control how the Magnifier interacts with your system.

Narrator

The Narrator reads everything onscreen to you. I find that it does a relatively good job, and I use it when I need to "read" documents online. I'll get the document placed onscreen, and then I'll kick back and let Narrator do the work while I concentrate on the information contained on the Web site. This application also acts as a sanity check for my Web site. I'll see if Narrator stumbles on the content. If it doesn't, I'm sure that no one else will have trouble, either. Of course, its main purpose is to help those with low vision make more sense of what they see on screen.

Tip

Narrator, like many Windows XP multimedia features, relies on a working soundboard to perform its work. If Narrator fails to work, check Sound, Video, and Game Controllers folder of Device Manager for an operational soundboard.

The Narrator dialog box contains four options. The Announce events onscreen option tells Narrator to announce when you successfully complete an action, such as changing windows. The Read typed characters option tells you which character you typed last, including control characters, such as backspace. The Move mouse to active item option moves the mouse cursor so that you can see which item onscreen has the focus. Finally, the Start Narrator minimized option starts the program with the Narrator dialog box minimized.

The Voice button takes you to the Voice Settings dialog box. This dialog box allows you to choose a new voice for Narrator. The default setting is Microsoft Sam. You can also change the speed, volume, and pitch of the voice. Nothing you do will make Narrator sound completely human. However, adjusting the pitch and speed does make Narrator friendlier. Adjust the pitch and volume settings to make Narrator easier to understand.

On-Screen Keyboard

The On-Screen Keyboard shown in Figure 6.9 is a replica of the keyboard attached physically to your system. It allows you to type text by using a mouse or other pointing device. You can adjust the appearance of the keyboard using the options on the Keyboard menu. For example, you might want to use a 106-key keyboard instead of the 101-key default. You can also choose between a standard and an enhanced keyboard.

FIGURE 6.9

You can use the On-Screen Keyboard as an alternative means for inputting data.

The Settings menu controls how the On-Screen Keyboard interacts with the system. For example, you might want to use a different font for the keys. You can also choose whether the keyboard always remains on top. The Use Click Sound option comes in handy if you're used to a regular keyboard and miss the sound it makes. Finally, the Typing Mode option displays the Typing Mode dialog box. You'll use the options on this dialog box to control how the user inputs data. You have a choice between clicking, hovering, or using a joystick (or other recognized device).

Utility Manager

The Utility Manager is a special application for managing your accessibility applications. It controls the Magnifier, On-Screen Keyboard, and Narrator. All three of these applications appear in the field at the top of the dialog box (along with any other accessibility applications you may install).

To stop an application, highlight it and click Stop. Likewise, click Start to restart the application.

You can also set the startup options for each application. The three options will start the program when you log in, lock the system, or start the Utility Manager when they're checked.

6

A New Way to Collaborate

Using the Internet for collaboration purposes is becoming more popular as more people connect. The proliferation of high-speed connections in some areas of the world helps collaboration along by making it easier to perform high bandwidth activities, such as voice communication. Finally, collaboration over the Internet has always been popular because it's easier than traveling. In fact, one of the initial purposes of the Internet was to support collaboration between individuals at universities.

The following sections won't make you a collaboration guru—only experience can do that. However, you'll learn about the new features of Windows XP that make collaboration easier. We'll discuss the new Remote Desktop Connection utility and see how it makes it easier to provide assistance as well as train other users. Remote Desktop Connection also comes in handy for sharing applications and performing other collaboration-oriented tasks.

Microsoft has also bundled MSN Explorer and MSN Messenger Service with Windows XP. These two utilities make it easier to find other people with similar interests online and then chat with them.

We'll also discuss some of the downsides of these products. Unlike NetMeeting (discussed during Day 4), these products require you to give up more than a little control over your system and at least some of your privacy. While you had a choice over these issues with NetMeeting, the following sections show how these new additions provide better functionality in a few areas, at the cost of flexibility and privacy in others.

Note

At the time of this writing, Microsoft plans to release Windows XP with all of the features that I describe intact. However, everyone from privacy groups to the government is concerned about the ramifications of these products. The courts may force Microsoft to change the way these products interact with the user as a minimum, or remove them completely. Of course, there's no way my crystal ball can see so far into the future in such murky waters. With this in mind, you may find that these products work a little differently in your version of Windows XP.

Making a Remote Desktop Connection

One of the most interesting features of Windows XP is Remote Desktop Connection. This application allows you to view and control someone else's machine from your workstation. You use this application to provide training and support for other users. It's also the suggested method for managing servers. However, more than a few users have already suggested that the security risks of using Remote Desktop Connection on servers far outweigh any benefits the network administrator might receive. We'll discuss networking issues from Day 14 to Day 18.

FIGURE 6.10

Remote Desktop Connection allows you to control the amount of information you see.

When you first start Remote Desktop Connection, you'll see a simple connection dialog box. Click Options, and you'll see the advanced form shown in Figure 6.10. This is the dialog box you use to configure Remote Desktop Connection. If you've already configured Remote Desktop Connection, open a remote desktop parameters (RDP) file using the Open button and click Connect.

The first time you use Remote Desktop Connection (and every time you want to create a new connection), you'll want to configure it. The utility won't ask you to configure your system, but the default settings rarely work. The first thing you'll want to do is enter the computer name, your username, your password, and the domain (if applicable).

The Display tab contains the parameters for how the remote desktop will look on your machine. Microsoft assumes that you want to use your whole desktop. However, you may find that using only part of the desktop works better, especially if you want to access files or utilities on your own machine while you access the remote machine.

The Local Resources tab tells Remote Desktop Connection how much of the remote computer you want at your desktop. Microsoft assumes that you want to bring everything

6

over, which means you'll use the maximum network bandwidth. You can safely reduce the load on your network by selecting the Do Not Play option for the Remote computer sound option. You can usually get by without remote access to peripherals, such as the printer. The use of Windows key combinations does come in handy.

The Programs tab tells Remote Desktop Connection which program to start when you initiate the connection. This can be a double-edged sword. On the positive side, you can automate part of the setup process for working with the remote computer. On the negative side, you may find that the remote application fails and causes the remote connection to fail as well. In short, the default setting of not starting any remote applications is probably the safest choice.

The Experience tab controls the remote desktop environment. It enables you to see elements on the remote desktop, such as the desktop background and any changes made by themes. However, using any of these elements will increase network bandwidth use, and you generally don't need them for a training or configuration session. This dialog also contains a special entry for optimizing the performance by choosing a connection type. Always choose the connection type you'll actually use for this connection.

Now that you've configured the connection, select the General tab. Click Save As to display a Save As dialog box. Type a descriptive connection name and click Save. Except for the password, this save file will always restore the connection settings for you. Click Connect to take control of the remote desktop.

Using MSN Explorer

The MSN Explorer utility allows you to explore the Internet in a comfortable environment. When you first start this application, it will ask if you want to use MSN Explorer to get on the Internet and to check your e-mail. Unless you want MSN Explorer as the only means to log on to the Internet, choose No.

During your first use of MSN Explorer, you'll need to configure it, so you'll see a Welcome screen. The following steps will help you to configure MSN Explorer for use:

1. Click Continue. MSN Explorer will ask you to enter your location.

2. Select a country from the list and click Continue. MSN Explorer will ask if you want to sign up for Internet access. You don't have to have an MSN account to use MSN Explorer. If you already have an Internet service provider (ISP), you'll likely want to choose the No, I already have Internet Access option. The remainder of this procedure assumes that you already have an ISP.

3. Select an Internet Access option and then click Continue. MSN Explorer will ask if you have an MSN dial-up account. If you use a third-party ISP, you'll want to say No in this dialog box.

4. Select a connection method and then click Continue. You'll see a Connecting dialog box. After MSN Explorer connects, you'll see dialog that asks if you have an MSN or Hotmail e-mail account. If you don't have one of these two accounts, you must create one to use MSN Explorer. Select the Create new e-mail address for me option. The Hotmail accounts are free. You can read about them at `http://lc2.law13.hotmail.passport.com/cgi-bin/login`. You can read about the MSN accounts at `http://www.msn.com`.

Note

At the time of this writing, there's more than a little controversy concerning MSN Explorer and the need to use Microsoft's e-mail account with it. To gain access to a Hotmail or MSN account, you need a Passport, which is essentially a description of you and your personal information. Privacy advocates feel that Passport is too invasive, and they don't like the fact that Microsoft stores this information on their server. You'll need to decide if a Passport is too invasive for your needs.

5. Select an e-mail option and click Continue. MSN Explorer will ask you a series of personal questions. Fill each form out and click Continue. None of the information is optional, which means that you need to include personal information such as your age and gender. Eventually, you'll see an MSN Terms of Use screen.

6. Read the MSN Terms of Use screen, select I accept the agreement (if you do), and click Continue. You'll see a password screen.

7. Type a password and click Continue. MSN Explorer will ask you to enter a secret question.

8. Select a secret question category, type a secret question answer, and click Continue. MSN Explorer will ask you to choose an e-mail name. Note the option to share your e-mail address with other MSN partner sites.

9. Type an MSN e-mail address, choose whether you want to share this e-mail address with the MSN partner sites, and click Continue. At this point, MSN Explorer will tell you that you must change your Internet Explorer privacy settings to medium. This setting allows sites to use cookies on your machine and your personal information in some cases. (If your privacy settings are already at medium or below, you won't see this dialog box.)

10. Select a lower privacy policy if necessary or choose not to use MSN Explorer. Click Continue. MSN Explorer will check your e-mail address. If it conflicts with another e-mail address, MSN will give you a few seconds to change to a new e-mail address or MSN will automatically choose a new e-mail address for you

6

based on your old entry (usually by adding a number). You'll see the MSN
Explorer Tour dialog box shown in Figure 6.11.

FIGURE 6.11

*After you configure
MSN Explorer, you'll
see the Tour-Welcome
dialog box.*

MSN Explorer can replace Internet Explorer as your browser. Nothing you see in the
viewing area (except for MSN sites) will differ from what you see in Internet Explorer.
You type URLs in the Address bar at the top of the display and then click Go. The
Favorites menu still appears at the top of the display, and you'll still organize it using the
same technique you use with Internet Explorer. Look at MSN Explorer as a friendly,
MSN site-enabled form of Internet Explorer.

Contacting Others Using the Windows Messenger Service

Windows Messenger is the instant messaging feature of Windows XP. It allows someone
to call you over a network or the Internet instead of using a telephone. If you have MSN
Explorer running when you start Windows Messenger the first time, you'll see the window shown in Figure 6.12. Otherwise, you'll need to configure an e-mail address first.

Windows Messenger will offer to import names and addresses from Outlook Express if
you used it in the past. You can also add names by clicking Add on the toolbar. Windows
Messenger offers two methods for entering new addresses. You can manually type the
address information or use an online search to locate the person and enter the information automatically.

FIGURE 6.12

Windows Messenger allows you to send and receive both text and voice messages over the Internet.

Sending an instant message is easy. Select an option on the Send menu to begin. Type the address of the person you want to contact and then click OK. You'll see a Conversation dialog box that contains a transcript area at the top for the message traffic. The bottom third of the dialog box contains the field where you type your message, a Send button, and the address of the person you've contacted. The Options menu in the upper right corner of the dialog box allows you to set the instant messaging options, send a file, set the font used to display message traffic, and start the Audio Tuning Wizard. Use the Invite button in the upper left corner to invite other people to the conversation.

You can also use voice communication. However, this means using the Audio and Video Tuning Wizard to tune your microphone to Windows Messenger. The following steps show you how to complete this process. I'll assume that you're at the Welcome screen of the Audio and Video Tuning Wizard.

1. Click Next. The Audio and Video Tuning Wizard will ask which camera you want to use.

2. Select a camera from the list (or None if you don't want to use a camera) and then click Next. You'll see a set of instructions for tuning the audio.

3. Read the audio recording instructions and then click next. The Audio and Video Tuning Wizard will ask which device you want to use for the microphone and your speakers.

4. Select a device for both record and playback and click Next. The Audio and Video Turning Wizard will ask to test your speakers.

5. Test the speakers by clicking Click to Test Speakers. When you're finished, click Stop. Click Next. The Audio and Video Tuning Wizard will ask to test your microphone.

6

6. Talk into the microphone and adjust the level as needed. Click Next. You'll see a Success screen.

7. Click Finish.

The Voice tab of the Conversation dialog box looks similar to the Text tab. The only additions are a Mute button for your microphone and a volume switch. Windows Messenger will attempt to automatically initiate communication with the other party, rather than wait until you click Send after you type your first message.

Sending and Receiving Faxes

Many home users and small businesses rely on a fax modem to send and receive faxes. Windows XP doesn't install fax support by default, so you'll need to install it using the Add/Remove Programs applet. Click Fax Services on the Windows Components Wizard dialog box and then click Next. Follow the prompts to complete the installation process.

 Note

If you plan to use the Windows XP fax services, you must have a device that supports fax transmission. Most dial-up modems include this support as a standard feature. However, many cable, DSL, and satellite modems lack fax support. In short, the ability to create a connection isn't enough, your machine must feature built-in fax support to send and receive faxes.

After you install fax support, you'll find a new Fax folder in the Start | Programs | Accessories | Communications folder that contains three icons. Select the Fax Cover Page editor if you want to create a new fax cover page. The editor looks like a simple graphics editor. You can add text, draw lines and other basic shapes, and perform object-related tasks, such as aligning various cover page elements.

The Fax Console application forms the core of the Windows XP faxing feature. The first time you start this application, you'll see a Fax Configuration Wizard. Configuring your fax requires four steps (it requires more than four screens). First, enter your personal information. Second, select a device for faxing the information. You'll need to decide if the modem should simply send faxes or both send and receive faxes. Third, provide a Called Subscriber Identification (CSID) and Transmitting Subscriber Identification (TSID). Finally, you'll need to choose some routing options. For example, you could print all of the faxes out or send them to a folder on your hard drive.

When you complete the configuration process, you'll see the Fax Console. The Fax Console contains four folders: Incoming, Inbox, Outbox, and Sent. The Incoming and

Outbox folders contain faxes in transit, and the Inbox and Sent folders contain completed faxes.

Click File | Send a Fax to begin sending a fax. You'll see the Send Fax Wizard. This wizard will take you through the steps of sending a fax. First, you'll need to select one or more recipients. You can type the names in by hand or use the entries in your Outlook Express address book. If you choose an address book entry that lacks a fax number, the wizard will tell you and leave the contact out of the recipient list. Second, you'll need to select the fax cover page and add content. Third, you'll need to schedule the fax delivery. Finally, you can preview the fax, add any required annotation, and send it.

Text Processing Aids

One of the most common needs for computer users is the ability to process text quickly. Everyone from developers, to managers, to network administrators, to common users need to process text at one time or another.

However, text isn't always plain text. Sometimes a user needs formatted text to provide output with a nice appearance. In other cases, having any formatting codes in the text would wreak havoc with computer operations. As a result, the one-size-fits-all approach won't work for text processing.

Users also need to use special characters in their writing. Not only do users have languages other than their own to consider, but they may also have special icon and mathematical formatting requirements. In short, users need some way to select special characters and put them where they're needed on the printed page.

This section of the chapter addresses all of these requirements. We'll discuss two text-processing utilities. Notepad outputs pure ASCII text, which means there aren't any formatting codes to consider. Wordpad provides simple formatting features so that you can create output with a pleasing appearance. Finally, Character Map is the utility to use if you need to find out more about special characters. You'll be surprised at what you can find in some of the fonts on your machine.

Notepad

Notepad is a simple text editor. You can use it to create batch and script files because it doesn't add any formatting to the text. It's also the editor that Internet Explorer typically uses to display the source code for Web pages.

> **Tip**
>
> Notepad is a simple utility that performs its task well. However, most users want something a little more capable. Notepad+ from RogSoft (http://www.mypeecee.org/rogsoft/) fits the bill. It still works exclusively with plain text, but you can directly open additional plain file types, such as HTML. Notepad+ also includes more formatting features. Of course, the problem is replacing Notepad with Notepad+ without Windows XP interfering. Rename Notepad.EXE in the System32 directory to Old Notepad.EXE. Windows won't let you delete this file, but you can rename it. Copy Notepad+ to the System32 directory. After you successfully copy it there, you can also copy it to the Windows directory.

When you open this utility, you'll see a main menu with five options. Of course, the one requisite entry for every Windows application is a Help menu.

The File menu allows you to open and close files. You can also create new text files. This menu contains a Page Setup feature that controls how Notepad outputs text to a printer and a Print option that sends the data to the printer. The page layout features include the capability to create a header and a footer. You can use special commands as shown below to add content to the header or footer (along with standard text).

- **&&**   Inserts an ampersand into the printed output.
- **&c**   Aligns the text to the center.
- **&d**   Inserts the date.
- **&f**   Inserts the filename.
- **&l**   Aligns the text to the left.
- **&p**   Inserts the page number.
- **&r**   Aligns the text to the right.
- **&t**   Inserts the time.

The Edit menu contains all of the usual entries for a simple program. You can undo one action. The menu also contains entries to cut, copy, and paste text. Use the Find and Find and Replace options to locate and modify text. Finally, the Time/Date option types the time and date into the file. I find this option exceptionally handy when I'm using Notepad to create a log file.

The Format menu contains options for changing the viewing font and enabling word wrap. Note that the font change only affects the viewing area. It doesn't change anything within the file.

The View menu contains an option for displaying the Status bar. This feature tells you information about the file, such as the current cursor position.

Wordpad

This is the utility to use for formatted text. Figure 6.13 shows an example of the types of input you can provide. As you can see, Wordpad provides toolbars that allow you to format the text directly without having to use the menus. These features work very much like those found in Microsoft Word, so anyone who knows that interface will be able to use this one as well.

FIGURE 6.13

Wordpad provides simple, but useful, text-formatting capabilities.

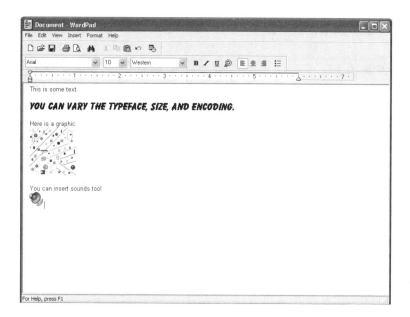

Because Wordpad outputs in rich text format (RTF) files, it will save any formatting you do with the file. Word and other word processors can import RTF files, which means you can use Wordpad to create simple documents and then embellish them when you return to the office. Wordpad can also output text files, but many people consider Wordpad unsuitable for pure text needs because there's a chance of adding formatting to the document by accident. Wordpad can also read a variety of document formats, including text, Word DOC files, Microsoft Write WRI files, and RTF files.

Character Map

Unlike the other text processing tools in this section, Character Map appears in the System Tools folder under the Accessories folder. Character Map doesn't actually process text; it allows you to create special text by exposing the entire content of the font files on your system. The characters you can access directly only account for a small number of the characters that the font file contains.

Figure 6.14 shows a typical example of a Character Map display. You should notice several things about this display. First, the characters appear in numeric order. The font file assigns each character a number that appears in the lower left corner of the display. In this case, we're looking at Unicode number 00E7h (for hexadecimal). This is a hexadecimal (base 16) number, so it will use the letters *A* through *F* to represent the values not found in the base-10 system you're used to using. This entry also includes the human readable name for the character. You can also see this information by hovering the mouse over the character. Balloon help containing the character name will appear over the character.

FIGURE 6.14

Character Map displays the full content of a font file.

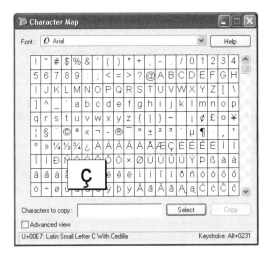

The second element you should notice is the Alt-0231 on the right side of the dialog box. Not all characters will include this entry, but this one does. If you hold the Alt key down while pressing 0231 on the numeric keypad, this special character will appear in your favorite word processor and many graphics applications. However, you must use the numeric keypad on the right side of the keyboard, not the numbers across the top immediately above the letters.

The standard character entries in Character Map are hard to see. If you click on a character, Character Map will expand it to four times its normal size. This allows you to see the character in more detail, an especially important feature when working with some special characters. How many special characters will a font file have? It depends on the vendor. However, Arial has entries from U+0021 to U+FFFC or 65,499 total entries. You'll find everything from smiley faces (of various sorts) to mathematical symbols in this file.

Using the characters if you don't have an Alt key substitute is easy. Highlight the letter you want to use and click Select. After you have selected the string of characters you want to use, click Copy to place them on the clipboard and then Paste within your favorite application.

Summary

Today you've learned about three important elements in Windows XP. The first is the use of the Accessibility features. Many people never even try out this feature, but it really can make life simpler for the Windows XP user. The second is the use of collaboration under Windows XP. The new Microsoft strategy does offer some advantages to the NetMeeting strategy used in the past, but you need to consider the drawbacks as well. Finally, we discussed some techniques to manipulate text without even installing a word processor. Of course, you'll want to invest in a high-end product if you work with documents for a living.

Q&A

Q: What happens if I return to my desk, only to find someone has left the high contrast display on?

A: Instead of attempting to change the settings on the Appearance tab of the Display Properties dialog box, open the Accessibility Options dialog box from the Control Panel. Select the Display tab and clear the Use High Contrast option.

Q: How do I know if my modem is capable of sending a fax?

A: The easiest way is to check the vendor documentation that came with your system. Normally, the documentation tells you the capabilities of your modem. If your documentation has taken a hike, you can always check the Fax Console to see if your modem appears in the list. If it does, you're usually safe in assuming that the modem has fax capability.

If all else fails, you can ask the modem if it can send faxes. Right-click My Computer and select Properties to display the System Properties dialog box. Select the Hardware tab. Click Device Manager to display the Device Manager dialog box. Right-click the entry for your modem under the Modems folder and choose Properties to display the Modem Properties dialog box. Select the Diagnostics tab and click Query Modem. After a few seconds you'll see the Response field fill up with data about your modem as shown in the Figure 6.15. Look for the Fax Options entry. If you see this entry and it contains options such as Class 1/Class 2.0, then your modem has fax capability.

6

FIGURE 6.15

One of the easy ways to determine modem capabilities is to query it.

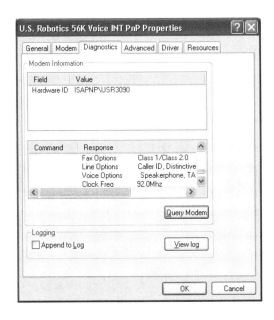

Workshop

It's the end of the fifth day. It's time to see how much you know about using Outlook Express for both e-mail and newsgroup communications. You can find answers to the quiz and exercise questions in Appendix A at the back of the book.

Quiz

1. How can the MouseKeys feature help the average user?

2. What are the two ways to set the Accessibility features?

3. Microsoft provides two text-editing applications with Windows XP. What are their names and how do you use them?

Exercises

1. Try out the various Accessibility features, especially after you've had a long day in front of the computer screen.

2. Play with Character Map to see what entries the font files on your machine contain.

3. Try the Remote Desktop Connection utility if you have a network.

WEEK 1

DAY 7

Playing with Multimedia and Games

Sounds, visual effects, even tactile feedback have all become standard parts of the Windows computing environment. Only gamers used to enjoy these elements, but today, you run into them constantly. Windows contains a wealth of multimedia—you find it on the Internet, some people use their computer DVDs to play movies, and of course, games have only gotten more multimedia oriented as time has passed. In short, the Windows user of today needs to know something about multimedia, and it helps to know a little about games, too.

We'll begin our whirlwind tour of multimedia today by looking at the Windows offerings. We'll look at old standby applications such as the CD Player and Sound Recorder. Of course, the versions Windows provides today bear only a passing resemblance to the first versions of these utilities. We'll also discuss some new features such as the Windows Movie Maker and how to work with both cameras and scanners. One of the best new features is the ability to record CDs without using a third-party utility.

You'll also see the games that Microsoft provides as part of Windows. The old standbys (Mine Sweeper, Pinball, Solitaire, and FreeCell) are present. You'll also find a series of new Internet games that you can play with friends online. These new Internet games also provide a method for checking your Internet connection for problems. Also, look for a new and very addictive game called *Spider Solitaire*.

Finally, we'll discuss some troubleshooting tips for your multimedia and games. Nothing is worse than spending leisure time diagnosing problems with your system instead of playing with it. We'll look at both local and networking problems.

The Standard Windows Multimedia Add-ons

Windows XP comes equipped with many of the same multimedia add-ons found in other versions of Windows. You'll find most of these utilities in the Start | Programs | Accessories | Entertainment menu. However, as with all those previous editions, Microsoft has made a few improvements to this version of the product. In this case, you'll notice that some of the applications look nicer, while others provide enhanced features. For those of you who like neat looking gizmo applications, the Windows Media Player is the big news. The following sections tell you about the standard multimedia add-ons for Windows XP.

Sound Recorder

The Sound Recorder you see today is much the same as the one you saw yesterday. It looks the same and acts the same as the one that appeared in both Windows 9x and Windows 2000. Figure 7.1 shows what this utility looks like. The Sound Recorder still allows you to record a sound into memory, modify it a little, annotate it, and then save it to disk. The biggest change from Windows 9X is that you can make longer recordings.

To begin a recording, click Record. You'll see the time position bar move across the front of the utility. The Sound Recorder makes recordings in 60-second increments. When the time position bar reaches the other side, the recording will stop. Click record again and you get another 60 seconds of recording time.

Sound Recorder allows you to modify the recording using entries on the Effects menu. This includes increasing/decreasing the recording speed and increasing/decreasing the recording volume. Unfortunately, changing the recording volume tends to introduce noise that most users find undesirable.

You can add echo to the recording, which gives it a fuller sound when used in moderation. You can also increase echo to the point where the recording sounds ridiculous. The Reverse option on the Effects menu allows you to play the recording backward.

FIGURE 7.1

The Sound Recorder allows you to record sounds from your system and save them to disk.

The Sound Recorder enables you to perform some types of sound editing. For example, you can insert a sound clip into the current click by using the Edit | Paste Insert or Edit | Insert File commands. You can mix two files together using the Edit | Paste Mix or Edit | Mix with File commands. Finally, you can cut the current sound click using either the Edit | Delete Before Current Position or Edit | Delete After Current Position commands.

The final piece of this application appears under the File menu. Select Properties, and you'll see a Properties for Sound dialog box. Click Convert Now, and you'll see the Sound Selection dialog box shown in Figure 7.2. Notice that this dialog box lets you convert the sound into other formats.

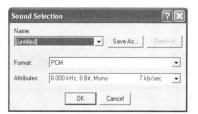

FIGURE 7.2

You can use the Sound Recorder to convert sounds from one format to another.

The Name field contains a list of named formats. For example, if you choose the Telephone format, you'll get a small sound file with mediocre quality at best. The Sound Recorder will set the Format field to PCM and the Attributes field to 11.025kHz, 8-bit, mono, and 10 kb/sec. The last attribute tells you how much file space this format requires for each second of recording time.

You can change the Format and Attributes fields by hand to achieve specific effects. The Format field supports 13 different formats. The content of the Attributes field will change to match the format you choose. The highest quality PCM format of 16-bit stereo at 48,000kHz requires a whopping 187 kb/sec of storage space. The "lossy" Motion Picture Experts Group (MPEG) layer 3 format of 48,000KfHz stereo only requires 15 kb/sec, but you also lose data. The recording isn't as good as the PCM version, even though they're both recorded at the same quality level.

7

Volume Control

You can access the Volume Control by using a number of techniques. The fastest method is to click, right-click, or double-click the speaker icon in the notification area of the Taskbar. If you simply click the icon, you'll see a single slider dialog box that you can use to change the volume for the system as a whole.

Note

If you don't see the Volume icon in the notification area of the Taskbar, open the Sounds and Audio Devices applet in the Control Panel. You'll see a Place volume icon in the taskbar option on the Volume tab of this dialog box. Check this option, click OK, and the Volume icon will appear in the notification area.

Double-clicking or right-clicking and choosing Open Volume Control from the context menu displays multiple sliders as shown in Figure 7.3. Notice that each slider also has a Mute or Mute All checkbox. Clicking Mute will turn off sound for that feature no matter where you have the volume slider set. This is good for turning the sound off temporarily, so you don't lose the volume setting.

FIGURE 7.3

The Volume Control allows you to set the volume level for the system as a whole or the separate components.

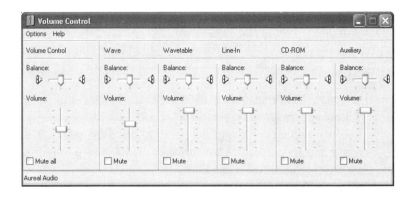

Tip

Use the Mute button as a diagnostic tool. Sometimes a sound system will develop hiss or noise that's hard to locate. Mute the features one at a time until you locate the culprit. You can look for the problem with this feature, which is normally a bad cable, but could be faulty circuitry as well. If you can't locate the source of the noise within that feature and you don't normally use the feature, you can simply keep it muted to keep the sound out of your system.

The Volume Control normally hides at least a few of the features that you can access. In addition, the view you see initially controls playback, not record. Use the Options Properties command to display the Properties dialog box. You'll see three areas of control. The Mixer Device field selects the device you use for mixing purposes. Normally, you have just one sound card in your system, so there isn't must to see in this area.

The Adjust Volume For group includes three options: Playback, Recording, and Other. The option you select determines the content of the Volume Control. It also controls the content of the Show the following volume controls list box.

You'll use the Show the following volume controls list box to determine which features appear in the Volume Control. Select the features you plan to use and leave the other clear to reduce the complexity of the Volume Control.

If you select Recording and then click OK, the Volume Control will change to a Recording Control. The same sliders are present as before. However, the Mute check box changes to a Select check box. You can only select one device at a time for input. Windows XP normally selects the microphone, but you can also select from the CD-ROM, line-in, video, and other ports.

Tip

If you hear noise or hissing while recording, you already know the culprit. Because you can only select one recording device at a time, only that device could produce the noise you hear. However, to ensure that you try to fix the right device, select another input device to see if the hiss or noise goes away. In most cases, if the hiss goes away, the problem is with a cable or input device such as a microphone, and not with the circuitry. If you still hear the noise and hissing, then the problem is likely in the soundboard.

Windows Media Player

Microsoft added so many improvements to the Windows Media Player that you'll hardly recognize it the first time you see it. Figure 7.4 shows a typical example of this utility with a CD loaded. Notice that the Windows Media Player automatically identifies the CD and provides track information. The following sections describe how to use the Windows Media Player. I'm describing the default Media Player configuration, except where noted. Each Windows Media Player "skin" places the controls in a different position. If you use something other than the default configuration, your screen and control positions will differ from the ones discussed in this section.

7

FIGURE 7.4

*The Windows Media
Player sports both new
looks and updated
features.*

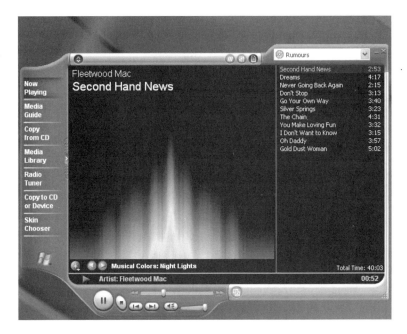

| Note | For those of you who were looking for the venerable CD Player with its interesting quirks, this particular utility no longer appears in Windows XP. You'll find that the Windows Media Player does a far better job than the CD Player could ever do. However, if you absolutely must have the CD Player to feel comfortable, the version from Windows 2000 works just fine under Windows XP. |

Windows Media Player General Operation

You can adjust every aspect of your Windows Media Player experience. For example, you can adjust the graphic in the center of the display. Click Select visualization or album art (the button with the asterisk in the lower left corner of the display area). You'll see a list of visualizations, plus an Album Art option. Interestingly enough, quite a few of my CDs were able to display the album art, even though I didn't supply this information to the computer (nor did I supply anything else about the CD). Choose the visualization you want to see (or the album cover). If you choose a visualization, you'll see two arrow buttons next to the visualization button. Click these arrows to see different versions of that visualization. If you want to see your visualization full screen, click View Full Screen in the lower right corner of the display area. This is the button with a window in the center and four arrows pointing outward from the edges of the window.

Tip

If you choose the album art visualization and then click on the album art, a copy of Internet Explorer will open. You'll go to the `http://windowsme-dia.com/` site where you'll see a list of all the albums available by the same group. The site will help you explore these other options. For example, you can play samples from many of the albums to determine if you'd like to hear more. You can buy the albums directly online if want with a few additional clicks. (The site links to CD-NOW.)

At the bottom of the screen, you'll see a set of ten controls. These controls allow you to control the current position in the CD by using pause, stop, next song, previous song, a position-seeking pointer, a rewind function, and a fast forward function. You can also control the volume of the music and mute it when necessary. The final button, Switch to skin mode, changes the appearance of the Windows Media Player to the selected skin. Figure 7.5 shows just one of the many skins you can choose.

FIGURE 7.5

Select the skin that suits your personal preferences.

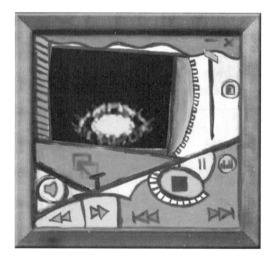

Yes, that's a Picasso-like picture and all of the painted buttons do work. You'll find quite a few skins for your Windows Media Player, and I anticipate that people will want to create their own.

Three of the four buttons at the top of the display control window will be displayed. The Show/Hide Menu Bar button controls the window surrounding the Windows Media Player. Normally, this window is invisible so you can see the effect of the skin. The Show/Hide Equalizer and Settings in Now Playing button displays a window immediately below the visualization window shown in Figure 7.4. This new window can display

7

the SRS WOW effect, graphic equalizer, video settings, media information, captions, and lyrics. The Show/Hide Playlist in Now Playing button shows a list of the songs you plan to play. Double-clicking a song in this list automatically changes the player to that song. The fourth button at the top, Turn Shuffle On/Off, automatically selects tracks at random when set to on. This means that the CD won't play end-to-end, but it will continuously play random selections.

The Lyrics option won't work right out of the package. Because the lyrics are copyrighted, Microsoft can't supply them for you. However, you can type them into the Windows Media Player yourself. Right-click the song you want to modify in the play list and choose Properties from the context menu. You'll see a Properties dialog box. Select Lyrics, and you'll see a field for the lyrics. Type the lyrics and click OK. Every time you play this song with the Lyrics option selected from this point on, the lyrics will be displayed.

The play list has a lot more to offer than allowing you to select the tracks on the CD and add lyrics. The context menu contains options to play the selected song, enable sections, and disable selections. Disabling a selection means Windows Media Player will skip it when playing the CD in either random or sequential order. The Edit option allows you to change the name of the song in the play list. You can also change the order of songs in the list using the Move Up and Move Down options. The context menu contains several other options that we'll discuss as part of performing other tasks.

Searching the Internet for Media Content

We haven't discussed many of the buttons on the left side of the Windows Media Player yet. You'll find several of them enable you to find media on the Internet. The main Internet button is Media Guide. Click this, and you'll go to WindowsMedia.com. This is Microsoft's main site for all things media.

The Radio Tuner feature also relies on the Internet. You click this option and after a few seconds, Windows Media Player displays the radio station page of WindowsMedia.com. Select a radio station and Windows Media Player will begin streaming content from it.

Using the Media Library

The Media Library helps you organize all your media. The first time you select it, you'll see a dialog box that asks if you want to search your hard drive for media. Click Yes, and Windows Media Player will begin the search. Of course, you can always conduct the search later using the Tools | Search for Media Files option (you can also press F3). After you click Yes, Windows Media Player will ask where to search for media on your system. However, unless you click Advanced, you won't see the additional options shown in Figure 7.6.

FIGURE 7.6

The Windows Media Player helps you find media on your system and helps eliminate media you don't want in the library.

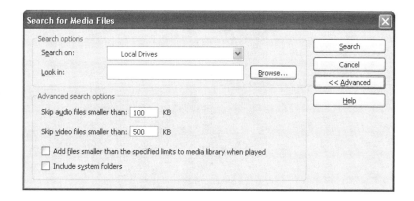

Select the search criteria you want to use for searching. The default settings may not work in all cases. For example, you may want to keep track of your sound bites in the library. The size options may prevent this by excluding files that are too small, yet fit within the sound bite category.

Notice that the default search criteria doesn't include system folders. If you want to include Microsoft supplied media in your list, you'll want to check the Include system folders option. In some cases, you might want to add files that you play to the media library even if they're smaller than the limits you set. The Search for Media Files dialog box also includes an option to address this concern. Once you're happy with the search settings, click Search, and Windows Media Player will begin searching your system for media. After the Windows Media Player finds all of your media, you'll need to click Close to exit the Search for Media Files dialog box.

The Media Library will categorize your audio and video data with a hierarchical format like the one shown in Figure 7.7. Notice that this library shows the video clips by author. Other selections present the data in other ways.

Creating a database of your media selections makes it easier to see what you have and to work with the data. You can play everything in your library. The Windows Media Player also allows you to copy the data to an audio CD or work with it in other ways. For example, you can use this screen to create and manage play lists.

Note

Some of the elements on the left side of the hierarchical list don't support a context menu. The choices for the selection normally appear at the top of the window, so you need to highlight the element before you can do anything with it. For example, if you want to create a new play list, you have to highlight My Playlists and click New Playlist at the top of the window.

7

FIGURE 7.7

*Use the Media Library
to organize your media
selections.*

Creating Your Own Audio CD

The Windows Media Player makes it possible to create your own audio CDs. The CDs
could contain anything you have recorded. You can also copy tracks from CDs that you
own and make your own "best of" compilations. Of course, you'll want to ensure that
you observe all copyright laws when you work with copyrighted materials.

The first step in creating an audio CD is to compile the content. Make any required
recordings as part of the first step. All WAV files must use the 44 KHz, 16-bit setting. If
you're making a CD compilation, you'll need to copy the songs from your CD to your
hard drive as a first step. All you need to do is place the CD into the drive. Windows
Media Player will automatically load it. Select the Copy from CD option, and you'll see
a list of songs like the one shown in Figure 7.8.

Place check marks next to each song that you want to copy. Click Copy Music. Windows
Media Player will display a message asking if you want to override the settings
Microsoft has put in place for protecting copyrighted music. If you say no, you won't be
able to copy music from most CDs. After you change the copyright setting for Windows
Media Player, it will copy the songs from the CD to the My Music folder on your hard
drive. It will create two levels of folders. The first level is for the group, while the second
is for the album. The songs will appear within the album folder.

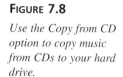

FIGURE 7.8

Use the Copy from CD option to copy music from CDs to your hard drive.

Now you need to collect all of the data in one place. Click Media Library. Select My Playlists and then New Playlist. Type a name for the new Playlist; then click OK. You can use the same technique that you use for Explorer to drag recordings from other folders and place them in your new play list.

At this point, you're ready to record. Click Copy to CD or Device. Select your play list from the drop-down list box. Make sure that all the entries say Ready to copy in the Status column. Click Copy Music. Windows Media Player will convert each of the files before it copies them. If it experiences any error, you'll see an error message along with instructions for fixing the problem.

Using the Windows Movie Maker

We already talked about the Windows Movie Maker to a limited extent in the "Windows Movie Maker" section of Chapter 1. The Windows Movie Maker allows you to create your own animations and movies. You can add sound to your movies by mixing a sound track with the pictures you capture. Given the capabilities of this product, you can use it for four purposes:

- **Animations** A series of hand drawn pictures that you use to create the effect of motion.

- **Movies**   A succession of real life images captured with a device such as a camera.
- **Analysis Tool**   If you have the equipment to capture live action video, you may not use Windows Movie Maker as an output device. You might use it to analyze the movie you captured.
- **Slide Shows**   Still life or hand drawn pictures placed in a sequence. The slide show presents a progression or set of related images without motion.

The reason I presented these three typical applications is that many people will look at the term, Windows Movie Maker, and envision a studio in Hollywood. This isn't a professional tool, but it does make a nice addition to the amateur's arsenal.

For many people, the slide show is going to be the most common use of the Windows Movie Maker. You can create everything from self-running presentations to a picture show for loving grandparents of your children's latest escapades. The point is that you can make Windows Movie Maker into your "soap box," your way to present you to the world.

A Look at the Controls

The Windows Movie Maker provides a reasonably easy set of controls to create your presentation. Figure 7.9 shows a typical display for a slide show.

FIGURE 7.9

The Windows Movie Maker provides a limited set of controls for creating a presentation.

Let's begin with the toolbars. Windows Movie maker provides four toolbars. The Standard Buttons toolbar contains buttons you might find in any applications such as New Project, Open, Save Project, Cut, Copy, Paste, and Delete. The Project toolbar contains the Save Movie (creates the movie), Send (email or Web server), and Record (from live video source such as a camera or video capture board) buttons. The Collections toolbar contains the Up One Level, New Collection, Collections (shows or hides the collection tree view), and Views buttons. Finally, the Location toolbar contains the Collection drop-down list box that allows you to switch between collections.

The Collections tree view shows a hierarchical view of your collections area of the hard drive. A collection is a folder that holds all of the data for a movie. This definitely means still images and captured video. However, you can also add sound bites and other audio files that you have on hand. In short, the collection is your central location for storing everything for your presentation.

The center pane in Figure 7.9 contains the collection. The folder you highlight in the Collections tree view appears in detail in this pane. The left and right panes have the same relationship in Windows Explorer. Notice that the figure shows the thumbnails view of the data. You can also use a details or list view. The thumbnails view is extremely practical while putting your presentation together because there are fewer chances for making mistakes.

The right pane contains an enlarged view of the highlighted object or objects. It also contains controls for playing your presentation. They're the same VCR-style controls you use with your home entertainment system. However, this control set also includes a Previous Frame and Next Frame button so that you can play the presentation one frame at a time. You'll also find Full Screen and Split Clip buttons. The Full Screen button comes in handy for a realistic look at the output from your presentation.

You'll find a combination of the storyboard and timeline on the bottom third of the screen in Figure 7.9. The storyboard and timeline are mutually exclusive. You can select between the two using the Timeline/Storyboard button. The Zoom In, Zoom Out, Record Narration, and Set Audio Levels buttons are only active when using timeline mode.

Part of the controls for the Windows Movie Maker are the options you can set for the application as a whole. Use the View | Options command to display the Options dialog box shown in Figure 7.10.

The Default Author field should contain the name of the person creating the movie. Windows Movie Maker defaults to the current username, but you can use any value you like.

7

FIGURE 7.10

Use the options to change the default Windows Movie Maker behavior.

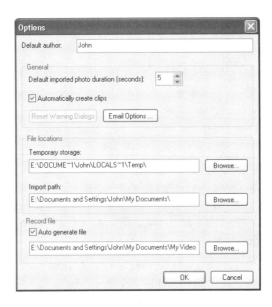

Notice the Default imported photo duration (seconds) field. Adjusting this value before you import data for your collection can save time later when you need to create a time-line. If all the images will take the same amount of time, then setting this value now means that you won't have to fiddle with the timeline later. Unfortunately, this setting only allows full seconds. It won't help much when working with animation.

You'll also want to check all of the file storage locations. Windows Movie Maker assumes that you want to use your personal directory for all storage needs. This works fine unless you're sharing the data with someone else. You'll want to change these settings to a common directory for collaboration purposes.

The E-mail Options button displays the E-mail Movie dialog box. This is the service that Windows Movie Maker will use if you create a movie and then use the File | Send Movie To | E-mail command to send it to someone on the Internet. Make sure that you select the correct service if you have more than one e-mail account. Windows Movie Maker will give you another opportunity to change this value when you actually send a movie to someone on the Internet.

Creating a Movie

How do you make a "movie" using Windows Movie Maker? First, you need to decide what kind of presentation you want to create. In Chapter 1, I showed you a series of images you could easily turn into animation. The clock hands would move around and simulate time moving too fast for words. The time interval between pictures would create the animation effect. In this case, we're looking at a faster time interval of about a second or less. You have to give the viewer time to see the image, but not enough time for the animation to look jumpy. In fact, cartoons and other forms of professional animation use extremely small movements between pictures and present the images at 30 frames per section or higher.

If you decide to make a slideshow, the time between pictures is much longer. You need time to tell about the picture before the image changes. Of course, you don't want to drone on about the same picture for hours, so it's important to choose between speed and presentation content.

Finally, if you do have the equipment to capture live video, the camera decides the interval between pictures for you. The most you want to do is touch the pictures up, if necessary.

The second step is to create a collection and fill it with content. To create the new collection, click New Collection; then type the collection name and press Enter.

You can use several methods to collect data for your presentation. The easiest method is to import existing data. Use the File | Import command to display the Select the File to Import dialog box. You can use the Ctrl-Click method to select multiple files within this dialog box. If you plan to acquire still images from a scanner, you'll need to scan the images first and then import them into the Windows Movie Maker (see the "Acquiring Images" section of this chapter for details).

The Windows Movie Maker also provides the means to collect live data from a camera or a video capture board. Click Record to start the process. You'll see the Record dialog box shown in Figure 7.11.

You'll need to select several options in this dialog box before you can begin a recording. First, make sure that you select an option in the Record field. Windows Movie Maker enables you to choose between video only, audio only, or both video and audio. It's also important to configure the input devices. Click change to display the Change Device dialog box. Notice that you have to choose both a device and an input line for both video and audio. Some video devices provide video composite, video tuner, and video SVideo input (among others). The Record Time Limit field helps you keep track of disk usage by limiting the size of the file you can create. Make sure that you also set a quality setting. The Windows Movie Maker provides high, medium, and low, along with another setting that allows you to set your own parameters. Finally, you can click Record to collect live images. When you click Record, Windows Movie Maker will begin recording the live data. Click Stop to end the recording and save the file on disk.

7

FIGURE **7.11**

The Record dialog box allows you to choose settings for recording live video for your presentation.

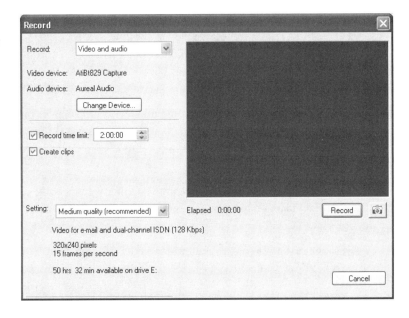

Note

You can also use the Record dialog box to collect still images from a camera. Instead of clicking Record, click Take Photo next to it. This is the button with the little camera on it.

The third step is to tell a story. Good presentations interest an audience because they draw the audience into the presentation. The audience has to care about what they're seeing. A storyboard allows you to set the sequence of events for your presentation. It doesn't tell when the events will happen, just that they'll happen and in what order. You want to create the storyboard first because it allows you to concentrate on the sequence of events for your movie.

To create a storyboard using Windows Movie Maker, drag objects from the collections area to the Storyboard. (Make sure that the bottom third of the screen is in storyboard mode.) You can change the order of the pictures by dragging them to a new location.

Tip

When creating the annotation for your presentation, place the audio for each graphic in a separate file. This enables you to synchronize audio and video better. The audio files provide clear end-of-file indicators that you can use with the pictures.

The fourth step is to create a timeline. This step can get tricky because you have to coordinate both video and audio elements. Click Timeline to display the timeline view of your presentation. Figure 7.12 shows a typical timeline example. If you can't see the trim points, then use Zoom In to enlarge the picture. The trim points are the two triangles on the timeline. They control the start and end times for each picture.

FIGURE 7.12

Use the timeline to coordinate the elements of your presentation.

You'll need to play your presentation several times to get the timing correct. To play the presentation, select the first image on the timeline, press Shift, and select the last image on the timeline. The Windows Movie Maker will highlight all of the pictures in your presentation. Click Play to start the presentation. Adjust the trim points of your presentation as needed to synchronize the pictures with the audio.

The final step in creating the movie is to create a copy and watch it. Click Save Movie. You'll see the Save Movie dialog box. Select a quality level in the Setting field. Type any information you want to appear with the movie. Finally, click OK. Windows Movie Maker will output the presentation at the quality level you requested. It will ask if you want to watch the presentation. Click OK and enjoy.

Scanner and Camera Support

At one time, scanners were rare PC peripherals and cameras were unheard of, even on expensive setups. Today, both scanners and cameras are common devices. Users have found that the camera and scanner are money-saving devices in the long term. You can capture as many pictures of the family get-together as you want with a digital camera—and development is free. Likewise, scanning both images and text is a requirement for many home and business users today.

The following sections will help you install, configure, and use these new peripherals that have found their way onto many systems. Fortunately, Windows XP does a superior job of detecting these devices, so you may not even have to worry about device installation. I won't tell you which devices to buy or about any quirks for a particular device. You'll need to consult the vendor documentation for any oddities that come with your device.

7

Installing a New Device

Before you can scan the first article or capture your first picture, you'll need to set your system up to recognize the device. Normally, Windows XP will perform this detection automatically. This is especially true if Windows XP provides built-in support for the device. You may have to configure the device by hand if your scanner or camera is so new that Windows XP shipped without support for them. The following steps tell you how to install a new camera or scanner.

1. Open the Scanners and Cameras folder in the Control Panel. Double-click the Add Device icon. You'll see the Welcome screen of the Scanner and Camera Installation Wizard.

2. Click Next. Unlike other installation wizards for Windows XP, the Scanner and Camera Installation Wizard will normally display the "Which scanner or camera do you want to install?" dialog box shown in Figure 7.13 immediately.

FIGURE 7.13

You'll need to know your scanner or camera vendor name and model number.

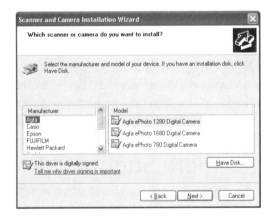

3. Select a vendor and the scanner or camera model number. You can also click Have Disk and follow the prompts to read installation information from a floppy or CD-ROM if necessary. Click Next. The Scanner and Camera Installation Wizard will ask for connection information. You can choose the port if you know it, or ask the wizard to detect it for you automatically.

4. Select a connection option and then click Next. The Scanner and Camera Installation Wizard will ask for a name for the device.

5. Type a device name; then click Next. You'll see a completion dialog box.

6. Click Finish.

At this point, you should see the new device in the Scanners and Cameras folder. It's still not ready to use because you don't know if the device will work. Right-click the device and select Properties from the context menu. You'll see a Device Properties dialog box. The General tab of this dialog box normally contains a diagnostic section with a Test button. Click Test. Windows XP will test the unit and report success or failure. If the system reports success, you're ready to go. Otherwise, make sure that you check cables, port settings, and the device itself for potential problems. You must turn the device on to test it.

Configuration Tips

Scanners and cameras are normally simple devices from a configuration standpoint. Most devices will provide a Color Management tab on their Device Properties dialog box. You can add or remove color schemes as needed to obtain good image captures from the devices. Generally, the default color settings will work just fine.

Some devices also include vendor specific tabs. You'll need to consult the vendor documentation for usage instructions on these tabs. However, the custom tabs are often the source of problems with these devices. The vendor will provide a custom tab so the user can configure the device for optimal performance. The default settings may work, but normally you have to "tweak" the device to get it to work properly.

Acquiring Images

The purpose of installing a scanner or camera is to obtain images for your computer. Both devices require some type of image acquisition software. Fortunately, Microsoft built this software right into Windows XP. The following steps show you how to use the built-in software to scan an image. (Other image capture procedures are similar to this one.)

1. Double-click the device entry in the Scanners and Cameras folder found in the Control Panel. You'll see a Scanner and Camera dialog box.

2. Click Next. You'll see a Choose Scanning Preferences dialog box like the one shown in Figure 7.14. This dialog box looks deceptively simple, but it contains hidden settings that you need to adjust to get a good image capture. The first thing you need to do is select an image type.

3. Select an image type. Use the appropriate type for the image you want to capture. For example, while you must use the color setting for color images, the black-and-white setting actually produces images with higher definition. The second thing you need to do is to tweak the scan area and settings.

7

FIGURE 7.14

*The Choose Scanning
Preferences dialog box
contains options for
choosing scanner and
camera settings.*

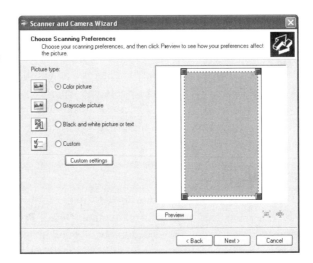

4. Click Preview. Windows XP will scan the entire bed the first time. This will allow you to grab just the part of the image that you need.

5. Use the sizing squares to adjust the size of the scanning area to match your image. Notice the two buttons on the right side of the dialog box. You can use these buttons to see the entire scanning area to adjust the sizing squares and then zoom into the capture area to see how it fits with the scanned image. After you size the image, you need to check image quality. If the image quality is less than perfect, you'll need to set some custom settings.

6. Click Custom Settings, if necessary. You'll see the Properties dialog box. Notice that you can adjust the resolution of the image, as well as the image type. It pays to adjust the image resolution to match the output resolution of your printer. For example, most laser printers offer 600 dpi resolution, compared to the 150 dpi default resolution of the Windows XP capture software. You can also adjust the image contrast and brightness—a must for color images.

7. Make any required custom setting changes. Click Preview after each change to verify image quality. Click Next. You'll see a Picture Name and Destination dialog box. This dialog box allows you to choose an output file type. Make sure that you use an appropriate file type so you don't lose information during an image conversion. The JPG and PNG file formats work well on the Internet. The PNG format may not work with older browsers, so use JPG for highest compatibility. You should use the TIF or BMP formats for local storage. The BMP format offers maximum compatibility with Windows applications, but TIF is more efficient.

8. Select the image storage options, type an image name, and click Next. You'll see a Scanning Picture dialog box. After the scanning process completes, you'll see an

Other Options dialog box. You can use the options on this dialog box to send content to the Internet or order copies of the pictures from a photo Web site.

9. Choose one of the other options or tell Windows XP that you're finished for right now. Click Next. You'll see a completion dialog box.

10. Click Finish. You now have an electronic copy of the scanned image.

Multimedia Hardware Support

It's important to know how to configure multimedia support on your system. For example, Windows XP assumes that you have standard desktop speakers. If you don't change this setting, you'll never receive the full value from your speaker purchase. Windows XP provides multimedia hardware support through the Sounds and Audio Devices applet in the Control Panel. The following sections describe the tabs in this dialog box and tell you how to use the controls they contain to configure your system.

Controlling Volume

The Volume tab appears in Figure 7.15. The Device Volume slider serves the same purpose as the single slider version of the Volume Control that you can access from the notifications area of the Taskbar. Click Advanced, and you'll see the full Volume Control dialog box. Notice the Place volume icon in the taskbar option. Check this option if you want to see the speaker icon in the notification area.

FIGURE 7.15

Use the Volume tab to set the output options for your soundboard.

Click Speaker Volume, and you'll see a Speaker Volume dialog box. This dialog box allows you to adjust the output volume for the speaker, not the soundboard. Many speakers are unaffected by these settings. However, when the setting does affect your

7

speaker, you can use it to balance out the sound for specific purposes. For example, one speaker may sit closer than the other and changing this setting will equalize the volume level.

One of the dialog boxes you'll want to check is Advanced Audio Properties. Click Advanced to see this dialog box. The Speakers tab enables you to adjust the type of speaker that Windows XP optimized the output to handle. There are settings for everything—from no speaker at all to 7.1 surround-sound speakers. The laptop speaker settings are nice change from previous versions of Windows. This setting seems to help many laptops produce reasonable sound, although the small speakers found in most laptops will always sound tinny compared to full-sized, surround-sound speakers.

The Performance tab contains sliders that adjust the performance of your system. The first slider adjusts the level of hardware acceleration used for special features such as 3D sound. The higher you adjust this level, the more Windows XP relies on the soundboard to handle the sound processing requirements. The second slider adjusts the sample rate conversion quality. This setting, more than any other, can make a big difference in the sound you hear. Use the best setting your system will support to get high quality output.

Selecting Sounds

The Sounds tab shown in Figure 7.16 contains the list of system events and corresponding sounds that you hear as you work with Windows. The number of events you see in the Program Events list depends on the operating system features and applications you have installed on your system. You'll always see some event categories such as Windows in this list.

FIGURE 7.16

The Sounds tab contains the list of program events and associated sounds you hear while working with Windows XP.

You can change sound settings by selecting an entry from the Sound Scheme list. Windows XP also allows you to store your favorite setups as sound schemes. Simply make adjustments to the entries in the Program Events list and click Save As. You'll see a Save Scheme As dialog box. Type a name for the scheme and click OK.

To assign a new sound to a program event, highlight the event name in the Program Events list. Select a sound from the Sounds drop-down list box or click Browse to locate the sound you want to use. If you want to hear what the sound is like, click the arrow key. Windows XP will play the sound selected in the Sounds drop down list box.

Configuring Audio

The Audio tab allows you to assign a device to the playback, recording, and musical instrument device interface (MIDI). To change a device, select a new option from the appropriate drop-down list box. Windows XP normally selects the best device for a particular task if you have one soundboard. However, you'll normally need to adjust these settings if you have multiple soundboards or a specialty device such as a MIDI board installed in your system.

You'll also notice that the devices have a Volume and Advanced button. Click Volume to display the Volume Control or Recording Control dialog boxes. Click Advanced if you want to change the settings on the Advanced Audio Properties dialog box.

Adjusting Voice

Like the Audio tab, you'll use the entries on the Voice tab to adjust your hardware settings. However, in this case, the settings adjust voice recording and playback. The Volume and Advance buttons work the same as the Audio tab.

The one difference on this tab is the Test Hardware button. Click this button if you want to adjust the voice settings for your system. You'll see the Sound Hardware Test Wizard. Click Next to get past the Welcome screen. The wizard will perform a diagnostic on your hardware and then display a Microphone Test dialog box. Speak into the microphone and adjust the volume; then click Next. You'll see a Speaker Test dialog box. Talk into the microphone again, adjust the volume, and click Next. You'll see a completion dialog box. Click Finish.

Verifying Hardware

The Hardware tab provides a complete list of the multimedia hardware on your system. You'll want to check this list to ensure that Windows XP recognizes all your devices. Click Troubleshoot if you see a non-functional device listed. Click Properties if you want to adjust the settings for a device or update its driver.

7

Text to Speech Support

The Text to Speech support provided by Windows XP may sound like a separate feature at first, but it's really Narrator (discussed in the "Narrator" section of Chapter 6) in disguise. You can access the Speech Properties dialog box shown in Figure 7.17 by using the Speech applet.

FIGURE 7.17

The Speech Properties dialog box contains a single tab, Text To Speech.

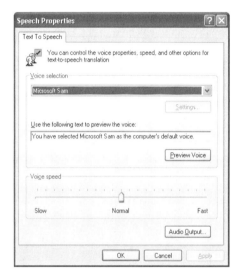

The Voice Selection field allows you to choose a new default voice from the drop-down list box. However, Windows XP only ships with one voice, Microsoft Sam. Eventually, third-party vendors will ship other voices. As you can see, Text To Speech disables the associated Settings button because Microsoft Sam doesn't use it. A third-party voice could use this button to configure special voice features.

The voice preview feature includes a text field and the Preview Voice button. Microsoft supplies a default line of text, but you can type anything you'd like to hear. Click Preview Voice, and Microsoft Sam will talk to you.

Microsoft Sam doesn't have the most pleasant voice in the world, but it's definitely usable. You can adjust Microsoft Sam for your personal likes by adjusting the Voice Speed slider. You can also adjust the volume of the voice by clicking Audio and then clicking Volume in the Text To Speech Output Settings dialog box. Note that the Speech Properties dialog box doesn't offer the pitch setting found in the Narrator setup, so you may prefer to set the voice settings that way.

Recording Your Own Data CDs

Unlike previous versions of Windows, you no longer have to have a third-party application to burn CDs in Windows XP. Considering that many computers come with CD drives capable of burning CDs today, this is an especially useful feature. The CD burning capability is automatic. The moment you place a blank CD (one you can burn) into the CD drive, Windows XP will display a dialog CD Drive dialog box similar to the one shown in Figure 7.18. The following steps will show you how to record your own data CD.

FIGURE 7.18

The CD Drive dialog box appears automatically when you place blank media in a recordable CD drive.

1. Highlight Open writable CD folder using Windows Explorer and click Ok.

2. Place all of the files you want to write into the single pane view of Explorer. You can create folders to organize the data by right-clicking the folder area and selecting New | Folder from the context menu. Theoretically, you can also create new data files within the folder, but normally you'll drag completed files into the folder for copying. The content for your CD should appear in finished format before you try to create the CD.

3. Use the File | Write these files to CD command to start the writing process. You'll see the CD Writing Wizard. The first thing you need to decide on is a name for your CD. Use a descriptive name that will tell you the content of the CD. For example, Sams Data is less descriptive than Proj 101 Data. Use the most precise short name you can think of for the CD.

7

Caution   CD writing is a one-time process under Windows XP. Verify the files in the temporary folder before you commit them to the CD-ROM. The burning process creates a physical change that you can't undo.

4. Click Next. The writing process will begin. Check your CD drive to ensure that it's actually writing data (normally the light on the front of the CD drive is a different color for reading than writing). Be patient and don't touch the CD drive until the CD Writing Wizard tells you to do so. The progress indicator tells you how long the writing process will take. When the CD Writing Wizard is complete, the drive will open. You'll see an option to write the data files to another CD. If you check this option, you'll need to add another CD to the drive.

5. Click Finish to complete the CD writing processing.

6. Verify the content of the CD by closing the drive door and viewing the contents using Windows Explorer. After you verify that the CD contains the data you want, you can get rid of the temporary files.

7. Close the initial Explorer single pane view. Windows XP will automatically remove the temporary files from your system.

Game Controller Configuration

Unlike most devices, Windows XP won't normally detect your game controller because it won't be able to detect it through the game port on your machine. This means that you have to install support for your game controller separately. The following steps tell you how to install a new game controller.

1. Open the Game Controllers applet found in the Control Panel. You'll see the Game Controllers dialog box. Check this dialog box to ensure that the game controller doesn't appear in the list. If it does, check the status column; you may find that the device is already recognized and functional. Adding a device twice can have undesirable results.

2. Click Add. You'll see the Add Game Controller dialog box. Notice the Custom button in this dialog box. If you click this button, you'll see the Custom Game Controller dialog box shown in Figure 7.19. As you can see, you'll need to configure all of the specifics for the custom game controller.

3. Choose a standard game controller or configure a custom game controller. Click OK. Windows XP will add the new game controller to the Installed Game Controllers list on the Game Controllers dialog box. You need to test and adjust the game controller before you can use it.

4. Click Properties. You'll see a Properties dialog box for your game controller. The Test tab will help you check the buttons and the positioning capability of the controller. The Settings tab will help you calibrate the controller. To calibrate the game controller, click Calibrate and follow the prompts provided by the Game Device Calibration Wizard.

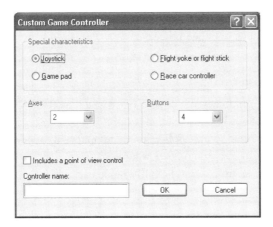

FIGURE 7.19

Windows XP provides options for configuring a custom game controller.

5. Test and calibrate your device. Click OK. Click OK a second time to close the Game Controllers dialog box.

Configuring Windows Games

Windows has always had a love/hate relationship with games for a variety of reasons. With the advent of DirectX, gaming became better for Windows 9x users, but not for Windows 2000 users. You had to choose between a secure system and one that would run your games. Windows XP breaks this mold for the most part by providing some innovations that Windows 2000 users could only dream about.

Unfortunately, game users will experience one problem that defies an instant fix. Those of us who are lucky enough to have dual processor machines will also find that many games won't work. You can play them for a while, but will eventually find yourself back in Windows. The problem is easy to fix once you know what it is. All you need to do is make the game think you have one processor by following these steps.

1. Start your application as normal. However, as soon as it gets to a menu or other stable location, use Shift+Tab to get back to Windows.

2. Right-click the Taskbar and choose Task Manager from the context menu. You'll see the Windows Task Manager dialog box.

3. Select the Applications tab and locate the game within the list.

4. Right-click the game entry and choose Go to Process from the context menu. Task Manager will highlight the appropriate entry on the Processes tab.

5. Right-click the process and choose Set Affinity from the context menu. You'll see a Processor Affinity dialog box. This dialog box tells Windows XP which

7

processors to assign to an application. Remember, we want to fool the game into thinking we have only one processor.

6. Clear the CPU 1 checkbox. Click OK.

7. Close the Windows Task Manager. Enjoy your game.

Some games won't run under Windows XP because they think it's Windows NT/2000 or there's something about Windows XP they don't like. You can get around this problem in many situations by running the application in compatibility mode. Windows XP will fool the game into thinking it is some other version of Windows. The following steps show you how to set a game up for compatibility mode use.

1. Locate the game shortcut on the Start Menu. Right-click the entry and choose Properties from the context menu. Select the Compatibility tab, and you'll see a dialog like the one shown in Figure 7.20.

FIGURE 7.20

Use the Compatibility tab to fool your game into thinking that it's running under another version of Windows.

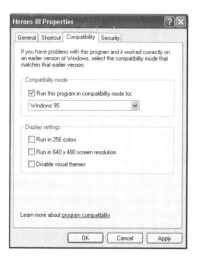

2. Check the Run this program in compatibility mode for option. Select one of the operating system versions you think will run the application.

3. Check any required display settings. For example, many pieces of educational software require you to set the display to 256 colors. Unfortunately, Windows XP doesn't support this mode, so you need to emulate it.

4. Click OK. Windows XP will apply the new settings to your game.

5. Test the game by selecting its entry in the Start Menu. If the game plays correctly, then the compatibility settings have helped. Otherwise, it's unlikely that you'll be able to run the game under Windows XP.

Always start the game using the shortcut you just set up. Otherwise, Windows XP won't know how to run it using compatibility mode. Some games offer to start immediately when you place the CD in the drive and close it, but this won't work with games that need to run in compatibility mode.

Troubleshooting DirectX

Most games rely on DirectX today, so if DirectX isn't working on your system, then the games probably won't work either. If Microsoft has a deep dark secret for gamers to discover, it's that DirectX doesn't have to be impossible to troubleshoot. All you really need to know is where to look and how to understand what to do with the information you find.

The first step is to start the DirectX diagnostic utility. You won't find it on your Start Menu. Open the Run dialog box, type DXDIAG, and click OK. You'll see a DirectX Diagnostic Tool dialog box like the one shown in Figure 7.21.

FIGURE 7.21

The DirectX Diagnostic Tool checks your DirectX installation for problems.

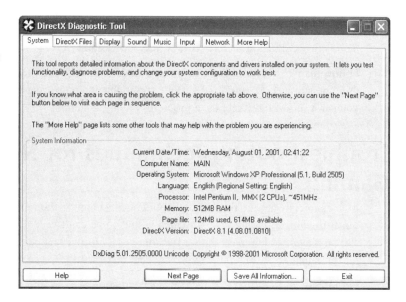

The first setting I always check is the DirectX Version entry near the bottom of the dialog box. You need to go to the DirectX Web site (`http://www.microsoft.com/direc-tx/default.asp`) to verify this version number against the current version that Microsoft supports. If you see that the Web site contains a newer version, download it, install it,

7

and restart your machine. Check the game again to see if it works. If the game still doesn't work, you'll need to perform some additional troubleshooting.

Notice the Next Page button at the bottom of the screen in Figure 7.21. You'll find a button like that one on most of the DirectX tabs. What the button doesn't tell you is that clicking it runs a test on your system. Try clicking it now, and you'll advance to the DirectX Files tab. If you see No Problems Found in the Notes section, you know that the test passed.

Click Next Page again, and you'll advance to the Display tab. The same success or failure message will appear in the Notes field again. However, this time you'll also see some diagnostic buttons. For example, you can disable Direct3D Acceleration by clicking the associated Disable button. Before you cripple your system, however, you'll want to test its compatibility with DirectX. Click Test DirectDraw, and the DirectX Diagnostic Tool will perform extended tests on your system. If everything goes well, click Test Direct3D. These tests will verify that your display adapter can work with DirectX and therefore work with the games on your system. If you do run into problems, the DirectX Diagnostic Tool normally provides enough information for you to fix the problem yourself or ask intelligent questions of a support person. In some cases, you have to disable a hardware acceleration feature to gain true compatibility.

Follow the Next Page and testing process until you get to the More Help tab. If everything passes at this point, your system is completely compatible with DirectX. The game you can't run would likely have problems on any system.

Troubleshooting Techniques for Network Gaming

Many gamers want the thrill of competing against another human being today. Generally, the artificial intelligence (AI) provided with a game can't keep up with the mind of a skilled player, which makes the game somewhat boring. The only problem with multiplayer games is getting the network connection to work.

Let me say up front that you'll experience situations on the Internet when no amount of screen banging will result in a good connection. Sometimes Internet connections fail, and you can't do anything about it. The tips in the following sections skip over some of the impossible and esoteric problems I've heard about. We'll discuss common problems that gamers experience.

Adjusting Your LAN for Games

You have full control over your LAN, but sometimes it seems to fight harder against playing a game than any Internet connection. The good news is that you can fix any non-performance or non-game related problem that you'll experience with your LAN. If the problem is hardware or configuration related, you won't have a problem fixing it.

The first thing to do is check the simple problems. For example, if the machines aren't on the same network segment, you'll find it difficult to play. Check your network addresses to make sure they're in the same subnet. Right-click My Network Places and choose Properties from the context menu. You'll see the Network Connections dialog box. Right-click Local Area Connection and choose Status from the context menu. Select the Support tab. Look at the IP Address and the Subnet Mask entries. The subnet entries must match. So, if your machine has an IP address of 192.168.0.5 and the other machine has an IP address of 192.168.0.25 and the subnet mask is 255.255.255.0, the two machines should be able to communicate. The subnet for both machines is 192.168.0. If the two machines aren't on the same subnet, you'll need to configure one of them by using the instructions in the "TCP/IP Configuration" section of Day 14.

After you establish that the two machines can talk, you should check to ensure that they actually do have a connection. Open a command prompt and type **PING <Other Machine Name>**; then press Enter. The other machine should respond. PING will test the connection four times for you. If the connection fails, you need to check problems such as a failed network interface card (NIC), a bad cable, a disconnection, or even a bad hub.

If the two machines can communicate by using PING, then there's nothing wrong with your hardware or machine specific configuration. It's time to recheck the game manual and see if there's a problem with your game configuration. Generally, games will ask you to provide the address of the other machine. You could make a mistake entering the address. "Close" doesn't work with TCP/IP, so you must configure it exactly right. If nothing else, type everything back in again and pay close attention to problems such as replacing a 0 (zero) with an O.

Sometimes, the game is broken, and there's no doubt about it. Unfortunately, the game developer won't call your house and tell you about the problem. In addition, game product support may not know about the problem or any existing fixes. You may find that a third party has released the fix and the game vendor doesn't even know about it. That's when you need to get online and check the game newsgroups online. Someone is almost certain to know about the problem. If there's a fix, they can usually tell you where to find it.

7

Configuring Internet Games

Getting Internet games to talk is about the same as working with LAN games; only the players are different. You still need to check your local setups first. However, the IP address for your machine will vary from that of your friend. It's important to get the right IP address. Make sure that you use the number from your dial-up or cable connection instead of the one for the local connection.

You also need to check with your Internet Service Provider (ISP). In some cases, a game will fail to run because the connection is extra slow. The ISP support staff can generally tell you if there's a problem with the line. If there is, you'll probably have to wait to play your game another day.

Don't assume that because a game's LAN connection works that the Internet connection also works. It would seem like the software used to make a direct connection would also make the remote connection, but this isn't always true. So, if you have doubts about the vendor's ability to deliver a solid product, you'll want to check online again and see if there's a patch that fixes the problem.

Playing Windows Games

Windows XP comes packed with more games than any previous version of Windows. These aren't long or complex games, they're the type you play while the boss isn't looking or during a break. You'll find all the usual favorites: Solitaire, Mine Sweeper, Free Cell, and Pinball. All of these games play the same as they always did in the past. Microsoft has also included Hearts in the mix. You can play this game locally against three computer opponents.

One of the most addictive new games is Spider Solitaire shown in Figure 7.22. This is another form of the popular game where you place like suits on top of each other instead of alternating red and black. When you have a complete set of 13 cards, the game automatically picks them up and puts them aside. The draw pile works differently than other versions of solitaire. You select an entire set of cards, one for each row of the game board. One of the features I like about Spider Solitaire is that you get to choose the level of difficulty. The hard game really is hard to play.

Microsoft also includes a series of Internet games with Windows XP. To play these games, you must have an MSN account. There isn't any way to play them across a LAN or with other users who don't have an MSN account. You'll find old favorites such as backgammon, reversi, checkers, spades, and hearts.

FIGURE 7.22

Spider Solitaire is one of the most addicting forms of solitaire that you'll ever play.

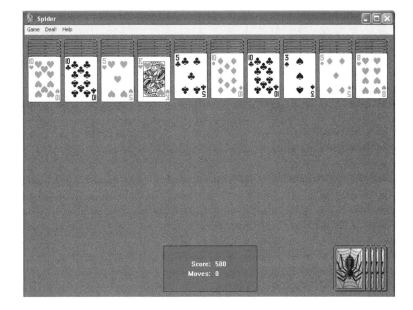

Summary

Today you've learned about multimedia on your computer. I hope you agree that Windows XP includes a wealth of new multimedia features, some of which will affect everything form the way you tell people about your latest vacation to the way you run your business. The level of multimedia support you obtain with Windows XP is better than any previous version of Windows.

Q&A

Q: Why doesn't the Windows Media Player list the statistics for my favorite album?

A: You may be running into one of several problems. The first problem is that Windows Media Player requires a connection to the Internet before it can supply your system with media data. The first place to check is your Internet connection to ensure that the Windows Media Player can grab the data it needs. The second problem is the level of content on the Microsoft Web site. It contains information for many CDs, but not every CD. If a CD is too old or too new, your chances of obtaining any information about it are slim. Finally, you won't ever see some types of information from the Windows Media Player without a little work on your part. For example, you won't see any lyrics unless you type them in yourself.

7

Q: Why does the animation I created using the Windows Movie Maker look jerky?

A: I'm not a professional in this area. However, the animation books I've read show that animators use many pictures with evenly spaced amounts of movement. The interval between each picture must remain constant or the viewer's eye will notice the discrepancy. Early animators were so concerned about the even movement and constant time problems that they would study live action video for hours to detect how the real world moves. Because I'm not a professional, I use graphics I can control easily, such as the clock example in Chapter 1, to create an animation with a somewhat smooth appearance.

Q: Why doesn't the live video capture seem to work on my system; the clip is always blank?

A: Make sure that you can see the live video in the window in the Record dialog box before you begin recording. If you can't see the live video, check the cabling and ensure the device is on. It's also important to install any device drivers you need. For example, the tuner on most video boards won't work by using the default Windows XP drivers; you need a special driver from the vendor.

Q: Why do sounds sometimes repeat on my system or disappear completely?

A: You'll normally see odd sound system behavior when the hardware acceleration settings on the Performance tab of the Advanced Audio Properties dialog box are set too high. Make sure that you set these sliders as high as they can go without affecting system performance or sound quality. In some cases, this will mean accepting lower quality sound output to ensure you get any output at all.

Workshop

Welcome to the end of the first week! We've covered a lot of ground this week—everything from installing Windows XP, to using the product, and beyond. It's time to test your knowledge of multimedia and games. You can find answers to the quiz and exercise questions in Appendix A at the back of the book.

Quiz

1. What's the easiest way to discover the source of hiss or noise when playing back a sound on your system?

2. You want to record a WAV file onto a CD. What are the recording attributes for such a file?

3. Does the Windows XP CD Writing Wizard allow you to create music CDs? How many times can you write a single CD?

Exercises

1. Learn to use the Windows Media Player.

2. Try creating your own slide show or animation.

3. Try burning your own data CD.

4. Tune your audio system for best performance.

7

WEEK 2

At a Glance

This week we'll discuss Windows management issues. You'll begin by looking at what you need to do to work with users. The discussion will move on to software and hardware issues. As the week progresses, you'll learn how to configure services, work with the registry, and take care of the special needs of laptops and handheld devices. The week ends with the first discussion of networking topics. You'll learn the prerequisites for setting up a network, such as installing the proper Windows XP support.

- Day 8, "Working with Users," is the first day in the "basic configuration" section of the book. It contains an overview of the Computer Management Microsoft Management Console (MMC) console, which provides a centralized place to manage most computer activities. The user management section begins by looking at the process for setting up users and groups on the local workstation. The next section looks at the process of sharing data with other users. Finally, we'll look at how to set up a single workstation to accommodate multiple users.

- Day 9, "Working with Software," looks at how you can install and remove both third-party and Microsoft-supplied applications. We'll also discuss how you can monitor application performance using the Event Viewer and the performance monitoring MMC snap-ins. The day ends by looking at ancillary application setup requirements.

- Day 10, "Working with Hardware," begins with a simple look at the installation and configuration of hardware as a whole. The "Using Device Manager" section is important because it tells you how to manage your hardware. The sections that follow examine specific types of hardware in detail.

- Day 11, "Configuring Services," looks at services in general—how to install, configure, and manage them. This day's goal is to provide general information and to discuss services that don't fit well in other days. For example, we'll discuss the Indexing service and how to work with the power management options.

- Day 12, "Working with the Registry," focuses on working with the registry. The day begins by looking at the RegEdit utility Microsoft provides for modifying the registry. I'll show you how to perform every registry-oriented task by using this single utility. The remainder of the day shows how to perform common registry editing tasks. The final section discusses how the reader can reverse certain types of registry entries by looking within INF files.

- Day 13, "Using Laptops and Handheld Devices," discusses laptops and handheld devices from a Windows perspective. One of the issues we'll discuss during this day is how to make these devices perform optimally. During this day, we'll discuss several techniques for transferring data and keeping shared data synchronized. Finally, because these devices often rely on battery power, I include a special power management section.

- Day 14, "Setting Up a Network," begins with a discussion of network setup and configuration in general. The second goal of this day is to look at special networking features, such as firewall support. Finally, we'll look at Microsoft Message Queue (MSMQ), which Microsoft has changed to Queued Components.

DAY 8

Working with Users

Today we're going to look at user management. The entire purpose of creating a network is to make users more efficient, in order to enable them to do more than they could in the past. The network has to answer the needs of users, yet protect them from themselves. Many network administrators consider users the toughest part of the networking picture because users are unpredictable, and you can't lock them in a closet like you can a server.

It's important to have good tools when managing a network and the users it serves. Good management tools help you see the big picture. They also help you monitor the network for problem areas and perform configuration tasks quickly. The Microsoft Management Console (MMC) is an application that can help you do all this and more. You'll learn how MMC works today. We'll begin by looking at the issue of computer management. One tool allows you to manage both local and remote computers, so the process is essentially the same for either task.

Security is one of the tools that network administrators use to ensure that users obtain what they need from the network. The security policies you set determine how a user interacts with the system as a whole. It also affects a user's attitude toward the network. If you set a security policy that's too strict, the user will constantly fight with the system to gain access to the most basic of resources. Users on a restrictive network are often unhappy and don't mind telling everyone why. On the other hand, networks that have lenient security policies set themselves up for failure. I'll show you how to create network policies today and help you understand the ramifications of certain configuration choices you'll need to make.

Finally, users require access to resources. Most network resources are difficult to abuse because you maintain a security policy that controls access. However, users always find a way to abuse the hard drives on a network. Every byte of space will disappear in short order if you're not careful. We'll look at some management policies that help users understand the cost of the network resources they use, so they can manage them with greater care.

An Overview of Computer Management

Windows XP relies mainly on the MMC for computer management tasks. You'll find the MMC in one form or another in most of the management tools provided with Windows XP. However, Windows XP also relies on other tools. For example, the backup application is still stand-alone; it isn't part of the MMC. The point is that you don't have to use an MMC console to perform every type of maintenance, but most people find that MMC consoles are easy to use and understand.

The following sections discuss a special "one size fits all" MMC console named Computer Management. It allows you to perform many types of computer maintenance and this one console may be all you need to perform most of the maintenance tasks on a small network. (You'll always need other tools, but probably not every day.)

One MMC Console for Many Uses

As previously mentioned, the MMC is the central tool in the Windows XP management arsenal. However, it's important to understand that MMC is really a container application. You place snap-ins inside the container. The combination of snap-ins and the container is a console. The MMC console is the actual tool you use to maintain some part of the network.

You can create your own MMC consoles; just run the MMC command at the Run dialog box (use Start | Run to access it). You'll see a blank container that you fill with snap-ins using the File | Add/Remove Snap-in command. Click Add in the Add/Remove Snap-in dialog box, and you'll see an impressive list of snap-ins from which to choose. (Not every snap-in has a home in a console right now.) This command generally isn't available when using predefined consoles, especially those created by Microsoft. Begin with a blank console if you want to create something special for your administrator toolbox. You can see a list of the predefined consoles in the Administrative Tools folder (found in the Control Panel or the Start | Programs menu).

Fortunately, many of you will never have to worry about creating an MMC console because Windows XP ships with so many of them. The emphasis of the Microsoft console creating effort is the corporate workstation or home system. Consequently, you'll find an MMC console to manage local security policies, but not a group policy manager. These "world view" consoles will arrive with the next version of Windows server.

In the meantime, you do have direct access to a wealth of consoles for your local needs. The Computer Management MMC console is the Swiss knife of the console world. As you can see from Figure 8.1, this console contains a little bit of everything needed to maintain your system.

FIGURE 8.1

Use the Computer Management console as your view to system configuration and performance.

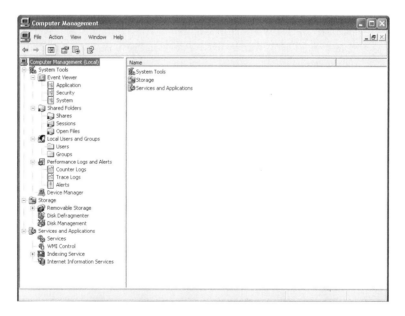

As you can see, this truly is a central repository of tools for the small network. You can manage the three computer system areas: System Tools, Storage, and Services and Applications. In addition, you can manage more than your own system by right clicking Computer Management and choosing All Tasks | Connect to Another Computer from the context menu. The Select Computer dialog box contains the Another Computer field you use to select another machine on the network. Use the Browse button if you don't know the other computer name. Click OK, and you'll see the same information for the other machine. The location information (seen as "Local" in parenthesis beside the Computer Management entry in Figure 8.1) will change to show the new computer name.

The main entries you see in Figure 8.1 will remain the same when you switch to another computer. However, you may see a difference in subentries. For example, if you connect to a server, Event Viewer will contain several new logs including Directory Service, DNS Server, and File Replication Service. The entries you see depend on the capabilities of the machine you monitor.

Some entries will stay intact, but you won't be able to use them. For example, you can't use the Disk Defragmenter on a remote drive. The entry stays in place, but you'll see an error message instead of the local display. Fortunately, the situations where you can't perform a task on a remote system are rare.

System Tools

The System Tools folder of Computer Management helps you configure and maintain your system. This folder doesn't contain every snap-in you'll ever need, but you'll find that you can spend most of your time using this folder for system specific needs. For example, while the System Monitor snap-in doesn't appear in this folder, the Performance Logs and Alerts snap-in does. You only need System Monitor when tuning your system for optimal performance, but you might use Performance Logs and Alerts daily to ensure that your system stays in shape. The differentiation in purpose is important.

Now that you know why particular tools appear in the System Tools folder, let's talk about their purpose. The following list provides an overview of each tool and tells why you might use it on a regular basis. Some of these tools receive a complete description section today; we'll discuss others on other days.

- **Event Viewer**   The Event Viewer helps you keep track of special occurrences on your system. The three folders this snap-in contains track application, security, and system events. Event Viewer provides three levels of tracking: information, warning, and error. Depending on which machine you're monitoring, you might see more logs. It's also possible (but unlikely) that a vendor will use special message types. You should check Event Viewer each day because it normally provides the first indication that something is wrong with your system. In fact, a well-written application can alert you to conditions long before they become problems. We'll discuss this snap-in in more detail in the "Using Event Viewer" section during Day 9.

- **Shared Folders**   Networking involves sharing resources with other people. For example, you might have a project folder on your system that requires the efforts of several people to complete. It's important to share the data, but you also want to monitor access to ensure that people don't abuse their privileges. The three folders provided by this snap-in (Shares, Sessions, and Open Files) help you track which resources are available, who's using them, and for how long. We'll discuss this snap-in more in the "Shared Drive and Folder Monitoring" section today.

- **Local Users and Groups**   This snap-in contains two folders. The Groups folder contains a list of all the groups that can access your machine. The Users folder contains a list of all the users who can access your machine. You'll use the groups to define the same level of access for more than one person. In both cases, you want to provide access to other users, but limit that access to ensure your data remains safe. We'll discuss this snap-in in more detail in the "Managing Local Users and Groups" section today.

- **Performance Logs and Alerts**   Some people view performance tuning as a one-time task that they'll begrudgingly do someday. Performance tuning begins when you monitor system performance, select a course of corrective action for problem areas, and implement the changes as needed. However, this is just the beginning. If you don't continue to monitor your system, performance will eventually decline as the system state changes. This snap-in helps you track system performance on a continuous basis. You can create alerts to tell you when specific events occur, such as a significant drop in disk space or performance. In short, System Monitor is the tuning tool you use occasionally, while Performance Logs and Alerts is your helper for daily performance tuning. We'll discuss this snap-in in more detail in the "Performance Logs and Alerts" section during Day 9.

- **Device Manager**   The Device Manager contains a complete list of the devices on your system. It displays the devices by type, making them easier to find. You can tell if a device has failed because Windows XP will mark it for you. This snap-in also allows you to check how Windows XP uses system resources, update device drivers, and perform some device configuration tasks. We'll discuss this snap-in in more detail in the "Using Device Manager" section of Day 10.

Storage

Your system has three essential resources you must control in order to get good performance: memory, processing cycles, and hard drive space. A lack of any of these three items will result in a system that performs poorly. You can control memory by configuring applications to use only the features you need and by opening only the applications that will fit within memory. Of course, you can always take the "add more memory" route because it does work. You can control processing cycles by keeping processor intensive applications to a minimum. We'll also explore a more interesting technique in the "Processes" section during Day 9.

The Storage folder contains utilities you need to maintain the hard drive space requirement for good performance. You'll find that it provides access to three snap-ins that are specifically designed to make managing storage easier. The following list discusses these options and tells you where you can learn more about them.

- **Removable Storage**   Computers have many removable storage options today. For example, you can use permanent removable media such as CD-ROMs and DVDs. Some removable media is semi-permanent. The CD-RW and DVD-RAM drive both fall into this category. Still other devices, such as ZIP drives, look just like hard drives. This snap-in helps you keep track of your removable drives by checking the media they contain and their status. We'll discuss this snap-in in more detail in the "Working with Removable Storage" section of Day 10.

- **Disk Defragmenter**   The Disk Defragmenter snap-in reorganizes the data on your hard drive so your system can find it faster. Defragmenting your hard drive removes some of the costs of working with physical devices such as head movement. We'll discuss this snap-in in more detail in the "Disk Defragmenter" section of Day 21.

- **Disk Management**   Use this snap-in to create new partitions, format a drive, change the drive letter, and determine the drive status. You'll also use this utility to create special drive setups, such as using a redundant array of inexpensive disks (RAID) to increase system reliability. We'll discuss this snap-in in more detail in the "Using Disk Management" section of Day 10.

Services and Applications

The Services and Applications folder contains a minimum of one folder, Services. The Services folder contains a list of services on your system, plus a status for each service. It also provides two views: standard and extended. The standard view contains the list of services in a details type view. The columns include name, description, status, startup type, and logon as. The extended view contains the same information, along with a secondary pane that extends the description so you can see it. Unfortunately, you can't adjust the size of the secondary pane, which means you need to move items around to see all of the column entries properly. Figure 8.2 shows a typical example of the extended view. We'll discuss services in more detail during Day 11, "Configuring Services."

Figure 8.2 shows three applications in addition to the Services folder. Sometimes these applications will show up in the folder even if you haven't activated them. In this case, only the Indexing Service is active. The WMI Control and Internet Information Services entries will produce error messages when you click on them.

FIGURE 8.2

The extended view of the Services folder allows you to see the entire service description at a glance.

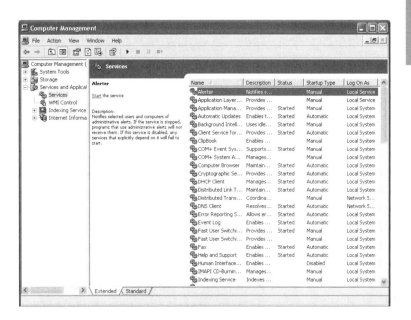

You should also notice that the applications aren't applications in the standard sense of the word. These are background, service-related applications. For example, the Indexing Service keeps track of your hard drive content in the background. It comes into play when you need to find data on your hard drive. The Indexing Service can provide answers to the search engine much faster than a real time search.

Managing Local Users and Groups

Windows XP provides several interfaces for managing users and groups on your machine. The first method is the simplified interface provided by the User Accounts applet. This interface has the advantage of using a task-based approach to user management. You don't need to worry about which menu has the option you need. The disadvantage is one of flexibility and access. This interface is somewhat rigid and doesn't provide full access to user information. In addition, using this technique doesn't allow you to manage groups.

The second method is the Local Users and Groups MMC snap-in. You saw this snap-in loaded in the Computer Management console in Figure 8.1. This method does allow you to manage both users and groups, but at the expense of a more complex interface and increased management time. Problems aside, this is the method that you'll want to use to create users, in most cases, because it allows you to assign a password and group permissions. The following sections discuss both interfaces.

Using the User Accounts Applet

The User Accounts applet helps you manage user accounts without the complexity of an MMC snap-in. In addition, it consolidates several functions, such as changing the way users log into the system, and uses a task-oriented management approach. Figure 8.3 shows a typical view of the User Accounts dialog box from the network administrator perspective. You'll see in a few moments that the average user sees something different.

FIGURE 8.3

The User Accounts dialog box provides an easy interface for many of your user management needs.

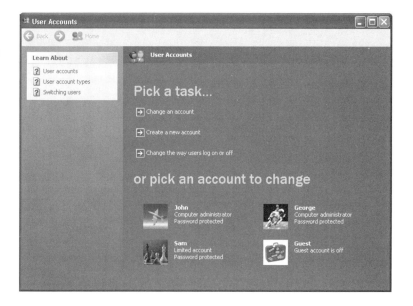

The User Accounts dialog box doesn't provide access to the Local Users and Groups MMC snap-in. It also limits the tasks you can perform on a user account. Making this applet accessible to users allows them to change some of the characteristics of their account, such as the picture displayed on the Welcome screen, without leaving any security holes. This is a good solution for network administrators who want to give users freedom without leaving the network open for attack. With this applet in place, there's no reason to expose the Local Users and Groups MMC snap-in to anyone but network administrators.

Click Change Account, and you'll see a Pick an Account to Change dialog box that lists the accounts the user can access. Select an account, and you'll see the *What you do want to change about your account?* dialog box shown in Figure 8.4. You can also reach this dialog box by clicking the account you want to modify on the Users Accounts dialog box shown in Figure 8.3. You can also choose other people's accounts. Again, this is the network administrator view of the User Accounts applet. The average user won't see any accounts but the one that he or she normally uses.

FIGURE 8.4

Select Change an Account or click on an account entry if you want to modify the account settings.

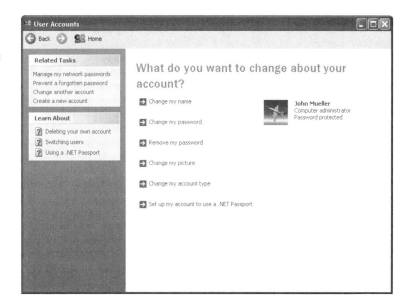

As you can see, you can change or remove your password, change your picture, and set your system up to use a .NET Passport. The User Account applet will always enable these options. The availability of the other options depends on the rights of the user and the local security policy settings. For example, average users can't change their network names assigned to them or their account types.

How does the average user's view differ from the one seen by the network administrator? Figure 8.5 shows what the user will see when he first opens the User Accounts dialog box. As you can see, the user's choices are limited, and he can't access anyone else's account. This simplified interface makes it easy for any user to change his password and Welcome screen picture as needed or desired.

Using the various links is easy. If you change your name, the User Account applet will present your current name and ask for a new one. Changing your password involves typing the old password, the new password twice, and a phrase or a word used to provide a password hint. Generally, you're better off enforcing a policy that prohibits the use of hints. Removing your password is almost too easy. All you need to do is type the old password and click Remove Password. Windows XP won't complain unless you set the Minimum password length policy to something other than 0 (the default). The Change my account type setting is also simplistic. You choose between a computer administrator or a limited account.

FIGURE 8.5

Select Change an Account or click on an account entry if you want to modify the account settings.

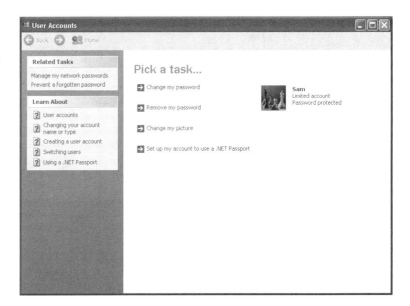

> **Caution**
>
> The password hint is visible to anyone on the network. Some users will almost certainly try to use their password as a hint. Unfortunately, Windows XP doesn't check for this potential problem. It accepts the user's password as a perfectly acceptable hint. This means that you could have passwords that are completely visible to anyone on the network. The problem is more serious than you might think. No local security policy bans this practice, so you can't enforce the user's password and hint choice. A written policy might help, but it's difficult to enforce considering the network administrator doesn't know the user's password.

When you click Change my picture, Windows XP will display a list of new pictures for your account. Many of the pictures are generic, and you may want something special. Click Browse for more pictures if you want to use your own picture for an icon. The important thing to remember is that the picture is going to be small, so you have to choose a picture that looks good in a small size. Windows XP allows you to use any picture in a BMP, RLE, DIB, JPG, GIF, or PNG format.

Using the Local Users and Groups MMC Snap-in

The Local Users and Groups MMC snap-in provides you with the greatest flexibility in changing the accounts for a specific machine. In addition, you can use this MMC snap-in on more than one machine by connecting to it. You won't find these features in the User Accounts applet.

You can use the Local Users and Groups snap-in in two essential areas: *users* and *groups*. The Users folder contains individuals in your company, while the Groups folder contains settings for groups of individuals who perform similar tasks. The following sections will help you learn to work with both users and groups, and better define the differences between them.

Working with Users

When you open the Users folder of the Local Users and Groups snap-in, you'll see a list of users currently set up for the local machine. This doesn't represent the users for a domain unless you connect to a server. In addition, Active Directory provides another set of snap-ins to perform work with it. The list includes the name (login), full name, and description for each user.

To create a new user, right click an open area in the details window and choose New User from the context menu. You can also use the Action | New User command to perform this task. Figure 8.6 shows the New User dialog box that you'll see. It allows you to enter the user's login name, full name, description, and preliminary password. A network administrator should force the user to change his password during the login so that the user can never say the administrator used the account for illegal purposes.

The New User dialog box only contains the essentials for defining a user. If you right-click the new user entry and choose Properties from the context menu, you'll see a User Properties dialog box with several tabs of information. The General tab contains the information we just defined for the user.

Click the Member Of tab, and you'll see a list of groups. Click Add if you want to add a new group to the list. You'll see a blank Select Groups list, which is something that confuses many people. Microsoft listed the groups in previous versions of Windows, but doesn't for Windows XP. Click Advanced, and you'll see a Select Groups dialog box like the one shown in Figure 8.7. Click Find Now, and Windows XP will provide a list of groups on your local machine. Notice that I've already conducted a search using the entries in this dialog box.

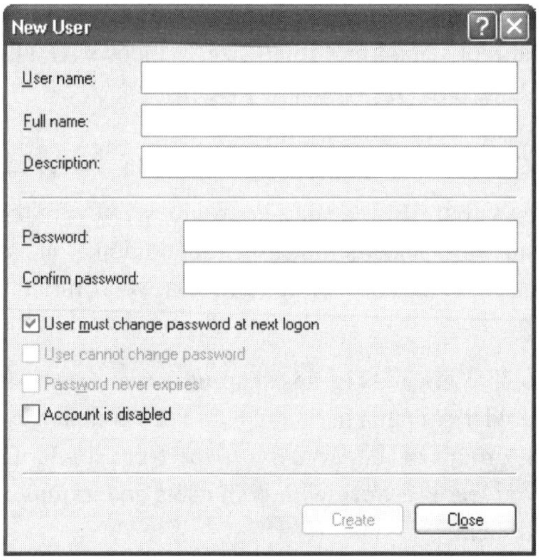

FIGURE 8.6

Creating a new user is as easy as opening this dialog box and typing a few basics.

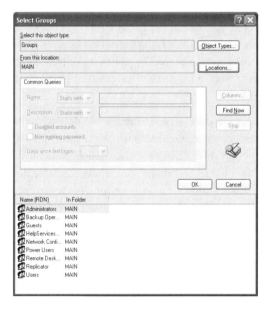

FIGURE 8.7

Use the Select Groups dialog box to find groups for your users to join.

The Profile tab contains login settings for the user. The Profile Path field enables you to assign a profile located on a server to the user, which allows the user to roam from machine to machine and still use the same setup. Windows XP supports two types of profiles: roaming and mandatory. In both cases, the user downloads a profile from the server when he or she logs in. In the case of a roaming profile, Windows XP will update the

8

profile settings on the server when the user logs out. The mandatory profile doesn't allow any changes, so Windows XP won't update it when the user logs out.

The Dial-in tab shown in Figure 8.8 is only active for server-based accounts. These settings determine if a user can call into the server. They also determine how the user can call into the server. Generally, Windows XP relies on whatever remote access policy you set for dial-up connections. Fortunately, you can override those settings to always deny or allow access.

FIGURE 8.8

The Dial-in tab defines the dial-in connection settings for a particular user.

If you check the Verify Caller-ID option, the user must call in from the same number every time he or she uses the dial-in connection. This setting also sets limits on the features the user can add to his or her remote connection because some telephone services will hide the number.

A more traditional method of checking the remote caller's identity is to use the callback system. In a callback system, the user calls the server and provides identification. The server hangs up the telephone, validates the user's identity, and then calls the user back to establish a connection.

The least secure callback method is to allow the user to set the callback number. Using this technique allows you to track the receiving number and allows the user to call in from more than one location. The most secure method is to call back to a specific number. In this scenario, the user must call in from the same number every time. Unless the user changes numbers, the callback ensures the user's identity by calling the same number every time.

You'll use the Assign a Static IP Address and Apply Static Routes options to remote networks that call into a main network number. For example, a satellite office might need to call into the office to establish a connection each morning. Assigning the caller a static IP address enables communication between the two networks and users of the two networks. Using static routes also allows communication between two individual machines by allocating a static route for all machines on the remote network.

Working with Groups

Groups are an organizational tool, and you'll find they're simpler to understand than the use settings. Click the Groups folder in the Local Users and Groups snap-in, and you'll see a list of groups for the system. The groups don't contain much in the way of settings. Figure 8.9 shows a typical setup.

FIGURE 8.9

Groups are a simple organizational tool containing one or more users or objects.

As you can see, the Group Properties dialog box contains the group name, a description, a list of users and objects, and buttons for adding and removing members. The New Group dialog box looks similar to the one shown in Figure 8.9. The main difference is that the New Group dialog box allows you to change the group name.

Shared Drive and Folder Monitoring

Sharing hard drives and folders is an essential part of networking. It's the basis for every network in existence. In fact, early network operating systems (NOSs) built their reputation on file and print sharing.

Windows XP provides file and drive sharing, just like almost every version of Windows before it. The model used for file and drive sharing is similar to the one used in Windows 2000, rather than the less secure model used in Windows 9x. This means that you set specific levels of security at an individual or group basis. We'll discuss security in detail during Day 16, "Configuring Security."

Today we'll discuss the Shared Files MMC snap-in. This snap-in helps you keep track of user connections and other information about your drives. We'll also talk about auditing and quotas— two methods to tracking drive resource usage. Auditing creates a record for disk accesses, while quotas limit the drive space each user can access.

Using the Shared Files Snap-in

The Shared Files snap-in contains three folders: Shares, Sessions, and Open Files. You'll use each of these folders to monitor drive usage on your system.

The Shares folder, shown in Figure 8.10, shows which drives you've shared and the number of connections people have made to them. Don't assume that this means one person for each connection. The same user can connection to more than one drive, and Windows XP counts each drive connection separately. Notice that this list includes both standard shares and default or administrative shares (those with a "$" in their name). This allows you to monitor all system activity.

FIGURE 8.10

The Shares folder shows the number of connections people have made to your shared drives.

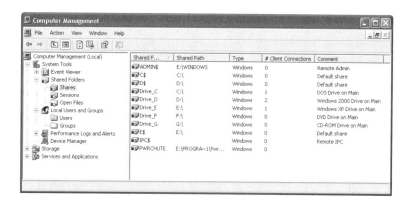

Tip

You can use the Shared folder display to perform a number of not-so-obvious tasks. For example, a Stop Sharing entry on the context menu will remove the share from the system. Click Properties, and you'll see a Drive Properties dialog box containing tabs that allow you to adjust caching, share permissions, and security. The Security tab has an Advanced button that provides access to the auditing features of the drive. Unfortunately, you can't adjust the quota from this drive.

The Sessions folder appears in Figure 8.11. Notice that it contains the name of each person using your system. The entries also include the number of files the person has open, the time they connected, and the amount of idle time since their last activity. The Guest column tells you if the user logged in using the guest account.

FIGURE 8.11

Use the Sessions folder to see how many users have logged onto your system.

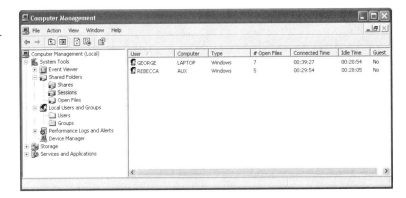

The only task you can perform in this folder is to end the user's session by using the Close Session option found on the context menu. Using this feature can have undesirable results. For example, users could lose data because their session ended with a file in an uncertain state. Normally, you'll want to contact the users first and ask them to disconnect from your system. You do this by right-clicking Computer Management and Selecting All Tasks | Send Console Message from the context menu.

You'll use the Open Files folder shown in Figure 8.12 to monitor the files opened by other people on your system. Notice that the columns list the user's name, the type of file access, the number of locks on the file, and the type of access requested. A file lock indicates some type of shared access. For example, two people can share a database file. It's important to use locks in such a case to ensure that one user doesn't infringe on the edits make by another user.

FIGURE 8.12

The Open Files folder tells you which files other people opened on your system.

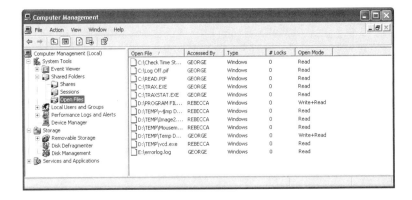

As with the Sessions folder, you can only perform one action on files in the Open Files folder, Close Open File. Closing a file opened for Read access is usually safe. The action might inconvenience the other user, but is unlikely to harm the file. However, closing a file opened for either Write or Write+Read access could damage the file, cause data loss, and will definitely do more than irritate the other user. Again, it's always better to send a console message to ask the other party to close the file, rather than close the file yourself.

Setting Drive Quotas

You can enable drive quotas under Windows XP in a number of ways, but one way is easier than all the rest. Open a copy of Windows Explorer, right-click the drive you want to modify and select Properties, and select the Quota tab. You'll see a display similar to the one shown in Figure 8.13. The first step in using drive quotas is to check the Enable Quota Management option as shown in the figure.

FIGURE 8.13

Use the Quota tab to control user access to drive resources.

You'll want to decide if new users should have an automatic quota set on their accounts, or if you want to set the limit as necessary. You can also choose to log any excessive use of disk space. The log can contain just the users that exceed their limit, or you can include those that reach the warning level as well.

Enabling quotas and setting a default limit isn't enough to ensure good resource management. You also need to review the users who have a quota. To do that, click Quota Entries. You'll see a Quota Entries dialog box like the one in Figure 8.14 that contains a list of users who have a quota for this drive. The list indicates their warning level and quota limit. You'll also see how much space these users have already used and learn if they've exceeded their limit.

FIGURE 8.14

*The Quota Entries dia-
log box tells you how
much space each user
has used on the drive.*

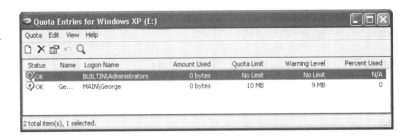

To add a new user to the list, click New Quota Entry. You'll see a Select Users dialog
box. Type a user's name or locate it by using the Advanced button. Click OK, and you'll
see a New Quote Entry dialog box. Select a quote limit and warning level for the new
user and click OK. Their name will appear in the Quota Entries list.

Auditing Drive Access

Auditing, for the purpose of this discussion, is the act of creating a log of user activity on
your system. You can audit all kinds of user activity. For example, if you want to know
every time a user successfully deletes a file, you can create an audit entry for it. These
logs are useful if you want to monitor user activity or check for illegal actions.

You can enable auditing in a number of ways, but the easiest method is to right-click a
drive in Windows Explorer and choose Properties from the context menu. Select the
Security tab in the Drive Properties dialog box and then click Advanced. You'll see an
Advanced Security Settings dialog box. Select Auditing, and you'll see a dialog box similar to the one shown in Figure 8.15.

FIGURE 8.15

*The Auditing tab
allows you to observe
user activity on your
local hard drive.*

As you can see from the dialog box, you can monitor users for success, failure, or both success and failure in performing certain tasks. Windows XP helps you monitor everything from taking full control of the drive to deleting files to simply changing the file attributes.

To Add a new entry, click Add. You'll see a Select User or Group dialog box. Click Advanced and then Find, to display a list of local user and group names. Select a user or group from the list and click OK. You'll see an Auditing Entry dialog box. Select the tasks you want to monitor and click OK. Windows XP will add the new auditing entry to the drive. The audit will remain in place until you remove it.

Multi-user Workstation Setup Tips

Many of the offices I've set up in the past use multi-user workstation setups. One user has possession of the computer during the day; another by night. Several users might share the same computer because one user won't use it all day. A manager might need access to an employee computer because the one in his or her office is too far away. The reasons could go on forever, but multi-user workstations are common. The following tips help you set up a multi-user workstation up in the most convenient way.

- Create a default user setup. The \Documents and Settings\Default User directory contains a complete set of empty folders. Every user you create for a local machine will use this set of folders as a starting point. The user will only receive input from this folder during the creation phase. Don't confuse this set of folders with the All Users folder.

- Use the all users folder (\Documents and Settings\All Users) to hold all common elements. For example, if everyone needs access to the word process, you'll want to place the icons for it in this folder, rather than duplicate those icons for every user. However, if you have a situation where most, but not all users, require access to an application, you can place it in the default user setup. This allows you to remove the icons from those users who don't need it.

- Implement Start Menu security. You might have a machine where all employees need access to some icons, but guest users shouldn't have access. Assigning security to those icons allows you to place them in the all users folder, but still restrict access. Icons normally inherit rights from their parent, so you need to click Advanced on the Security tab of the Object Properties dialog box. Clear the Inherit option and then click OK before you begin setting a new security policy. Note that everyone can still see the icon, but only those with the required permissions can use it.

- Create common desktop elements as needed. For example, everyone might work on the same project together, so placing the folder for that project in the \Documents and Settings\All Users\Desktop folder makes sense. This way you can ensure that everyone will use the same folder, and that all of the data is changed at the same time.

- Set security to assume that the user will always fail to log out when leaving the area. For example, you can set the screen saver to log the user out automatically and return to the login screen. This forces the user to log back into the system and protects it from prying eyes.

Summary

Today you've learned about some of the MMC snap-ins provided with Windows XP. You also learned about the User Accounts applet in the Control panel. Each of these management tools affects the user environment in some way. In some cases, the user receives access to resources. In other cases, you restrict the user from entering sensitive areas of the computer. These management tools allow you to monitor user activity in a way that maintains both user privacy and system security. Finally, you can look at these tools as a performance aid. By managing the user's access to resources, you also optimize the use of those resources and enhance overall system performance.

Q&A

Q: The set of consoles provided with Windows XP seems limited when compared to Windows 2000 and Windows XP won't let me add the tools from a Windows 2000 Server. How do I get these other tools back?

A: The consoles and snap-ins provided with Windows 2000 are incompatible with Windows XP. That's why you can't install the old snap-ins on your system. Windows XP ships with a limited number of predefined consoles because Microsoft views the role of Windows XP as a corporate workstation or home system. However, when Windows .NET Server appears on the market, it will provide the same (or extended) set of tools that Windows 2000 Server provided. In addition, if you look through the list of snap-ins provided with Windows XP, you'll notice it does include the server snap-ins such as group policy and those required to manage Active Directory. You can still create your own tools from the snap-ins as needed. Microsoft simply doesn't provide the predefined consoles.

Q: Is setting up a .NET Passport a requirement of using Windows XP?

A: The .NET Passport is a completely optional part of Windows XP. You do have to set one up if you want to use the bundled features, such as Windows Messenger,

8

supplied by Microsoft. The choice of using these features is up to you, but the implementation of these features is something that Microsoft decided.

Q: Is it always necessary to use groups on a network?

A: Some network administrators would use groups even on a network with two people. Groups provide such an essential service that they'd look at the cost of setting the group up as minimal compared to managing two accounts. However, most network administrators would agree that using groups becomes more valuable when you have more than one group to manage. For example, if your company has departments, then you should also use groups. If a number of people perform one task and another group performs a completely different task, then using groups makes sense. Using groups does become somewhat ridiculous if you have four lawyers and a secretary in an office. There's little chance of creating a group environment in such a situation, so individual settings probably work better.

Workshop

It's the end of the eighth day. By now, you should consider yourself a network guru, or at least a guru in training. It's time to see how much you know about working with users on a network. You can find answers to the quiz and exercise questions in Appendix A at the back of the book.

Quiz

1. How do you create you own MMC consoles?
2. What are the three user-controlled performance elements in a computer?
3. Why do some of the entries in the Services and Applications folder produce error messages?
4. What's one of the biggest password security hole that users can implement in Windows XP?
5. Which is the most secure type of dial-in callback?
6. The Shares folder allows you to access special features for each drive on your system. You can use it to set one type of resource management feature, but not another. What's the name of the feature you can set; which feature do you set by using another utility?

Exercises

1. Create your own MMC console and use it to work with your network for the next week.

2. Try creating a user account with both the User Accounts applet and the Local Users and Groups MMC snap-in.

3. Use the Shared Folders snap-in to monitor your system.

4. Set auditing and quotas for your system as required.

WEEK 2

DAY 9

Working with Software

After you get the operating system installed and updated, and you verify that everything is working as anticipated, you'll want to install some applications. It may seem like a long road from clean system to completed operating setup, but if you perform it correctly, the installation should remain stable for a long time. Applications, on the other hand, represent a constant investment in time. As applications age or your computing needs change, you'll find yourself removing the old and installing the new. As a result, application installations eventually become something you can perform in your sleep.

Today we'll discuss the mechanics of application installation, configuration, maintenance, and troubleshooting. You'll perform all of these tasks—some of them on a regular basis. It's important to know how to perform these tasks correctly because the alternative is to spend hours figuring out what when wrong with your setup. As part of learning to perform application installations correctly, you'll learn some tips that will save you both time and effort.

Performance is another area of the application picture. Each application has individual resource needs and therefore performance tuning requirements. In addition, each application will require a different set of tuning goals. For example, you'll look at disk tuning more when working with a database management application than you would with a spreadsheet.

Finally, we'll talk about data sources today. A *data source* is a pointer to a source of information on another machine. The data source defines the type of data, as well as your access requirements for that data. The only time you'll need to worry about data sources is when you work with a database application that relies on Open Database Connectivity (ODBC). However, because ODBC was the technology of choice for many years and some developers still use it to the exclusion of everything else, your chance of running into this technology is good.

Adding and Removing Programs

Windows has always differentiated between operating system and standard applications. The operating system applications require special installation and removal. In most cases, the operating system requires special handling, which warrants the extra effort. However, the extra work is still a source of concern for the network administrator.

The following sections will discuss the two procedures needed to add and remove applications under Windows XP. We'll discuss the standard application process first and the special Windows process second. We'll also discuss a special feature of the Windows installation that may save you a lot of work. It seems that Microsoft doesn't make all of the Windows features readily accessible for removal, but you can change this situation when desired. In both cases, you'll start with the Add/Remove Programs applet in the Control Panel.

Applications

You have to install and configure your applications before you can use them. The installation process begins when you place the CD or floppy into the appropriate drive and Windows XP automatically detects the setup sequence, or when you manually double-click Setup (or install). The installation procedure varies by vendor and applications. You'll need to read the vendor instructions that come with your product before you install it. I stress the "before" part of this scenario because many people will try to install a product before they read anything.

One of the most important parts of the installation process is to read the vendor documentation. At the very least, you'll learn how to detect a failed install. In many cases, the vendor also includes some pre-install instructions that you need to follow to ensure a successful installation. Many products also come with a README or other documentation file on the disk. Failing to read this documentation can also cause the installation to fail. The on-disk documentation represents the latest information the vendor had at the time of product shipment. You'll learn about product incompatibilities and other problems that could affect the way you install the product.

When Compatible Isn't

Microsoft has determined that some applications require a higher level of compatibility than others do when it comes to Windows XP. I'm not sure I can say that I blame them for wanting applications, such as disk management utilities and firewalls, to provide the absolute highest level of compatibility. After all, these applications do change the way the operating system works.

However, some industry pundits are already saying that this measure is another way of Microsoft forcing its will on the unsuspecting public. Some have already mentioned the compatibility messages Microsoft included with Windows for products such as DR DOS in the past (the compatibility problems didn't exist). In many minds, it's also a means for forcing users to pay to upgrade products they could get free within Windows XP (making the free software more attractive). Fortunately, the authors of products such as Zone Alarm and Black Ice are already working on products that will address the product blocking Microsoft put in place. It isn't known whether products such as Voice Express and Web Booster Ninja have compatible versions on the way at this time.

The question, then, is how do you know if an installation problem is product blocking induced or a real problem with the application? If you look in the \WINDOWS\AppPatch directory, you'll see a file with the name APPHELP.SDB. This file contains a list of the applications that won't run with Windows XP due to product blocking. Open the file using a hexadecimal editor such as WinVI (http://www.winvi.de/en/), and you'll see a list of applications starting about a third of the way through the file. Each of these entries will also include a Web page that contains test information at the time of this writing, but will hopefully contain an explanation of the incompatibility somewhere along the way.

At this point, you have an application installed and can use it for anything it's designed to do. Which brings up the point of why you need to worry about the Add/Remove Programs applet in the Control Panel if you don't use it to add applications to your system? Obviously, you need the Add/Remove Programs applet to remove the application. However, look at Figure 9.1, and you'll see another reason to use this applet.

As you can see, the entry contains a lot more information than a simple application removal. One of the most important features is the Click here for support information link. Figure 9.2 shows a typical Support Info dialog box.

Click the URL in this dialog box, and you'll go to the support site for that application. This dialog box also contains the vendor name and the product build information. A support person will likely require the build information, so it's nice to have this information so handy.

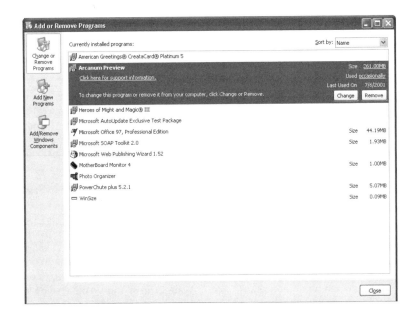

FIGURE 9.1

The Add/Remove Programs applet contains a few features you might want to use even if you're not removing an application.

FIGURE 9.2

The Support Info dialog box tells you where to get help with an application.

Notice the *Repair* button in this dialog box. Click this button, and the application will begin a repair installation. For some vendors, this means performing the last installation over again, so you need to have your application CD-ROM handy. At least a few vendors will perform a check on the application and associated DLLs and only update those that don't match the installed conditions.

The Add/Remove Programs dialog box (Figure 9.1) also contains entries for the application size and frequency of use. Some applications also include the date of last use. The frequency indicates whether you use the application rarely, occasionally, or frequently. However, I find that this indicator doesn't work well if you use a data-oriented approach to working with your application. In other words, if you normally open the application by double-clicking a data file, the indicator may not give a true indication of usage. At least this entry provides you with some method for gauging application use if you're unsure. A large application that you use rarely is a good candidate when you're trying to free hard disk space.

Some applications will also have a Change/Remove or separate Change and Remove buttons. In some cases, you may find that you don't use all of the features that an application has to offer. The unused features can waste processing cycles and definitely waste hard drive space. Click Change if you want to remove these extra features or add features you may have removed in the past.

You can use the Add/Remove Programs applet to add new applications to your system. Normally, you won't need to go this route, but sometimes it comes in handy. Click Add New programs, and you'll see two options. If you click CD or Floppy, Windows XP will search these drives for suitable applications. It won't show you all of the available options if you have setup programs in more than one drive. Windows XP will search the floppy drive first and then the CD-ROM drives in drive letter order. Windows XP will display the first setup program it finds. Use this option if you want to add an application, but don't want to open a copy of Windows Explorer to look for the setup program.

Click Windows Update, and you'll see a copy of Internet Explorer open. Eventually, you'll see the Windows Update Web site. In short, clicking this button is the same as selecting Windows Update from the Start Menu. The only difference is this method takes longer. The only time you'd use this feature is if you were in the Add/Remove Programs applet anyway.

Windows Features

As previously mentioned, you'll use a separate installation dialog box to install Windows applications. Click Add/Remove Windows Components in the Add/Remove Programs applet, and you'll see the Windows Components Wizard dialog box shown in Figure 9.3.

FIGURE 9.3

The Windows Component Wizard helps you install and remove Windows applications.

You should notice a couple of features about this dialog box. First, every entry has a description to tell you about that Windows feature. If you select a new item from the list, the Total disk space required field will tell you how much space the feature requires. Likewise, clearing an option will show a negative number showing how much space you'll save.

Some entries in this list are folders for other entries. If you want to choose one or two features from the list, click Details. The Windows Component Wizard list will open a new dialog box to show just the items in the folder.

After you select all of the features you want within the Windows Component Wizard, click Next. Windows XP will install the new features you requested. It may prompt you to insert the Windows XP disk or a third party disk at some point in the installation.

One thing you may not know about the Windows Component Wizard is that it's unlikely you're seeing all of the possible options. For example, you may have noticed that you can't remove some of the games from the system. Look in the \WINDOWS\inf directory on your system, and you'll see SYSOC.INF in the file list. Open this file, and you'll see a list of entries like the one shown in Figure 9.4. Notice that I've highlighted the word "HIDE" in the list. If you see an entry with the word "HIDE" in the position shown in this list, you won't see that entry in the Windows Component Wizard.

FIGURE 9.4

The SYSOC file contains entries that control the contents of the Windows Component Wizard.

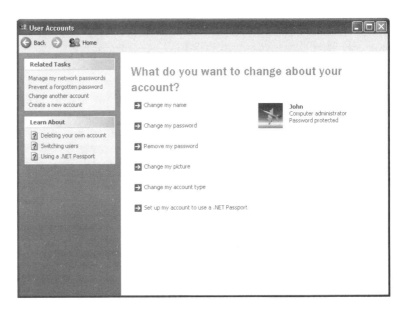

Modifying the SYSOC.INF file after you've made the requisite backup will allow you to see the entry in the Windows Component Wizard. In many cases, exposing the entry will enable you to remove an unwanted feature from the system. Of course, you want to retain the original version of the file to ensure that you can return the system to its original state.

Fortunately, making an entry visible doesn't always allow you to remove the feature from the system. The list contains a few features you must have to make the operating system work properly. Attempting to clear these entries in the Windows Component Wizard won't work. This is a safety feature that prevents someone from removing required entries.

Using Event Viewer

The Event Viewer helps you track special conditions on your computer, generated by either the operating system or an application. You open Event Viewer by using the Event Viewer entry in the Administrative Tools folder found in the Control Panel or in the Start menu. When you open Event Viewer, you'll see anywhere from three to six folders (and more, in some cases, when working with a server). The three common folders are Application, Security, and System as shown in Figure 9.5. You'll see these three folders for a Windows XP Home Edition or a Professional Edition setup.

FIGURE 9.5

The Event Viewer provides a list of messages generated by application or the operating system.

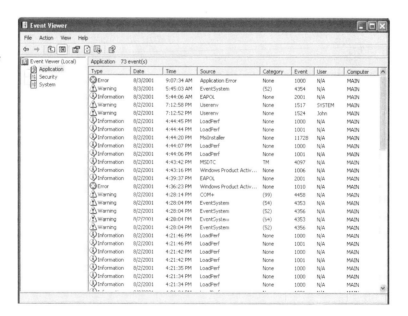

Notice there are three levels of message. The *informational* message tells about a non-critical event, such as an application starting or stopping. In fact, background applications such as the Indexing Service will use the event logs to ensure that you know they completed a task or started a new one. The idea is to allow the application to communicate with you without disturbing your normal work.

The *warning* message tells you about a non-critical event that will cause loss of functionality within the system. For example, if the system needs to install a component and doesn't succeed, it may generate a warning message to warn you of the loss of the functionality the component normally provides.

The *error* message tells you about a critical event. You need to take care of these messages immediately because ignoring them can result in undesirable side effects such as data loss. Generally, error messages aren't so critical that they'll cause an instant system shutdown. For example, if the system experiences a sudden loss of power, the UPS won't bother with the event log. It will send an immediate message telling you to check the power supply.

When you look at a folder in the Event Viewer, you're seeing a summary of the message. This summary tells you the criticality of the error, the date and time of the error, the error source, the message category, the event that generated the message, the name of the user, and the computer. The Computer column isn't particularly useful because all the entries in an event log come from the same computer. The User column is interesting because it tells who was responsible for the offending application. If the operating system or a background application is the cause of the problem, you'll see N/A in the user column. The Source column is a better indicator of the responsible party because it tells you the application that generated the message.

Double-clicking a message displays an Event Properties dialog box similar to the one shown in Figure 9.6. Notice that this dialog box contains all of the information shown in Figure 9.5 with some important additions.

The two big changes are the addition of a Description and a Data field. The Description field contains any additional information the application designer provides. In many cases, this information will tell you the events that led to the generation of the message. The description may also tell you where to find additional information about the message.

The Data field contains any data that the vendor chooses to share about the event. In many cases, the data is simply an error number or a success indicator. If you call the vendor's support number to get additional help, knowing the contents of this data field can be helpful, even if you don't understand what it means.

This dialog box also contains three buttons. The up and down errors take you to the previous and next messages. This allows you to view all the messages within the log

Figure 9.6

Figure 9.6

The Event Properties dialog box displays details about a message entry in the Event Viewer.

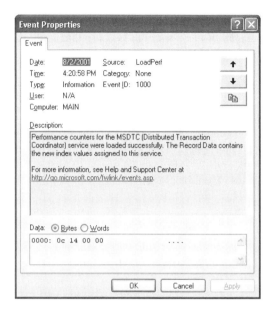

9

without opening them one at a time. The third button copies the content of the Event Properties dialog box to the clipboard. You can use this feature to create a text log of important events or to print a copy of the message before calling technical support.

Checking Performance

At some point during your use of Windows, you'll want to check system performance. In some cases, you'll check system performance out of curiosity to see if you need to perform maintenance. Performance monitoring can also work as a diagnostic to help you locate problems in your system. Of course, the traditional purpose of performance monitoring is to find ways to gain a little extra performance. No matter what the reason, eventually most people need to know how to use the performance monitoring features that Windows XP can provide.

The two performance monitoring snap-ins found in the Performance console look quite simple, but can actually perform complex monitoring tasks. They might not be as good as some third-party products, but you'll discover a lot about your system by using them. The combination of the System Monitor and Performance Logs and Alerts snap-ins allow you to perform both short term and long term monitoring using a variety of display types. Both snap-ins rely on the use of counters—little applications designed to keep track of performance statistics. To find the Performance Monitoring snap-ins, open the Performance Console in Administrative Tools.

The following sections provide you with an overview of performance monitoring. We won't discuss every detail of these snap-ins because that could require an entire chapter or a small book. However, you'll learn how to perform both short and long term performance monitoring and use all of the displays. You'll also learn about some of the most important performance counters.

System Monitor Usage

System Monitor is the short-term, performance-monitoring tool. It provides all of the displays used for analysis of performance data. The following sections describe some essential areas of System Monitor usage.

Using Counters

A monitoring session begins with the selection of performance counters. The easiest method to add counters is to click the Add button (the plus sign) on the toolbar. You'll see an Add Counter dialog box like the one shown in Figure 9.7.

FIGURE 9.7

The Add Counters dialog box is the starting point for every System Monitor session.

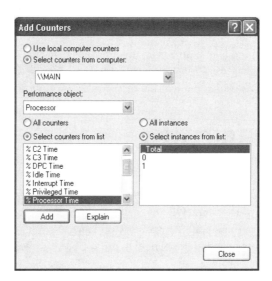

The dialog box shows that you can choose four levels of performance monitoring. The following list describes each level.

- **Machine**   The machine you choose to monitor depends on the circumstances. For example, one performance-monitoring scenario is to compare two machines with the same characteristics and application load. If one machine performs substantially slower than the other, the statistics might indicate the presence of a problem on the slower machine.

- **Performance Object**   This is the name of an application that contains counters. There's a performance object for each major category of device or application on your machine. For example, Figure 9.7 shows the Processor object. You'll also find objects for the physical and logical disk drive, memory, and network. Applications appear in objects such as browser, job, and thread.

- **Counter**   A specific performance measuring thread within the object. The counter is the portion of the performance monitor that acquires the data. The term *counter* is accurate in this case. The counters actually do count the number of occurrences of an event within a given time interval. For example, when determining the percentage of CPU cycles used to handle user requests, the counter counts both the total processor clock cycles and those used to handle user needs. It then performs a mathematical computation to calculate the percentage.

- **Instance**   In some cases, saying you want to count something doesn't define the problem. For example, if you have two processors and want to determine the percentage of user time, you have to indicate whether you want the user time for one or both processors. You also need to indicate which processor you want to work with if you choose only one.

As you can see, the potential number of performance monitoring combinations for a single system is immense. A typical system provides a minimum of 40 performance objects. Each of these objects has a number of counters (2 is a minimum and 30 is common). Many of these counters have at least two instances and a _Total instance (the combination of all instances of a counter). In addition, many applications such as SQL Server add their own counters to the mix. If you add multiple machine scenarios into the mix, you can see that System Monitor has a lot to offer.

Tip

> Click Explain in the Add Counters dialog box if you want to know the meaning behind a particular counter. The explanation is relatively short, but usually helpful. It will always provide you with enough information to conduct additional research into the counters.

This brings up an important point. You don't want to overload a single display with too many counters. Tracking five or six of these counters is difficult on some displays. Adding more than that makes the information hard to track. Select the counters you want to see carefully. If you find that you've selected too many counters, remove a few by highlighting them in the listing and clicking Delete (the X next to the Add button).

After you add the counters, click Close. You'll return to the Performance console and see the counters you selected displaying data. Figure 9.8 shows a typical example of a

Performance console display. The line extending from the top to the bottom of the chart area is the current drawing position.

FIGURE 9.8

The Performance console displays the output from the counters you selected.

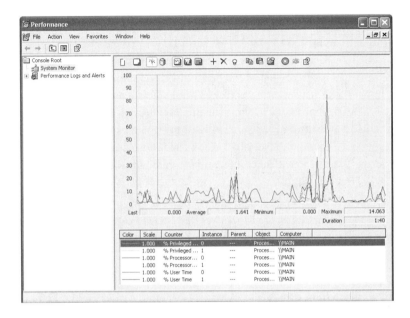

After you find settings that you like, you can save the settings to disk and reopen them later. You can also study the settings if you want, because the Microsoft Console (MSC) files are actually eXtensible Markup Language (XML) in disguise. If you open the file in Internet Explorer as shown in Figure 9.9, you can learn a lot about the way Microsoft structures these files. In some cases, you might be able to tweak a console setting after the fact to make the console more appealing.

Even with the few counters displayed in Figure 9.8, you still might have a hard time seeing a particular counter line. System Monitor fixes this problem with the Highlight button, which looks like a little light bulb. Click Highlight, and the associated counter line will turn dark.

Sometimes, you need to study the information you're seeing onscreen for a while without interruption. If so, click Freeze Display (the red circle with an "X" in it). Click Freeze Display a second time to restart the display. Freeze Display just stops the display; System Monitor continues to collect data in the background. If you want to update the display quickly, click Update Data (the camera next to Freeze Display). Click Clear Display if you want to start the entire sequence over again. This allows you to see an entire screen without interruption.

FIGURE 9.9

MSC files actually contain XML data.

FIGURE 9.9

MSC files actually contain XML data.

Setting Graph Properties

Graph appearance is important. For example, you might want to add horizontal or vertical graph lines. Click Properties if you want to change any of the settings. Figure 9.10 shows the General tab of the System Monitor Properties dialog box.

FIGURE 9.10

The General tab allows you to set graph elements such as the graph type.

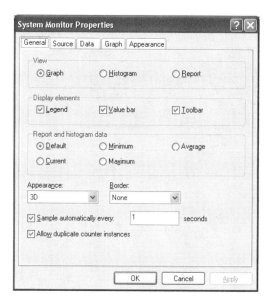

As you can see, this tab allows you to select a view. System Monitor supports three views including graph, histogram, and report. You can also select a view by using the appropriate button on the toolbar (as we'll see in the "Selecting Another View" section).

Below the views are three options for displaying the Toolbar, Value Bar, and Legend. The toolbar contains all of the buttons we've discussed to this point. The Value Bar contains a list of all the vital statistics for the counter highlighted in the Legend. For example, you can learn the minimum, maximum, and average values for a particular counter. The Legend lists the selected counters. Each counter entry includes the instance, parent, object, and computer information.

The report and histogram views support only instantaneous data values. Often, it's beneficial to see something other than the default data. For example, you might want to see the average data value. The next section of the General tab allows you to change the histogram and report view values. The default setting displays the current (instantaneous) values.

The Sample automatically every setting permits you to update the display more or less often than the default setting of 1 second. Clearing this entry will freeze the display. The Allow duplicate counter instances option tells System Monitor that it's okay to display more than one instance of the same data. This feature comes in handy in report view, but is actually detrimental in other views.

The Data tab shown in Figure 9.11 helps you configure the data display. You begin by selecting one of the entries in the Counters list. This view allows you to change the color of the data, along with the width and style of the line. The scale determines how the lines scale in comparison with the rest of the lines onscreen. Using a larger scale can often bring out details about the data, especially if variations are small.

FIGURE 9.11

Use the Data tab to change the appearance of the data onscreen.

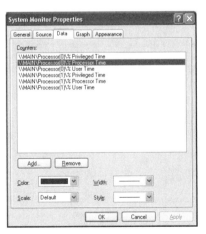

The Graph tab contains settings that change graph display elements. This includes the use of a vertical and horizontal grid. You can also give your graph a title and assign a name to the vertical element (the horizontal element is always the time). The Vertical Scale properties offer another chance to optimize the graph display. You can set the graph so it displays the data a little larger or smaller than the default settings allow.

Finally, the Appearance tab contains settings that change the colors used to display certain elements such as the graph background and time bar. This tab also enables you to choose a new font for the display. The use of a different font may make the information more legible or easier to print.

Selecting Another View

The default graph isn't the only view of the data you can get. System Monitor also provides histogram and report views of the data, both of which serve different purposes. To select a different view, click the appropriate button on the toolbar. There are three buttons: View Graph, View Histogram, and View Report.

The histogram view shown in Figure 9.12 is best for comparing instantaneous values between similar elements. For example, you might want to compare the statistics for two processors. The large bars make it easy to see how to values compare with relative ease.

FIGURE 9.12

Use the histogram view to compare values between similar counters or counter instances.

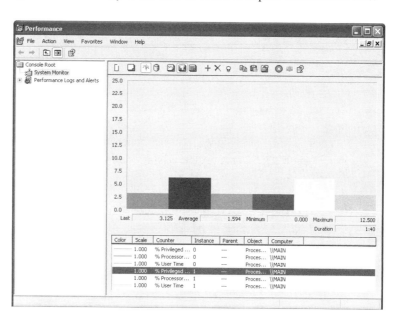

To gain the full benefit from the histogram view, you need to keep the number of bars small. Lots of pencil-thin bars are hard to compare, and they defeat the purpose of using this view. Remember that you do lose the time element in this display, so you may have to resort to a display of average values instead of instantaneous values.

The Report View appears in Figure 9.13. Notice that System Monitor organizes this view by counter and instance. The System Monitor doesn't provide any means for changing the method of organization, so you'll need to consider the counters you use carefully.

FIGURE 9.13

Use the report view to organize large numbers of counters into an easy-to-read report.

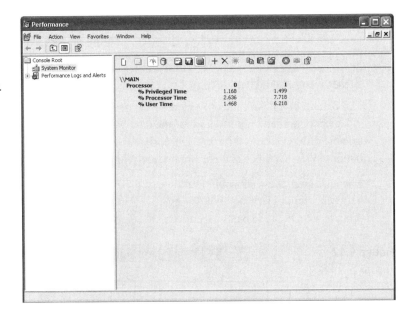

The strength of the report view is the organization that it provides. You can view a large number of counters with this view without going crazy comparing the different lines or bar heights. The report view is also best when you select something other than an instantaneous value. The average value display works well, but you could also use minimum or maximum values in some cases.

Performance Logs and Alerts

The Performance Logs and Alerts snap-in performs long-term event monitoring. This snap-in performs three different tasks by using three folders: Counter Logs, Trace Logs, and Alerts.

The Counter Logs folder performs essentially the same task as System Monitor. It relies on the same counters as the System Monitor, but stores the data it collects on disk, rather than displaying it immediately. You'll view the data created by this snap-in by using the System Monitor and a few special settings that we didn't discuss earlier.

Trace Logs perform detailed system monitoring. You can choose the types of events it monitors. A trace log can help you see the flow of data on a system or determine when an application is creating too many threads. This part of the snap-in creates special logs that you have to convert into human readable format by using the TraceRpt utility. You can read the resulting output in System Monitor or within an application such as Excel (the preferred method in this case).

You'll use the Alert folder to warn you of system conditions. For example, you can use it to warn you that system memory or hard drive space is low. An alert can create event log entries, send you a console message, or run an application as part of the alerting process.

Now that you have a quick overview of the tasks you can perform with these three folders, let's look at them in detail. The following sections will show you how to use the three Performance Logs and Alert snap-in elements to help maintain your system.

Creating Counter Logs

As mentioned earlier, Counter Logs are essentially a long-term version of the System Monitor. You begin creating a log by right-clicking Counter Logs and choosing either New Log Settings or New Log Settings From. If you choose New Log Settings From, you'll see an Open dialog box from which you can choose an HTM or HTML file containing the appropriate settings. You'll generate this HTM or HTML file by right-clicking an existing Counter Log entry and then selecting Save Settings As from the context menu.

The New Log Settings entry displays a New Log Settings dialog box. Type a name for the counter log and click OK. You'll see a properties dialog box like the one shown for My Counter Log in Figure 9.14. Notice that I've already added a counter to this dialog box. Normally, you'd see a blank dialog box and would need to add counters to it.

FIGURE 9.14

Creating a log means defining one or more counters as a source of information.

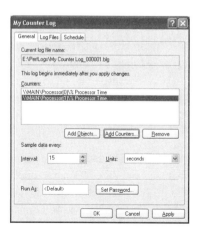

The counters and objects used with the Counter Logs are the same as those used for System Monitor. In fact, when you click Add Counters, you'll see the same Add Counters dialog box as shown in Figure 9.7. Click Add Objects, and you'll see a dialog box that only allows you to select a machine and a performance object. If you select a counter, then you're selecting just that counter or even a counter instance. When you select an object, it includes all the counters within that object.

Tip

> You need to consider the tradeoffs between counters and objects. An object will require more hard drive storage space, and it will consume more processing cycles. However, you'll have all of the counters for that object, so you don't need to worry about finding a particular piece of data. Using counters is more efficient, but lacks flexibility. If you don't store a critical piece of data, it won't appear in the log later for analysis. Generally, it's best to use objects when you can spare the hard drive space and lost processing cycles.

After you select some objects or counters, you can set the sampling interval. Short intervals produce more data, so you'll get results that are more precise. However, using short intervals also makes the impact of performance monitoring more severe. Again, it's a matter of balancing system resources and performance against the performance monitoring requirements.

Notice the Run As field on the dialog box. In some cases, the person running the performance monitoring software won't have the credentials required to perform all tasks. The monitoring will fail in this situation, preventing you from obtaining good readings. To overcome this problem, type the name of a person with the correct rights, click Set Password to display the Set Password dialog box, type the password twice, and then click OK. The counter can run now because it isn't relying on the user's credentials.

The Log Files tab of the properties dialog box contains fields that adjust the output log. You can choose from several output formats including text, binary, and SQL Server. The last entry is helpful if you want to store the results in a database for complex analysis and archival. The Example field shows what the output filename will look like; you can monitor this entry as needed. Finally, you can add a comment to the file and choose to overwrite the old log file each time you restart the Counter Log.

You'll use the Schedule tab to define a starting and ending time for the Counter Log. The Start Log field contains entries that start the logging manually or a specific date and time. The current time is the default setting. The Stop Log field contains entries that will stop the logging manually, after a specific time interval (seconds, minutes, hours, or days), a specific date and time, or when the log is full. The default setting stops the logging manually. Finally, you can set the Counter Log to perform a task automatically when the log file closes. This includes creating a new log and running an application.

After you set everything up, click OK. If you're using the default Start Log settings, the Performance Logs and Alerts snap-in will begin the logging immediately. Otherwise, you'll need to start the logging manually by right-clicking the Counter Log object and selecting Start, or waiting until the predefined conditions occur.

Viewing Counter Logs

You have a log that you created of processor activity or some other performance object. Having the log and doing something with it are two different things. You need to know how to view the log after you create it. As previously mentioned, this means setting System Monitor to use the log containing static data, rather than collecting the data in real time.

To view the content of a log file, open System Monitor and click View Log Data (the icon that looks like a database symbol). You'll see the Source tab of the System Monitor Properties dialog box. Click Log Files (or database, if you saved the data in that form). Click Add and then select the log file(s) you want to view. Note that you can add more than one log file to the list to see a longer interval. Make certain that all the logs come from the same Counter Log. If you think you might want to limit the interval viewed onscreen, click Time Range. Figure 9.15 shows an example of the Source tab with the Time Range feature enabled.

FIGURE 9.15

Selecting a log to view is as easy as changing the data source for System Monitor Properties.

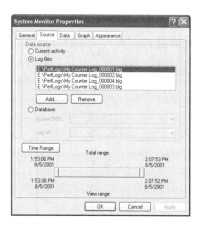

Click OK, and you'll see the static data collected in the log. Of course, this means you won't see the Time Bar moving across the screen—System Monitor only uses the Time Bar when it has active data to read. All of the other options that you use for active data apply when working with a log. For example, you can display a graph, histogram, or report version of your log.

Note

One change that you'll notice is that the content of the Add Counters dialog box will change. You can only view data that you've recorded, which means the list of objects and counters will change. In addition, you can only select counters for computers that you logged. Any other computers will fail to appear on the list.

There's an interesting alternative way to view the content of the Counter Log. Right-click the Counter Log and choose Save Settings As from the context menu. Because the file you create is a true Web page, you can place it and your log file on a Web server. You need to modify the LogFileName entry in the Web file to match the new log file location and read the data from your Web site. Figure 9.16 shows an example of this alternative viewing method in action.

FIGURE 9.16

Internet Explorer works as an alternative log file viewer.

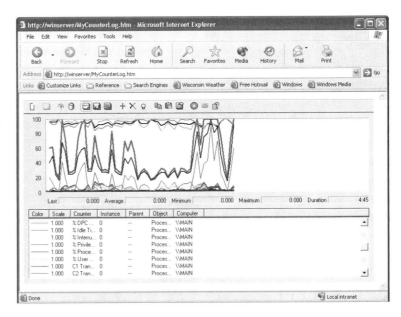

This method has three drawbacks. First, it only works on counter log files. You can't use it on a trace log. Second, there doesn't appear to be any way to sort the data out with any ease. At least, you can't do it automatically. All of the System Monitor controls are available, though, so you can modify the data presentation to suit your needs. Third, for some reason, Internet Information Server (IIS) and Internet Explorer make this scenario harder than it needs to be. Make sure that you set the directories up properly so the file will download to your local system. If you can't download the files automatically, then set the Web site up to allow download of the log file to the local drive. With the log file loaded on the local drive, open a Web page configured to look for data on a local drive. This still allows remote monitoring of the data, but you have to perform the log file download step separately.

Creating and Converting Trace Logs

As previously mentioned, Trace Logs allow you to record system events. For example, you can record every time someone creates a new process on your system, even if that someone is the system. Trace Logs are the diagnostic portion of Performance Logs and Alerts because they help you see the flow of activity on a system. In addition, you can look for unusual or aberrant behavior on the part of applications or the user.

The process to create a Trace Log is similar to that of a Counter Log. You begin by right-clicking Trace Log and choosing New Log Settings From, or you can choose New Log Settings from the context menu. I'll assume you've selected New Log Settings in order to create the Trace Log object from scratch.

When you see the New Log Settings dialog box, type a name for your Trace Log and click OK. You'll see the properties dialog box shown in Figure 9.17. Note that I've selected Events logged by system provider to show those options clearly in the figure. You can also choose non-system providers to track. In most cases, you'll need to provide a Run As entry to ensure that the Trace Log works as anticipated since few users have the rights required to perform this low-level work.

FIGURE 9.17

You'll need to define what type of system events you want to trace.

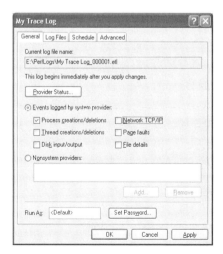

The Log Files and Schedule entries work just like those for the Counter Log. One difference that you'll note is that Trace Logs use different log file types. You can't read either log file type directly; both require the use of the TraceRpt utility.

The Advanced tab contains the buffer settings for the Trace Log. A Trace Log gathers a large amount of data. The log service saves data to temporary buffers in order to improve performance. If the settings you choose don't meet minimum requirements, the log service will override them. Normally, the log service saves data in the buffers to disk when the buffers are full. However, you can also set the number of seconds between data transfers to reduce the risk of losing data.

Tip

The settings you use for the buffers will affect the performance of your machine and the activities of the Trace Log. In some cases, providing a larger number of buffers or using a larger buffer size will allow the log service to work more efficiently and reduce system load. However, adding too many buffers increases the risk of data loss or corruption should the machine freeze or act in other unexpected ways.

Click OK. Performance Logs and Alerts will attempt to start the Trace Log if you used the default settings. Otherwise, you'll need to start the logging process manually or wait for the conditions you set to occur. If the Trace Log lacks the proper permissions to start, the indicator will remain red, and you'll see a warning message in the Applications folder of the Event Viewer indicating the problem. Fix any problems and restart the Trace Log manually.

After you collect the required data, stop the Trace Log from running. Right-click the Trace Log entry; then select Stop from the context menu. The indicator will turn red. Open a command prompt in the \PerfLogs directory. Type **TraceRpt <Name of Trace Log>** and then press Enter. TraceRpt will process the files and create two outputs for you. The first is SUMMARY.TXT, which contains a summary of the number and type of events. The second is DUMPFILE.CSV, which contains the detail data. Note that you can use wildcards in your arguments to TraceRpt in order to process more than one file.

Note

TraceRpt accepts other command line switches, but you normally won't need to use them unless you perform multiple traces on one system and don't want to overwrite the default files. Use TraceRpt /? to see a list of other command line arguments and switches.

Figure 9.18 shows a typical SUMMARY.TXT file. Notice that I processed multiple log files, in this case, by using a wildcard character for the input file. The Total Events Lost statistic is important because it can indicate problems with your system or a configuration problem with the Trace Log buffers. The table at the bottom of the SUMMARY. TXT file indicates the events trapped by these logs. The Event Name and Event Type columns specify the events. The Event Count column tells you how many of that particular event occurred during the monitoring period. Finally, the globally unique identifier (GUID) column tells you which object generated the event.

FIGURE 9.18

SUMMARY.TXT tells you about the events generated in the log file.

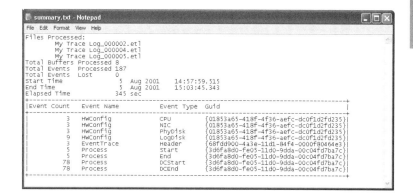

You can open the DUMPFILE.CSV file in a number of ways, but the two best ways are with a spreadsheet or a database manager. This file will contain a lot of information and working with it any other way will prove to be difficult. Sorting the data is going to be a necessity. Figure 9.19 shows a typical DUMPFILE.CSV file output displayed within Excel.

In this case, I set the Trace Log to monitor process creations and deletions. As you can see from the figure, I created a few new processes, but the system generated a lot more. Much of the trace data remains hidden in the figure. For example, you can't see the event name or type columns.

One column contains the thread identifier (TID) for the process. Windows XP assigns every instance of an application a unique TID. For example, if you open two copies of Notepad, they'll both have a different TID. It's safe to ignore this column for troubleshooting and performance needs.

You'll also see columns for clock time (indicates the process priority), user time, and kernel time. These are the three columns of most interest for performance needs. The priority tells you how the application shared CPU cycles with other applications. If you see an application that sets a high priority, you might want to explore further and ensure that

FIGURE 9.19

The DUMPFILE.CSV file contains the detailed trace information.

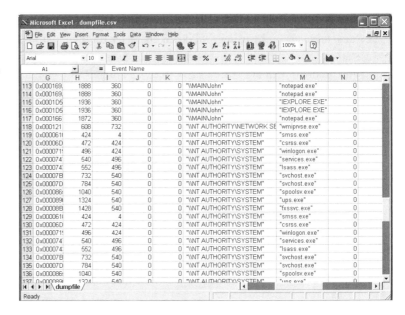

the application warrants the extra processing cycles. The user time indicates how much time the application spent in user mode, generally serving user needs. The kernel time shows how much time the application spent in protected mode accessing system resources.

Creating Alerts

Alerts should be a favorite tool for network administrators because they can tell you about system problems before they cause the system to fail. For example, you can set an alert for low memory or hard drive space. These alerts will tell you when there's a system overload, long before the overload causes problems. The fact that you can ask for alerts in several forms only makes this feature more valuable.

To create an Alert, right-click Alerts; then choose New Alert Settings From or New Settings Alert from the context menu. Type the name for your Alert in the New Alert Settings dialog box and click OK. You'll see a properties dialog box.

Alerts work by monitoring performance counters on your system, so you need to add at least one counter to the Counters list before you can do anything else. Click Add, and you'll see an Add Counters dialog box. I chose processor idle time as an example because it's easy to generate an alert by using this counter. Figure 9.20 shows the General tab for the sample Alert. You'd use something practical such as the Available KBytes counter from the Memory performance object. An Alert can rely on more than one counter, but you should create one Alert for each major event so that you can detect which Alert went off.

Figure 9.20

The General tab helps you configure the alert conditions.

You also need to select an alert condition. For example, if you're monitoring memory, you might want to set an alert when the amount of available memory falls below a certain level. As you can see, this tab also allows you to set the monitoring frequency and the Run As field.

The Action tab contains options for telling you when an event occurred. The following list discusses each option and tells what they mean.

- Log the event to the application event log. This is the best solution for non-critical alerts. You want to know the event happened, but you don't have to fix the condition immediately.

- Send someone a message. Reserve this option for critical alerts that require immediate attention. For example, if a lack of memory or hard drive space will cause the system to fail, then you want to send someone a message. There are two odd requirements when sending a message. First, the message must go to a machine other than the current machine. Second, the message must go to the machine and not the person. If more than one person uses a machine, this second requirement could become a problem. If the message sending option looks like it won't work, then you could always write a script to send the message in another way.

- Start a performance data log. Some events require monitoring because you know they already exist, but don't know how to fix them. Starting a performance data log can give you the information needed to track the problem and fix it.

- Run an application. You'll reserve this action for situations when an application can fix the problem automatically. For example, you might set an alert for a near hard drive capacity problem that starts an application to clean up temporary and other unneeded files. A higher-level alert could tell you that the action was ineffective, and you need to look at the machine.

The final tab, Schedule, works the same as every other performance-monitoring tool we've looked at. Just set a starting and ending time. You can also set the Alert for a manual start or stop. Once you complete the Alert setup, click OK, start it, and hope you don't see a message.

General Windows Performance Tips

The place to begin tuning your system is with Windows. Unless the operating system is working at full capacity, you'll never get your applications to perform well. Of course, once you get the operating system working, you'll want to move on to application tuning. The following list is by no means inclusive of every tuning tip around, but it does provide you with some ideas on where to start. We'll discuss other tuning tips as the book progresses.

- **Performance versus Productivity**   Not every performance change you make to your operating system is worth the effort. Whenever you trade productivity for performance, you're actually reducing system performance as a whole. The time of the user is the most valuable resource you have, so it's important to make performance changes that don't affect productivity.

- **Visual Effects**   Just in case you haven't noticed, Windows XP includes a wealth of visual effects. The problem with visual effects is that they kill the performance of your machine. They could cost some productivity as well. You can turn off some visual effects by clicking Effects on the Appearance tab of the Display Properties dialog box. You'll find more visual effects on the Visual Effect tab of the Performance Options dialog box (click Settings in the Performance area on the Advanced tab of the System Properties dialog box).

- **Applications**   Sometimes, you can enhance performance by getting rid of the applications you don't need. For example, some people keep a game of solitaire running on their system. Sure, this is a small game and hardly consumes any resources, but it hurts both user productivity and system performance. Make sure that you need all of those icons in the notification area of the Taskbar as well. You can experiment removing some of the icons using the settings found in the MSCONFIG utility (open the Run dialog box, type MSCONFIG in the Open field, and then click OK).

- **Memory**   The number one performance enhancement you can make to a system is to add more physical memory, especially if you notice that Windows is creating a large swap file (PAGEFILE.SYS) on disk. Of course, there are practical limits to how much memory you can and should add to your system. Many desktop machines currently allow you to add up to 1 GB of RAM. However, 512 MB is probably a practical limit for most desktop users.

- **Virtual Memory**   Windows XP needs a certain amount of virtual memory to work properly. Virtual memory doesn't really exist—it is hard drive space that the operating system configures to look like memory to applications. Windows XP swaps information the application isn't using to virtual memory so it has enough physical memory to handle work it's performing. Generally, you should configure virtual memory to the same size as physical memory (less, if you have lots of physical memory). In addition, making the minimum and maximum swap file sizes the same can produce a performance boost.

- **Processes**   You can gain a temporary performance boost for an application by giving its process a higher priority. However, giving the foreground application a performance boost means everything else will run more slowly. To give your application a boost, open Task Manager and click Applications. Locate the application you want to tune, right-click on that application, and choose Go to Process from the context menu. Right-click the process that Task Manager selects and choose one of the options from the Set Priority menu. You'll find that using AboveNormal or High is enough to give your application a boost. Never use the Realtime setting because it can cause your system to freeze or act in an unanticipated way.

Performance Tuning with Multiple CPUs

If you're fortunate enough to have a system with two or more CPUs, you know that the extra processing horsepower can make a big difference in system performance. However, you can also run into a couple of problems using multiple CPUs.

One of the problems you'll see is that the application will refuse to run. This is especially true of game applications because the vendor never designed them to use more than one CPU. If you run into this problem, you can fix it with relative ease.

Start the application that has the CPU problem. Don't do anything with it. Open Task Manager and click Applications. Right-click on the application, and choose Go to Process from the context menu. Right-click the process that Task Manager selects and choose Set Affinity from the context menu. You'll see a Processor Affinity dialog box. Clear all but one CPU entry. The application should run fine now because all it can see is one CPU.

The second problem you'll run into is the greedy application that tries to grab everything. Again, you'll want to set the processor affinity so it sees fewer CPUs. However, in this case, you might want to tune other essential applications to use the CPU that you freed from the clutches of the greedy application.

Managing Data Sources

Most businesses run on database management applications. Major applications require some method for storing data on a permanent storage device such as a hard drive. The database represents the most flexible method for storage of large quantities of repeating data.

Creating a connection between your application and the data it needs is important, especially if the data resides on a server. An application can't find the information itself. Modern applications use a variety of methods for finding and manipulating data, one of which relies on Open Database Connectivity (ODBC).

ODBC requires that you define the connection between the application and the data on your machine. Each vendor provides a similar, but different technique for defining this connection. The following sections show you how to work with the Data Sources (ODBC) applet in the Control Panel.

Creating DSNs

A data source name (DSN) defines a connection between your machine and a database. The DSN is database management system (DBMS) specific, so a DSN for an Access database won't work with SQL Server. The DSN defines every aspect of the connection including the database name, connectivity specifics, database options, and user statistics.

ODBC defines three types of DSNs. The following list tells you about each type.

- **User**   This connection is only visible to you. It's a private connection to the database. User DSNs work best for personal data or information that only a select group of users should access.
- **System**   This connection is visible to all users on the same machine. It enables anyone on your machine to use the same connection that you use to the database. This DSN works best for common databases where the connection information varies by machine.
- **File**   You can transfer this connection from machine to machine. This DSN works best in situations when you use generic connection information for all machines and rely on the user to provide details such as username and password.

Creating a DSN may seem confusing at first, but it's quite simple once you know how DSNs work. The first thing you need to decide is which type of DSN to create: user, system, or file. Second, you must know which database manager you're using. Third, you need to know the location of the data. Once you know these three pieces of information, you have almost everything needed to create a DSN (you'll also need some custom items such as a username, password, and any special options required for the connection). The following steps show how you'd create a user DSN for an Access database. The steps for any other DSN would be about the same, with small differences to account for differences in DBMS or connection visibility.

9

1. Open the Data Sources (ODBC) applet. Click the User DSN tab. You'll see an ODBC Data Source Administrator dialog box that contains a list of connections (if any) and three buttons (Add, Remove, and Configure).

2. Click Add. You'll see a Create New Data Source dialog box that contains a list of ODBC drivers installed on your machine. If you don't see the driver for your DBMS vendor on this list, it means the vendor didn't supply a driver or you need to install it.

3. Locate the ODBC driver you want to use (the Microsoft Access Driver entry, in this case). Click Finish. This is all there is to the generic portion of the DNS configuration. However, now you'll need to perform the vendor specific portion of the configuration. In this case, we're working with Access, so you'll see an ODBC Microsoft Access Setup dialog box.

4. Type a value in the Data Source Name field. Making this field one word or combining multiple words so they appear without spaces is helpful in maintaining compatibility with some applications. This field contains the name you'll use to refer to the connection within the application.

5. Type a string in the Description field. Make this entry relatively long and descriptive so you can identify the connection within the ODBC Data Source Administrator later.

6. Click Select. You'll see a Select Database dialog box. This is where you'd normally select a database. If you have an Access database handy, you can select it. Even an empty file containing an MDB extension will work since we're not using this connection.

7. Select a database and click OK.

At this point, the connection is usable. You've defined everything you have to define for the connection to work. However, you might need to add a few more options before you click OK to create the connection. If you click Options, you'll notice you can set the connection to create a read-only or an exclusive connection. The Page Timeout field changes the time before a timeout occurs—a handy feature for problematic connections to a remote server. The Buffer Size field helps you tune the database connection.

Creating a buffer the exact size of one or more records reduces memory cost and improves network bandwidth usage. In practice, you have to weigh the cost of the buffer in memory against the gains that you receive.

Click Advanced, and you'll see a Set Advanced Options dialog box. The most common entry in this dialog box is the username and password so you don't have to supply it when accessing the database. However, making this entry also opens the database to possible penetration by crackers. The Options list varies by database vendor and even by database version. Only experts should make changes in this list. When you're finished looking at this dialog box, click OK to close it. Click OK again to close the ODBC Microsoft Access Setup dialog box. The new connection will appear in the ODBC Data Source Administrator dialog box.

To ensure that you won't use the connection we just created for anything, highlight it and click Remove. This will remove the entry from the list and ensures that it won't come back to haunt you later. Make sure that you erase any fake files you created and close the ODBC Data Source Administrator dialog box.

Checking Drivers

Database connections are complex, so it's possible that you'll experience problems with them. One of the most common problems is having the wrong driver installed. The ODBC Data Source Administrator dialog box contains a Drivers tab that you can use to check that status of your drivers.

Every entry on the Drivers tab will include a driver name, version, company, filename, and date. The driver name isn't unique. Any number of drivers could have the same driver name and usually only one will work efficiently.

In some cases, even the version number isn't unique. This is a better indicator of the driver you have on your system, but it isn't an absolute indicator. What you need to do to verify your driver is look at the combination of the filename, version, and date. If any of these values differ from what you need to create a connection, then you need to download a new driver from the vendor's Web site.

ODBC also has a problem where newer isn't always better. If you find that your new driver isn't working right, install the old one. Looking for the exact version number, filename, and date is always a good idea if compatibility is the problem.

Fortunately, ODBC drivers are easy to replace. Some come with an installation program. However, in other cases, you'll need to copy the new file to the \SYSTEM32 directory on your machine. Make sure that you make a backup of the old driver before you install the new one.

Tracing Database Activity

The ODBC Data Source Administrator dialog box contains a Tracing tab. What you see when you click this tab depends on the applications you have installed on your system. Generally, you'll see two fields and a Start Tracing Now button. The Log File Path field contains the filename and path of the log file. Make sure that you use something easy to remember. If you want to use a different existing log, you can use the Browse button to find it.

The Custom Trace DLL field contains the default trace program for Windows XP. Unless your vendor provides a special DLL for tracing purposes, you should always leave this entry alone. If your vendor does provide a special DLL, you can find it using the Select DLL button.

When you finish configuring the trace setup, click Start Tracing Now. Windows XP will begin filling the log with data. You can tell the action took place because Start Tracing Now will change to Stop Tracing Now, and you'll see the log created on the hard drive. (Don't worry if the log says it contains 0 bytes because Windows XP uses a buffer to hold the log entries.) The log will continue filling until you click Stop Tracing Now.

If you're knowledgeable enough about the way your DBMS works, you can read the log entries and see the actions the driver took to create a connection and exchange data. The vendor support personnel might ask for a copy of the log as well to help troubleshoot problems with your system. The log doesn't contain any personal information—just database events.

Summary

Today you've learned about managing software on your system. We explored everything from application installation to performance tuning. You also learned how to use three more tools: Event Viewer, the Performance console, and the ODBC Data Source Administrator. These three tools are essential parts of your application management strategy. While we didn't explore every aspect of these tools, you should know enough to perform most system maintenance tasks and to tune your machine for optimum performance.

Q&A

Q: Why don't all Event Properties dialog boxes contain entries in the Data field?

A: Sometimes there's no error data to share with the user or the vendor didn't design the application to provide such information. In other cases, the application shared the information as part of a pop-up error message and the event log entry only acts as a reminder to the administrator to perform some action. Finally, the error data may appear as part of the information in the Description field, so the use of the separate Data field isn't necessary.

Q: What are the best ways to sort CSV files to gain the most information?

A: It depends on what you're trying to accomplish. If you're looking for performance information, you might want to sort by one of the performance columns or by application name. Sorting by user name allows you to see how the system uses resources and how you're interacting with the system. For example, you can see the effects of closing and opening applications too often. Sorting by event name and type helps you see the categories of process use on your system.

Workshop

It's the end of the ninth day. You should have a much better idea of how to install, configure, and manage software on your system. It's time to see how well you've learned the lessons this chapter has to teach. You can find answers to the quiz and exercise questions in Appendix A at the back of the book.

Quiz

1. Which file do you modify to make new entries visible in the Windows Component Wizard?

2. Which command line utility do you use to convert a trace log into human readable form?

3. What's the main difference in viewing active data in System Monitor versus viewing logged data?

4. What are the two requirements for sending a message using an alert?

Exercises

1. Spend time in the Add/Remove Programs applet learning more about the applications installed on your system.

2. Use System Monitor to explore the performance monitoring capability of your system.

3. Use some of the application tuning tips in this chapter to tune your applications. Check the results by using System Monitor.

4. If you have a database installed somewhere on your network, try creating a DSN for it.

DAY **10**

Working with Hardware

The computer system you use today won't be the system you use tomorrow. A PC is only as good as the next upgrade that makes it obsolete, in the eyes of a computer industry bent on constant upgrades. According to many of the surveys that abound in the PC industry, your system will exist in one form or another for about three years. At which time you'll dump it and get a new one. That is, if you believe the polls.

Part of the reason for this view of hardware is the corporate strategy that says it's less expensive to get a new system than it is to upgrade an old one. (Many of these systems are $2,000 or less.) In fact, given that many corporate machines use mediocre components to save on cost, this idea is probably true. The corporate machine requires less work if you configure it to meet the needs of the majority at the outset and then leave it alone if possible. However, parts still fail, so the network administrator will likely need to reconfigure the hardware at some point.

Another reason for this view of hardware is the computer gamer, who also tends to be the hot rod enthusiast of the computing industry. An industry pundit once proclaimed that the computer you want (not necessarily the one you need) always costs $5,000. At one time, I thought that statement would lose its validity as the computer became a commodity. The fact is, for a gamer, the computer you want still costs $5,000. Other computers cost less because vendors design them to different specifications than what a gamer would find acceptable. Because the initial investment for a gaming computer is so high, gamers are positively motivated to tinker with their machines so long as it makes economic sense to do so.

This leaves the home user and small- to medium-sized business owner. I've seen some of these computers age to the point that the paint is wearing off. A home user and small business has every reason to make incremental upgrades and save cash on the parts that still work acceptably. After all, some typing from work and a few educational games hardly tax today's computer. The business requirements of the small- to medium-sized owner are higher than the home user, but economics play a large role in the decision to upgrade. These businesses have few machines when compared to a large corporation, so making incremental upgrades can save money.

If you haven't guessed yet, we're going to discuss hardware from a variety of perspectives today. The fact is that everyone will need to tinker with his system, at least occasionally, so knowing something about your system is important. We'll talk about all of the major hardware categories, and you'll learn what you need to do to install and configure each type of hardware. I'll also include a few configuration and usage tips. We won't discuss troubleshooting today; that topic will wait until Day 21.

Configuration Issues

One of the most common problems for anyone working with hardware is configuration. The manuals that arrive with your new product are often written in a combination of first year engineering student and broken English (substitute your favorite language). I find that some of the information defies logical explanation. For example, why should I care if ratcheting the slingbob by the light of a new moon causes the machine to hiccup uncontrollably?

Fortunately, most of the hardware you buy today is self-configuring, which means that you stick it in your machine and hope for the best. The problem is that the hardware often doesn't self-configure itself; it merely sits in your machine looking pathetic. The hardware doesn't care how angry or frustrated you get; it'll continue sitting there, looking out of the box hoping you won't notice its presence.

Tip

Make sure that you read the entire user guide for your new piece of hardware. Vendors often place the one piece of information you need in the most inconspicuous place in the manual. Check the disks that accompany the hardware and read the README files as well. The README files contain last minute information about your hardware that doesn't appear in the manual. If you don't read the README, it's unlikely that you'll get a good installation. Look on the vendor Web site for new drivers and updated information. Never assume that the manuals and drivers you have are up-to-date. Finally, see if the vendor offers some support through a newsgroup and ask any questions you might have. Peer support is often better than the information you get from support personnel on the telephone. If the vendor doesn't provide support through a newsgroup, try one of the generic newsgroups such as `alt.comp.hardware`, `alt.computer.hardware`, `alt.ibm.pc.hardware`, or `microsoft.public.win2000.hardware` (or a Windows XP alternative when it becomes available). You can find all Microsoft newsgroups on the news.microsoft.com server if your ISP doesn't carry them.

10

Your first clue that there's a problem with your new hardware is when you start the machine and you don't see it listed with the plug-and-play hardware during the BIOS check. Of course, this assumes that you can read fast enough to see the chart containing this information. If the chart passes you by and Windows starts, you still have another clue that there's a problem. If Windows supports a piece of hardware that you install on your machine, yet doesn't automatically detect it during startup, it's likely that you have a configuration problem.

The fact is that Windows XP should always detect your hardware. It should ask you to install a driver for the new hardware except under two conditions. The first is if you install an older, but simpler device, such as an extra serial (COM) or parallel (LPT) port. My machine came equipped with one parallel port, and I have two printers, so I installed a second port. The second is if the device is newer than Windows XP. In most cases, Windows XP should still detect the new device, but you'll have to supply a driver for it.

What happens if the device doesn't fit into these two categories, and you still can't get Windows XP to recognize it? The following list contains some fixes that I've used in the past. They work most of the time, and you'll find that you get a lot less frustrated if you try them first. Remember that kicking your machine isn't an option!

- Verify that the hardware doesn't require any setup. If you see any jumpers on the board at all, spend some time in the manual figuring out what they do. If the manual doesn't document the jumpers, try to find an answer online. Jumpers always perform some function, even if it's vendor-specific testing.

- Ensure that you connect all cables to the right location and that the cables are firmly seated on their posts. If you can place the cable in more than one place, check the manual to ensure that you've connected them to the correct place.

- Try exchanging this board with another board in your system. The BIOS reads boards nearest the power supply first. In addition, rearranging the boards will force the BIOS to update the system configuration. Finally, this technique will reveal "dead" or non-operational expansion slots on the motherboard. Be extremely careful when doing this because the boards are somewhat fragile, and you don't want to break any of the fingers within the expansion slots on the motherboard. The boards will require a firm push into the expansion slots, just don't force the board and break it.

- Check all boards to make sure that you fully seat them in the expansion slots. A properly seated board makes good contact with the expansion slot fingers, which allows good contact with the motherboard. Make certain you place the boards in the proper slot—a PCI board requires a PCI slot.

- Remove any boards that you don't need to start the system. For example, your system does require a hard drive controller and a display adapter, but it doesn't require a soundboard. Sometimes, starting the system with the minimum number of boards plus the problem board forces Windows to recognize it. Once Windows recognizes the board, you can add the other boards back into the system.

- Try installing the device driver anyway. If you've tried everything else, then this is the option of last resort. It generally won't work because Windows won't know which piece of hardware you're trying to install. The recognition process is important.

At this point, a call to the vendor is in order. You've tried installing the board according to vendor instructions without success. The process we just tried has eliminated common causes of setup failure, such as a board that requires setup. You've eliminated the motherboard, interactions with other boards, and bad expansion slots.

You only have three possibilities to consider. First, the board requires some "magical" setup that the vendor will tell you about for this system. For example, some CD-RW drives require special assistance before the recording application will work. Second, the board is incompatible with your system and won't ever work with it. This is rare, but it does happen. Third, the board is non-operational. In some cases, a board gets jostled just enough during transit to cause it to fail. A weird form of this third failure is a board that develops small fractures in the solder joints. Heat closes the fractures, so the board runs fine as long as it's warm. You should consider replacing such a board as soon as possible because there is no way to tell when it will fail permanently.

Using the Add Hardware Wizard

You'll normally use the Add Hardware Wizard for hardware that's newer than Windows XP or too old for Windows XP to recognize reliably. The hardware recognition features of Windows XP are much better than previous versions for hardware that Microsoft decided to support. Therein lies the problem for many users. You may have hardware on your system that doesn't appear in Microsoft's hardware compatibility list (HCL) found at http://www.microsoft.com/hcl/default.asp. If you have a Windows XP specific driver for that hardware, Windows XP will still be able to use the hardware, but it may not recognize the hardware when you start your system after installation.

The following steps will show you how to use the Add Hardware Wizard. It assumes you started the Wizard by double-clicking the Add Hardware applet found in the Control Panel.

10

1. Click Next. The Add Hardware Wizard will automatically search for any new plug-and-play hardware. If it finds the hardware, you'll see a dialog box telling you that Windows XP is installing the required support. Windows XP may also ask you to provide a third-party vendor disk for the hardware. Make sure that you have both the third-party vendor and the Windows distribution disk available. If Windows XP doesn't find a plug-and-play device, it'll ask if you've connected the hardware to the system.

2. Click Yes or No. If you select No, the Add Hardware Wizard will tell you it can't continue and ask you to connect the hardware to the system. This is the point when you may need to read the vendor instructions again. Some hardware, such as PDAs, requires that you install the software first and then the device. However, when working with a PDA, you'll install the software by using the Setup program on the vendor disk, not the Add Hardware Wizard applet.

    If you select Yes, Windows XP will display a list of hardware it detected on your system as shown in Figure 10.1. Notice the hardware with the question mark in this list. Hardware with a question mark lacks a driver or is inoperative for some other reason. If you can't find your device in the list, the device with the question mark may be the one you're looking for.

3. Select one of the hardware items from the list. If you don't see the item you want to install, select Add a new hardware device (found at the end of the list).

4. Click Next. If you selected an exiting device, the Add Hardware Wizard will show you the device status, but not offer to install any new drivers for you. Non-functional devices require troubleshooting. (Try the Reinstall Driver option on the General tab of the Device Properties dialog box first.) You'll use the Update Driver

option on the Driver tab of the Device Properties dialog box to install a new driver for an existing device.

FIGURE 10.1

The Add Hardware Wizard will ask you to identify the hardware you want to install from this list.

If you selected the Add a new hardware device option, the Add Hardware Wizard will ask if you want to search for the device automatically or perform a manual installation. It normally pays to perform the automatic installation because the Add Hardware Wizard will offer to use the manual installation if the automatic search doesn't work. The only time you want to avoid the automatic search is if experience shows that Windows XP will incorrectly detect the hardware.

5. Select Search for and install the hardware automatically (Recommended); then click Next. The Add Hardware Wizard will search for a device on your system. However, this time it isn't just looking for plug-and-play devices; it's also looking for older devices listed in the INF files. If the Add Hardware Wizard finds a device, it will prompt you to install it. Just follow the prompts and exit this procedure. Otherwise, the Add Hardware Wizard will ask if you want to install the device manually.

6. Click Next. The Add Hardware Wizard will display a list of device categories. You can also choose the Show All Devices option if none of the device categories look appropriate.

7. Choose a device category and click Next. You'll see a device driver selection dialog box like the one shown in Figure 10.2. At this point, you have a choice. You can select the vendor and device from the list and use the default Windows XP driver (if one is available), or you can click Have Disk and install a vendor-specific driver for your device. If you choose the Have Disk option, provide a driver location and follow the vendor-specific prompts to install your device.

Figure **10.2**

You'll need to choose a device driver from this list or use a vendor-supplied disk to add support for your device.

8. Select a vendor and then select a device from the list. Click Next. Follow the prompts to complete the device installation.

10

Using Device Manager

Device Manager provides you with an overview of your system from a hardware perspective. It lists every major device in your system, the drivers the device uses, the operational state of the device, and other facts about the device such as the system resources that it uses. In some cases, you'll also find rudimentary diagnostics for your device in the Device Manager, so this is one of the first places you should look if you think you're having a problem with Windows. The following sections tell you the details about using Device Manager.

Understanding the Device Manager Views

You can open Device Manager in a number of ways. For example, this is one of the snap-ins listed in the Computer Management console found in the Administrative Tools folder in the Start Menu or Control Panel. The easiest way to open Device Manager if you're working at the desktop is to right-click My Computer, select Properties, choose Hardware in the System Properties dialog box, and click Device Manager. You'll see a list of devices on your system in the Device Manager dialog box like the one shown in Figure 10.3.

Note that Figure 10.3 shows only one view of the data, and it doesn't even show all of the available entries. If you look at the View menu, you'll notice a Show Hidden Devices entry. Click this entry, and you'll see new device categories such as Storage Volumes appear in the list. You won't have to interact with hidden devices very often (if ever), so it's a good idea to keep them hidden.

FIGURE **10.3**

*Device Manager lists
all of the major
devices in your system.*

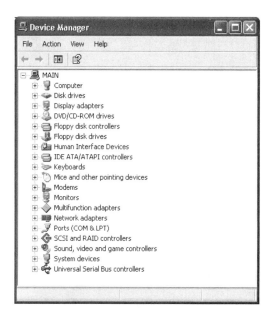

The initial Device Manager display assumes that you want to see the devices on your system. However, if you're troubleshooting a problem, you may not be as worried about the devices as you are about the resources they use. Resource conflicts are a common cause of hardware problems. For this reason, Device Manager provides two resource views. Figure 10.4 shows the Resources by Type view with the Interrupt Request (IRQ) folder open so you can see how the resource view works.

FIGURE **10.4**

*Use a resource view to
troubleshoot some
hardware problems.*

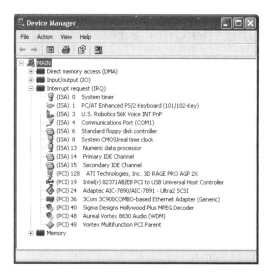

It's more common to use the device views as a starting point for any investigation of hardware problems. Each entry in the Devices by Type list is a device category that will contain one or more device entries. Every entry on this list has a context menu associated with it. For example, if you right-click on the computer name entry (MAIN, in this case), you'll see an option to scan your system for new devices. Most device entries have multiple context menu entries, including the usual Properties entry.

Working with Device Properties Dialog Boxes

Every device on your system provides a Device Properties dialog box. Modems are one of the most common devices installed on any machine, and they make a good device to look at because they include a few uncommon features. Figure 10.5 shows the U.S. Robotics Properties dialog box for my machine. You might want to open the Modem Properties dialog box on your machine to see what it contains as well. Most devices will include the General, Driver, and Resources tabs shown in Figure 10.5. The following sections describe the common and special tabs shown in Figure 10.5.

10

FIGURE 10.5

The Modem Properties dialog box contains the common and a few unusual tabs.

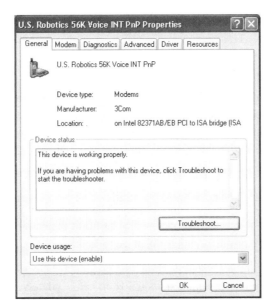

General Device Tab

The General tab tells you about the device. For example, it tells you where the device is physically located in the machine and the manufacturer. This is also the tab where you'll find status information. Click Troubleshoot if the device isn't operating correctly, and Windows XP will attempt to help you locate the problem.

One of the more important entries on this tab is the Device Usage field. You can choose to enable or disable the device. Depending on how you configure your system, the Device Usage field may contain a simple two-entry Enable or Disable option. Those using hardware profiles will have an option to enable the device in the current profile, disable it in the current profile, or disable it in all profiles.

> Most laptop users will want to create more than one profile for their system and then use the General tab to configure the various devices. I have three profiles set up for my laptop: docked, undocked, and unplugged. (See the "Using Profiles" section for details.) The unplugged profile disables any device that I can remove and still run the computer. For example, you don't have to have sound while on the road, so why enable this feature? You can also get by without a network interface card (NIC) and a modem while on the road in battery mode. Personal experience shows that I can increase battery life by about 12% using this technique. The battery on my laptop normally runs between 100 and 120 minutes with a standard profile. Using the unplugged profile extends that time to 130 to 140 minutes. No, that's not a lot of extra time, but it does help.

Driver Device Tab

The Driver tab contains information about the drivers used to enable device communication. This information includes the name of the provider, the driver date, the driver version, and the signing authority for the driver. These entries tell you about the main DLL associated with the device, but not any supplementary DLLs.

To find the details about all DLLs, you'll need to click Driver Details. The Driver File Details dialog box contains a list of all the drivers used with the device. You can find information about each file by highlighting it. The information about that device displays in the fields before the driver list. If you suspect file corruption or an old DLL as the cause of a hardware problem, this is the place to look.

The other buttons on the Driver tab allow you to update, rollback, and uninstall the drivers. The Update Driver button starts the Hardware Update Wizard. Those who have used this wizard will know that it looks similar to the Add Hardware Wizard we discussed earlier.

Whenever you install a new driver, Windows XP records the changes it makes. If you click Rollback Driver, Windows XP will try to restore the last known good driver state, making it possible to recover from a bad hardware installation. The rollback feature doesn't always work, but it does work more often than not.

Resources Device Tab

The Resources tab contains a list of the resources used by the device, including the IRQ and input/output (I/O) range. The important field on this tab is the Conflicting Device List. It contains a list of the devices attempting to use the same resources. If there aren't any conflicts, the field will say there aren't any conflicts.

If you do see a conflict, you can try to fix it by using another setting. The first step is to clear the Use Automatic Settings option. This will enable the Setting Based On field and the Change Setting button. The first repair you should try is to use a different standard setting. Select the options in the Setting Based On field until you find one that doesn't conflict with any other device or you run out of standard options.

At this point, you'll need to try some non-standard options. The first thing you'll need is the vendor manual. It doesn't pay to try a setting if the device doesn't support it. Highlight the conflicting resource. For example, if the IRQ is the conflicting resource listed in the Conflicting Device List, then select that entry in the Resource Setting list. Click Change Setting, and Windows XP will allow you to try another setting in most cases.

What happens if you can't find a standard setting that will work and Windows XP won't allow you to change the setting manually? You have several choices. First, you could try to change the settings for the other device. If this won't work, then you can try the risky process of modifying the device INF file.

The option of last resort is to remove one of the conflicting devices. Generally, you want to remove older, less flexible devices first. This allows you to upgrade the device to something newer. It isn't a perfect solution, but it may be the only solution if resource conflicts prove especially difficult.

Special Device Tabs

Many of your devices will contain special tabs that allow you to do more than enable or disable the device and manage resources. A modem is a classic example of the value added Device Properties dialog box. It contains Modem, Diagnostics, and Advanced tabs.

Some people wonder how to control the volume of a modem during the calling phase. They find the dialing annoying. The Modem tab contains the answer in the form of a Speaker Volume slider. This tab also contains settings for the maximum speed at which the modem can communicate and an option for forcing the modem to wait until it "hears" a dial tone before dialing.

10

Tip

Listening to your modem can become the best diagnostic tool in your arsenal. Knowing how a modem sounds as it dials a remote connection can save
you a lot of troubleshooting time. For example, you should hear the dial
tone, then the individual tones of each number, and then the modem signaling. If you don't hear a dial tone, then you know to check the telephone
line for a connection. The problem could be as simple as a disconnected line
or a bad cable. You should also learn the modem signaling sequence. Each
modem connection speed uses a different set of tones. You can detect subtle
differences in this sequence after a while. This technique comes in handy if
you suspect the part of the modem circuitry is bad, but not all of it.

The Diagnostics tab is the most important troubleshooting aid for any device because it
contains the vendor-recommended diagnostic routines. Figure 10.6 shows a typical
example for a modem. To obtain this screen, click Query Modem. The list of information
you get back from the modem (when it works) tells you a lot about the capabilities of
that modem. For example, you can check the list to see if the modem provides fax capability and the level of capability offered. The returned information will also tell you
about standards that the modem supports and a few unexpected surprises. For example,
some modems keep track of the last number that you dialed, making it relatively easy for
someone to check on your dial-up access habits.

FIGURE 10.6

*Use the Diagnostics
tab to troubleshoot
your modem and find
out more about it.*

Note that this Diagnostics tab also contains an option to log modem activity. Keeping track of modem activity through a log is another way to diagnose problems. You can detect what problems the modem encounters as it calls another location.

The final special tab is Advanced. This tab contains a field for typing advanced commands and two innocent looking pushbuttons that most people would bypass without a second look. However, these two pushbuttons enable some of the most important features of the modem.

Click Advanced Port Settings, and you'll see an Advanced Settings dialog box. This dialog box contains an option to use the first in first out (FIFO) buffers, which optimizes modem use in a multitasking environment. A modem contains two buffers, one for *send* and another for *receive*. Setting the buffers high allows the modem to collect more data between interrupts to the operating system. Using the high setting helps the operating system to work faster because it spends less time attending to the needs of the modem. Using a lower setting is safer because there's less of a chance of a modem buffer overflow. When the modem buffer becomes too full, it simply tosses the extra characters and you lose data. This dialog box also allows you to select the modem communication port setting. This is another important option for resolving conflicts. However, the modem is about the only device that offers such as setting.

Click Change Default Preferences, and you'll see a Modem Default Preferences dialog box. This dialog box contains two or more tabs, depending on your modem model. The two common tabs are General and Advanced.

The General tab adjusts the modem connection settings. It controls how long the modem will wait to create a connection and determines how long the modem will hold an idle connection. This tab also controls the connection speed and features such as error correction (EC). You can also use it to enable data compression, a feature that helps the modem work more efficiently, but introduces compatibility problems that may not work with all modems. You'll also find flow control options on the General tab. The default setting usually works best, but you may need to change it for compatibility reasons as well.

The Advanced tab contains the hardware settings that used to be important but have faded into obscurity. You can select the data bit, stop bits, parity, and modulation type. The only time these settings come into play anymore is if you're trying to connect to an older bulletin board system (BBS). Even so, you'll find that most communication software allows you to change these settings by using connection parameters so changing entries in this dialog box is unnecessary.

10

Using Profiles

Profiles may be the most underused part of Windows because users view them as difficult to configure and even harder to use. A profile is nothing more than a declaration of
the hardware you want to use. It allows you to configure your system for different situations without physically removing unneeded hardware. As we saw in the General Device
Tab section, all you need to do to configure a profile is to enable or disable the device.

 Note   You must log on as an administrator equivalent to create, modify, or delete
hardware profiles. Windows XP does allow everyone to choose a profile during the boot sequence.

To create and manage profiles, you'll need to open the Hardware tab of the System
Properties dialog box. You can access this dialog box by right-clicking My Computer and
selecting Properties from the context menu or through *System* option found in the
Control Panel. Click Hardware Profiles on the Hardware tab, and you'll see a Hardware
Profiles dialog box like the one shown in Figure 10.7.

FIGURE 10.7

*The Hardware Profiles
dialog box helps you
create new profiles for
your system.*

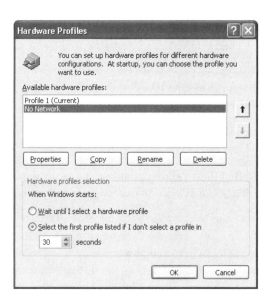

Notice that this dialog box contains a list of profiles. The profile listed at the top of the
list is the default. If you choose to display a menu for profiles for a limited time (as
shown in the figure), Windows XP will automatically choose this option after the time
lapses without a profile selection.

Creating a new profile is as easy as highlighting the profile you want to copy and then clicking Copy. You'll see a Copy Profile dialog box. Type a name for your new profile in the To field and click OK. Windows XP will create a new profile. You can't create an empty profile because the system won't boot with this selection. That's why Windows XP only allows you to copy existing profiles.

Click Properties, and you'll see a Profile Properties dialog box. Laptop users will want to select this option because it allows you to designate the profile as laptop enabled. You can choose three docking status indicators: docked, undocked, or unknown. The unknown setting forces Windows XP to perform extra checks that slow the boot sequence, so this is another reason to provide specific boot options for the docked and undocked state.

For some reason, Microsoft assumes that you'll create a profile and then not use it. The Always include this profile as an option when Windows starts option is always cleared by default. This means that you can create a new profile, but you won't see it the next time you boot the machine. Make sure that you check this option so you'll see the profile. The only time you'll want to clear the option is if you lend your laptop to someone and don't want him or her to use the profile.

After you create the new profile, boot the system using it. Use Device Manager to enable and disable devices as needed. Check the setup by booting your machine again. The new profile is ready for use as needed to save boot time, power, and help maintain your sanity (no more network missing messages).

10

Hard Disk Configuration

The hard drive is one of the most important, yet difficult to configure resources for your system. The reasons for hard drive problems are many, but you can sum them up as follows:

- **User Access**   Unlike memory, processor cycles, network bandwidth, and other performance factors, the hard drive is under direct user control. This means that the activities of the user directly affect the efficiency of this resource and users tend to abuse resources without considering the impact of such abuse. Many network administrators feel that user files will automatically expand to fill any increase in hard drive capacity. This axiom is true if you don't manage the hard drive carefully, but you can usually get around the problems.

- **Variety**   Hard drives and other permanent storage solutions come in many shapes and sizes. Managing a permanent hard drive mounted in the system is different from managing a removable device such as a ZIP drive. A network drive differs from a local drive. Working with Network Attached Storage (NAS) and Storage

Area Networks (SANs) is different from working with drives permanently attached to a single server. The list goes on. The problem of hard drive management is so significant that many trade press organizations now offer special magazines that keep network administrators updated on new storage technology and the management methods the administrator will need to use it.

- **Disk Formats** Windows XP supports several different formatting techniques for disk drives. You have a choice between the File Allocation Table (FAT), 32-bit FAT (FAT32), and NT File System (NTFS) methods of formatting the drive. Each of these formats brings with it different management problems. For example, an NTFS drive offers higher levels of data compression and security than FAT, but it isn't as compatible with other systems.

- **Tools** Hard drives enjoy a profuse overflow of management tools, more than any other component on your system. With so many tools to choose from, some network administrators feel they need a special school just to learn about the tools at their disposal. Of course, the administrator has to decide whether the Microsoft supplied tools will work. In the past, most network administrators assumed that the Microsoft offerings wouldn't work. Today, Windows XP offers tools that will work for many companies, so network administrators should take a serious look at this issue.

- **Accessibility Requirements** No one has to decide if the user should access the processor or use memory. While network bandwidth throttling is a common requirement today, network administrators decide this issue on a network wide basis. Only the hard drive requires complex accessibility schemes to ensure that no one sees anything they shouldn't see.

Now that you have a better idea of the problems you'll face, let's look at the solutions. The following sections describe the majority of the disk management tools provided with Windows XP.

Working with Removable Storage

Removable media requires special handling by Windows XP. For one thing, you never know when someone is going to remove the media from the drive and make it inaccessible. You'll also find that removable media comes in many non-standard formats, which is one reason you have to add special support for it when booting a machine using DOS. The BIOS can provide information about any standard drive, but removable media tends to follow different rules born of the consumer market for CDs and DVDs.

You can view and manage your removable storage with the Removable Storage snap-in found in the Computer Management console. This view of the snap-in contains two folders: *Media* and *Libraries*. However, you might want to look at the full version of this snap-in, which is unavailable in the Administrator Tools folder. To access the full Removable Storage console shown in Figure 10.8, you need to open a Run dialog box, type **NTMSMGR.MSC** in the Open field, and click OK. The advantage of this view is that you see all of the available snap-in features. The disadvantage is that you can only work with local drives. If you want a version of the Removable Storage console that works with remote drives, then you need to create your own console.

FIGURE 10.8

You'll want to use the full version of the Removable Storage console for many tasks.

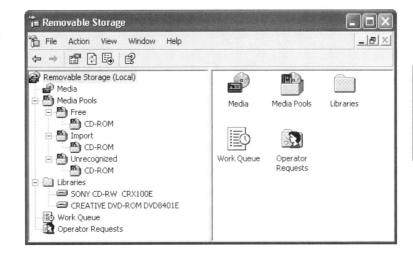

10

In both cases, the snap-in allows you to track the allocation of media used for storage. In the case of a tape, you can allocate and use the media more than once, and Removable Storage will track each use. The same holds true for other types of storage such as read/write drives. You can only allocate a CD once, so you'll see just the current CD unless you make changes to the various folders.

Let's discuss the common elements of this snap-in first. You'll see a Media folder. The folder will contain all of the current media in use on your system. This includes media used in the past for read/write operations. Figure 10.9 shows a typical Media folder when you have a tape drive attached to the system. Notice that each entry contains the name and type of the media. You'll also find a device entry, the device state, the mounted portion of the media, and the way Windows uses the media. Notice that the device name falls under the Library column. A device such as a tape drive can have more than one tape or other media assigned to it. The media that isn't mounted has a device entry of Offline Media.

FIGURE **10.9**

FIGURE **10.9**

*The Media folder con-
tains a list of media on
your system, plus
offline media in some
cases.*

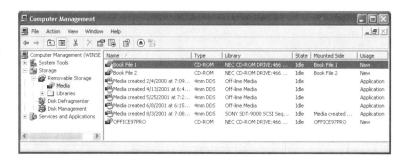

The Libraries folder contains one entry for each device on your system. Each device
folder contains a list of the media loaded on that device. Because most devices provide
room for just one disk or tape, you'll see a single entry in the folder. However, when
working with jukeboxes or other types of multiple disk drives, you'll see more than one
entry.

Now that we've discussed the common folders, let's talk about the additional Removable
Storage folders. The Media Pools folder contains three subfolders. The first is Free, and
it contains a list of the freed media. In other words, this media is no longer in use.
Normally, Windows XP will delete media found in the Free folder, but you can configure
the folder to hold these entries by right-clicking Free, selecting Properties, and clearing
the Delete Offline Media entry on the General tab. The Import folder contains a list of
the currently mounted media. The Unrecognized folder contains a list of new media such
as a blank CD. This folder could also contain entries for damaged media that Windows
XP can't identify.

Tip

> The Media Pools folder can contain other entries. For example, if you have a
> tape drive on your system, you might see a Backup folder. This folder would
> contain a list of all the media used for backup purposes. Note that this fold-
> er won't automatically delete offline media because tape drive applications
> tend to have more than one tape they need to track.

The Work Queue folder contains a list of all the tasks that the removable drives on your
system performed during a given time frame (normally, 72 hours). This entry enables
you to see tasks such as ejects, disk inventories (normally due to a media change),
mounts, dismounts, and media identification. You can change the recording period by
right-clicking the Work Queue folder, selecting Properties, and changing the Delete After
field on the General tab of the Work Queue Properties dialog box.

The Operator Requests folder contains a list of pending operator requests for the drive. Normally, this list is clear if the drives are idle. If you see an entry in this list for an idle drive, it could indicate a drive failure or other problem. Normally, Windows XP will report failures to answer operator requests with an error message or event log entry.

Using Disk Management

The Disk Management snap-in displays the logical and physical layout of your hard drives. Figure 10.10 shows a typical example of this window. The upper half of the window contains the logical drives, their status, capacity, free space, and fault tolerance, among other statistics. The lower half of the window contains the physical drives and their layout. Notice that one physical drive can contain more than one logical drive.

FIGURE 10.10

Use the Disk Management snap-in to view the layout and status of your drives.

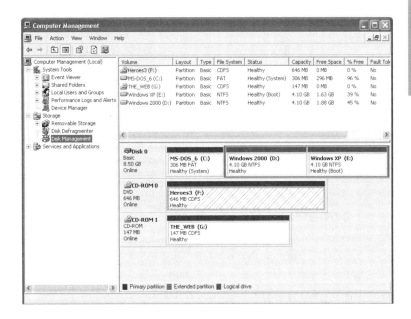

10

Each of the entries in this snap-in provides context menus that help you manage the drives. Most drives will allow you to create or delete a new partition (set aside or recover storage space), set the partition active (so you can boot from it), and format the partition (so it can hold data). You can also open or explore the drive. Opening the drive displays a single pane details view of the data that it contains, while exploring the drive will display the more familiar two-pane view.

One of the more interesting features is the ability to change the drive letters used to access each drive. You can also assign a path to a drive so you can access it as part of another drive (creating one large volume). To perform this task, right-click the logical drive entry and select Change Drive Letter and Paths from the context menu. Click Add, Remove, or Change in the Change Drive Letter and Paths dialog box to modify the drive information.

Using Data Compression

Windows XP provides data compression features that decrease the space consumed by each file. This feature doesn't work with FAT or FAT32 drive; you can only use it on an NTFS formatted drive.

To use this feature, open a copy of Windows Explorer, right-click the drive you want to compress, and select Properties. You'll see a Drive Properties dialog box. Select the General tab and check the Compress Drive to Save Space option. Click Apply. Windows XP will ask if you want to apply the change to just the root directory or to the entire drive. Select the entire drive. The drive compression phase will last several minutes, depending on the size of your drive.

> **Tip**
>
> After you compress your drive, you'll want to be able to tell the difference between compressed and uncompressed files. Select Tools | Folder Options to display the Folder Options dialog box. Select the View tab. Check the show encrypted or compressed NTFS files in color.

Formatting Disks

Sometimes, you'll need to format a disk while using Windows XP. You can format new hard drive partitions by using the Disk Management snap-in. However, floppy drives require some other means of formatting. You can format them using the FORMAT command at the command prompt, or you can use Windows Explorer.

To use the Windows Explorer method, right-click the floppy drive and select Format from the context menu. You'll see the Format Disk dialog box like the one shown in Figure 10.11.

You can't change most of the settings listed on this dialog box for a floppy disk, but they do come in handy for hard drives. The only settings you need to consider for a floppy are the capacity, volume label, whether you want to perform a quick format, and if you want to create a bootable floppy containing DOS.

The Quick Format option initializes the floppy without performing a complete format. The disk looks clean when you view it with Windows Explorer, but someone with the proper software could recover at least part of the old data. Unfortunately, even a complete format won't rid you of this problem.

FIGURE 10.11

The Format Disk dialog box formats a disk for you.

10

After you make your selections, click Start. Windows XP will format the drive for you. It will add DOS if you ask. You can watch the progress of the format by using the bar at the bottom of the Format Disk dialog box. You'll see a Format Complete message when Windows XP completes the task.

Setting Quotas

Quotas help prevent data bloat on your system. Each user receives a specific amount of space for data and application use. If the user attempts to exceed the amount of allocation space, Windows XP will tell them about the problem and notify the network administrator as well.

Only NTFS drives can use the quota system provided by Windows XP. You access this feature by right-clicking the drive and selecting Properties from the context menu. Select Quota, and you'll see a dialog box similar to the one shown in Figure 10.12.

Before you can do anything, you'll need to check Enable quota management. This will enable the rest of the selections on the dialog box. Notice the Deny disk space to users exceeding quota limit option. You must check this option if you actually want to protect the drive from abuse. Otherwise, the user can simply ignore the Windows XP plea to control disk usage.

The next series of options make it easy to set a default quota for every new user. However, in practice, you'll probably find that you need to set each user's quota separately, unless every user has precisely the same needs.

FIGURE 10.12

The Quota tab enables you to create quotas for an NTFS formatted drive.

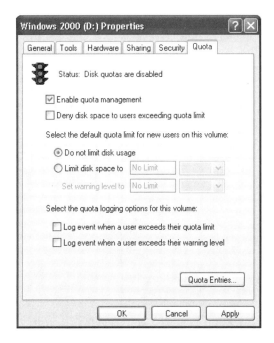

The final set of options enable logging of user abuses. Again, if you really want to protect the disk, then the best way to accomplish this is to log the user excesses so you can keep track of who regularly uses more than his fair share of disk space. You can set Windows XP to notify you when the user reaches his warning level and again when he exceeds his limit.

We haven't added any users yet, so no one has a quota. Click Quota Entries, and you'll see a Quota Entries dialog box containing at least the Administrators group. Use the Quota | New Quota Entry command to add a new user or group to the list. Type or select the user name or group that you want to assign a quota in the Select Users dialog box; then click OK. Select the user quota limits in the Add New Quota Entry dialog box. Note that this dialog box contains separate entries for both the maximum level and warning level. Click OK when you're finished, and you'll see a new entry in the Quota Entries dialog box. To remove an entry, highlight it and press Delete.

Printer Installation and Configuration

Despite the rapid expansion of the Internet and all kinds of electronic media, the printer is still a mainstay in most offices today. You need a printer to output any document that needs to remain in permanent form. In addition, printed documents form the basis of legal contracts, and they might be the only way to communicate with someone who doesn't have a computer.

The following sections tell you about printers. We'll discuss printer installation and configuration. You'll also learn how to manage print jobs. Since fonts are part of the world of printing, you'll learn about them as well.

Printer Installation

Windows XP provides a myriad of ways to install a printer. Of course, many printers come with a setup disk today. All you do is place the CD in your drive, answer a few quick questions, and you're ready to go.

Another method to add a printer to your system is to use the *Add Printer Wizard*. You can access the Add Printer Wizard in several ways. For example, you can double-click the Add Printer icon in the Printers and Faxes folder found in the Control Panel. If you find a printer on the network, you can right-click it and choose either Connect or Install from the context menu. In many cases, the server will download the required files immediately. However, if the server doesn't provide you with the required files, Windows XP will show a short form of the Add Printer Wizard.

No matter how you access the Add Printer Wizard, you'll need to provide some basic information about the printer. The following steps lead you through the process of creating a new local printer connection. I'll assume that you've clicked the Add Printer icon, and you're seeing the Welcome screen.

1. Click Next. The Add Printer Wizard will ask if it's a local or a network printer. Select Local printer attached to this computer. Notice that you can tell the Add Printer Wizard to look for a plug-and-play printer. Generally, if you select the option and Windows XP detects the printer, installation is close to automatic.

2. Click Next. If you chose the plug-and-play option, then Windows XP will look for the printer. A failure message means you'll have to configure the printer using the standard method. You'll need to click Next to get past the failure message. In either case, the Add Printer will ask you to select a printer port.

Note In rare cases, you'll need to create a new port because the Use the following port list box won't contain the port you need. For example, you might need to connect to a TCP/IP connection instead of a parallel or serial port. Many printers come network-enabled today, which means they don't consume a port on the back of your machine. However, it also means they require special handling. Select the Create a new port option, choose a port type, and

> then click Next. The Add Printer Wizard will ask you a question or two and place you back in the port selection dialog. Only this time you'll see the new port you created selected in the Use the following port list box.

3. Select a printer port; then click Next. The Add Printer Wizard will ask you to select the vendor and model for your printer.

4. Select a vendor and model. You can also use the Have Disk or Windows Update options to locate a printer driver in those ways. The Windows Update option is new. It takes you to the Windows Update Web site where you can search through the latest drivers for your printer. Click Next. The Add Printer Wizard will ask for a name for your printer. It'll also ask if you want to use this printer as your default printer; the one that applications use for print shortcuts.

5. Type a printer name, choose whether this will be the default printer, and click Next. The Add Printer Wizard will ask if you want to share this printer. If you choose to share the printer, the Add Printer Wizard will also ask for location and description information.

6. Choose a sharing option and click Next. The Add Printer Wizard will ask if you want to print a test page. This is normally a good idea because it allows you to see if the printer will work.

7. Check Yes; then click Next. The Add Printer Wizard will show you a completion dialog.

8. Click Finish. The Add Printer Wizard will install the printer drivers and output a test page. Make sure that the test page prints. If it doesn't, you'll need to troubleshoot the connection between your machine and the printer. For example, make sure that you turn the printer on and connect the cable.

Quick Printing Techniques

Sometimes you don't want to waste a lot of time opening a document to print it. Windows XP offers several shortcuts you can use to avoid opening an application to print a document using the default settings. For example, you can right-click the document and choose the Print option from the context menu. This first method has the disadvantage of limiting you to one printer, the one you set as a default.

Another technique is to place a shortcut to the printer on the desktop. You can then place documents you want to print directly over the printer shortcut. In this case, the document will go to the selected printer, rather than the default printer. However, you have to drag the document to the printer, which isn't quite as automatic as right-clicking, but faster than opening the application in some cases.

Whenever you choose a quick printing technique, you'll see the document open for a few moments as Windows sends it to the printer. The application still has to format and print the document, but at least Windows will close it automatically for you. Some applications also provide a print module that's separate from the rest of the application, so using this technique can save system memory. However, the most important aspect of using quick printing techniques is the time and effort it saves you.

Managing Print Jobs

No matter where your printer is located, you'll need to know how to manage the print jobs you create. For example, you might need to pause a print job or give another print job a higher priority.

The main resource for performing this task is the printer management dialog box you see when you open a printer (double-click its icon or choose Open from the context menu). You'll see a list of print jobs, if you have any printing. Each print job tells you the name of the file, the application that created it, the status (if paused), the owner name, number of pages printed so far, the time submitted, and the port number used to print the job.

This dialog box gives you a lot of control over the printer, at least in the way it works with your system. You can change the way the printer outputs documents using the File | Print Preferences command. The resulting dialog box contains all of the preferences for your printer, such as printing in landscape or portrait mode, the paper and print quality, and printer options. The File | Pause Printing command pauses all print jobs going to the printer. If you want to pause an individual print job, you'll need to right-click the print job and select Pause from the context menu. If the printer is experiencing problems and you want to clear the print queue, you can use the File | Cancel All Documents command to remove all print jobs from the queue. Finally, you can use the File | Properties command to display the Printer Properties dialog box. This dialog box gives you access to all of the physical printer settings such as sharing, the printer port, security, and any advanced printer settings.

As previously mentioned, you also have control over any documents you output to the printer. Right-click the document, and you'll notice that you can pause, cancel, or restart it. The restart option comes in handy if you've printed part of a document, had a printer jam, and need to restart the printer to get a clean printout.

If you right-click the document and select Properties, you'll see a simple Properties dialog box. The first entry in this dialog box allows you to enter the name of a person to notify when the print job is complete. Normally, Windows XP will notify the person who printed the document. The priority slider gives your document a higher priority than other documents in the list. The base priority for all documents is 0, or the lowest priority. The Schedule setting changes the time that the printer will accept the document for printing. Normally, the document doesn't have a time restriction, but you can use this setting to ensure that the print job doesn't complete after you leave work for the day.

Installing Fonts

You'll probably find a font for every need. However, you probably won't find all of them on your hard drive. At some time or another, you'll need to install a new font on your system. Of course, that means knowing the location and name of the font before you begin.

Once you know which font to load, open the Fonts applet in the Control Panel. You'll see a list of fonts that your system contains. Use the File | Install New Font command to display the Add Fonts dialog box. The Folders and Drives fields will help you find the location of the fonts you want to install. As soon as you locate a drive with fonts, the List of Fonts field will begin to fill with font names. Highlight the font you want to use and click OK. Windows XP will display an Install Font Progress dialog box. When the copying is complete, both the Install Font Progress and the Add Font dialog boxes will go away.

Removing Fonts

How many people can honestly say they need all 2,000 fonts on their hard drive? For that matter, how many of them can honestly say they know where all of them came from? Not many people use all of the fonts on their system and even fewer actually installed all of them, so it makes sense that you'll eventually want to remove a few of them.

Windows XP makes this task easy. Simply locate the fonts you want to remove and press Delete.

Caution | Note that deleting fonts is permanent. Unlike other areas of Windows, deleting a font removes it from your hard drive and doesn't place it in your Recycle Bin, so you have to exercise some care in pruning your font burden.

Viewing and Printing Fonts

Finding just the right font can be difficult. For one thing, you might know the name of a font that is almost correct, but not quite right. The Fonts folder includes several ways to make the task of finding the right font easier than printing them out one at a time from your word processor.

The first tool you'll want to use is to list fonts by similarity. Click Similarity on the toolbar, and the display will change to a list view containing two columns. The first column tells you the font name, while the second tells you how similar it is to the target font. Select your font in the List fonts by similarity to field. The Fonts dialog box appearance will change automatically to list any fonts with similar characteristics to the one you selected.

You'll want to view the selected fonts. Double-click any of the font icons, and you'll see a dialog box similar to the one shown in Figure 10.13. This dialog box won't show every character in the font. To see every character you'll need a utility such as Character Map. However, this view does show what the font looks like at various sizes and tells you something about the font creator.

FIGURE 10.13

You can view and print fonts using this dialog box.

Notice the Print button in the upper right corner of the dialog box. Click Print, and you'll see a Print dialog box. Select the printer and options you want to use; then click Print to send a copy of the window to your printer.

Keyboard Optimization

The keyboard is the main input device for most people. As a result, the keyboard is the one device that you need to fully optimize. Using a cheap keyboard or one that's arranged poorly will definitely impact your efficiency. However, the feel and arrangement of your keyboard aren't the only factors that affect your ability to work with Windows. You'll also find that the Windows settings for your keyboard affect your efficiency. The following sections show how to configure your keyboard for most efficient use.

Changing the Settings

Open the Keyboard applet in the Control Panel, and you'll see the Keyboard Properties dialog box. This dialog box contains two tabs: Speed and Hardware. The Hardware tab displays information about your keyboard, provides the means to troubleshoot it, and contains an option that will access the device settings.

The Speed tab contains three sliders that control the way Windows interacts with the keyboard. Use the Repeat Delay slider to control the amount of time Windows will wait before it repeats a key you press. The Repeat Rate slider controls how fast the key will repeat. A test area enables you to test the interaction of these two sliders.

The third slider controls the cursor blink rate. This setting is more important than you think. Certain cursor blink rates can cause physical reactions in people. For example, some people react negatively to a fast cursor blink rate, others to a slow blink rate. The cursor blink rate can also affect your ability to see the cursor on devices such as laptops. Use a slower blink rate in sunny locations, and you'll see the mouse better.

Installing Regional and Language Support Options

Windows XP provides support for a vast range of languages. Of course, it only installs a modicum of this support during installation because most people only need one language to begin using Windows. This means that you'll need to install support for additional languages once you have Windows set up.

You access both regional and language choices by opening the Regional and Language Options applet in the Control Panel. Windows XP separates regional choices, such as the way you format numbers and display currency, from language choices. The regional choices appear on the Regional Options tab. You can choose a predefined language option, such as English, from the list box, or you can customize the display to meet specific needs.

Click Customize, and you'll see the Customize Regional Options dialog box shown in Figure 10.14. This dialog box contains tabs for numbers, currency, time, and date. Within each tab you'll find customization options for various formatting needs. For example, when formatting the time you'll need to decide on a time display format, a time separator, the symbol for AM, and another symbol for PM.

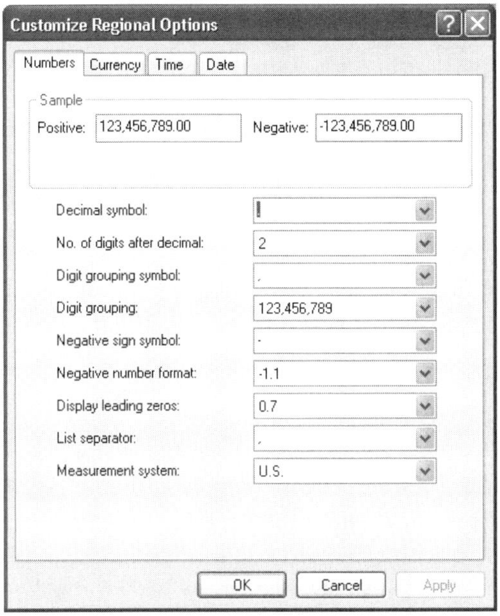

FIGURE 10.14

Use the Customize Regional Options dialog box to tune the way you display numbers, currency, time, and date.

The language options appear on the Languages tab. This tab contains options for loading the scripts required to support script and right-to-left languages. It also contains an option for installing East Asian language support.

Click Details, and you'll see the Text Services and Input Languages dialog box. This is where you can add other languages to the keyboard. In other words, you'll be able to select a new language, and the keyboard will reconfigure itself for that language. Click Add, and you'll see an Add Input Language dialog box. This dialog box contains two fields. The Input language field controls the Windows language options, while the Keyboard layout/IME field controls the keyboard layout.

If you install two or more languages, you'll also notice that Windows enables the Remove, Key Settings, and Language Bar buttons. Highlight a language and click Remove to remove it from the system. The Language Bar helps you to change between languages quickly by displaying language options in various places. For example, you can place the Language Bar on the Desktop for easy access. Click Key Settings to display the Advanced Key Settings dialog box. Use this dialog box to change the key settings used to move between languages.

Mouse Setting Configuration and Adjustment

The mouse has long been the alternate input device that people love to hate. The mouse forces you to move your hand from the keyboard, which costs you time and efficiency. On the other hand, the mouse saves you time by making it easier to move around Windows.

You can adjust your mouse settings by opening the Mouse applet in the Control Panel. You'll see a Mouse Properties dialog box that contains the Buttons, Pointers, Pointer Options, Wheel, and Hardware tabs. The Wheel tab is optional, depending on the type mouse you own.

The Buttons tab helps you adjust the way Windows interacts with the mouse. You can switch the left and right buttons so the mouse will work on either side of the keyboard. The Double-click speed slider controls how fast you have before Windows will execute the default action, rather than select an object. Finally, this version of Windows includes a new ClickLock feature. Turn ClickLock on, and you'll find that holding the left button down for a few seconds locks it in place. You can then drag the mouse across the screen without holding the button in place. Click the left button again, and Windows will release it.

The Pointers tab contains a list of the pointers that Windows will use for various situations. For example, when Windows is busy, it normally turns the mouse cursor into an hourglass. You can change the pointers in a number of ways. First, you can select a new entry in the Scheme field. This changes all the pointers at once. You can also highlight individual pointers, click Browse, and choose a new pointer from anywhere on your hard drive.

The Pointer Options tab shown in Figure 10.15 contains settings that define pointer operation. For example, you can change the pointer speed or display pointer trails to make the mouse more visible on a laptop. Special features such as Snap To make the mouse perform tasks automatically. For example, enabling Snap To will force the mouse to point at the default button in a dialog box. One interesting feature will place a bulls-eye around the mouse pointer when you press the Ctrl key, while another hides the mouse pointer as you type.

The Wheel tab controls the action of the mouse wheel. You can choose to move the screen up or down a certain number of lines for each move of the mouse wheel, or you can have display move one screen at a time.

FIGURE 10.15

The features on the Pointer Options tab can make working with your mouse a lot easier.

Finally, the Hardware tab tells you about your mouse hardware. Click the Troubleshoot button if you're having problems using your mouse. The Properties button displays the Device Properties dialog box where you can change features such as the device driver.

Video Advanced Settings

One of the more difficult set of hardware settings to find in Windows are those for your display adapter. If you look in the Control Panel, you'll find a Display applet, but nothing for your display adapter. It turns out that you have to go through the display settings to locate those for the display adapter. Right-click the desktop and choose Properties to show the Display Properties dialog box. Select the Settings tab; then click Advanced to display the Display Adapter Properties dialog box. This dialog box contains five tabs including: General, Adapter, Monitor, Troubleshoot, and Color Management.

The General tab contains settings that adjust the font size that Windows uses for general purposes. Normally, you'll want to adjust the font using the features on the Appearance tab of the Display Properties dialog box instead. Changing the font size here can have undesirable affects on some of the applications fond in the notification area of the Taskbar. You'll also find compatibility settings on this tab. These settings determine if Windows XP will reboot the computer before it makes changes to the display. In most cases, modern display adapters don't require a reboot.

The Adapter tab contains detailed information about your display adapter. For example, you'll find out how much memory Windows XP thinks your display adapter has by looking at the information on this tab. Click Properties, and Windows XP will open the Display Adapter Properties dialog box from Device Manager. Click List All Modes if you want to know which modes your display adapter supports. The listing normally includes resolution, color depth, and refresh rate for each mode.

The Monitor tab contains a list of the monitors connected to your system. One oddity about display adapter with tuners is that Windows XP always assumes you have a television attached to the machine. Click Properties, and Windows XP will display the Monitor Properties dialog box from Device Manager. If you have more than one monitor attached to your machine, Windows XP will display the properties for the highlighted monitor. The Screen refresh rate drop-down list box tells you the current refresh rate. Higher refresh rates present a cleaner screen appearance and tend to reduce both eyestrain and headaches. Avoid the 60-hertz setting if you work in an office with fluorescent lights. This refresh rate can cause subtle flickering effects that result in headaches for many people.

The Troubleshoot tab actually contains the hardware acceleration settings. The Hardware Acceleration slider determines how many hardware features Windows will use—the higher the setting, the more hardware acceleration features that Windows will use, and the better your performance. Lower the setting if Windows appears to have problems with some of the features of your display adapter. You may see other acceleration options on this tab, such as using write combining. This setting can cause screen corruption, so you'll want to use it carefully.

Finally, the Color Management tab affects the color management settings for your display. Color management is a process where Windows XP tries to match the color you see onscreen to the color output on other devices such as a printer. Normally, Windows detects and sets this option for you automatically. However, you may need to set it manually in some cases. To add a new color profile, click Add, select one of the available profiles, and then click OK.

Phone or Modem Configuration

The phone or modem attached to your system usually requires little in the way of configuration. These are simple devices with well-known features and capabilities. You'll find the hardware configuration settings for your phone and modem in the Phone and Modem Options applet in the Control Panel. The Phone and Modem Options dialog box contains three tabs that we'll discuss in the following sections.

Dialing Rules

Windows XP will ask you to create a location for yourself as part of the installation process. The dialog that you see only presents a few of the location settings, so you don't get a chance to use this feature fully. The Dialing Rules tab contains the initial entry you create, plus any locations you want to add to Windows.

Let's discuss the location entries first. Highlight the New Location entry and click Edit. You'll see an Edit Location dialog box. The General tab of this dialog box contains the name of the location, your country of origin, and the area code where you live. Windows requested these settings during setup. The remainder of this tab contains dialing rules. Each entry contains a key code that you'd normally dial to perform the requested action. For example, many companies require that you dial 9 to get an outside line. This tab also contains a special entry to disable call waiting.

The Area Code Rules tab enables you to create dialing rules for your location. These rules tell Windows XP to dial normally within an area code for some prefixes, dial 1 for others, and use both 1 and the area code for still other prefixes. The prefix for a telephone number is the first three digits. If your telephone number is 555-1212, then the prefix is 555.

You'll use the entries on the Calling Card tab to set your machine up for long distance dialing. The Card Types field of this tab includes a large number of predefined calling card types. Note that you can create your own calling card if necessary. The predefined cards act as examples. After you select a calling card type, you enter your account number and personal identification number (PIN). This allows your machine to make long distance calls automatically.

Modem

The Modems tab of the Phone and Modem Options dialog box contains a list of modems and three buttons. Use the Add button to add a new modem to your system. When you click this button, you'll see a special form of the Add Hardware Wizard. The first option is to let Windows XP detect the modem automatically. Normally, you'll want to let Windows perform the detection phase because if the detection fails, the Add Hardware Wizard will ask you if you want to add the modem manually anyway.

If Windows XP detects the modem automatically, you can follow the prompts to install the modem normally. Otherwise, Windows XP will ask if you want to select the modem manually. Click Next, and you'll see the usual list of modem vendors and associated products. Select a vendor and modem from the list; then click OK to begin the installation process. If you have a disk from the vendor, click Have Disk and follow the prompts.

10

Removing a modem is easy. Simply highlight the modem in the list and click Remove. Windows XP will ask if you're sure you want to remove the modem. Click Yes to remove the modem.

We've already discussed the Properties button in the Working with Device Properties Dialog Boxes section of the chapter. Click this button, and you'll see the same Modem Properties dialog box you can access from Device Manager. Make sure that you read about the special features that modems provide. For example, the Modem Properties dialog box contains a special Diagnostics tab that helps you find problems with the modem connected to your system.

Advanced

The Advanced tab contains a list of providers for telephone and modem use. Normally, you won't need to do anything with the providers. However, this dialog box contains options to add new providers, remove existing providers, or configure a provider. Not all providers allow every choice. For example, some providers don't include any configuration options, and you can't delete others. Every provider included on this list is different, so you'll need to know more about the provider before you modify it.

Summary

Today you learned a lot more about the hardware in your machine and saw how it interacts with Windows. Many users treat hardware as a dark mystery that only hardware gurus know or care about, but hardware is something that everyone should know about because it affects your entire computing experience.

Knowing some simple tricks can save you considerable time and money. Some hardware technicians don't even open the box when they get a new machine to troubleshoot. The first thing they do is check Windows and then they run diagnostics. A good technician can fix up to 65% of all hardware problems without replacing any hardware. (Statistics are based on a telephone survey of 15 computer stores and independent computer repair stores where the service technician works exclusively on hardware related problems.) Many problems are the result of simple configuration or resource errors. In other cases, an updated driver is all that the technician needs to restore the system to full functionality.

Q&A

Q: I've installed the vendor-supplied drivers for my device and Windows still says it's non-functional. What should I do next?

A: The first thing you'll want to do is ensure that your hardware is configured correctly. Many of the tips in the "Configuration Issues" section will help. You'll want to check the vendor's Web site for an updated driver. Also, make sure that you visit Windows Update for new additions to Windows. Ensuring that you have the latest software on your system makes finding a problem easier. In some cases, it's possible for gremlins to attack your system during an installation. Try installing the driver software again to ensure that you receive a good installation. Use the information we will discuss during Day 21 to diagnose your problem. Finally, check with the other users and the vendor to see if this is a common problem. The device may actually be non-functional or completely incompatible with your system or Windows XP.

Q: Why do some vendors provide several special tabs in the Device Properties dialog box and others provide little more than the standard tabs?

A: Generally, what you're seeing is the difference between a generic driver and a vendor-specific driver. The vendor-specific drivers tend to provide more special configuration tabs so you can enjoy all the features the device provides. Microsoft usually includes just enough functionality in the generic drivers to power the device. Creating full-featured drivers for every potential device would prove too time-consuming in most cases. However, even Microsoft provides special tabs on occasion. The Modem Properties dialog box we explored today is an example of special tabs offered by Microsoft.

Q: Should desktop computer users configure profiles for their system, or is this a laptop user only feature?

A: Profiles do have more to offer the laptop user because their configuration changes more often than any other machine. However, desktop machine users can create usable profiles as well. For example, there are days when I want to use my machine in stand-alone mode, so I configured a No Network option for my desktop machine. Admittedly, this isn't often, but it does happen. The use of the No Network option raises performance and allows applications such as games to run faster. You can also use profiles for diagnostic purposes. For example, you might want to create a profile that excludes devices you don't need for maintenance purposes to keep the operating system environment as pure as possible.

Workshop

It's the end of the tenth day. Today should have been one of those eye-opening experiences where you learn why things don't work the way the vendors say they will. It's time to see how much you know about installing, configuring, and maintaining your hardware. You can find answers to the quiz and exercise questions in Appendix A at the back of the book.

Quiz

1. When working with hardware, should you install the vendor-supplied drivers immediately, even if Windows doesn't recognize the hardware?
2. What are the three device management tabs provided by most devices in Device Manager?
3. What types of drives will use disk compression?
4. How do you add new language support to your keyboard?
5. What's the difference between the Pointers and the Pointer Options tab on the Mouse Properties dialog box?

Exercises

1. If you own a laptop computer, create several profiles to correct boot problems and enhance battery life.
2. Format a floppy using the Windows XP method.
3. Locate and record all of the devices in Device Manager that provide trouble-shooting or diagnostic aids.

WEEK 2

DAY 11

Configuring Services

Getting a handle on your operating system is important. You need to know about the tools at your disposal to manage the system. In the case of Windows XP, what you really need is a means to manage services. The operating system depends on modules called *services* to perform just about every task. When you install a new application, you often install a service as well.

Services reside in the background where you can't see them. They manage everything from the flow of power in your system to the indexing of files so you can search for data quickly. The operating system starts some services when the system boots, others when the system needs them, and a few won't start at all. An application could install the service on your machine until you need it later. Of course, you have final say over all these services, but only if you know how to manage them. This chapter looks at one service management tool in particular, the Service console.

Some of the power to work with services and to configure the operating system as a whole resides with the Control Panel applets. You'll find there are applets that affect just about every part of the operating system, from the way you dial a phone to the method used to display data on screen. We'll discuss the Control

Panel and its contents in this chapter. While the chapter won't discuss any of the applets
in detail, you'll know which applet to use the next time you need to change something.
Of course, we'll discuss the applets in more detail as the book progresses.

An Overview of the Control Panel

You can look at the Control Panel as a toolbox. It provides a place to store the tools you
use to manage Windows. Like most toolboxes, the Control Panel has a variety of tools,
each of which has a special purpose.

The Windows XP Control Panel can present your list of tools in a number of ways. The
two main views are the classic view used by previous versions of Windows and the category view.

The category view shown in Figure 11.1 is a new addition to Windows XP. It groups the
applets by functional area. You'll select a category of use first and then choose a particular applet within that category. Using this two-layer approach makes it easier to find the
right applet the first time. It also reduces the complexity of the Control Panel.

FIGURE 11.1

*The category view of
the Control Panel
makes it easier to
select the right tool
and simplifies the
Control Panel inter-
face.*

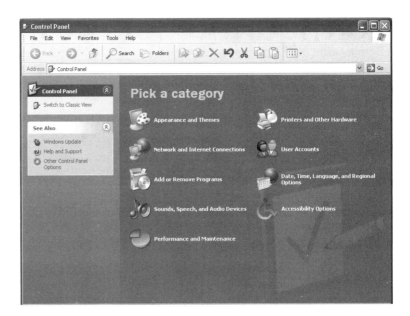

The category view doesn't stop at grouping applets; it also provides a task view of the
Control Panel. For example, if you select the Network and Internet Connections category,
you'll see two applets: Internet Options and Network Connections. In addition, you'll see
several task entries such as creating a connection to the network at your office or chang-

ing the configuration of a home network. The use of tasks puts the management options provided by the applets into words.

The classic view of the Control Panel shown in Figure 11.2 provides a list of applets and depends on the user's knowledge to make the right selection. An experienced user will probably use this view more often because it requires fewer clicks. Someone who already knows which applet to use has little to gain from the task-based approach of the category view.

FIGURE 11.2

The classic view simply lists the contents of the Control Panel and allows you to make your own decision.

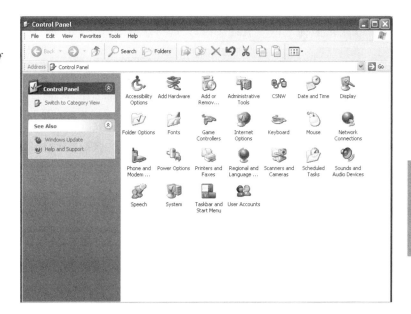

11

The Control Panel contains many standard applets. You'll see most of these applets on any machine you want to use. Table 11.1 lists these applets and provides a quick overview on how you'd normally use the applet to manage the system.

TABLE 11.1 Control Panel Applet Overview

Applet Name	Book Location	Description
Accessibility Options	"Working with the Accessibility Features" Day 6	These options enable you to change some Windows XP features to make them easier to operate for people challenged in various ways. For example, this applet helps you to enable the StickyKeys option for the keyboard.

TABLE 11.1 continued

Applet Name	Book Location	Description
Add Hardware	"Using the Add New Hardware Wizard" Day 10	This applet adds hardware to your system. Windows XP can automatically detect most modern hardware. You can also manually install the hardware when Windows XP can't detect it. This includes vendor-supplied disks for hardware that arrived on the market after Windows XP.
Add/Remove Programs	"Adding and Removing Programs" Day 9	This applet checks the status of your applications and enables you to manage them. In many cases, the software will provide options to add or remove features, perform updates, and remove the application completely. In some cases, the entry will also help you obtain technical support for the application.
Administrative Tools	Many areas of the book.	This is a folder, not just a single applet. It's the repository of other utilities that, in some cases, (Data Sources, for example) used to be in the main Control Panel folder. In addition, this folder contains many of the MMC snap-ins you'll use to manage Windows XP.
Client Service for NetWare	"Using the CSNW Applet" Day 8	This applet provides additional configuration options for your NetWare connection. For example, you'd use this applet to set the default tree and context. This applet also configures NetWare printing options. (You'll only see this applet if you have the NetWare services installed.)
Date and Time	"Date/Time Adjustment" Day 3	This applet helps you keep the date and time current on your machine an important task as your machine makes more connections to other resources. Users rely on the clock to schedule automated tasks, to keep track of appointments, to schedule automatic downloads from the Internet, and to carry out a variety of other responsibilities.
Display	"Managing the Desktop" Day 3	This applet enables you to perform tasks such as changing the display resolution and colors. You can also use it to enlarge the display fonts

TABLE 11.1 continued

Applet Name	Book Location	Description
		and change the wallpaper on the desktop. All these features add up to an incredibly flexible and easy-to-modify display system.
Folder Options	"Folder Options" Day 3	This applet displays the same properties dialog box that you see when you choose Tools | Folder Options in Windows Explorer. These options define the way Windows Explorer looks and acts.
Fonts	"Printer" Day 10	This applet manages the fonts on your system. Some applications include hundreds of fonts and most include at least a few, so your system can quickly fill with unwanted fonts.
Game Controllers	"Game Controller Configuration" Day 7	This applet tests and configures joysticks and similar input devices.
Internet Options	"Setting the Internet Options" Day 4	This applet displays the same properties dialog box you get when you choose Tools | Options in Internet Explorer. It sets Internet Explorer options such as privacy, security, and connection settings.
Keyboard	"Keyboard" Day 10	This applet sets a variety of keyboard options, including language and keyboard layout settings. A simple click of the International icon on the taskbar enables you to choose from any of the installed keyboard layouts. This applet not only installs support for these languages, but it provides other forms of keyboard support, such as repeat-rate adjustment, as well.
Mouse	"Mouse" Day 10	This applet helps you configure the mouse. This doesn't mean just the double-click speed and other mouse-specific features; it also includes the actual pointers the mouse uses and whether Windows XP displays mouse trails.
Network	Connections	"General Network Setup" Day 14 This applet enables you to install new network components or get rid of old ones. It's also where you set how the network controls access to your resources, as well as where you see Dial-up connections. TCP/IP users will use this

11

TABLE 11.1 continued

Applet Name	Book Location	Description
		applet to configure the various addresses needed to make their network functional.
Phone and Modem	"Phone or Modem" Day 10	This applet creates and modifies dialing locations. You can also defeat call waiting. The Modems tab is where you can add, remove, or change the properties of modems attached to your system. The Advanced tab contains a list of your telephone and modem service providers.
Power Options	"Setting Power Usage" Day 11	This applet configures system features that help conserve power by turning off system components after a period of inactivity. The suggested settings determine the time interval before Windows XP turns off system components such as the monitor and hard drives. The Hibernate feature is similar to the "sleep" feature found on some portables—it stores the current contents of RAM to your hard drive and then shuts down.
Printers and Faxes	"Printer" Day 10	This applet enables you to configure existing printers and faxes, or add new ones. It also enables you to maintain control over any print jobs the printer is processing.
Regional and Language Options	"Installing Language Support" Day 10	This applet manages all the text-formatting information required to make the output of an application correct. It includes the actual time zone. You also use this applet to change the numeric, currency, time, date, and regional settings.
Scanners and Cameras	"Scanner and Camera Support" Day 7	This applet helps you maintain your scanners and cameras. You can also use it to add new scanners and cameras to the system manually.
Scheduled Tasks	"Scheduling Tasks" Day 19	This applet configures Windows XP to run applications or utilities at scheduled times automatically. Click the Add Scheduled Task button and the Scheduled Task Wizard opens up, guiding you through the process of choosing a program and then telling Windows XP how often, or when, to run it.

TABLE 11.1 continued

Applet Name	Book Location	Description
Sounds and Audio Devices	"Multimedia Hardware Support" Day 7	This applet controls everything relating to the sound features supported by Windows XP. It not only controls the actual drivers and their settings; it helps you configure the interface as well.
Speech	"Narrator" Day 6	This applet controls the settings for the text reader provided with Windows XP.
System	Many areas of the book.	This applet enables you to maintain your computer as a whole. It enables you to select hardware profiles and configure the system environment. You'll also use it to select some shutdown features and determine which operating system appears as the default on the boot menu.
Taskbar and Start Menu	"Selecting and Configuring the Start Menu" and "Working with the Taskbar" Day 3	This applet configures your Start Menu and Taskbar options.
Users Accounts	"Using the User Accounts Applet" Day 8	This applet provides a simple method to create, configure, and maintain user accounts.

11

Understanding the Active Directory Connection

If you're working with a large network that uses Windows 2000 Server or Windows .NET Server, and has Active Directory installed, you'll need to learn about a few additional management tools. These tools don't affect the local computer as much as they change your connection to the server. For example, you won't use the Local Users and Groups snap-in found in the "Using the Local Users and Groups MMC Snap-in" section of Chapter 8; you'll use the Active Directory Users and Computers snap-in instead.

Active Directory is a large database that the server shares across all compatible servers on the network. All of your user, configuration, and preferences information appears in this database. In addition, Active Directory tracks your computer setup, and many applications use it for settings storage as well. In short, it's the central repository of information on the network.

The first thing you need to understand about Active Directory is that it invalidates many of the tools we've discussed so far in the book. You must use the Active Directory equivalent of a tool when working with Active Directory on the server. The snap-ins we've discussed will still work on your local machine. However, some of the changes you make won't take effect. For example, the group policy settings stored in Active Directory override your local policy settings. The settings are intact, and you can configure them if you like, but the group policy takes precedence when configured.

You'll run into several problems when working on a system that uses Active Directory, given the current Windows XP setup. As previously mentioned, you can't run ADMIN-PAK.MSI to install the Windows 2000 server tools on your local Windows XP machine. The snap-ins used by Windows 2000 are incompatible with the tools used by Windows XP. You'll also find that the set of consoles in the Administrative Tools folder lacks anything with an Active Directory name in it. The easiest way around this problem is to create your own MMC consoles by using the techniques found in the "One MMC Console for Many Uses" section of Chapter 8. Figure 11.3 shows the list of Active Directory snap-ins you'll find for your local machine in the Add Standalone Snap-in dialog box.

FIGURE 11.3

Build your own Active Directory tools for Windows XP by using the snap-ins in this list.

Another problem for any Windows administrator working with Active Directory is knowing the directory structure of your system. This is a giant database, and any changes you make will affect the network as a whole. The number one snap-in you need on a local machine for administering Active Directory is Active Directory Users and Computers. This snap-in works similarly to the Local Users and Groups snap-in we discussed during

Day 8. However, unless you know the Active Directory schema for your system, it's probably best to leave the Active Directory Schema snap-in off your local machine.

Modifying Service Settings

A *service* is an application that runs in the background and augments the operating system environment in some way. The service may not always affect the operating system directly, but it helps the operating system provide additional services. No matter how Windows uses a service, it always appears in the Services console (shown in Figure 11.4). You'll find the Services console in the Administrative Tools folder located in the Control Panel or on the Start | Programs menu. In this case, you're looking at an extended view of the Automatic Updates service. The standard view looks similar, but doesn't include the description pane.

FIGURE 11.4

The extended view of the Services console presents the service description in a secondary pane.

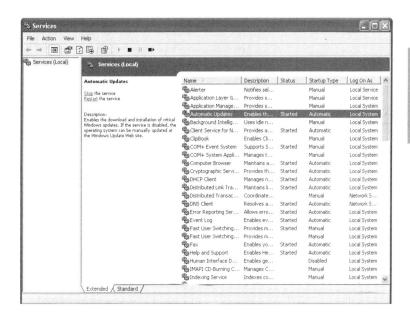

This view of the Services folder tells you three important pieces of information. First, it tells you if the service is running right now. You can compare the list of started services with the list of processes in Windows Task Manager to discover which file is associated with a particular service.

Second, this view tells you how the service will start. The automatic setting means Windows XP will try to start the service during the boot process. The manual setting means that you have to start the service or rely on an application to do it for you. Windows XP won't start a disabled service.

Third, this view tells you what account the service will use to log on to the system. The account determines the amount of risk the service presents if a cracker compromises it. You can often reduce some of the risks of using a service by creating a special account that limits its access to system resources.

Right-click any service in the Services Console, and you'll see options to stop, start, pause, resume, and restart the service. A server can configure itself to disable any of these options. In some cases, such as the Event Log service, you can't do anything with the service unless you reconfigure it. The operating system requires constant access to these services, so changing their status can result in unusual behavior.

You also need to consider the differences between the stop, pause, and restart options. Use stop when you want the service to stop any processing and unload itself from the system. The pause option stops processing, but allows the service to start where it left off when you click resume. Finally, the restart option stops and then starts the service. You use this option if the service appears to operate incorrectly and you want to reset it.

If you select the Properties entry on a service context menu, you'll see a Service Properties dialog box. The General tab of this dialog box contains the name of the service, the service description, the executable path, the startup type (automatic, manual, or disabled), the service status, and the service startup parameters. You can click any of the buttons (Start, Stop, Pause, and Resume) in the Service Status area to change the status of the service. The Path to Executable field is interesting because it helps you learn more about the services start.

The Log On tab determines which account the service will use to log onto the system. The standard entry is the local system account, which may leave you system open to attack by crackers in some cases. You can create a new account with limited security as long as you understand the resources the service needs.

Tip

> The Log On tab contains entries that enable or disable a service based on hardware profile. (You create profiles using the options on the Hardware Profiles dialog box that's accessible through the Hardware Profiles button on the Hardware tab of the System Properties dialog box.) Use the Hardware Profile setting to tailor a set of services for a specific need, just as you do with your hardware in the Device Manager. For example, when creating a "No Network" profile for a laptop, you'd normally disable the network interface card (NIC). You could save additional processing power by disabling any network-related services for that profile. (Make sure that you enable them for other profiles that require network access.)

The Recovery tab shown in Figure 11.5 contains settings that determine what will happen if the service fails. Windows XP allows each service to try to start three times (which explains long startup times when you're having problems with failed services). As you can see from the figure, there's a field for each attempt. You can choose not to take any action, restart the service, run a program, or restart the computer. If you choose to restart the computer, you can use the Restart Computer Options dialog box to compose a message that Windows XP will send to all computers on the network. You can also choose the amount of time Windows XP will wait before restarting the computer. You can also run any program that supports a command line interface. This means that you have access to the vast majority of the Windows XP utilities.

FIGURE 11.5

Use the Recovery tab to adjust the way your system responds to service failures.

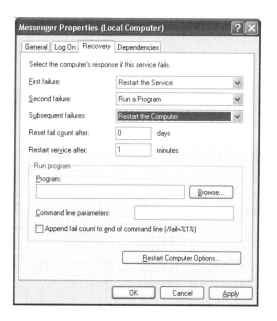

11

The Dependencies tab shown in Figure 11.6 provides a hierarchical display of the services that the current service requires when performing its work. Stopping the required service will stop this service and any services that rely on it. Notice that the dialog box contains entries for services that depend on the current service. If you stop this service, any dependent services will stop as well. It's important to look at the Dependencies tab before you stop a service. Otherwise, you may stop a service only to find that other functions on your workstation have stopped too. Fortunately, Windows XP normally warns you before it stops services with dependencies.

FIGURE **11.6**

A quick check of the Dependencies tab will help you understand how this service relates to others on your machine.

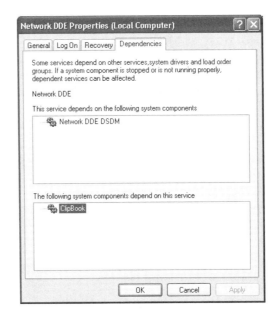

Configuring the Indexing Service

Windows XP features an Indexing Service that creates an index of specific areas of your hard drive. This means that you can search for files faster because the Indexing Service has already searched for the files for you. The whole purpose of the Indexing Service is to ensure that you can find information fast. Real-time searches worked well in the past because drive sizes were small, but today's large hard drives require something better. Indexing is the process of creating an organized list of pointers based on key words and byte sequences.

You'll find the Indexing Service in the Computer Management console. It resides within the Services and Applications folder. Figure 11.7 shows a typical example of the Indexing Service displayed in its own window.

Windows XP doesn't start the Indexing Service by default. You need to start it by right-clicking the Indexing Service entry and choosing Start. As with most services, you can also stop and pause this one. The pause feature comes in handy when you need to perform disk intensive tasks on your system and you want to disable the Indexing Service to make your system perform faster. Normally, the Indexing Service will turn itself off if it registers a high level of system activity.

After you turn the Indexing Service on, you'll want to optimize its operation for your specific needs. Right-click Indexing Service; then choose the All Tasks | Tune

Performance option. You'll see an Indexing Service Usage dialog box. This dialog box has three default performance levels of often *used*, *used occasionally*, and *never used*. The best way to tune the Indexing Service is to select the *Custom* option. You'll see a Desired Performance dialog box that controls the level of indexing and querying that the Indexing Service will support. Higher levels of performance cost you more in system resources, but also yield better results. The Indexing slider controls how fast the Indexing Service can rebuild an index, while the Querying slider controls how fast you'll get an answer.

FIGURE 11.7

The Indexing Service creates pointers to data on your system, making key word searches faster and more efficient.

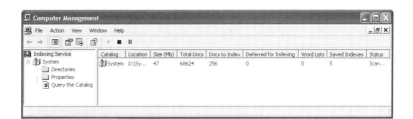

The System folder displayed in Figure 11.7 is a catalog. You can create other catalogs, but let's look at the System catalog first. Indexing Service builds this catalog by default because the Windows Explorer search routine will use this catalog for searches you conduct. Each catalog also has performance settings that you need to set.

Right-click the System catalog, choose Properties, and you'll see a System Properties dialog box. The General tab on this dialog box contains information about the catalog such as the catalog name, size, location, and cache size. The Tracking tab determines if you create a network share for the catalog automatically. The catalog can also inherit settings from the service. The Generation tab controls some of the indexing features for the catalog. For example, the Indexing Service normally generates entries only for files with known extensions, but you can set it to index files with unknown extensions as well. If you do any development or low-level management at all, then make sure you select this option. A second option tells the Indexing Service to generate abstracts for each index entry. An abstract tells you what the file contains and makes the process of looking for a specific file easier. You can also inherit these settings from the service.

You'll notice that the catalog has three subfolders. The Directories folder tells the Indexing Service where to look for files. Each entry either adds or subtracts information from the index. For example, you might decide you don't want to look in the \Temp folder because you never search there. You add a new directory to the list by right-clicking the directory entry and choosing New | Directory from the context menu. The Indexing Service will display the Add Directory dialog box. Type the directory path (use the

Browse button if desired), a universal naming convention (UNC) alias, and a username
and password. (A UNC alias normally contains the machine name and path like this:
\\MAIN\TEMP.) You also need to tell Indexing Service whether you want to include or
exclude the directory from the index.

The Properties folder contains a list of properties for the index. The properties control
precisely what the Indexing Service tracks and how it tracks the information. Normally,
you'll never need to change the entries in this folder. The only time you'll need to add a
property is if you use the Indexing Service Query Language as part of an application to
create specialized query forms or background search routines.

The Query the Catalog folder contains a Web page you can use to work with the catalog
once you optimize it. Figure 11.8 shows a typical Indexing Service Query Form with
some search results. Notice that the display looks more like the results of using a Web
search than a local search.

FIGURE 11.8

*Use the Indexing
Service Query Form to
test your catalog set-
tings.*

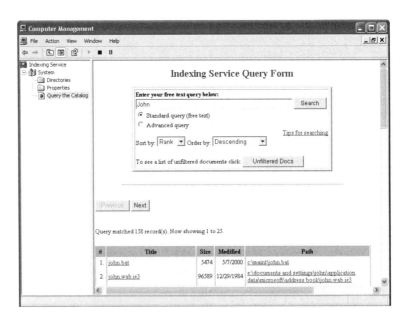

The query language you can use to find information is quite complex and offers greater
flexibility than the standard search methods. For example, if you want to find a specific
document author, you'd use a query that contains the @DOCAUTHOR property like
this:

```
@DOCAUTHOR = John Mueller
```

The query language depends on the properties defined in the Properties folder. However, you can't simply define a new property and expect the Indexing Service to fill it with useful information. Each property requires code behind it to perform a useful task. Click the Tips for Searching link if you want to know more about the query language.

Setting Power Usage

It's important to maintain good power usage habits in an era of rolling blackouts and other power concerns. Windows XP comes equipped to help you save power by automatically shutting some parts of the system off when you don't need them. Used correctly, you can save power without the inconvenience of setting your desktop up again each time you want to step away from your desk. The following sections discuss the Power Options applet found in the Control Panel.

> The Power Options Properties dialog box is one area where some vendors tend to specialize, especially laptop vendors. You may see tabs other than the ones listed in this section. If you do, check the documentation for your system for usage details. For example, you may need to learn how to set alarms for your laptop or how to use a power meter feature. These advanced options allow you to manage your system better and get more life from the battery.

11

Creating Management Schemes

Using power wisely saves not only precious resources, but helps maintain your machine in peak condition as well. Of course, you could always have the system turn itself off after ridiculously short periods of inactivity, but this tends to negate the effects of using automatic power-saving measures. The problem is that most of us use our computers for more than one task, which means our power usage changes over the course of a day.

The Power Schemes tab of the Power Options Properties dialog box contains settings for standard desktop configurations. You can choose one of these schemes to configure your desktop for a standard use. However, you may find that none of these schemes will work for your needs. For example, it's a good idea to create a maintenance scheme. Maintenance tasks usually require little human interaction after you set them up, yet you want to see the screen at a glance. Turning the screen off is normally a good idea, but you might want to keep it on while performing a maintenance task.

To create a new scheme, select the power settings for each device listed on the Power Schemes tab. Some systems provide more settings than others do. Most modern systems provide settings for the monitor and hard disks as a minimum. Some also let you set the time before the system goes into standby mode. Laptops usually provide more settings than desktop machines because the vendors design them to conserve power, and you usually have to set normal and battery configurations. After you set the power settings, click Save As. You'll see a Save Scheme dialog box. Type a name and click OK. You can select the scheme any time you need it from the Power Schemes list box.

Setting the Advanced Options

The Advanced tab can contain a number of settings. The most common setting is the Always show icon on the taskbar. Check this option if you want to see the Power icon in the notification area at all times. Laptops normally show the icon while on battery power, but hide it during operation on a standard electrical current.

You may also see settings that tell Windows XP to prompt for a password when the system goes off standby. This prevents someone from grabbing your machine while you're at a meeting. Standby mode saves considerable power, yet allows you to resume your work in a modicum of time.

Enabling Hibernate Support

The Hibernate tab contains a single option that enables hibernation support on your machine. However, before you can enable hibernation, you need to compare the memory storage requirements of your system with the amount of free hard drive space. If you don't have enough hard drive space to store the entire contents of memory, you can't use hibernation. The reason for this requirement is that Windows XP doesn't know how much memory is in use. It has to assume that all system RAM contains useful information.

Hibernate mode differs from standby mode. When you use standby mode, the system is in its lowest power on state. System RAM still contains all your data and the system maintains the contents of RAM as needed. When a user presses the spacebar or moves the mouse, Windows XP returns the system to a fully powered state. The time to return from standby mode is minimal.

When you use hibernate mode Windows XP copies the contents of memory to the hard drive. It also records any required environmental data. The system powers down, power is no longer applied to any part of the system. Moving the mouse or pressing the spacebar no longer returns the system to an active state. You must turn on power using the power switch, as normal. However, instead of going through the normal power on sequence, Windows XP reads the saved data and settings from the hard drive into memory. You return to your previous setup without having to reopen application or do anything with the desktop.

Summary

Today you've learned about services, the background applications that do so much for your Windows XP experience. A service is actually a special type of application designed without an interface. It sits quietly in the background doing the work the system asks of the service. You'll find services work automatically, in most cases, and learn that the number of services on your system will vary with the applications you install. Finally, it's important to know how to manage your services because they do require help to complete their tasks from time-to-time.

Q&A

Q: **My Control Panel contains more than the usual number of applets. Where did they come from and why should I care to know about them?**

A: Many enterprise applications (large and complex) will add applets to the Control Panel. These applets manage operating system extensions the application installed in order to perform its work better. You'll use these added applets just as you would any other applet in the Control Panel. Because I can't predict which applets you'll see in advance, Table 11.1 contains only the applets that Windows XP provides in the default configuration.

Q: **What happens if I need to stop a service and can't because the Services console won't let me?**

A: First, it's important to know if you actually need to stop the service. Windows XP generally won't allow you to stop services that it needs to perform basic or critical tasks. If you're working with a support technician, he or she should be able to tell you how to stop the service (otherwise, you have to wonder about the qualification of this person).

Second, if you verify that the system can get along without the service, you'll need to disable it by making a change in the registry. You need to find the command line for starting the service, save this entry to disk by exporting it, and then delete the line from the registry. Restart your system to make the change take effect. This move is extremely dangerous, and you should use it only if you know for sure that the system will restart and function properly without the service.

Q: **Is there always a requirement to create new power schemes?**

A: You don't have to create new power schemes, but you should always select a power scheme that's compatible with your usage requirements. Some people perform the same task all day and rely on someone else to perform maintenance for them. In this case, it's possible you could set the power scheme for your system once and leave it set that way until conditions change.

11

Workshop

It's the end of the eleventh day. You should have a good understanding of the contents of the Control Panel and know a lot more about services. It's time to see how well you can work with both the Control Panel and the services on your system. You can find answers to the quiz and exercise questions in Appendix A at the back of the book.

Quiz

1. What task does the Administrative Tools applet perform?
2. What makes a server with Active Directory installed special?
3. How many times can a service fail before Windows XP stops trying to start it?
4. How does standby mode differ from hibernate mode?

Exercises

1. Try the classic and category method of working with the Control Panel.
2. Explore the Services console to learn about the background applications on your machine. Compare the started services in the Services control with the entries on the Process tab of Windows Task Manager to see if you can make the connection between the started service and its process.
3. Modify the System index so you can search your drives with the search features of Windows Explorer faster. Try creating ancillary indexes, as well, so that you can search other parts of the network.
4. Create several power schemes to help manage system power better.

WEEK 2

DAY 12

Working with the Registry

The *registry* is a large centralized database of information for your computer. Every configuration setting for your system appears in the registry, along with your personal data (at least the data that you provide as input to the computer) and application settings. You'll also find the startup information for your system in the registry; Windows XP reads this information to locate files used for services and other operating system features. In short, the registry is one of the most important parts of Windows to protect because without it, the system won't run.

Today we're going to spend some time in the registry. You'll learn about the tools used to work with the registry, the way the registry is constructed, and a few of the safe edits you can perform on the registry. I'll also help you understand some basic registry concepts and show you ways to avoid common editing mistakes.

Although you can safely edit the registry, and even improve the performance of Windows by doing so, there's always a risk when editing the registry. An incorrect edit can cause your system to act strangely or cause damage to your applications. Some edits can even cause your system to stop booting. We'll explore many safe areas to make changes today, but always keep the potential danger to your system in mind when making edits of any kind.

Using RegEdit

The Registry Editor (REGEDIT.EXE) is the main tool you need when viewing the registry contents or making changes to it. This tool doesn't appear on the Start menu, and I can fully appreciate Microsoft's reason for keeping it hidden. You'll find this file in your \WINDOWS folder. If you plan to work with the Registry Editor regularly, you'll want to place a shortcut to it on your Start menu. Otherwise, you can easily start it from the Run dialog box whenever you need to make a change.

The Registry Editor doesn't require any command line parameters. The same editor under Windows 9x could use command line parameters to load and unload registry files. You can't use the Registry Editor at the command line in Windows XP, and we'll see during Day 21, "Maintaining Your System and Finding Problems," that there really isn't a need to use it at the command line.

The registry is a hierarchical database of information contained in several "hives." Figure 12.1 shows a typical view of the Registry Editor. You can see the five key handles (the HKEY entries in the list) that hold the hives. This view also shows the hierarchical nature of the registry.

FIGURE 12.1

The Registry Editor displays the five HKEYs used to store your system configuration settings.

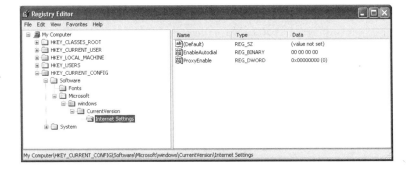

You need to know about several new terms when working with the registry. A *hive* is a collection of like data. For example, it makes sense to group all user data in one place for safe storage, but you wouldn't place NIC configuration information in that file. Each hive exists in a separate file. The location of the file varies according to the data stored. For example, the hive containing HKEY_CURRENT_USER appears in the \Documents and Settings\<User Name> folder as NTUSER.DAT.

Don't get the idea that HKEY is an equivalent of the term *hive*. For example, the HKEY_LOCAL_MACHINE\Security key is in the Security hive, while the HKEY_LOCAL_MACHINE\System key is in the System hive. Both hives appear in the \WINDOWS\System32\Config folder of your machine. HKEY is actually a programmer term that indicates an entry the developer can access from within an application. It's short for "handle to a key."

A *key* is a storage container. It can contain other keys or values. Figure 12.1 shows the hierarchical arrangement of keys you might see when working with the registry. Keys usually have names that describe their position within the hierarchy. For example, Internet Settings in Figure 12.1 is a key. Values within the key act as *key descriptors*. They tell you about the key and contain data that Windows or an application will use for configuration purposes. For example, EnableAutodial in Figure 12.1 is a value.

Values consist of three parts. The *value name* describes the data that the value contains. The *value type* determines the kind of information that the value stores, such as a string or number. The *value* itself is the data used for configuration purposes. The following list tells you about the data types:

- **REG_SZ (String)**   This value type contains a string in human readable format. The very end of the string has to have a 0 (null) attached to it. The "SZ" part of this type stands for "string zero." The registry uses the string value for everything from file paths and user configuration to the globally unique identifiers (GUIDs) used for components and other low-level references.

- **REG_BINARY (Binary)**   This value type contains a binary value displayed in bytes using hexadecimal format. You can create binary strings of any length, and they can contain any type of data. Binary values normally contain data that the computer can't represent in string form or as a DWORD, such as an image or compiled macrocode.

- **REG_DWORD (DWORD)**   This value type contains a double-word value, which is any number between 0 and 4,294,967,295. You'll normally find DWORDs used for anything that requires a count or a precise numeric value. For example, an application might allow you to configure the number of "last used" file entries in the File menu. If you request 10 entries, there might be a value 10 for a FileEntries value under the File key for the application.

12

- **REG_MULTI_SZ (Multi-String)**   This value type contains multiple strings in human readable format. The developer will separate each string with a null character. The developer uses this type of string for special purposes, such as list box entries. The developer may not know how many entries the list box will require in advance, so using a multi-string is the only answer.

- **REG_EXPAND_SZ (Expandable String)**   This value type contains a string that includes expansion values. For example, you could see an expansion value of %ProgramFiles% that equates to the position of the Program Files folder on your machine. A developer will often use this entry type for files that always appear in a certain directory. For example, a DLL might appear in the \SYSTEM32 directory. Because the user can give the Windows directory different names, the only way to refer to the \SYSTEM32 directory is using an expansion string. The system always knows where the Windows directory is, but the developer may not know at the time of program creation.

Every key also has a special "(Default)" value. It's always a value of the REG_SZ type. The system will provide the application with this string if it asks for a key value without specifying the value name. Consider this a special entry that ensures that an application will receive a value for an existing key, even when there are no values associated with the key.

Whatever Happened to REGEDT32?

Windows NT/2000 provided two versions of the Registry Editor. The first is REGEDIT.EXE, the version we'll use today. The second is REGEDT32.EXE found in the \SYSTEM32 folder of your system. Some developers liked the second form of the Registry Editor because it provided an interface consisting of cascading windows like the one shown in Figure 12.2.

Windows XP still supplies the REGEDT32.EXE file, but double-clicking it presents the standard REGEDIT.EXE interface shown in Figure 12.1. You don't have to use the new interface if you don't want to. The REGEDT32.EXE file found on Windows 2000 machines appears to work fine under Windows XP. However, I haven't tested it extensively, so you'll need to use it at your own risk.

The alternative version of Registry Editor does the same things as the version you see in Figure 12.1. The arrangement of some menus is different, and the interface is a little more cryptic. Using a separate window to display each hive tends to keep the display a little cleaner. You can also find the hives faster when you have a number of keys displayed on screen. In short, you don't gain anything by using the old version, but for some people, it's like getting rid of an old and comfortable pair of shoes.

Figure **12.2**

Windows NT/2000 pro-
vided an alternative
Registry Editor that's
missing in Windows
XP.

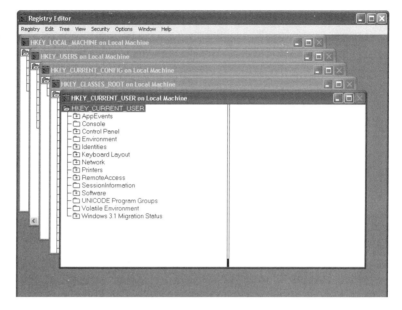

Importing and Exporting Registry Data

You'll import registry data far more often than you'll export it in most cases. Registry (REG) files contain text that describes one or more registry entries. You can view a registry file using a simple text editor. To edit a registry file, right-click the REG object in Windows Explorer and then choose Edit from the context menu. The file will normally load into Notepad or another default text editor.

Registry files appear in a number of situations. For example, when you export the registry as a whole or a single registry branch, you create a REG file. Some application programs supply REG files as part of the installation. You can use these REG files to restore a corrupted installation in many cases. In some cases, you'll also see registry files as part of a hardware installation. Finally, you'll download some registry files as patches from the Internet. In some cases, an application error is nothing more than an incorrect registry entry.

Microsoft provides a number of ways to import registry files into your registry. For example, if you double-click a registry entry, Windows XP will ask if you want to import it. Click Yes, and Windows XP will import the data. You can also right-click the registry file and choose Merge from the context menu. Windows XP will still display the import message before it imports the data. Finally, you can use the Registry Editor to import the data. Use the File | Import command to display the Import Registry File dialog box. Select the registry file you want to import and then click OK to complete the process.

12

The Registry Editor won't ask if you're certain about importing the registry file; it will simply complete the action for you. Registry imports always succeed unless the Registry Editor finds damage in the registry file or you don't have sufficient rights to add the requested entries to the registry.

You can only export the registry from the Registry Editor. Use the File | Export command to display the Export Registry File dialog box shown in Figure 12.3. Notice the option to export the entire registry or a single branch near the bottom of this dialog box. In addition, when you choose to export a particular branch, you can type the branch location. The left side of the dialog box will always contains common locations on your hard drive to act as a storage page for the registry information.

FIGURE 12.3

Use the Export Registry File dialog box to save the registry or registry branch to disk.

The Export Registry File dialog box defaults to export a branch of the registry. It uses the currently highlighted branch as input to the dialog box, which means you can save time by highlighting the registry branch you want to export before opening the dialog box.

Unlike application REG files that can contain entries from multiple registry branches, the REG files you create using this method will only contain a single branch. This makes the files excellent sources of information for studying the registry, as well as a means for saving the data.

Loading and Unloading Hives

As previously mentioned, the Windows registry contains several hives. Some of these hives affect the entire system, while others, such as the user hives, affect only a single part of the system. The two parts of the registry most affected by loading and unloading hives are HKEY_USERS and HKEY_LOCAL_MACHINE. Of the two, you'll work with HKEY_USERS most often. For example, you might need to load the hive of another user on the network to make low-level changes to the settings for an application or to view settings before invoking a policy change.

As previously mentioned, the hive containing HKEY_CURRENT_USER appears in the \Documents and Settings\<User Name> folder. You need administrator rights to load the hive belonging to another user. The following steps tell how to load a hive:

1. Select the HKEY entry you want to use as a starting point for the new hive.

2. Use the File | Load Hive command to display the Load Hive dialog box.

3. Locate and highlight the hive you want to load and then click Open. The Registry Editor will display another Load Hive dialog box that asks you to enter a name for the hive because two hives at the same level of the registry hierarchy can't have the same name.

4. Type the name of the new hive and then click OK. You'll see the new hive appear in the registry hierarchy.

After you complete an edit, you'll want to unload the hive to save the changes you made. You might want to unload a hive to clear viewing space in the Registry Editor. Whatever your reason for clearing the hive, the following steps show how to do it:

1. Highlight the hive you want to unload. Make sure that you select the correct hive.

2. Use the File | Unload Hive command to begin the unloading process. The Registry Editor will display a dialog box asking if you want to unload the hive.

3. Click Yes. The hive will unload. The entry will disappear from the list of keys in the Registry Editor.

Working with Network Registries

The ability to work on network registries using a local copy of Registry Editor is important because you may not want to travel to the next building to make a simple change to a user's registry. The less time that a network administrator spends traveling, the more time he or she has to fix network problems, so it pays to use remote connectivity whenever possible. Some remote connectivity options for Windows XP are obvious. For example, the Computer Management console includes features that help you connect to a remote machine and manage its resources from your desktop. However, not all of the Registry Editor remote connectivity options are obvious; Microsoft doesn't even document some remote connectivity options as being available.

The obvious remote connectivity option is the File | Connect Network Registry com-

12

mand. Use this command, and you'll see a Select Computer dialog box. Type the name of the computer you want to work with and click OK. Windows XP will make the connection if you have the proper rights. Figure 12.4 shows a typical remote connection. Notice that the original connection remains intact. The only difference is that you have added the remote connection.

FIGURE 12.4

Typically, the Registry Editor adds a remote connection to an existing connection.

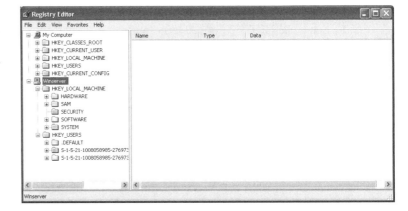

You should also notice that you gain access only to HKEY_LOCAL_MACHINE and KEY_USERS. The loss of HKEY_CLASSES_ROOT means you can't make any file association changes using a remote connection, but there are many other ways to make these changes on a Windows XP system. For example, you could make the required change using an entry in a user's login script. However, the lack of direct registry editing capability could be troublesome.

Although you do gain full access to the user entries, you need to know the security ID (SID) for the user. Notice that the entries in Figure 12.4 don't show names. Normally, Windows XP interprets the SID for you. That's why you'll see names instead of a SID in dialog boxes. Of course, this leaves you with a problem figuring out which user account to edit if the machine has more than one user attached to it. The best way to find the user name without memorizing the SIDs for every user on the network is to look at the \Software\Microsoft\Windows\CurrentVersion\Explorer key. The Logon User Name value will normally contain the name of the user. If this key doesn't have the right name, check the next account in line. Note that this technique only works when you see the full SID; otherwise, Windows XP hides the information.

Another technique to connect to the remote machine is to use the hive loading method shown in the "Loading and Unloading Hives" section. This technique works on both local and network drives, as long as you have the required administrator privileges. This method is also more selective than loading the entire remote registry and can save time when using a low-speed connection.

Caution	Always check for user activity on the remote machine before you open the registry. Opening the registry for an account that's in use may cause user confusion in some cases. The changes you make will affect the user in real time. In addition, some changes could cause side effects, such as data loss. A remote change makes life easy for the administrator, so long as the change doesn't adversely affect the user.

When you finish your remote edits, you need to disconnect from the remote registry. Use the hive unloading technique when appropriate. If you connected to the remote registry using the technique in this section, use the File | Disconnect Network Registry command to display the Disconnect Network Registry dialog box. You'll see when you display the dialog box that you can't disconnect from the local registry. Highlight the remote registry of interest and then click OK. Windows XP will save any changes you made and close the remote registry. The Registry Editor won't ask if you're certain about making this move, so make sure that you're actually finished with remote registry before closing the connection.

Editing and Creating New Keys and Values

At some point, you'll stop viewing the registry and begin editing it or creating keys of your own. Of course, it's most likely that you'll edit existing keys. Adding keys or values that an application can't read doesn't make much sense. Some users also make their worst mistakes as they move from viewing the registry to editing it. The number one rule to remember is never to edit a value using the Registry Editor that you can change in some other way. Always use application-supplied methods whenever possible.

Most beginning users will find registry edits from reliable sources, such as the Microsoft Knowledge Base (http://search.support.microsoft.com/kb/c.asp). Some of the Knowledge Base articles will direct you to make registry changes or supply a REG file that makes the change automatically. In some cases, a support person will also ask you to make changes in the registry.

After you gain a little experience and confidence working with the registry, you might be tempted to begin making your own registry hacks. A *registry hack* is a change that enhances Windows in some nonstandard way. In many cases, Microsoft doesn't recommend the change or is simply unaware of the benefits of making it. Registry hacks

12

always come with a price, a potential loss of system stability or data. While the registry changes that Microsoft provides in Knowledge Base articles are relatively safe, the hacks you find in a newsgroup online aren't. It normally pays to test a registry change of dubious origin on a test system, not the workstation you rely on to earn a living.

Tip

We won't cover every potential registry key today. Some books require a hundred or more pages just to provide an overview of the subkeys. You can find documentation for standard registry keys online. For example, the documentation for HKEY_CURRENT_USER appears at http://msdn.microsoft.com/library/en-us/regentry/51211.asp. The documentation also applies to HKEY_USERS, so you won't see an HKEY_USERS entry on the Microsoft Developer Network (MSDN) Web site. You'll also find documentation for HKEY_LOCAL_MACHINE at http://msdn.microsoft.com/library/en-us/regentry/17.asp.

You'll always use the same process for creating a new key or value. In both cases, it's best to highlight the key you want to use as a starting point. Right-click the target key and then choose one of the options on the New menu. When creating a key, select the Key entry. Otherwise, select one of the value entries. As soon as you select an entry, type the name you want to use for that entry. If you make a mistake, select the new entry and choose Rename from the context menu. This is all you need to do to create a new key.

When working with values, you also need to set the value. The easiest way to do this is double-click the value name. You'll see one of several dialog boxes depending on the value type. For example, if you select a REG_SZ or REG_EXPAND_SZ, you'll see an Edit String dialog box that contains a field for the data value. Just type the string you want to add.

Although the dialog boxes for these two types look the same, the output is completely different. I created a temporary key like the one shown in Figure 12.5. Notice that every entry, except the DWORD entry, is the same. You can do the same thing in your registry. Just make sure that you remove the temporary key later.

If you export this key and look at the results in a text editor, you'll see something like Figure 12.6. (Right-click the resulting file and choose Edit from the context menu to see the output, rather than add the REG file to the registry.) Notice that the output of REG_SZ is completely different from any other value in this list because it uses plain ASCII text. The other entries use binary or double-byte character set (DBCS) entries. DBCS relies on 16-bit characters, rather than the 8-bit characters used for ASCII text. This allows a DBCS to represent a myriad of languages, including both English and Japanese.

FIGURE 12.5

Sometimes it pays to create a temporary key and experiment.

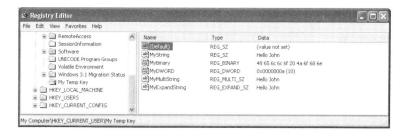

FIGURE 12.6

Looking at a saved registry file tells you something about the way values are stored.

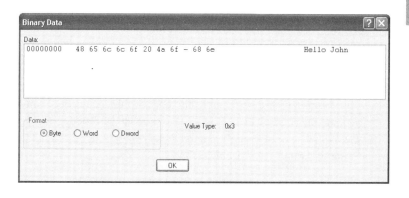

If you look at the hexadecimal representations, you'll find that the 48,65,6c,6c,6f sequence is "Hello," 20 is a space, and 4a,6f,68,6e is "John." The REG_MULTI_SZ (multi-string) value contains a 00,00 or NULL value instead of the space to separate the two words because I created that sting as two strings instead of one.

Let's get back to changing values. Binary values provide more editing methods than other value types. Double-click this entry, and you'll see a simple Edit Binary Value dialog box that contains the binary value on one side and the string value on the other. You can also highlight the value and use the View | Display Binary Data command to display the Binary Data dialog box shown in Figure 12.7.

12

FIGURE 12.7

The Binary Data dialog box offers more freedom in viewing binary values.

Notice that this dialog box also begins with the dual data display—binary on one size and ASCII text on the other. However, this dialog box doesn't allow you to edit the data. This dialog does offer a bonus of viewing the data in WORD or DWORD format.

When you double-click a REG_DWORD value, you'll see an Edit DWORD Value dialog box. This dialog box contains a Value Data field that receives the number you want to store. The Base option selects between decimal and hexadecimal entry. Type a value into the Value Data field, select the other base option, and observe the value change. Notice in Figure 12.5 that the default REG_DWORD display shows the hexadecimal value with the decimal value in parentheses behind it.

The final value type is REG_MULTI_SZ. Double-click a value of this type, and you'll see the Edit Multi-String dialog box. This dialog box contains a multiline Value Data field. Any words placed on the same line will use spaces (value 20) as separators in the registry. Any words placed on another line will use NULLs (value 0) as separators in the registry. To understand the importance of this differentiation, consider a list box in your favorite application. Anything you type on the same line will appear as a single entry in the list box, but entries on separate lines will appear on separate lines in the list box.

Deleting, Renaming, and Copying Keys and Values

You'll perform some common tasks with registry keys and values. For example, you may need to copy a value from one location to another. Unfortunately, Microsoft doesn't make this task very easy in many cases. For example, if you highlight a key that you want to copy from one place to another, you won't find any options for copying that key and associated values. The best you can do is copy the key name, not much of a help when you need to create a long branch of key values. It does help if you only need to copy a few keys.

Note that you can also rename and delete keys. When you delete a key, it automatically deletes all subkeys and associated values. The delete operation is one way, but you can't undo it. Always export a copy of the key before you delete it. That way, if you notice a problem with an application later, you can easily restore the missing key.

Values offer even less than keys when it comes to copying them somewhere else. However, you can also rename and delete values as needed. Unfortunately, you can't rename the (Default) value, but you can delete it. Deleting the (Default) value simply clears the value; you can't remove the (Default) entry from the list. The (Default) value is the one value you can't delete.

This leaves open the question of moving or copying information from one part of the registry to another. The technique I use for copying registry values from one place to another is to export the registry branch. Use a text editor to open the resulting REG file. Look at Figure 12.6 again, and you'll see the file includes the full key path. If you edit this path, you change the location of the resulting import into the registry. After you edit the path, save it and double-click the REG file. Windows XP will import it into the new location. Verify the results of the copy before you do anything else. After you verify the copy, you can complete a move by deleting the key from its original position in the registry. Always perform this procedure with care.

Setting Permissions

The registry, as with any other part of Windows XP, provides security. Registry security works much the same as hard drive security. Any security setting at a high level in the hierarchy will flow down to the lower levels unless you specifically disable inheritance.

Editing permissions in the registry can become tricky because you never know when a user will require access to a key. Applications read the registry using the user credentials in many cases. If you want the application to behave normally, the user must have permission to read the registry key and associated values as a minimum.

Tip

> It's possible to trick some applications into preventing the user from making changes to company-required application settings by making the application keys read-only. The application can read the settings but can't change them because it doesn't have write permission. However, this strategy will backfire with some applications. Instead of presenting the user with a simple error message, the application will crash. If you use this technique, make sure that you thoroughly test the resulting change on the application.

12

The user doesn't need access to some hives, unless you make them a power user or administrator. For example, entries under HKEY_LOCAL_MACHINE typically require system-level access, not user-level access. Securing this information from prying eyes doesn't represent a problem for the user and can increase system security.

After you determine the type of security you want to enforce, you can set it by highlighting the key in question and using the Edit | Permissions command to display the Permission dialog box. The Group or User Name field contains a list of groups and users with access to the key. You can add or remove users by clicking Add or Remove. Click Add, and you'll see a Select Users or Groups dialog box. Type the name of the user or group and click OK. To remove a user or group, highlight the entry and click Remove.

The Registry Editor provides a simple rights display in this dialog box. Highlight a particular group or user, and you'll see their basic level of access in the Permissions field.

Rights include Full Control, Read, and Special Permissions. When you add a new user, the Registry Editor assumes that you want to give them read access.

You won't see the full security picture until you click Advanced to display the Advanced Security Settings dialog box shown in Figure 12.8. As you can see, the registry provides many "hidden" security settings. The Permissions tab repeats the basic security settings shown in the Permissions dialog box. It also contains options for setting inheritance. The first option automatically sets the child object security to match that of the parent. The second option ensures that any changes you make to the parent also appear in the child after you click Apply. You can also add and remove users from this dialog box.

FIGURE 12.8

Use the Advanced Security Settings dialog box to make significant registry security changes.

Click Edit, and you'll see a Permission Entry dialog box similar to the one shown in Figure 12.9. That's right, you have to tunnel this far down into the security dialog hierarchy to obtain fine control over the registry security settings. Notice that you can control every aspect of registry access using this dialog box, but the cost in time is relatively high. This is one of the biggest reasons to start using groups as soon as possible on your network.

It's also important to note that you can apply this change to the current key and all its subkeys, or just to the current key. This makes it possible to restrict user access to a main key but allow access at the subkey level. In many cases, you can use this technique to keep the registry safe from user interaction without affecting the user's ability to work. An application can still access the lower-level keys.

The Auditing tab works much the same as the Auditing tab for a disk drive. You add lists of users to the Auditing Entries field. Windows XP will record successful or failed attempts to perform the same tasks as shown in the Permission Entry dialog box in Figure 12.9.

FIGURE **12.9**

You can gain fine control over registry security settings, but Microsoft doesn't make it easy.

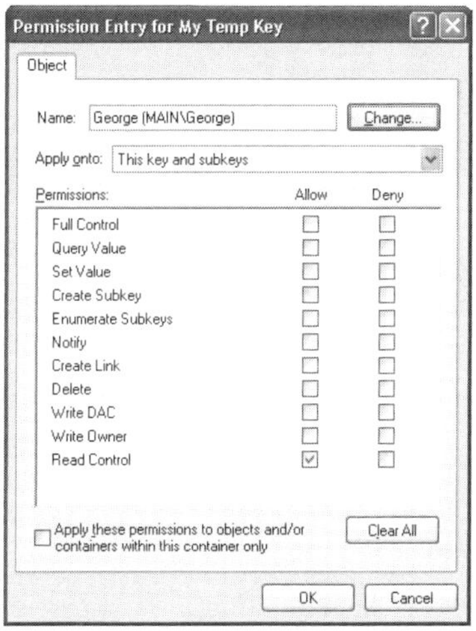

The Owner tab allows you to take control over a key if you have the proper permissions. It also lists the current owners of the key. The registry follows the same rules of ownership that a disk drive will follow. The Administrators group will always have full access to a registry key no matter who owns it and will appear on the Owner tab.

The Effective Permissions tab is a diagnostic for the registry. A registry entry can become so complex that knowing who can access it becomes difficult. You use this tab by clicking Select to display the Select User or Group dialog box. Type the username or group you want to check and click OK. The Effective Permissions list will fill to show which rights the selected user or group has to the currently selected key.

Locating Specific Data

By now, you have some indication of the size of the registry. It may seem impossible to find a particular piece of information that you need. However, like many Microsoft utilities, the Registry Editor includes Find and Find Next entries on the Edit menu.

When you select Find, you'll see a Find dialog box like the one shown in Figure 12.10. Type the value you want to search for in the Find What field. You also need to select the Find options. The Registry Editor enables you to look in keys, values, and data. It also includes an option for searching for whole strings only.

FIGURE 12.10

The Find dialog box enables you to find data values by location.

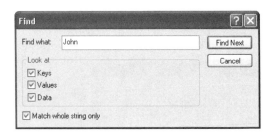

The easiest way to use Find Next is to press F3 when you've found the first value that matches your search criteria. The Registry Editor only searches down. If you start your search in the middle of the registry, the Registry Editor will only look for the search value from that point down. Find Next won't automatically wrap to the beginning of the registry to start the search again. The following list contains other registry search tips:

- Provide specific search criteria, whenever possible, because the registry is case insensitive when it comes to searches.

- Vendors often combine words when creating keys, so try several versions of multi-word keys when performing a search.

- Select only the search criteria you need. For example, it takes less time to search keys than it does to search keys and values. Whole word searches increase search time but can reduce the number of hits you obtain on a particular search.

- Choose human readable strings over other data types, whenever possible, to reduce the potential for typing errors. In addition, copy and paste matching key or data values when performing searches based on another key or value.

- Use partial words (or other data values) when searching the registry for complex values. The partial value will increase the number of hits (and therefore your search time) but also makes it more likely that you'll find what you need the first time.

Keeping Track of Favorite Locations

The Registry Editor includes its own Favorites menu. Explore doesn't provide a link to this menu, so it will be empty the first time you use the Registry Editor. The Registry Editor doesn't provide any means to organize the favorites, so you'll want to keep the list short. Long lists of favorites tend to reduce the usefulness of this feature.

To add a new location to the Favorites list, use the Favorites | Add to Favorites command. You'll see an Add to Favorites dialog box. Type the name of the location in the Favorite Name field and click OK. You'll see the name you typed added to the Favorites menu (this doesn't have to be the same as the key name).

Using a favorite is easy—just select it on the Favorites menu. The Registry Editor will locate the selected key. It will also expand the key hierarchy so that you can see any subkeys. However, the Registry Editor only expands one level of subkeys so that you don't fill the display.

A favorite will remain on the list, even if you delete or rename the associated key. The problem is that the favorite won't work. The Registry Editor won't find a renamed key. When you rename a key or delete it, you also need to change the Favorites list. Use the Favorites | Remove Favorite command to display the Remove Favorites dialog box. Highlight the favorite you want to remove and click OK. The Registry Editor will remove the favorite from the Favorites list.

Modifying File Associations

File associations are one of the easiest registry changes to make. In addition, they're one of the most noticeable changes, so they're easy to test. You can also easily fix a file association problem in most cases using Windows Explorer.

Why would you want to use the registry to work with file associations? In many cases, using the registry can save you time and effort. For example, you might have a file type that already has all of the definitions you require for a second file type. A graphics editor may handle both PCX and BMP files, but the registry only contains the association for the PCX file. You can change all of the entries manually, or you can make one change in the registry. You can learn more about manual file association modification in the "File Types" section during Day 3.

However, before you can make even a small change, such as a file association to the registry, you have to understand a little more about how it works. A file association entry consists of several parts. For the purposes of this discussion, we'll discuss the two most important parts.

The first part is the file extension entry. This appears at the beginning of HKEY_CLASSES_ROOT. For example, if you want to change the .BMP file extension behavior, you'd first look for the .BMP key. Figure 12.11 shows a typical example of this key.

Notice the (Default) value in Figure 12.11. This value defines the file type, how it's associated with a particular application. In this case, we're looking at the Paint.Picture application type. If you look down the list of applications in the second half of HKEY_CLASSES_ROOT, you'll find the Paint.Picture application key shown in Figure 12.12.

12

FIGURE 12.11

The first part of a file association is the file extension key.

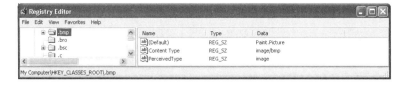

FIGURE 12.12

The second part of a file association is the application key.

This key contains many subkeys that have meanings, but you don't need to worry about them. However, if you look at the shell key entries, you'll see a list of actions for this application type. If you expand this further and look at individual commands, you'll see that they look very much like the application used to perform action entries for that action in Windows Explorer. The main difference, in this case, is the value is an expandable string. If you look at that same entry in Windows Explorer, you'll see the expanded version.

Let's say you don't want to use Microsoft Paint to open these files. You may have an application that normally works with PCX files that you prefer for this file association. Look up the .PCX key in the registry. Make a note of the (Default) entry for this file extension. Remember that the (Default) entry determines the application type. Go to the .BMP key, double-click the (Default) entry, and type the application type entry from the PCX application into this file extension as well. Click OK and you'll see the new application type in the .BMP key.

At this point, if you try to open the application in Windows Explorer, the new application will open—not the original Microsoft Paint. Right-click the application icon and you'll see all of the PCX file options. However, the application icon will remain the same as before.

Windows XP performs a process known as *icon caching*. The icon you see is stored in memory and in a cache file on the hard drive. To change the application, use the Tools | Folder Options command to open the Folder Options dialog box. Select the File Types tab. Locate the BMP file type. Click Advanced to display the Edit File Type dialog box. Notice that the icon is already the right type in this dialog box; Windows Explorer just doesn't know about the change yet. Click Change Icon and then click OK to close the Change Icon dialog box. Click OK again to close the Edit File Type dialog box. The icon will change in Windows Explorer because these steps reset the cache file.

Saving and Restoring Application Settings

The registry contains a wealth of information about your applications. Most applications store your personalized settings in the registry. Unfortunately, every time you need to reformat the drive or make some other major system change, those settings are lost and you spend time reconfiguring the applications all over again.

Creating a backup of your system only goes so far in recreating your old environment. Many users will reformat their drives to get a fresh start. They want to rid their system of those old drivers and registry entries. However, the user can still experience a benefit in saving the personalized settings for applications that the user intends to reinstall on the updated system.

Applications store their data in two areas of the registry. Personalized settings normally appear in HKEY_CURRENT_USER\Software as shown in Figure 12.13. As you can see, most vendors create a company entry and store the application settings by name in subkeys. The best way to approach the application data-saving problem is to select the application key as the export branch.

If you stop with the personalized settings, the application may not work. You also need to look in HKEY_LOCAL_MACHINE\SOFTWARE for global application settings. These settings generally affect all users. Again, you'll want to save the application branch settings to the hard drive.

12

Note

Just saving the registry settings might not work for all applications. You also need to look for data files. For example, if you save the Outlook Express registry entries, you have to save the associated data files as well. It's also essential to look for INI files because some applications still use them. Finally, look for special application requirements. For example, some applications require the installation of a server during startup. You can find these servers using the MSCONFIG utility. Look for the server entries first in the Startup folder. Also look at these four registry keys:
HKEY_CURRENT_USER\Software\Microsoft\Windows\CurrentVersion\Run,

```
HKEY_CURRENT_USER\Software\Microsoft\Windows\CurrentVersion\
RunOnce,
HKEY_LOCAL_MACHINE\SOFTWARE\Microsoft\Windows\CurrentVersion
\Run, and
HKEY_LOCAL_MACHINE\SOFTWARE\Microsoft\Windows\CurrentVersion
\RunOnce.
```

FIGURE 12.13

Personalized settings normally appear in HKEY_CURRENT_US ER\Software.

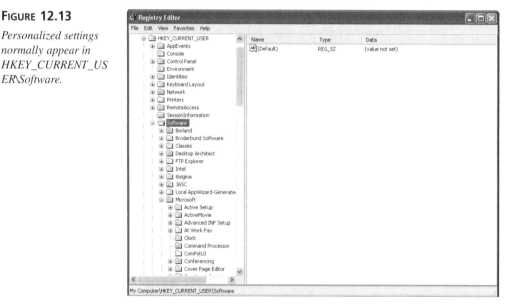

After you create the required backups, format the drive, reinstall the operating system, and reinstall your applications. Before you open the applications the first time, double-click the registry settings you've saved. In most cases, you'll find that the registry settings restore application environment when you start the application the first time.

Registry Settings Located in INF Files

For many people, the INF file represents the most mysterious part of Windows. Part of the problem is that vendors fill them with what appears to be unreadable text. However, you can understand INF files if you take them apart one piece at a time.

The most important piece of the INF file to understand from a system repair perspective is the registry settings. When you install a device, Windows XP makes changes to the registry based on INF file content. Unfortunately, a failed device may leave registry entries in place that can cause problems with a replacement device. You end up with a mass of equally bizarre registry entries and a machine that doesn't work right.

Sometimes you need to manually remove the registry entries made by a device to restore proper system operation. Figure 12.14 shows a simple example of registry settings in an INF file. In this case, you're looking at the entries made for an uninterruptible power supply (UPS).

FIGURE 12.14

These registry entries will active a UPS on your system.

Each column of information in this file serves a special purpose. Every entry begins with the location of the HKEY. For example, HKLM represents HKEY_LOCAL_MACHINE. The next entry is the path to the target key. For example, if you look at Figure 12.14, there's a path to a BattC key (SYSTEM\CurrentControlSet\Services\BattC). If an entry doesn't supply a path, Windows XP assumes you want to place the entry in the default registry location. Most devices use a default location of HKEY_LOCAL_MACHINE\SYSTEM\CurrentControlSet\Control\Class\ with the ClassGuid entry at the beginning of the added file. The next entry is the value name. If the entry doesn't supply a value name, Windows XP assumes you want to use the (Default) entry. Next, you'll see the value type and finally, the value data.

The device in our example has entries in three areas of the registry. The INF specifically spells out the last two areas. The first four entries appear in the default registry location as shown in Figure 12.15. Notice the full path for this entry appears in the status bar. The GUID is the unique identifier for this device.

FIGURE 12.15

Some INF file entries will appear in the default location in the registry.

Tips for Avoiding Registry Disasters

You can't spend too much time working with Windows before you hear about a registry disaster that a friend of a friend experienced some time ago. Some of these editing mistakes have been around so long that they take on the guise of an urban legend. Network administrators tell stories of terrifying registry incidents to scare new users into submission.

The point is that you can avoid most registry accidents. In many cases, all you need to follow are some simple rules when working with the registry. The following list tells you about the rules that you should follow every time you work with the registry:

- **Always Make a Backup**　The number one error that people make is assuming the changes they make to the registry will produce the desired results. In many cases, the edit won't work as anticipated, and you'll need a backup to return Windows to normal.

- **Use Reliable Information**　A registry edit that works for someone on a newsgroup may not work on your system at all. Your system is unique in many ways. A seemingly innocent change that works on one machine may not work on every Windows machine. Remember to use the Microsoft Knowledge Base and online documentation as sources of information whenever possible.

- **Know What You're Doing**　Changing a value in the registry without knowing what you're doing is like performing surgery without a medical degree and both eyes shut. If someone asks you to make a change to your registry, ask how the change works. It's important to know what a change will do before you make it.

- **Use a Test Machine**　Even if you understand a registry change and obtain the information from a reliable source, there's still risk involved in making a registry change. Sometimes, the registry change will affect a portion of the boot process or security, both of which offer little flexibility. A mistake in either area could render your machine unbootable. Making the change on a test machine limits your risk and increases the chance of success on a production machine.

- **Double-Check Your Entries**　This may seem like an obvious part of editing the registry, but all too often, the user's mind is on the effects of the change, not the change itself. A simple misspelling can spell disaster for a registry edit because the registry is notoriously unforgiving on even small entry errors. Make sure that the entry is complete. It's essential to verify that all keys and values are in place.

Summary

The registry is an essential part of Windows. You can't even start the operating system unless the registry is intact and fully functional. This means that the registry is a powerful element of the operating system to learn and a fragile component you don't want break. The registry information you learned today represents some of the safer things you can do. Many people will attempt to perform other tasks with the registry in ways that Microsoft didn't design it to work. The result, more often than not, is a nonfunctional operating system or damaged data files. You should know how to work with the registry, but you should also learn to treat it with respect.

Q&A

Q: **The registry seems to be bits of this and parts of that without any logical order. Is there any order to the registry at all?**

A: As discussed today, the registry does have some order in that like pieces of data appear in the same areas of the registry. For example, all of the HKEY entries contain some specific type of registry data. The hives are also used to group information by type. Microsoft also arranged the registry in a hierarchical fashion. Each major key has subkeys that describe it. Values describe individual keys. It takes time to learn registry construction, but eventually you begin seeing patterns. In short, don't expect to learn where data appears in the registry overnight; only continued registry use will help you understand the elements it contains. Until you do know the registry construction better, use a copy of the Windows XP/2000 Resource Kit as a guide to the registry.

Q: **Why didn't Microsoft place all of the hives in the same location on the hard drive?**

A: The arrangement is logical if you look at the way Windows uses hives. Most of the hives do appear in the \WINDOWS\system32\config folder of the hard drives. The user profile information appears with the user data in the \Documents and Settings\<User Name> folder. This way, when you move a user to another machine, you can also move that user's hive. Using a separate folder for each user also enhances security and makes it easier to find the data for a particular user.

Q: **How do I search for binary and DWORD values? Will the Registry Editor find strings in expanded and multi-strings without special formatting?**

A: You can't search for either binary or DWORD data values in the registry. All you can search for are the key or value names associated with the data. This makes it difficult to look for some types of data. However, the Registry Editor does provide

12

full string search capabilities no matter what type of string you look for. This means you can search both expanded and multi-string data values without special formatting.

Q: Why do some vendors provide application settings in HKEY_LOCAL_MACHINE, others in HKEY_CURRENT_USER, and still others in both?

A: It often depends on how the vendor views their product. An entry in HKEY_LOCAL_MACHINE often speaks of an application with global system impact. On the other hand, an entry in HKEY_CURRENT_USER reflects a personal application. Vendors often use both areas when an application provides global services but allows each user to customize their environment. In some cases, the reasoning behind a placement choice is obscure. The best policy is to assume that you'll find data in both locations.

Workshop

It's the end of the twelfth day. At this point, you understand the basics of working with the registry. Now it's time to see how much you know about using the registry to enhance your computing environment. You can find answers to the quiz and exercise questions in Appendix A at the back of the book.

Quiz

1. What's the most important registry editing tip you can learn?

2. Which registry value can you change but not rename or delete?

3. What are the two parts of a file association needed to change the application that a file uses?

4. What's the number one error when making a registry edit?

Exercises

1. Start a copy of RegEdit and view the sections of the registry we discussed today.

2. Create a temporary registry key and add some values to it. Export the key and view the resulting REG file in a text editor. Delete the temporary key when you finish working with it.

3. Try using the Find and Find Next features of the Registry Editor to search for keys, values, and data.

4. If you've wanted to use a different application for one of the file extensions on your machine, it might be a good time to perform a file association edit.

DAY **13**

Using Laptops and Handheld Devices

At one time, corporate users considered laptops unusual devices in the workplace that required special attention. Administrators considered them difficult to work with because they often required special drivers. Today, most people consider laptops common devices, and many people have replaced their desktop system with a laptop. Reliability and dependability are no longer concerns.

However, a new arrival in the workplace has replaced the laptop for some users. The handheld device offers users on the road an even smaller computer for handling tasks such as e-mail. The most popular version of the handheld device is the personal digital assistant (PDA). Cellular telephones are also becoming more popular, especially in countries such as Japan. Needless to say, many users consider these new computers somewhat unusual, and administrators believe that they're difficult to maintain. Eventually, vendors will standardize both PDA and cellular telephone devices so that they become workplace standards.

Portable devices in general still require special treatment. A laptop still requires special devices designed to fit together into a small package. PDAs are even more limited, and cellular telephones are the most limited of all. Today you'll learn how to circumvent some of the problems caused by these specialty devices and learn how to make them more efficient.

You'll also learn about some special applications designed for portable device use. Some of these applications, such as Briefcase, extend your work environment. Other applications, such as ActiveSync, create a bond between your PDA and your desktop machine.

 Note

All of the screenshots in this chapter use the Windows XP classic view for a reason. If you want to find out why I'm using classic view, read on. The new interface isn't quite as laptop friendly as Microsoft would lead you to believe. In fact, as we'll see later today, the new interface is downright hostile in a few ways.

Special Configuration Issues for Laptops

Laptops today are fully loaded computers. Users don't suffer from the lack of features that laptop users of yesterday had to deal with. You gain a wealth of connectivity features with most laptops, making them good replacements for desktop machines in many cases. The two problem areas with the laptop continue to be the mouse and the keyboard. The use of odd mouse devices and tiny keyboards are the only legacy problems you'll need to deal with. Vendors have produced a number of solutions for both problems, so even these issues are no longer a concern for many users.

Laptops do require special configuration when compared with a desktop machine. The very nature of this device means you'll use it in places that you never considered for a desktop machine. For example, I'll often take my laptop in the car. I work on articles while my wife drives. It's a good method for me to find additional work time in between stops on the road. Because of the way I use my laptop, I configure it in special ways.

The one configuration change that all laptop users should consider is the use of profiles. My laptop contains a modem, a video adapter, and a network interface card (NIC). All three of these devices perform essential tasks when I connect to my network at my office. Only one of the devices serves a useful purpose when I work in a motel. The soundboard can actually be a hindrance in this environment because I'm in close quarters with other people. Using three profiles allows me to adapt my laptop to meet the needs of these three environments. You can learn how to create profiles in the "Using Profiles" section during Day 10.

Laptops often have special devices included with them. For example, most desktop machines don't include a Personal Computer Memory Card International Association (PCMCIA) port. These ports normally appear on the side of the machine, and you use them to hold credit card-sized devices, such as modems and NICs. Some desktop machines have this port, but it's still rare. Even rarer is an infrared port. This port makes it easy for a laptop to connect to devices such as a printer without using a network connection. You can also use this port to download data from your PDA while on the road. Both of these ports require special configuration. We'll discuss both issues later in the chapter.

Another special consideration for laptops is the docked versus undocked status. A docked laptop will have different needs than an undocked laptop. For one thing, a docked laptop normally contains additional devices. This means you may need yet another profile to handle the docked state of the machine.

Tip Unlike machines that use standard cathode ray tube (CRT) displays, liquid crystal displays (LCDs) work well with Microsoft's new font technology. If you need font smoothing to see characters clearly, try the Clear Type option. To add Clear Type to your LCD display, right-click the desktop and choose Properties from the context menu. Select the Appearance tab. Click Effect to display the Effects dialog box. Check the Use the following to smooth edges of screen fonts option and select Clear Type from the drop-down list box. However, be aware that Clear Type isn't battery friendly. If you want to optimize battery life at the expense of screen clarity, don't enable the Clear Type technology.

Special Configuration Issues for Handheld PCs

Handheld PCs, or PDAs, represent the smallest platform you can use for computing purposes. Some devices, such as the Palm, include an extremely simple operating system. You'll normally use these devices for your e-mail, contact management, and appointment calendar.

Devices like the Pocket PC include a more robust operating system, so you can perform additional tasks, such as simple word processing. These devices usually include a simple database and a spreadsheet. You can download a wealth of third-party add-ons as well. For example, my Cassiopeia has a special screen capture program installed.

No matter which PDA you use, there's one special application you have to install on the host machine: some type of synchronization. For the Pocket PC, this normally means installing Microsoft ActiveSync. Other handheld PCs, such as the Palm, will use a similar application. The synchronizing program enables the PDA to exchange various types of information with the desktop machine. At the very least, you can exchange data files. Advanced PDAs also allow you to download static copies of Web pages. The bottom line is the PDA and the host machine form a symbiotic relationship, and you have to configure them to account for this relationship.

> **Tip**
>
> Microsoft upgrades its software on a regular basis, so it pays to check for the latest version of ActiveSync. You can find the latest version at `http://www.microsoft.com/mobile/pocketpc/default.asp`.

PDAs require a special connection to the host machine as well. In many cases, this means placing the PDA in a cradle that provides power for charging the PDA batteries and a connection to the host machine. Some PDAs rely exclusively on a serial port. Other PDAs use a faster universal serial bus (USB) connection. In both cases, you must reconfigure the bus on the host machine to ensure maximum transfer speed. In the case of the USB connection, you may also have to perform some level of troubleshooting before the connection will work. We'll discuss this issue in more detail in the "Tips for Circumventing Data Transfer Problems" section today.

Another PDA configuration issue is the use of alternative input devices. Vendors produce fold-up keyboards and special mice that plug into the PDA. Obtaining a device that will work with your particular PDA is hard enough; finding one that will also work when connected to the host machine might seem impossible. As a result, you need to choose add-on devices with care to ensure that they'll work for all your needs.

The final configuration problem for PDAs is one of updates. A PDA offers connectivity options that pale in comparison with the average laptop or desktop machine. Just loading the update information on the PDA can be a time-consuming and error-prone task. Performing the update is more difficult still because PDAs often lack the configuration options found on fully loaded machines.

Data Transfers

Transferring data from a desktop machine to a laptop or from a PDA to a full-sized computer is important. You take work with you on a trip and then need to transfer the results back to your main system. If you can't connect the two devices, the usefulness of each one diminishes. While a desktop machine can get both without connectivity to a laptop or PDA, reduced communication for these two devices does have a detrimental effect on their usefulness in the workplace. As a result, you'll want to know about every connectivity option at your disposal.

The following sections discuss data transfers, the connectivity between two machines. We'll discuss two common applications that come with Windows XP. The first is HyperTerminal, an application that has found a place in Windows for a number of years. The second is infrared data transfers. Using infrared eliminates the need to use wireless or direct connections with a portable device. Unfortunately, as we'll see in this section, infrared also comes with a few penalties that make it unpopular with some users.

Using HyperTerminal

Many people have used HyperTerminal over the years to promote communications between computers. This is one of the older products available for Windows XP. You can use it for a variety of communication needs, including file transfers.

When used for server communications, HyperTerminal is the graphical version of the text mode TELNET application. In fact, HyperTerminal will ask if you want to make it your default Telnet program when you start it the first time. HyperTerminal also has the capability of creating peer connections between two computers.

The following sections discuss ways you can use HyperTerminal to transfer data between your laptop and your desktop machine. In many cases, you're limited to simple file transfers, which may be all you actually need. These sections concentrate on how to perform common data transfer tasks using HyperTerminal.

Creating a Telnet Connection

One of the prerequisites for using HyperTerminal for a server connection is an operational Telnet server on the host machine. Microsoft turns the Telnet server service off by default because many people don't require Telnet, and it represents a hole in your security if left open to crackers.

Windows NT/2000 Server includes an actual Telnet Administration entry in the Administrative Tools folder. Select this option, and you'll see a command prompt open with a menu. One of the options on the menu will start the service. When using Windows XP Professional Edition, you need to open a command prompt. Type **TLNTADMIN START** and press Enter to start the service. Make sure that you stop the Telnet server when you finish using it by typing TLNTADMIN STOP and pressing Enter.

Before you can use HyperTerminal to create a server connection, you need to create a connection with it. If HyperTerminal detects that you don't have any connections defined, it will ask you to create one as part of the startup process. You can also use the

13

File | New Connection command to display the Connection Description dialog box. The following steps tell how to create a new connection:

1. Type a name for your new connection and select an icon to associate with it. Click OK. You'll see the Connect To dialog box.

2. Select the TCP/IP (Winsock) option in the Connect Using field of the Connect To dialog box. The Connect To dialog box fields will change to include entries for the host address and port number.

> **Tip**
>
> One way to enhance Telnet security is to use a nonstandard port. The Telnet Server Administration utility will allow you to change this port number to something else. You'll want to avoid other common ports, such as port 80, which most servers use for the Web server.

3. Type the required connection information. Click OK. HyperTerminal will attempt to make the connection. If HyperTerminal is successful, you'll see a login screen like the one shown in Figure 13.1. Otherwise, you'll see an error message and will need to try again.

FIGURE 13.1

HyperTerminal displays a login screen if you make a successful connection.

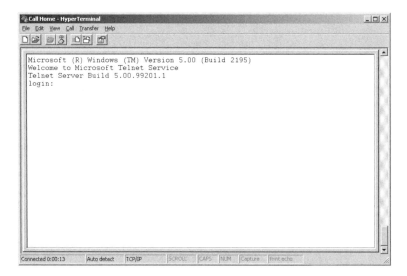

4. Use the File | Save command to save the connection to disk.

The Telnet connection limits you to tasks you can perform with Telnet. For example, you have full access to the command prompt using the default server settings. Unless the administrator changes the default shell, you'll be able to access any character mode utility that you have permission to access. However, you can't upload or download files using HyperTerminal because there's no server that allows this capability.

Creating a Peer Connection

The Telnet server option for HyperTerminal offers an automated interface at the server end. If you want to use HyperTerminal in peer mode, you'll need two people working at the computers, one at each end.

A peer session begins when one person sets up a machine to receive a call. To ensure that the previously loaded settings don't contaminate the environment, use the File | New Connection command to display the Connection Description dialog box. Click Cancel to clear all of the settings. Use Call | Wait for Call to begin waiting for the call. You'll see the Connection Description dialog box again. Type any name and click OK. The dialog box will go away, and your system will begin waiting for the call.

Now that we have someone waiting for a call, it's time to create a connection to it. The following steps show you how:

1. Use the File | New Connection dialog box to display the Connection Description dialog box.

2. Type a name for your new connection and select an icon to associate with it. Click OK. You'll see the Connect To dialog box. This dialog box contains the country, area code, and telephone number used to make the call. You can also choose a device to use for the connection.

3. Type the required connection information. Click OK. You'll see a Connect dialog box with the current location settings for your system.

4. Change the location settings, if required. Click Dial at the Connect dialog box. HyperTerminal will attempt to make the connection. If HyperTerminal is successful, the cursor in the window will become active. Anything you type will appear on both systems. You'll also see a connected indicator on the left side of the status bar. Otherwise, you'll see an error message and will need to try again.

5. Use the File | Save command to save the connection to disk.

Setting Connection Properties

The initial connection properties you see on the Connection Description dialog box don't fully describe the connection. HyperTerminal assumes that you want to use certain defaults for the connection. Click the Properties button, and you'll see a Call Properties dialog box. The properties on the Connect To tab should look familiar because they're the ones you entered in the Connect To dialog box.

13

Select the Settings tab, and you'll see a dialog box like the one shown in Figure 13.2. The figure shows the default settings that HyperTerminal uses. For example, HyperTerminal assumes that you want to send function, arrow, and Ctrl keys to the server for control purposes. If you select the Windows Keys option, HyperTerminal will use the function keys locally.

FIGURE 13.2

The Settings tab enables you to select various terminal settings.

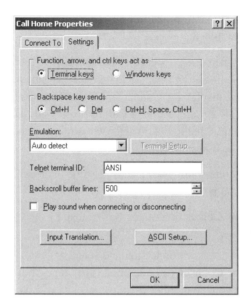

The Emulation field determines which terminal type to emulate when making a connection to the server. This setting hails back to the days when the only connection was one made to a mainframe. HyperTerminal still has to emulate a terminal to create the connection to the host machine. The Auto Detect setting is the safest selection, unless the host machine is looking for something specific and doesn't provide the proper "handshaking" to allow auto detection.

Use the Backscroll Buffer Lines field to determine the number of lines of text that HyperTerminal saves during the session. Using fewer lines saves memory, while more lines will permit you to scroll back further in the session. The 500-line default works for most situations, but you might want to increase this number if you need to capture the screen buffer for a long session. Capturing the screen buffer creates a record of the session that you can store in a text file for later analysis.

Click ASCII Setup, and you'll see the ASCII Setup dialog box shown in Figure 13.3. As you can see, this dialog box controls the manner in which HyperTerminal handles ASCII communication between client and server. The ASCII Setup dialog box includes separate settings for sending and receiving data.

FIGURE 13.3

Use the ASCII Setup dialog box to set special ASCII communication parameters.

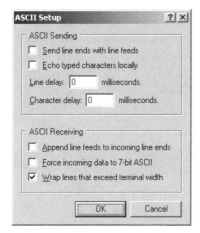

Each of these settings helps communication with older systems. For example, some systems won't acknowledge input unless HyperTerminal sends both a carriage return and a line feed as part of the end-of-line communication (when you press Enter). Selecting the Send Line Ends with Line Feeds option resolves this problem.

Sending and Receiving Files

When using HyperTerminal in peer mode, you can send and receive files using the Transfer | Send File and Transfer | Receive File commands. The normal sequence is for the receiving computer to use the Transfer | Receive File command to display the Receive File dialog box, select a location for the file, and then click OK. The system will enter a wait state.

The sending computer uses the Transfer | Send File command to display the Send File dialog box. The user locates the file to transfer using the Browse button (or typing the name directly into the dialog box). Both users can choose from a number of send and receive protocols, but the Zmodem with Crash Recovery option is the best in most situations.

After the two machines complete their setups, the sending machine clicks Send in the Send File dialog box. Both the sending and receiving machines will see the dialog box shown in Figure 13.4. This dialog box will disappear as soon as the file transfer is complete.

13

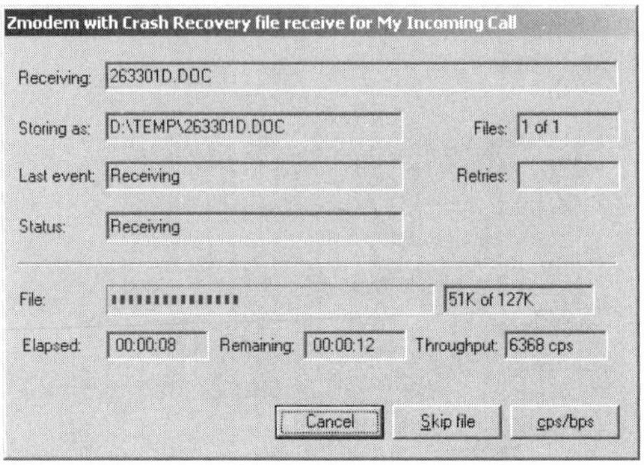

Figure 13.4

The sending and receiving computers will see this transfer dialog box.

Zmodem with Crash Recovery file receive for My Incoming Call

Receiving:	263301D.DOC
Storing as:	D:\TEMP\263301D.DOC
Last event:	Receiving
Status:	Receiving

Files: 1 of 1
Retries:

File: .... 51K of 127K
Elapsed: 00:00:08   Remaining: 00:00:12   Throughput: 6368 cps

[Cancel]   [Skip file]   [cps/bps]

Capturing a Session

You can capture a session to a text file using the Transfer | Capture Text File command. You'll see a Capture Text dialog box. Type the name of the text file you want to use to store the session information and then click Start. When you complete capturing the session, use the Transfer | Capture Text | Stop command. HyperTerminal will save the file to disk so that you can review the session later.

Sending Text

You can send files back and forth between computers. However, you might want to display a large block of text on screen at certain times. You can use the Transfer | Send Text File command to transfer the text onscreen. You'll see a Send Text File dialog box. Select the file you want to send and click Open. The text will appear on both screens.

Testing Your Modem

Windows XP provides a number of obscure methods for testing the condition of your modem. For example, you can use the options on the Diagnostics tab of the Modem properties dialog box. HyperTerminal is another option. Instead of running predefined tests, you can run vendor-specific tests that appear in your modem manual.

 Tip

> If you can't see what you're typing at the HyperTerminal window, you need to enable the "echo" feature of your modem. Type **ATE1** at the HyperTerminal window and press Enter. You'll begin to see everything you type.

To begin testing, type the **"AT"** command you want to run in the HyperTerminal window. For example, if I type "ATI4" and press Enter in HyperTerminal, my modem responds with a list of modem settings. If you've somehow lost your manual, you can always type AT$H and press Enter to see a display of the various AT commands supported by your modem. A modem usually provides multiple pages of help, and you may have to execute other commands to see a test command menu.

Using Infrared

Infrared ports first became popular with Windows 95 users. It's a technology that showed great promise at one time but has faded into obscurity in some areas. Essentially, an infrared port works about the same as the remote control for your television. It uses light at a frequency you can't see to transfer data between the portable device and a second device, such as a printer or a desktop machine. As far as the laptop is concerned, the infrared port is another serial or parallel port.

Given today's computing environment, infrared has two benefits to consider. The first is that you can create a direct connection between two machines without using wires. This makes using infrared relatively easy when your laptop or other device doesn't require long-term connectivity. The second benefit is privacy. Unlike wireless, an infrared connection focuses on a single destination and doesn't exist outside the local building, unless you want it to. An infrared connection is point-to-point. Finally, you'll save money by using infrared. You'll find infrared ports on most laptops and PDAs. This means you only need an infrared port for the other machine, and it's a low-cost item in most cases.

Everything comes with a price, unfortunately. Infrared has several problems you need to consider. One of the most important problems is availability. You're more likely to find an infrared port on a laptop than on a desktop machine. Most desktop machines don't feature an infrared port, which means you must obtain it as an add-on. You can say the same thing for other devices, such as printers.

Another problem with infrared is compatibility. There are several versions of infrared ports and not all versions are compatible with each other. Many of the early implementation infrared ports are still around, making communication somewhat difficult. Fortunately, the standards for the infrared port have stabilized, so compatibility should become less of a problem in the near future.

13

Directivity is another problem. One of the big advantages of using infrared is that you don't have to worry as much about others listening in on your connection. However, this also means you need a line of sight connection with the other machine (no using infrared between two rooms), and you have to aim the two devices at each other to gain the maximum connection. This is inconvenient if the two devices are at different heights or if the infrared port is on the back of the host machine.

Now that you know the pros and cons of using an infrared connection, let's look at some connectivity issues. Windows XP provides two configuration dialog boxes for infrared data association (IrDA) connections. The first is the IrDA Protocol Properties dialog box that you'll see when you open the device found in the Infrared Devices folder in Device Manager.

The IrDA Protocol Properties dialog box has the standard General and Driver tabs. You'll also find an IrDA Settings tab. Depending on the vendor that created your IrDA port, you may see any number of settings on this tab. However, all IrDA ports support two entries. The first is Maximum Connection Rate. Windows assumes that you want to use the maximum rate of 115,200bps. However, if you find that you have connection problems, you'll need to use a lower rate. The second setting is the Communications Port field. Select the port you want to use for communications purposes with IrDA.

> **Tip**   Some vendors support both serial and parallel connections with their IrDA port. If this is the case, you might see a second entry under the Infrared Devices folder or in the Ports folder. The parallel connection normally supports printer communications, and you can't use it for data transfers without special software.

After you install an IrDA port on your machine, you'll also see a new Control Panel applet named *Wireless Link*. As you can see in Figure 13.5, this applet helps you configure wireless communications for your system. It works with other types of wireless communication, not just IrDA ports.

The Infrared tab contains all of the settings for your IrDA port. You can use this tab to control the appearance of an IrDA icon in the notification area that shows current port activity. You can also set options, such as when to play sounds for port activity. In most cases, the use of sound is important because of the need to point the IrDA-enabled device in the right direction. The Infrared tab also has a Default location for received files field. This field is blank by default, but you'll want to provide a default download location. This ensures that file transfers will work smoothly, and the user won't have to worry about where the files will end up on the drive.

The Image Transfer tab defines the IrDA interface with devices such as cameras. The options on this tab enable image downloads from alternative devices. Again, you'll want to set a default download directory for image information. A special feature on this tab automatically opens a copy of Windows Explorer so that you can see the pictures after the download completes.

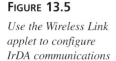

Figure 13.5

Use the Wireless Link applet to configure IrDA communications for your machine.

The final tab, Hardware, shows all of the wireless hardware on your system. The tab also includes Properties and Troubleshoot buttons you can use with the highlighted device. The Properties button will take you to the device's Properties dialog box in Device Manager. Troubleshoot opens a copy of Help and Support Center to assist in finding problems with your setup.

Tips for Circumventing Data Transfer Problems

Transferring data from one machine to another is always problematic. The problem is far worse when you only have one means of connectivity and the usability of that connection is dubious at best. For example, talk to anyone who's tried to connect a Pocket PC to a host machine using a USB port and Microsoft ActiveSync. Yes, the connection works lightning fast (at least when compared to a serial port) when it works. However, users have come up with all sorts of odd solutions to problems with this connection. The problem is so significant that several trade press columnists have written articles containing solutions to the problem.

Tip

The number one cause of connection problems for most first-time PDA users is a failure to follow the confusing vendor instructions. Some PDAs require that you connect the device first, install the drivers, and then install the software. Other vendors require that you install the drivers first, connect the PDA to the host machine, and then install the software. Make sure that you

> understand the vendor instructions before you begin installing your PDA. If
> you don't understand the instructions, give the vendor a call before you do
> anything. Obtaining a good first-time installation is key to making your PDA
> experience a good one.

Not every connection is a disaster waiting to happen. In some cases, the user will complain that the connection is slow or difficult to use, but at least the connection works reliably. However, the fact that the connection works won't appease some users, especially if they've seen a fast connection to the host using the same device. With this in mind, the following list tells you about common data transfer problems and offers some solutions:

- **Slow Connection**   This is one of the most common problems that users complain about. If you're using a serial connection, check the serial port configuration on the desktop machine. In many cases, an application or even Windows will set this port to a slow speed for use with a modem. Make sure that you configure the port to offer the maximum connection speed that it's capable of providing. This same point holds true for both USB and wireless connections. Host port configuration problems are a major cause of slow connection speed.

- **No Connection**   USB connections are most likely to have problems in this area. Windows has a significant problem with nonstandard USB configurations to begin with (as defined by rigid Microsoft standards). A number of users also find that ActiveSync provides less than stellar support for USB. Make sure that you begin by checking all the usual problems, such as a bad cable or a poor connection between the Pocket PC and the cradle. After you explore these problems, disconnect the Pocket PC from the host, uninstall the USB port, allow Windows to detect USB port and install support for it, and then reinstall the Pocket PC according to vendor instructions.

- **Missing Data**   Many PDA synchronization applications provide an optional desktop folder for storing data. The optional folder isn't optional. Make sure that you install the desktop folder to make it easy to find your data. Otherwise, you can't be sure where the PDA will place the data on the host drive. In addition, the folder makes it easy to send data from the host machine to the PDA. A lack of this folder means you have to figure out the secret handshake for performing the data transfer.

- **Corrupted Data**   The applications supplied with a PDA aren't full versions of the desktop machine that you normally use. Unfortunately, this sometimes means the data files aren't compatible. The PDA application may open the file, but what you'll see is corrupted data. The data isn't really corrupted; the PDA application just can't read it. The problem gets worse if you create the data file on the PDA, move it to the desktop for further editing, and then try to read the edited version on the PDA. A desktop application will often place formatting codes in the data file that the PDA version of the program doesn't understand. The bottom line is that you need to test application compatibility between the host and the PDA before you assume anything about the capability to transfer data.

- **Connection Loss or Intermittent Connection**   In some cases, the source of this problem is easy to figure out. If you move the PDA at all when using an infrared connection, you'll experience dropouts. However, some problems aren't quite as obvious. For example, if you set the read ahead buffer on your serial port too high, you could drop characters and experience connectivity problems.

Working with PCMCIA

The Personal Computer Memory Card International Association (PCMCIA) bus on your laptop does a lot more than work with memory. PCMCIA (PC Card or CardBus) takes the form of a credit card-sized circuit card that you plug into the side of a laptop or other compatible machine. PCMCIA or *PC Card* refers to this type of card in general. Vendors normally use the term *CardBus* to refer to the 32-bit version of the card. Some forms of this card support bus speeds of 33MHz and advanced features, such as *bus mastering* (the ability to perform a task without processor intervention).

Generally, Windows XP will automatically detect the PCMCIA bus on your machine. You won't find any special settings in the Device Manager. The PCMCIA bus does support the General and Driver tabs, so you can update the device driver as needed.

Some PCMCIA implementations also support a Control Panel applet. This applet generally allows you to stop cards before you remove them and start them after you insert them in the PCMCIA slot. The stopping and starting process ensures that Windows recognizes hardware changes you make to the system. The Control Panel applet will also contain settings that place a PCMCIA icon in the notification area of the taskbar.

13

Using Briefcase

Briefcase is one of the best tools made for laptops. This part of Windows XP is largely hidden, but you can still access it by right-clicking the desktop and choosing New | Briefcase from the context menu. You can have more than one Briefcase, but most users find that one works just fine.

The Briefcase is actually a special form of file. When you place an object within the briefcase, you make a copy of it that you can take home or on the road to work on. After you return from your trip, you can synchronize the contents of your Briefcase with the original files on your hard drive. The process works extremely well because you don't need to worry about lost edits or keep track of which files you updated. Briefcase manages a two-machine setup so that your data remains safe.

You can place any data object that Windows XP can handle in Briefcase. This means you can place both individual files and folders in Briefcase. To place a file in Briefcase, right-drag it to the briefcase on your desktop. Drop the object on Briefcase, and you'll see a menu containing options to Make Sync Copy, Make Sync Copy of Type, Move Here, Create Shortcut(s) Here, and Cancel. What you want is a sync copy of the object.

Using folders to hold your data is actually better, in this case, than working with individual files. If you move an individual file to Briefcase, that file will remain in sync with the copy on your hard drive. However, any new files you create will become orphans. They'll stay within Briefcase, but won't have a connection to the original location. Using a folder places the files in a container. Briefcase transfers any new files in the container to your hardware along with the updates of existing files. Figure 13.6 shows a typical example of Briefcase with a folder loaded.

FIGURE 13.6

Briefcase is a special type of folder that helps you keep data on your laptop synchronized with your desktop machine.

As you can see, Briefcase offers many of the same features as a standard folder. What makes Briefcase different is that it includes a Briefcase menu that contains the synchronization options. You can also use the buttons on the toolbar for synchronization. However, the menu includes a Split from Original option that orphans a file that you don't want to update on the desktop machine.

Files in the briefcase include the filename, location of the sync copy, the synchronization status, and the size of the file. Folders entries include everything but a size. You can do everything with a Briefcase copy of a file that you can do with it on the original drive.

When a file or folder requires updating, you'll see Needs Updating in the Status column of the Briefcase. Highlight the file and then click Update Selection to update it. You can also choose Update All to update all of the files in the Briefcase. In both cases, you'll see an Update Briefcase dialog box like the one shown in Figure 13.7.

Notice that this dialog tells you the name of the affected file, the source location, the action Briefcase will perform, and the destination file. If you want to update the files and

FIGURE **13.7**

Use Update Selection or Update All to display the Update Briefcase dialog box.

folders listed in the Update Briefcase dialog box, click Update and Briefcase will do the rest. The status column will change from Needs Updating to Up-to-date.

Installing Microsoft ActiveSync

Microsoft ActiveSync is one of the most common applications used to create a connection between a PDA and a desktop machine. It has a reputation of causing more than a few problems. However, you can take a few steps to avoid problems. The first step is to ensure that your system can actually see the PDA. Open Device Manager, locate the USB Root Hub entry, and open it. Look at the Power tab. If you don't see the PDA listed (see Figure 13.8), you need to check your connections before you attempt to install the ActiveSync software.

FIGURE **13.8**

Make sure that your system can actually see the PDA before you install support for it.

13

After you verify that Windows XP can see the PDA, it's time to install ActiveSync. The following steps take you through the process that I normally use to install ActiveSync:

1. Start the ActiveSync Setup program. You'll see a Welcome screen.

2. Click Next. You'll see a Select Installation Folder dialog box. The default folder normally works well.

3. Choose an installation folder (if necessary) and then click Next. Windows XP will copy the files to the hard drive. At this point, the setup program will disappear. You still need to configure ActiveSync to use your PDA.

4. Double-click the ActiveSync icon on the desktop. You'll see the ActiveSync dialog box.

5. Remove the PDA from its cradle. Windows XP should make a sound signifying that it noticed the PDA is unplugged.

6. Place the PDA in its cradle. Windows XP should make another sound signifying that it sees the PDA. Microsoft ActiveSync will display a New Partnership dialog box.

7. Select Yes when asked if you want to create a partnership and then click Next. If you already have a partnership with another computer, ActiveSync will ask if you want to maintain it. Choose Yes or No and click Next. You'll see a Select Synchronization Settings dialog box like the one shown in Figure 13.9. Notice the highlighted Files entry. Having a synchronization folder can prevent many problems with your desktop-to-PDA communication. Place a file in this folder and ActiveSync will copy it to the PDA during the next synchronization. This is a "must have" feature for all PDA users.

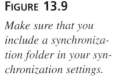

FIGURE **13.9**

Make sure that you include a synchronization folder in your synchronization settings.

8. Select the synchronization settings that you want and then click Next. You'll see a Setup Complete dialog box.

9. Click Finish. ActiveSync will begin the synchronization process with your PDA. When the process is complete, your dialog will look like the one in Figure 13.10.

FIGURE 13.10

The completed ActiveSync installation process leaves your PDA in a synchronized state.

Power Management Strategies

Making the battery on a laptop last long enough to perform one more calculation is often on the minds of most users. Even five more minutes is helpful. That's why power management strategies are so important for the laptop user. A power management strategy answers the question of how to get five more minutes out of the laptop's battery.

The problem is to figure out just how to tune your system for maximum battery life without making it impossible to use. Of course, some configuration changes cause more problems than others. For example, one of the first changes that many users make is turning off all of the fancy screen effects that Microsoft insists on including with Windows XP. Many of the screen effects are superfluous, and you can live without them. However, a screen effect such as font smoothing is a "must have" option for some users.

After running more than a few tests with Windows XP, I found that my laptop runs better with the classic interface. At first it was difficult to figure out why the classic interface worked better, but it turns out that the reason is simple when you think about it. All of the special effects provided with Windows XP require processing horsepower. The additional processing cycles come from the supply available to your application, so the system runs slower. In addition, the constant increase in processor usage keeps the processor from stepping down into a lower clock rate during periods of inactivity. Finally, all of

13

these features require additional disk access, something you want to keep to a minimum on a laptop. The net result is that a laptop that ran for an hour and 56 minutes using unoptimized Windows 2000 only runs for an hour and 5 minutes under Windows XP using the new interface.

You can reduce the battery performance hit by switching to the classic interface. We discussed this process during Day 3, "Exploring the Interface." It's also important to remove any unneeded special effects. The special effects are located in two places. First, right-click the desktop and choose Properties from the context menu. Select the Appearance tab and click Effects. Clear all of the options in the Effects dialog box. Click OK twice to make the changes permanent.

Second, right-click My Computer and choose Properties from the context menu. Select the Advanced tab. Click Settings in the Performance area, and you'll see a Performance Options dialog box. Notice that the Visual Effects tab contains three preset performance options. Select the Adjust for Best Performance option. Click OK twice to make the changes permanent.

This isn't the only speed boost you can add to your system, but it's a start in the right direction. At this point, you need to add a profile to your laptop that disables all of the devices that you don't use while on the road. We discussed profiles in the "Using Profiles" section during Day 10. I performed an extreme disable of devices on the same laptop that ran Windows XP unmodified for an hour and 5 minutes. The new results were nothing short of spectacular. The new configuration ran for 3 hours and 32 minutes.

Unfortunately, to obtain this increase in battery life, I had to give up quite a bit. For example, I disabled the serial and parallel ports, PCMCIA (which meant no expansion cards), the modem, soundboard, infrared port, and the network interface card (NIC). All I ended up with was a basic system.

I also changed my application setups. For example, I normally set Word to save my file automatically every 10 minutes. The new laptop setup uses a 15-minute interval, which might be too long in some circumstances. Now that you have some idea of what works for most systems, here are some additional power management strategies:

- **Reduce File Saves**   Every time you save a file on your system, it starts the hard drive. The hard drive is one of the biggest power draws next to the back lighting for the display. Some users constantly hit the Save button. They don't mean to click it all the time; the action becomes a habit. Breaking bad usage habits can make a significant difference in battery life.
- **Realistic Power Options Properties Settings**   The default power-down settings for a laptop are based on someone typing all the time. However, some people

aren't typing all the time; they might be reading a report or performing some other activity. If you find yourself constantly moving the mouse pointer or pressing the spacebar to get your screen back, the power settings are too aggressive. You want to set them so that the laptop saves power but also uses power wisely. My laptop has several power schemes so that I can quickly set it to the work I have to do.

- **Keep Applications to a Minimum** Desktop machines often have several applications open at once. A communications program monitors the Internet for e-mail, a day planner provides you with your schedule, and a word processor helps you write a report. Keeping all of these applications open on a desktop machine isn't problematic because the desktop doesn't have a power problem. A laptop doesn't have unlimited power. Decide which application you need to use and keep everything else closed. The idea is to reduce processor, memory, and hard drive use as much as possible.

- **Avoid Standby Mode for Long Breaks** Standby mode does use less power than the full power mode. However, it still uses power. You'll want to use standby mode for short breaks (10 to 15 minutes) because it doesn't require as much power as shutting the machine down and restarting. For long breaks, use the hibernate mode or shut the machine down and restart it from scratch.

- **Use Small Applications Whenever Possible** Sometimes, the choice of application makes a difference. If you plan to view a file but not change it, you might want to use one of the viewer programs available on the Internet. They're small and efficient. You can also use the Windows XP utility programs. Notepad and Wordpad both provide useful displays for a variety of text documents.

Summary

Today you learned about mobile devices. We concentrated on the laptop and the PDA because they're the devices that you'll use most often today. Future computer connectivity options will include cellular telephones and perhaps something as small as a watch or pager. The limiting factor in size today is the ability to create a connection between the device and the user. We also discussed some connectivity applications and hardware. Finally, you learned about power management, an especially important consideration for devices that run on batteries.

13

Q&A

Q: Why are so many people replacing their laptops with PDAs?

A: Laptops represent a major cost increase over the PDA. Many people who can't afford to maintain a laptop can afford to use a PDA. In addition, PDAs are both smaller and lighter than laptops, making them easier to carry. Finally, PDAs use a writing recognition interface, which is easier than a keyboard for some people to use. One of the major problems with using a PDA is that it can't replace a full PC due to limitations in application flexibility and performance. In addition, some people do prefer having a full (complete) keyboard and mouse to work with.

Q: When can I expect the major compatibility problems with PDAs to become a thing of the past?

A: The role of the PDA is evolving. In the past, people expected their PDA to manage contacts, appointments, and e-mail. Today, people expect more from their PDA, which means the underlying PDA technology must evolve as well. Several recent studies show that the Pocket PC is now becoming more popular than the Palm simply because it offers more features. The compatibility problems with PDAs won't disappear until the technology matures and people's expectations become better known.

Q: What do I do if I try to use the AT$H command and it doesn't work?

A: Older modems don't support this command. However, some do support the AT&V command, which provides similar information. In some cases, the modem vendor may provide online documentation, but this is doubtful with an older modem. Another alternative is to use the standard Hayes modem command set found at `http://www.modems.com/glossary/extend2b.html`. This is an abbreviated command set, and you may find that your modem doesn't support all of these commands. You'll find other pages of commands on this site as well.

Workshop

It's the end of the thirteenth day. You now have a good understanding of how to interface Windows XP with the devices you take on the road. Now it's time to see how much you know about laptops and handheld devices. You can find answers to the quiz and exercise questions in Appendix A at the back of the book.

Quiz

1. What's the main reason to use profiles with a laptop?
2. What's the number one problem for novice users trying to create a data connection for their PDAs?
3. How do you test a modem using HyperTerminal?

4. Which Control Panel applet controls IrDA communications?

5. How does Briefcase differ from a standard folder?

Exercises

1. If you own a laptop, create one or more additional profiles for it. Test each profile and determine how well it works in a given situation.

2. Try using HyperTerminal to create a connection between your laptop and desktop machines. If you have a Windows XP Professional Edition installation, try both the peer and the Telnet techniques.

3. Create a briefcase on your laptop and use it to move data files from work to home for the next few weeks.

13

DAY 14

Setting Up a Network with Windows XP

Most computers are part of a network in some way today. Even home users have networks so that the parents have one machine and the children another. The fact that you make a connection to the Internet to pick up e-mail, visit Web sites, and chat with other people means you're part of the world's largest network. No matter what size your network is, you'll need to manage it in order to gain the greatest benefit from it.

Today we'll look at setting up a network from a Windows XP perspective. Networking is such a complex topic that we'll spend the next five days discussing it. Today we'll discuss nuts and bolts issues. For example, you'll learn how to install protocols, clients, and services. You'll also learn how to configure low-level network resources, such as the network interface card (NIC) and Transmission Control Protocol/Internet Protocol (TCP/IP).

You'll also want to know about security issues. We'll have a whole day on security during Day 16, but today you'll learn how to configure a firewall.

Some of the best security is the type that you can configure once and then monitor from that point on. You don't need to do a lot of work to use it, just check occasionally to ensure that things are still working the way they should.

A final section will discuss *Microsoft Management Queue (MSMQ)*, also known as *Queued Components*. The two terms aren't precisely the same, but they're close enough from a user perspective that we can discuss them as a single entity. MSMQ allows you to work with specially designed applications in disconnected mode. For example, you could take orders from clients in the field and never worry about your connection with the company.

General Network Setup

It pays to know how your network is set up because you'll find that you need to change a configuration or fix some settings during your use of the computer. Your network will break down at some time. Even the best, most secure network in the world will break down because the lines of communication between computers are fragile at best.

The following sections look at four important network configuration tasks. First, you need to know the basic software used by every network to create a communication stream. Second, you need to know how to remove and disable features you don't want on your network. Third, the Achilles' heel of many networks is the Network Interface Card (NIC), so we'll spend some special time with this feature. Finally, you'll learn some basics about the Transmission Control Protocol/Internet Protocol (TCP/IP). The problems you'll experience configuring this one part of the network can often dwarf any other part.

Installing Protocols, Clients, and Services

Every network consists of three pieces of basic software: protocols, clients, and services. It's important to know what roles each piece plays in the overall network picture. The following list provides you with an overview of each piece:

- **Protocol**   A *protocol* is a set of rules that defines behavior. Protocols exist for everything in the computer world and many things in the real world as well. The purpose of a software protocol is to enable communication using a standard set of rules. Think of the protocol as a diplomat between two nations. It ensures that the two nations (computers) can communicate. Most networks have several layers of protocols that perform different tasks, so you need to be aware of the protocols that your network requires.

- **Client**   A *client* is a user of resources. Networks use clients to create an endpoint for communication. For example, when you install the Microsoft client, you're creating an endpoint for resources received from other Microsoft Windows machines. Likewise, a NetWare client acts as an endpoint for resources received from a NetWare server. Clients work by making requests that the server answers. In short, they coordinate two-way communication between your workstation and the server.

- **Service**   A *service* is a background task the network needs in order to provide resources to a client. Some services facilitate data transfers between two different operating systems. Other services monitor the client computer and send data back to the server for statistical analysis. Special services help a machine advertise the resources it can provide, while others browse the network looking for resources the client needs. In short, the service is the workhorse of the network.

Now that you have a better idea of what the three networking components are, it's important to understand that they interact with each other. For example, many older NetWare networks rely on the Internet Packet Exchange/Sequential Packet Exchange (IPX/SPX) protocol. If you install Client Services for NetWare, Windows XP will automatically install IPX/SPX support as well, even if you don't need it. (We'll see how to overcome this problem in the "Removing Versus Disabling Features" section.)

Note   Many of you will be looking for Network Basic Input/Output System (NETBIOS) Extended User Interface (NetBEUI) support in Windows XP. This protocol doesn't appear as one of the standard options because Microsoft is phasing out support for it. You can find the required installation files in the \VALUEADD\MSFT\NET\NETBEUI folder of the distribution CD. To add NetBEUI support, copy the NBF.SYS file to your \WINDOWS\SYSTEM32\DRIVERS\ folder and the NETNBF.INF file to your \WINDOWS\INF\ folder. Follow the standard installation process found in this section to install NetBEUI support.

All of this background leads to the discussion of installing and removing network protocols, clients, and services. You must exercise care when working with the network. Removing a service you don't need seems like a good idea until it also removes a client that you do need. Suddenly, the network stops working, and you need to get it back in operation. The following steps show you how to add a service, client, or protocol:

1. Right-click My Network Places and choose Properties from the context menu. You'll see the Network Connections dialog box.

2. Right-click the Local Area Connection icon and choose Properties from the context menu. You'll see the Local Area Connection Properties dialog box shown in Figure

14

14.1. The Local Area Connection Properties dialog box contains a list of all the clients, protocols, and services installed on your system. Notice that this dialog box allows you to install and uninstall network components. You can also configure network components and the NIC for your system. Finally, the option at the bottom of the dialog box enables you to display a network icon for this connection in the Notification Area of the taskbar.

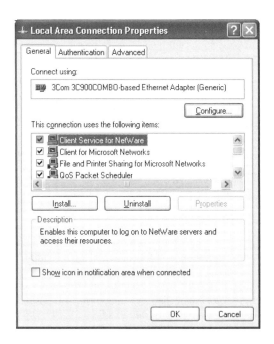

3. Click Install. You'll see a Select Network Component Type dialog box like the one shown in Figure 14.2. Notice the symbols next to each component type. You can use these symbols to identify network component types later. The names that Microsoft and third-party vendors use aren't always descriptive, so knowing the symbols may be your only way of identifying a network function.

4. Select a component type. Click Add. Windows XP will display a list of components of the type that you want to install. The Have Disk button enables you to choose third-party components from another location.

5. Highlight the component you want to install and click OK. Windows XP will begin the installation process. You may have to select configuration options during the installation process. Windows XP may also ask you to supply disks. It always pays to have the Windows XP CD available, as well as any third-party products you might have installed in the past.

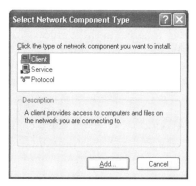

FIGURE 14.2

Knowing the symbols for clients, services, and protocols can help identify entries later.

6. Follow any remaining installation instructions. Reboot the machine if necessary. Note that Windows XP will seldom ask you to reboot the machine. This is one of the benefits of using this operating system.

Removing Versus Disabling Features

As previously mentioned, you need to remove networking features with care under Windows XP. A component you don't need may have a connection to a component you do need. Removing one component will remove them both.

Generally, it's safe to remove components that you install as add-ons to the networking environment. For example, the Service Advertising Protocol (SAP) service and the Network Monitor Driver protocol both fall into this category. It's also safe to remove features when your network configuration changes. For example, you no longer need a NetWare client when you retire the last server on your network.

To remove a networking feature, open the Local Area Connection Properties dialog box, highlight the feature you want to remove, and click Uninstall. In most cases, Windows XP will simply remove the component after it verifies that you want to do so. You may have to reboot your machine in some cases. It's also important to disconnect from any mapped drives or any other resource provided by a discontinued client connection, such as a printer.

Windows XP also provides a means for disabling a network component that you need to leave installed but don't require for normal network operation. For example, Windows XP will always install IPX/SPX support for a NetWare network, even if you set up your server for TCP/IP operation. In this case, you can't remove the unneeded support because Windows XP will also remove the NetWare client. However, you can clear the check mark for the IPX/SPX support to disable it.

14

Disabling a network feature means that the driver remains installed, but Windows XP doesn't load it into memory or start it during the boot process. You save the memory and processing cycles used by the network feature. The only thing you lose is the drive space required for the feature and associated files.

NIC Configuration

You normally configure your NIC one time, during installation. In fact, Windows XP normally configures the NIC for you. However, you may run into situations where you need to reconfigure the NIC to allow addition of a new feature on your machine. Some NIC vendors provide diagnostics as part of the configuration dialog box. Most NICs also include advanced features that you can use to improve machine performance. Windows XP turns these features off by default.

You access the NIC configuration features by clicking Configure in the Local Area Connection Properties dialog box. The Device Manager also provides access to the NIC configuration features. Figure 14.3 shows a typical example of the Advanced tab of the NIC Properties dialog box. (This NIC doesn't provide any diagnostics as part of the driver setup.)

FIGURE 14.3

The Advanced tab of a NIC Properties dialog box is where you set up advanced features.

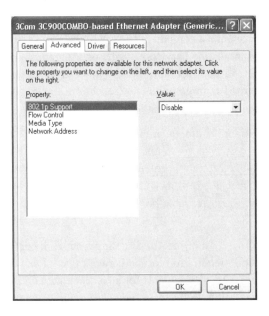

Figure 14.3 shows several interesting features for this NIC, which is using the default Windows XP configuration. The first entry is for 802.1p Support. This works with the Quality of Service (QOS) Packet Scheduler support that Windows XP installs in a default

configuration. (You can read more about 802.1p support in the Windows operating system at `http://support.microsoft.com/support/kb/articles/Q222/0/20.ASP`.) Notice that Windows XP turns this support off by default. If you turn this support on when using a switched Ethernet network, you'll notice a very small improvement in network traffic. On today's heavily loaded networks, even a small improvement is helpful. However, make sure that you have an Ethernet switch, not an Ethernet hub, on your network.

Combo NICs, those that support more than one connection type, will often provide a Media Type entry on the Advanced tab of the NIC Properties dialog box. The options for this setting will select a particular media feature for the NIC, including the connection type. Sometimes, Windows XP will tell you that the NIC is working, but it has no connection to the network. Try using the Media Type entry to direct Windows XP's attention to the correct connection on the NIC. Normally, Windows XP will make the correct connection after you make the change.

Tip

Figuring out all of the entries on the Advanced tab takes time because Windows XP provides little assistance in this area. For that matter, you won't find much help in many vendor manuals. However, using the same model NIC in all your workstations often helps reduce the work required to research these settings. If you can't obtain the same model for all of the workstations in your network, using NICs from the same vendor will often help. Vendors tend to support a specific set of features across their product line. In addition, the vendor will often provide the same functionality in their drivers, making it easier to transition from one model to the next.

Another interesting feature is flow control. You'll want to make sure that you enable this feature. Using flow control prevents a variety of packet errors. Fortunately, Windows XP normally enables this setting by default.

TCP/IP Configuration

Let's begin this discussion by saying that Windows XP will normally take care of TCP/IP configuration needs for small networks without any input from you. I say normally because I've seen more than my share of strange TCP/IP occurrences over the years. In fact, I've seen TCP/IP connections work one day and fail the next without any apparent reason (there always is a reason; it just remains hidden). With this in mind, you need to know about basic TCP/IP configuration if for no other reason than to fix your system when it does fail.

14

Many administrators make TCP/IP configuration a dark secret that only they can understand. Actually, TCP/IP is relatively easy to understand after you learn a few basic principles.

The two parts of a TCP/IP configuration are the address and the subnet mask. The address consists of four fields with values from 0 to 255. The subnet mask also contains four fields, but each field only has values of 0 or 255. Figure 14.4 shows a typical example of the Internet Protocol (TCP/IP) Properties dialog box with an address and subnet mask. (Normally, this dialog box doesn't contain any information because you'll select the Obtain an IP address automatically and Obtain DNS server address automatically options.) You can access this dialog box by highlighting the Internet Protocol (TCP/IP) entry in the Local Area Connection Properties dialog box and clicking Properties.

FIGURE 14.4

The Internet Protocol (TCP/IP) Properties dialog box contains configuration settings for your TCP/IP connection.

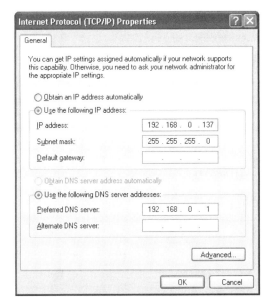

> **Tip**
>
> This section describes the version of IP currently used by Windows XP. Microsoft plans to support IP Version 6 when it becomes generally available. You can read a primer on IP Version 6 at http://www.microsoft.com/ TechNet/itsolutions/network/maintain/security/ipvers6.asp. IP Version 6 will provide a wealth of new features, including a larger address space. The current IP implementation is running out of addresses as the Internet expands.

The combination of address and subnet mask entries defines specific elements of the IP connection. The IP connection consists of an organization and an individual computer within that organization. The IP address contains the organization and computer number, and the subnet mask determines the purpose of each number. For example, if you have an IP address of 192.168.0.112 and a subnet mask of 255.255.255.0, the organization number is 192.168.0 and the machine number is 112. The value 255 in a subnet mask specifies an organization, and a value of 0 specifies a machine number.

You can delve a lot deeper into IP addresses, but there are only two other pieces of information that you really need to know to configure most computers. The first is that the Internet assigns two numbers for internal organization use: 192.168.0.XXX and 169.254.XXX.XXX. Windows will default to the 169.254.XXX.XXX setting if you have TCP/IP installed, but no Domain Name Server (DNS) or Dynamic Host Configuration Protocol (DHCP) server. It defaults to the 192.168.0.XXX setting for systems with a DNS and DHCP server. This includes systems with Internet Connection Sharing (ICS) installed and enabled. Of course, nothing stops you from using other addresses on your network; these are simply the recommended addresses and the ones that Windows uses as a default.

Note

> Although ICS includes a DHCP allocator and a DNS proxy, you can't adjust them to other settings. ICS uses a "hard-wired" setting because Microsoft designed it to work on small networks. If you want full control over the DNS and DHCP setups, you'll need to install these features on a Windows server.

Notice that the bottom of the Internet Protocol (TCP/IP) Properties dialog box shown in Figure 14.4 contains preferred and alternate DNS server entries. If you're using ICS, the Preferred DNS Server field will always contain 192.168.0.1 when you configure the fields manually. Otherwise, check with your network administrator for the TCP/IP address of the DNS server. Depending on the size of your network, the DNS server address might be the same as the address for the server that you use for every other purpose.

Configuring a Personal Firewall

Windows XP includes a new feature called a *personal firewall*. A *firewall* prevents certain types of access to your machine. It isn't unstoppable; a firewall just delays some crackers and keeps honest people honest. In other words, look at a personal firewall as a hurdle the cracker must jump, rather than the ultimate in personal security. Only by using a combination of tools and keeping a close eye on your network can you keep it safe.

14

You enable the personal firewall by checking the firewall option on the Advanced tab of the Local Area Connection Properties dialog box. However, enabling this option isn't the end of the road. You still need to configure the personal firewall by clicking Settings at the bottom of the Advanced tab. You'll see an Advanced Settings dialog box similar to the one shown in Figure 14.5.

FIGURE 14.5

The Advanced Settings dialog box helps you configure the personal firewall.

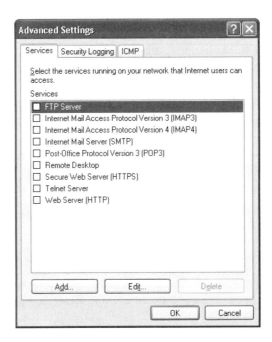

The Services tab shown in Figure 14.5 contains a list of standard Web services. Why are these services important? Previously, I mentioned that you contact other machines using an IP address. The address enables contact with the machine but doesn't provide access to services the machine may provide. To do that, you need a port number. Every service monitors one or more ports on your machine. For example, if you run a Web server on your machine and want other people to access it, you need to open port 80. A personal firewall protects your machine by keeping as many ports as possible closed. Opening a port exposes your machine to risk, but the risk is necessary if your machine provides services that other people need. The reason that the Services tab contains these entries is that they use standard port numbers. If you have a small network and don't provide any Web services to anyone outside the company, leave all of these options cleared.

Sometimes, you need to add an entry to the Services tab. For example, many Web sites include an Administrator site that uses a different port number than the main Web site does for security reasons. If you want to allow the administrator to access this site from home, you need to add a new entry to the Services list by clicking Add. The Service Settings dialog box will ask you to provide a name for your service, the IP address, the internal port number, and the external port number. You can also choose between the TCP and the User Datagram Protocol (UDP) transport methods. For small networks, the IP address is the same as the IP address of your server. The internal and external port numbers are normally the same. You'll find the port number on the configuration tab for the service. Most small networks rely exclusively on TCP as a transport protocol, but it pays to check the configuration for the service.

The Security Logging tab appears in Figure 14.6. Notice that this tab contains entries for logging both dropped and successful connections. Knowing who's logging onto your system is important in an age when crackers appear to jump the firewall hurdle with little effort. At least a log entry will tell you who's accessing your system so that you can stop them. Monitoring is part of the security process that's essential today. Notice that the Size Limit field helps keep the size of the log under control so that you don't find your hard drive filled with connection entries.

FIGURE 14.6

The Security Logging tab is one key to monitoring your system for break-ins.

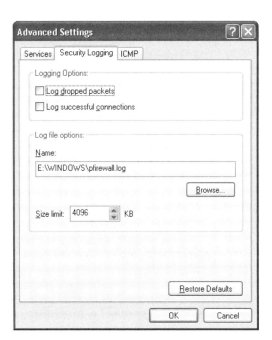

14

Tip

Crackers often look for the defaults on your system. They look for default accounts with poor security to break into your system. They look for default settings that allow them to thwart your security. Finally, they look for default logs they can edit to hide their tracks. Always use logging to track access to your system. However, hide the log in something other than the default directory and use a different filename that only you know. If you have multiple machines to maintain, use a different log name on each machine to make it harder for the cracker to find your logs. Don't make one machine the key to your entire system.

The Internet Control Message Protocol (ICMP) tab appears in Figure 14.7. Use this tab to control the types of information that a remote computer can request. IP is notoriously unreliable, so vendors require a method for gathering status information. In short, ICMP doesn't make IP more reliable; it just makes it possible for others to find out if IP failed to do its job.

FIGURE 14.7

ICMP provides a means for determining the IP status of your system.

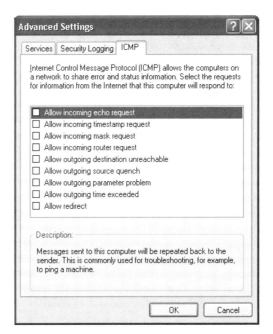

Note

ICMP is a standardized means of accessing IP status. You can find out more about it by reading RFC792 (http://www.faqs.org/rfcs/rfc792.html). IP Version 6 uses the RFC1885 version of ICMP

> (http://www.faqs.org/rfcs/rfc1885.html). If you'd rather know just
> the basics from a Windows perspective, check the Knowledge Base article at
> http://support.microsoft.com/support/kb/articles/Q170/2/92.A
> SP. Another excellent write-up appears at
> http://lib.nevalink.ru/tcp_stevens/icmp_int.htm.

One of the ways that crackers will begin a Denial of Service (DoS) attack on a computer system is to issue ICMP requests. The computer ends up spending all of its time trying to answer these requests. The result is a system that's incapable of doing anything because there isn't any bandwidth. Unless you actually need remote status information for your computer, always leave these options cleared. Of course, there are many other ways to start a DoS attack. All you're doing is removing one more tool from the cracker arsenal by setting up your system correctly.

Configuring Authentication Options

Authentication, knowing who's at the other end of the wire, is a critical part of the security setup for a computer. Windows XP provides authentication options on the Authentication tab of the Local Area Connection Properties dialog box. This tab looks relatively simple, but it's important to know how it works to ensure that you authenticate others before you trust them with access to your system.

Windows XP assumes that you want at least a modicum of authentication to take place, so it always enables the first option on this dialog box, Enable network access control using IEEE 802.1X (http://www.ieee802.org/1/pages/802.1x.html). All this means is that someone needs some form of identification to access your system, which includes a smart card, digital certificate, password, or biometrics. The RFC2284 Extensible Authentication Protocol (http://www.faqs.org/rfcs/rfc2284.html) or EAP field contains entries that determine the type of authentication that Windows XP allows. The default type is using a smart card or other certificate. You can also choose the RFC1994 MD5 challenge mechanism (http://www.faqs.org/rfcs/rfc1994.html), also known as the Point-to-Point Protocol (PPP) Challenge Handshake Authentication Protocol (CHAP).

You can further define the Smart Card or Other Certificate option by clicking Properties. You'll see a Smart Card or Other Certificate Properties dialog box. The first option on this dialog box chooses between certificate and smart card operation, with certificate as the default. The Validate Server Certificate option forces the server to provide credentials to your computer. Other options include the capability to set a specific server name as a

14

connection point, a choice of trusted root authority, and the capability to use another username for the connection.

The Authentication tab contains two additional options. You can choose to authenticate the user and the computer. This means that someone can't pose as the user unless they also copy the machine credentials. In addition, you can force a guest logon when you can't identify the user or when computer information is unavailable. This still allows users access to your machine but limits what they can do (the more limited, the better).

Identification Alternatives to Logging In

A user name and password are normally the only forms of identification that a user needs to gain access to your server. In most cases, that's all you really need to ensure that the data on your system remains secure. However, crackers easily compromise passwords, so they may not be secure enough. Users often choose easy passwords, forget them, or, worse yet, write them down for the whole world to see.

Even if everyone at a company does his best to protect security, crackers often find ways around the security measures you have in place. Just the fact that your security relies on a password means that someone can guess the password, given enough time and opportunity. In other words, using the name and password method of security is problematic at best.

Some companies are combating these problems by using other methods. One of the more common methods is the use of smart cards. A smart card is a credit card-sized device with some processing power built in. The user swipes the card in a special reader to gain access to the network. The card provides a digital certificate that identifies the user instead of a password.

A smart card eliminates the problem of compromised passwords. Without a password lying around, it would take a concerted effort by a cracker or inside party to break network security. However, a smart card can still be lost and used by someone who knows where the card is used and to whom it belongs. In addition, the issuing company has to bear the cost of providing and maintaining the cards, which could be an expensive proposition.

Biometrics is another alternative for many companies today. It's a statistical method of scanning an individual's unique characteristics and using these characteristics for identification. Some of the scanned characteristics include voiceprints, irises, fingerprints, hands, and facial features. The two most popular elements are irises and fingerprints because they're the two that most people know about. The advantages of using biometrics are obvious. Not only can't the user lose their identifying information, but also crackers can't compromise the identifying information.

There are two main problems with using biometrics: quality and price. Some managers don't want to use biometrics because of the time it takes to create quality scans that ensure absolute accuracy. In addition, the price for a single scanner can range from $100.00 for something simple to thousands of dollars for complex solutions. Considering the number of access points a typical company has, the price of using biometrics for all but the most stringent security requirements could be prohibitive.

One of the most popular systems, the IriScan System, can scan the iris of an individual using a camera instead of direct contact. The codes for the scanned individuals are stored in a Microsoft Access database. You can find out more about IriScan, Inc. at: `http://www.iriscan.com/main.html`.

If your company prefers to use fingerprints instead of other biometric techniques to enforce security, you might want to look at the fingerprint reader solutions provided by Veridicom, Inc. (`http://www.veridicom.com/`).

A few other biometric product dealers include Saflink Corp. (`http://www.saflink.com/`), Visionics Corp. (`http://www.faceit.com/`), and Keyware Technologies (`http://www.keyware.be/`). All of these companies provide various biometric products that can make your network just a bit more secure from prying eyes.

Special Hardware Considerations

Networks often use special hardware that you won't find on a stand-alone machine. We've already discussed one type of special hardware, the printer with a direct Ethernet connection (see the "Printer" section of Chapter 10 for details). We won't discuss some types of hardware in this book because they require special handling under Windows XP or you'll manage them using special software. For example, we won't discuss the inner workings of hubs and switches.

We'll discuss two types of special hardware that Windows XP does control directly in the following sections. The oldest type of network device is a common peripheral, such as a printer that includes an Ethernet card. Generally, you have to tell Windows XP that these devices exist, perform some type of specialized configuration, and hope that everything works as expected. Newer network hardware provides automatic configuration features similar to those found in peripherals for your machine. Universal Plug and Play makes it possible for Windows XP to discover compatible network hardware and configure it automatically.

Working with Network-Ready Devices

Network-ready devices are often standard peripherals, such as printers and scanners, which include a built-in network card. A few vendors also distribute shared disk systems that fall into this category. The two defining characteristics for a network-ready device are that it provides its own network connection and it's platform independent. In addition, Windows XP users can add the requirement for special configuration to the list. The device has a name of some sort that you use to access it through a TCP/IP connection.

14

Most people would also consider a generic use requirement for a network-ready device. For example, while disk storage technology, such as a Storage Area Network (SAN) or Network Attached Storage (NAS), might connect directly to a network, many people wouldn't consider them network-ready devices because you still access them through a server. In this case, the disk storage provided by a SAN or NAS requires the protection the server can provide. They don't represent generic devices that anyone can use.

The reason that network-ready devices are so popular is that you can share a device with everyone on the network without buying a server. All you need is some cable, a hub, and the devices you want to share. When you connect your workstation to the network, you have access to the new device. These devices usually provide a simple interface for configuration and don't cost very much. In short, this is the perfect solution for many small business and home user needs.

Whenever you work with a Network-Ready Device, you're working with a client/server relationship. Your workstation is a client making a request of the server (the device). The same types of problems that occur in any client/server relationship can occur with your network-ready device. For example, you need the proper rights to use the device. Security is the same no matter where you implement it.

You'll find that network-ready devices do impose a few additional problems that you need to consider when working with them. The following list represents the problems that most people run into, although you may find a few problems not listed here:

- **Special Configuration Software**   Most network-ready devices use specially optimized operating systems that allow them to work faster than a device attached to a server. Because the device lacks a console of the type you'll find on a server, you normally have to configure the device by using a control panel or special software. In many situations, the special software creates havoc on the client and doesn't communicate well with the server (the network-ready device). For example, a browser-based setup program might be incompatible with your browser, denying you direct access to the device. Make sure that you can obtain support for the device software before you buy the device.

- **Odd Hardware Requirements**   Surprising as it may seem, you have to exercise extreme care when buying network-enabled devices. For example, you need to verify what type of network connection the device will support at the time of purchase. One person I know needed a network printer that would work on a coaxial Ethernet (10Base-2) network. The picture of the product showed the BNC connection needed for the network connection, and the description said that the device provided this connection. When the device arrived, it only provided a twisted pair (10Base-T) connection, not the anticipated coaxial connection. It turns out that the vendor's Web site contained outdated information, and the vendor had discontinued the required connection. This problem happens in other ways to other network-ready devices.

- **Lack of Windows XP-Specific Drivers**   Many people will buy network-ready devices thinking they'll use them with every version of Windows on their network. The problem is that these devices still require drivers on your system in order for you to use them. Unfortunately, unless you buy a mainstream product, you might find that driver support is lacking. This is especially true for Windows XP because it's the new kid on the block. Don't assume that Windows 2000 drivers will work with your Windows XP installation, either. In many cases, you'll need a Windows XP-specific driver to use the network-ready device.

- **Difficulty Locating the Device**   One of the most common problems that people run into with network-ready devices is finding them. Sure, you can physically see the device connected to the network, and you know that it's on, but for some reason, you can't connect to it. In many cases, the problem is relatively simple to locate and fix. The vendor may not have seated the network card properly in the device, the device may have powered down automatically, or the network cable may be broken. In other cases, you need to reconfigure the device using the control panel because it has the wrong IP address or other problems. However, some devices will drive you crazy finding what's wrong. For example, it may have a power-down mode where it looks like it's on, but it refuses to acknowledge network requests.

- **Special Requirements or Needs**   Vendors keep producing more network-ready devices all the time. The good thing about innovation is that you gain additional flexibility from your network. The bad thing about innovation is that it usually turns out to be a nonstandard way of accomplishing the task. For example, many companies today produce home control systems that use your PC. You control lights and other house elements using computer software and some sensors. At least a few of them use the standard X-10 home automation system. However, innovations abound, which means compatibility problems abound.

Tip

Home automation isn't just for electronics enthusiasts; it also comes in handy for home businesses or even small businesses that want to get a handle on energy costs. An automation system can help you improve the energy efficiency of your business by intelligently controlling lighting and other systems. For those of you who are interested in home automation, check out http://www.x10.com/ for ideas on what's available. You can read a discussion of someone who's actually implemented an energy-efficient design at

14

http://www.redoak.co.uk/. Another interesting X-10 site that contains tips and links is http://www.leroygibbons.com/.

Using Universal Plug and Play

Windows XP includes support for Universal Plug and Play (http://www.upnp.org/), which is actually a step up from a network-ready device. The device has the same requirements that we discussed in the "Working with Network-Ready Devices" section. You still need a network connection, and the device is usually of the general-purpose printer, disk drive, or scanner type. Some vendors even plan to create Universal Plug and Play versions of CD jukeboxes.

You can sum up the difference between Universal Plug and Play and network-ready devices in one word: automation. Instead of actively looking for the device, the device actively looks for you. All that your workstation needs is the ability to detect the Universal Plug and Play device. As soon as the operating system and the device make contact, Windows XP presents a message in the notification area of the taskbar telling you the device is available. In addition, Windows XP displays any Universal Plug and Play devices that it finds in My Network Places.

Some of the same problems that plague network-ready devices also plague Universal Plug and Play devices. For example, broken network cables or odd configuration software will cause problems because you still need the connectivity they provide. However, you won't have as many problems finding the device because it actively searches for your machine. In addition, because these devices are newer, you'll run into fewer problems finding Windows XP-specific drivers.

Universal Plug and Play devices have several advantages for mobile users as well. When using a network-ready device, the mobile user needs to install support by locating the device, just as any desktop user would. However, when using Universal Plug and Play, the devices are automatically available to the mobile user with sufficient rights to use them. This means that guests using your network won't have to entirely reconfigure their systems just to access a network printer.

Windows XP doesn't come with Universal Plug and Play support installed. You'll find it in the Networking Services folder of the Windows Component Wizard. You don't have to perform any special installation steps; just use the procedure found in the "Adding and Removing Programs" section of Day 9. Universal Plug and Play doesn't require any configuration beyond that needed for the device.

When you install Universal Plug and Play, you'll notice that Windows XP doesn't start the Universal Plug and Play Device Host service right away. That's because this technology relies on the Simple Service Discovery Protocol (SSDP) Discovery Service (http://www.globecom.net/ietf/draft/draft-cai-ssdp-v1-01.html) to search for new devices. SSDP is a multicast protocol that provides two message types: OPTIONS and ANNOUNCE. The client issues the OPTIONS message to ask all of the servers on the network if they provide a certain service. The server uses the ANNOUNCE message to tell all of the clients that it provides a given service. Between the two message types, your machine will locate a service that it needs in the form of a Universal Plug and Play device. When the SSDP Discovery Service sees a Universal Plug and Play device, it starts the Universal Plug and Play Device Host.

Simple Network Management Protocol

The Simple Network Management Protocol (SNMP) is a means of monitoring the status of network devices. For example, you can use SNMP to monitor the status of your server over a TCP/IP connection. It doesn't matter if the server uses Windows or not, just that it supports SNMP. The use of agents allows the server to gather information about client status and collect it for administrator use as well. In short, SNMP enables you to learn more about your network using a platform-independent communication protocol.

Tip   Microsoft provides a wealth of information about Windows XP SNMP in the form of Knowledge Base articles. You'll find a good overview of SNMP at http://www.cisco.com/univercd/cc/td/doc/cisintwk/ito_doc/snmp.htm. This site includes some SNMP 2.0 information, as well as the SNMP 1.0 support provided by many older systems. You'll also want to learn about the standards documents including RFC1157 (http://www.faqs.org/rfcs/rfc1157.html).

You should consider SNMP as part of the basic TCP/IP package, even though Microsoft supports it as an add-on for Windows XP. SNMP is an older technology that first appeared in the computer world in the early 80s. SNMP 1.0 provides a simple response that indicates whether a piece of equipment is operating correctly. Standards efforts for SNMP 2.0 are under way, but the usual politics have stalled efforts on that front. SNMP 2.0 will provide a greater range of device information, enabling network administrators to proactively monitor device status. Because of the SNMP 2.0 delay, at least a few vendors now rely on a related technology called *Remote Monitoring (RMON)*.

14

Installing SNMP Support

Installing SNMP is easy. You'll find the Simple Network Management Protocol option in the Management and Monitoring Tools folder in Windows Component Wizard. You don't have to perform any special installation steps; just use the procedure found in the "Adding and Removing Programs" section of Day 9. SNMP doesn't require any special installation configuration. However, you'll want to perform a few service-related configuration tasks after you complete the installation.

Let's begin with the SNMP Service. The SNMP Service Properties dialog box contains the same General, Log On, Recovery, and Dependencies tabs as every other service. You'll also find a Security tab that works much the same as the security tabs found in a few of the other services. However, the Security tab also has a special purpose, in this case, that we'll discuss later in the section. Windows XP defaults to allowing the public read-only privileges to any information that SNMP can provide.

The Agent tab shown in Figure 14.8 is one of the main points of interest for the SNMP Service Properties dialog box. Figure 14.8 shows the Windows XP defaults for this service. As a minimum, you'll want to add contact and location information to the appropriate fields of the dialog box. SNMP sends this information along with any status information it provides to a remote location.

Notice the list of services on the Agent tab. The default settings show what Windows XP installs for you. However, if you install any third-party agents, you'll likely need to change these settings. For example, if you add an agent for controlling the hard drive, you'll want to check the Physical option.

The SNMP Service Properties dialog box also contains a Traps tab that you use to configure traps for your system. A trap is a piece of software that captures an event, such as an error, from one of the devices on the network that supports SNMP. In short, a trap is a way to receive system events. Windows XP will normally use the event log to hold trapped events. However, many third-party utilities, such as SNMP Trap Watcher

FIGURE 14.8

Use the Agent tab to configure the SNMP service to provide additional information about your system.

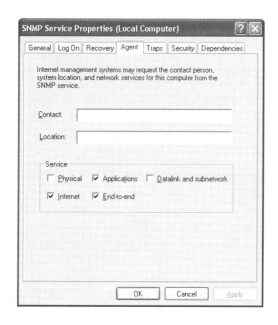

(http://www.bttsoftware.co.uk/snmptrap.html), will filter trapped SNMP messages and display them in an easy-to-read format reminiscent of Event Viewer.

The Traps tab contains two fields. The Community Name field acts as a sort of password. If another machine wants to trap the messages sent by the SNMP host, it must know the community name that you use in this dialog box. After you add a community name, you can add a list of machine names or IP addresses to the Trap Destinations field. These machines will receive every trap message generated by your machine.

If you want to receive trap messages from other machines, you configure them on the Security tab. To add a new community to the list, click Add. You'll see an SNMP Service Configuration dialog box. Type the community name in the Community Name field and select a level of access for that community from the Community Rights list box.

You'll see a second SNMP service in the Services MMC snap-in called *SNMP Trap Service*. Normally, Windows XP stops this service because the system doesn't need it. However, if you set a trap, the service should start to provide monitoring for that trap. This service doesn't provide any configuration options beyond those normally provided for a service.

14

Note

You normally can't run the SNMP Trap Service and a third-party product, such as SNMP Trap Watcher, at the same time. If you see a message from the third-party product saying it can't bind to the trap port (162), then you need to stop the SNMP Trap Service. Make sure that you restart the third-party product to ensure that it hears any trap message sent by a server.

Creating Traps

At this point, you have a service that's ready to trap some events and pass them along using SNMP. The only problem is that you don't have any traps configured, and it's apparent that none of the entries on the Start menu will help. Open the Run dialog box and type **EVNTWIN** in the Open field. Click OK, and you'll see the Event to Trap Translator dialog box. Select the Custom option so that you can create some traps for your machine. Figure 14.9 shows a typical Event to Trap Translator display.

FIGURE 14.9

The Event to Trap Translator helps you to create traps for your system.

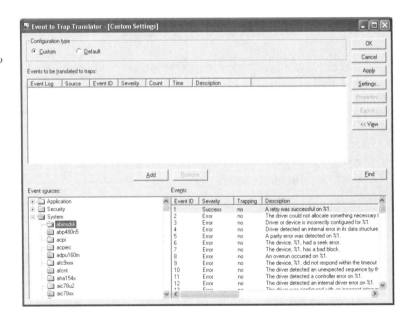

Notice the Event Sources list, which is a hierarchical display of event sources that follows the logs in Event Viewer. Select any of the entries in this list, and you'll see a list of events in the Events list. You can trap any of these events using SNMP, which includes a lot of ground.

Of course, figuring out what to monitor can boggle the mind, especially when you go into the Application folder. For example, many motherboard-monitor utilities, such as Motherboard Monitor (http://mbm.livewiredev.com/), include events that you can monitor by using SNMP. This utility works with many vendor motherboards, including those from Asus, and provides detailed information about motherboard status. You could set up an SNMP message for every machine on your network that tells you when the motherboard experiences an error. However, you can monitor everything from the starting and stopping of services to the documents that users print. The choice is up to you.

When you find an event that you want to monitor using SNMP, highlight it and click Add. You'll see a Properties dialog box. Use this dialog box to set the number of events required to generate an SNMP message (the default is 1). It also allows you to set a time interval within which the event count has to reach the specified level. Click OK.

While Event to Trap Translator is a great tool for creating SNMP entries, it's not the end of the line. You need to export the entries you create to a text file. Event to Trap Translator uses a default of EVENTS.CNF as the output file. You'll find it easier if you use EVENTS.TXT as the output file because then you can create the required changes using Notepad. Highlight all of the entries that you want to export, click Export, type a filename, and then click Save. Event to Trap Translator will export the entries to a text file.

Tip

Asking SNMP to track certain events is only good as long as the device generates events. For example, if you want to track form changes for the printers on your system, you need to select the Log spooler information events option on the Advanced tab of the Print Server Properties dialog box. You access this dialog box using the File | Server Properties command in the Printers and Faxes applet.

At this point, you have a text file containing what you'd like SNMP to track. However, we still need a destination for the information. The community you set up on the Traps and Security tab is the destination for the information we're creating now. The way to add a destination is to add a special command to the text file created by Event to Trap Translator. Here are the source entries I'm using as an example:

```
#pragma add System "Print" 2147483654 1 0
#pragma add System "Print" 1073741834 1 0
#pragma add System "Print" 1073741839 1 0
#pragma add Application "MBM" 2147483906 1 0
#pragma add Application "MBM" 1073742081 1 0
#pragma add Application "MBM" 3221225728 1 0
#pragma add_trap_dest MySNMP Main
```

14

Event to Trap Translator generated all of the source entries in this text file except the last one. That line tells SNMP where to send the information. All you need to provide is the name of the community you created and the name of the machine that hosts that community. Make any required changes to your file and save it to disk.

You need to learn about one last utility for SNMP. The character mode EVNTCMD utility makes the changes to SNMP. Simply type **EVNTCMD <Name of Event File>** at the command prompt and press Enter. EVNTCMD will read your file, perform the required commands, and restart SNMP. Figure 14.10 shows some typical SNMP output from SNMP Trap Watcher when using the source entries shown earlier in this section.

FIGURE 14.10

Using an SNMP monitor, such as SNMP Trap Watcher, shows you just the SNMP output from your machine.

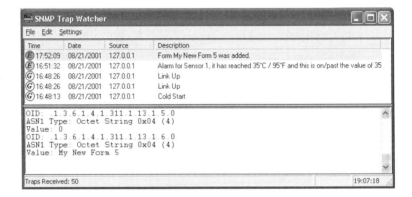

Using the Routing Information Protocol (RIP) Listener

Network traffic management means transferring data from a source to a receiver. Large networks typically include *routers*, devices that transfer data from one network segment to another. Each router has routing tables that help it determine where to send the information. Think of the routing tables as telephone directories for the router. Routers and servers use routing information protocol (RIP) to output routing table information at regular intervals, or if there's a change to the network topology.

Tip

You can learn the details about RIP from a variety of sources. For example, you'll find a detailed discussion of RIP at http://www.cisco.com/uni-vercd/cc/td/doc/cisintwk/ito_doc/rip.htm. RIP comes in two versions. The version 1 specification is defined in RFC1058 (http://www.faqs.org/rfcs/rfc1058.html), while the version 2

specification appears in RFC1723
(http://www.faqs.org/rfcs/rfc1723.html). Unfortunately, the RIP Listener only works with RIP Version 1. You'll need to use the Routing and Remote Access Service (RRAS) to gain RIP Version 2 support.

Your machine also includes a routing table. It's not responsible for outputting routing tables, but it can listen to the routing information and use it to update its internal routing tables. The RIP Listener serves this function. It enables your machine to communicate faster with remote network machines in some circumstances. For example, if your machine is in a satellite office, the RIP Listener could help it talk to the main office a bit faster.

Windows XP doesn't install RIP Listener support by default, and you should check with the network administrator before installing it on your machine. Remember that this technology is only useful for large networks. RIP Listener support appears in the Networking Services folder of the Windows Components Wizard dialog box. You don't have to perform any special installation steps; just use the procedure found in the "Adding and Removing Programs" section of Day 9.

Working with Queued Components

Microsoft has so many names for Queued Components that you might get dizzy just thinking about it. Older versions of Windows use Microsoft Management Queue (MSMQ) to refer to a related version of this product that's actually bundled in as part of Queued Components. From a user perspective, both Queued Components and MSMQ perform the same tasks. Under Windows XP, you'll install a feature named *Message Queuing*, which Windows calls Queued Components. You'll see at least three names for this technology that does one thing well—it creates a messaged environment for disconnected applications.

Queued Components could revolutionize the way you work with Windows XP. For that matter, it could become the basis of an entirely new way to write applications. The fact that many companies are already creating and using disconnected applications shows that this is a viable technology. Consider the case of PeopleSoft support for sales people on the road. The use of disconnected applications allows employees to work even when they lack a network connection. You can find out more at http://iwsun4.infoworld.com/articles/hn/xml/01/08/20/010820hnpsoft.xml.

Now that you have a better idea of why Queued Components are useful, let's discuss them in a little more detail. The following sections will help you understand what

14

Queued Components can do for you as a user. In addition, we'll discuss what you need to do to use applications that rely on Queued Components.

What Are Queued Components?

Queued Components are the messaging arm of the COM+ strategy for Microsoft. It allows applications to do things that would have been impossible in the past. One of the areas in which Queued Components helps is communications. Windows XP sends and receives COM+ requests and responses as messages. This means that all COM+ really needs is a message queue in which to place the message. Queued Components places such queues on both the server and the client and then provides a method for transferring data in these queues between the two machines without the user's assistance. The server and the client don't really need to connect directly as long as they pick up their messages.

As a user, you'll first learn about Queued Components as a means for creating a disconnected application, one that doesn't require a server connection to perform tasks such as order entry. It helps to look at this messaging arrangement in the same way that you look at e-mail on the Internet. You can have a conversation with an associate using e-mail without directly contacting that associate. The use of e-mail allows both of you to communicate ideas and learn new ways of doing things. Likewise, disconnected applications can use the Queued Components queues to hold a conversation with the server. Obviously, there has to be some way to exchange the information between the queues. Again, it's easy to look at Internet e-mail as a means for understanding how Queued Components works. Although you can answer your e-mail offline, you eventually need to go online to upload the responses that you create to the ISP's server. The same thing happens with a disconnected application using Queued Components.

Microsoft had to provide four features in Queued Components to make it a useful technology. The following list describes these four features and tells you why they're important:

- **Delivery Guarantees** Unless Queued Components guarantees delivery of messages, there's no way to ensure that the server or client will actually receive query responses. Without a guaranteed communication, the application would be unreliable. In sum, a guarantee of delivery, no matter how long such delivery takes, is a requirement for robust, reliable applications that ensure that you obtain the same results whether you're connected to or disconnected from the server.

- **Routing** *Routing* is the process of moving messages from one location to another without knowing which path they'll take. You might require a dial-up connection over a modem on one day and a direct network connection the next. As a result, it's up to Queued Components to ensure that messages go from the client to the server and vice versa. Routing these messages is an important part of the background processing Queued Components performs on your behalf.

- **Connectionless**   The whole reason to use Queued Components is so that you can use an application without worrying about connections or manually performing uploads to the server. Disconnected applications allow you to complete the work that you need to do and not worry about learning more than one way to do it. In addition, the application is inherently more reliable because there are fewer points of failure.

- **Security**   Like everything else in a distributed application, your data must remain secure. In this case, Queued Components provides the means for ensuring that the application keeps messages secret. Queued Components encrypts data on both the client and server so that prying eyes don't gain access to your company's data by looking through the messages that Queued Components stores on the hard drive.

Queued Components actually contains three discrete components that include the message queues, a queue manager, and the Application Programming Interface (API) used to request data from the queue manager. The developer who creates the application for your network will need the API to access Queued Components functionality. In other words, you can't install an application on your network and ask it to use Queued Components. The application must include support for this feature.

There's a fourth Queued Components element that you also need to be aware of that has little to do with the actual handling of the messages. It's the Queued Components Information Service, also known as Message Queue Information Service (MQIS). This database holds the definitions for Queued Components sites, machines, queues, and users. Queued Components implements the database using SQL Server, which is why the Windows server provides a "limited" version of SQL Server as part of the package. You won't find MQIS on every machine and definitely not on any client. MQIS is a central repository of data and is therefore found on just a few servers (at least one) on the network.

Installing Queued Components

Before you can use Queued Components, you have to install the Message Queuing portion of Windows XP. Microsoft doesn't install this support by default because you need a server to use it. In addition, you have to decide what level of Queued Components support to install on your machine. For example, you can create a dependent version of MSMQ for machines that always require local access and an independent version for machines that may require disconnected application support.

14

When you open the Message Queuing folder, you'll see at least four entries as shown in
Figure 14.11. Check Active Directory Integration if your machine belongs to a domain
that uses Active Directory. In other words, you won't want to check this option if all of
the servers on your network use Windows NT. You always select the Common option
because it includes the base components for Message Queuing. You'll add the MSMQ
HTTP Support option if you plan to transfer messages over the Internet. For example,
your company might set up a virtual private network (VPN) for the purpose. Finally, add
Triggers if your application will rely on a COM (not COM+) component or stand-alone
application to handle incoming messages.

FIGURE 14.11

Make sure that you
select the correct
Message Queuing
options for your
machine.

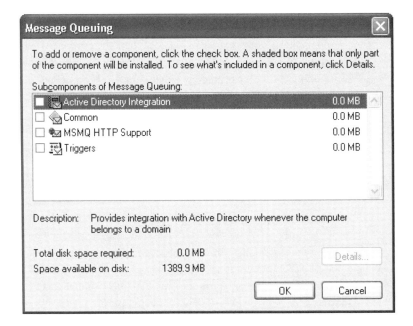

After you select the options you want, click OK to close the Message Queuing dialog
box. Click Next. Windows XP will begin installing the Queued Component files for you.
At some point, the installation process will complete, and you'll be ready to use Queued
Components.

Configuring Queued Components

Before we begin this section, it's important to understand that you'll seldom need to configure a queue directly. COM+ applications create and configure all of the queues they
require automatically. Generally, even a simple Queued Component application should
configure the queues for you. However, you'll probably want to know information about
the queues on your machine. You may also need to repair the application on occasion by

fixing the queues it relies on. Finally, you may need to tweak the settings in order to obtain acceptable application performance.

Most of the MSMQ configuration tasks occur in the Computer Management console shown in Figure 14.12. Notice that the Message Queuing snap-in (the friendly wrapper around MSMQ) appears under the Services and Applications snap-in. In addition, the Computer Management console defaults to the local machine. You can always connect to another machine if you have the proper rights by highlighting the Computer Management snap-in and then using the Action | Connect to another computer command. The Select Computer dialog box will display a list of computers from which you can choose.

FIGURE 14.12

The Computer Management console is where you'll configure MSMQ for use.

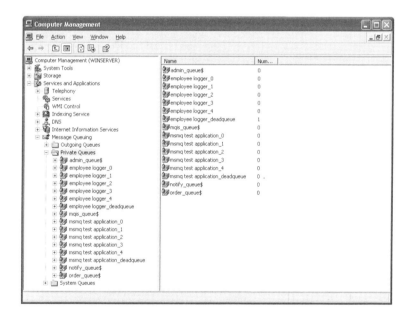

Message Queuing can contain four folders that group the queues by use, including private, public, outgoing, and system queues. You'll have to look in the right folder for the queue you want to find. In most cases, you'll need to look at either the Outgoing Queues or Public Queues folders for application data, and the Private Queues folder for administrative queues. The System Queues folder contains the dead letter queues and other system-related queues.

When you initially look at a queue folder, you'll see a list of the queues that it contains, the label for each queue, and the number of messages each queue holds, as shown in Figure 14.12.

14

Fortunately, you aren't limited to this list of information. Right-click a queue folder and choose View | Choose Columns from the context menu. You'll see a Modify Columns dialog box. Notice that this dialog box allows you to add everything from the number of journal messages for the queue to the queue's globally unique identifier (GUID). The Modify Columns dialog box will also allow you to change the order of the various columns using the Move Up and Move Down buttons. In most cases, it pays to display all of the available columns unless desktop space is at a premium. Doing so allows you to better track queue conditions without opening each queue separately.

Manually adding new queues to a queue folder is easy; just right-click the queue folder and then use the New | <Queue Folder Name> Queue command. You'll see the Queue Name dialog box. Type a queue name, determine if you want to make the queue transactional, and click OK. Transactions help keep data safe by adding checks to the data-handling process. The application developer will need to tell you if the application requires transaction support. You'll need to configure the queue settings manually using the queue Properties dialog box.

Configuring the queue is important. Right-click the queue you created and choose Properties from the context menu to see the settings for that queue. Figure 14.13 shows the General tab of the Queue Properties dialog box.

FIGURE 14.13

The General tab of the queue Properties dialog box contains performance and identification properties.

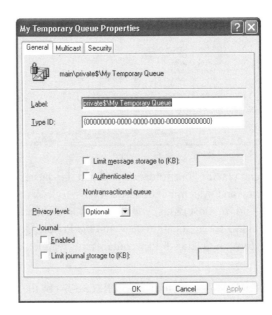

As you can see, the General tab provides quite a bit of information about the queue. The following list describes the fields in this tab:

- **Label** Defines the name of the queue. This is the name that a developer typically uses within an application to access the queue.

- **Type ID** Contains the GUID for the queue. The GUID is used to identify the type of service offered by the queue or the queue's function. A GUID containing all zeros indicates a general-purpose queue. When a queue is assigned a GUID, it's usually associated with a specific application or component.

- **Limit message storage to (KB)** Determines if the queue has a size limit. If so, the associated field allows you to define how many KBs the queue can hold. When the queue reaches this limit, it will no longer accept new messages.

- **Authenticated** Specifies if the queue will accept only authenticated messages. This is another queue security feature.

- **Transactional** Contains the transactional state of the queue. Queued Components makes this setting when you create the queue. You can't change the transactional status of a queue.

- **Privacy Level** Determines the amount of encryption the queue will accept. Queues will normally default to Optional, which means they accept either encrypted or unencrypted messages. The Body option forces the queue to accept only encrypted messages, while the None option forces the queue to accept only unencrypted messages.

- **Enabled (Journal)** Determines if the target journal is enabled. The journal holds messages that an application removes from the queue. It doesn't store messages that the application removed because their timeout value elapsed or as a result of administrative removal using directory services. You must manually remove messages from the journal when they are no longer needed.

- **Limit journal storage to (KB)** Limits the amount of disk space used to store journal messages. This is an important setting because journal and dead letter queue messages count against the computer's storage quota.

Figure 14.13 shows a Multicast tab. This is a new feature for Windows XP. It allows an application to send a message to multiple recipients. You probably won't see many applications that use this feature until developers begin using Visual Studio .NET to create most applications.

The Security tab of the queue Properties dialog is a standard security configuration dialog box. It allows you to set the level of access to the queue. Clicking Advanced displays the Access Control Settings dialog box, which allows finer control over the security

14

settings. In addition, you can use the Access Control Settings dialog box to set security auditing for the queue and change the queue owner.

Beneath each queue entry are two folders: Queue Messages and Journal Messages. (You may see a Triggers folder, as well, if you installed Triggers support.) As with other folders we've talked about so far, right-clicking on the folder and choosing the View | Choose Columns command will allow you to specify the amount of information you see for each message. Clearing unneeded messages from the queue message folder is relatively easy. Right-click the queue message folder and then choose All Tasks | Purge from the context menu.

Caution Purging messages from a queue message folder will result in the loss of all messages. Queued Components won't place the messages in a journal queue from a message queue. In addition, you can't select which messages to purge. This action removes all of the messages. The only way to provide selective message removal is to ask the developer to add a removal code to your application.

Managing Message Queues

You need to perform certain kinds of administrative tasks on your message queues. For example, you need to know how to create and configure new queues as needed. It's also important to know how to read the messages that your application creates and determine if there's any problem with them. The following sections will touch on a few additional issues. None of these tasks are earth shattering, but it's handy to know about them so that you can fully test and maintain the applications you create.

Exporting Queue Data

There are times when it would be nice to have some status information about the queues that you're dealing with. Unfortunately, the Computer Management MMC snap-in does not provide much in the way of quick documentation. However, you can create a quick overview of the queues on a specific machine using the Export List command on the context menu for the various folders in Message Queuing. Selecting this option will display a Save As dialog that you can use to export a list of entries at that level.

The exported list doesn't provide you with very much information, but it does provide the names of the queues that are currently in use and the number of messages that each queue contains. This is enough information, in most cases, to at least track the ebb and flow of message traffic on the network and determine if messages are moving along as anticipated. You can use this snapshot of the queue status to detect when certain events happened. For example, these snapshots could tell you when a component is getting overloaded or even stops working.

Dead Letter Messages Queue

Checking the Dead letter messages queue (or the dead letter queue associated with your application) is important because it contains the messages that Queued Components couldn't handle. After a while, the dead letter queue can fill with messages and slow system performance. You can receive a number of false indicators when this occurs, none of which will seem obvious at the time. For example, in one case, an application reported security errors when the Dead letter messages queue overflowed with messages. In short, if you're having a weird application problem, check for some non-obvious problems with an overfilled Dead letter messages queue.

Checking the Event Viewer

COM+ doesn't always display error messages that you can use to detect problems in your application. In fact, you'll see several situations where your application will appear to work just fine, but there will still be a problem. If you don't think to look in the Event Viewer, you might miss the information required to fix the problem. For example, there are situations when the message recorder will report problems, yet you'll never see them at the application level.

At first, you may question why Microsoft would take this approach. Consider for a moment that like the components executing on your server, Microsoft can't assume the application is still around to receive an error message. It's also in poor taste to display error messages on the server because you can't be sure that the network administrator will find them anytime soon. Therefore, the only place that Microsoft could report some application errors was within the Event Viewer.

Queued Components' Limitations

Some people look for the "silver bullet" for application deficiencies. Queued Components won't fix every problem that you may have with your application today, and, because of the way it's designed, it actually introduces a few new limitations. Anyone who tells you that Queued Components will fix every distributed application need for your company should seriously rethink their statement. While Queued Components is the greatest new application technology on the horizon, you need to know that this technology represents one piece of the whole picture. The following list describes what I consider the important user issues for Queued Components (developers have far more to consider):

14

- **One Way Message Transport**   Applications use a modular design approach today that relies on components. Remember to think of a component as a programmer's Lego, and you'll have a good idea of how they work. Most applications contain components that require one or more inputs and produce some type of output. However, an application developed for use with Queued Components can create components with only inputs and no outputs. The reason for this one-way transfer of information is easy to understand—the server may not be accessible when you use your application.

- **No Synchronous Result**   Queued Components provide asynchronous data transfer through messages. This means you can't expect instantaneous results from it. For example, you may query the database for recent customer orders. If your application downloaded that information to your local hard drive, you can expect to get a response even in disconnected mode. On the other hand, if the information only appears on the server, you need to create a server connection that allows your application to retrieve the information you need. In short, there are some situations when a connection is required. In other cases, you'll have to be a little more patient when waiting for a response.

- **Complete Messages Only**   Because the requestor may be unavailable when the server begins processing a request, the messages that your application sends to the server's message queue have to contain complete information. For example, if you want to enter new orders into the fulfillment database, all of the data required for the orders have to appear within the individual order messages. Unfortunately, this means your application is going to become less forgiving of entry errors and other issues that might not be a problem when using a standard application.

As you can see, most of the Queued Components' limitations occur for the same reasons that make this technology so attractive in the first place. When you use a disconnected application, you have to assume certain things about the user interface and the server, such as the inability to talk with the server whenever you want. Hopefully, the developer will think ahead and provide the information you need as part of a download.

At this point, you're probably thinking that you may not be able to use Queued Components because of your need to receive a response for every transaction. Actually, there are many situations when you don't require an immediate response. For example, when you input orders, you really don't need any response from the server. All you need is a response from the server after it makes the order, something a disconnected application can handle with ease. If you require an update on order status, you can always issue a status request that will be answered during a later connection. As an alternative, the server can always assume that it needs to provide order status information and provide it during the your regular connection time.

Summary

Today you learned about networking. You learned about general networking components. You also learned how to install and configure them, and how to use them. As part of this basic network training, we also discussed a little about security. That discussion will continue during Day 16.

We also explored a distributed computing technology called *Microsoft Management Queue (MSMQ)*. Newer Windows installations bury MSMQ within a new technology, Queued Components. Both technologies accomplish the same purpose from the user perspective. However, they do differ from a developer perspective. It's likely that you'll run into either MSMQ or Queued Components if you use distributed applications in a large network environment, so it pays to know a little about this technology.

Q&A

Q: Why doesn't Microsoft design protocols, clients, and services so that you can install them separately? For example, I don't need IPX/SPX for my NetWare setup, so why install it in the first place?

A: Microsoft has two good reasons for installing the services, protocols, and clients the way they do. First, there's user confusion to consider. Many people don't know which protocols go with what client. If Microsoft kept the elements separate, it would create problems for most users performing an upgrade. The second reason is operating system design. Microsoft has to make certain assumptions when they design an operating system as complex as Windows XP. One of those assumptions is that if File A is present, File B should also be present. The interrelations between components makes it necessary to bundle certain operating system elements together.

Q: If Windows users have access today to high-end scanning techniques, such as biometrics, why is security still such an issue?

A: User identification is only part of the security picture. A cracker gains access to your network through many openings. In fact, stolen passwords are often the domain of the disgruntled employee, not the cracker. Many of the most devastating cracks in recent history have nothing to do with user identity and everything to do with security holes in software. Network configuration also plays a big part in gaining access. Many network administrators make life too easy for the cracker by retaining default settings and accounts. Unfortunately, even if you have perfect user identification, software without holes, and an administrator who does everything right, the determined cracker can still break into your system. The only real

14

security measure is one where a network administrator combines security tools with constant network monitoring.

Q: When will I be able to upgrade my existing, non-Windows XP machines to use Universal Plug and Play?

A: You might already have the required support if you own Windows Millenium Edition. The Knowledge Base article at `http://support.microsoft.com/support/kb/articles/Q262/4/58.ASP` tells you about the support that Microsoft provides for this version of Windows. You should also read how to enable Universal Plug and Play support at `http://support.microsoft.com/support/kb/articles/q276/5/07.asp`. Unfortunately, it doesn't appear that Microsoft will provide Universal Plug and Play support for other versions of Windows right now. This could change in the future as third-party vendors begin to support Universal Plug and Play as a standard feature.

Q: How do you remove SNMP entries after you add them to the registry?

A: Create another text file containing a #pragma delete <Event Log Filename> <Event Source> <Event ID> entry for each event monitor that you added. You can use the file you generated to add the events as a source. Just change all of the "add" entries to "delete" entries. Likewise, you need to remove the message destinations you created using a #pragma delete_trap_dest <Community Name> <IP Address or Machine Name> entry for each destination.

Workshop

It's the end of the fourteenth day. By now you're a networking guru and able to take on any networking problem at your organization (or, at least, you have a better understanding of why the network administrator looks so pained all the time). Now it's time to see how much you know about network elements such as protocols, clients, and services. You can find answers to the quiz and exercise questions in Appendix A at the back of the book.

Quiz

1. In networking terms, what is a client?

2. What are biometrics?

3. Why would you want to use a network-ready device?

4. What's the importance of the RIP Listener?

5. What's the main benefit of installing Queued Components on your machine?

Exercises

1. Check the configuration for your NIC. Determine if you have the NIC setup for optimal use with Windows XP.

2. If you have a newer network-ready device, try installing Universal Plug and Play to see if Windows XP will redetect the device automatically.

3. Try creating your own SNMP setup to monitor events on your system.

14

WEEK 3

At a Glance

This is the networking and problem solution week of the book. You'll begin by learning how to set up a basic Windows network. The week continues with a discussion of security issues. You'll move on to viewing both NetWare and Linux networks from the Windows perspective.

The problem solution portion of the book begins by showing you how to create scripts. You'll also learn how to automate many Windows tasks. The next topic is Web site management. Not only will I show you how to set up an extremely basic Web site, but you'll also learn how to create your own Web pages. Part of this day's discussion includes trouble-shooting common Web site problems. The week ends with an in-depth discussion of Windows XP hardware and software troubleshooting.

- Day 15, "Using Windows Networking," covers three levels of Windows networks: home, small business, and enterprise. The day begins with a look at the new Home Networking Wizard feature of Windows XP. It ends with a discussion of essential Windows network configuration issues.

- Day 16, "Configuring Security," begins with a discussion of the need for a security plan. Next, we'll discuss how to manage user accounts from a security perspective. One of the more important discussion topics is a summary of local security policies. The day finishes with some tips on overcoming security deficiencies in Windows.

- Day 17, "Working with Linux," discusses how to make Linux servers accessible to Windows clients. It shows a variety of Linux networking issues, such as using Linux as a print server and a Web server. You'll see how to manage a Linux server using both GUI and command line (character mode) techniques. Finally, I'll discuss how to maintain security when working with a Linux server.

- Day 18, "Working with NetWare," discusses all of the NetWare usage essentials. This includes working with the Client Service for NetWare (CSNW) applet within the Control Panel. We'll discuss the use of NetWare Administrator for user and other Novell Directory Service (NDS) object needs. A special section will show how to use RConsole to manage NetWare servers remotely because the administrator can't perform some maintenance tasks anywhere but the system console. The day also includes a full discussion of the NetWare client, print features, and long filename support. Finally, we'll look at special issues, such as installing the NetWare documentation locally and optimizing NetWare use within the Windows environment.

- Day 19, "Creating Scripts and Automating Tasks," discusses basic scripting during the first half of the day and automation techniques during the second half. You'll see how to run scripts using the both Windows GUI and the command line. Of course, I'll provide a technical discussion of the various scripting objects and show how to use them within an application. The first automation section looks at using the Migration Wizard to move settings from one machine to another. The second section discusses the techniques for scheduling tasks. Finally, we'll look at how to use Synchronize to automate data updates from remote sources, such as the Internet.

- Day 20, "Developing a Web Page," begins with a discussion of Web server setup. It shows how to create a simple Web site using IIS and Web development tools. We'll also learn about issues such as the use of virtual directories and security.

- Day 21, "Maintaining Your System and Finding Problems," is the basic hardware and software problem troubleshooting day of the book. The first part shows how to prevent many common hardware failures by maintaining your machine. Not only does this section show how to make a machine last longer, but it also demonstrates how regular maintenance can increase machine efficiency and reduce the possibility of data loss. The software problem resolution section discusses software failures in detail. It looks at everything from device drivers to configuration errors. The hardware problem resolution section focuses on how to detect and fix most common hardware failures. It begins with some basics on hardware installation and configuration and then shows how to detect errors before they become major problems. The network problem resolution section looks at the potential sources of network failures and methods for fixing them.

WEEK 3

DAY 15

Using Windows Networking

Just about everyone who's reading this book will eventually use some form of Windows networking. You may have a Linux, NetWare, or other server on your system, but eventually you'll want to use the peer capabilities that Windows provides. In fact, many people use Windows networking as their only form of networking.

You'll run across several forms of Windows networking. For example, there's the pure peer-to-peer network designed so that every machine acts as a workstation without a server. A second form of Windows networking relies on a single Windows Server machine to provide file, print, and communication services. The third form of Windows networking relies on more than one server connected in one of several ways to provide services to a large network.

Microsoft might want you to believe that there are serious differences between these configurations, but they all rely on the same basic networking principles. You'll want to start with the pure peer-to-peer network, but building up to large networks isn't that hard. Yesterday you learned some of the principles for building and working with a Windows network. Today we expand that conversation to specific Windows networking areas.

We'll begin with a look at Microsoft's attempt to automate networking using the Network Setup Wizard. You'll find that this effort wasn't as successful as it could have been, but it does help a little. Someone who's never put a network together before has the most to gain from using the wizard but will also suffer the most confusion regarding the interesting choices it makes.

The remainder of our discussion today focuses on what you need to do in order to create a network using manual methods. It's important to realize that even if you do get the Network Setup Wizard to work as expected, you still have to perform tweaks to your network to gain full functionality from it. In addition, you'll need to make changes as your network changes. For example, if someone leaves your organization, changes jobs, or receives a promotion, you'll likely need to make a change to the network.

Using the Network Setup Wizard

Let me say at the outset of this section that creating any form of automated network installation is difficult because the vendor can't guess the specifics of your network while designing the wizard. Even if the vendor writes software that correctly determines the capabilities of every device on your machine (something Windows XP does well), a network isn't about one machine. Networks consist of several machines connected together using cable. Many networks require add-on devices, such as hubs or switches, for even basic network functionality. In short, attempting to guess the specifics of your network from the clues left in the machinery is nearly impossible.

The Network Setup Wizard does a reasonably good job at setting up small (two- or three-machine) networks where your computing needs are light. Microsoft designed it to meet the needs of the home network, not the corporate environment or even the small business environment in many cases. In fact, Microsoft originally called this tool the Home Networking Wizard.

You'll find the Network Setup Wizard in the Start | Programs | Accessories | Communications folder. When you start the application, you'll see a Welcome screen that tells you the tasks the wizard can perform. It pays to read this list so that you know precisely how Network Setup Wizard can help you. The following steps tell you how to complete the process:

1. Click Next. You'll see a list of tasks that you need to perform before you use the wizard. Make sure that you perform all of these asks before proceeding; otherwise, the wizard won't perform as expected.

15

> **Tip**
>
> Some of the bullets on the Before you continue dialog box are unclear. When Microsoft says that you need an Internet connection, it means you must have a live connection. If you're using dial-up networking, make sure that you can interact with the Internet (the telephone is connected) before you begin this wizard. In addition, you need to verify that all printers and other peripherals have a connection to the network and are turned on and active. Windows XP seems to have a problem detecting printers and other peripherals in the "power saving" state. The printer will still accept print jobs, but it doesn't always provide a response to Windows XP queries for information.

2. Complete the preparatory steps requested by the wizard and click Next. You'll see a Select a connection method dialog box. This dialog box contains options for three types of Internet connection. Essentially, you need to decide if your computer connects directly to the Internet, or if you use another machine to make the connection. If you select the direct Internet connection option, the wizard assumes that you want to install Internet Connection Sharing (ICS). The Other option takes you to another screen with three more options: using a hub, establishing a direct connection without any network support, or having no connection at all.

3. Choose an Internet connection option and click Next. You'll see a Give this computer a description and name dialog box.

   You must provide a name for your computer. However, the description is optional, and some people find the description more trouble than it's worth on a small network. Older versions of Windows would display the actual name of the machine, and you could obtain the machine description if desired. Windows XP provides the machine description first, with the machine name in parentheses afterward as shown in Figure 15.1 for the Aux machine. If the network administrator uses an inconsistent description or leaves out the description on some machines, you'll see the flawed network setup shown in the figure.

4. Type a name for your computer in the Computer Name field. Type a description in the Description field, if desired. Click Next. You'll see a Name your network dialog box. Every computer on your network has to use the same network name. Otherwise, the computers will act as if they're on different networks and won't talk with each other. Make sure that you select a name you'll remember to use for all computers on your network.

5. Type a network name and click Next. You'll see a Ready to apply network settings dialog box like the one shown in Figure 15.2. This is your last chance to verify the

network settings before you begin the network installation. Make sure that you check every entry on the list before proceeding.

FIGURE **15.1**

Windows XP displays computer descriptions differently than older versions of Windows.

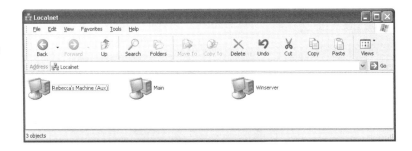

FIGURE **15.2**

Make sure that you check your network settings before proceeding.

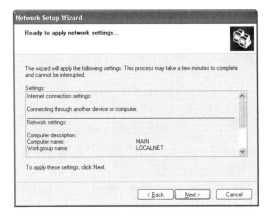

6. Check the network settings and click Next. The Network Setup Wizard will perform some analysis and setup on your system. This process can take a long time. Be patient and wait for it to complete. A small two-machine network requires about 5 minutes for this step to complete; larger networks will require more time. When the configuration process is complete, you'll see a You're almost done dialog box. This dialog box contains four options for saving your network settings. Generally, using the floppy will work best.

7. Select one of the setup disk options. The procedure assumes that you'll select the Create a Network Setup Disk option. Click Next. You'll see an Insert the disk you want to use dialog box.

8. Insert the floppy disk in the drive. Click Format Disk, if required. Click Next. The Network Setup Wizard will copy the setup information to the floppy disk and then display a dialog box containing instructions for using it.

9. Write or type the instructions in a safe place so that you can find them later. Click Next. You'll see a completion dialog box.

10. Click Finish. At this point, your network setup should be ready to go, at least on this machine.

Building a Network

If you decide to go the manual-networking route, the first thing you'll need to do is create a design of your network. You need to decide that the printer goes in one place and your workstation in another. Write everything down so that you can document your network and make it easy to work on. Decide how you plan to run cabling before you actually begin to do it. Measure everything so that you know precisely how much this network will cost (the estimate will probably be off a little, but you can come very close if you plan your system well).

One of the most important tasks in building a usable network is deciding up front who will serve which functions on the network. A network administrator is a requirement on even a small network. If someone doesn't take responsibility for the network, you'll experience problems with it. Even a home network requires a network administrator in the form of Mom or Dad. The network administrator is the person who takes care of the network as a whole—the person who has the greatest access but also the greatest responsibility. On a small network, the network administrator is also the person who takes care of maintenance tasks, such as performing backups and cleaning the machines.

Workgroups function because they have structure. Not everyone should access every resource; they should access only the resources they need to access. Even on a small network, the network administrator has to maintain control over portions of the system. For example, on a small network, no one should have access to the network administrator's machine except the network administrator. If this isn't possible, at least secure the machine to hide the networking features from view and secure them from misuse. In short, security begins with the design and setup of your system. It shouldn't be an afterthought. (I'll show you how to create a security plan for larger networks in the "Creating a Security Plan" section tomorrow.)

Of course, a written design does much more than assign tasks and tell where to place equipment. It can also help keep you on budget when the salesperson tries to tempt you with just one more gizmo. The whole design process should help you think things through—to find potential problems in the way you want to configure the network.

At some point, you'll finish your network design and purchase all of the required equipment. It's important to put all of the equipment in place, connect it to the network, and test everything as much as possible in a stand-alone mode. Take time to learn about any special configuration requirements for the equipment. Make sure that you have optional features, such as network cards, loaded. Finally, make sure that you download all of the latest drivers for every piece of equipment on your system.

Part of the network setup also involves documentation. I've worked with small businesses for many years. The number one problem when I walk through the door is that no one has any documentation for anything. Every piece of equipment becomes a mystery to solve because I don't have the documentation required to work with it. In addition, no one knows when the machine was maintained last (if ever).

Keeping the documentation for a machine *with* that machine is the best way to make life easy. Toss out old documentation when you replace it with something new. Keep the documentation in order so that you can find it when needed (large businesses tend to store their documentation in a central area but identify the associated machine on the documentation. It also helps to maintain logs for every machine containing the following information:

- Part replacement
- General maintenance, such as cleaning
- Backups
- Updates
- Software installation and removal

When you get all of this prepared, you're finally ready to install the operating system and associated network software. We discussed installation procedures during Day 2, "Windows XP Installation and Configuration." Make sure that you understand how to work with Windows Explorer (Day 3, "Exploring the Interface") before you proceed to the Sharing Resources section that comes next.

Sharing Resources

You can share many of your resources with other people on the network. However, before you can share anything, you'll need to install the File and Printer Sharing for Microsoft Networks service shown in Figure 15.3. Generally, you'll install this service during the installation process. However, you can also install it later using the procedure found in the "Installing Protocols, Clients, and Services" section of Day 14. Make sure that you disable this service or remove it if you decide not to share any resources later. We discussed this process in the "Removing Versus Disabling Features" section of Day 14.

FIGURE 15.3

*You must install the
File and Printer
Sharing for Microsoft
Networks service to
share resources with
other people.*

Every printer or disk resource you can share will have a Sharing tab on its property dialog box (see Figure 15.4) and a Sharing entry on the context menu. As you can see, this
drive has at least one "share" that people with the proper rights can use to access it. In
many cases, you'll create several shares for drives and may even create shares for lower-
level objects, such as folders. Unfortunately, you can't share individual files within a
folder, so it's important to create shared folders on the drive. These folders don't even
have to contain the original file; you can place file shortcuts within them. We'll discuss
sharing and security issues in detail in the "Managing File/Folder Access" section
tomorrow.

FIGURE 15.4

*Shareable resources
will contain a Sharing
tab like this one.*

Windows XP also provides a method for sharing data over the Internet (or, at least, the company intranet). You can't share an entire disk drive over the Internet. Actually, it isn't safe to share this much of your system over a connection that a cracker could use. However, you can share individual folders on a drive using the Web Sharing feature shown in Figure 15.5. This feature works with Internet Information Server (IIS). Of course, you must have a Web server installed in order to use this feature. The Windows XP Professional Edition comes with a simple version of IIS that you can use.

FIGURE 15.5

The Web Sharing feature helps you to share a network folder across the Internet as long as you have a Web server installed.

> **Note**
>
> Generally, it's safer to share resources using an e-mail connection. This one-way data transfer helps keep your network secure because the recipient never has access to your system (barring a Trojan Horse or back-door program). Collaboration using NetMeeting is also safer than using a Web share. Even a remote desktop is safer than a Web share in some respects. In short, use this feature with caution because you never know who will try to access your network.

While printers and disk drives both use the sharing methods just described, you also have to consider other resource-sharing scenarios. Some of these scenarios are under your direct control. For example, Internet Connection Sharing (ICS) permits you to share a connection with other people on the network. (See the "Connecting with Dial-Up Networking" section for details.) We'll also discuss Remote Access Server (RAS) in the "Using Remote Access Server (RAS)" section. RAS is another means to create a remote connection.

In other cases, the resource sharing hides within the dark recesses of applications. For example, a developer can create an application that looks for resources on your machine. Using technologies such as simple object access protocol (SOAP) and distributed component object model (DCOM) allows applications to share remote resources. Don't worry; you still have full control over your machine. The security settings you use either permit or deny access to the remote application. You can also control the level of access that the remote application obtains.

Using Remote Access Server (RAS)

The Remote Access Server provides an external connection for someone to use to access your system. RAS supports a number of connection types; most of them are secure. Some of these connections provide straight access, while others require your machine to call the user back. In short, there's a type of connection for just about every need.

You'll normally use RAS for an extremely small number of people when working with Windows XP Professional Edition. (This service is unavailable to Windows XP Home Edition users.) For one thing, Microsoft didn't design this version of the operating system for heavy server use. Another consideration is that you don't want to give the entire world access to your system data.

The one thing you won't want to do is confuse the RAS support provided with a server with the support provided in Windows XP Professional Edition. Microsoft turns the support on by default for server products, and servers support many options not found in Windows XP Professional Edition. You may also have problems using the Routing and Remote Access MMC snap-in with the Professional Edition. Yet, this is the main utility for working with RAS on a server. Professional Edition users will find that Microsoft has provided other means for working with RAS and the connectivity it provides.

There are two phases for creating a RAS connection. First, you have to create the connection using the special Incoming Connections applet. Second, you need to configure the user account to use the RAS connection by using either the Incoming Connections applet or the User Properties dialog box. You can use the Routing and Remote Access snap-in to monitor the connections you create. The following sections discuss all three issues. In addition, we'll discuss some command line utilities that help you to work with RAS.

Configuring RAS

Configuring RAS for Windows XP Professional Edition is different from using RAS under Windows Server. Microsoft assumes that you aren't going to use RAS on your machine, so they disable this support. To use RAS, you need to start the Routing and Remote Access server manually in the Services snap-in. Right-click the Routing and Remote Access entry and then Properties. You'll see a Routing and Remote Access Properties dialog box. Change the Startup Type field from Disabled to Manual or Automatic. Windows XP will enable the Start button. Click Start to start the service. Click OK to close the Routing and Remote Access Properties dialog box. Reboot your machine.

Note

Starting the Routing and Remote Access server will disrupt all of your network connections, especially those for Linux and NetWare. Although you don't need to reboot the machine to start working with RAS, you do need to reboot it to reestablish contact with the rest of the network. In some cases, you'll find that the network still won't respond, and you may have to work with the various protocol and service settings to get things working again. If you have problems with your NetWare network, ensure that you have the NWLink NetBIOS protocol installed and enabled. You'll also notice a significant decrease in network speed when using NetWare or Linux in combination with RAS.

You'll know that you're successful in starting RAS when you see the Incoming Connections icon in the Network Connections window. In some cases, this means creating an outgoing connection using the New Connection icon first. You need to perform the extra step to set up security and other internal settings.

When you see the Incoming Connections icon, double-click it to open the Incoming Connections Properties dialog box shown in Figure 15.6. The first configuration step is to select a device for the incoming connection on the General tab. Windows XP will list the devices in the Devices field. Check every device you want to use to create a connection. Note that you can click Properties to set the properties for each device.

If you plan to use RAS to enable Internet connectivity using a Virtual Private Network (VPN), you also need to check the Virtual Private Network option. On the other hand, keep this option clear if you only plan to support dial-in connections. Checking this option could open your system to security risks and will definitely result in a performance hit.

At this point, someone could access your system, but no one has permission to do so. Select the Users tab, and you'll see a list of users on your machine as shown in Figure 15.7. If you want to allow a user to create a remote connection, check their name in the list. You can also use the New and Delete buttons to add and remove users. Note that adding or removing a user here also adds or removes on your machine as a whole.

FIGURE 15.6

The Incoming Connections Properties dialog box enables you to configure RAS support on a Professional Edition machine.

FIGURE 15.6

The Incoming Connections Properties dialog box enables you to configure RAS support on a Professional Edition machine.

FIGURE 15.7

Use the User tab to determine who can access your network.

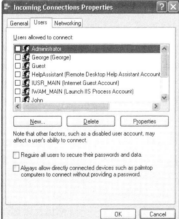

It's important to click Properties for each user that you add to the list of those who can remotely access your system. The General tab of the User Properties dialog box contains the username, full name, and password. Make sure that every user has a password. The Callback tab contains the options for setting callback. The following list explains these important options:

- **Do Not Allow Callback**   This is the least secure way to make a remote connection. Users can call in, provide stolen credentials (no doubt obtained from someone in your organization), and do whatever they like on your system without any verification. However, this may be the only option, in rare circumstances, when someone is calling from a location where it isn't easy to call back, such as a motel room with a central switchboard.

- **Allow Callers to Set the Callback Number**   This is a good solution for people who spend a lot of time on the road. Users call in, supply a callback number, and then wait for the system to call them back. This option has two advantages over the no-callback option. First, you verify the location of the remote user. Second, you can usually obtain lower long-distance rates, making the remote connection less expensive to operate.

- **Always Use the Following Callback Number**   This is the most secure option but also the least flexible. Someone calls into your system, provides identification, and waits for the system to call back. Always use this option if someone will always call from the same location. For example, if you have an employee who will call from home and from no other location, it's best to use this option. This method provides positive verification that the caller is actually the person granted access. There are still ways to thwart this access method, but someone has to be both determined and skilled in order to do it.

Notice the two options at the bottom of the Users tab of the Incoming Connections Properties dialog box. The first option is an essential aid to security. It requires that all users use encryption for their passwords and data. If you allow connections with this option disabled, Windows XP will send all passwords and data in clear text. That's akin to leaving the key to your system under the doormat. If you select this option, make sure that you also select the Require Data Encryption option for the user account.

The second option is a security risk. If you check this option, any computer that looks like it has a direct connection can access your system without a password. Unfortunately, this means that a cracker posing as someone on your network by using techniques such as spoofing has direct access to your system. Of course, if you clear this option (the default), local users will have to supply a password, which is a small inconvenience to maintain network security.

The Networking tab controls the clients, services, and protocols available to the incoming call. Changing these options won't change your settings for the machine as a whole. You'll notice that you can install and uninstall network features. This does appear to affect the network as a whole, so exercise caution when using these buttons. You'll also notice that some clients, services, and protocols have grayed-out check boxes. You can't deselect these items. However, you can disable any item that has a normal check box, disabling that feature for the remote caller. When you complete configuring the RAS connection, click OK and users will be able to call into your system.

Using the Routing and Remote Access MMC Snap-in

For those of you who normally work with Windows Server for RAS connections, you'll find the Routing and Remote Access snap-in almost useless for Windows XP Professional Edition. As shown in Figure 15.8, the information that you obtain from Professional Edition versus any version of Windows Server is paltry indeed. Because of the lack of support for Windows XP Professional Edition in this snap-in, I'll only provide an overview of Routing and Remote Access snap-in functionality. You'll also want to spend some time reading specifics at

`http://www.microsoft.com/windows2000/en/server/help/sag_rasstopnode.htm`.

FIGURE 15.8

The Routing and Remote Access snap-in helps you to create remote connections to your computer.

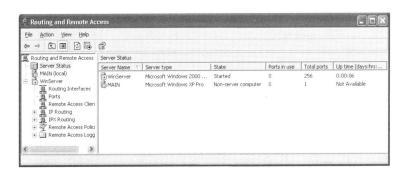

The main reason for the Routing and Remote Access snap-in limitation is that Windows XP Professional Edition limits the connection types that you can create. If you try to configure Windows Server for a basic RAS connection (the only type available under Windows XP Professional Edition), you'll find that you have to use the same process as for a Windows XP Professional Edition connection. The fact that you can't create an advanced connection under Windows XP Professional Edition is the reason the Routing and Remote Access snap-in is less than helpful.

The Routing and Remote Access snap-in provides access to other servers, much like other snap-ins. To add a server, right-click the Routing and Remote Access entry and then choose Add Server from the context menu. You'll see an Add Server dialog box. Use the options in this dialog box to add the server from the current computer, a server from a specific computer, or all of the Routing and Remote Access computers from a domain, or to browse Active Directory.

Windows servers don't provide RAS support by default. However, you can enable the support by right-clicking the server name and choosing Configure and Enable Routing and Remote Access from the context menu. You'll see a Connecting dialog for a few moments, and then the Routing and Remote Access Server Setup Wizard will appear.

Follow the prompts to create a connection. Note that this wizard only works if you want to create an advanced RAS connection. Otherwise, you need to configure the RAS connection locally on the server. Creating an advanced RAS connection may require that you install other support on the server, such as Dynamic Host Configuration Protocol (DHCP).

After you install the required support on a server, you can use the Routing and Remote Access snap-in to add additional routing and remote communication features. You can also configure the server properties (something you can't do for a Windows XP setup). These properties include security, protocol setup (IP and IPX in most cases), point-to-point protocol (PPP) options, and event logging. The Routing and Remote Access snap-in also helps you monitor the server status. For example, you determine the port status and monitor which users have logged in.

Configuring the User Account

I wanted to include this section because many administrators use the user account as the means to configure RAS support. This feature only works on Windows servers, not on Windows XP. You can use your local computer to configure a user account on the server, but attempting to configure a user account on a local machine will display an error message telling you that the feature is unavailable. The only way to configure a local user account for RAS access is to use the Incoming Connections Properties dialog box mentioned earlier.

However, you may want to configure a user account directly on a server. In this case, open the Users folder in Local Users and Groups (or use the Active Directory equivalent). Right-click the user account that you want to modify and choose Properties from the context menu. Select the Dial-in tab, and you'll see a display similar to the one shown in Figure 15.9.

The Remote Access Permission section of the User Properties dialog box determines if the user can call in. Normally, Windows controls access through a policy unless you specifically give the user access. You won't find the Verify Caller ID option when working with Windows XP Professional Edition. This feature verifies caller identify through the telephone number used to contact the server. As you can see, the User Properties dialog box provides callback options similar to those found in Windows XP. The last two options are also unique to Windows Server. The first assigns the same address to the user for every call. The only time you need this feature is if people on the main network need that specific IP address to contact the caller. The Apply Static Routes option is a performance feature. By setting a static route for the caller, people on the main network can make contact with fewer routing errors.

FIGURE 15.9

You can configure the User Properties dialog box for dial-in connections when using Windows Server.

An Overview of the Command Line Utilities

Windows XP provides two RAS-related command line utilities you should know about. The NETSH utility provides invaluable information about your RAS setup. You can also use this utility to make configuration changes. The RASDIAL utility enables you to call a remote server. It provides command line entries for most of the RAS features we've discussed, such as a callback number. Both utilities are important because you can access them from batch files and scripts. You can perform every task using command line arguments, which means you can automate many of your RAS tasks. The following sections describe both utilities.

Using NETSH

NETSH is the more complex of the two command line utilities. It comes in most helpful for viewing statistics. If you decide to use scripts in place of the GUI tools that Microsoft provides for managing your RAS connections, NETSH is also the tool of choice. The scripting features of NETSH come in most handy for large networks because writing and debugging a script is no small undertaking where RAS is concerned.

You start NETSH at the command prompt. If you type **NETSH** and press Enter, you'll see a NETSH prompt where you can type additional commands. This is an interactive mode. The first command you should learn when using NETSH is Help. This simple command displays all of the other commands you can use in the current NETSH context.

A special section called "Commands in this context" displays context-specific commands.

NETSH has several contexts or areas of control. One of those areas of control is RAS. If you type **RAS** at the NETSH prompt and press Enter, the prompt will change to NETSH RAS. At this point, you can access RAS statistics and make changes to its configuration.

One of the more useful commands for verifying your RAS setup is Show user. Figure 15.10 shows the output for this command on my text machine. As you can see, it provides a quick overview of the RAS user account settings. You can gain the same information by typing **NETSH RAS SHOW USER** at the command prompt and pressing Enter. If you want to send the output of this command to a text file for further processing, you can extend it even further by typing **NETSH RAS SHOW USER >> MYOUTPUT.TXT** and pressing Enter. In short, you can use NETSH interactively or automate the process.

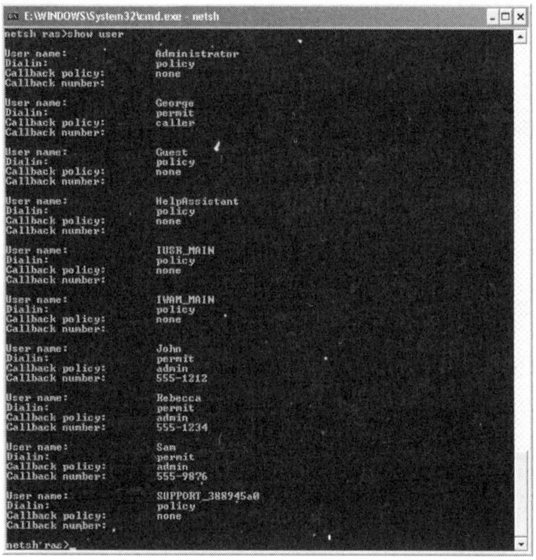

FIGURE 15.10

NETSH can tell you all about your RAS user configuration.

NETSH can show you a lot more than just the user information. For example, you can display a complete list of all the helper files that RAS uses. This is helpful information when you're trying to troubleshoot a problem with your RAS configuration. If you want to see a complete list of SHOW commands, type **SHOW** at the NETSH RAS prompt and press Enter.

Some of the benefits of NETSH won't be apparent at first. For example, if you type **NETSH RAS DUMP >> MYSCRIPT.TXT** and press Enter at the command prompt, you'll generate a NETSH script that you can edit and move to another machine. Type **NETSH -f <Script Name>** and press Enter at the second machine to configure it automatically. As you can see, all you really need to do is configure RAS once and then move the configuration to other machines as needed. Of course, you'll still need to configure machine-specific information, such as the list of users who can make remote connections.

When you finish using NETSH, type **BYE or QUIT** at the prompt and press Enter. You'll exit to the command prompt. NETSH will also recognize the Ctrl+Break key combination as a signal to quit.

Using RASDIAL

RASDIAL is a simple command line utility for making a remote connection. The benefit of using RASDIAL is that you can include it within scripts. This means you can create automated connections to other servers to download information during periods of inactivity. Of course, you can use it to automate user connections as well.

Before you can use RASDIAL, you need to create a phonebook of connections using the RASPHONE utility. This utility displays a Network Connections dialog box that contains a list of your current connections. Click New, and you'll start the New Connection Wizard. Use the Properties button to display the properties of an existing connection or click Connect to dial an existing connection.

You use RASDIAL by specifying the name of the phonebook connection that you want to use. For example, if the name of your connection is MyPlace, type **RASDIAL MyPlace** at the command prompt and press Enter. RASDIAL also includes command line arguments to specify the username and password, telephone number, callback number, and the location of a phonebook you want to use. The default phonebook appears in the \Documents and Settings\All Users\Application Data\Microsoft\Network\Connections\Pbk folder as RASPHONE.PBK.

Connecting with Dial-Up Networking

Dial-up networking is the means to connect to a number of server types using a standard modem. Generally, you'll create the one connection you need to your ISP during Internet Explorer configuration. We explored this configuration process in the "Creating a Connection Using Internet Connection Wizard" section during Day 4.

Sometimes, you'll need to create an additional connection to another server. Perhaps you use more than one ISP, or you need to connect to an older remote system. To start this process, you'll start the New Connection Wizard found in the Network Connections applet of the Control Panel. Click Next to get past the Welcome screen, and you'll see that you can create four new connection types. As we've already discussed the Internet connection type, I won't discuss it again here.

We've also looked at another one of the options listed on this dialog box. The Set up a home or small office network option starts the Network Setup Wizard described in the "Using the Network Setup Wizard" section. The following sections describe the remaining two connection types.

Creating a Workplace Network Connection

You can create two types of connections with this option. The first is a Virtual Private Network (VPN), and the second is the more traditional dial-up connection. The VPN option enables you to create a connection through the Internet. The following sections show you how to create both connection types.

Dial-up Connections

When you create a dial-up connection for your workplace, you'll use a telephone to dial out to a RAS server (or any other server that allows telephone communication). The following steps show you how:

1. Select Dial-up Connection in the Network Connection dialog box and click Next. You'll see a Connection Name dialog box.

2. Type a name for the connection. The New Connection Wizard suggests your company name, but any name will do. Click Next. You'll see a Phone Number to Dial dialog box.

3. Type the telephone number. Include the area code if necessary. Click Next. You'll see a completion dialog box. This dialog box contains an option for placing a shortcut to the connection on your desktop.

4. Click Finish. The New Connection Wizard creates the connection for you.

VPN Connections

The VPN connection works by creating a connection through the Internet. Think of the Internet as the land and VPN as the tunnel that data travels through. The data still travels across the land, but no one can see it because the data travels in a tunnel. The following steps show how to create this connection type.

1. Select Virtual Private Network connection in the Network Connection dialog box and click Next. You'll see a Connection Name dialog box.

2. Type a name for the connection. The New Connection Wizard suggests your company name, but any name will do. Click Next. You'll see a Public Network dialog

box. Use this dialog box to choose either a dial-up connection or a connection through a proxy using the Do not dial initial connection option. If you use the Automatically dial this connection option, you can also choose an existing dial-up connection for your ISP. Unfortunately, this dialog box doesn't allow you to create new connections.

3. Select a connection option and click Next. You'll see a VPN Server Selection dialog box.

4. Type a server name or the server IP address and click Next. You'll see a completion dialog box. This dialog box contains an option for placing a shortcut to the connection on your desktop.

5. Click Finish. The New Connection Wizard creates the connection for you.

Creating an Advanced Connection

When you select the Set up an advanced connection option on the Network Connection Type dialog box, you'll see the Advanced Network Connection Options dialog box containing two options. The Accept incoming connections option is really the Incoming Connections Properties dialog box in disguise. We discussed this dialog box in the "Configuring RAS" section.

The second option, Connect directly to another computer, enables you to connect to other computer systems, even those running other operating systems. You can use a parallel, serial, or infrared port to make the connection. Of course, when using the parallel or serial port options, you need the proper cable setup to make the connection between machines.

A serial port connection is especially practical if you need to access machines with other operating systems. Most computer systems support a serial communication program that helps someone to transfer data files. Of course, text files are the universal format for most machines, but this form lacks any type of formatting.

I've used serial connections on many systems to perform hardware upgrades when the two systems wouldn't talk to each other any other way. You need a standard serial cable, a NULL modem, and an RS-232 gender changer. The serial cable makes the connection possible. The NULL modem simulates the action of a modem and aids in the data transfer. The gender changer modifies one end of the serial cable so that it will plug into the second machine.

Now that you have some idea of how you can use a direct cable connection, let's see how to create one. The following steps help you to configure a direct connection. It helps if you make the cable connection (if required) before you create the connection.

1. Select the Connect directly to another computer option and click Next. You'll see a Host or Guest? dialog box. It doesn't matter which machine is the host or which one is the guest. All you need is one machine configured as a host and another as a guest. I normally make the machine sending data the host.

2. Select the Host or Guest option and then click Next. If you select the Guest option, you'll see a Connection Name dialog box. Type the name of the connection and click Next. Both connection types will lead to a Select a Device dialog box.

3. Select a device to use for the direct computer connection and click Next. If you selected the Host option, you'll see a User Permissions dialog box. Select the users who can make a connection and click Next. Both connection types will lead to a completion dialog box.

4. Click Finish. The New Connection Wizard creates the connection for you.

Networking Services and Other Features

Windows XP provides a wealth of other networking features. We discussed some of these features yesterday. Others will appear during the next three days. The following sections contain services and features that you'd consider Windows networking-specific. They can work with other networks, but you'll use them most often to meet the specific needs of Windows.

SNMP Support

The Simple Network Management Protocol (SNMP) has been an important part of remote computer management for a long time. This protocol allows someone to monitor specific events on remote computers using agents. If your network is large enough that you don't want to check each computer individually on a daily basis, SNMP might be the answer you're looking for. It allows you to track the status of all the machines on your network, no matter which operating system they use. We discussed this feature in detail in the "Simple Network Management Protocol" section of Day 14.

SLIP and CSLIP Support

Windows XP provides support for SLIP (Serial Line Internet Protocol). However, unlike earlier versions of Windows, you won't find CSLIP (Compressed Serial Line Internet Protocol) support, which means that you lose the performance benefits a CSLIP connection can provide. Both protocols support remote network connections, such as those supported by older UNIX remote servers over a serial port. You can find a detailed description of SLIP in RFC1055 (http://www.faqs.org/rfcs/rfc1055.html) and

CSLIP in RFC1144 (http://www.faqs.org/rfcs/rfc1144.html). The operator of the host machine should let you know if you require this level of support.

The first thing you need to do to make a SLIP connection is open Dial-Up Networking and create a new connection using the procedure in the "Connecting with Dial-Up Networking" section. After you complete this task, right-click the new connection and select the Properties option. Select the Networking tab and choose SLIP: Unix Connection from the Type of dial-up server I am calling drop-down list box.

After you select a SLIP server, select the Internet Protocol (TCP/IP) entry. Click Properties. You should see the Internet Protocol (TCP/IP) Properties dialog box. Notice that it contains all the familiar TCP/IP address information required by the host computer. Configure these settings as needed for your connection.

Desktop Management Interface (DMI) Support

Desktop Management Interface (DMI) is part of Systems Management Server (SMS) (http://www.microsoft.com/smsmgmt/default.asp) that works as the hardware-auditing component of Windows XP. It follows the standards set by the Distributed Management Task Force (DMTF) (http://www.dmtf.org/).

A vendor writes a Management Information File (MIF) that contains all the particulars about a piece of equipment. When the SMS looks at a workstation and finds this file, it adds the file contents to an SQL database that you can open with any number of products. In addition to the hardware information, SMS adds the software auditing information that it finds to the database. The combined software and hardware information gives you the data required to know whether a particular workstation can run a piece of software without an upgrade.

You need a Windows server working with Windows XP as a client to use this feature. The Windows server will need a copy of SQL Server and SMS installed.

Remote Procedure Call (RPC) Support

Remote procedure calls (RPCs) begin with the network transport layer of your network. The complexity of your setup and the requirements of the protocol determine number of pieces in a network transport installation. There are four elements within the network transport: the transport driver interface (TDI), the transport protocol, the network device interface specification (NDIS) interface, and the NIC driver.

Microsoft first added RPC to Windows NT 4. However, it wasn't until Windows 2000 that Microsoft made tools available to make use of this technology. Windows XP implements RPC as a network-transport mechanism using named pipes, NetBIOS, or WinSock to create a connection between a client and a server. RPCs are compatible with the Open Software Foundation (OSF) Data Communication Exchange (DCE) specification.

So what do RPCs do for you? OLE uses them, for one. Actually, OLE uses a subset of RPCs called *light RPCs* (LRPCs) to enable you to make connections that you couldn't normally make in complex documents. You'll also find that RPC makes technology such the distributed component object model (DCOM) possible. Developers use this technology to execute application code required by a local application on a remote machine.

Windows Sockets (WinSock) Support

Windows Sockets (WinSock) is a developer support tool that helps applications make TCP/IP connections. The developer plugs an application into a WinSock (socket) to create a connection. The only requirement is that the developer writes the application to make WinSock calls properly. WinSock makes all of the required connections, leaving the developer free to concentrate on the tasks that the application must perform. Microsoft includes two WinSock applications with Windows XP: SNMP and FTP.

Besides making the interface easier to use, WinSock provides another advantage. Normally, an application has to add a NetBIOS header to every packet that leaves the workstation. The workstation at the other end doesn't really need the header, but it's there anyway. This additional processing overhead reduces network efficiency. Using WinSock eliminates the need for the header, and the user sees better performance.

Sockets are an age-old principle (at least in the computer world), but they're far from obsolete. The WinSock project proved so successful that Microsoft began to move it to other transports. For example, Windows XP includes a WinSock module for both the IPX/SPX and NetBEUI transports.

Summary

The most important lesson you could learn today is that networking with Windows isn't an impossible task. Given a little time, most people can set up and configure at least a pure peer-to-peer Windows network. Many of you will have the knowledge required to perform complex setups.

You learned three networking skills today. First, we examined the automated method of installing a Windows network using the Network Setup Wizard. Second, we discussed the tasks that you'll perform to manually create a Windows network. Finally, we looked at some features that Windows XP provides to make networking easier.

Q&A

Q: Why does Microsoft provide so many ways to share resources? Why not use a Sharing tab for all resources to make it easier to share just the resources I want to share?

A: The problem is one of configuration. Printers and disk drives lend themselves to the Sharing tab. However, creating a shared resource connection with ICS or RAS requires more work. You need to specify how to create the connection as well as how to share the resource. In the case of a Web share, you need to configure the resource for use with a Web server (generally IIS). In short, it would be nice to have a consistent way to share resources, but it simply isn't possible given the diversity of resources you can share.

Q: How do I determine which remote connection to create using the New Connection Wizard?

A: Microsoft bases connections on the destination you want to reach. Breaking the problem down into destination types is the best way to determine which connection to use. For example, you'll use the Connect to the Internet option for all Internet connections, even those that involve a connection to the office. The Set up a home or small office network option is actually the Network Setup Wizard in disguise. You'd use it to create a network at home. You'll use the Connect to the network at my workplace option for all dial-up connections to a company site, even if it isn't your workplace. For that matter, you'd use this connection type to dial your home computer from the office. The Set up an advanced connection option helps you create incoming connections (described in the "Configuring RAS" section) or create a direct connection to another computer using infrared, parallel, or serial port connections.

Q: How many applications actually use WinSock? I've never heard of it before.

A: Most communication programs today use WinSock or rely on a component that implements the WinSock code for them. The ability to create connections quickly and easily in our connected world becomes more important every day. WinSock represents one of the best choices for developers. The reason you need to know WinSock exists is that communication applications will occasionally display a WinSock error message. Knowing the source of this message can help you diagnose and fix the problem.

Workshop

It's the end of the fifteenth day. You should know how to perform most essential Windows networking tasks. Now it's time to see how well you can perform Windows network configuration tasks. You can find answers to the quiz and exercise questions in Appendix A at the back of the book.

Quiz

1. When is the best time to use the Network Setup Wizard?
2. What's the most secure callback method for mobile users on the road?
3. Which command line utility helps you configure RAS?
4. What's the difference between a dial-up and a VPN connection?
5. How does DMI record information about your equipment?

Exercises

1. Create a network design and management plan for your network.
2. Try creating a RAS setup for your system.
3. Experiment with the different connection types that the New Connection Wizard makes possible.

DAY 16

Configuring Security

Security is front-page news today because of break-ins at various Internet sites. People also suffer at the hands of crackers in their e-mail. Computer systems suffer death due to lax security, or, at least, the user suffers loss of data. Let's just say that security is a passionate subject for some, but a requirement for all.

The press often maligns Microsoft as being too slow in their security efforts. In addition, many members of the press point to every flaw and failed attempt to fix problems to indicate that Microsoft is incompetent. It's true that Microsoft's track record isn't the best in the industry and their solutions for problems are often dubious at best. However, you'll also find plenty to say about the negligence of network administrators and users alike. For example, Microsoft released a fix for the Code Red worm weeks before it appeared on the scene, yet the worm infected many computer systems because the network administrator failed to apply the patch. The fact that Microsoft makes such a large target for crackers to attack doesn't help either. Most people use Microsoft products, and crackers want to affect the largest number of people they can.

We're going to discuss security issues today. The information you obtain will help you organize your security efforts. You'll also learn how to make the best use of the security features that Microsoft provides. In addition, I'll tell you about a few techniques that you can use to sway the security war in your favor. Crackers use well-known techniques because they work. You can use that to your advantage by ensuring that you don't fall into traps.

However, the two things we can't do today are predicting the future and making your system completely airtight. You don't know what new viruses and worms crackers will create tomorrow. In fact, even if you did know, it would be hard to prevent an attack on an unmonitored system. This is the second part of your security responsibility. Not only do you need to be aware of security threats and fixes for your software, but you also need to monitor your system for security problems. Only monitored systems have a chance to survive in a world filled with security threats.

Creating a Security Plan

Every network should have a security plan. Even if you put two computers together to play games with your friends on the weekend, you need a security plan. Some security plans are quite formal, while others appear on a single sheet of paper in a maintenance log. The important thing is that you know what security measures are in place on your system and what to do in case someone breaks in. Think of it this way—it doesn't matter *what* data you lost as the result of a cracker attack. The only thing that matters is that you *did* lose data.

The following sections will discuss the requirements for a security plan. They help you design a security plan that really maintains a system security. While the security plan won't lock your system up, it does help with security because it helps you understand the security process in place in your organization.

Breaking the Company into Groups

Breaking the company into securable groups seems like one of those things that every network administrator should know about, and yet I've seen more than a few networks that assign security on an individual basis. Always break your company into groups that you can manage easily. The group mentality will save you time and effort because groups take less time to configure. Groups also reduce the chance that you'll forget to change someone's account when you need to make a change to network security. All you need to consider is the needs of the group and change the group settings.

Of course, the big question is how you break the company into nicely packaged groups. You might look at your company and see a multitude of people who all do different tasks. It might not be easy to break them into groups. You can use the following list of grouping suggestions as a guide, but sometimes you'll just have to become creative in your approach to the problem.

- **Department**   This is the easy grouping choice. Everyone in the same department should have similar security needs at some level. Some users will have other requirements, but you can consider their department security needs as essential. For example, everyone working in accounting will require access to some level of accounting files. All you need to do is find out what that level is and create a group that will answer that need.

- **Rank**   Another easy grouping choice is rank. Even if you have the smallest company in the world, some users will fit into the worker category, while others fit into the manager category. Managers often have network needs greater than those assigned to a department because of their position within the company. The larger your company, the larger the number of rank-based groups you'll need to consider.

- **Team**   Many companies have a team mentality. Users from different departments join together to create a product or perform some other task. The members of the team often require access to special files. In addition, you normally want to keep people outside the team from knowing what the team is doing. The team approach keeps files in the hands of those that need them. This particular grouping is rank independent. A manager may not have access to some of the files used by a subordinate if he or she isn't part of that team.

- **Skill Level**   If your company is large enough, you'll have a constant influx of new people. You don't want to give these people access to everything the network has to offer until they've completed a training period. Of course, skill levels can go well beyond the trainee. You need to consider other skill levels in the organization. For example, a new manager may not know enough to work with all of the management files. You may want to train them first or give them time to adjust to their new position.

- **Sensitivity Level**   Companies have secrets, and you only want those you can trust to know them. You might need a special grouping for the company's inner circle. It might seem at first that this group would include only managers, but politics often play a role in the sensitivity setting. It pays to keep your options open on the groups so that it's easy to make changes. Don't assume that all managers will have access to every company secret.

- **Temporary Groups**   This group could contain just about anything that you don't plan to keep around for very long. It could even include temporary employees hired on for a specific purpose and let go after the job is complete. A temporary group works well when you have company training that requires user interaction with the network.

16

> Everyone outside of IT is going to complain about any security plan you create if you don't involve them in the decision process. Part of the group creation process is to present the list of groups to those involved. You might be surprised at the ideas that users come up with when you ask them to brainstorm your security plan. In addition, you can be a little more certain that you're not forgetting a major security need.

What happens if you can't fit every user need within a group? In some cases, you'll have to assign an individual user a unique set of network privileges. The unique settings you make can come back later to haunt you, however, so it's important to take some precautions when you need to go outside the group mentality. It pays to maintain a log of individual user settings so you can find them quickly when needed. Otherwise, you don't know where those little "security bombs" will show up.

Part of the group creation process should involve diagramming the groups to show how they relate to each other. If you don't want to diagram the security on your network, at least make a list of the groups and provide a reason for the existence of each group on the list. Eventually, the user and group entries on your network will create clutter that you'll want to clean up, and you may find yourself wondering why you created a particular group. Good notes now prevent head scratching later.

Security Plan Considerations

Once you have a list of groups and a structure for your security plan, you need to begin work on the security plan itself. A good security plan considers some basic needs. The following list shows what I normally include in a security plan. Depending on the size of your company, you may need to add other provisions to the security plan.

- **Responsibilities**   Many companies today stress the team concept toward managing projects. The concept works well on projects because the entire team can pull together to complete the task. However, the team concept in security is a mistake and a disaster waiting to happen. One person has to have responsibility for each security area. In addition, the plan should assign a second person to check the first person's work. However, the first person is ultimately responsible for a particular well-defined area of security and only that person will "fry" when something happens.

  Responsibility extends to the user realm. Every user is responsible for maintaining his or her password. They're responsible for keeping their part of the information puzzle confidential. Finally, each user is responsible for reporting anomalies to the network administrator. A good security plan begins with personal responsibility.

- **Policies**   Every security plan should consider how the company manages resources. The plan needs to spell out the policies the network administrator implements within the network setup in the form of local or group policies. For example, the plan should consider the frequency of password change within the organization. See the "Setting Local Security Policy" section for additional policy settings that Windows XP supports.

- **Normal Event Handling**   One of the biggest problems with security plans that I've seen is that they don't spell out normal procedures. Simple questions, such as how a user requests additional access to system resources, remain unanswered. Without a list of standard procedures, users are apt to conceive their own unique solutions to problems. Unfortunately, the solutions often put user needs first, the needs of the company second, and security requirements dead last.

- **Emergency Event Handling**   Quick! Someone has spotted a virus on the network! Do you know what to do? If you have a good security plan, you do. On the other hand, if you're like most companies, your system is now dead in the water, and your data is at risk. Everyone has a headache, and no one wants to face the extreme task of fixing the system. In short, most companies manage by crisis. A little forethought in the form of emergency procedures can keep the situation calm and damage to a minimum.

- **Penalties**   This is one area where most security plans do have an entry. However, the penalties are often weak or extreme. They don't reflect the idea of, "Let the punishment fit the crime." Firing someone who forgot his password is akin to capital punishment for jay walking. Likewise, a slap on the wrist for someone who brought a virus to work on that floppy from home isn't strong enough. Make penalties for minor infractions a teaching experience. For example, you could ask the person to write a paper on the topic and present it before their workgroup. The process of researching and presenting the paper is a lesson the person is unlikely to forget. Of course, infractions that damage the company in a major way require a major response—up to and including firing the person for cause.

- **Review Process**   The world is changing and so is your company. A security plan that fulfilled every need six months ago is unlikely to work today. You need to spell out a review process. The parties responsible for security should meet regularly to review changes in technology, external and internal threats, and company needs.

The preceding list tells you about the mechanics of a security plan and what this plan should contain. However, you need to consider other needs as part of the security plan. For one thing, you need the full support of management for a security plan, which means involving management in the creation process. Make sure that management reviews and

16

approves your security plan. In addition, you need to get approval to add "teeth" to the penalties of your security plan.

Another axiom for security plans is that it won't work without user cooperation. Some users will fight tooth and nail about every provision in a security plan because they don't want their "freedoms" taken from them. That's the reason you need a penalties section. However, the vast majority of users, the proverbial 95% of them, will want to cooperate. All they need is training on the new security plan. After you create a security plan, make sure that you schedule training time and show the users how Windows XP will help them implement the tenants of the plan. It's important to stress that the security plan will actually give the user more freedoms, not less. For example, users won't constantly worry about virus attacks if they follow the requirements of the plans.

Security Considerations for User Accounts

We began discussing user management issues, including user security, during Day 8, "Working with Users." Today we'll explore the security aspect of user management in detail. The discussion begins with the Local Users and Groups snap-in of the Computer Management console.

Working with Groups

Figure 16.1 shows the Groups folder, which contains a list of the default groups for Windows XP along with an explanation of each group. You'll want to check this list out when creating your own group list because the default groups will serve some of the generic requirements. In addition, looking at the default groups will present you with some ideas for your own.

FIGURE 16.1

The Groups folder contains a list of the default groups for your system.

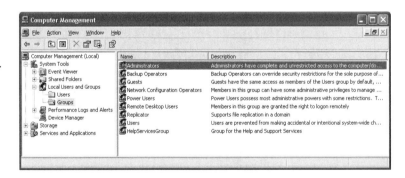

To create a new group, right-click anywhere in the Details pane and select New Group from the context menu. You'll see a New Group dialog box. Type a group name in the Group Name field and a description for the group in the Description field. Click Add to display a Select Users dialog box. Type or find the names of the users you want to add to the group and then click OK. Click Create to create the group. From this point on, every time you assign a right to the group, you also assign it to the users of that group.

Tip

Always provide detailed descriptions for groups. The default groups will provide you with ideas on what type of information to include in a group description. The description should always tell precisely what purpose the group serves and indicate why you created it. Temporary group descriptions should begin with the word "Temporary" to make them easier to find. Documentation is extremely important when security is involved.

If you need to rename or delete a group, right-click the group name within the Details pane. Select the appropriate action. If you're deleting a group, Windows XP will warn you of the consequences of deleting it. Group deletions are permanent, and you can't restore them later. If you select the Rename option, then the group name will change into an edit box where you can change the name. Changing the name doesn't affect the users assigned to the group or the resources the group can access.

Sometimes, you'll need to change the group description or add or remove users. You'll do this in the Group Properties dialog box. Right-click the group entry in the details pane; then choose Properties from the context menu. Note that the Group Properties dialog box won't allow you to change the name of the group; you must do this with the Rename option on the context menu. You'll use the Add and Remove buttons in the Group Properties dialog box to add and remove users as needed.

Working with Users

Figure 16.2 shows the Users folder. The list contains a few default users such as Administrator and Guest. You'll also find the initial user that Windows XP requested you create as part of the installation process. Microsoft also includes a SUPPORT_<Some Number> and a HelpAssistant account with Windows XP for the newer features it supports. Either you or an application created the remaining accounts in this list.

Notice that many of the users in this list have a red circle with an X on them. This indicates that the account is disabled. You don't want to delete default accounts you'll need later. In fact, you can't delete them in some cases, because Windows XP will prevent you from doing so. You can disable any account, including the Administrator account. Disabling the account makes it unavailable and a less likely target for compromise.

FIGURE 16.2

The Users folder contains a list of default and created users for your system.

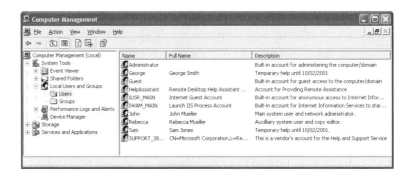

Crackers always look for defaults. You can rename any of the accounts including the Administrator account. It pays to rename any default account that you can in order to protect the account from prying eyes. Although I haven't renamed the accounts in Figure 16.2 for clarity, I normally rename all of the default accounts in a manner consistent with my security plan. For example, one good naming scheme that I saw on a system was to combine the name of the machine with a shorter version of the default account name. For example, Administrator might become MyMachineAdmin. The name is easy to remember, yet doesn't use the default name.

Note   Always check the documentation for applications that create default accounts on your system. For example, a UPS may create a default account that only has privileges for UPS information. You can't rename these accounts, in some cases, because they're "hard wired" into the application. If you can't change the account name in the application, you can't change it in the Users folder either.

We already discussed adding and removing users in the Users folder in the "Working with Users" section of Day 8. Let's look directly at the security issues for users. The General tab of the User Properties dialog box shown in Figure 16.3 contains account and password settings. The option that you should *never* check is Password never expires. This is like saying that you don't care how long a cracker uses the account to create havoc on your system. Forcing users to change their password regularly increases security in a big way. Likewise, I've never come up with a good reason for network administrators to disallow user password changes; a good administrator wants users to change their passwords regularly.

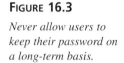

FIGURE 16.3

Never allow users to keep their password on a long-term basis.

Use the User must change password at next logon option whenever you make a change to the account. Generally, you want users to be responsible and in control of their accounts. Security begins when someone takes responsibility for his or her actions. If users know you can't access their accounts, then they begin to build a sense of ownership over the account.

The Member Of tab contains a list of the groups to which the user belongs. Use Add to add new groups to the list and Remove to remove the accounts. The user always has access to anything the group can access.

Managing File/Folder Access

The most difficult resource on your network to manage is the disk drive. Anything the user can use to store data becomes the target of abuse on every network. Users don't even know they're using the resource incorrectly in most cases. All they know is that they want to keep that report from five years ago, even if they'll never use it again.

We've already discussed some disk-related issues in the "Disk" section during Day 10. The following sections focus on the security elements of disk management. You'll learn how to protect your disk resources and make them a less tempting target for abuse by everyone on the network.

Creating Shares

One of the bigger security concerns you'll have is how much of a resource to share. We discussed quotas during Day 10, but quotas only protect the use of the resource, they don't protect the data the resource contains. To do that and still allow users access to the data they need, you need to create one or more shares on a host drive.

Every host drive already has one share defined at the root level. This is an administrative share designed to provide access for backups and other administrative tasks. No one else should have access to this share and even the administrator should never use it directly. Administrative shares commonly have the device name and a dollar sign ($). For example, the C drive will have an administrative share name of C$.

Many shares will occur at the folder, not the drive level. You want to share the minimum level of drive resources that will satisfy a user's needs. The smaller you make the share, the better from a security perspective.

To manage a share, right-click the drive or folder icon and then choose Properties from the context menu. Select the Sharing tab, and you'll see a Drive Properties dialog box similar to the one shown in Figure 16.4. Notice that the dialog box contains sections that determine the sharing status of the resource, the user limits, and caching status. The areas we're interested in for this section are the Permissions, the Remove Share, and the New Share buttons.

FIGURE 16.4

Use the Sharing tab to manage the shares for resources on your system.

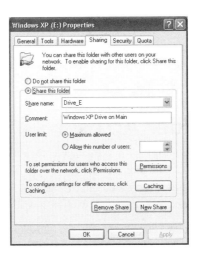

You can create a new share by clicking New Share. Windows XP will display a New Share dialog box. Type an easy-to-remember single word share name. You can use underscores to connect words if desired such as My_Drive. Add a comment that describes the share. I normally include the drive type, location, and reason for the share. For example, the comment might look like this: "Windows XP hard drive on John's machine for general data storage." If the share appears on a user machine, then you'll also want to select Allow this number of users and set a reasonable number that will reduce the burden of data sharing on the user. Click OK to make the new share permanent.

Removing a share is as easy as selecting the share in the Share Name drop-down list box and clicking Remove. However, Windows XP doesn't provide any warning when you take this action. Removing the share is permanent and Windows XP doesn't save any of the settings for you. In short, use the Remove option with care.

Working with Permissions

In the previous section, we discussed the mechanics of creating a share. However, the share isn't complete until you assign permissions to it. Windows XP always assumes that you want the Everyone group to access the share with full permissions. Always remove this permission unless you really need it because it's too broad for most purposes. Of course, you'll also find that you need to reassign permissions to a share from time-to-time. In most cases, you want to add specific group permissions and only give them the level of access they require.

To change the permissions for a share, click Permissions, and you'll see a Permissions for Share Name dialog box. Windows displays this same dialog box when you click Permissions in the New Share dialog box. The Group or User Names field contains a list of the users and groups that can access the share. Click Add to add new entries and Remove to remove existing entries.

When you click Add, you'll see a Select Users or Groups dialog box. Type or find the name of the user or group you want to add to the permissions list. Click OK. Check boxes in the Permissions for field for the new entry that determines the level of access the user or group will have.

Adding Security

Creating a share for your drive makes it accessible by others on the network. You can determine which groups have access to the drive, but creating the share doesn't mean they'll actually enjoy all of the access you provide in the share. The Security tab shown in Figure 16.5 determines the precise level of access every group and user has to use the drive. It overrides the settings in the share.

FIGURE 16.5

The Security tab is the true indicator of access for a drive or folder share.

You'll still see a list of groups or users that can access the drive in the Group or User Names field. However, notice that the list of rights in the Permissions for field is more extensive and offers finer control over drive access. When working with a folder, you'll notice that Windows XP automatically checks the permissions at the folder level that you checked at a higher level unless you disable permission inheritance.

Notice the Advanced button at the bottom of the dialog box. Click this button, and you'll see the Advanced Security Settings dialog box shown in Figure 16.6. We've already discussed the Auditing tab of this dialog box in the "Auditing Drive Access" section of Day 8. Today, we'll discuss the uses for the other tabs in the dialog box.

FIGURE 16.6

The Advanced Security Settings dialog box offers maximum control over resource security.

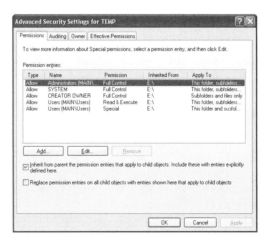

Note

The Advanced Security Settings dialog box shown in Figure 16.6 is for a folder. The inheritance option at the bottom of the dialog box forces the folder to use the settings of the parent resource when checked. Clear this option to set the permissions for the folder individually. The drive version of this dialog box lacks the inheritance check box because drives are at the top of the resource hierarchy.

16

The Permissions tab contains a list of every group and user that has permission to access the resource. To add a new user or group to the list, click Add. You'll see a Select User or Group dialog box where you can type or find the name of the user or group that you want to add.

After you add the user or group, click OK, and you'll see a Permission Entry dialog box similar to the one shown in Figure 16.7. Note that this is the same Permission Entry dialog box you'll see when you click Edit in the Permissions tab. As you can see, the list of permissions is very detailed and allows you to set security for a wide range of needs.

FIGURE 16.7

The Permission Entry dialog box offers fine control over user and group permissions.

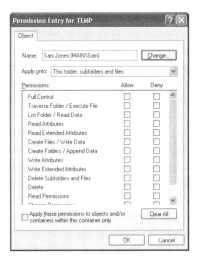

Notice the Change button next to the Name field. This button enables you to change the name of the user or group that the settings will affect. Use the entries in the Apply Onto list box to control what effect the changes you make have on the directory structure. For example, you can choose just this folder, just the subfolders, or just the files in the folder, or any of a number of other combinations. After you make the required changes, click OK.

The Owner tab displays the current owner of the objects within the drive or folder. You can take ownership of the objects by checking the Replace owner on subcontainers and objects option and then clicking Apply. If you have the required permissions, Windows XP will change the owner on every object at the current level and below in the hierarchy.

The Effective Permissions tab is an essential security diagnostic tool. So far, we've looked at a number of ways to set security, and it would be easy to get confused, especially if more than one administrator makes changes to the same drive. To use this tab, click Select. Type or find the name of the user or group whose security you want to test. Click OK. You'll see the effective permissions (the combination of all permissions) checked in the Effective Permissions field. Using this feature can help you locate users and groups with too many permissions for a given area of the resource.

Setting Local Security Policy

The Local Security Policy console shown in Figure 16.8 helps you set the security policies for your system. A policy is a general rule that Windows XP applies to everyone who uses the computer. In addition, some policies apply to objects and not just users. For example, you can specify how much access the UPS account has to the system as a whole.

FIGURE 16.8

Use the Local Security Policy console to make your system more secure.

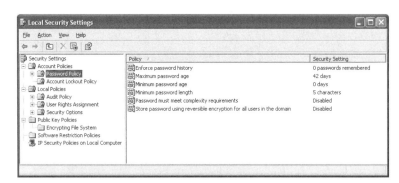

Windows XP includes an impressive list of policies for you to use in securing your system. One of the biggest problems with the initial Windows XP setup is that most of these policies are either undefined or have a default setting that leaves the system open to attack. In short, one of the first security tasks you need to perform is changing the security policies so they work in your favor.

If Windows XP simply presented you with a list of policies, you'd spend a lot of time trying to find the one you need, so Microsoft grouped the policies into functional areas.

The following sections tell you how to use the four standard policy folders: Account Policies, Local Policies, Public Key Policies, and IP Security Policies on Local Computer. I won't discuss the Software Restriction Policies because these policies are application specific. The application designer has to create and document them for you.

Note

This section doesn't discuss every policy in detail because you can find a detailed description of every policy in the Windows Help and Support Center. The purpose of this section is to show you how to use the policies to your benefit. In short, we'll focus on the practical aspects of using the policies, rather than determining what they do.

16

The Account Policies Folder

The Account Policies folder affects everyone's ability to log into the system. It consists of the Password Policy folder shown in Figure 16.8 and the Account Lockout Policy folder.

The Password Policy folder contains entries that affect the way that users log into the system. Figure 16.8 shows the default settings for this folder. As you can see, the settings aren't very challenging. To make these settings a little tougher for a cracker to break, you'd want to enforce the Password History option to ensure that users have to change their password. In addition, I recommend a maximum of 30 days between password changes. However, even a weekly change isn't too much if you're working with secure data. (Daily changes might become annoying after a while.)

Notice the Password must meet the complexity requirements option. Select this option, and users will need to select unique passwords that contain three categories of characters that include numbers, uppercase letters, lowercase letters, and special symbols. When you add this requirement to a minimum password length of at least six characters, the passwords are much harder to break.

Tip

Some people's idea of a hard to break password is something long and difficult to remember such as xyz@2aBC$928. I'm sure that most users are just going to roll their eyes at such a password and write it down somewhere—I know that I would. Of course, the problem is creating a difficult to guess password that's also easy to remember. How about using two words and a special symbol? For example, My$Password uses all of the criteria for a complex password, is relatively hard to figure out, and yet easy to remember. If

> you don't want users to write their password down, then give them some-
> thing they can remember. Of course, it also helps if you add some thing to
> your security plan that details penalties for writing their password down.

Windows XP provides three account lockout policies for your system. The Account lockout threshold policy is the key to these settings. The default setting of 0 means users can
enter the wrong password all day long, and you'd never know about it. A policy of 3 or 4
incorrect logins usually assures that the system can handle typos, but leaves crackers
with little room for invading your system. The other two policies set the lockout duration
and the amount of time that must pass between incorrect logins before the lockout
counter resets. The default of 30 minutes really isn't long enough to discourage crackers.
In addition, it might tempt employees to wait before reporting problems. I normally set
both counters to 1,440 minutes or 24 hours as a minimum.

An account lockout occurs when a user types his password incorrectly a given number of
times. When this occurs, Windows XP will display a message telling the user that the
system has locked him out, and he needs to contact the network administrator. Figure
16.9 shows the results of a lockout. You enable the account by removing the check next
to the Account is locked out option. Whether you clear the User must change password at
next login will depend on the reason for the lockout. In most cases, you'll want the user
to create a new password for his account.

FIGURE 16.9

*One of the effects of
the account lockout
policy is that the user
must change his pass-
word afterwards.*

The Account lockout threshold setting also shows another part of the Local Security
Settings console. Whenever you change a policy that affects other policies, you'll see a
Suggested Value Changes dialog box like the one shown in Figure 16.10. This dialog box

tells you what Microsoft suggests as minimum policy settings to go with the change you want to make. You can always set the policy settings higher than suggested.

FIGURE 16.10

The Local Security Settings console automatically suggests new settings for related policies when you make a key policy change.

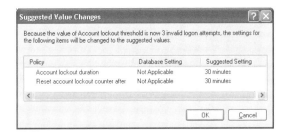

The Local Policies Folder

The Local Policies folder contains three major folders: Audit Policy, User Rights Assignment, and Security Options. This is the heart of the local security policy for your system because it contains the settings that the user will rely upon while working with Windows XP.

The Audit Policy folder contains the main audit settings for your system. Windows XP doesn't cover the entries in this list in other areas. For example, you'll see options to audit account logon events. Double-clicking these entries displays a dialog box that contains a Success and Failure option. You can audit none, either, or both of the options.

The User Rights Assignment folder is misnamed. It actually contains settings that control the access provided to every object in the system. Figure 16.11 shows an example of the entries in this window. Notice that you can change settings such as the user's right to change the priority of applications. When you double-click any of these settings, you'll see a dialog box containing a list of the users that have the right in question. It contains the usual Add and Remove buttons for management purposes.

You'll want to observe the user additions in this folder carefully, because changes could indicate cracker activity. For example, if the Everyone group suddenly has the power to deny local logins, you can bet that someone has tampered with the settings. You'll also want to modify a few of the standard settings. For example, even if you disable the Guest account, the Log on locally policy will still contain Guest as one of the people that can log on. Removing Guest from the list adds a little more security to your system.

FIGURE 16.11

The User Rights Assignment folder affects the rights of every object on your system, not just the user.

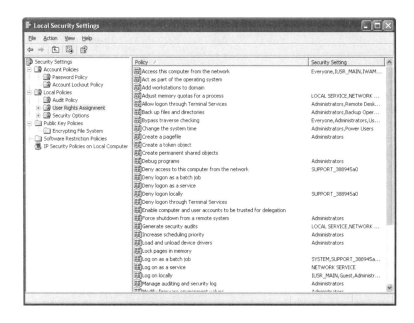

The Security Options folder shown in Figure 16.12 contains policies that affect system processes. For example, you can restrict access of the CD-ROM drive on your machine to users who log on locally. No matter how you change Windows Explorer, this policy won't change (unless you change it with a global policy).

FIGURE 16.12

The Security Options folder contains policies that affect system processes.

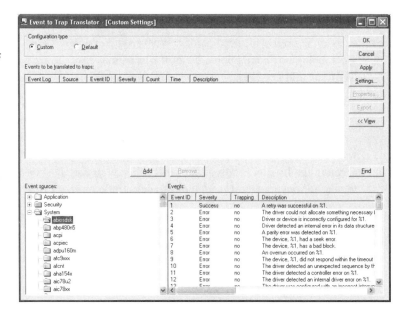

Some of the more important security settings reside in this folder. For example, you'll find the Interactive Logon settings in this folder. Use the Do Not Require CTRL-ALT-DEL setting to determine if users go directly to the logon screen when they start the machine. Other settings change the logon message and title. You can also delete the name of the last user who logged in with an Interactive Logon setting.

You'll also find some convenience items in the list. Look at the Shutdown group, and you'll find the Allow system to be shut down without having to log on policy. This policy adds a convenience factor if you enable it for regular workstations. Of course, you'll want to keep it disabled for public machines such as those used for kiosks. Otherwise, you'll find users who will shut your system down and annoy the person running the kiosk.

Notice that this folder contains yet more audit options. It's important to realize just how much auditing you can perform on a Windows XP system. Windows XP provides the means to monitor just about every form of system activity.

The Public Key Policies Folder

The Public Key folder normally contains just one folder, Encrypting File System. The Encrypting File System folder contains all of the certificates for your system. A certificate is a form of identification that you can present to someone else to validate your identity. This listing tells you who owns the certificate, who issued it, the date the certificate expires, how the system uses the certificate, the certificate's friendly name, the certificate status, and the template used to create the certificate. Generally, you won't need to do anything with the certificates on this tab.

You can delete, export, and open certificates. Because Windows XP generally keeps certificates even when they're out-of-date, your major housekeeping task is to delete the certificate. Opening a certificate enables you to view its contents. Sometimes, you'll find useful information about the issuer within the Details tab of the Certificate Properties dialog box.

The only time you need to export a certificate is to send it to someone else or to move the user to another machine. Right-click the certificate and choose All Tasks | Export from the context menu. You'll see a Certificate Export Wizard Welcome screen. The following steps show how to export a certificate.

1. Click Next. You'll see the Export Private Key dialog box. Always export the private key if you're moving the certificate to another machine or creating a backup. Never export the private key if you're going to share the certificate with someone else.

2. Choose a private key option; then click Next. You'll see an Export File Format dialog box. The options you see in this dialog box will vary by your machine setup, the network configuration, and whether you chose to export the private key. If you're exporting the certificate to share with someone else, choose a file format that's compatible with their machine setup.

3. Choose an export file format and then click Next. You'll see a File to Export dialog box.

4. Type or choose a filename; then click Next. You'll see a Completion dialog box. Notice that the dialog box contains all of the settings for the file export.

5. Verify the certificate output settings; then click Next. The Certificate Export Wizard will create the file for you.

The IP Security Policies on Local Computer Folder

Windows XP provides the means for creating a secure IP computing environment. The IP Security Policies on Local Computer folder contains the following three entries.

- **Client**   Describes how the client will react to requests from the server and what type of information the client supplies to the server. The standard settings allow the client to communicate if unsecured (plain text) mode. If the server requests a secure connection, the client will negotiate the type of security used.

- **Secure Server**   Defines the settings for a secure server environment. The default setting requires secure communication with the client, preferably using Kerberos. The server won't allow any form of unsecured communication.

- **Server**   Defines the settings for a normal server environment. The standard settings ask the client to use Kerberos for a secure environment. If the client doesn't respond, then Windows XP will use clear text communication.

If you double-click on any of these entries, you'll see a Policy Properties dialog box. The General tab contains the name and description of the policy. It also contains a setting that determines how often Windows XP checks for new security policies. You can also click Advanced if you want to change the key exchange settings.

The Rules tab contains the rules used to administer the policy. If you want to add a new rule, click Add. You can also edit and remove rules by using the associated buttons. Whenever you add a new rule, you have a choice of creating the rule using the New Rule Properties dialog box or using the Security Rule Wizard. Both methods produce the same results and most people find the Security Rule Wizard (the default setting) easier to use. The following steps tell you how to create a new security rule using the Security Rule Wizard.

1. Click Next. You'll see a Tunnel Endpoint dialog box. This dialog box contains the address of an endpoint (the remote machine) for a communication. If this is a general rule, you won't want to provide an endpoint value.

2. Enter an endpoint value, if necessary, and then click Next. You'll see a Network Type dialog box. Windows XP divides the rules into three types: those that affect all networks, those that affect the local network, and those that affect remote communications of any type.

3. Select a network type option; then click Next. You'll see an Authentication Method dialog box. Windows XP doesn't support Kerberos without domain controller (Windows Server) that has Active Directory installed. If you have a smaller network without the required support, you'll need to choose one of the other authentication methods.

4. Choose an authentication method. Type any required information. Click Next. You'll see an IP Filter List dialog box. Unless you want to install a new file, Windows XP provides you with a choice of standard IP or Internet Control Message Protocol (ICMP) filtering. Even if you choose one of the standard filtering choices, you can highlight the option and then click Edit to change the settings. Never remove a default filtering option.

5. Select or create an IP filtering option; then click Next. You'll see a Filter Action dialog box. The filter normally allows three actions. The first is to allow unsecured transactions. The second requests a secure transaction, but will allow an unsecured transaction if the client or server doesn't provide the required support. The third requires secured transactions. You can add other actions as necessary using the Add button.

6. Select or create an IP filtering action and click Next. You'll see a Completion dialog box.

7. Click Finish. The Security Rule Wizard creates the rule for you.

Encrypting Data on Your Hard Drive

Encryption is one of the easiest ways to secure data on your system if you're using the NFTS file system. If you want to secure a file or folder, right-click the file or folder and choose Properties from the context menu. On the General tab, you'll see an Advanced button. Click Advanced, and you'll see an Advanced Attributes dialog box. Check the Encrypt contents to secure data option. Note that encrypting the file and compressing it is mutually exclusive, so Windows XP will automatically clear the compressed attribute if you select encryption. Click OK twice to make the change. Windows XP will encrypt the file for you.

Tip

> If you choose to display encrypted and compressed folders in an alternate color, Windows XP will normally use blue for compressed files and green for encrypted files. This helps you determine what type of file you're viewing just by looking at the color.

Overcoming Windows Security Deficiencies

Microsoft has spent considerable time and money trying to convince everyone that Windows XP is secure. Likewise, many other vendors have spent an equal amount of time and money pointing out the flaws in Microsoft's operating system in the hopes that you'll buy their product. The fact of the matter is that Microsoft is unlikely to make Windows XP secure in our lifetime, and it's equally improbable that anyone else will introduce a completely secure operating system. The reason that Windows appears in the news so often is that they're such a large target that no cracker can resist.

The biggest Windows security deficiency is one of perception. If you buy into the Microsoft hype, you'll eventually get hurt. It's safer to assume from the outset that anyone who really wants to is going to break into any operating system out there. Once you assume this mind-set, many Windows security deficiencies won't only become apparent, but you'll be able to stop them by using third-party tools, patches, and intense system monitoring as well.

Anyone who's observed Microsoft recently will admit that they've gotten better about reporting bugs in their system. The problem is that they often hide the information so no one knows about it. This is the two-edged sword of being a marketing-driven company with a large target product. The best way around this problem is to take a proactive approach and search the Microsoft Knowledge Base (http://search.support.microsoft.com/kb/c.asp) for new articles on a weekly basis.

A final way to overcome Windows security deficiencies is to use third-party products. Many of the major trade presses include product reviews you can use to determine the relative merit of third-party offerings. What most people don't realize is that these reviews often alert you to security problems you didn't know about. In short, not only can the third-party product solve security problems you do know about, but it can help you better understand security requirements based on the current security environment as well.

Tips for Thwarting Crackers Inside and Out

Some people are under the assumption that all crackers are brilliant computer specialists in disguise. It's true that many crackers are smart computer users. However, the one thing that a cracker needs in abundance is time. Crackers are patient, and they'll wait for an opening in your network before they attack, unless they have a good reason to force their way in. An opening created by someone in your company requires less work on the part of the cracker and definitely hides their activity.

Crackers are also opportunistic. If you fail to apply a patch to your system or fail to remove a default account that everyone knows about, it's like hanging a sign on your network saying, "Attack here, I really don't care!" However, we've already discussed these issues as part of the chapter. You already know that you need to close the holes in your network. What can you do to keep crackers at bay once you fix the major problems?

16

Tip

Privacy is a major concern for most users of the Internet. Several recent surveys by large consulting companies show that about 86% of users consider privacy a major concern and one of the reasons they don't trust Internet commerce. A few companies such as Anonymizer.com (http://www.anonymizer.com) have set up secure servers you can use to surf the Web in privacy. You must click a button on your Internet Explorer toolbar to enable the service and can disable it at any time. The way the service works is you send the URL you want to surf to Anonymizer, who then obtains the data for you and sends it back to your machine. Therefore, it's impossible for anyone to track you, your personal information, your IP address, or send cookies to your machine. This means that you can't use Anonimizer to access a financial institution or to shop online. Anonymizer (and sites like it) is currently grappling with the issue of keeping its site safe from use by crackers to hide their activities. In addition, these privacy services plan to provide secure service to financial institutions.

The first mistake that every network administrator makes is assuming that you can seal your network up tight so that no crackers can get through. Many people have tested this theory and none of them has succeeded. If a cracker wants to access your system, he'll find a way to do it. Therefore, your best friends as a network administrator are the monitoring tools you use to check your system for leaks. After you have your system fixed and your monitoring tools in place, you might want to try some of the following suggestions. Just remember, there isn't a network made that someone else can't break into.

- **Kill the Default Setting**   The default setting is your worst enemy. Crackers spend a great deal of time learning all of the default settings for a network they want to invade. They look for anything that might help them, including the small things like log files. It always pays to change the default settings if possible. Move your log files to another directory to make them harder to find. Use something other than the default name for your administrator account. Keep the number of default configuration settings to a minimum.

- **Limit Resource Access**   If a cracker does break into your system, make sure that he gains a minimum level of access. The user does require enough resource access to accomplish his tasks, but you don't want to give him anything more than the minimum. This also makes it easier to ascertain the level of risk after a cracker breaks into your system.

- **Never Work with the Administrator Account**   You have to use an account with administrator privileges to manage your system. However, always use a standard user account when performing other tasks. Crackers often try to steal the administrator account information, so the less you use it, the less exposure the account has to compromise.

- **Read the Trade Press Alerts**   Electronic newsletters often provide valuable information long before you see it anywhere else.

- **Take Threats Seriously**   I don't know of a more effective cracker than a disgruntled employee with a modicum of knowledge. Some of the worst damage you'll ever see comes from within. However, it's a mistake to consider any threat so much hot air. Every threat is serious, and you need to deal with it.

- **Don't Make Brash Statements**   At least one person has made the mistake of saying his site was cracker-proof to a member of the press. The crackers proved this person wrong by launching a major DoS attack. Several days later, the person in question begged the crackers to leave the Web site alone and admitted that it was wrong to make such a brash statement. If you want crackers to leave you alone, keep a low profile and don't make yourself a target.

- **Use the Latest Tools**   Some network administrators install a firewall on their system and never look at it again. They just assume that the firewall will continue to work as anticipated. Sometimes, you need to do more than just patch your security software. In many cases, it gets outdated, and you need to replace it.

Summary

Today is only the beginning of an education in security. A knowledgeable network administrator keeps track of new threats and knows how to recognize them. Education isn't an option today; you must continually look for the threats that will affect your system.

You did learn about the security features that Windows XP can provide. Crackers often attack because they find the door to your network wide open. Closing the door will at least discourage the cracker. Some will still sneak in through the windows, but you'll keep many crackers at bay.

Finally, there's no such thing as a secure system. The best you can hope to achieve is a system that has all of the required patches installed and security barriers in place. You must maintain vigilance over your network if you want to ensure that you detect the first appearance of crackers on your system.

Q&A

Q: I'm confused about the role of local and group policies on the network. Where does one begin and the other end?

A: Windows XP actually provides four policy levels. Windows XP won't implement some policies until you specifically set them. Other policies have a default value that defines their effect on the system. Local policies that you specifically set come next. Setting a local policy means that you've taken a stance on a particular security measure. However, local policies affect only one machine— the one on which you define them. Finally, group policies affect the system as a whole. You set a group policy when the entire organization observes a rule. Group policies override all other policy settings.

Q: Why doesn't Microsoft make all of the permissions for a resource available at one level, rather than using so many levels?

A: The main reason for all of the levels of security settings is simplicity. If someone doesn't understand the detailed security settings, or a network administrator only wants to set a basic level of permissions, the upper-level dialog boxes work just fine. Only when you want to perform a detailed setup do you need to access the lower-level dialog box as we did today.

Q: There are so many security alerts, at times, that turn out to be hoaxes. How can I tell the difference?

A: Reliable news sources generally check their facts before they pass a virus alert along to their readers. In addition, you'll find several places online that specialize in presenting virus information. One of the better sources of information is to subscribe to an online newsletter such as InfoWorld (`http://www.iwsubscribe.com/newsletters/`) and eWeek (`http://enewsletters.ziffdavis.com/pc_subscribe.asp`). You can also check several Web sites devoted to revealing hoaxes for what they are. Some of the more popular sites include:

- Forum of Incident Response and Security Teams (`http://www.first.org/`)
- Stiller Research (`http://www.stiller.com/`)
- Symantec AntiVirus Research Center (`http://www.symantec.com/avcenter/`)
- University of Michigan Virus Busters (`http://www.itd.umich.edu/virusbusters/`)
- Computer Incident Advisory Center (`http://www.ciac.org/ciac/`)
- VMyths.com (`http://www.vmyths.com/`)

Workshop

It's the end of the sixteenth day. You should have a better understanding of how security works now. Of course, it will take time for you to understand security fully, and I doubt that anyone can ever say that he is completely ready for a cracker attack. Now it's time to see how well you understand security-related tasks. You can find answers to the quiz and exercise questions in Appendix A at the back of the book.

Quiz

1. Why do you need to break users in your company into groups?
2. Which two user account options should you avoid using?
3. How do you test your security settings for errors?
4. How do you create a disk copy of a certificate?

Exercises

1. Create a security plan for your network.
2. Spend time reviewing, validating, and verifying the user accounts on your system.
3. Verify that your hard drives and other media resources are safe.
4. Review your local security policy and make any required changes.

WEEK 3

DAY 17

Working with Linux

More and more, users are finding that the appeal of Linux is becoming stronger. A good portion of you have already integrated Linux into your own networks. Businesses are still reluctant, though, to bring Linux fulltime into a network. Most of the reasons for this stem from a lack of knowledge of Linux and a hesitation on the behalf of network administrators to trust their networks and data to a "free" operating system.

Linux has been around for quite some time now and is no longer the domain of computing gurus. Some will say that Linux is a mainstream product now and deserves a place among the enterprise network operating systems. In light of this, you may find yourself needing to integrate Linux into your Windows networks or you may just want to integrate it for the sake of seeing how it performs.

Whatever your reasons for wanting to put Linux in your network, it's a decision you won't regret since it's an excellent server in any network for file or printer sharing or as a Web or FTP server. You can even use it as a Primary Domain Controller (PDC) in a Windows NT network with some configuration, but we won't delve into that here.

The discussion in this chapter will focus on using Linux as a file and print server in your Windows network and accessing the file and print shares provided by Linux from Windows XP Professional.

 Tip

> The Internet abounds with interesting sites containing Linux software. However, one of the best places to find great software and tips to go with it is Dave Central (http://linux.davecentral.com/). You'll find a lot of great software here, including a version of Quicktime for Linux.

Installing and Configuring Samba

Samba started life as the brainchild of Andrew Tridgell back in 1991. Andrew was looking for a way to access files that resided on a Sun computer from his own PC, which was running Digital's PATHWORKS for DOS.

Samba is a tool that allows for resource sharing from a Linux computer with a Windows computer. This sharing works both ways. You can use Samba to provide shares on a Linux server to Windows clients, and you can access shares on Windows computers from Linux by using the client portion of Samba.

Samba uses the server message block (SMB) protocol that's found in Windows and other network environments. Samba isn't just for Windows/Linux integration, however. It's widely available as a free software package that allows file and printer sharing among many disparate computing platforms such as MacOS and Unix variants. Currently, Samba runs on the following operating systems:

- AIX
- AmigaOS
- BSD (FreeBSD and OpenBSD)
- BeOS
- Coherent
- HP-UX (Hewlett Packard)
- Irix (SGI)
- MVS
- OpenVMS
- OS/2
- Tru64 UNIX (formerly Digital UNIX now Compaq)
- ULTRIX (formerly Digital)

Many products and networks have used SMB over the years. The first implementation was in IBM's PC Network Program—a broadband Ethernet network. Since that inception, IBM's LAN Server, Microsoft LAN Manager, Windows NT, Windows for Workgroups and Windows 9x, as well as LAN Manager for UNIX and Advanced Server for UNIX, have all used SMB.

Most Linux distributions come with a version of Samba on the install CDs or downloads. Samba gets installed during the OS install if you choose it from the available packages. One of the first things you may want to do before continuing with this chapter is to acquire and install the latest version of Samba. This ensures that you have the latest bug fixes.

You can download the current version from `http://www.samba.org`. Look for your Linux distribution link and download the latest version there. As of this writing, version 2.2.0 is the latest version.

After you've acquired the latest version of Samba, you can install it. For some distributions of Linux such as RedHat and Mandrake, a software installation package, called *RPM*, is available. RPM stands for RedHat Package Manager and is perhaps one of the easiest ways to install software on a Linux computer. Check your distribution of Linux as many more are starting to use RPM.

Note

If you have a distribution that uses RPM, be sure to download the RPM version of Samba. In addition, after you install Samba, check the version number using the smbstatus command in a terminal session. It's important to verify the version number before you proceed.

To use RPM to install Samba, locate the version of Samba that you downloaded; it normally resides in the user directory you were in when you logged into the Linux computer. For example, if I logged in as jmueller, then the file should be located in /home/jmueller.

RPM comes with many commands and options for software installation, removal, upgrading and verification; but we only need to look at the installation and upgrade options here. To see the available options, issue the RPM command in a terminal session by itself and press Enter. The options are displayed onscreen. Alternatively, you can read the manual pages by specifying man RPM. If you don't have any version of Samba installed yet, issue this command to install the new package that you've just downloaded.

```
rpm --install samba-2.2.0-200010417.i686.rpm
```

This command causes the RPM application to install the files in their required location to run Samba on your Linux computer. If you already have a version of Samba installed, you can either install the new version or upgrade the existing installation.

 Caution

> You may receive errors when trying to upgrade over an existing version of Samba. These errors usually indicate conflicting file versions. Use the—force option with RPM to force the installation of the newer files. The—force options is used immediately after the—upgrade or—install switches. Example;
>
> ```
> rpm --install --force samba-2.2.0-200010417.i686.rpm
> ```

Making Linux Visible to Windows

After you install Samba, you need to configure it before it will perform any useful functions on your network or even be visible to a Windows network. Samba is configured by using a text file called smb.conf. You'll find this file located in the /etc directory. An example of a smb.conf file as shown in Listing 17.1.

LISTING 17.1 Main Samba Configuration File

```
#=======================GlobalSettings===============================
[global]
# workgroup = NT-Domain-Name or Workgroup-Name
 workgroup = MDKGROUP
# server string is the equivalent of the NT Description field
 server string = Samba Server %v
# This option is important for security. It allows you to restrict
# connections to machines which are on your local network. The
# following example restricts access to two C class networks and
# the "loopback" interface. For more examples of the syntax see
# the smb.conf man page
; hosts allow = 192.168.1. 192.168.2. 127.
; encrypt passwords = yes
; smb passwd file = /etc/smbpasswd
```

This isn't the complete smb.conf file, since it's considerably longer than this. Not that it has to be, but you'll notice the comments throughout the file. The commented lines are prefixed with # and ; symbols. As the introductory text in the file mentions, the # symbol is used to indicate comments for information and the ; symbol is used to indicate lines that the user can edit or enable a certain feature by removing the ; symbol.

Most Linux and Unix users are familiar with a command line text editor called *vi*. *vi* has been around for quite some time in the Unix community and was included with Linux. As previously mentioned, it's a command line text editor, and it's very powerful. You can use *vi* to edit the smb.conf file by changing to the /etc directory and issuing the command:

```
vi smb.conf
```

Editing the smb.conf file manually certainly isn't the easiest way to get Samba working for you. You need to know what each section is responsible for, what parameters are correct, and the settings for those parameters. This chapter can't cover all the aspects of Samba, since it's very complex. We'll use *vi* to set a few options that will allow your Samba server to be visible to Windows. With the smb.conf file open in the *vi* editor, make the following changes to the file.

1. Using the arrow keys, scroll down to the line that contains the workgroup = MDKGROUP option and place the cursor on the M. Press the letter x to delete the entire MDKGROUP word.

Tip Using x in this fashion in *vi* will delete the characters under the cursor.

2. After the entire word is deleted, press the "i" key to cause *vi* to go into "insert" mode. Press the spacebar once and then enter your workgroup or domain name. When you're finished, press the ESC key to exit "insert" mode.

3. Once you're out of "insert" mode, you can move around the document again. Using the arrow keys, scroll down to the section that contains the options:
```
encrypt passwords = yes
smb passwd file = /etc/smbpasswd
```

You'll notice two semicolons (;) at the beginning of these lines. Using the "x" key, delete both semicolons. This ensures that Samba will use encrypted passwords, which is now the default in Windows.

Tip Setting encrypt passwords to yes means that Linux and Samba will recognize the passwords transmitted across the network in encrypted format, rather than plain text. This is important because if your sent passwords are plain text, they can be intercepted in transmission by packet sniffers or network analyzers, which compromises security.

That's all that's required in terms of configuring Samba to be seen by a Windows computer on the network. All you have to do now is restart the Samba server or start if it isn't already running. You do this by issuing the following command from the /etc/rc.d/init/d directory on the Linux computer.

```
./smb start
```

You should see a status message indicating that both the SMB and NMB services have started. This will be evident by the bracketed OK indicators after the name of each service as it starts.

To verify that you can see the Samba server, open Network Neighborhood on your Windows computer. You should see the Samba server listed, as shown here in Figure 17.1, where you can see my server listed as Samba Server 2.2.0(Linux_One).

FIGURE 17.1

The Samba server visible in Network Neighborhood.

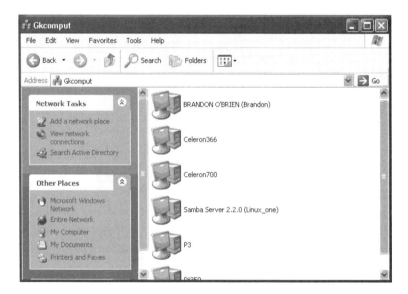

Encrypted versus Clear Text Passwords

Before we can go any further into the configuration of Samba, we need to discuss the use of passwords. There have been some issues surrounding how passwords are used for Linux and Windows. Versions of Windows 95 prior to OSR2 used plain text passwords. This meant that your passwords were passed across the network to the Linux server as plain text, which obviously caused some security concerns. Later versions of Windows switched to using encrypted passwords. These two styles will be discussed in the following sections.

Using Encrypted Passwords

As mentioned before, Windows clients use encrypted passwords to satisfy login requests across the network. When a Windows client attempts to connect to a Samba share, the Samba server will first check the username and password that the requesting client used if he logged into a Windows domain, such as Windows NT or a Windows 2000 Active Directory domain. If you don't have Encrypted passwords specified in the Samba configuration file, the login or access to the Samba share will fail.

When we talk about encrypted passwords, we mean that the password itself is hashed (identified using string that is generated by a mathematical formula). This prevents any network snoopers from getting the password when it's sent across the network. All they'll see is the hashed password; and without the correct hashing algorithm, they can't decipher the password.

It's a good idea to use encrypted passwords in your network unless you're absolutely certain that nobody can tap into your network and monitor the transmissions. Also, by default, Windows uses encrypted passwords; so, you need to enable this option in the smb.conf file. You'll see how to do this in the section in configuring Samba.

Using Clear Text Passwords

Samba can use clear text passwords if you have Windows clients earlier than Windows 95 OSR2, or if you decided you wanted to use clear text passwords. Samba comes configured by default to use clear text passwords so you only need to make changes to the smb.conf file if you don't want to use clear text. That will be explained shortly in the section on configuring Samba.

There's one caveat in using clear text passwords. If you have newer Windows clients, later than OSR2 or Windows 95, you'll have to make a change in the registry to enable this on the Windows clients.

To change this parameter in Windows XP, go to this key in the registry:

```
HKEY_LOCAL_MACHINE\SYSTEM\ControlSet001\Services\lanmanworkstation\parameters
```

You'll see a value called enableplaintextpassword with a data type of REG_DWORD. Double-click this value to open it for editing. Change the HEX value to 1 to enable the use of plain text passwords, and set it to 0 to disable plain text passwords and use encrypted passwords instead.

From a security point of view, enabling clear text isn't a good idea. I highly recommend, especially since you're using Windows XP, that you enable encrypted passwords in your smb.conf file.

Configuring Samba

The methods that you used in the previous sections won't allow you to browse any resources on the Samba server until the rest of the options are set. Editing the smb.conf by hand with a text editor isn't the best method to get the job done. The easiest way to configure Samba is to use the Samba Web Administration Tool (SWAT) and Webmin.

Using SWAT

In order to use SWAT, open your favorite Web browser on the Linux computer and type `http://localhost:901` in the address bar. This will cause Linux to load the SWAT tool into the browser and ask for a username and password to access it. You must have root access to use SWAT, so enter root as the username and then enter the root password. SWAT will present you with the screen shown in Figure 17.2 upon successful login.

FIGURE 17.2

SWAT loaded into Netscape on the Linux computer.

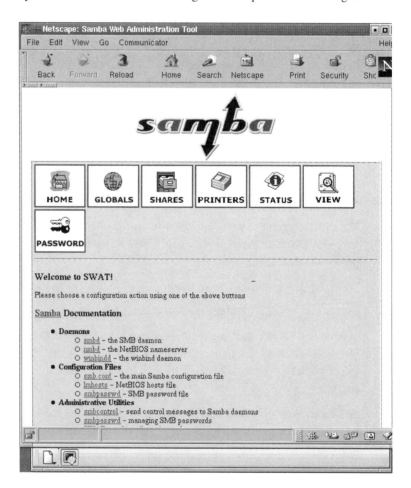

As you can see in this figure, the SWAT tool is a graphical environment running in a Web browser. This allows you to easily configure settings for Samba by clicking graphics and hyperlinks.

The first section you need to be concerned with is the Globals section. Clicking on the Globals image at the top of the page opens the Globals page ready for editing.

Each of the options that are available on this page correspond to the Globals section in the smb.conf file. SWAT will write those values to the file when you click the Commit Changes button on this page. You'll configure some of these options now.

The first set of options you see fall under the Base Options group and are listed and explained here:

- **workgroup**   This setting is used to specify the Windows workgroup or domain that this Samba server will participate in. Enter your workgroup or domain name here.

- **netbios name**   Using this setting gives the Samba server a netbios name that will be visible when users browse the network neighborhood applet of Windows. Provide a computer name that you want to use here.

- **server string**   Use this setting to give the server a descriptive name that appears in the description field when browsing the network. You can check the manual pages for Samba to determine the available options for this setting but the default is fine. The &v option is used to indicate the version of Linux that's running on the computer.

- **interfaces**   Using this setting indicates which network interfaces the Samba connection will work over if you have multiple NICs installed in the computer. We won't set this value here, since it's not explicitly required.

The next section that you come across is the security section. This section deals with securing the Samba server from users and computers that aren't allowed access. There are various ways to secure your server, and we'll look at each in turn here.

The first option is the security and has USER specified next to it. This is the default, and we'll leave it at USER. USER simply means that when a client attempts to connect to the Samba server, Samba will check to see if there's a user account with a password for that user. If so, the user is allowed access and the home directory is displayed in the network neighborhood window, as shown in Figure 17.3.

FIGURE 17.3

The home directory for the user account gobrien is displayed after that user attempts to connect to the Samba server.

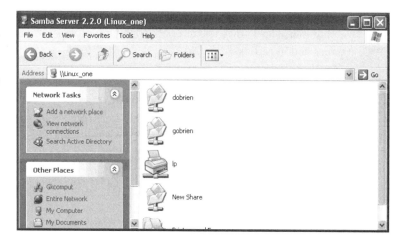

We'll look at specifying users a little later. For now, we'll look at the remainder of the security settings. The next option after USER is the encrypt passwords option. You know about encrypted and clear text passwords from our discussion earlier in this chapter. Here's where you enable that option. Ensure that you select Yes next to encrypt passwords.

Directly under this option is the update encrypted option. This option is used to specify whether a user logging on with a clear text password will have his encrypted password updated with the clear text password. This password resides in the /etc/smbpasswd file. Remember to set this option to Yes if you have encrypt passwords set to No.

Under the update encrypted option, you'll notice the guest account option. You use this option to specify the guest account to use. Linux will use the guest account for users logging into the Samba server that have no valid user account on the server. The default is nobody, which tells Samba not to allow any guest logins.

You can set up a guest account on the server and limit the permissions that the account has and then assign that account here for guests to use. This is a security risk and not recommended, since it allows anonymous user access to your Samba server.

The next two options are the *hosts allow* and *hosts deny* options. You use these two options to specify which IP addresses or workstation netbios names to allow or deny access to the Samba server. The default is no entries in either of these options, which means that all workstations will have access to the Samba server, providing they have a valid login username and password.

One reason for using these two options is to limit access to clients that can connect to your Samba server by checking the IP address or range. You can use this feature if you connect your Samba server to the Internet through an internal network or make it available across the Internet. Using this technique allows remote sites within your organization to access your network across the Internet or a WAN.

You can specifically allow only certain clients by specifying an IP address or partial IP address to include a subnet, or you can also specify workstation names. For example, if you wanted to allow all workstations in the 192.168.0 subnet to access this Samba server, you can enter 192.168.0. in the hosts allow text box. This tells Samba to allow all IP address in the range 192.168.0.1 to 192.168.0.254.

You can specify more than one subnet or IP address by separating each entry with a space, as in the following example.

```
192.168.0. 192.168.1. 192.168.3.1
```

This example will allow all workstations that have an IP address in the 192.168.0 and 192.168.1 subnets plus the workstation with the IP address of 192.168.3.1.

The *hosts deny* works the same way. You can allow all workstations access and explicitly deny access to certain workstations by specifying the workstation name or IP address in the hosts deny text box. For our discussion, leave these options empty to allow all workstations access so as not to interfere with our examples.

The next section of the configuration deals with Logging Options. Samba can log all activity that takes place on the server when clients connect to and use the resources on the server. You can specify the location for the log file in the log file text box. Samba defaults to placing the log file in the /var/log/samba directory with a filename of log.%m where %m is used to specify the machine name that's making the connection. If you don't specify the %m variable in this text box, Samba will log all activity to the log.samba file.

If you look at the log file, you'll notice a few things. First, there's a time and date stamp placed on every activity that has taken place. You'll also see status messages and error messages. The log files are a great Samba troubleshooting tool. You should enable them to help troubleshoot individual workstation connect issues.

The last option in the Logging Option section is the max log size. This setting allows you to specify how large, in Kilobytes, you want to allow the log file to be. The default is 50 Kilobytes.

The tuning options that are available in the section after logging deal with the communication over the network that Samba will use. Samba isn't capable of automatically tuning itself for your network, so you may need to experiment with the available settings. Check the manual pages for Samba to get an understanding of all the available options for tuning.

17

One that I recommend that you add to the default is the SO_KEEPALIVE option by specifying it as:

```
SO_KEEPALIVE=1
```

This option will maintain your network connection to the client if left idle. If you don't specify this option, a timeout will occur and cause your connection to be lost.

The default options that are shown in the Tuning section are designed to prevent any transmission delays on TCP/IP and set the size, in bytes, of the send and receive buffers.

Next, you'll see the Printing options section. Here's where you set the options relating to the display of printers in Samba. Most Linux systems are using the System V style of file and print systems. For this reason, the default entry in the printcap name option is lpstat. I recommend that you leave the default option of lpstat, unless you have reason to change it, since it will automatically provide a list of available printers on the server.

The next option in the Printing section is simply called *printing*. This option deals with the style of printing system used on the Samba server. Samba 2.0.6 uses CUPS (Common Unix Printing System) by default. There's a list of available printing systems displayed when you click the arrow on the option drop-down. You can use these to select the printing system used by your Samba server if you've changed it to a different printing system. The available options are listed here for your convenience.

- sysv
- aix
- hpux
- bsd
- qnx
- pnp
- lprng
- softq
- cups
- nt
- os2

After you've set the printing options, you can move on to the Browse options. These options deal with how Samba will behave in your Windows network in terms of announcing itself to browse masters and if it will behave as a browse master. Browse masters are used to contain lists of workstations, servers, and resources available on a Windows network.

The first option you'll see is the OS-level option, which is used to set how aggressively Samba will announce itself to the Windows network in terms of browser elections. By default, Samba will win browser elections over Windows 9x workstations, but not over NT or Windows 2000 domain controllers. The higher the number, the more aggressive the announcement. The default is 20.

The next option is titled *preferred*. Setting this option to True will cause the Samba server to force an election and attempt to become the preferred master browser. The default is Auto, and it should be left at auto if you have domain controllers or other master browsers in your network. The reason is that Samba could force the election and cause a continuous round of browser elections with other master browsers. This will result in excess network traffic and network resources becoming unavailable or not visible at all. If you don't want Samba to be a browser, set this option to False.

After the preferred option is the local master. This option is defaulted to Yes, which means that Samba will attempt to be the master browser for the local subnet. Once again, the same cautions apply as for the preferred option.

The last available setting in the Browsing section is the domain master. This option determines if Samba will be a domain wide master browser. Again, use this option with caution if you have Windows NT/2000 domain controllers on your network.

The last section to configure on this page is the WINS Options section. This section deals with name resolutions from NetBIOS names to IP addresses.

The first option specifies whether Samba will attempt to look up the NetBIOS name as a DNS name if it doesn't find it listed in the WINS database. The default is No, and unless you have a DNS server running on the network, it's recommended that you leave this at the default setting.

The next option, wins server, allows you to specify a WINS server on the network to perform the NetBIOS to IP name resolution. For Windows NT networks, WINS servers were a common occurrence; however, with Windows 2000 Active Directory reliant on TCP/IP and the fact that NetBEUI is no longer recommended or supported in Windows 2000, WINS support is slowly dwindling. The Samba server itself can act as a WINS server, which is discussed in the following paragraph. This option is normally specified as an IP address, but it can also be a DNS name. For the most part, you can use the LMHOSTS file on the Windows clients to specify the NetBIOS to IP address mappings.

The last option is the wins support option, and it is used to indicate if the server will act as a WINS server. Setting it to Yes will cause this server to act as a WINS server for the network. There are a couple of cautions to be aware of here. First, don't enable more than one Samba server on the same network with WINS support. Second, this option shouldn't be enabled unless you're running multiple subnets on your network. The reason for this is the amount of network traffic that's generated by WINS servers to maintain the mapping lists.

Once you've configured the necessary changes on this page, be sure to go back to the top of the page and click the Commit Changes button to make the options take effect. It may also be necessary to restart the Samba services to cause the changes to take effect.

Now that you have the network options configured, you can select the Share button at the top of the page to display the Share page as shown here in Figure 17.4.

FIGURE 17.4

The Share page in SWAT that allows you to create new shares on the Samba server.

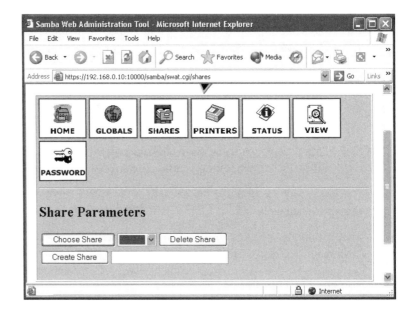

Creating Shares

In order to create a new share, simply type in a name for the new share in the box provided and click the Create Share button. The new share will be created. If you want to configure the new share or any other share, select the share name from the drop-down box and then click Choose Share. SWAT will display the share options for the selected share.

Since the options on this page are self-explanatory, I won't cover them here. It's important to note that the home directories are available by default for users as they log in.

There's a page available on configuring printers, but we'll discuss that a little later in this chapter when you'll learn how to use Linux as a print server.

The button immediately to the right of Printers is the Status button. This brings up the status page for the Samba server, as shown here in Figure 17.5.

FIGURE 17.5

The status page from SWAT shows the current status of the Samba server.

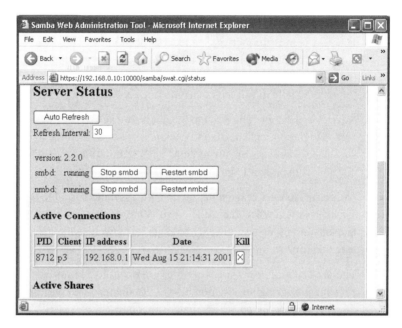

You'll notice a few things from this page. First, the top button allows you to have the status page refresh automatically according to the interval specified in the interval box. This gets boring fast, since the entire page needs to reload for each refresh.

Next, you'll see the version number of Samba that you're running. Then you'll see two sets of buttons each for the smbd and nmbd services. You can stop, start, or restart each service with these two buttons.

Note

> The current screenshot shows that the smbd and nmbd services are running, which is why the first set of buttons state "stop smbd, stop nmbd". If the services weren't running, the buttons would say "start".

You can use the Status page at any time to view the current status of your Samba server. Most times, simple connectivity issues are a direct result of the Samba service not running when you think it is.

Tip

> You only need to issue the restart smbd command to cause an implicit restart of both the smbd and nmbd services when both are running.

The next item is the Active Connections section, which is where you can see what computers are connecting to your Samba server. The available information tells you what PID is (process ID) assigned to the client for the connection. The PID is necessary for Linux to be able to kill the connection, if need be.

Next, you'll see the client name, which is the NetBIOS name of the client computer connected to the server. The client IP address follows; then the date and time the connection was made. The last column contains an X button titled *Kill*. This allows you to "kill" or disconnect the client from the server.

Under the Active Connections section, you see another table that lists the Active Shares. This shows you what shares the client computer has open and provides the share name, the user and group that the user belongs to, as well as the PID, client NetBIOS name and date and time stamp.

The last section shows you what files are open. It also provides information such as the PID again, sharing information along with the read and write aspects of the file, oplock information, the filename, and date it was opened.

You'll access the next available page by clicking the View button at the top of the page. It's a view of the smb.conf file as you've configured it to this point.

The last page that you can access using SWAT is the Passwords page. This page allows you to add, delete, and configure Samba users. Figure 17.6 shows an example of this page where the user account jmueller is about to be created.

After you click the Add New User button, the user is added to the /etc/smbpasswd file. The user can now access the Samba server.

What you've just stepped through is the basic requirements to set up and configure Samba for access by Windows XP. You can use advanced features that are available by choosing the Advanced View button on the Globals page in SWAT. The advanced features aren't important for our discussion here, so I suggest that you experiment and read more in the advanced features on your own.

So far, you've seen how to configure Samba using the smb.conf file and a text editor, as well as using the SWAT utility. You can configure and manage your Samba server with another Web-based interface that allows even more security. That interface is the Webmin interface.

FIGURE 17.6

Creating a Samba user with the Password page in SWAT.

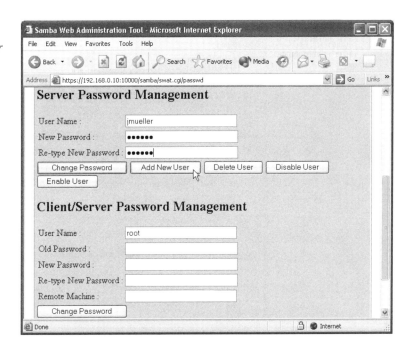

Using Webmin

Webmin is a Web browser based interface that enables you to manage your Linux computer using SSL (secure sockets layer). In order to use Webmin, it must be installed on your Linux computer. Most Linux distributions come with Webmin, which you can install using the method utilized by your version of Linux. Mandrake 8.0, which the distribution used for this example, allows you to install Webmin when you set up the operating system. If your version of Linux doesn't have Webmin, you can download it from `http://www.webmin.com/webmin`.

You can only gain access to Webmin by issuing a particular URL in your browser's address bar. To access Webmin, you use the https protocol and specify the DNS name or IP address of the Webmin server along with the port number of 10000. For example, to access Webmin on my Linux computer, I enter this URL, https://192.168.0.10:10000. You'll also need to enter a username and password, which appears as root until you create a new Webmin user.

You'll notice that there are six tabs across the top of the page. These tabs allow you to configure certain aspects of your Linux computer. Since Samba is a server, you'll find it under the Servers tab. If you click that tab, a list of servers appears that are installed on your Linux computer. Selecting the Samba Windows File Sharing server at the lower left corner will bring up the screen shown in Figure 17.7.

FIGURE 17.7

The Samba configuration screen shown using Webmin.

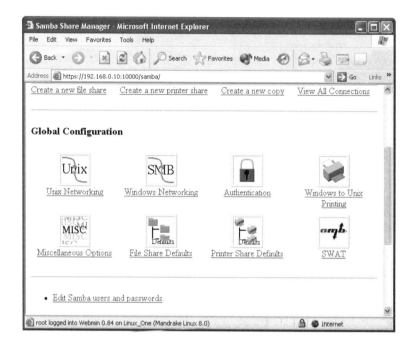

Selecting the various options on this page allow you to configure that aspect of Samba. Note that there's also a SWAT entry at the bottom of the options. By using SWAT in this way, you have secure remote access to configure your Samba server.

Working with Linux

Once you have the configurations set, as mentioned in the previous sections, you can begin to use Linux in your Windows XP network. Linux can exist as either a server or client in your network. It can serve as both at the same time also.

As a server, Linux can be used as a file and print server, as a Web server, or an FTP server. However, we'll concentrate on using it as a file and print server, as well as a client for use in your network to access shares and resources on your Windows XP computers.

Using Network Neighborhood

If you're familiar with Windows networking in Windows 95 and later, you're familiar with the Network Neighborhood applet that allows you to browse and access file and printer shares on other networked computers. Network neighborhood allows you to view shares on Linux Samba servers as well.

You've already seen the use of Network Neighborhood earlier in the chapter when you browsed the network to see the Samba server listed. After you set the necessary user accounts, as mentioned in the preceding sections, you can gain access to the home directory for the username you logged in as. Once you have access to your home directory or the share on the Samba server, you can gain access to the directories and files just as you would a Windows-based computer.

Take some time right now to browse the files and directories on your Samba server. You also have to remember that Linux and Windows store files differently. Samba allows a transparent interaction of the two computing platforms that will allow you to copy, move, and delete files on either machine without needing to worry about how they're stored.

Note

Even though you can copy a Linux executable file to a Windows computer or vice versa, that doesn't mean that the file will execute on the opposite computer. The executable files are compiled for different operating system platforms and aren't compatible.

An ongoing software project called *WINE* is currently being developed. This Windows emulator project runs on Linux and allows you to execute Windows applications. You can get more information on WINE, including downloading working versions at `http://www.winehq.com/`.

Note

One thing you'll notice with XP in comparison to other versions of Windows is that once you've accessed a share on the samba server for a username, that username becomes the default share. Network Neighborhood will display this each time you try to access the Samba server. You'll need to log off the XP computer and back on again to clear the network mapping, allowing you to see the entire Samba server share list.

Command Line Using NET Utility

You can also gain access to your Samba server through the use of the NET utility at the command line. Some of you may be familiar with this utility and use it quite often. This section will discuss using NET to access the Samba server.

One of the first things that you might want to do with the NET command is to view what resources are available on the server you want to connect to. In our case, this would be the Linux_One server, so you'd issue the command net view \\Linux_One. This will display the information shown in Figure 17.8.

The results of issuing the net view command for the Linux_One server.

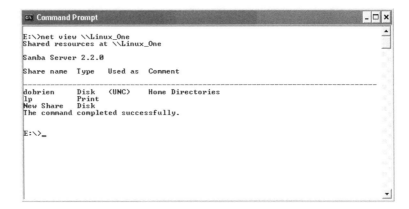

Net view is used to display the available resources or shares on a server. All of the shares may not be accessible to you since some require passwords for authentication or user accounts that may differ from your own.

Once you have a picture of what's available on the remote server with the use of the net view command, you can connect to those directories and access the files that reside in them. To do this, you use the net use command and assign a drive letter to the directory that you want to access on the server. Issue the "Net use k: \\Linux_One\foldername" command to map a drive letter to the desired share folder.

Replace k: with an available drive letter on your computer. This will associate the drive letter k: with the share on the Samba server. You can now gain access to the files in that share by using the cd command to change to the directory as you would on the local computer.

The Net utility that comes with Windows has many more commands available. Some of them, such as net group, which deal with adding or modifying groups in a domain, don't pertain to a Samba server and therefore aren't usable. A list of the usable commands for XP and Samba interactivity is found here with brief explanations of each. The reader can view the online help to make the best use of these commands.

- **net continue** Used to continue a service that has been paused by the pause command.
- **net file** Displays the open file shares on the server and allows you to close files.
- **net name** Used to add or delete messaging names used to accept messages (local computer).
- **net pause** Used to pause the specified service on the local computer.

- **net print**   Used to view information about the specified print queue.
- **net share**   Used to display the shares on the local computer.
- **net time**   Used to check or set the time on the remote or local computer.
- **net use**   Connects to or disconnects from a shared resource on a remote computer.
- **net view**   Allows you to view shared resources on a remote computer.

As you can see, this list of commands comprises quite a few capabilities for the network with a command line utility. This list isn't comprehensive, but it does include the commands that are useful in a Windows/Samba network.

Using Linux as a Print Server

17

Using Linux as a print server in a Windows network is made possible by the Samba software. There are a few issues that you need to be aware of in terms of using Linux as a server. The first is support for the printer hardware itself. If Linux doesn't have a driver for your printer, you can't use it on the Linux server. You may also find that the drivers available for certain printers don't cover all models, but will still work with limited functionality. Contact your printer manufacturer or other sources such as drivers.com, for up-to-date drivers for Linux.

Another issue is the availability of drivers for the XP computer. Linux drivers aren't compatible with Windows drivers and vice versa. Therefore, you must have a driver available for the Windows XP computer that you want to print from.

When you install a printer on the Linux computer, the drivers for XP computers aren't made available on the Linux server as they are with Windows servers. You must install the drivers for the printer from a source other than the server.

To install a printer under Linux, ensure that you have the drivers and then run the printtool application. Printtool is a utility that's available on Mandrake and RedHat systems that allows for easy installation of printers. If you have a distribution other than one of these, check the documentation for a printer installation utility.

When you issue the command printtool at a terminal on Mandrake 8.0, the screen shown in Figure 17.9 will appear.

You can see here that the queue lp, which is the default printer queue in Linux, is already installed. You can add a new print queue here to attach to a printer by selecting the Add option and clicking the OK button. You'll see a message that Linux is bringing up the CUPS system. CUPS is the *Common Unix Printing System* that's used by Mandrake 8.0 and later versions of other distributions are starting to use it as well. Once CUPS has come up, you have the option to select a printer connection.

The local printer option is used to specify a printer that's attached to the local printer port (LPT1 usually). Use the remote printer to select a printer that is located on another Unix or Linux server. The last option, SMB/Windows is used to install the drivers for a printer that resides on a Windows computer such as Win9x/NT/2000/XP. If you have a printer installed on the local LPT port, select local and click OK.

FIGURE 17.9

The printtool application allows you to edit or install new print queues.

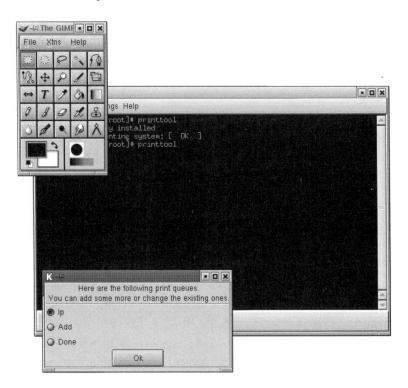

Next, a dialog box appears asking you to name the printer and give it a description and location. Each printer in Linux needs a name. The names default starting at lp and then increment such as lp1, lp2 and so on for each successive printer. Name your printer with a descriptive name such as OfficeJet or AcctLaser. Enter a description and location if desired and click OK.

CUPS will then try to detect the printer that you have installed. It may not detect it automatically, at which time you'll see a list of printer manufacturers and models from which to choose. Find your printer in the list or a model number that closely matches the printer that you have. Click the OK button, and Linux will ask if you want to test printing. It's a good idea to print the test page to ensure that the printer is functioning correctly locally first. If the test page prints satisfactorily, you have your printer installed and ready to use.

If not, try another model number or review the troubleshooting options for your specific distribution of Linux.

Now that you have the printer installed on the Linux computer, you can connect to and install the printer on your Windows computer from across the network. To do this, open Network Neighborhood. You should see the newly installed printer.

You can't print to this printer without installing it onto the local Windows XP computer. Run the Install Printer wizard from Windows XP to install the printer and correct drivers on your XP computer.

The wizard will list the available printers on the network, including the printer shared on the Linux computer. You may also notice that it states that no drivers are available for this printer. This is because Linux doesn't install the Windows drivers for the printer. You must install the drivers by using the installation media that accompanied the printer.

After the driver is installed, you can access and print to the driver from your Windows computer. All other operations, such as canceling documents and pausing document printing, are available on the printer.

Linux Security Differences

It's important to understand the difference between how Windows and Linux handle security. This comes in terms of user accounts and file and directory access.

For most users of Windows, security isn't an issue until you step into a networked environment where you need to log onto servers and can only gain access to resources that are made available to your user account or group. Linux operates in a similar fashion, with the exception that you must log into a Linux system every time you want to use it. That differs from older versions of Windows, where anybody could use the computer if networking wasn't installed. Even Windows 9x allows users to press the cancel button on the network login screen to bypass login and gain access to the computer. This is no longer the case with Windows XP.

Linux treats security seriously. You can't gain access to the computer without first logging in. In order to log in, you must have a user account with a password. An administrator is responsible for setting up user accounts. Linux is similar to Windows NT/2000 in that it has an administrative account that has complete power over the user accounts and system. Windows calls this account the Administrator account. Linux refers to it as root. If you have root access, you have complete access to the Linux computer.

17

Caution If you do have root access on a Linux system, don't use that account for day-to-day operations of the system. You can cause some harm to the files or systems by inadvertently issuing an incorrect command and rendering the system unstable or unusable. Always create a user account for yourself and use that for day-to-day operations. You can issue the su command, (discussed shortly), to perform most administrative tasks from your own user account.

We've already discussed user accounts for XP in "Day 8, Working With Users," so we won't discuss it in detail here. Instead, I'll introduce you to how Linux uses user accounts and determines access to files.

A user account in Linux is similar to one in Windows in that the user is assigned a username, a password, and a group to belong to. The user must sign in with the username and password to access the system. The user's password is stored in a file in Linux that's located in the /etc directory and is called passwd. An example password file is shown here.

```
root:x:0:0:root:/root:/bin/bash
bin:x:1:1:bin:/bin:
daemon:x:2:2:daemon:/sbin:
adm:x:3:4:adm:/var/adm:
lp:x:4:7:lp:/var/spool/lpd:
mysql:x:416:417:MySQL server:/var/lib/mysql:/bin/bash
gobrien:x:501:501:Gerry O'Brien:/home/gobrien:/bin/bash
jmueller:x:504:508::/home/jmueller:/bin/bash
```

One of the first things that you may notice is that there are no passwords listed in this file. The reason is that Linux hashes the password. For security reasons, they're not visible. Let's gain an understanding of this file by taking apart one entry in it, the entry for jmueller, which happens to be the last entry. You'll notice that the first entry is the username. This is what the user logs into the system with. Following the username is the colon. You'll also notice that the colon is used to separate fields of the entry.

Next you see a letter x. This is where the password would be if it were to be displayed in plain text. After the password field comes the user ID. Every user has a user ID. Normal user IDs start at 501 and increment by one for each new user added. Following the user ID is the group ID. This is the group that the user belongs to. If the user belongs to more than one group, each group will be listed in this field.

The next field is the user's full name. The jmueller account doesn't have the full name specified, in this case, but the gobrien account above it does. This demonstrates that any field not present will be blank, but the colon separator is still used.

After the full name field, the user's home directory is listed. On most Linux systems, this directory can be found under /home and is labeled with the user's login name.

The last field indicates what shell the user will use when logged into the system. Linux uses shells to provide the functionality to the user for interacting with the operating system. This isn't the same as a DOS shell from Windows.

So, as you can see from this example, user accounts are treated differently than they are in Windows. NT/2000 make use of domain controllers and SAM(security accounts manager) databases to keep track of users. Linux uses the /etc/passwd file.

In terms of file security, Windows uses what is known as ACLs (access control lists) and ACEs(access control entries) to determine if users are allowed to access a file or resource. Each time you try to access a resource, Windows compares your ACE with the ACL of the resource to determine if you have access to it.

Linux treats file access a little differently. Linux uses the same method of securing files as those used by Unix. The file contains attributes that determine the access allowed. For example, list the files in a directory by using the ls -l command to display the files like those shown in Figure 17.10.

FIGURE 17.10

Directory listing in Linux showing the file's access attributes.

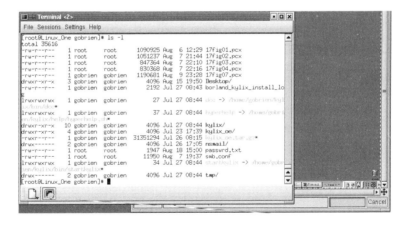

Look at the image shown. Note the beginning of each entry. You'll see a group of letters and dashes. These are the attributes of the file, and they determine the file type and access allowed to the file.

The attribute section is broken down into four sections. These sections, from left to right, are File type, user access permissions, group access permissions, and everyone else's access permissions. Let's look at an example.

Looking at Figure 17.10, locate the file entry under the .pcx files that is titled *Desktop*, (the sixth file down). The file attributes are Drwxr-xr-x. The four sections are divided in this fashion. The first section is one letter wide and indicates the file type. The meanings of each letter that can be present are as follows:

- **-** This indicates a normal file
- **b** This indicates a block-special file
- **c** This indicates a character specific file
- **d** This indicates a directory
- **l** This indicates a symbolic link

Of these entries listed, you only need to be concerned with the dash (-) and the directory (d). The others are special types of files that we need not go into here. You can see from this list that our entry is a directory.

The next three sections each contain three characters. These three characters can only be r, w or x and they must appear in that order in the field. r Stands for read access, w is for write access, and x is for execute permission. The first group is used for the file's owner, the second sets the permissions for the file's group and the third sets the permissions for everyone else.

For our example directory file, we see that the owner of the directory, which, in this case, is the gobrien account, has read, write and execute permissions. The group and everyone else have read and execute permissions.

To set the permission on files, Linux users must understand a bit about the Octal numbering system. The reasons for this date back to when UNIX was originally create on DEC (Digital Equipment Corporation, now Compaq) minicomputers. These computers used the octal numbering system.

To set permissions, you use the chmod command and perform some simple addition of the octal numbers to achieve the permission. Table 17.1 shows how it works.

TABLE 17.1   Octal Numbers Used for Various Permissions

Octal Number	Permissions
0001	Execute permission for owner
0002	Write permission for owner
0004	Read permission for owner
0010	Execute permission for group
0020	Write permission for group

TABLE 17.1 continued

Octal Number	Permissions
0040	Read permission for group
0100	Execute permission for everyone
0200	Write permission for everyone
0400	Read permission for everyone

So, to set the appropriate permissions for a file, you simply add the columns as needed. For example, to assign execute, read and write for the owner, and read only for the group and everyone else, you'd take the columns for the owner which is 0001, 0002 and 0004 and add them to the columns for the group which is 0040 (read), and then the column for everyone else 0400 (read) and come up with the result of 0447. Lop of the leading zero to get 447. You would then issue the command, "chmod 447 filename." That's how you set or change the permissions for a file in Linux. Of course, you must have root access to do this or be the owner of the file.

So, in terms of the two most important aspects of security, user login and resource permissions, you now know how Linux treats these topics. and you can understand some of the differences in the Windows XP and Linux.

Tips for Optimizing Linux Use with Windows

For the most part, Linux and Windows XP should co-exist perfectly fine without too much intervention after the necessary configurations have been made. Accessing shares on each platform should be seamless, and end users should have no idea of what takes place behind the scenes. Sometimes, that just isn't enough.

If you're a network administrator, or just concerned that your network is performing at its possible best, you may want to tweak a few things here and there to enhance the performance of the interaction between the two systems. The concepts discussed in this section will help you to increase the performance of your Linux and Windows XP network.

One of the areas that we touched on earlier in the chapter dealt with log files that Samba creates. These log files are a great source of information when it comes to troubleshooting Samba connectivity. However, having Samba log every activity that takes place will have an impact on your network performance. The reason is the Samba server is busy writing the log file events as they happen. For one or two clients, the impact may be negligible, but if you have many clients, you can understand how the impact can increase substantially.

The logging for Samba is specified as a level in the smb.conf. Located in the [global] section, it has an entry that reads:

```
log level = 3
```

Most distributions of Samba default to level three, which causes Samba to log every packet that is exchanged between the two computers. If your Samba server is installed and running with no issues, I recommend that you reduce the log level to 1. This level causes Samba to only log connect and disconnect packets, which will substantially reduce the logging activity, as well as the log file size.

Another area that can be tweaked for performance gains is in the TCP options used in network communication. Linux uses TCP/IP as its default network protocol and, as a result, has to endure the overhead that's inherent in this protocol suite. TCP is a connection-oriented protocol, and it requires acknowledgement for each packet sent. This, of course, increases network traffic.

You can't get away from this fact, so the best you can do is to tweak the TCP stack to gain the best performance you can. The way you specify the various options for TCP is to modify the socket options section in the smb.conf file, located in the [global] section. The various settings for the socket options are specified on the same line separated by spaces as shown in this example.

```
socket options = TCP_NODELAY SO_RCVBUF=8192 SO_SNDBUF=8192
```

You can see by this example that the no delay option has been specified and the buffers are set at 8192 bytes. Table 17.2 explains these options.

TABLE 17.2   Delay Options for the TCP Stack

Option	Parameters	Description
TCP_NODELAY	None	Causes Samba to send network packet segments as soon as they're sent by the application. This one option can cause Samba performance to increase substantially, and it is definitely a recommended option to enable.
SO_KEEPALIVE	None	This option is used to send periodic packets to keep the connection alive. This option doesn't have an impact on performance.
SO_SNDBUF	# bytes	Specifies the size of the transmit buffer. The smaller you set this size, the more restrictive it is on throughput. Therefore, it will have a negative impact on performance. Newer builds of the Linux Kernel default to 32768, and you should never set it below 2048.

TABLE 17.2   continued

Option	Parameters	Description
SO_RCVBUF	# bytes	Specifies the size of the receive buffer. This has the same impact on performance as the send buffer and should be set accordingly as well.
SO_SNDLOWAT	# bytes	Used to specify a minimum value for bytes free in the socket send buffer before allowing a select or poll call to return writable for the socket. This setting has no impact on performance.
SO_RCVLOWAT	# bytes	Same as for the SO_SNDLOWAT buffer above, but used for the receive buffer instead.
IPTOS_LOWDELAY	None	Used on LAN style connections to time the connection for low delays or network latency. Can have a minimal effect on performance.
IPTOS_THROUGHPUT	None	Same as LOWDELAY above but used for WAN connections.

Each of these options has some recommendations that are somewhat generic and offer only guidelines. You need to make the adjustments to suit your networks to achieve the best performance for your connections.

If you're in the habit of transferring large files over your network between Linux and XP, you can gain a performance increase by using RAW reads and writes. Enabling these options provide the capability of Samba to transfer information in chunks of 65,535 bytes in size. This helps to speed up the transfer of the data because the files take less time to reassemble on the receiving end and less time to break up on the transmitting end. To enable this feature, set the following options in your smb.conf file [global] section:

```
write raw = yes
read raw = yes
```

Note that not all SMB clients support raw reads and writes. You have to experiment with this if you're running other operating systems in your network besides Linux and Windows XP.

Although small in number, these areas of Linux/Windows interoperability can help you eke out some performance gains in your network and make the communication between the two operating systems just a little bit faster. After all, fast performance is a goal that's sought after on a regular basis. The more you can do to reach that goal, the better.

17

Working with Linux Clients

So far in this chapter, we've talked about accessing Linux from Windows XP clients. This section will discuss the use of the smbclient utility for the purpose of accessing Windows XP computers from Linux.

The smbclient program is only one of many that Linux users can utilize to access resources or functionality from a Windows computer. The client utilities are listed here with a description of each.

- **smbclient**   Command line program used to access windows clients.
- **smbprint**   This is a print filter used for printing from Linux clients to Windows systems printers on a Windows server.
- **smbtar**   Tar is a Unix/Linux archiving program. Smbtar is actually a shell script used for backing up Windows systems on a Linux computer.
- **smbmount**   Used to mount SMB file systems as native file systems. Mount is the Linux term used to describe making access available to a drive or device.
- **smbsh**   A program that's used to emulate the mounting of file systems for computer systems that don't support smbmount.
- **rpcclient**   This is a command line program that you can use to invoke RPC (remote procedure call) services on computer supporting RPC.

As you can see, there are quite a few applications that allow you to access Windows computers from Linux. This chapter and section will only be discussing the use of the smbclient program.

One of the first things you can do with the smbclient application is to simply issue smbclient at the command line to get a list of available options and some help on the command.

You may want to find out what resources are available on a Windows computer. If you know the NetBIOS name of that computer, this is an easy task. Simply issue the following command, "smbclient –L \\computername -U username%password," to get a listing of available resources on the computer as shown in Figure 17.11. Replace the computername, username, and password variables in the above command with that of your XP computer. The username and password must be a valid user account on the XP computer.

As you can see from this figure, there are 8 shared resources available. In actuality, the shares with a $ sign are, for all intents and purposes, hidden shares. These won't show up on Windows computers. Therefore, you can gain access to the three driver letters C, D, and E from your Linux computer.

In order to access a specific share or drive on the Windows computer, you need to issue
another smbclient command. To access the E drive from the previous listing in Figure
17.11, you can issue the command, "smbclient '\\computername\D' -U username%pass-
word." This will produce an output similar to that shown in Figure 17.12. Note the use of
the single quote surrounding the \\computername\D entry. This is necessary because of
the way some versions of Unix and Linux treat the backslash character. If you don't
include these, you'll be given an error message indicating that there aren't enough
\ characters.

FIGURE 17.11

*The list of available
resources on the XP
computer called P3 as
displayed from the
Linux command line.*

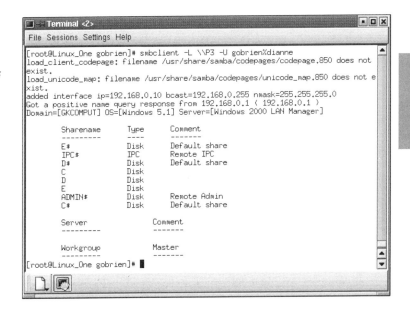

17

As you can see from Figure 17.12, you're placed at the SMB: \> prompt. This is an indication to you that you can now issue commands and gain access to the files on the
remote XP computer. The available commands are listed here.

- **dir**   Same as Windows and DOS dir command, gives a listing of the files
  in the directory.

- **cd**   Used to change directories on the remote computer.

- **get**   With the smbclient program, you can't use the copy or move commands on files. Instead, you use get to retrieve a file (works the
  same as an FTP get command).

- **put**   Used to send a file from the Linux computer to the remote
  computer.

- **del**   Used to delete a file on the remote computer.

- **!shell**   Allows you to gain access to Linux commands on the local Linux computer. You may want to issue a command, such as ls, to get a listing of files in a local directory.

- **lcd**   Used to change the local directory on the Linux computer.

FIGURE 17.12

The SMB: \> prompt greets you after connecting to a remote share on the XP computer.

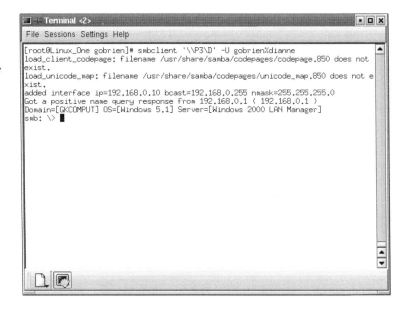

smbclient has more command options than what are used here. You've already seen the two most commom options, -L to list the available resources on a host and –U to specify a username and password for the connection. You can issue the smbclient command by itself, as mentioned earlier in this section, to obtain the list of options for the program. These will include a brief explanation of each. If you still need more information, you can use the manual pages on the Linux computer and issue the command man smbclient.

Summary

Even with Microsoft's newest operating system offering the features and benefits it does, Linux is still a popular optional operating system and becoming more popular as time goes on. This chapter has presented you with the opportunity to learn how to connect to a Linux computer with Windows XP and allow the two to interact seamlessly.

Q&A

Q: What is Samba?

A: Samba is a tool that's used to allow the sharing of files and resources on SMB compliant computers.

Q: Are all shared resources displayed when you browse to the Samba server using Network Neighborhood?

A: If you have a valid user account on the Linux computer, you'll only be able to see those shared resources that are available to that user account.

Workshop

Let's see how well you've been paying attention to this chapter with a few questions and exercises for you to try. These will help reinforce what you've learned in day 17. The answers can be found in Appendix A at the end of the book.

Quiz

1. What platforms is Samba available for?

2. What does SMB stand for and why is it important?

3. What's the easiest way to install Samba on a RedHat or Mandrake Linux computer?

4. What's the name of the program that you use to access Windows servers from a Linux client?

5. What's the numbering system that Linux uses for setting user permissions on files and directories?

Exercises

1. Using the appropriate command, stop and then restart the samba server on your Linux computer.

2. Using your Windows XP computer, access the SWAT utility for configuring Samba and add a new user account.

3. Using the smbclient program, connect to a share on your XP computer; get a directory listing and copy a file from XP to Linux.

WEEK 3

DAY 18

Working with NetWare

NetWare was the first usable network operating system for PC networks. Other vendors had created networks, and some had looked at the PC, but Novell got there first. While NetWare is no longer the company to beat for networking, it still has a large loyal following of users. The main reason is that NetWare is extremely reliable, and it works with multiple platforms.

Today we'll look at how to work with NetWare when using Windows XP. Fortunately, unlike Linux, Microsoft provides some support for NetWare right out of the box. This support is enough to access NetWare resources but not enough to perform configuration tasks. Because of this limitation, we'll also discuss how to install the NetWare client.

NetWare provides several means of making changes to the server configuration. None of the methods provides complete access, so you need to know at least two access methods. We'll look into NetWare Administrator, the GUI method of accessing NetWare, and RConsole, the character mode interface. You'll use NetWare Administrator most often because it enables you to perform tasks such as adding and removing users.

Finally, we'll discuss some maintenance issues. For example, you'll learn how to install long filename support on your NetWare volume. We'll also discuss how to work with printers, and you'll learn about the various types of printer support that NetWare provides.

Using the CSNW Applet

The *Client Service for NetWare (CSNW)* applet in the Control Panel is one that people often overlook when they're having trouble with the NetWare connection. Figure 18.1 shows what this applet looks like when you open it. (Note that you won't see this applet in the Control Panel until you install the Windows XP version of the NetWare client. We discussed client installation in the "Installing Protocols, Clients, and Services" section during Day 14.)

FIGURE 18.1

Many people overlook the CSNW applet when working with NetWare connections.

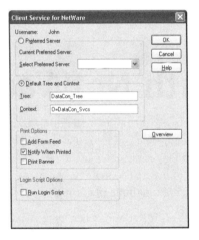

The CSNW applet is Microsoft client-specific. If you install the Novell client, the CSNW applet will disappear. The NetWare client offers other ways to control all of the items in the CSNW applet, along with features the CSNW applet doesn't provide. See the "Using the NetWare Client" section for details on using the NetWare client from Novell.

Depending on how you set up your NetWare server, you'll use the Preferred Server or Default Tree and Context option. Normally, you set this option as part of the installation process for your machine or during the initial network setup. However, you may need to change the options after you perform a server update or if you move the machine to a different location.

Setting Login Options

The CSNW login options determine your location on the NetWare network. Some people don't know whether they should use the Preferred Server or the Default Tree and Context option. Generally, if your server uses the bindery (NetWare 3.x and older) or bindery emulation, you need to select a default tree. On the other hand, if your server uses NetWare Directory Services, you'll use the Default Tree and Context option.

Some users run into a problem working with the context for their server. As a minimum, you need to enter the name of the tree that you created during installation. Every tree also has an organizational level, so in that context, you'll provide an O=<Organization Name> entry. Figure 18.2 shows a NetWare Directory Services (NDS) tree. George would have a context of O=DataCon_Svcs, while Sam would have a context of OU=Editorial.O=Datacon_Svcs. You can usually abbreviate the context as DataCon_Svcs or Editorial.DataCon_Svcs.

FIGURE 18.2

Look at the NDS tree to discern how to log into the system.

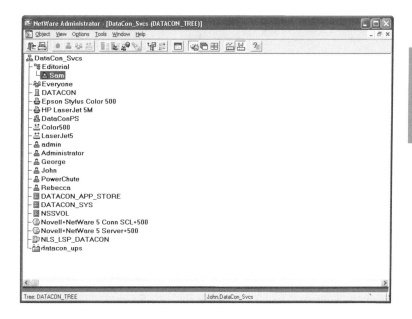

18

After you set up the server or tree and context, you should be able to contact the server as needed for logins. All you need at that point is the correct permissions.

Getting Rid of Banners

Banners are a helpful aid for large companies because they identify the person who printed a document. On the other hand, banners waste paper in small companies because you already know who printed a document. Unfortunately, Windows XP assumes that you always want to output a banner for a network printer because Microsoft assumes that most people work in a corporate environment.

For many users, eliminating banners when working with NetWare is a major problem because Windows help always refers you to the Advanced tab of the Printer Properties dialog box (shown in Figure 18.3). If you click Separator Page, you'll see a Separator Page dialog box. Make sure that the Separator Page field is blank. This is the first step in getting rid of banners on your system.

FIGURE 18.3

Make sure that the Printer Properties dialog box is set to leave the separator page blank.

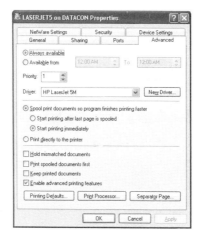

The next step is to check the CSNW applet. Make sure that you clear the Print Banner check box in the Printer Options area. If you don't clear this option, NetWare (not Windows XP) will continue to print the banner.

Running Login Scripts

The Run Login Script option in the CSNW applet tells Windows XP to run the NetWare login script. This option doesn't control the content of the login script, nor does it do anything else for you. It only turns login script processing on or off.

NetWare actually provides four levels of login script. The login script that runs when you select the Run Login Script option depends on your server configuration. The following list describes each of the login script types:

- **Container** The login script at the organization or organizational unit level will execute before any other script that you might create. (A container login script replaces the system login script found in NetWare 3.x setups.) You'll normally use this level of scripting for settings that affect everyone in the container. Only the script in the highest-level container executes, so large organizations normally place the script in the lowest organizational unit level.

- **Profile**   NetWare has a profile object. You can say that a user fits within a specific profile in order to reduce the number of settings you create. A user can only belong to one profile. The profile script executes after the container script but before the user script.

- **User**   Every user can have an individual script that executes last in line of all other scripts on the system. This script contains the user's individual settings. For example, you could print a message for that user alone, install applications the user needs, or create special drive mappings.

- **Default**   If the user has no container, profile, or user script, NetWare uses the default script. The network administrator can't modify this script, so it always behaves in the same way. As a minimum, the user will see drive mappings for the SYS volume and \PUBLIC and personal user folders.

You must run NetWare Administrator to change any of the login settings for a user. Figure 18.4 shows the login script for a user. To access this setting, right-click the container, user, or profile object and then select Details. Click Login Script. The precise display varies by object, but you'll always see a list of login script entries.

FIGURE 18.4

This is an example of a NetWare user login script.

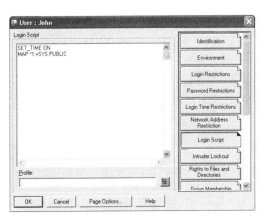

Notice that Figure 18.4 also shows a Profile field. This is where you assign a user to a specific profile. The profile affects the user's security settings, security equivalencies, and login script. It can also affect certain identification information, such as the user location, department, and organization.

18

Using the NetWare Client

This section tells you about the NetWare client. The NetWare client is an alternative to the Microsoft client that Windows XP installs by default. As mentioned in the "Installing the NetWare Administrator Without the Client" sidebar, you can work with NetWare without installing the client, but you'll find it a lot easier if you do.

 Note

> You must install the NetWare client if your server uses IP instead of IPX. The Microsoft client only supports IPX.

The reasons that people don't want to use the NetWare client vary. In some cases, it's the fact that the NetWare client is larger than the Microsoft client. This means the NetWare client runs a little slower and consumes more memory than the Microsoft equivalent. However, the performance differences are slight, as are the memory differences in a world where workstations commonly have 256MB of RAM installed (if not more).

Another complaint is that the NetWare client tends to cause compatibility problems. It's true that the client that comes with NetWare will normally turn your machine into scrap right after the installation completes—if the installation completes. Of course, the first thing you'll want to do is download the latest client from NetWare so that you can be sure that it will work with Windows XP. Look at the product support Web site at `http://support.novell.com/products/psMenu.jsp` for the latest NetWare downloads, including client software.

 Note

> If you can't find a Windows XP-specific driver and you don't what to use the procedure in the "What, No Windows Client?" section, don't download the driver for any other version of Windows. Only the Windows XP driver will work with Windows XP. In addition, Novell doesn't intend to support Windows XP Home Edition with a client. The Windows XP Professional Edition client won't work with Windows XP Home Edition due to limitations Microsoft has placed in the product. In short, if you want to use NetWare, you must also use Windows XP Professional Edition.

Some people don't like all of the additional features that the NetWare client provides. They prefer the simplicity of the Microsoft client. In that case, you could always set aside a laptop or other machine that you don't use on a daily basis for maintaining the NetWare portion of your network. Unless you have a large network where the staff changes daily, you'll find that NetWare is very stable, and you'll only need to check it occasionally for problems.

Because of the features the NetWare client provides, I normally recommend using the NetWare client on all administrator machines and the Microsoft client on all user workstations. Of course, all workstations require the NetWare client if you want to use one of the Novell add-on products, such as ZENworks. Using the Microsoft client on user workstations is actually an insurance policy of sorts given that the NetWare Administrator program won't run on a default Microsoft setup. The following sections show you how to install the NetWare client and how to configure it.

What, No Windows Client?

Novell often lags behind in getting new software out the door. Of course, they're also cautious about releasing software, so perhaps the two issues represent a trade-off. The fact remains that you might not find a Windows XP client for NetWare right away.

The following procedure will enable you to install the current Windows NT/2000 client version 4.8 or higher. You must have an installed copy of Windows 2000 to make this procedure work because it relies on one of the Windows 2000 files. Don't try to use this procedure with an older client. In addition, this procedure doesn't come with any guarantees; it could fail. Make sure that you test it on a clean system.

1. Open the User Accounts applet in the Control Panel. Click Change the way users log on or off.

2. Clear the Use the Welcome screen option (if selected) and click Apply Options. The default NetWare client won't work with the Welcome screen. If you leave this option checked, you'll still install the NetWare client, but the desktop will be blank when you start the system. To recover from this problem, start the system in Safe mode, clear the Welcome screen option, and then restart the system.

3. Create a NetWare client directory that has all of the setup files. The client file you download from the Internet will ask for an installation directory. I used the root directory of my Windows XP drive, but you can use any convenient location.

4. Copy the SETUPDLL.DLL file from Windows 2000 \SYSTEM32 folder or the source CD (expand it if necessary) to the \NOVELL\ENGLISH\WINNT\I386 folder. Make sure that this is the folder with the SETUPNW.EXE file.

5. Rename SETUPNW.EXE to SETUP.EXE.

6. Follow the steps in the "Installing the NetWare Client" section to complete the process.

18

Installing the NetWare Client

Before you can use the NetWare client, you need to install it on your system. It pays to install the client as early as possible after you install Windows XP to reduce compatibility problems. As mentioned earlier, you should obtain the newest copy of the client that you can. Using an old client will almost certainly result in problems in usage or configuration. Also, be certain that you obtain information about the server before you begin the installation. In some cases, the client will ask for information in addition to the data that it collects from the Microsoft client. Finally, copy the client files to the local drive to ensure that any loss of network connection won't affect the installation.

After you copy the client locally and obtain the required information, you can start the installation. The following steps show you how. (I'll assume that you've already started the client installation program.)

1. Read the license agreement and click Yes if you agree with it. You'll see a Select an installation option dialog box. Generally, most people can use the Typical Installation option if they only need the client services. However, most administrators or those familiar with special NetWare features will want to use the Custom Installation option. The remainder of the procedure assumes that you're using the Custom Installation option.

2. Select Custom Installation and click Next. You'll see a list of custom options as shown in Figure 18.5. The options you see checked in the list are the options that the Setup program installs for a Typical Installation.

FIGURE 18.5

Use this dialog box to choose one or more custom installation options.

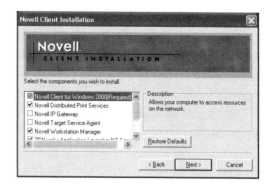

3. Select one or more custom installation options, depending on your networking needs. Make certain that you select the Novell IP Gateway if your server has IP installed in place of IPX. Click Next. You'll see a Protocol Preference dialog box like the one shown in Figure 18.6. This dialog box determines how the client will access NetWare. If your server has only IPX installed, it's best to use the IPX option.

However, if you have IP installed, always use the IP with IPX compatibility or the IP and IPX option to ensure that you have a backup protocol when working in mixed environments.

FIGURE 18.6

The Protocol Preference dialog box contains options for installing the NetWare access protocol.

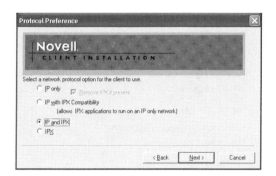

4. Select a protocol and click Next. You'll see a Login Authenticator dialog box. The two options on this dialog box help you select between NDS and Bindery operation. In most cases, newer systems use NDS, but verify this setting before you make a choice.

5. Select an authenticator and click Next. You'll see a Workstation Manager dialog box. This dialog box contains a single field that contains the same tree information that you'd enter in the CSNW applet discussed earlier today.

6. Type the tree information for your network and click Next. You'll see a completion dialog box.

7. Click Finish. Setup will begin copying files to your system. If it sees the Microsoft client installed, Setup will ask if you want to remove it. Click Yes. The installation process will take some time, so be patient as Setup copies the files. You'll then see an Installation Complete dialog box.

8. Click Reboot. The client is ready to use.

Configuring Your Novell Client

Depending on which client features you chose to install, you'll see one or more new icons in the notification area of the taskbar. The most common icon is the NetWare client icon, which helps you manage your connection to the server. This icon is a red *N* that contains a wealth of options, as shown in Figure 18.7, when you right-click it.

Most of the options on the list in Figure 18.7 are self-explanatory. For example, if you select NetWare Connections, you'll see a dialog box listing your current NetWare connections, including both the NDS tree and the physical server connection. Likewise, the

NetWare Login option displays a Novell Login dialog box that you can use to log into another server.

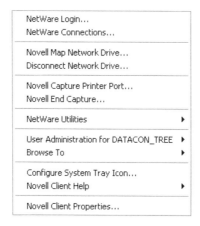

The User Administration menu contains options for maintaining your personal information on the network. This includes personal, work, and mailing information. You can also modify your login script, login account information, password, and group membership. Of course, you'll need the proper rights to perform some tasks.

Whenever you select the Novell Client Properties option, you'll see the Novell Client Configuration dialog box shown in Figure 18.8. This is the Novell version of the CSNW applet we discussed earlier. As you can see from the figure, you have more control using the Novell client than you could ever achieve using the Microsoft client.

FIGURE **18.8**

The Novell Client Configuration dialog box contains all of the configuration options for your NetWare connection.

We won't discuss every potential configuration feature provided by the NetWare client. However, notice the context options on the Client tab shown in Figure 18.8. Unlike the Microsoft client, you can log into multiple trees and contexts by adding their values to the Tree and Name context fields and then clicking Add. You can remove trees and contexts with equal ease.

If you're wondering where the banner settings from the CSNW applet have gone, look at the Default Capture tab. You'll find that you can enable up to two banners for your print jobs. In addition, the Capture tab contains special settings, such as Enable Tabs, that make it easy to print formatted text files. This option even allows you to set the number of spaces for each tab.

Another benefit of using the NetWare client isn't obvious at first. Open a copy of Windows Explorer and right-click a NetWare drive. You'll notice many new options, including the ability to salvage and purge deleted files. The Properties dialog box also contains a wealth of new features, such as those shown in Figure 18.9. Notice that you can now tell a lot more about your NetWare drives, including how the space on the drive is used.

FIGURE 18.9

The NetWare client provides access to all sorts of new information through Explorer extensions.

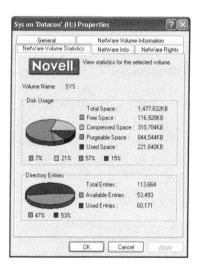

18

As an administrator, you can manage the drives right from this display. The NetWare Info tab contains options to set the NetWare-specific attributes for a drive, such as Don't Compress or Immediate Compression. You can also set the Rename Inhibit and Delete Inhibit attributes. The NetWare Rights tab tells about both user and group names and their rights to use the drive, folders, or files. You can also use this tab to set those rights.

Using NetWare Administrator

NetWare Administrator is the main utility you'll use when configuring a NetWare system. You'll find this utility in the \PUBLIC\WIN32 folder of your NetWare server under the name NWADMN32.EXE. Adding a shortcut to this utility in your Start menu is a good idea if you want quick access. If you're on a large network, you might even consider adding it to the Quick Launch toolbar of the taskbar. Whenever you start the NetWare Administrator, you'll see a directory tree similar to the one shown in Figure 18.2.

Every icon in the NDS tree is an object on your NetWare server. You'll always see organization, group, volume, and user objects. As you add security and organize your system, you might see profile and organizational unit objects, along with more group objects. Finally, as you add printer support, you'll see one of several series of print objects in your tree.

We can't discuss every element of a NetWare server today. It's important to realize that NetWare is a complex operating system that has been around at least as long as Windows. However, as the day progresses, you'll work with many of the objects in NetWare Administrator.

Working with RConsole

All versions of NetWare provide the means to access the server console from a remote location. Of course, providing remote access without any form of protection would be an invitation to a breach of security by crackers. Therefore, Novell doesn't provide remote access support by default at any NetWare server. However, adding this support is easy. Just type **LOAD RSPX** at the server console. NetWare will load the remote access server and then ask you to provide a secure access password. Type a password and press Enter. You're ready to access the server from a workstation.

 Caution   After you load RSPX, anyone who knows the server password can access the server console. Access isn't limited to network administrators. Therefore, the best policy is to unload RSPX after you complete a remote access scenario to ensure that the required server side support is disabled. You'll also want to use a truly secure password. Make sure that a cracker won't guess the server password with ease. Finally, never use the same password twice. Change the server access password every time you load RSPX.

Getting to the server from the workstation is easy. The following steps will get you going:

1. Open a command prompt and change directories to the file server's \Public directory.

2. Type **RCONSOLE** at the command prompt and press Enter. If you're working in Windows, RConsole might display an error message saying that Windows may cause RConsole to destabilize. Press Enter to get past the error message. RConsole will ask what type of connection you want to use. In most cases, you'll want to use a LAN connection for local servers and an Asynchronous connection for remote servers.

3. Choose a connection option and press Enter. You'll see a list of available servers.

4. Choose one of the servers from the list and press Enter. RConsole will ask you to enter the password for that server.

5. Type the password and press Enter. You'll see the server console.

Note RConsole works fine if you're using character mode utilities at the server console. Unfortunately, some of the new configuration options for NetWare 5 and above rely on the X-Server Graphical Console. You won't be able to access the graphical console using RConsole, which means you'll need to go directly to the server console to perform some tasks.

18

Remote Monitoring of Server Status

After you create an RConsole session, you can see the system console prompt. Of course, this tells you little about anything, much less the server status. You can start the System Monitor by typing **MONITOR** and pressing Enter. The initial window will present you with general system information, such as the example shown in Figure 18.10. Notice the Available Options list. This list tells you all of the statistics you can see for your NetWare server, which is an impressive list.

Let's say you already know that a copy of monitor is running. You can switch to that screen within RConsole, but you need to do something special. Press Alt+F1, and you'll see an Available Options menu that contains all of the special tasks you can perform with RConsole. Choose the Select a Screen to View option and press Enter. You'll see a list of active screens on the server. Select the one you want and press Enter.

FIGURE 18.10

*RConsole provides
access to server
statistics using the
System Monitor utility.*

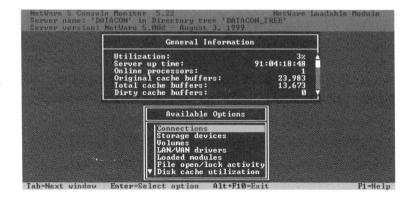

You'll find other options on the Available Options menu. For example, you can perform a
directory scan of the NetWare drives using options on this menu. You can also transfer
files to the server. Of course, the one option that you'll always use is End Remote
Session With Server.

RConsole makes every NetWare utility except graphic utilities available for your use.
You can use features such as TRACK to monitor the actual traffic on your server. Other
displays show volume information and configuration options. You can also load new
files, as we'll do in other sections today. In short, you don't need to use the system console at the server very often if you know how to use RConsole.

Making Configuration Changes

One of the reasons to use RConsole is to access various server utilities. We won't have
time to look at every utility today, but one utility is special. You'll use the NetWare
Configuration utility quite often to configure your server. It allows you to add new features, change the automatic configuration files, and perform other tasks, such as partitioning and formatting hard drives.

To start the NetWare Configuration utility, type **NWCONFIG** at the system console and
press Enter. You'll see the NetWare Configuration utility window shown in Figure 18.11.
Notice that the Configuration Options menu contains entries for everything from adding
new features to controlling the drivers.

You'll learn about adding new features as the day progresses. The configuration feature
we'll discuss in this section is the NCF File Options. Select this entry, and you'll see an
Available NCF File Options menu. Notice that this menu contains options for creating
and editing both the AUTOEXEC.NCF and STARTUP.NCF files. In most cases, you'll
want to select an edit option so that you can change the files. If you select either of the
create entries, NetWare will erase the old files.

FIGURE 18.11

*The NetWare
Configuration utility is
the workhorse for
making changes to
your NetWare setup.*

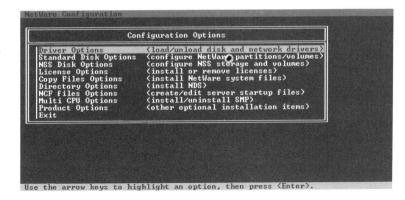

Installing Long Filename Support

Most modern versions of Windows provide long filename support. Using long filenames for files allows you to find what you need more quickly, and you no longer have to come up with those interesting short names for files. Unfortunately, standard NetWare volumes don't support long filenames unless you do a little extra work. The following procedure tells you how to install long filename support:

> **Note**
>
> You'll need to shut down your server by typing **DOWN** at the server console and pressing Enter to implement this change. You'll probably want to do it on a weekend. Because this procedure won't take you more than a few minutes per server to perform, you won't need to take the network offline for a long time.

1. Make sure that you have the most current OS2.NAM (pre-NetWare 5) or LONG.NAM (NetWare 5 and above) name space file. You can download the most current drivers from Novell support at
   `http://support.novell.com/products/psMenu.jsp`.

2. After you get the needed driver, copy it from a local drive to the \SYSTEM directory on the server. There are two console commands that you'll need to use to install name space support at the server console.

3. Type **LOAD OS2.NAM** or **LOAD LONG.NAM** at the file server console and then press Enter. After NetWare loads the name space, you'll need to tell NetWare to use it.

4. Type **ADD NAME SPACE OS2 TO <Volume Name>** or **ADD NAME SPACE LONG TO <Volume Name>** to tell NetWare which volume to use long filename

support on. For example, if you wanted to add long filename support to volume SYS, you'd type ADD NAME SPACE OS2 TO SYS. Press Enter. You need to add long filename support to each volume separately.

5. Shut down the server by typing DOWN at the system console and pressing Enter.

6. Add the OS2.NAM or LONG.NAM file to the DOS directory containing the rest of your server software.

7. Restart the server. NetWare should install the long filename support automatically as the server boots. (The message may pass too quickly for you to see it, so you'll have to test the installation to be sure that the long filename support was loaded.)

8. Check the long filename support from a Windows workstation. You should be able to create a file or folder containing a long filename. Don't try to change the name of an existing file—use a blank file or folder for the purposes of testing long filename support.

Understanding NetWare Printer Support

NetWare performs two tasks extremely well: file management and printer support. This section addresses the second of those two tasks, printing. We'll discuss the two levels of printer support that NetWare provides, and I'll tell you the basics for installing the support so that it works properly with Windows XP. The first section discusses the reliable queue-based method for printing, and the second section discusses the newer Novell Distributed Print Services (NDPS).

Configuring Print Support with PServer

Using PServer or the queued printer setup is the easiest way to configure printer support under any version of NetWare. It's true that NDPS provides many features now found in the queued approach and that NDPS is also faster, but if you're looking for an easy setup, this is it. Every queued setup includes three elements: the printer, the queue, and the print server. The following sections show you how to create all three objects in the easiest manner possible.

Print Queue Setup

The first step in setting up the printing environment for NetWare is to create a print queue. A print queue holds all of the data that users send to the printer. Using a queue enables the server to handle more than one user at a time. In addition, using the queue is fast because the data spools at the speed of the hard drive, rather than the speed of the printer. Because you can assign priorities and other configuration to a print queue, you might use more than one queue per printer. Generally, you'll use at least one print queue per printer to keep the print jobs separated. The following steps show you how to create a print queue:

1. Right-click any organization or organizational unit object and choose Create from the context menu. The New Object dialog box opens.

2. Double-click the Print Queue object. The Create Print Queue dialog box will open. Print queues can use either NDS or the bindery. In addition, this dialog box will ask you to provide a print queue name and the name of a volume used to store the queued print data.

3. Type the print queue name. Type or select a print queue volume. You can use the Browse button to locate a volume in the NDS tree. Click Create. NetWare will create the print queue. At this point, you could double-click the print queue entry in the NDS tree and perform additional configuration.

Printer Setup

The second step in setting up the printing environment is to create the printer object. A printer object represents the printer within NDS. The configuration changes that you make to this object affect how the NetWare configures and interacts with the physical printer. You need one printer object per printer on your system.

1. Right-click any organization or organizational unit object and choose Create from the context menu. The New Object dialog box opens.

2. Double-click the Printer (Non NDPS) object. Make sure that you don't choose the NDPS version of this object. The Create Printer dialog box will open.

3. Type the name of your printer in the Printer Name field. In most cases, you'll want to use a printer name that matches the physical name of the printer. You may want to include the printer model number in the name and a printer number if there's more than one printer of that type on your network. Select Define Additional Properties and click Create. You'll see a Printer (Non NDPS) dialog box.

4. Select the Assignments page shown in Figure 18.12. You'll use this page to select one or more queues to service this printer. This page also contains the default queue option so that NetWare knows which queue to use if the user doesn't make a particular selection.

5. Click Add. You'll see a Select Object dialog box.

6. Double-click the queue that you want to associate with this printer. Assign a priority to the queue (NetWare defaults to the next available priority number). Continue adding queues as needed. Select a default queue in the Default Print Queue field.

18

FIGURE 18.12

Use the Assignments page to connect a printer to a queue.

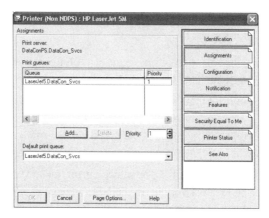

7. Select the Configuration page shown in Figure 18.13. You'll use this page to set the printer interface options, such as the connection type, service interval, and buffer size. Note that NetWare supports much more than just the normal parallel and serial port. You also have connectivity options such as Unix and AppleTalk.

FIGURE 18.13

The Configuration page contains printer interface options, such as the port you'll use for the connection.

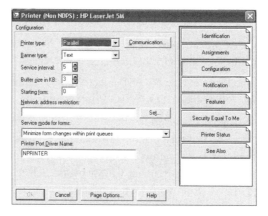

8. Select the printer configuration options that you want. Make sure that you click Communication to set the printer port options after you select a printer port type.

9. Click OK to close the Printer (Non NDPS) dialog box.

Print Server Setup

The third step in setting up the printing environment is to create a print server. You only need one print server per physical location, so if your printers all attach to ports on the server, you'll only need one print server. The print server manages the print jobs. It sends data from the print queue to the printer. The following steps show you how to create a print server:

1. Right-click any organization or organizational unit object and choose Create from the context menu. The New Object dialog box opens.

2. Double-click the Print Server (Non NDPS) object. Make sure that you don't choose the NDPS version of this object. The Create Print Server dialog box will open.

3. Type the print server name in the Print Server Name field. Check the Define Additional Properties option. Click Create. NetWare will create the print server. You'll see the Print Server (Non NDPS) dialog box.

4. Select the Assignments page shown in Figure 18.14. You'll use this page to select one or more printers to service using this print server.

FIGURE **18.14**

Select printer assignments for the print server using the Assignments page.

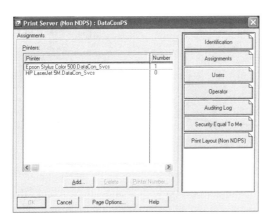

5. Click Add. Select one or more printers from the list and click OK. NetWare will add the printers to the print server.

6. Highlight each printer as needed in the Printers list. Click Printer Number. Assign the printer the number you want and click OK. Click OK to close the Print Server (Non NDPS) dialog box. At this point, the printers are ready to go; you just need to start the print server on the server console.

7. Type **LOAD PSERVER <Name of Print Server>** at the server console and press Enter. NetWare will load the print server. After the print server loads, you'll see a NetWare Print Server window like the one shown in Figure 18.15.

8. Verify the print setup. Double-click the print server entry in the NDS tree. Select the Print Layout (Non NDPS) page. You'll see a connection between the various print elements. Figure 18.16 shows a typical example of a print layout.

FIGURE 18.15

Starting the NetWare Print Server enables access to the printers.

FIGURE 18.16

A typical printer layout for NetWare includes a print server, printer, and print queue.

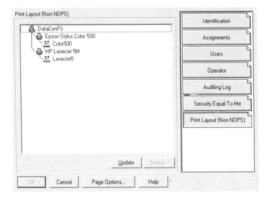

It's time to install printer support on your workstation. Access the printer through My Network Places, just as you would any other network printer. Use the procedure found in the "Printer Installation" section of Day 10 to install the printer on your workstation. You'll always need to install the printer driver from the Windows XP distribution CD or the vendor CD in order to complete the installation.

Using Novell Distributed Print Services (NDPS)

Novell doesn't force you to use the new NDPS feature of NetWare 5. In fact, many systems benefit from the simplicity provided by the queue system presented in the previous section. However, NDPS does provide extra flexibility that large organizations require and theoretically provides a speed boost as well. The following procedure shows how to install NDPS support:

1. Start the NWConfig utility at the server console. You'll see the NetWare Configuration dialog.

2. Highlight Product Options and press Enter. You'll see an Other Installation Options dialog box. This dialog contains a list of NetWare-specific products or products provided by third-party vendors.

3. Choose the Install Other Novell Products option and press Enter. NWConfig displays an Other Installation Items/Products dialog box if it finds the NetWare Operating System CD mounted on the server. Otherwise, you'll need to provide alternative path information that NWConfig can use to find the NetWare Operating System CD.

4. Press Enter. NWConfig will turn control over to the X-Server Graphical Console. You'll see an Additional Products and Services dialog box.

5. Check the Novell Distributed Print Services option and click Next. After a few moments, you'll see a Novell Login dialog box.

6. Type the fully qualified name and password of a user with administrator privileges and then click OK. NetWare finalizes the installation and displays a Summary dialog box.

7. Click Finish. NWConfig will install the required support, which includes all of the files required to use NDPS, some basic resources, an NDPS snap-in for NetWare Administrator, and some miscellaneous files. It will also create the Broker object for you. When the software installation is complete, you'll see an Installation Complete dialog box.

8. Press Esc twice. You'll see an Exit NWConfig dialog box.

9. Highlight Yes and press Enter.

At this point, you've installed the NDPS service and created a Broker object. We're ready to configure the print setup. The following steps show you how to initialize an NDPS setup:

1. Start NetWare Administrator at the workstation. Notice the Broker object added to the NDS tree. In a few moments, you'll see the new NDPS-related objects added to NetWare Administrator as well. These new NDPS objects will help you to configure your system to use NDPS.

2. Right-click the Organization object and choose Create from the context menu. You'll see a New Object dialog box like the one shown in Figure 18.17. Notice the three new NDPS object types listed in this dialog box.

3. Highlight the NDPS Manager option and click OK. You'll see a Create NDPS Manager dialog box. This dialog box contains options for defining the NDPS manager name, resident server, and database volume name.

FIGURE **18.17**

Adding NDPS support to your server adds new objects to the New Object dialog box.

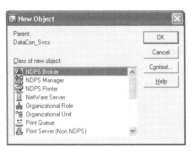

4. Type **Printer Manager** (or another suitable name) in the NDPS Manager Name field. Type the name of your server in the Resident Server field. You can also use the Browse button to find your server. Type the database volume name (such as SYS) in the Database Volume field. You can use the Browse button to find a volume.

5. Click Create. NetWare Administrator will create the new object for you. We're ready to add some printers. However, before we can create those printers, we'll need to start NDPS.

Tip

> If you're upgrading from a queued system, make note of the old printer settings. Delete the old printer objects before you create new printer objects for the NDPS setup.

6. Type **LOAD BROKER "<Name of your Broker object>.<Name of your Organization object>"** at the server console. For example, I used LOAD BROKER "DATACON_BROKER.DataCon_Svcs" for my server. You'll see an NDPS Broker dialog box like the one shown in Figure 18.18 on the server console after the broker is loaded.

FIGURE **18.18**

The NDPS Broker helps you work with various broker services.

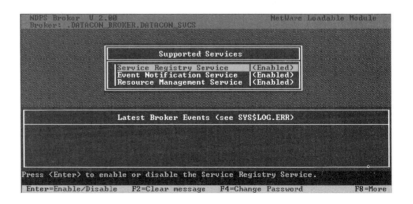

7. Right-click the Organization object within NetWare Administrator at the workstation and select Create from the context menu. You'll see a New Object dialog box.

8. Highlight the NDPS Printer object and click OK. You'll see a Create NDPS Printer dialog box. This dialog box contains options for configuring the printer name, printer agent source, and printer object creation options, such as defining additional properties.

9. Type a name for your printer. The example will use one NDPS Printer object that has a name of HP LaserJet. The names you choose for your NDPS Printer objects should reflect the kind of printers attached to your network.

10. Select the Create a New Printer Agent option because we're creating new printers and check the Define Additional Properties checkbox. Click Create. You'll see a Create Printer Agent dialog box. This is where you'll define the linkage between the new printer and the Print Manager object.

11. Type a name for your agent in the Printer Agent field. I normally use some form of the printer name. Type the name of the NDPS manager object in NDPS Manager Name field. You can also use the Browse button to select the name from a list. Click OK. You'll see a Configure Novell PDS for Printer Agent dialog box. Use this dialog box to choose the printer and port handler types.

12. Choose the Print Device Subsystem (PDS) that matches your printer and click OK. For example, I have a Hewlett-Packard LaserJet 5M attached to my network, so I chose that PDS. You'll see a Configure Port Handler for Printer Agent dialog box. This is where those settings from the previous installation will come in handy. You need to select a printer port (either local or remote).

13. Choose the correct settings for your printer. Depending on the printer and its connection to your network, you may see several additional dialog boxes. Make appropriate setting changes on each dialog box and click Next. When you reach the final dialog, the Next button will be grayed and the Finish button enabled.

14. Click Finish. The Printer Agent will load. You'll see a Select Printer Driver dialog box. This dialog box contains a list of drivers that will automatically load on the user's workstation when they choose to use the selected printer.

15. Choose a printer driver for each of the supported Windows operating systems and click Continue. You'll see a status and configuration dialog box. Note that your version of NetWare may not support every version of Windows, especially Windows XP.

You can now access the printer through My Network Places, just as you can any other network printer. Use the procedure found in the "Printer Installation" section of Day 10 to install the printer on your workstation. In many cases, you'll need to install the printer

18

driver from the Windows XP distribution CD or the vendor CD in order to complete the installation. At the time of this writing, Novell hasn't released the Windows XP-specific client, so it's hard to know what level of printer support they'll provide.

Tips for Optimizing NetWare Use with Windows

We've covered a lot of material today. Trying to discuss an entire operating system in one day is difficult (make that impossible). However, we've hit the highlights of the Windows view of NetWare. It's time to look at a few more interesting facts about the NetWare to Windows XP connection.

- **Use NetWare Administrator Whenever Possible**   You can accomplish some tasks using either NetWare Administrator or a system console utility. The fact is that RConsole is less stable than NetWare Administrator. Using NetWare Administrator, whenever possible, reduces the likelihood that a Windows XP crash will leave your NetWare server in a state of limbo.

- **Monitor Often, Change Little**   NetWare is an extremely stable operating system. I've seen some configurations continue operating without a reboot for several years. It pays to monitor NetWare so that you can catch any problems before they cause the server to crash. However, you'll find that you need to make few changes after the initial configuration process.

- **Avoid Using Odd NLMs**   Almost every NetWare horror story that I've heard involves adding a third-party NLM of dubious origin. In many respects, Windows Server provides better application server capabilities than NetWare. You'll find that you begin to have problems with NetWare after you begin to move away from its core capabilities.

- **Use a NetWare Security Model**   NetWare is way ahead of Windows XP when it comes to security flexibility. You have extremely fine control over every element of NetWare security, making it both easier and harder to configure. It's important to realize that NetWare provides a lot in the way of file, folder, and drive security.

Summary

Windows XP provides the standard Microsoft client as the default NetWare connection. In many cases, this is all you need to use NetWare successfully. If you get creative, every machine on the network could conceivably use the Microsoft client to the exclusion of everything else. However, the NetWare client does work better with the Novell utilities, such as NetWare Administrator, so you should consider using it for the administrator workstations as a minimum.

Most companies use NetWare servers for file and print services. In a few cases, they also use NetWare for a Web server (although Linux is actually a better operating system platform in this situation). We also viewed many ways to work with both print and file services today. This is only the tip of the iceberg, and you'll want to spend more time with NetWare if you plan to use it extensively. Consider today the Windows eye view of NetWare.

Q&A

Q: When will Novell produce a client specifically for Windows XP?

A: The precise date is up in the air right now; no one knows for certain. However, according to the product support Web site information at `http://support.novell.com/cgi-bin/search/searchtid.cgi?/10061913.htm`, testing will begin this fall. Based on previous experience with Novell, you probably won't see a Windows XP-specific client until sometime in the first quarter of 2002.

Q: Why use the outdated queued printer setup when NDPS is obviously superior?

A: NDPS is the right choice for large installations because it provides greater flexibility and better performance. However, most small- to medium-sized business installations will never use the features that NDPS has to offer. In this case, the simplicity and reliability of the queued printer setup is more appealing and practical.

Q: My copy of NetWare Administrator has objects not shown anywhere in your description. How do I use these icons to configure my system?

A: You might see other objects for a number of reasons. For example, a third-party vendor may have installed the object on your system to help you maintain features of that product. UPS vendors often provide add objects as part of their installation. In addition, NetWare provides many objects that we didn't discuss today. For example, we didn't delve into the intricacies of Service Location Protocols (SLPs) and the two objects associated with them (SLP Directory Agent and SLP Scope Unit).

Workshop

It's the end of the eighteenth day. At this point, you should feel more comfortable with NetWare. Now it's time to see how well you can perform NetWare network configuration tasks. You can find answers to the quiz and exercise questions in Appendix A at the back of the book.

Quiz

1. Which option of which applet should you use for controlling banner pages on a NetWare network?

2. How many levels of login script does NetWare provide? What are they?

3. What's the namespace used for long filename support when working with a NetWare 4.x machine?

4. What elements does a typical non-NDPS print server include?

Exercises

1. Try installing the NetWare client from Novell and using it for a test period.

2. Spend some time working with NetWare Administrator.

3. Add long filename support to your NetWare server if necessary.

4. Install or update your printer support on a NetWare server with attached or remote printers.

DAY 19

Creating Scripts and Automating Tasks

Windows XP provides several automation features that help you perform tasks quickly, easily, and best of all, with little effort. The Task Scheduler is a great example of a tool that tells the system to perform a task for you automatically. All you need to do is perform a little task configuration, and the system will get it done.

However, what happens if you can't package the task neatly into something that Task Scheduler will understand? For that matter, what happens if the task isn't one that you perform on a regular basis? That's where scripting can come in handy. It allows you to execute tasks when you need to perform them.

Scripting is more flexible than using Windows automation. It allows you to perform tasks that Microsoft might not have thought essential. You can create your own utilities that help you work faster and more efficiently.

Today, we'll discuss both scripting and automation, with an emphasis on scripting because it's more flexible. You'll learn enough about scripting to create some basic utilities. These utilities won't astound the world, but they'll make your life easier.

Script Essentials

Scripting, as people currently view it, is relatively old. A *script* is simply some human words that an interpreter changes into data that the computer can understand. *An interpreter* is a special type of application that performs conversions; it comes in many different forms. If you use this definition for scripting, it's been around since the beginning of computers, for all practical purposes.

Windows XP includes the Windows Scripting Host (WSH). The combination of WSH and a scripting engine form an interpreter that accepts a script file as input and outputs application data from the computer. Of course, WSH and its associated scripting engines are more complex than any previous interpreter. You can read about Microsoft's original vision for WSH at http://www.microsoft.com/mind/0698/cutting0698.htm.

Before you can do much with scripts, you need to understand how to work with them. This means at least learning to run the scripts. The following sections show you how to run scripts.

Note

> The Internet includes many useful WSH resource sites. One of the more interesting sites is LabMice.net (http://www.labmice.net/WSH.htm). If you want to learn about books about WSH, check http://ourworld.com-puserve.com/homepages/Guenter_Born/WSHBazaar/USBook.htm. You'll find quite a few other resource sites throughout the following sections. Make sure that you check them out to get the most out of the material presented today.

Running Scripts

You can start scripts from a variety of places. Scripts permeate every part of Windows XP. For example, you'll find scripts in your browser and most likely your word processor as well. A script can make the difference between an application that works well and one that only performs simple tasks.

Scripts use something known as the Windows Scripting Host (WSH) to run. WSH is an interpreter, something that reads human words and converts them into machine language that the computer can understand. WSH is extremely flexible. It can run a number of languages if you install the required support. Windows XP comes with support for both JavaScript (JS files) and VBScript (VBS) built in. The VBS files normally have a Visual Basic Editor (VBE) extension in Windows XP.

Note

You'll see several different names for JavaScript. The most popular alternative name right now is JScript. It also appears under the name of ECMAScript (`http://www.ecma.ch/ecma1/stand/ecma-262.htm`) because this organization is producing a standardized form of the language. The big thing is not to confuse JavaScript with Java. The two are completely different. You'll find JScript in Windows XP, but Java support has gone by the wayside due to Microsoft's legal loss to Sun. For the purposes of clarity, I'll always use JavaScript in the book.

All of the scripts we'll use in this section will run at the command prompt. However, it's important to realize that the scripting skills you develop now will also work in other areas of Windows. As long as you have an interpreter that understands your script, it will run in any environment. You'll find Command Prompt in the Start\Programs\Accessories folder. Here are the two command lines you can use to start a WSH script:

```
CScript <Script Name> [<WSH Command Line Switches>] [<Script Arguments>]
WScript <Script Name> [<WSH Command Line Switches>] [<Script Arguments>]
```

As you can see, there are actually two different commands you can use to start WSH. CScript is the character mode version of WSH, and WScript provides a dialog interface. Both forms of WSH accomplish the same tasks. The only difference between the two commands is the interface.

FIGURE 19.1

The standard script icon is blue for JS files and yellow for VBE files.

19

CScript and WScript use the same command line. You must provide a script name as the first command line argument. Most scripts have a VBE or a JS file extension, but any extension is acceptable. For example, you can still use VBS files with WSH, but the icon won't look right and you can't double-click it to start the execution. Figure 19.1 shows the standard script icon. The icon is yellow for VBE files and blue for JS files. Other languages will potentially use other icons or other colors.

WSH provides a wealth of command line switches that you can use to modify its behavior. Table 19.1 shows a list of the command line switches that WSH provides. Notice that all of these command line switches start with two slashes like this: //. The slashes differentiate them from switches you may need for your script. WSH passes script arguments to your script for processing. Script arguments can be anything including command line switches of your own or values needed to calculate a result.

Note   Users of older versions of CScript and WScript may remember the //C and the //W switches used to switch the default scripting engines. Newer versions of CScript and WScript replace these switches with the //H switch. You'll also find the //R (reregister) and //Entrypoint switches missing because with WSH the functionality is no longer needed by script developers.

TABLE 19.1   WSH Command Line Switches

Switch	Description
//?	Displays the currently documented command line switches. The newest versions of WSH tend to reject older switches, even those of the undocumented variety.
//B	Use this mode when you don't want the user to interact with the script. Batch mode suppresses all non-command line console user interface requests from script. It also suppresses error message display (a change from previous versions).
//D	Activates debugging mode so that you can fix errors in a script.
//H:CScript	Makes CSCRIPT.EXE the default application for running scripts. (WScript is the default engine.)
//H:WScript	Makes WSCRIPT.EXE the default application for running scripts.
//I	Allows full interaction with the user. Any pop-up dialog boxes will wait for user input before the script continues.
//Job:<Job Name>	Executes a WSH job. A WSH job has a WSF extension. This file enables you to perform tasks using multiple scripting engines and multiple files. Essentially, this allows you to perform a "super batch" process. We'll discuss WSH jobs in more detail in the "Creating Script Job Files" section.
//Logo and //NoLogo	WHS normally prints out a logo message. You'd use the //NoLogo switch to prevent WSH from displaying this message.
//S	This command line switch allows you to save current command line options for a user. WSH will save the following options: //B, //I, //Logo, //Nologo, and //T:n.
//T:nn	Limits the maximum time the script can run to nn seconds. Normally, there isn't any timeout value. You'd use this switch in situations where a script might end up in a continuous loop or unable to obtain the requested information for other reasons. For example, you might use this switch when requesting information on a network drive.
//X	Starts the script in the debugger. This allows you to trace the execution of the script from beginning to end.

TABLE 19.1 continued

Switch	Description
//U	Outputs any console information using Unicode instead of pure ASCII. This is a CScript-only option.

Some of the switches in Table 19.1 may not make a lot of sense right this second, but I'll explain them as the day progresses. Let's look at a couple of the switches right away, though, so that you'll have some idea of how they work.

As shown in Table 19.1, you can work with WSH in either interactive or batch mode. You use batch mode when you need to perform tasks that don't require user input. For example, you might want to run Scan Disk every evening but use different command line switches for it based on the day. You could use Task Scheduler to accomplish this task, but using it in conjunction with a WSH script will improve the flexibility you gain when running the task.

Another kind of batch processing might be to send log files to your supervisor or perhaps set up a specific set of environment variables for a character-mode application based on the current user. On the other hand, interactive mode requires user interaction. You'd use it for tasks such as creating a form letter script. Such a script could ask the user a set of general questions and then create a form letter based on the user's input. The form letter would follow company guidelines and save the user time. All the user would need to do is tweak a few of the lines to make the letter complete.

Tip

Because batch processing doesn't require any form of user input, I normally include the //T:nn switch with the //B switch. This allows me to stop the script automatically if it runs too long. In most cases, this allows me to stop an errant script before it corrupts the Windows environment or freezes the machine. However, you can't time some tasks with ease. For example, any Web-based task is difficult to time because you can't account for problems with a slow connection. In this case, you'll need to refrain from using the //T:nn switch or provide a worst-case scenario time interval.

19

The next set of command line switches that I'd like to talk about are //Logo and //NoLogo. There aren't any right or wrong times to use these switches, but I usually use the //Logo switch when testing a script and the //NoLogo switch afterward. The reason is simple. During the testing process, I want to know about every potential source of problems in my script environment, including an old script engine that might cause problems. On the other hand, I don't want to clutter my screen with useless text after I debug the script. Using the //NoLogo switch keeps screen clutter to a minimum.

Host and Property Page Options

You don't have to rely exclusively on command line switches to configure WSH; you can configure two WSH options from the Windows Script Host Settings dialog box. Run WScript by itself, and you'll see the dialog box shown in Figure 19.2.

FIGURE 19.2

WSH will allow you to set certain configuration options permanently without the use of command line switches.

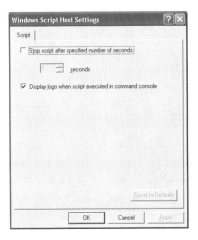

The first check box allows you to set WSH to stop executing a script after a certain time interval has elapsed. The edit box below it contains the number of seconds to wait. Setting this option is like adding the //T:nn command line switch to every script that you run.

The second check box determines whether WSH displays WSH logo when running scripts from the DOS prompt. Normally, this option is checked, which is the same as adding the //Logo command line switch to every script that you run. Clearing this option tells WSH that you don't want to display the logo, which is the same as using the //NoLogo command line switch.

You can get the same dialog as shown in Figure 19.2 for individual scripts. All you need to do is right-click the script file and select Properties from the context menu. Select the Script tab to see the options. Changing the WSH options when looking at a script file Properties dialog changes the options for that script, but the options for WSH in general remain the same.

Use Reset to Defaults to change all of the settings back to their Microsoft defaults. The default settings include no time out period and will always display the WSH logo.

Creating Script Job Files

Job files can help you create a modular script environment and yet automate tasks. Modular scripts perform a single task. You can use them alone or with other scripts to produce certain effects. Using a modular approach saves time because you only have to create and debug a script to perform a specific task one time. After that, you just add it to your application. Think of modular scripting as a way of creating applications with script Lego's.

The script job file is a form of eXtensible Markup Language (XML), which looks similar to the code in HTML pages. The job files have a specific format. The following WSF file executes a single script named TEST1.JS:

```
<Job ID=MyJob>
    <Script Language="JScript" Src="TEST1.JS" />
</Job>
```

Every job begins with the <Job> tag. You have to assign an ID to your job to make it easy to identify. Notice that the <Script> tag includes an ending slash (/). XML requires that you include the slash so that all of the entries are symmetrical.

You can use a mix of languages within a job. Every entry identifies the language it uses so that WSH doesn't have to guess how to run it. If the code is in a file, you add an Src attribute to the <Script> tag.

WSH also provides support for code within a job file. You can mix languages if desired. Anything you can do with a script file, you can also do with a job file. For example, the following job runs a JavaScript script and then executes some internal script (don't worry too much about understanding the code for now):

```
<Job ID=MyJob>
    <Script Language="JScript" Src="TEST1.JS" />
    <Script Language="VBScript">
        WScript.Echo("Hello World")
    </Script>
</Job>
```

In this case, the job file outputs the results of the TEST1.JS file first and then outputs "Hello World." If the user started the script with WScript, there would be dialog boxes for each output. CScript places all of the output on separate lines of the command window.

Let's say you wanted to create a single file containing all your jobs. That way, all you really need to know is the name of your file and the name of your job. Everything is located in one place on the hard drive, so there's nothing to lose. The following example shows how to create a file with multiple jobs:

19

```
<Package>
    <Job ID="MyJob1">
        <Script Language="JScript" Src="TEST1.JS" />
    </Job>

    <Job ID="MyJob2">
        <Script Language="JScript" Src="TEST1.JS" />
        <Script Language="VBScript">
            WScript.Echo("Hello World")
        </Script>
    </Job>
</Package>
```

Notice that we've added a <Package> tag to the mix. The <Package> tag serves to bundle all of the jobs together. Each job still requires an ID, but you don't assign an ID to the package. You'll use the //Job:<Job Name> switch as shown below to access a specific job in the package:

```
CSCRIPT MyJob3.WSF //Job:MyJob1
```

That's all there is to job files. You'll use a combination of XML and script to combine script files together. Using this approach enables you to create some interesting scripts for your system.

Working with Scripting Objects

I can't provide you with a complete tutorial on scripting in one day. Some developers require months to learn everything there is to know about the scripting language and the objects the language controls. Today you'll learn a little about the scripting language as you work with various objects that WSH supports. By reading through the examples, you'll learn the basics of scripting. You won't become a guru overnight, but you could create some simple scripts. As you learn more, you'll be able to create scripts of increasing complexity. Scripting isn't hard to learn, but you need to take your time and learn it a bit at a time.

Note

> Earlier versions of Windows used to include a samples directory for scripts. Windows XP doesn't include this directory. However, you can still download the script samples from Microsoft's site at http://msdn.microsoft.com/ scripting/. Select Windows Script Host and then Overview from the menu on the left side of the page. Click Download the Samples to obtain a variety of scripting examples.

WSH depends on objects that Microsoft supplies as part of Windows XP to perform tasks such as outputting text to the display. An *object* consists of two elements: properties and methods. A *property* describes the object and determines its functionality. For example, you can say an apple is red. In this case, red is a property of the apple. However, you can also paint the apple blue. In this case, you changed the color property of the apple to another value.

Methods are actions you can perform with an object. For example, looking at an apple again, you can say that it has a grow method. As the tree applies the grow method, the apple becomes larger.

Writing scripts in Windows XP means knowing the object you want to work with, the properties that object provides, and the methods you can use with that object. You don't have to learn about every object. In fact, you'll find it easier to learn about one object at a time. The following sections will tell you about the main scripting object, WScript, and some of the supporting objects it contains. We'll also look at some scripting examples in both VBScript and JavaScript.

Using the WScript Object

The WScript object is the main object for WSH. You'll access every other object through this one. The following list tells you about the properties that the WScript object supports:

- **Application**   Provides you with access to a low-level interface for WScript. An *interface* is a pointer to a list of functions that you can call for a particular object. Only advanced programmers will need this property because WSH exposes all of the basic functions for you.

- **Arguments**   Provides a complete list of the arguments for this script. Applications pass arguments on the command line. WSH passes the argument list as an array. You create a variable to hold the argument list and then access the individual arguments as you would any array. The Arguments.Count property contains the total number of array elements.

- **FullName**   Contains the full name of the scripting engine along with the fully qualified path to it. For example, if you were using CScript, you might get C:\WINDOWS\SYSTEM32\CSCRIPT.EXE as a return value.

- **Interactive**   Returns true if the script is in interactive mode.

- **Name**   Returns the friendly name for WScript. In most cases, this is Windows Scripting Host.

19

- **Path** Provides just the path information for the host executable. For example, if you were using CScript, you may get a return value of: C:\WINDOWS\SYS-TEM32\.
- **ScriptFullName** Contains the full name and path of the script that's running.
- **ScriptName** Provides just the script name.
- **Version** Returns the WSH Version number.

Remember that all of these properties tell you about the WScript object. You can also use methods to perform tasks with the WScript object. The following list provides a brief overview of the more important methods you'll use with the WScript object. Note that most of these methods require that you pass one or more parameters as input.

- **CreateObject(strProgID)** Create the object specified by strProgID. This object could be WSH specific, such as "WScript.Network" or application specific, such as "Excel.Application".
- **GetObject(strPathname [, strProgID])** Retrieves the requested object. The filename for the object you want to retrieve is contained in strPathname. In most cases, this is going to be a data file, but you can retrieve other kinds of objects as well. As soon as you execute this command, WSH will start the application associated with that object. For example, if you specified "C:\MyText.TXT" as the strPathname, WSH may open Notepad to display it. The optional strProgID argument allows you to override the default processing of the object. For example, you may want to open the text file with Word instead of Notepad.
- **Echo(AnyArg)** Displays text in a window (WScript) or to the console screen (CScript). AnyArg can contain any type of valid output value. This can include both strings and numbers. Using Echo without any arguments displays a blank line.
- **GetScriptEngine(strEngineID)** Registers an alternative script engine, such as the PERL script engine we talked about earlier. The identifier for the script engine that you want to retrieve is contained in strEngineID. You'll need to register the engine using the GetScriptEngine.Register method before you can actually use it. A script engine also requires you to provide a default extension.
- **Quit(intErrorCode)** Exits the script prematurely. The optional intErrorCode argument returns an error code if necessary.

Using the WScript.WshArguments Object

Whenever you start a script, you have the option of passing one or more arguments to it on the command line. That's where the WshArguments object comes into play. It helps you determine the number of arguments and retrieve them as needed. You'll always use the WScript.Arguments property to access this object; it's not directly accessible. The following list describes the properties for this object:

- **Item(intIndex)**   Retrieves a specific command line argument. The index of the argument that you want to retrieve is contained in intIndex. The array used to hold the arguments is 0 based, so the first argument number is 0.
- **Count()**   Returns the number of command line arguments.
- **Length()**   Returns the number of command line arguments. This property is provided for JScript compatibility purposes.

Using the WScript.WshShell Object

You'll use this object to access the Windows shell (the part of Windows that interacts with applications and creates the user interface) in a variety of ways. For example, you can use this object to read the registry or to create a new shortcut on the desktop. This is an exposed WSH object, which means you can access it directly. However, you need to access it through the WScript object like this: WScript.WshShell. The following list describes the WshShell methods:

- **CreateShortcut(strPathname)**   Creates a WSH shortcut object. The location of the shortcut, which will be the desktop in most cases, is contained in strPathname.
- **DeleteEnvironmentVariable(strName [, strType])**   Deletes the environment variable specified by strName. The optional strType argument defines the type of environment variable to delete. Typical values for strType include System, User, Volatile, and Process. The default environment variable type is System.
- **GetEnvironmentVariable(strName [, strType])**   Retrieves the environment variable specified by strName. Default environment variables include NUMBER_OF_PROCESSORS, OS, COMSPEC, HOMEDRIVE, HOMEPATH, PATH, PATHEXT, PROMPT, SYSTEMDRIVE, SYSTEMROOT, WINDIR, TEMP, and TMP. The optional strType argument defines the type of environment variable to delete. Typical values for strType include System, User, Volatile, and Process. The default environment variable type is System.
- **Popup(strText [,intSeconds] [,strTitle] [,intType])**   Displays a message dialog box. The return value is an integer defining which button the user selected. It includes the following values: OK (1), Cancel (2), Abort (3), Retry (4), Ignore (5), Yes (6), No (7), Close (8), and Help (9). The text that you want to display in the dialog box is contained in strText. How long WSH displays the dialog box before it closes the dialog box and returns a value of −1 is determined by intSeconds. The title bar text is contained in strTitle. The intType argument can contain values that determine the type of dialog box that you'll create. The first intType argument

19

determines button type. You have a choice of the following: OK (0), OK and Cancel (1), Abort, Retry, and Ignore (2), Yes, No, and Cancel (3), Yes and No (4), and Retry and Cancel (5). The second intType argument determines which icon Windows XP displays in the dialog box. You have a choice of the following values: Stop (16), Question (32), Exclamation (48), and Information (64). Combine the intType argument values to obtain different dialog box effects.

- **RegDelete(strName)**   Removes the value or key specified by strName from the registry. If strName ends in a backslash, RegDelete removes a key. You must provide a fully qualified path to the key or value that you want to delete. In addition, strName must begin with one of these values: HKEY_CURRENT_USER, HKEY_LOCAL_MACHINE, HKEY_CLASSES_ROOT, KEY_USER, HKEY_CURRENT_CONFIG, or HKEY_DYN_DATA.

- **RegRead(strName)**   Reads the value or key specified by strName from the registry. If strName ends in a backslash, RegDelete reads a key. You must provide a fully qualified path to the key or value that you want to read. In addition, strName must begin with one of these values: HKEY_CURRENT_USER, HKEY_LOCAL_MACHINE, HKEY_CLASSES_ROOT, KEY_USER, HKEY_CURRENT_CONFIG, or HKEY_DYN_DATA. RegRead can only read specific data types including REG_SZ, REG_EXPAND_SZ, REG_DWORD, REG_BINARY, and REG_MULTI_SZ. Any other data types will return an error.

- **RegWrite(strName, anyValue [, strType])**   Writes the data specified by anyValue to a value or key specified by strName to the registry. If strName ends in a backslash, RegDelete writes a key. You must provide a fully qualified path to the key or value that you want to write. In addition, strName must begin with one of these values: HKEY_CURRENT_USER, HKEY_LOCAL_MACHINE, HKEY_CLASSES_ROOT, KEY_USER, HKEY_CURRENT_CONFIG, or HKEY_DYN_DATA. RegRead can only write specific data types including REG_SZ, REG_EXPAND_SZ, REG_DWORD, and REG_BINARY. Any other data types will return an error.

- **Run(strCommand [, intWinType] [lWait])**   Runs the command or application specified by strCommand. You can include command line arguments and switches with the command string. The type of window that the application starts in is determined by intWinType. You can force the script to wait for the application to complete by setting lWait to True; otherwise, the script begins the next line of execution immediately.

- **SetEnvironmentVariable(strName, strValue [, strType])**   Sets the environment variable named strName to the value specified by strValue. The optional strType argument defines the type of environment variable to delete. Typical values for strType include System, User, Volatile, and Process. The default environment variable type is System.

Using the WScript.WshNetwork Object

The WshNetwork object works with network objects such as drives and printers that the client machine can access. This is an exposed WSH object, which means you can access it directly using the WScript.WshNetwork object. The following list describes properties associated with this object:

- **ComputerName**   Returns a string containing the client computer name.
- **UserDomain**   Returns a string containing the user's domain name.
- **UserName**   Returns a string containing the previous name that the user used to log on to the network.

As with any other WSH object, the WshNetwork object uses methods to work with network resources. The following list describes the methods associated with this object:

- **AddPrinterConnection(strLocal, strRemote [, lUpdate] [, strUser] [, strPassword])**   Creates a new printer connection for the local machine. The local name for the printer specified by strRemote is contained in strLocal. The strRemote value must contain a locatable resource and usually uses a UNC format, such as \\Remote\Printer. Setting lUpdate to true adds the new connection to the user profile, which means Windows XP will make the connection available each time the user boots the machine. Optional user name and password values required to log onto the remote machine and create the connection are contained in strUser and strPassword.
- **EnumNetworkDrives()**   Returns a WshCollection object containing the list of local and remote drives currently mapped from the client machine. A WshCollection object is essentially a 0-based array of strings.
- **EnumPrinterConnections()**   Returns a WshCollection object containing the list of local and remote printers currently mapped from the client machine. A WshCollection object is essentially a 0-based array of strings.
- **MapNetworkDrive(strLocal, strRemote [, lUpdate] [, strUser] [, strPassword])**   Creates a new drive connection for the local machine. The local name for the drive specified by strRemote is contained in strLocal. The strRemote value must contain a locatable resource and usually uses a UNC format, such as "\\Remote\Drive_C." Setting lUpdate to True adds the new connection to the user profile, which means Windows XP will make the connection available each time the user boots the machine. Optional user name and password values required to log onto the remote machine and create the connection are contained in strUser and strPassword.

19

- **RemoveNetworkDrive(strName [, lForce] [, lUpdate])**   Deletes a previous network drive mapping. If strName contains a local name, Windows XP only cancels that connection. If strName contains a remote name, Windows XP cancels all resources associated with that remote name. Set lForce to True if you want to disconnect from a resource whether that resource is in use or not. Setting lUpdate to true will remove the connection from the user profile so that it doesn't appear the next time that the user logs on to the machine.

- **RemovePrinterConnection(strName [, lForce] [, lUpdate])**   Deletes a previous network printer connection. If strName contains a local name, Windows XP only cancels that connection. If strName contains a remote name, Windows XP cancels all resources associated with that remote name. Set lForce to True if you want to disconnect from a resource whether that resource is in use or not. Setting lUpdate to true will remove the connection from the user profile so that it doesn't appear the next time that the user logs on to the machine.

Scripting in VBScript and JavaScript

Now that you have some idea of how Windows XP supports scripting, let's look at a simple script. I'm presenting these examples in both VBScript and JavaScript so that you can see the differences between the two languages. In addition, some people prefer one scripting language to another, so this is your chance to see both in action. The following code shows a basic example in VBScript:

```
' Test1.VBS shows how to use functions and subprocedures
' within a WSH script.

WScript.Echo("The value returned was: " + CStr(MyFunction(1)))

function MyFunction(nSomeValue)
    WScript.Echo("Function received value of: " + CStr(nSomeValue))
    Call MySubprocedure(nSomeValue + 1)
    MyFunction = nSomeValue + 1
end function

sub MySubprocedure(nSomeValue)
    WScript.Echo("Subprocedure received value of: " + CStr(nSomeValue))
end sub
```

As you can see, the sample code uses the WScript object to send some information to the screen. I thought it important to introduce you to the idea of functions and subs, the two building blocks of VBScript. The following code shows a similar example for JavaScript:

```
// Test1.JS shows how to use functions within a WSH script.
```

```
WScript.Echo("The value returned was: " + MyFunction(1));

function MyFunction(nSomeValue)
{
   WScript.Echo("The value received was: " + nSomeValue);
   return nSomeValue + 1;
}
```

JavaScript only provides functions, so that's all this example demonstrates. It's also important to notice that VBScript requires you to convert numeric values to a string, while JavaScript performs the conversion automatically.

At this point, you know a little about scripting and a little about the WScript.Echo() method. Let's look at some other methods that the WScript object provides. The following JavaScript code retrieves information from the command line. It also retrieves information about the application environment.

```
// ProgInfo.JS determines the specifics about your program and then
// displays this information on screen.

// Create some constants for display purposes (buttons and icons).
var intOK = 0;
var intOKCancel = 1;
var intAbortRetryIgnore = 2;
var intYesNoCancel = 3;
var intYesNo = 4;
var IntRetryCancel = 5;
var intStop = 16;
var intQuestion = 32;
var intExclamation = 48;
var intInformation = 64;

// Create some popup return values.
var intOK = 1;
var intCancel = 2;
var intAbort = 3;
var intRetry = 4;
var intIgnore = 5;
var intYes = 6;
var intNo = 7;
var intClose = 8;
var intHelp = 9;

// Create a popup display object.
var WshShell = WScript.CreateObject("WScript.Shell");

// Create a variable for holding a popup return value.
var intReturn;
```

19

```
// Get the program information and display it.
WshShell.Popup("Full Name:\t" + WScript.Fullname +
        "\r\nInteractive:\t" + WScript.Interactive +
        "\r\nName:\t\t" + WScript.Name +
        "\r\nPath:\t\t" + WScript.Path +
        "\r\nScript Full Name:\t" + WScript.ScriptFullName +
        "\r\nScript Name:\t" + WScript.ScriptName +
        "\r\nVersion:\t\t" + WScript.Version,
        0,
        "Program Information Demonstration",
        intOK + intInformation);

// Ask if the user wants to display the argument list.
intReturn = WshShell.Popup("Do you want to display the argument list?",
          0,
          "Argument List Display",
          intYesNo + intQuestion);

// Determine if the user wants to display the argument list and
// display and appropriate message.
if (intReturn == intYes)

    // See if there are any arguments to display.
    DisplayArguments();
else
    WScript.Echo("Goodbye");

function DisplayArguments()
{

    // Create some variables.
    var strArguments = "Arguments:\r\n\t";    // Argument list.
    var intCount = 0;              // Loop counter.

    // See if there are any arguments, if not, display an
    // appropriate message.
    if (WScript.Arguments.Length == 0)
       WshShell.Popup("There are no arguments to display.",
           0,
           "Argument List Display",
           intOK + intInformation);

    // If there are arguments to display, then create a list
    // first and display them all at once.
    else
    {
        for (intCount = 0; intCount < WScript.Arguments.Length; intCount++)
            strArguments =
                strArguments + WScript.Arguments.Item(intCount) + "\r\n\t";
        WshShell.Popup(strArguments,
```

```
        0,
        "Argument List Display",
        intOK + intInformation);
    }
```

When you run this script, you'll see a dialog box containing all of the information about the script engine. When you click OK, the program will ask if you want to display the command line arguments. If you say yes, you'll see anything you typed at the command line. Otherwise, the script displays a Goodbye message.

You should notice a few things about this example. First, I create an object in this code. You need access to the WshShell object for many of the tasks you'll perform with scripts. The code also shows how to use the Popup() method to obtain information from the user. Finally, the code uses the Arguments object to access the command line information. Notice the object hierarchy used in this example.

The final example shows how to use VBScript to access information in the registry. You don't want to change information unless you have to, but seeing what's available in the registry is a good way to build your knowledge of both scripting and the registry. Note that this example uses the command line argument to determine which file extension to look for in the registry.

```
' RegRead.VBE will display the application extension information
' contained in the registry.

' Create an icon and button variable for Popup().
intOK = 0
intInformation = 64

' Create a popup display object.
set WshShell = WScript.CreateObject("WScript.Shell")

' Create variables to hold the information.
strExtension = ""     ' File extension that we're looking for.
strFileType = ""      ' Holds the main file type.
strFileOpen = ""      ' File open command.
strFilePrint = ""     ' File print command.
strDefaultIcon = ""   ' Default icon for file type.

' See if the user provided a file extension to look for.
' If not, assign strExtension a default file extension.
if (WScript.Arguments.Length > 0) then
    strExtension = WScript.Arguments.Item(0)
else
    strExtension = ".txt"
end if

' Get the file type.
```

19

```
strFileType = WshShell.RegRead("HKEY_CLASSES_ROOT\\" +_
              strExtension + "\\")

' Use the file type to get the file open and file print
' commands, along with the default icon.
strFileOpen = WshShell.RegRead("HKEY_CLASSES_ROOT\\" +_
              strFileType +_
              "\\shell\\open\\command\\")
strFilePrint = WshShell.RegRead("HKEY_CLASSES_ROOT\\" +_
              strFileType +_
              "\\shell\\print\\command\\")
strDefaultIcon = WshShell.RegRead("HKEY_CLASSES_ROOT\\" +_
              strFileType +_
              "\\DefaultIcon\\")

' Display the results.
WshShell.Popup "File Type:" + vbTab + vbTab + vbTab + strFileType +_
        vbCrLf + "File Open Command:" + vbTab + strFileOpen +_
        vbCrLf + "File Print Command:" + vbTab + vbTab + strFilePrint +_
        vbCrLf + "Default Icon:" + vbTab + vbTab + strDefaultIcon,_
        0,_
        "RegRead Results",_
        intOK + intInformation
```

When you run this script, it reads the command line. If you haven't supplied a value, the script will assign a default extension of .TXT. The script uses the extension to locate information in the registry such as the file open and print commands. Finally, the script uses the Popup() method to display the output.

You should notice several differences between this example and the JavaScript example we looked at previously. First, the method for creating an object requires the use of a "set"—you can't simply assign the object to a variable. You'll also notice that VBScript has access to all of the standard Visual Basic constants, such as vbTab and vbCrLf. Finally, VBScript handles many of the method calls as subs, not as functions. You need to exercise care when working in a mixed environment.

Using the Files and Settings Transfer Wizard

The main purpose of the Files and Settings Transfer Wizard is to move your Windows settings from one machine to another. Microsoft developed this tool to make it easier to upgrade to a new machine. You could also use the Files and Settings Transfer Wizard for a number of other tasks. For example, some people have used it to move their settings from one partition on a machine to another. This allows you to create a Windows 2000 setup, for example, and transfer those settings to a Windows XP partition on the same machine

> **Tip**
>
> A few people have mentioned that they use this wizard to create a backup of their system. All you need to do is select the network file save option found in the "Working with the Old Computer" section. Of course, the best option is to create a backup of your system using a standard backup application, but this serves as an interesting alternative for those on a budget.

You'll find the Files and Settings Transfer Wizard in the Start\Programs\Accessories\ System Tools menu. When you first open the program, you'll see a Welcome Screen. Data transfers using media such as a hard drive or floppy disk occur in two steps. You move the data from the old machine to the media and then from the media to the new machine. Serial cable transfers occur in real time on both machines. The following sections show how to use this utility to move data from an old machine to a new one.

Working with the Old Computer

You'll always transfer files from the old computer first. In many cases, you'll create what amounts to a backup of your old computer on a floppy or removable media and then transfer it to the new computer. The wizard also provides an option for moving the settings using a serial cable between the old and new machines. The following steps show you how to use the wizard to save the old computer settings:

1. Click Next. You'll see a Which computer is this? dialog box.

2. Select Old Computer. Click Next. You'll see a Select a Transfer Method dialog box. Notice that you have a choice of using a serial cable, floppy or other removable media, or a network drive.

3. Select a transfer method. Make sure that you select an empty folder if you select a location on a network. You'll see the What do you want to transfer? dialog box shown in Figure 19.3. Notice that you have three default settings: settings only, files only, and files and settings. The defaults assume that you want to transfer everything. If you check the option at the bottom of the dialog box, you can perform a custom selection of files and settings. Note that this is the best way to use this wizard to backup your system if you don't plan to restore everything.

4. Select the information that you want to transfer. If you select the custom option, click Next and you'll see a Select Custom Files and Settings dialog box. Choose the files and settings that you want to transfer and click Next. In all cases, you'll see an Install programs on your new computer dialog box.

19

FIGURE 19.3

You can use this dialog box to select the settings and files that you want to transfer.

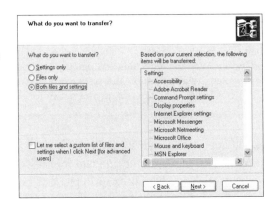

5. Make note of the programs that Microsoft recommends you install on the new machine (for that matter, you may want to install them at this point). Click Next. The Files and Settings Transfer Wizard will collect information about your machine. At some point, you'll see a completion dialog box. Make note of any files or settings that the wizard couldn't move and move them manually if possible.

6. Click Finish. The files and settings are now ready to move to the new computer.

Working with the New Computer

After you backup the settings from the old computer, you can transfer them to the new computer. The following steps show you how to transfer the old computer settings to the new computer:

1. Click Next. You'll see a Which computer is this? dialog box.

2. Select New Computer. Click Next. You'll see a Do you have a Windows XP CD? dialog box. Use the options in this dialog box to create a wizard disk that you can place in the new machine. The wizard disk creation method depends on the options you choose. Follow the instructions that the Files and Settings Transfer Wizard provides.

3. Select a wizard disk creation option and then click next. If you choose the last option, the wizard won't create a wizard disk. Click Next. You'll see a Where are the files and settings? dialog box. This dialog box contains options that help you choose a transfer method. You can use options such as transferring data from a floppy.

4. Select a file and setting transfer option and then click Next. You'll see a Transfer in Progress dialog box. Eventually, the Files and Settings Transfer Wizard will display a completion dialog box.

5. Review the list for any files or settings that the wizard couldn't complete. Click Finish. The Files and Settings Transfer Wizard will ask you to log off so that the settings can take effect.

6. Log off and then back on. Try to restore the missing files or settings manually.

Scheduling Tasks

The Task Scheduler is one of the handier utilities provided with Windows XP. It helps you create automated jobs that will run on a predefined schedule. This means that you can schedule work for your computer and not worry about it afterward.

You can use the Task Scheduler for a number of tasks. In fact, some people end up overusing this utility in an attempt to reduce their work. The Task Scheduler works well for repetitive tasks that rely on a single application. In addition, the application must perform the same steps every time you use it because the Task Scheduler can't think. In other words, the Task Scheduler is quite useful, but it can't replace the human on the other side of the monitor.

One of the best uses for Task Scheduler is machine maintenance because this task uses the same precise set of steps every time you do it. I normally schedule a disk defragmentation every morning before I start work. Once a week, the Backup program runs automatically to preserve my local settings. (My system also uses a network backup on a daily basis.)

In some cases, Task Scheduler is actually redundant and can't perform as well as the application. For example, Outlook Express will faithfully check your e-mail every half hour (or other selectable interval) using settings on the General tab of the Options dialog box (accessible using the Outlook Express Tools | Options command).

Task Scheduler provides two distinct interfaces. Actually, they're separate commands, but the effect is the same. The graphical user interface (GUI) is the easiest way to use Task Scheduler for manual entries. Use the AT command line (character mode) utility for scripts and batch files.

Now that you have a better idea of what Task Scheduler is like, it's time to learn how to use it. The following sections discuss both the GUI and command line interfaces for Task Scheduler. You learn how to use both so that you gain the extra flexibility that both interfaces provide. We'll also discuss using scripting and the Task Scheduler together.

19

Using the GUI

The easiest way to learn about Task Scheduler is to start the program found in Start\Programs\Accessories\System Tools. You'll see the Scheduled Tasks entry. Figure 19.4 shows what this program looks like when you first start it. As you can see, the Task Scheduler includes entries for each scheduled task. The entries include the task name, run interval, the next run time, the time the Task Scheduler last ran the task, the last result, and the task creator. Note that the Task Scheduler (using the Scheduled Tasks window) shows all of the scheduled tasks—even those of other users.

FIGURE 19.4

The Scheduled Tasks window shows a list of tasks for your machine and provides statistics about them.

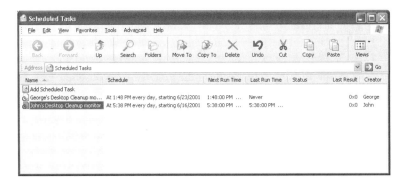

The Task Scheduler interface is relatively easy to learn. All you need to know is how to work with the tasks and modify the behavior of Task Scheduler. The following sections tell you about both activities. We'll start with the simple part of the interface, changing the Task Scheduler behavior.

Setting the Task Scheduler Options

Figure 19.4 shows many menu options. However, the only menu you're interested in for Task Scheduler is the Advanced menu. The following list describes the menu entries:

- **Stop Using Task Scheduler**   Select this option and Windows XP will stop the Task Scheduler service on your machine. It will also prevent the Task Scheduler service from running automatically. The menu entry will change to Start Using Task Scheduler and you'll notice that several other options are grayed out. Normally, you'll use this option only if you decide not to use Task Scheduler at all.

- **Pause Task Scheduler**   Select this option if you want to temporarily stop the Task Scheduler. Windows XP will simply pause the Task Scheduler service. The menu entry will change to Continue Task Scheduler, and you can continue where you started. All of the other menu options remain enabled and Windows XP will automatically restart Task Scheduler the next time you boot the machine. You can use this feature if Task Scheduler wants to run a task at an inconvenient time. For example, Task Scheduler might decide to perform a disk defragmentation in the middle of a file download.

- **Notify Me of Missed Tasks**   Use this option if you want Task Scheduler to remind you of missed tasks. The notice you receive lets you run the missed task. Of course, this feature can become a nuisance if you already know that you missed the task and don't want Task Scheduler to remind you.

- **AT Service Account**   The AT command line utility can add entries to the Task Scheduler. You'll find the entries aren't the same as those created using the GUI. We'll discuss these differences in the "Using the AT Command Line Utility" section. The account runs separately from the user account, a necessity if you want the AT utility to add tasks to everyone's account.

- **View Log**   To use this entry, you have to stop the Task Scheduler service. Otherwise, you'll receive a message that the file is in use by another application. Use View Log to see the log entries for the Task Scheduler.

As previously mentioned, the AT service account defaults to the system account. If you select the AT Service Account option, you'll see the AT Service Account Configuration dialog box. The dialog box contains two options: System Account and This Account. If you choose This Account, you'll also need to enter the name and password of the account you'd like to use. Generally, you'll never need to use this option unless you want to allow regular users access to the AT command.

The View Log option is a bit of a disappointment. This option actually opens the SCHEDLGU.TXT file found in the \WINDOWS folder. The only problem is that Windows associates the TXT extension with Notepad, so you see the messy display shown in Figure 19.5. If you looked at the SCHEDLGU.TXT file with a hex editor, you'd notice that it uses Unicode characters, a format that Notepad can't handle. While Notepad does a marvelous job with plain text, you won't want to use it for the Task Scheduler log file.

19

FIGURE 19.5

Use the View Log option only if you want to see this messy log display.

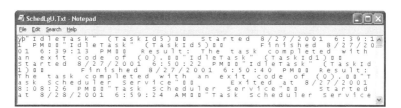

The alternative, in this case, is to open the file with WordPad. Of course, you'll still need to stop the Task Scheduler service before you can read the log entries. Figure 19.6 shows the readable display provided by WordPad. Notice that each task entry contains a TaskId value used to identify the task within the log. Unfortunately, unless you started the task with AT, there isn't any way to match the TaskId with an entry in the Scheduled Tasks window (at least, not without a lot of research). The best way to use this log is to match the starting times and dates with the entries in the Scheduled Tasks window.

FIGURE 19.6

Using WordPad to view the SCHEDLGU.TXT file produces a neat display that you can read with ease.

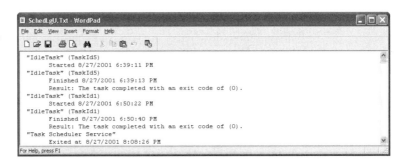

> **Tip**
>
> You can fix the View Log problem with Task Scheduler using a simple registry change. Locate the HKEY_LOCAL_MACHINE\SOFTWARE\Microsoft\SchedulingAgent key. This key contains a LogPath value that you can change to another extension. Instead of using SCHEDLGU.TXT, try using SCHEDLGU.DOC. You'll find that the View Log option now works as intended. If you have Word installed on your system, you'll find this fix even negates the need to shut down the service. Word will simply tell you that the file is in use by someone else and will ask if you want to make a copy. Click Yes and you'll see the existing logon screen. Because you won't make any changes to the log, this method of access is completely safe and won't interfere with normal Task Scheduler operation. Note that the key also contains values that enable you to change the default log size, the number of minutes before the Task Scheduler goes into idle mode, and the location of the scheduled tasks folder.

Creating Tasks

One of the first tasks you need to perform with Task Scheduler is creating some tasks to perform. Creating a task is easy. Right-click the Scheduled Tasks window and choose the New | Scheduled Task option from the context menu. Type a name for your task, and you're ready to go, except you haven't configured anything.

If you want to create a new task the easy way, double-click the Add Scheduled Task icon in the Scheduled Tasks window. You'll see the Welcome screen for the Scheduled Task Wizard. The following steps show you how to use the wizard:

1. Click Next. You'll see a list of applications on your machine. In some cases, the applications will also include version numbers so that you can choose a particular version.

Note

The interesting thing about the application list is that it contains all of the registered applications. If you have a script, an older Windows application, or even an old DOS application you want to run, you'll need to click Browse to find it. The list also contains some choices you'll want to ignore. For example, no one would want to schedule Minesweeper to run at a given time (except as a means to remind yourself to take a break). Finally, some obvious choices are missing. For example, if you want to defragment your disk, you'll need to locate the DFRG.MSC file in the \WINDOWS\SYSTEM32 folder.

2. Highlight the application you want to run and click Next. You could also click Browse and use the Select Program to Schedule dialog box to choose an application. In both cases, the Scheduled Task Wizard will display a dialog box that asks for a task name and scheduling time. You can choose intervals that include weekly, one time only, or when you log on to the system.

3. Type a name for the task and select a task interval. Click Next. You'll see the Start Time dialog box. The content of this dialog box varies according to the schedule you select. Figure 19.7 shows a typical example of a weekly interval. In most cases, you'll need to select a time to run the application. However, the other start time information will vary. For example, you might have to provide a list of months in which to run the application or the day of the week. Some options, such as When I Log On, don't ask for a starting time. In this case, you'll skip to step 5.

4. Select the start time information for your application. The Scheduled Task Wizard will ask for your name and password.

5. Type your name and password. Click Next. You'll see a completion dialog box. Notice the option for opening the Advanced Properties dialog box. The Advanced Properties dialog box helps you further refine your task options. In most cases, you won't need to do anything more at this point.

6. Determine if you need to modify any advanced properties (we'll see what they are in the "Modifying Tasks" section). Click Finish. The Scheduled Task Wizard will create your task.

19

Figure 19.7

*Select a start time for
your application based
on the interval you
chose.*

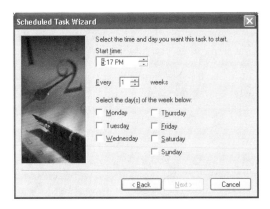

Modifying Tasks

What happens if you change your mind about a scheduled task or want to refine the
schedule you create for it? That's where modifying the task comes into play. Double-
click the task, and you'll see a task properties dialog box.

The General tab of the task properties dialog box contains application specifics. You'll
note that the Scheduled Task Wizard didn't allow you to add any command line parameters. This is where you add the parameters. Just type them into the Run field along with
the application path. This dialog box also contains fields for changing the starting directory, adding some comments, and changing the username and password. Notice the
Enabled option at the bottom of the dialog box. Clear this option if you want to disable
the task but want to retain it for future use.

The Schedule tab shown in Figure 19.8 determines when the application will run. The
figure doesn't show the default state of the dialog box. Notice the Show Multiple
Schedules option at the bottom of the dialog box. Check this option if you want to run
the application on more than one scheduled time. For example, you might want to run it
once a week and once a month at given times. To add a new scheduled run time, click
New. You can remove scheduled run times by selecting the entry and clicking Delete.

Figure 19.8 shows the setup for a monthly task. However, you can change the interval
using entries in the Schedule Task field. In addition to the normal entries provided by the
Scheduled Task Wizard, this list also includes a When Idle option. The When Idle option
is a great choice for tasks that you can perform a little at a time when the user isn't doing
anything else with the system. For example, the user might be reading a Web page. You
set the time interval that Windows will wait before it begins the tasks. As soon as the
user starts a new activity, the task will pause and wait for another idle period.

FIGURE 19.8

Task Scheduler offers to run an application on as many schedules as required to meet specific needs.

You'll find some differences on the Schedule tab when compared to the Scheduled Task Wizard. For example, the Schedule tab hides more items. In Figure 19.8, you'd need to click Select Months to change the month in which the application will run. You'll also see an Advanced button that displays the Advanced Schedule Options dialog box. Fields in this dialog box select the start date and end date. The Advanced Options dialog box also includes an option to repeat the task over a given interval.

Figure 19.9 shows the Settings tab. The options on this tab control task execution, rather than the application. Notice that you can set the task to delete itself automatically if you haven't scheduled it to run again. This keeps your Scheduled Tasks window from filling with old information.

FIGURE 19.9

Use the Settings tab to change the way the task runs.

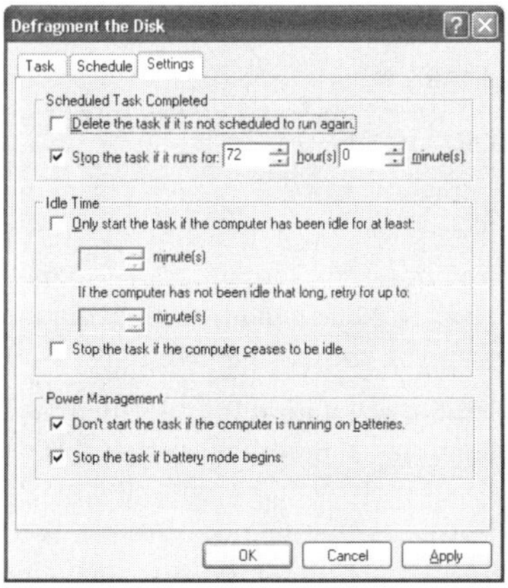

19

This tab also contains a idle time setting. However, this time the setting affects the task, not the application. When the application begins running, it will continue to run until it runs out of time or it completes its task. Use this option to ensure that the machine isn't in a high state of activity when you start the application.

Finally, this tab contains power management options. You'll use these options with laptop machines. For example, you wouldn't want to defragment the disk while the laptop is on battery power because excessive disk use drains the battery quickly. Task Scheduler will simply wait until you connect the laptop to AC power to start the task.

Deleting and Renaming Tasks

You rename and delete tasks much the same as you do anything in Windows Explorer. Right-click the task you want to delete or rename and select the appropriate option on the context menu. Deleted tasks remain in the Recycle Bin until you empty it. Unlike Windows Explorer, using Shift+Delete doesn't remove the task permanently; it still ends up in the Recycle Bin.

Using the AT Command Line Utility

As previously mentioned, the AT command line utility uses a character mode interface. You interact with it using the command prompt. The AT command use the following formats:

```
AT [\\Computer] [[<Id>] [/DELETE] | /DELETE [/YES]]
AT [\\Computer] <Time> [/INTERACTIVE] [/EVERY:<Dates> | /NEXT:<Dates>] <Command>
```

As you can see, the first format removes tasks, while the second adds them. Table 19.2 tells you about the switches and parameters the AT command accepts.

TABLE 19.2   AT Command Switches and Parameters

Switch or Parameter	Description
/DELETE	Removes a job from the list. If you omit the Id parameter, AT will remove all jobs that it created from the list. This command doesn't affect other jobs created using the GUI. However, AT will request confirmation for each deleted job unless you specify the /YES switch.
/EVERY:<Dates>	Runs the job during the specified day of the week or month. Adding more than one entry will run the job on multiple days of the week or month. If you omit the date parameter, AT assumes that you want to run the job monthly during the current day of the month.
/INTERACTIVE	Determines if the user can interact with the job (and vice versa). The default setting runs the job in the background without any interaction.

TABLE 19.2 continued

Switch or Parameter	Description
/NEXT:<Dates>	Runs the job during the next occurrence of the day of the week or month. Adding multiple dates runs the job during each of the specified dates. If you omit the date parameter, AT assumes that you want to run the job during the current day.
/YES	Prevents AT from asking whether it should delete each job in the list.
\\Computer	The name of a remote computer used to run the AT command.
Command	The path of the command you want to run including any command line switches. You must enclose the command in double quotes.
Id	The identifying number of the job. The AT command begins at 1 and moves up from there.
Time	Determines the starting time of the job.

Creating a job with AT is relatively easy. Earlier, we used the Scheduled Task Wizard to create a defragmenter job that runs at 6 p.m. every Friday. You can create a similar job using the following command line:

```
AT 6pm /Every:Friday "E:\WINDOWS\SYSTEM32\DFRG.MSC"
```

You don't obtain the same level of configuration features using AT that you would using the GUI method. Many of the special configuration features we discussed in the "Modifying Tasks" section are unavailable. If you modify an AT task using the Scheduled Tasks window, AT won't track it any longer. The second you apply the changes, AT removes the task from its list.

The Scheduled Tasks window tracks jobs created using both the GUI and the command line method. AT only tracks jobs that it creates. If you type **AT** at the command prompt and press Enter, all you'll see are the AT jobs. Figure 19.10 shows a typical example of the same jobs created using the GUI and AT. Notice that the AT job name has "at" and the number of the job.

As you can see, from a Scheduled Tasks window perspective, both jobs are the same. The only two differences are the job name and the creator name. Unless you change the default setting, the system creates all AT jobs. Any job created using the Scheduled Tasks window will appear under the user's name.

19

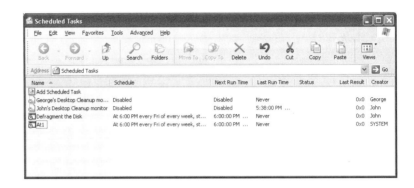

FIGURE 19.10

AT jobs appear in the Scheduled Tasks window as "at" jobs.

Combining Scripts and Task Scheduling

Today you've looked at scripting, and you've learned about automation. Some people never think to combine the two, but they're a natural fit. When you create scripts that perform a common task, adding the script to the Task Scheduler is a natural way to save time. Of course, you'll want to ensure that you debug the script fully. Otherwise, you can't be sure what the system will end up doing in your absence.

The powerful aspect of scripts and the Task Scheduler for the average user is that you're the one in control. You create the script and determine when it will run on your system. The combination of scripts and the Task Scheduler frees you from performing some of the mundane tasks you might otherwise perform.

Creating a task to run a script is precisely the same as creating a task for any other application. You have access to most of the settings as normal. For the most part, Task Scheduler looks at your script as an application to run and nothing else. However, Task Scheduler does appear to have a problem working with scripts that require switches or parameters. Sometimes, the job won't run as anticipated without a lot of fiddling.

It's also important to avoid user interaction within a script. The task will simply stop at the point of user input and wait for the user to do something. If the user is away from his desk at the time, the task could time out, and Task Scheduler will terminate it. The only thing you'll know when you look at the script entry is that it failed. This is one of those surprise errors that occur when you mix scripting and automatic execution.

Using Synchronize

Throughout the book, we've discussed synchronization. For example, you can set up a Favorites entry for offline viewing. Windows XP downloads a copy of the page to your hard drive so that you can view it as needed, even if you don't have an Internet connection to use. Offline viewing extends to other resources, such as network drives (if you enable the feature). No matter what the source of synchronized data, Windows XP provides the means to update it.

The Synchronize utility shows you the current synchronization settings for your system. You can access this utility using the Tools | Synchronize command of any Explorer-like utility provided with Windows XP including the Scheduled Tasks window. Windows XP will display the Items to Synchronize dialog box, which contains a list of items to synchronize. Click Synchronize, and Windows XP will begin the synchronization task.

Click Setup and you'll see a Synchronization Settings dialog box similar to the one shown in Figure 19.11. Each of these tabs tells Synchronize when to perform its work. You can synchronize data during the login or logout process. Windows XP will also update Web content during system idle time or at a time that you schedule using the Task Scheduler. (Use the entries on the Schedule tab to perform this task.)

FIGURE 19.11

The Synchronization utility will update your system during off-peak times, when the system isn't busy working with you.

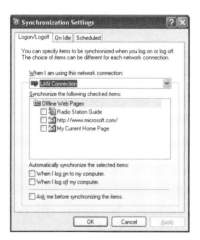

The Logon/Logoff and On Idle tabs work about the same. You select the connection you want to use for synchronization purposes and a list of offline content to synchronize. The options at the bottom of the dialog box tell when to perform the synchronization. If you choose to perform synchronization during the logon or logoff process, you can also tell Windows XP to ask before it performs the task.

The individual entries in the Synchronization utility also have settings. Highlight any entry and click Properties. You'll see a Content Properties dialog box. This dialog box contains the individual offline content settings for that site. We've already discussed these settings as part of Internet Explorer. See the "Browsing Offline" section of Day 4 for details.

Summary

As you saw today, scripting and automation are two sides of the same coin. You use both of them to make your life simpler. Scripting has the advantage of providing great flexibility, while automation is something you can configure and forget. Both scripting and automation are essential tools for the power user. If you use them together, you can create an impressive list of productivity aids that will help you stand above the crowd.

Q&A

Q: Where can I find a complete reference for WSH?

A: Microsoft provides a number of places that contain a WSH reference, but many of them aren't complete. The best place to find a complete reference is `http://msdn.microsoft.com/scripting/windowshost/doc/wshTOC.htm`. Not only is this online reference complete, but the reference is relatively easy to use as well.

Q: How many languages will actually run on WSH?

A: The number of languages is undefined. As long as you can find a script engine for WSH, you can use the associated language. From a practical standpoint, VBScript and JavaScript have the greatest support. Perl also garners support from Microsoft and third-party vendors (see `http://www.xav.com/perl/Windows/windows_script_host.html` or `http://pages.infinit.net/che/perlwsh/perlwsh0.html` for details). A REXX scripting engine is also available (`http://www-4.ibm.com/software/ad/objrexx/orx_sys.html`), but you may not find good support for it. Rumors talk of TCL and Python scripting engines, but you won't find much information about either of them. (See `http://aspn.activestate.com/ASPN/Cookbook/Python/Recipe/65108` for an example of a WSH script in Python.) Note that you can use WSH alternatives, such as PrimalScript (`http://www.sapien.com/Primalscript21.htm`), if you have specific language needs.

Q: What's the most practical use of synchronization?

A: Many people go crazy when they discover the Synchronize utility. However, this tool can quickly eat valuable computing time as it goes about updating every Web page that you tell it to update. Eventually, you can slow system access and use so many resources that Synchronize becomes a detriment, rather than a productivity aid. The best solution to this problem is to synchronize data you use every day. In addition, you should target data that you use offline and that's small enough to fit comfortably on your hard drive. Synchronize is a valuable tool, but like any other tool, you can misuse it.

Workshop

It's the end of the nineteenth day. By now you should have a better idea of what scripts can do for you and some idea of how to create and test them. Now it's time to see how well you can create, debug, and use scripts of your own. Of course, part of scripting is to automate tasks, so you'll see a few automation items in the list. You can find answers to the quiz and exercise questions in Appendix A at the back of the book.

Quiz

1. How can you use a network connection when using the Files and Settings Transfer Wizard?

2. Which scripting languages does Windows XP support by default?

3. Where can you store the information collected by the Files and Settings Transfer Wizard?

4. Where does Task Scheduler store its log entries?

5. What task does the Synchronize utility perform?

Exercises

1. Create a script in either VBScript or JavaScript.

2. Use Task Scheduler to automate one or more task that you perform regularly on your system.

3. Combine Task Scheduler and WSH to create a task automation setup that you couldn't accomplish with either product alone.

19

DAY 20

Developing a Web Page

The Web is an open environment for sharing information that attracts both novices and professionals. Every year, statistics show that more people have connected to the Internet to share information in some way. The fact that the Internet is slowly running out of addresses for Web sites only serves to tell you how quickly the Internet has caught on.

When some people think of the Internet, they think of businesses. It's true that you can find just about every business that exists in the real world on the Internet. In addition, the Internet supports some businesses you won't find out in the real world. For example, you can't buy electronic books at your local bookstore, yet.

For those who were with the Internet at the beginning, it represents an information store for scientists. In fact, that's the original purpose behind the Internet (if you haven't heard the story a dozen times before). The Internet still serves a purpose for academia. You'll find a myriad of standards groups and scientists sharing information in the same way they always have. In fact, the Internet probably contains more science today than it ever has.

The Internet is also about home users and communities. Many people that I know of create Web pages now. Most of them wouldn't consider themselves programmers. All they want to do is present a few pictures of the kids online or tell about their latest project.

Windows XP provides features that allow anyone to create and test Web pages. Theoretically, you could run an extremely small Web site with your Windows XP machine as well (although Microsoft doesn't recommend you do so). Windows XP could also serve the needs of a small intranet, making it easier to create paths of communication in a small company.

Today we'll learn about everything Windows XP has to offer with regard to Web page development and Web site setup. Mind you, Windows Server has a lot more to offer than Windows XP does, so you may not see everything you've seen in that environment.

Working with Internet Information Server

Windows XP Professional Edition includes a limited version of Internet Information Server (IIS). Generally speaking, you won't be able to run a Web site using this product, or, at least, not a very busy Web site. Microsoft places strict limits on the number of Web servers you can create with the version of IIS found in Windows XP Professional Edition. You'll also find there are limits on the number of connections you can create. In short, this version of IIS works fine for Web page testing and small intranets, but most people won't want to use it for anything on the Internet.

Note   Many ISPs offer Web site hosting for a reasonable charge, but make it up by charging exorbitant rates for services such as domain name registration. You can register your domain name for free at http://www.yournamefree.com/ and rid yourself of one more cost for starting a small Web site.

The copy of IIS found in Windows XP Professional Edition is complete in almost every other respect. Any practice you perform using this version of the product will transfer to the full version found in Microsoft's Windows Server products. This means you can practice on a workstation, before you move onto a real Web site on your server, reducing the usual risks in learning something new.

You do need to be aware of a few missing features from the version of IIS that comes with Windows XP Professional Edition. One of the most critical elements is a lack of bandwidth throttling. The lack of this feature means that a remote site could consume all the local processing cycles and network bandwidth with Web requests. You'll also notice a lack of support for operator entries (Windows XP assumes the local user) and server extensions. However, the property page tabs you do see under Windows XP are precisely the same as those on Windows Server.

The following sections will help you understand some of the basics of using IIS. By the time you complete this section, you'll know enough to set up a Web site for an intranet or test your personal Web paged hosted by someone else. This section won't make you an IIS guru. There are many issues that we won't cover such as creating an enterprise grade Web site with full security.

Installing New Components

Microsoft rightfully assumes that most people won't use IIS their first day with Windows XP. In fact, most people won't use IIS on their workstation at any time, so Windows XP doesn't install this feature by default. You'll find all of the IIS setup features in the Internet Information Services folder of the Windows Component Wizard dialog box. As you can see from Figure 20.1, the IIS installation requires a little more thought than setting up the games that Windows XP provides.

FIGURE 20.1

Windows XP provides a wealth of limited use IIS features you can use for practice.

Caution

The moment you install IIS on your workstation, it becomes vulnerable to the same viruses that a server can get. For example, a workstation that has IIS installed can get the Code Red virus. Make sure that you use safety features that include a firewall and virus scanner. Keep both products updated. You'll also want to patch IIS as needed to keep your network safe. For example, the Microsoft security bulletin at http://www.microsoft.com/technet/security/bulletin/MS01-044.asp makes you aware of fixes for the Code Red virus. Check the Windows Knowledge Base (`http://search.support.microsoft.com/kb/c.asp`) and Windows Update (accessible on the Start Menu) for patches on a regular basis.

20

With so many features to consider, you might find it hard to figure out just what to install. The one thing you don't want to do is install everything at one time. Taking it slow with IIS is a good idea because it's a complex product. Most people start by installing the World Wide Web Service and the Documentation. Make sure that you only install the level of World Wide Web Service you need. The folder has three virtual directories: Printers, Scripts, and Remote Desktop Web Connection. If you're using this setup for testing purposes, it's unlikely you'll need any of these features.

Some features that Windows XP provides are developer related. The only time you need to install the Visual InterDev RAD Remote Deployment Support is when you have Visual Studio installed on your system. Otherwise, this feature will waste drive space and opens your system to attack by crackers. Likewise, the FrontPage 2000 Server Extensions feature is only useful if you own the full copy of FrontPage.

A few of the features are growth items that you might want to consider sometime down the road. For example, many intranet Web sites also feature an FTP site where users can download files (or you can set scripts to download them for the users).

You might also need the Simple Mail Transfer Protocol (SMTP) Service. The mistake many people make is thinking this service provides full electronic mail support. The SMTP Service only provides the base electronic mail support; it doesn't include an e-mail server. To get full e-mail services, you need a server such as Exchange (`http://www.microsoft.com/exchange/default.asp`). In most cases, Microsoft provides a 120 day trial version of Exchange you can download and test with your Web Server. Considering the size of the download, you might want to take Microsoft up on its offer of obtaining Exchange through a CD shipped in the mail.

IIS installation is the same as any other Windows XP feature you've worked with in the past. Select the options you want; then click OK. Click Next and follow the prompts in the Windows Component Wizard dialog box. To verify that Windows XP installed IIS properly, open a copy of Internet Explorer. Type `http://localhost/` in the Address field and press Enter. You'll see a Web page similar to the one shown in Figure 20.2. Internet Explorer should also open a second window and display the IIS documentation.

FIGURE 20.2

After you install IIS, you should be able to open this default page on the localhost.

Exploring Configuration Issues

Before you can use IIS, you need to configure it. Microsoft makes some assumptions about the setup that you'd like, but they normally won't meet all of your needs. At a minimum, you'll want to perform the setups in the Global and Web Site sections that follow. These setups help you gain the most out of your intranet or test Web site.

Note

Windows XP Professional Edition doesn't support a news server (NNTP). However, in some cases you'll see an NNTP entry in the Internet Information Services MMC snap-in. You can right-click on the computer entry and choose the New | NNTP Virtual Server option. The New NNTP Virtual Server Wizard will even start. However, when you try to finish the setup, the wizard will fail with an ambiguous message. The only time you can use NNTP is if you see a Network News Transport Protocol (NNTP) entry in the Services MMC snap-in.

20

Unlike the full version of IIS that comes with Windows Server, you'll find that this version lacks an administration Web site. This means you can't use a remote Web interface to configure this setup, as you could with the server version. We'll use the Internet Information Services MMC snap-in shown in Figure 20.3 for configuration purposes throughout the day. The following sections address the basics of all IIS configuration requirements.

FIGURE 20.3

Use the Internet Information Services snap-in to administer your Web site.

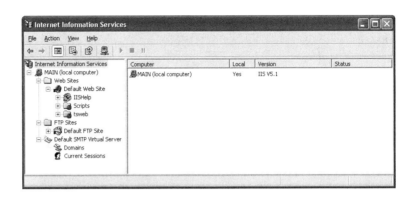

 Tip

IIS tends to cache site settings. This means you can make changes to a Web or FTP site configuration and not see the changes immediately. Stopping and then Starting the service usually makes the changes visible. Make sure that you also refresh browser and FTP utility displaces because these products also cache information. You might be looking at an old copy of the data on your own drive.

Working with Global Settings

The global setup affects all of the Web sites you create. You can override some settings at a lower level, but these settings will affect the starting setup for every Web site. To change the global settings, right-click Web Site and then choose Properties from the context menu. You'll see a Web Sites Properties dialog box similar to the one shown in Figure 20.4.

FIGURE 20.4

The Web Sites Properties dialog box contains settings that affect all Web sites on your system.

The ISAPI Filters tab contains a list of special applications for IIS. Figure 20.4 shows the default list of filters' simple IIS installation. Internet Server Application Programming Interface (ISAPI) Filters do just what their name says—they filter the information arriving at your server. Unless you buy a third-party package that includes ISAPI Filters, or you create an ISAPI Filter of your own, you'll never need to look at this tab except to ensure that the filters are all running. You can tell a filter is running because it has a green arrow that points up. If you see a red down arrow icon, you know the filter isn't running, and you need to find out why. Filters often cause IIS to act erratically, or you'll see a loss of functionality.

When you select the Home Directory tab, you'll notice that IIS grays out many of the features. Most of the features on this tab won't apply until you get to the Web site level. However, you can still assign global permissions such as read and write. It also pays to select the Log Visits option, at this level, so that you record all user visits to the site. Finally, make sure that you select the Index this resource option so the Indexing Service will create search entries for it.

Tip

> The Indexing Service handles Web sites separately from local hard drives or other indexing setups you might create. This allows search pages to report only the data that appears on your site and reduces the risk of inadvertent disclosure of critical information. In addition, this separation enables you to set the indexing features separately from the rest of your system.

The Default Document tab contains a list of default documents. IIS chooses a default document based on the capabilities of the requesting browser and the order in which the documents appear in the list. IIS uses a default document when you check the Enable Default Document option. If you don't enable this feature, then users will need to enter the name of a Web page precisely, or they'll receive an error message. You can add and remove default documents by using the Add and Remove buttons.

IIS also provides a feature for adding a default footer to every Web page. Default footers commonly contain contact information or other links on the Web site. To use this feature, check Enable Document Footer. You'll also need to supply the name of a footer file. A footer file is a standard HTML page that IIS adds to the bottom of the document.

The Directory Security tab contains the security settings for your site. The only setting you can change at the global level is authentication control. Click Edit, and you'll see an Authentication Methods dialog box. Windows XP provides three levels of access: anonymous, basic authentication, and integrated Windows authentication. You'll use anonymous access for a site that everyone can visit. Basic authentication works fine for

20

local sites, but presents a security problem for remote sites because the user passes their name and password in clear text. The Integrated Windows Authentication method is secure because it uses encryption for both the username and password. However, the problem with this method is that it limits access to Windows clients. This last limitation will have a greater impact on server setups than a workstation setup.

The HTTP Headers tab shown in Figure 20.5 controls content handling for your Web site. The Enable Content Expiration is especially important if your site handles time critical information. The browser will compare the cached copy on the user's local hard drive with the expiration date to determine if it needs to download a new copy of the page from the Web server. Using this feature effectively means reducing Web server demands, while ensuring the user always has fresh content.

FIGURE 20.5

Use the features found on the HTTP Headers tab to control content for your Web site.

The Custom HTTP Headers section contains a list of specialized headers for your Web server. An HTTP header contains information about the content that follows. For example, it can tell the client to use a particular helper application to display the content. The headers that IIS sends out are standard as of the time of release. However, as standards groups define new HTTP headers, you might want to add them to your server. This feature allows you to make the extension without much effort.

You'll use the Content Rating feature on sites that contain objectionable material that younger viewers might see. Click Edit Ratings, and you'll see a Content Ratings dialog box. The Rating Service tab tells you about the ratings service. It provides a link you can visit that provides additional information and has a questionnaire you can answer about your site. The Ratings tab has settings that you can use to set the content rating for your site. There are entries for violence, sex, nudity, and language. You'll rate the level of each of the entries by using a slider. The tab also contains fields for a contact address (the e-mail address of the person who rated the site) and an expiration date for the content rating.

The final setting on the HTTP Headers tab is the MIME Map. The Multipurpose Internet Mail Extensions (MIME) setting determines the types of files your site supports. IIS sends this information to the client, so the client knows what to expect concerning content types. Unless you use some unusual file types, you'll never need to touch this setting. However, if you do find that you need to change something, ensure that you add the standardized MIME entries for the file type available from RFC3161 (`http://www.faqs.org/rfcs/rfc3161.html`).

The Custom Errors tab contains a list of every error that the Web server can generate, along with an associated error message. In most cases, the generic error message is pretty generic and less than helpful. However, most users find them useful enough—at least they know there's a problem. You can use the entries on this tab to define custom responses for error messages. For example, users of your Web site might run into one error more often than any other error message. Defining a custom error message can provide useful help to users who need it and reduce the number of support calls you receive.

Configuring FTP Sites

FTP sites require fewer configuration settings than Web sites do, so I'll discuss both global and local FTP settings in one section. Figure 20.6 shows the Default FTP Site Properties dialog box. You'll use this dialog box for local FTP settings. The FTP Sites Properties dialog box (the one used for global settings) doesn't include the FTP Site tab. In addition, you'll find a few features missing on the Home Directory tab.

As you can see from Figure 20.6, the FTP Site tab contains the FTP site, address, and port. The default setting is port 21. If this is a private FTP site, using a different port can reduce the chance of cracker attack (or at least slow it down a little). The Connection properties are a little optimistic for Windows XP. In most cases, you'll want to set the number of connections to 2 or 3. The Connection Timeout value will probably work, but you may want to set it lower in order to avoid holding resources for failed connections.

The FTP Site tab also contains an option for logging all user access. The standard format is a World Wide Web Consortium (W3C) standard format. You can also use a custom IIS format. Click Properties, and you'll see an Extended Logging Properties dialog box like the one shown in Figure 20.7. The General Properties tab has settings that determine the interval that IIS uses the same log and the location of that log. The default settings

20

change the log daily and place it in the \WINDOWS\System32\LogFiles folder. You can increase security by changing the default log location to another secure area of your system. The Extended Properties tab shown in Figure 20.7 contains a list of standard log entries. The standard settings don't tell you much about the person using your site. If this were a public site, you'd want to save log space by using the Spartan entries shown in the figure. However, given that this is a private site and log size won't be a problem, you should log as much information about the individual as possible.

FIGURE 20.6

The Default FTP Site Properties dialog box contains settings for your local FTP site.

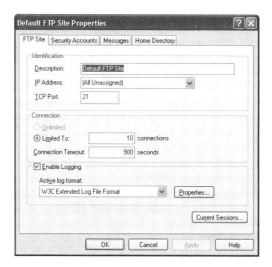

FIGURE 20.7

Use extended log entry information to help identify anyone using the FTP site.

Click Current Sessions at the bottom of the FTP Site tab, and you'll see a FTP User Sessions dialog box. This dialog box lists the name of the person(s) using the FTP site, the IP address of the remote connection, and the amount of time they have connected to the FTP site. You can use the Disconnect and Disconnect All buttons to remove users from the site as needed.

The Security Accounts tab controls access to your FTP site. Clear the Allows Anonymous Accounts option if you want to restrict someone from logging into the site anonymously. Unfortunately, this also causes problems because FTP passes the username and password in clear text. This means that someone with a network sniffer could gain access to the user's connection information. This tab also contains options that force IIS to use anonymous connections alone. Finally, you'll find a list of the FTP site operators.

FTP sites normally require the use of four messages for connecting users. The Messages tab contains Banner, Welcome, Exit, and Maximum Connections fields to handle all four messages. IIS doesn't include any default messages, so visitors to your site will see a blank screen until you define a message.

The Home Directory tab, shown in Figure 20.8, controls the location and security settings for the home directory. Notice that you can use a local directory or a share (directory or drive) on another machine. The FTP Site Directory information includes the path to the directory and the rights the user has to the directory. Notice that you only have a choice of read, write, and log visits. The Directory Listing Style is especially important. Many FTP utilities require the UNIX style of directory listing and won't show any subdirectories until you use it. If users have problems seeing the folders or files on your FTP site, you may need to make this change.

FIGURE 20.8

The Home Directory tab controls the location and security settings of the root FTP directory.

20

Working with Web Sites

Web Sites use settings that are similar to the Global settings we discussed earlier. However, as shown in Figure 20.9, you'll see at least one additional tab. The Web Site tab begins by defining the Web site identification. This includes a Web site name, IP address, and port number.

FIGURE 20.9

*Web site configu-
rations include a
Web Site tab that
determines the Web
site identity.*

The problem is that the TCP Port field is misleading. While this number does define the default port number, it doesn't tell you about other port numbers that IIS supports native-ly. Click Advanced, and you'll see an Advanced Multiple Web Site Configuration dialog box like the one shown in Figure 20.10. As you can see, IIS defines two ports for all Web sites: standard and secure. If you allow outside access to your Web site, you'll need to configure your firewall to accommodate both the standard port of 80 and the secure port of 443.

Note

You can create multiple standard host ports for your system. In fact, you can even remove the default setting of port 80 and use something else. However, the secure port setting of 443 is cast in stone, and you can't change it. In addition, you can't create additional secure port entries.

FIGURE 20.10

Web sites support both standard and secure connections, so they require multiple port numbers.

The Connections section of the Web Site tab determines the connection settings. The first point of interest is the HTTP Keep-Alives Enabled option. This setting tells IIS to maintain a connection with the client during the entire client session. The advantage of this setting is that the client won't need to reestablish contact for each request. The client and server both save time and server performance improves. The disadvantage of this setting is that IIS maintains the connection if the client inadvertently loses contact with the server. The server must wait the entire interval specified by the Connection Timeout setting before it releases the connection. The default setting of 900 seconds (15 minutes) is too long for a local connection. A setting of 400 seconds (or less) works better.

As with the FTP site settings, you can log all access to your Web site. You have the same logging choices of a W3C standard format or an IIS specific format. However, in this case, you also have a choice of a National Center for Supercomputing Applications (NCSA) common log file format. This format is compatible with servers running the Apache Web server, so it's a good choice in a mixed server environment. The remaining log file choices and options are the same as they are for FTP sites.

20

Tip

You might be tempted to think that once you select a log format you have to live with it forever. Fortunately, Microsoft provides the CONVLOG utility to convert IIS logs from any supported format to NCSA common log file format. The utility will convert IP address to DNS names. You can even convent logs from local time to GMT in order to synchronize entries from various parts of the world. Several Web sites have a description of this log file format including `http://ulysses.uchicago.edu/docs/LOGS.doc2.html`.

We discussed some of the other tabs found in the Default Web Site Properties dialog box in the "Global" section. The ISAPI Filters, Documents, HTTP Headers, and Custom Errors tab work the same as before. However, you'll notice some implementation differences. For example, the ISAPI Filters tab is unlikely to have any filters installed or active. You'll also find additional Web pages on the Documents tab for the default Web site.

The Home Directory tab shown in Figure 20.11 contains all of the information for the root location of the Web site. As with an FTP site, you can place the Web site on a local or remote drive. Unlike an FTP site, you can also redirect a Web site to another URL. Notice that Web sites provide a few more directory access options. You can tell IIS to index the Web site. Notice, also, that there's an option to protect your script source and to allow directory browsing. Directory Browsing is a nice feature to have if you want to make the Web site completely open. It enables users to search through all of the available files. However, this option is harmful if you want to hide anything on your site and probably isn't a good choice for public sites.

FIGURE 20.11

The Home Directory tab contains location and usage information for the Web site root.

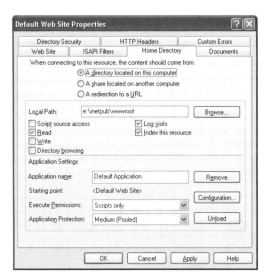

The Directory Security tab for the Default Web Site Properties dialog box differs from the Web Site Properties (global) version. It contains an option for creating a server certificate. When you click Server Certificate, you'll see the Welcome screen for the Web Server Certificate Wizard. The following steps show you how to use this wizard.

1. Click Next. You'll see a Server Certificate dialog box. This dialog box gives you three options for installing a server certificate. The first is to create a new

certificate, which is the option that you'll use when you first start working with IIS. The second is to assign an existing certificate to the server. You'll use this option after you receive a certificate from a third party such as Verisign. Finally, you can import a certificate from the Key Manager backup file.

2. Select Create a New Certificate; then click Next. You'll see a Delayed or Immediate Request dialog box. If you choose the delayed option, IIS will generate a request on disk that you upload to the third party. The immediate option sends the request directly to the certificate authority.

3. Select a request option; then click Next. You'll see a Name and Security Settings dialog box. This dialog box contains settings that determine the certificate name, encryption key length, and cryptography options. It also contains an option for choosing a cryptographic service provider (CSP)—the vendor that supports your server cryptography mechanism.

4. Type a name for your certificate. Select security settings as needed. If you decide to choose the CSP for the certificate, you'll see an Available Providers dialog box where you'll choose a CSP. Click Next. You'll see an Organization Information dialog box. Type the name of your organization and the name of your organizational unit. The organizational unit can reflect the organization of your company in any way, but normally contains a department or other workgroup name.

5. Type an organization and organizational unit name. Click Next. You'll see the Your Site's Common Name dialog box.

6. Type the name of your site. Windows XP normally uses your machine name, but you can choose any appropriate name. Click Next. You'll see a Geographical Information dialog box that contains fields for your country, state, and city.

7. Type the name of your country, state, and city. Click Next. You'll see a Certificate Request File Name dialog box.

8. Type a name for the request file. Click Next. You'll see a summary dialog box.

9. Read the summary and verify all of the information is correct. Click Next. You'll see a completion dialog box that provides additional information about your certificate.

10. Read the instructions; then Click Finish.

When you receive the certificate from the CSP, place it in an easy-to-find directory on your machine. Start the Web Server Certificate Wizard. You'll see an option to process the pending request and install the certificate. You'll need that option in this case. When asked for the certificate, provide the location on disk. After another question or two, IIS will install the certificate for you.

20

Working with Web Site Directories

IIS provides the means for you to create individual settings for your Web site directories. Generally, the Directory Properties dialog box contains a subset of those found for the Default Web Site Properties dialog box. The Documents, Directory Security, HTTP Headers, and Custom Errors tab entries work the same in both cases. The Virtual Directory tab is actually a renamed form of the Home Directory tab. In short, working with a Directory is easy once you understand how to work with a Web site.

Configuring Web Page Properties

The Web Page Properties dialog box is an even smaller version of the Default Web Site Properties dialog box. It contains the same HTTP Headers and Custom Errors tab. The File Security tab is a renamed version of the Directory Security tab with the same options. Finally, the File tab is a shortened version of the Home Directory tab. You'll see fewer options than before. For example, you can't use a share from another computer for obvious reasons. In addition, the security options only include read and write protection. The File tab also contains options for protecting your source code and logging user visits.

Creating Virtual Directories

It isn't always convenient to place data you want to see on your Web site on the local drive or even within the \Inetpub\wwwroot folder hierarchy. A virtual directory is essentially a pointer to the data, wherever it exists. The virtual directory makes it appear that the data is local to the Web server, although the data might exist on a network drive. Think of a virtual directory as a sort of shortcut for IIS.

Creating a virtual directory is relatively easy. Right-click the location you want to place the virtual directory. You can place the virtual directory at any level below the Default Web Site in the IIS hierarchy. Choose New | Virtual Directory from the context menu, and you'll see the Welcome screen of the Virtual Directory Creation Wizard. The following steps will show you how to complete the virtual directory setup.

1. Click Next. You'll see a Virtual Directory Alias dialog box. The name you assign here is the name that IIS will use to reference the directory. It's also the name the user will need to access the directory. Using single word directory names is usually best because using spaces causes problems for some browsers. In addition, you'll find single word directory names easier to work with when you create Web pages.

2. Type an alias for the virtual directory and click Next. You'll see a Web Site Content Directory dialog box. The Directory field contains the path to the physical directory location. Click Browse if you want to search for the directory.

3. Provide a content directory name and then click Next. You'll see an Access Permissions dialog box as shown in Figure 20.12. Notice that the access permissions don't directly correspond with the settings from any of the tabs that we discussed earlier. The security settings are easy to understand, but you'll always want to check the settings later.

FIGURE 20.12

The security settings on the Access Permissions dialog box don't correspond to settings in the Directory Properties dialog box.

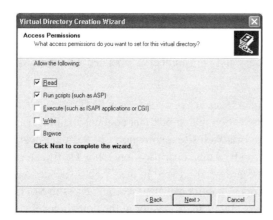

4. Choose security settings for your virtual directory and click Next. You'll see a completion dialog box.

5. Click Finish. IIS will create the virtual directory for you.

6. Right-click the new virtual directory; then choose Properties from the context menu. You'll see a Directory Properties dialog box.

7. Verify the settings for your virtual directory.

Working with the SMTP Service

As previously mentioned, you can't use the SMTP service in place of a standard e-mail program. However, you can use it to send and receive messages in some situations. For example, a developer can use the SMTP service to enable communication between applications. Some applications use SMTP as a means to deliver data to the company.

The SMTP service creates two folders: Domains and Current Sessions, as shown in Figure 20.3. The Domains folder contains a list of domains participating in SMTP. Generally, you'll see a single domain consisting of your machine when working with Windows XP. If you double-click this entry, you'll see a Domain Properties dialog box. The Drop Directory field of this dialog box specifies where IIS places incoming mail. The Enable Drop Directory Quote option determines if IIS automatically stops accepting incoming mail after the folder reaches the size specified by the directory quota.

20

The Current Sessions folder contains a list of users or applications connected to the SMTP server. Like the FTP server, you'll see a username, remote connection IP address, and the connection time. You can also disconnect one or all of the users as needed.

The only configuration for the SMTP server is the Default SMTP Virtual Server. Right-click this entry, choose Properties from the context menu, and you'll see the Default SMTP Virtual Server Properties dialog box. The General tab of this dialog box contains the IP address for the service, the number of connections, connection timeout, and logging options. If you click Advanced, you'll see an Advanced dialog box that contains the IP address and port numbers associated with the SMTP server (the default port number is 25).

The Access tab contains security options for the SMTP server. Click Authentication, and you'll see an Authentication dialog box that contains the three same authentication options you can use for a Web site (anonymous, basic, and integrated Windows). You can secure communication by using a certification. Click Certificate, and you'll see the Web Server Certificate Wizard we discussed in the "Web Site" section. The Connection and Relay buttons both open dialog boxes that restrict access to SMTP by IP address. You can restrict computers singly, in groups, or at the domain level.

The Messages tab shown in Figure 20.13 determines acceptable incoming message para-meters. As you can see, you can limit content per message and per session. You can also limit the number of messages sent by any one client and the number of recipients per message. The last two options on this tab determine how SMTP handles undeliverable mail. The default settings place the bad mail in the \Badmail folder. Considering the size of a Windows XP setup you should supply an e-mail address for the bad message reports. Otherwise, the directory can fill up without any advance notice.

FIGURE 20.13

Use the Messages tab to configure the parameters for acceptable incoming messages.

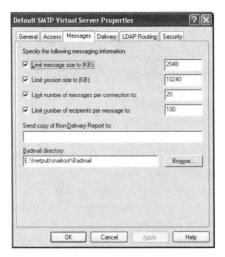

The Delivery tab shown in Figure 20.14 contains all of the settings that determine a delivery schedule for messages. Notice that SMTP will try to deliver each message four times. If the message is undeliverable after four attempts, it goes into the \Badmail folder. The settings shown in Figure 20.14 are more appropriate for an Internet connection, than a LAN setup.

FIGURE 20.14

The delivery settings you use will depend on the type of network setup you use.

Notice the Outbound Security and Outbound Connections buttons on this tab. Click Outbound Security, and you'll see an Outbound Security dialog box that contains the three levels of authentication we discussed earlier. This dialog box also contains entries for the name and password to use for authentication. You need these settings because SMTP uses these security settings to send messages to another location. You can also choose to use encryption to protect message content.

Click Outbound Connections, and you'll see an Outbound Connections dialog box. The settings in the dialog box determine the connection and timeout values for outbound connections. A special setting determines the number of connections per domain so you don't use all of the outbound connections on a single domain. The TCP Port field contains the port number of the outbound connection.

The LDAP Routing tab of the Default SMTP Virtual Server Properties dialog box contains settings for a lightweight directory access protocol (LDAP) connection. The only time you'll need this connection is if you decide to use Active Directory or another server database setup (such as Site Server or Exchange). The settings on this tab include the name of the server, the schema type of the database (Active Directory is the default), and the type of binding (security setup). If you choose a secure binding protocol, you'll also

20

need to supply a domain name, username, and password. The final field on this tab is Base. In essence, the Base field contains a description of the location you want to access in the directory service database with SMTP.

The Security tab contains a list of qualified SMTP operators. SMTP will use this list of names for notification purposes. In addition, the list contains the only people allowed to modify SMTP settings or perform other kinds of maintenance.

Creating Web Pages

Now that you have a functional server, you'll want it to do something for you, which means creating Web pages. A Web page contains a combination of tags and content. All the end user should see is the content. The browser reads the tags and uses them to perform tasks such as formatting the output so it looks nicer. Of course, learning all the tags is akin to learning a new language and a new way of thinking, which is why many people see Web page creation as a difficult task. If you obtain a good Web page editor, you can work with the content more than the tags.

 Note

This discussion looks at the simpler aspects of Web page design. Web pages can contain a lot more than just tags and content. For example, many people add scripts so that the Web page can do more than provide a static interface to the user. However, it's important to take small steps before you take large ones. Creating successful Web pages means knowing how to use tags and how to present content in an aesthetically pleasing way before you move onto the harder topic of scripts.

Internet Explorer versions before Version 6 (the one in Windows XP) provided FrontPage Express as a Web page editor. FrontPage Express isn't the best editor in the world, but it works and it's free. Most important of all, FrontPage Express is a good tool to learn simple Web page development because it doesn't overwhelm you with features you don't care about immediately.

Web page design is a popular topic, so you'll also find a wealth of third-party editors on the Internet. We'll also talk about a few of the editors. You'll definitely want to try them before you buy one because Web page editors tend to provide unique interfaces. One Web page editor might seem intuitive, while another with the same features seems cumbersome.

Finally, Web pages aren't about tags or scripts. If you design a Web page around the fancy gizmos you can include, you're missing the point. The whole point of Web pages is content. It's important to design Web pages in such a way that the user sees an immediate need for the content you have to provide. The content has to be easy to read and understand.

Using FrontPage Express

FrontPage Express is the first Web page editor that many people use because it comes with Internet Explorer. You can hardly beat a deal where the editor is free and delivered to you. In addition, FrontPage Express has the advantage of being simple to use and learn. You'll find that you're productive with it in just a few hours.

Tip

For those of you who've wondered where FrontPage Express went, you won't find it by searching Microsoft's Web site. For the obvious reasons, they want you to buy the full-fledged version of FrontPage. However, you can still download the required FrontPage Express CAB file from `http://mssjus.www.conxion.com/download/ie501sp1/install/5.01 _sp1/win98/en-us/fpsetup.cab`. This is part of Microsoft's download for Internet Explorer 5.01. You can view the contents of the CAB file after you download it from the Internet site. Create a folder where you'd like to extract the FrontPage Express files. Open the CAB folder, select all of the files in the CAB folder, and then drag them to the location you created. Windows XP will automatically extract the files for your and place them in the new folder. Open a command prompt in the folder where you placed the extracted files. Type **rundll32 advpack.dll, LaunchINFSection fpxpress.inf, defaultinstall**. Windows XP will install FrontPage Express for you and create a shortcut to it. You'll be able to uninstall this product by using the normal procedure.

Of course, FrontPage Express has problems, too. It lacks many of the features of modern editors, and Microsoft shows little interest in upgrading the product. Yes, you can do all of the basics, but you'll find a complete lack of support for advanced features, such as graphic mapping (associating areas on an image with links to other parts of the Web site). In addition, FrontPage Express lacks any kind of support for scripting. Because of these limitations, many people learn with FrontPage Express, and then they move on to something a little more functional.

20

An Overview of the Controls

Figure 20.15 shows what FrontPage Express looks like when you first start it. As you can see, it looks like a simple word processor or other editor. The three toolbars have very different purposes.

FIGURE 20.15

The initial FrontPage Express display looks like a simple editor.

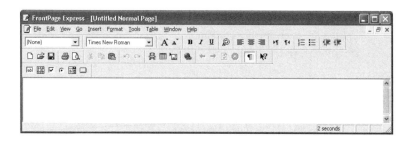

The long toolbar on the top controls text features. You can perform all of the basics you find in any editor including adding bold, italics, and underlined text. The text can appear left, right, or center justified—it can read from left to right, or right to left (left to right is the default). You can vary the font size and select a font face. The Increase Indent and Decrease Indent buttons help you position the text on the page. The Change Style drop-down list box leaves the formatting details to the editor—you simply select the paragraph style you want to create. This first toolbar also has buttons for creating numbered and bulleted lists.

The second toolbar contains many functional buttons. This is where you'll save existing files and create new ones. You'll find the usual Cut, Copy, and Paste buttons, along with icons for printing and previewing your document. The four interesting buttons on this toolbar include Insert WebBot Component, Insert Table, Insert Image, and Create or Edit Hyperlink. The WebBot components consist of Include, Search, and Timestamp.

The third toolbar contains the size components you'll use to create Web pages. They include a single line edit box, scrolling edit box, check box, radio button, drop-down menu, and a push button. Out of all these components, the drop-down menu is the only one that does something extraordinary.

In some respects, FrontPage Express uses Microsoft Word as a model for the user interface. For example, FrontPage Express provides a special Table menu that contains a wealth of entries for manipulating the tables you create. You can set individual cell properties, merge cells, insert cells, and change the overall table properties.

You'll also want to spend time looking at the Insert menu. It includes a few features that you might not see otherwise. For example, this menu includes an option for inserting a marquee on your Web page. The Insert menu also contains options for inserting ActiveX controls, Java applets, special plug-ins, a PowerPoint animation, video, and background sounds. The Insert menu also contains an option for inserting scripts, but you'll find it simplistic at best.

Starting a Simple Web Page

Every project begins with a new file. However, you don't have to start with the empty page shown in Figure 20.15. Use the File | New command to display the New Page dialog box, and you'll see a list of standard forms. FrontPage Express provides a few basics, such as a survey, confirmation, and a form page. You can modify these pages and add more of your own by working in the \Program Files\Microsoft FrontPage Express\ Pages folder. However, these forms are a good place to start working with Web pages.

Before you begin adding anything to the Web page, you should define the page properties. Use the File | Page Properties command to display the Page Properties dialog box shown in Figure 20.16. The Base Location field is especially important because it helps define the format of any links you create. This is one of the reasons you need to define the page properties early. FrontPage Express has a tendency to modify links incorrectly if you don't supply this value at the outset. You'll also use this tab to change values such as the background sound and the encoding used for fonts.

FIGURE 20.16

One of the important tasks to perform on your Web page is to define the page properties.

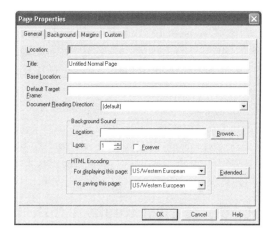

The Background tab contains entries for all the colors your Web page will use. You can change the background, text, hyperlink, visited hyperlink, and active hyperlink colors. If you want, you can also add a background image and make it into a watermark (a repeating image).

Normally, you won't specify margins for your Web page. Using margins limits the size of the page and causes problems with some browsers. If you do decide to add margins to your Web page, the Margins tab contains options for modifying both the width and the height.

20

The Custom tab enables you to add both user and system variables. In most cases, you won't need to worry about changing these values until you know a lot more about Web page design. For now, all you need to know is that these values appear at the top of the file. They're essentially comments that some search engines use for finding your Web page faster.

Adding Some Content

After you define a page, it's time to add some content. After all this effort, it's time for the main event. Unfortunately, some people damage their Web page design at this point. Start simply by outlining your ideas. Use the predefined Header styles to create an outline for your page.

The headers add structure to your Web page, but they don't really do much for the reader, except tell them what to expect. The second phase is to add any basic structures. For example, if you plan to use a table to hold some information, try setting it in place under the heading that will hold the information. You'll also want to insert any graphics and position them on the page.

It's time to add some text. You have all of the structural elements in place, so now it's time to tell the viewer what these elements mean. Make sure that you use short, descriptive paragraphs. Don't waste words, but at the same time, use enough text to describe your topic fully.

After you get to this point, you'll want to save the page to your test Web site and check it out in Internet Explorer. One of the problems that Web page designers run into is that they make their page too large. Many of your viewers will see the page in 800[ts]600 resolution. Shrinking your browser down to these dimensions helps you see your page from their viewpoint.

Shareware Products That Really Work

You'll find a wealth of shareware editors on the Internet. In fact, there are so many of these editors that you might invest considerable time figuring out which one you want to use. The problem isn't so much one of features (although feature set is important), it's one of interface. Web site design is essentially an artistic process. The tools you use have to reflect your style of working with content. This means that you might reject a perfectly acceptable editor because the interface doesn't work the way you'd like.

The following sections present some shareware products that seem to do a good job. Each product has a different slant on creating Web pages. If you don't find a product you like in this list, at least you'll have a better idea of what's out there so you know where to look.

Evrsoft First Page III

The feature that most intrigues me about this product is that it contains an interesting list of features. For example, the author includes graphic conversion tools and an image mapper, two tools you don't see in every shareware product. First Page III supports dynamic HTML (DHTML), so you can perform some interesting tricks with it. For example, you can create drop-down list boxes without resorting to script. You can obtain a copy of First Page III at `http://www.evrsoft.com/`.

MVD WebExpress

WebExpress is another basic Web page editor. It emphasizes simplicity above anything else. You won't find some of the gizmos offered by other products in this package, but you won't drown in excessive functionality either. One of the more interesting features of this product is that it supports so many graphic file formats. I checked the list and did not find anything that I'd need beyond the list WebExpress provides. This product also includes an excellent form wizard. Designing forms can be challenging, but this product makes them easy. You can find out more about WebExpress at `http://www.mvd.com/webexpress/index.htm`.

Allaire HomeSite

HomeSite is a little more complex than the previous two tools, but not quite in the professional category. It's a good, middle-level tool for those who have a little Web development experience and want to build on it. You'll find some interesting features in this product. For example, HomeSite is the only product in the section that provides both wireless and handheld support right out of the box. You'll also find support for productivity features such as cascading style sheets. HomeSite also supports a variety of scripting languages including JavaScript, VBScript, and Perl. You can find out more about HomeSite at `http://www.allaire.com/products/homesite/index.cfm`.

Trout Software Hippie

This is a moderately complex Web page editor. It includes all of the standard tools that you'd expect from a middle-level tool. For example, the editor provides color coding, and you'll find the project organizer is a snap to use. One of the more interesting features of this product is that it includes scripting wizards. The wizards won't make you a great programmer, but they do get you started. Think of the wizards as a way to get the mundane development tasks out of the way so you can concentrate on what you'd like the code to do. Hippie uses a side-by-side editor, which means you can see the code and the final Web page at the same time. Changes in either window automatically appear in both. You can find out more about this product at `http://www.hippie98.com/`.

20

Lorenz Graf's HTMLtool

This is a tool for professionals. HTMLtool has features that make many commercial products look like bumbling attempts by comparison. A pick bar helps you choose key words and tags to use in your Web page. All of the source code is color coded to make it easy to read. You'll even find a spelling checker that keeps track of problems as you type. The editor will underline incorrect spellings with a wavy red line. You'll also find tabs that lay your project out in hierarchical format. In fact, the display looks similar to the one used by many development products such as Visual Studio today. In short, this is the product to consider when you've gotten well past the basics and into advanced design. You can find out more about HTMLtool at

`http://members.nbci.com/htmltool/index.html.`

Web Page Design Basics

Web pages can be a lot of fun to design if you look at them as a means of expressing your inner thoughts. The content you deliver to the people who see your Web site should grab their imagination and leave them wanting more. Unfortunately, many Web sites go for the glitz and leave out the content. While this section won't replace the years of experience that many Web site developers have, it will help you avoid some of the pitfalls of poorly designed sites.

Tip

> You've probably seen Web sites that include their own icon as part of their link. When you save the URL in Favorites, the icon goes along with it, giving the Web site entry a distinctive look. It's reasonably easy to add an icon to any Web page. Find out more about this process at
> `http://hotwired.lycos.com/webmonkey/01/18/index1a.html?tw=design.`

One of the most basic principles of good Web site design is readability. If the person visiting your Web site has to squint to read the text, you've probably lost someone who might be interested in what you have to say. Likewise, you need to avoid using terms that the reader might not understand unless you also define them. Finally, it's important to use a spelling and grammar checker on your Web site. The text on some Web sites is so terrible that no one can understand it.

Tip

Sometimes, you can read your text a hundred times and never see the problems with it. That's when the Narrator comes in handy. Set up the Narrator, display your Web page, and listen. In many cases, you can hear a problem with the text on your site long before you spot it by reading. Using the Narrator will also point out potential problems in your setup. Narrator will have problems reading poorly formatted Web pages. Because many visitors with special needs will use a product like Narrator to interact with your site, you'll want to be sure to remove any flaws that might cause problems for these applications.

Organization is another problem you need to solve. I find that organizing my thoughts using an outline helps. Major topics go on separate pages. Any topics that belong together, but cover different aspects of the topic belong in separate sections on the same page. Use links as needed to put the pages together. Make sure that you include a link back to the home page so users don't have to back out of several levels of your Web page to find another topic. If a Web page is particularly difficult to construct, it helps to work on the outline down to the paragraph level. If you don't understand the organization of your Web site, neither will anyone else.

Use graphics sparingly or not at all on your Web page. Small graphics can dress up a Web page and make it look appealing, but lots of large graphics tend to clutter the Web page and increase the download time dramatically. The users of your site will click Stop long before they see the lovely images you've included. A better choice is to provide a small version of the image that the user can click to see a larger version on separate page.

Include a little white space on your Web page. The term "white space" refers to areas around the content. If you don't provide enough white space, the Web page looks cluttered and is hard to read. Try to make paragraphs small, use bulleted and numbered lists whenever possible, and present some information using tables as a visual organization aid.

20

If you follow these basic tips, you'll find that people get a lot more out of your Web site. More importantly, you'll find that your site is a lot easier to maintain. Good design pays many dividends.

Summary

The Internet has grabbed the attention of everyone. Many people are experimenting with ways to make the Internet personal. They use it as a means of communication. Not only do Web pages convey information to others, but your Web page also says a lot about who you are. It helps other people understand some facet of you and what you want to present to the world.

The Internet isn't only about Web pages; you need a Web server to display those Web pages. One of the things to consider about creating your own Web site is that it helps you gain a better understanding of how the Internet as a whole works. We've looked at some of the basics of creating a Web site today. You aren't ready to create a mega-site like Microsoft's, but you could create something small and experiment with it.

Q&A

Q: **Why does Microsoft provide such a confusing array of IIS features when most home and small business users won't use them?**

A: Microsoft assumes that network administrators and developers will use this product, too. It's easier to learn the basics on a local machine than it is to create a two-machine setup for working with the full product. Consequently, you'll find that Microsoft has packed IIS with features that you might not use, but others will.

Q: **How does the content rating system work? Why would I want to use them?**

A: The browser compares the content rating of a Web site with the content rating of the browser. If the rating is such that the user can view the site, then the browser loads the Web page. Otherwise, the user will receive an error message telling why the Web site is unacceptable. You can find out more about the ratings at `http://www.rsac.org/` (scripting enabled) or `http://www.rsac.org/lr_about.html` (plain text). The reason you want to use the rating system is to ensure that no one can enter your site if it contains material they don't want to see. This avoids problems with those who don't want to see or hear an abundance of sex, violence, nudity, or inappropriate language.

Q: **What's the best way to determine if people with color blindness can view my site?**

A: The easiest say to make your Web site color friendly is to use colors that everyone can see well, yet use colors that make the site look aesthetically pleasing. Of course, that's a difficult combination for anyone. A color selection that looks fine to you may make the site incomprehensible to someone else. Fortunately, you can find precise guidelines for this problem at `http://www.firelily.com/opinions/color.html` and `http://msdn.microsoft.com/voices/hess10092000.asp`.

Workshop

It's the end of the twentieth day. You've learned some of the basis of creating a Web page and maintaining an IIS Web server. Now it's time to see how well you can create Web pages of your own and maintain your Web server. You can find answers to the quiz and exercise questions in Appendix A at the back of the book.

Quiz

1. How does the Enable Content Expiration feature of IIS work?
2. What's the NCSA Common Log Format?
3. Which tab of the Directory Properties dialog box contains the location of the directory and the security settings for it?
4. Does Windows XP provide NNTP support?
5. What's one of the easiest ways to check your Web page for errors?

Exercises

1. Install and configure IIS on your machine.
2. Create a logical Web site design for your test setup.
3. Design and create several test Web pages.

20

DAY **21**

Maintaining Your System and Finding Problems

Computers have become faster, more efficient, and more reliable over the years. A computer today will outlive its useful life by several years if you take a modicum of care of it. This means doing the little things like keeping it clean and checking the status of the various components regularly. You'll also want to back your data up in case the nightmare of a hard drive failure occurs.

Of course, everything you do for the computer eventually pays dividends for you as well. Cleaning the mouse helps the mouse work longer, but it also makes the mouse less frustrating to use and more precise when you do use it. Cleaning (and optionally degaussing) the monitor reduces the potential for electric shock to both you and the monitor. (Only some monitors require manual degaussing, most modern monitors perform this task automatically as part of their power-on cycle.) A computer with clean fans tends to make less noise, allowing you to concentrate on your work.

Today, we'll delve into the not so mysterious world of computer maintenance. Maintenance is actually the least understood part of a computer setup because most people see the computer as an appliance they use to do work and play games. However, even a refrigerator needs maintenance. You wouldn't believe how much you can save by keeping it clean.

One of the nice features about Windows is that it does include a few maintenance programs to get you started. They might not be the best utilities, but you'll find they do the job for a small business. You'll still need to buy a few items, and I'll let you know what they are as the day progresses. For now, put on your coveralls, and let's get into some dusty places.

Maintenance Issues

As previously mentioned, Windows XP provides several pieces of software you need to know about. Each piece of software helps you maintain your machine in some way. The following sections provide an overview of each utility and help you understand how to use them. I won't be able to tell you how to use the utility on your specific system, but you'll learn enough to adopt the procedures I show into something you can use.

Using Error Checking

Most people who've used Windows 9x know that it provides the ScanDisk utility for checking your drive. However, if you look at Windows XP, you won't find a disk scanner, at least not on the Start Menu. You need to open a copy of Windows Explorer or My Computer. Right-click the drive icon and choose Properties from the context menu. You'll see a Drive Properties dialog box. Select the Tools tab. Figure 21.1 shows a typical example of the entries on this page. One of the features I miss about this tab is that it no longer shows the time since your last check of the system.

FIGURE 21.1

You'll find the disk maintenance utilities on the Tools tab.

Click Check Now, and you'll see a Check Disk dialog box. The first option determines if Windows XP tells you about the errors it finds on your hard drive or attempts to fix them automatically. In most cases, you'll want to know about the errors so you can record them in a maintenance log. This is one of the ways to track the health of your hard drives.

The second option on the Check Disk dialog box tells Windows XP to scan for bad sectors and attempt to fix them. Checking the option will increase the time required to error check the drive, but it's time well spent. You don't want a problem with bad sectors to begin killing your data. Bad sectors can sneak up on you, usually at the worst possible moment.

Select the options you want to use and then click Start. The indicator bar will show you the progress of the disk check. In most cases, you'll see several error-checking phases. Each error-checking phase requires another time interval measured by the progress bar.

Data Backups and Restore

Creating a backup of your hard drive is one of the more important maintenance tasks you can perform. If your machine fails or a disaster occurs, the backup protects your data investment, which is often more than the cost of your machine and associated software. Let's take a quick tour of the Backup utility that Microsoft has come up with for Windows XP.

 Note

> Make sure that you clean your tape drive regularly and inspect it before each backup. Open the tape drive door with a non-metallic screwdriver or other small non-metallic implement. Peak inside at the mechanism to ensure that everything is intact. One company I knew faithfully made backups of their system, only to discover that the tape head had detached from the tape transport. None of the tapes had any data on them.

The first time you start Backup, it will ask if you want to use the Backup Wizard (described in the "Creating a Backup with Backup Wizard" and "Restoring a Backup with Backup Wizard" sections). Advanced users will want to clear the Always Start in Wizard Mode option and then click the Advanced Mode link. Windows XP displays the Welcome tab of the Backup Utility dialog box. At this point, you can create a backup, restore and manage media, and schedule backup tasks. We'll discuss these options in the sections that follow the Backup Wizard section.

21

Tip

Replace your tapes when they become too old or you've used them too often. Most tapes wear well through 20 uses, but you need to monitor signs of problems such as an uneven tape pack, which usually indicates stretching. The adhesive used to secure the magnetic media on tapes also fails after a while. Most tapes last about two years under perfect conditions. DAT tapes last about five years. Check your tape vendor specifications for tape storage requirements.

Creating a Backup with Backup Wizard

The Backup Wizard is a great choice if you have no experience at all creating backups. The Backup Wizard starts automatically when you start the Backup utility. You can also access it from the Welcome tab of the Backup Utility dialog box. The following steps tell you how to use the Backup Wizard to create a backup. I'll assume that you can see the typical Welcome screen.

1. Click Next. Backup Wizard asks if you want to create a backup or restore previously backed up files.

2. Select Backup; then click Next. You'll see a What to Back Up dialog box. Select one of the four options. If you select the Let me choose what to back up option, Backup Wizard displays an Explorer-like dialog box that lets you choose the backup files. Select the files you want to backup and then click Next. Backup Wizard asks which device you want to use for backup purposes. You can use a dedicated tape drive, a floppy drive, or an area on another hard drive.

3. Select a backup device; then click Next. You'll see a completion dialog box. Notice the Advanced button at the bottom of the dialog box. This enables you to choose advanced backup features such as type of backup and the use of verification after the backup.

4. Choose advanced features if desired. Follow the prompts to make any changes to the standard setup. Click Finished. Backup will perform the backup you created.

Restoring a Backup with Backup Wizard

Backups are like insurance. You know you need to have them, but you hope never have to use them. Unfortunately, you'll eventually need the backup you created. That's when you perform a restore by using the Backup Wizard. The following steps show how to do that. I'll assume you can see the typical Welcome screen.

1. Click Next. Backup Wizard asks if you want to create a backup or restore previously backed up files.

2. Select Restore; then click Next. You'll see a What to Restore dialog box that looks similar to a two-pane view of Windows Explorer.

3. Select an entire backup, or just a single file in a backup, using the same techniques you've used to choose files in Windows Explorer.

4. Click Next. You'll see a completion dialog box. Notice the Advanced button at the bottom of the dialog box. This enables you to choose advanced restore features such as restore location and whether Restore should overwrite existing files.

5. Choose advanced features if desired. Follow the prompts to make any changes to the standard setup. Click Finished. Restore restores any required files on your system.

Creating a Backup

Advanced users will want to use the manual method for creating backups because it gives you better control over the backup settings. Always create backup jobs for your system. You'll perform the same backup process more than once, so saving your settings is always a good idea. Even if you have to modify the default settings, making small changes usually requires less time than creating a new backup.

It's important to create a backup strategy for your system. For example, many companies will store some tapes in a vault and others in an offsite location to ensure they always have a viable backup of their system. The following steps show how to create a backup job and start it. Begin the job creation process on the Backup tab of the Backup Utility.

1. Use the Explorer-like display to select the files you want to back up. Note that it's better to use My Network Places entries than to use network shares when selecting network files. You never know when a network share will go away or change—making your settings obsolete.

2. Select a backup destination and a backup media or filename. The backup destination can include a backup device or a file. You can use any accessible location when working with a file. It's best to use another machine for the purpose so you won't have the data stored locally.

3. Use the View | Options command to display the Options dialog box. Select a backup type on the Backup tab.

4. Select the Backup Log tab and choose one of the three logging options. You'll normally want to create a log to ensure that Backup can record any backup errors.

5. Select the Exclude Files tab and add or delete file specifications as need. Backup always includes files and directories that are active during backup. However, you'll want to add file specifications such as *.BAK to reduce backup time.

21

6. Select the General tab and perform any required configuration. For example, Microsoft assumes that you don't want to verify data after the backup completes; yet, this is an extremely important feature.

7. Click OK to close the Options dialog box.

8. Use the Job | Save Selections command to display the Save As dialog box. Give your job a name; then click Save.

9. Start the backup by clicking Start Backup. You'll see a Backup Job Information dialog box.

10. Click Start Backup. You'll see a Backup Progress dialog box. The Backup Progress dialog box will eventually tell you the backup is complete and allow you to view a report if desired.

11. Click Close to complete the backup process.

Restoring a Backup

Disasters happen to the best of us, which means you'll eventually need to restore a back-up. Unlike backups, you'll seldom perform a restore. For this reason, the Backup Utility doesn't provide the means to create a job for restores. The following steps show you how to restore a backup.

1. Select the Restore and Manage Media tab of the Backup Utility dialog box.

2. Select the backup media you want to use from the Explorer-like display. Choose one or more files from within that media. The Backup Utility won't restore files from more than one media at a time, so if you try to choose files from more than one media, it will ask if you want to clear the previous selections.

3. Select the files you want to restore. Make sure that you choose all of the required files so you restore everything needed on the first pass. Restores take longer than backups, so you'll want to get this step right.

4. Select a restore location. If you choose anything but the Original Location option, you'll also need to provide a directory name.

5. Use the Tools | Options command to display the Options dialog box. Select a restore option from the Restore tab. Microsoft recommends that you never replace an existing file with one from the backup. You do have the choice of replacing older files only, or replacing all files.

6. Click Start Restore. You'll see a Confirm Restore dialog box. The Advanced button on this dialog box enables you to change additional restore options, such as the restoring security. Generally, you want to leave these options alone.

7. Click OK, and you'll see a Restore Progress dialog box. This dialog box will tell you when the restore is complete and provide you with restore statistics. As with the backup, you can view a report containing any restore anomalies.

Optimizing Your Hard Drive

This section shows you how to optimize your hard drive. Just what is hard drive optimization? Your hard drive is a mechanical device that exacts a heavy toll on system performance. Anything you can do to make the hard drive run faster and work more efficiently nets large increases in system performance. The process of optimizing your hard drive includes moving data around so the hard drive can access it faster. You'll also clean up old files and delete the older files that slow your system down to a crawl. An optimized hard drive also increases your productivity by making data easy to find.

Tip

Keeping your hard drive clean and defragmented yields other tangible results. A drive lasts longer when it doesn't have to work as hard to find your data. Optimization can help where it counts most: in the cost operating your system. Keep your drive running faster by optimizing it regularly.

Now that you have some idea of what disk optimization is and why you'd want to do it, let's look at the two utilities you'll use to perform this task. The Disk Cleanup utility removes all of the old files from your system. It makes suggestions about the files you can remove safely. The Disk Defragmenter moves files around so the hard drive can access them faster. As you use your hard drive, the files become fragmented and the hard drive has to work harder to access them. The following sections show how to use both utilities.

Disk Cleanup

One of the best things you can do for your system is clean up the wealth of useless files that accumulate. For example, many applications generate temporary files while you work on your data. Internet Explorer is one of the worst offenders, in this case, but word processors often come in a close second. In some situations, junk files continue to lurk on your hard drive until you delete them manually.

You'll find the Disk Cleanup utility in the Start\Programs\Accessories\System Tools folder. The Disk Cleanup utility performs safe disk searches, in most cases, so the chances of error are low. However, you're still deleting files from your data drives, so data loss can occur when using this utility. Always create a backup of your system before you perform any disk maintenance task, especially one that removes "unnecessary" files from the system as this one does. The data you save will be worth the time expended to create the backup. The following steps show you how to use the Disk Cleanup Utility.

1. Start the Disk Cleanup utility. You'll see a Select Drive dialog box that contains a Drives list box.

2. Select the drive you want to check from the list; then click OK. Disk Cleanup will display a Disk Cleanup dialog box while it performs maintenance tasks such as compressing old files on your drive. The progress indicator will show how much time Disk Cleanup will require. When Disk Cleanup completes the first part of the process, you'll see a Disk Cleanup dialog box like the one shown in Figure 21.2.

FIGURE **21.2**

Disk Cleanup will search your drive for problem areas, perform a few mainte-nance tasks, and then display this dialog box.

The Files to Delete field contains options for removing unnecessary files from your system. Each entry contains a checkbox you use to select the item. It also tells you the location of the files and shows how much disk space you can save by using this feature.

3. Select one or more file groups to delete. Click OK. The Disk Cleanup Utility will remove the unneeded files.

Of course, this is a simple disk cleanup. You can perform a thorough cleanup by using special features provided by the Disk Cleanup utility. The More Options tab of the Disk Cleanup dialog box contains three areas that help perform additional disk cleanup. You can remove optional Windows components, installed programs, and restore points from System Restore. When working with System Restore, Disk Cleanup will save the last restore point, but remove all of the others.

You might still have reservations about deleting the files based on location alone. Click View Files on the Disk Cleanup tab, and you'll see an Explorer view of the files in that location. The view you'll see depends on the location. For example, when looking at the Downloaded Program Files folder, you'll see the status of the file, along with the date of last access. If you decide that you don't want to delete all of the files in a particular location, you can delete just those you think are outdated while in the Explorer view. Make sure that you clear the option in the Disk Cleanup dialog box when you're finished.

Disk Defragmenter

The first question many of you will have is "What is disk fragmentation?" As you work with a disk drive, Windows XP has to find new places to put files. At some point, all of the spaces available for holding files will get too small for the file you want to save, and Windows XP will have to place the file in two sections of the hard drive. The act of placing the file in more than two places is fragmentation.

Fragmentation affects performance in a big way. Every time the system needs to access a fragmented file, it will have to move the drive read head to two (or more) locations, which is expensive in computer time. Of course, this problem will begin affecting more than just one file. After a while, many of the files on your drive will experience some level of fragmentation, and you'll definitely see the performance drop.

Defragmenting your hard drive is one of the most important performance related maintenance actions you can do. The Disk Defragmenter utility reorders the content of your hard drive. It places the files back into one section of the hard drive and frees continuous space by moving all of the files to one end of the hard drive. A defragmented hard drive runs much faster. Unfortunately, this fix doesn't last forever; you have to defragment your hard drive on a regular basis.

21

There are some problems with the Microsoft solution to disk defragmenting. The biggest one is convenience. Disk Defragmenter only works on local drives; you can't start it on a local drive and hope to defragment remote drives. Disk Defragmenter is also Windows version specific. You need to use the version of Disk Defragmenter that comes with your system (or a compatible third party product).

Tip

The market for third-party disk defragmenter utilities is huge. This is an extremely important computer maintenance task, so administrators want to be sure they have the right tool for the job. Unfortunately, Microsoft changes the format of their drives every time they release a new product. This means that you need a new version of the third-party product if you want to run it on Windows XP. Unlike Microsoft, most third-party vendors make their product usable with all previous versions of Windows. They support features such as remote defragmenting, and they provide you with statistics that show the results of your activity. In short, while the Microsoft-provided utility is good, the third-party products tend to be better.

Now that you have a better idea of what Disk Defragmenter can do for you, let's look at the procedure for using it. The following steps show who you how to perform a typical disk defragmentation.

1. Start the Disk Defragmenter utility. You'll see a list of the drives on your machine. The statistics include the formatting method, capacity, amount of free space, and the percentage of free space. The first phase of defragmenting the drive is to make sure that you actually need to defragment it.

Tip

You can perform two tasks using Disk Defragmenter: analyze and defragment. Performing analysis first on large hard drives can save time. It pays to defragment drives smaller than 1 GB each time you perform maintenance.

2. Click Analyze. The Disk Defragmenter display will change as shown in Figure 21.3. Disk Defragmenter will check each file on the drive for fragmentation. When the analysis process is complete, you'll see a dialog box that either recommends you defragment your drive or leave it alone for now.

3. Click View Report. You'll see an Analysis Report dialog box. This dialog box provides information about the volume and lists the most fragmented files. Even if your drive doesn't require defragmentation, you may want to defragment the drive if one or two files have an exceptional amount of fragmentation.

FIGURE 21.3

Disk Defragmenter helps you check your drive for fragmentation.

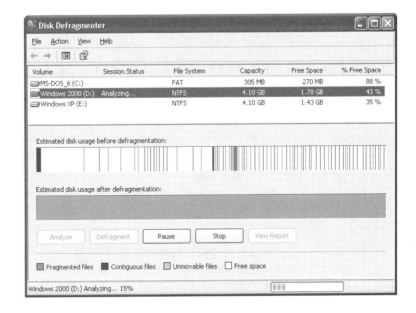

4. Click Defragment if you need to defragment a drive. Disk Defragmenter will perform a quick analysis and then begin the defragmenting process. You'll see the areas of fragmentation disappear as the program moves files around on your system.

Locating Software Problems

Everyone has problems with software from time-to-time, if for no other reason than buggy software. The problem is tracking the problem down so you can fix it. Some vendors make this nearly impossible by automatically starting parts of their application, hiding functionality in poorly named services, or using drivers that are incompatible with the rest of the software on the machine. However, using a logical troubleshooting process, knowing which tools Microsoft provides for analysis, and logging your installations all help to make the process a lot easier.

The following sections explore all three of these issues. You'll learn about utilities such as the System Configuration utility that Microsoft provides for diagnosing problems. We'll explore the drivers and how you figure out which ones Windows requires. Finally, we'll look at some hardware-imposed issues that disguise themselves as a software issue.

21

Using the System Configuration Utility

You can look at system configuration from a number of perspectives. For the purposes of this section, we'll look at system configuration as the setup that Windows XP uses to configure itself during the book process. In short, when you see an icon in the notification area immediately after startup, that's a part of the system configuration process.

Unfortunately, the startup applications don't always get along with every other piece of software on your system. For example, your disk detector utility might conflict with the CD burning software, making it impossible to create new CDs. While the disk detector is a great feature you'd love to keep around, it's bothersome when you want to create a CD. If the disk detector doesn't provide some convenient means for stopping, you might find yourself uninstalling the utility.

This is where the System Configuration (MSCONFIG) utility comes into play. It helps you modify the startup settings for your machine so you can start only want you need. To start the System Configuration utility, select Run from the Start Menu, type MSCONFIG in the Open field, and then click OK. You'll see a System Configuration Utility dialog box shown in Figure 21.4.

FIGURE 21.4

Use the System Configuration Utility to adjust the way Windows XP starts.

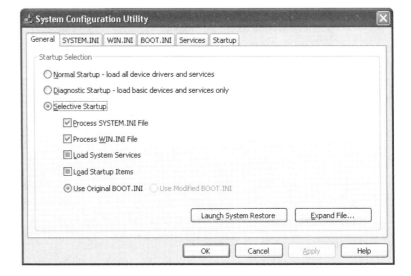

> **Caution** This section of the chapter discusses the boot options for your system. Enabling or disabling boot options is always risky because you can cause your system to freeze during the boot process by disabling a needed driver, service, DLL, or other part of the operating system. Use the content of this section carefully. Disable or enable entries one at a time, so you can see what effect the single entry will have on the system. Using MSCONFIG does offer safety because you can always boot in safe mode and enable an option you need—the option isn't gone forever.

As you can see, the System Configuration utility contains tabs that affect almost every part of the operating system boot process. You can use these entries to modify your setup. The following list provides an overview of each tab.

- **General**   Controls the way Windows XP launches the next time you start it. You can choose a normal, diagnostic, or selective startup. The Normal Startup option is the one that you'll use most often. It loads all the drivers and applications configured for your machine. You'll use the Diagnostic Startup option starts Windows XP with only the essentials so you can check for problems with the operating system. The Selective Startup option is the one that you'll use for performance and application compatibility purposes. However, you won't normally change the boot options from this tab. You need to select files using the other tabs and the System Configuration Utility will set the options on this tab automatically.

- **SYSTEM.INI and WIN.INI**   The SYSTEM.INI and WIN.INI tabs are leftovers from previous versions of Windows. Check these two tabs first for old 16-bit drivers and applications. Many of the entries on these tabs affect printer and font settings for old applications. You might find other surprises from antiquity here as well. Check the "Finding Unneeded Drivers" for additional ideas.

- **BOOT.INI**   Controls the boot process from an operating system selection perspective. The BOOT.INI file contains entries for every operating system on your machine that the boot manager controls. Use Move Up and Move Down to change the position of the boot partition in the list displayed during system startup. The Set as Default button controls the default operating system. Finally, you can use Check All Boot Paths to verify the usability of the BOOT.INI entries.

  The diagnostic functions go further than just validating the boot paths. You can use settings in this dialog box to change the boot type. For example, one option instructs boot manager to start the operating system in a non-GUI mode. Another option tells the system to create a boot log, while other settings change the default video or use the Safe Mode booting.

21

- **Services**   Determines which services Windows XP loads during the boot process. A check box indicator shows whether the service is in an enabled or disabled state. Notice the Disable All button on this dialog. Disabling all services just about ensures your system will have difficulty restarting. The Essential column is supposed to tell you if the service is essential. However, many essential services aren't marked, so exercise care when you make changes to this tab. The Status column shows the server state. For example, a service that's marked Stopped is loaded into the system, but isn't running at the time. A Hide All Microsoft Services option helps you see just the services installed by third party vendors.

- **Startup**   Determines which applications Windows XP will start, including those in the notification area of the Taskbar. This is one of the safest choices for performance changes. You can disable all of the entries in this list and still expect the system to boot properly. Of course, you may notice the loss of some functionality, but the operating system will work as intended.

Finding Unneeded Drivers

We previously discussed the SYSTEM.INI and WIN.INI tabs of the System Configuration utility. Both tabs have an entry marked ";for 16-bit app support." If this entry contains anything at all, then you have 16-bit applications on your machine that you should retire.

It also pays to look at the [drivers] entry on the SYSTEM.INI tab because these are normally 16-bit drivers. Note that most machines will have a 16-bit wave and timer driver for compatibility purposes that you can theoretically eliminate unless you play DOS games on your system.

Entries in the [driver32] section of the SYSTEM.INI tab are safe, but suspect. Only older 32-bit drivers use this section, so you might want to look for updates. Likewise, take a close look at the [386enh] section for potential problems.

Not every unneeded driver on your system will wave a red flag and shout that it's old and cranky. You can probably eliminate some of the entries on the Services tab of the System Configuration utility. The best way to know if you can disable a service is to research it first. Sometimes, you can tell a lot by just the service name. For example, if you see an entry marked NetMeeting Remote Desktop Sharing and you never use NetMeeting, you can probably save some memory by not loading that service. However, no matter what you think you know about the services listed in this dialog, always disable them one at a time, reboot, and test your theory before you make any other changes.

Setup or Configuration Errors

System glitches—they're annoying, and we all hate them. In some cases, the problem is a fault in Windows XP, and you can't repair it. In other cases, the problem is due to a number of causes that are under your control. You may not know how to fix the problem, but you could do something about it if you knew what to look for and how to get help fixing it.

The following sections look at the most common cause of system glitches. The solutions to many of these problems involve a system cleanup. You'll get rid of old drivers, set up an application correctly, or find a new way to access a device. In short, it's cleaning of the configuration portion of your machine.

Startup Problems

Many glitches occur during startup—the very worst moment to have them happen because the system doesn't have enough software installed to track the problem correctly. Startup problems can involve everything from a corrupted driver to a piece of hardware that decided it was time to call it quits. Sometimes, the startup problem occurs because you installed something yesterday, which is why logs are helpful in diagnosing problems.

We've already discussed some of the solutions to this problem. For example, you can use the System Configuration utility to disable a suspected problem. In many cases, you can find the errant program, reinstall it, and have the problem fixed (at least until the nest time corruption sets in).

It also helps to look at Device Manager. Non-functional devices appear in the list with a yellow exclamation point next to them. If you can get your machine running at all, the Device Manager entry will at least cue you to the problem. Of course, sometimes you can't get the machine running, so you'll need a diagnostic program to find the problem. We'll discuss this solution in the "Running Specialty Diagnostics" section.

You'll also find your share of subtle problems. Your machine might start one time and not another. Perhaps the problem is due to heat or other environmental stress conditions. Diagnostic programs can help find these problems. However, don't overlook the help that Microsoft provides in the form of the Event Viewer. Look for repetitive entries or those that happen when you experience the problem. Sometimes, a startup problem is the result of an odd combination of software. You might need to start some applications automatically and others manually to obtain a stable system.

21

Hardware Configuration Problems

The hardware configuration problem is one of the tougher problems to figure out. You install the hardware just like the vendor says, but it fails to work. If you install the same hardware on another machine, it works without a hitch. Of course, the vendors all engage in a major finger pointing session at this point, and you don't receive any help with your problem.

One of the more interesting problems that you'll see is one where a piece of hardware keeps another piece from working. For example, one brand of hardware decoder for a DVD installed fine as long as you didn't have a certain brand of soundboard. If you tried to install the DVD after the soundboard, Windows XP never found the hardware decoder. It recognized the DVD, but that didn't help you play movies on your system.

In this case, the solution to the problem was to remove every non-essential board from the system, which included soundboards and extra SCSI boards (you could have one specifically for your tape drive). If Windows XP suddenly saw the hardware decoder or other device, you could install support for it and then add the other boards back in. Generally, you'll find the device works fine from that point on.

Some software won't exercise the full range of hardware settings. This problem used to be common, but you'll rarely see it now. For example, a communications program might place an artificial limit on the serial port settings that it'll recognize. The device works, you can use it with other applications, but it won't work with the one application you need to use. The solution is to attempt to reconfigure the device. Unfortunately, that doesn't always work, so you might have to buy a new application that does provide the required support.

Memory-Related Problems

Memory, or the lack of it, is the number one problem you'll run into when working with large applications. Creating a larger swap file (or allowing Windows to create it for you) will only go so far in helping a memory problem. Windows XP requires real memory to function. The swap file is a means to offload parts of memory that an application has requested, but isn't using now. In short, the swap file can't fill in for a lack of system memory.

Both main memory and the swap file do have one thing in common. A machine that's running for long periods will experience fragmentation in both main memory and the swap file. The fragmentation causes a drop in performance. It could, in rare cases, cause Windows to deny an application request for additional memory. The fix for the memory problem is to reboot Windows occasionally in order to clear memory.

Fixing the swap file problem requires that you recreate the PAGEFILE.SYS file located in the drive's root directory. You can do this by changing the partition that the swap file uses, changing the size, selecting the No Paging File option, or setting the minimum size to 0. (You'll find the swap file options on the Virtual Memory dialog box accessed through the Advanced tab of the System Properties dialog box.) If you defragment the drive before you create a new swap file, you'll notice an incremental increase in speed.

Driver-related Problems

Drivers have been the bane of users everywhere for as long as Windows has existed (and before). The problems they cause range from a lack of support for hardware features to interference with other drivers and applications. Sometimes, the problems stem from using an old driver that doesn't follow the rules correctly or is no longer current with existing technology. In other cases, the design of the hardware is incompatible with the system as a whole or the application doesn't access the driver correctly.

Microsoft is trying to fix this problem by using signed drivers. Whenever you see a signed driver, it means that it has gone through extensive testing. Signing is akin to a certification process. Unfortunately, vendors are usually unwilling to go through the effort of signing for an older device, so you might be stuck with an unsigned driver.

Using the newest driver possible ensures that you have the benefit of any bug fixes the vendor may have provided. In many cases, the newer driver will also perform better than an older drive in the same circumstances.

In a very few cases, you might have to get online, check into the Microsoft newsgroups, and see if anyone knows of an alternative driver. For example, using a third-party driver fixed a problem with my DVD drive and hardware decoder. The original vendor didn't want to provide a fix, so a third party provided a solution. It doesn't always happen, but looking for solutions of this sort does work.

Problems Associated with Multiple CPU Machines

Sometimes, you'll run into odd problems associated with multiple CPU machines. For example, we looked at a common problem with games in the "Configuring Windows Games" section of Day 7. The solution in that situation was to turn one of the processors off for that application. You simply tell Windows XP to execute the application using only one processor. Of course, this problem can affect more than games, so you should always check for multiple CPU problems with problem applications.

The problems can become more severe than an application that refuses to work. For example, you may have a special utility program that refuses to work. Sometimes, programs such as Microsoft ActiveSync will refuse to recognize parts of your hardware

21

(the USB port in this case). If you find that these special programs won't work, you should look for a newer version of the product. Sometimes, these vendors will find the problem and fix it. You can also try the solution from Day 7, but that's problematic, in this case, because you have to make the change after every reboot for every affected application. In some cases, finding a third-party alternative application will work. Finally, you might simply have to move the problem application to another machine to get it to work.

Having multiple CPUs can cause other problems. An incorrect implementation of multiple CPU support can cause a motherboard to malfunction. For example, some Asus motherboards have a problem where you can't use Advanced Configuration and Power Interface (ACPI) support. These motherboards actually require a physical change you can't make at home (see `http://www.asus.com.tw/Products/Techref/Acpi/solution.html` for details). The only way to know about this problem is to spend time on the vendor Web site searching for the required answer, the vendor will almost certainly fail to contact you regarding the situation.

Locating Hardware Problems

I'm often amazed at how reliable hardware is today. There was a time when I replaced my hard drive annually, rather than face the problems of a crash. Today, hard drives run longer than the machine is viable. The machine and its hard drive are often in great shape a year or two after I turn it over to someone else. The point is that hardware reliability isn't as much of a concern as it once was (although hard drives will fail).

The problem with hardware today is that it interacts with the system in so many ways and has become so complex, that you often run into compatibility problems. The problems are so severe that the hardware may not work at all. For that matter, the system may not even see the hardware.

Standards are also a problem. By the time standards organizations produce standards that hardware vendors can follow, the technology is already out-of-date. It's as if we're in a constant state of using beta hardware for missing critical needs.

No matter what your hardware problem is, you can usually find a solution for it. The following sections discuss the methods for locating hardware problems on your system. In fact, the first section that follows will tell you one way to prevent the problems from occurring at all. We'll discuss cleaning your machine as a means to keep your hardware healthy and happy.

Quick Tips for a Clean Machine

One of the best things you can do for your hardware is to clean it. Dust is the mortal enemy of electronics and removing it can only extend your computer's life. Even if you plan to make a yearly computer upgrade, cleaning helps the machine run better and make less noise.

Unfortunately, most people don't know how to clean their machines properly. One person that I talked with had used a vacuum with a metallic nozzle no less to clean their machine. The resulting disaster sent them to the computer store in search of a new machine.

You should invest in a few cleaning essentials for your machine. A can of computer-quality compressed air is a requirement. It's also helpful to have static free wipes, a bottle of methyl (best) or isopropyl alcohol, some electronics grade cotton swabs, a floppy disk cleaner, CD cleaner, and a cleaning tape (if you have a tape drive). A small computer toolkit will help you with the screws that still permeate computer construction and an inspection mirror (think dentist) will help you look in tight corners. Now that you have your cleaning kit assembled, the following tips will help you use it.

- Carefully remove your computer from its hiding spot. If necessary, mark and then remove the cables. Marking the cables is important if you want the machine to work later. Moving your machine to an open area helps you do a better job of cleaning it and makes it easier to clean the resulting dust.

- Open the computer case. Use the compressed air to get rid of dust. Spray in the hidden areas too. Disk drives are notorious for hiding dirt in crevices. If some dirt is especially hard to get rid of, use a cotton swap soaked in alcohol to help remove it. For example, you'll find the blades of the various fans attract and retain dirt.

- Look for any damage such as frayed wiring or burned components. Sometimes, a computer component will show damage before it stops working. Use the inspection mirror to check places you can't normally see. Put your computer back together, but don't put it back into place just yet.

- Blow as much dust as you can from your monitor without removing the cover.

- Blow as much dust as you can from the printer. Make sure that you open the user accessible areas of the printer, but don't open the areas where you need a screwdriver for access. Look for areas of ink buildup. Clean them with fresh alcohol-soaked cotton swabs.

- Clean your mouse. If you have an optical sensor, clean the sensor opening with an alcohol soaked cotton swab. If you have a standard mouse, carefully remove the cover holding the ball in place. Blow dust from the inside of the mouse. Wash the

21

mouse ball carefully in plain water (no soap). Dry the mouse ball with a lint free cloth. Don't let the contaminants from the water supply stay in place, remove them with the cloth. Put the mouse back together.

- Clean your keyboard. Use the compressed air to get bits of dust and other material from between the keys. Clean the keys with a screen wipe or other slightly damp cloth. Don't use alcohol on the keyboard because you might rub the letters and numbers right off. In addition, use a soft cloth, rather than a paper towel, to remove dirt from the keys.

- Vacuum the dust you've dislodged from the computer and any surrounding areas. Don't use a vacuum on any piece of computer equipment or get the vacuum around recordable media such as floppy disks. After you clean the area up, put the computer back in place and reconnect any cables using your connection diagram or other documentation.

- Turn your machine back on. Use the vendor instructions for the floppy disk cleaner, CD cleaner, and tape cleaner to clean these devices. You now have a clean machine worthy of your use.

Running Machine Level Diagnostics

You'll eventually run into a situation when you need to perform diagnostics on your system. A piece of hardware might fail, the system will refuse to recognize a new piece of hardware, or you might run into a compatibility problem. The point is that you need some means for identifying the cause of the problem and fixing it. With hardware, this could mean everything from getting a new driver to replacing the old hardware with something new.

The following sections discuss diagnostics at several levels. You'll learn about the Microsoft provisions for gaining access to system information. We'll also discuss third-party products that you can use to augment your hardware diagnostic toolkit.

System Information (WINMSD)

System Information has been around in one form or another for many years. Originally, Microsoft called the product Microsoft Diagnostics (MSD). It was then renamed WinMSD to reflect a change to a graphical information. Today, we call an updated form of the same utility System Information. The System Information moniker is actually more accurate than calling this utility a diagnostic. It tells you details about your system, but doesn't tell you that anything is wrong with it.

You'll find System Information in the Start\Programs\Accessories\System Tools folder. Figure 21.5 shows the initial display for this application. Notice that you receive detailed information about your system from the very beginning. However, the utility can provide details at an even greater level. All you need to do is select one of the four categories of information that System Information can provide.

FIGURE 21.5

System Information provides in-depth information about your computer.

Generally, you'll use System Information to view the status of your machine. However, you an also export this information to a file on disk. This is one way to take a snapshot of your system state and save it for later use in diagnosing problems. In fact, this is the way that Microsoft originally used this program. It allows them to collect information about your system to aid in problem resolution.

You can export system data in two ways. First, you can use the File | Export command to create a text version of your system information. This is the most convenient way to transfer the information to a database for later analysis. Second, you can use the File | Save command to create a file on disk. This file has an NFO extension that permits you to view it within System Information later. This is the best way to store data if you simply want a snapshot of your system for later use.

21

> **Tip**
>
> The NFO files that System Information creates use XML. In some cases, this might be a better format for importing the data into your database. Of course, the database will have to know how to interpret the XML file. Many new database managers and associated languages use XML as a common form of data exchange, so you'll find that this method works better that straight text.

Like many other Windows XP utilities, System Information has a command line interface. Type **MSINFO /?** to display a complete list of the current switches. The switches that you'll commonly want to use within a script include those that output system data to disk in silent mode. You can save a text file by using the /Report <Filename> switch. Likewise, you can produce an NFO file using the /Info <Filename> switch. You can even switch to a remote computer using the /Computer <Computer Name> switch.

Now that you have a better idea of what System Information can do, let's discuss a few details. System Information uses a hierarchical format similar to Windows Explorer. The following list tells you about each of the entries in the display shown in Figure 21.5.

- **Hardware Resources**   Contains a complete list of hardware resources for your machine. You can use these lists to look for missing or misconfigured hardware. This list also tells you about hardware conflicts (two devices using the same resource) and shows free resources that aren't used by any hardware. The Forced Hardware entry is especially important because it shows hardware someone has forced to non-standard settings on the system. This could point to a problem that wasn't resolved, just sidestepped.

- **Components**   Describes the individual components of your system. For example, if you select the CD-ROM option, System Information will query your CD and DVD drives for vendor specifics. It will also test the drives and tell you about device characteristics such as data transfer rates. Some of the entries shown in Figure 21.5 had additional subentries. For example, you'll generally find two selections under the Input entry: Keyboard and Mouse.

- **Software Environment**   Describes every running application on your machine. You'll find entries for applications, services, and drivers. Notice from Figure 21.5 that System Information differentiates between signed and system drivers. The System Driver entry lists all drivers on your machine, signed or not. The information you receive will vary. For example, if you select Services, System Information will tell you if the service is stopped, the start mode, and the kind of service that you're viewing.

- **Internet Settings** Contains a list of the Internet settings for your machine. More specifically, you'll find information about Internet Explorer under this entry, unless you have another browser installed. The Internet Explorer information includes facts such as driver version numbers and a few of the settings. System Information seems most interested in security levels, not in the kind of rules you set for discarding junk mail or the last place you visited online.

The Importance of Maintaining a DOS Partition

DOS was once the only way you could start a diagnostic program and expect it to find out anything about your hardware. In some cases, having a DOS partition on your machine today is one of the best ways to ensure you can at least boot the system and find out what's wrong with it.

The DOS partition contains a simple operating system and works with a variety of low-level utilities, many of which come from the vendors that created your system. For example, DOS is the only environment in which many flash read-only memory (ROM) tools will run. You need a flash ROM tool to upgrade your machine basic input/output system (BIOS) if your machine has a supported configuration. You'll also find that some vendors still provide DOS-based diagnostic tools with this hardware.

At one time, I would have said that you needed a DOS partition no matter what operating system you used normally. Windows tends to hide the hardware so well that a diagnostic is nearly useless in that environment. Other operating systems such as NetWare have few diagnostic programs available for them. DOS was the one operating system where you could find a tool that would tell you about the problems with your system.

Today, many high-end diagnostic programs are self-booting, which means that you don't need DOS to run them. If your only concern is the ability to test your system for faults, then you might be able to rid yourself of that ancient DOS partition. However, until you know that you'll never need to run anything from the DOS prompt again, you might want to keep it around.

Running Specialty Diagnostics

Windows XP provides many useful tools for diagnosing problems with your system. For example, you can check your modem with relative ease by using the Query Modem button on the Diagnostics tab of the Modem Properties dialog box. The problem is that these utilities are scattered throughout Windows, they don't provide low-level analysis of problems, and they often fail to locate the real problems in your system. This last point is especially important because few people realize that Windows maintains an iron grip on the hardware that will block the efforts of any serious diagnostic.

21

The only way to test your hardware fully is to get outside of Windows. That means using a third-party product that loads in DOS or provides a self-booting feature. The following sections provide a brief overview of three such utilities. All three of these utilities are self-booting, so you don't need to maintain a DOS partition to use them. Some of these utilities are quite expensive, but you definitely get what you pay for. Anyone who has more than a few machines to care for will realize the value of having an application that can pinpoint even significant hardware problems quickly.

TuffTest

#1-TuffTest Pro (http://tufftest.pcdiag.com/tufftest.htm) is the least expensive diagnostic program you'll find on the market today (unless the diagnostic is free). This is the no frills solution for someone who wants to test just the basics and absolutely nothing else.

You'll want to avoid TuffTest when working with certain types of hardware. For example, it doesn't include anything for working with SCSI drives. You'll also find that the port support is minimal and that you can't test any of your buses. TuffTest doesn't provide any configuration utilities or any of the other add-ons that other diagnostic tools provide. In short, this is the Spartan configuration.

You'll also find some benefits when using this program. The diagnostic is extremely small and fast. The menu system is easy to understand, and the vendor didn't clutter it with many features you'll never use. Unlike many large diagnostic programs, you can test all of your memory using this product.

One of the features that doesn't stick out at first is the product support that you get with TuffTest. The author maintains a newsletter where you can find out more about the product. In addition, there's a mailing list where you can exchange information with other users. Overall, this is one of the better product support packages.

PC-Technician

PC-Technician (http://www.windsortech.com/pctech.html) is a basic diagnostic program at a reasonable cost. It emphasizes the essentials of your system. You can use it to test main components such as memory, the hard drive, and your ports. One of the advantages of using this product is portability. PC-Technician is small and executes within about 200 KB of RAM. This enables PC-Technician to test all of main memory and perform a few other tricks that larger diagnostic programs can't perform.

What you won't find with PC-Technician is the capability to test some of the newer hardware on the market. For example, this program won't test the expansion bus on your machine. If you have a problem with your PCI or AGP setup, PC-Technician won't find it. Generally, PC-Technician won't work with newer ports. For example, you can't use it to test your USB port.

This program does have similarities to other offerings on the market, but the simple interface makes the features easy-to-use. For example, you can use PC-Technician to perform burn-in and certification testing. You can also perform certain types of performance tests.

Finally, PC-Technician helps you perform system configuration, as long as the configuration is within the range of PC-Technician capabilities. You can perform all of the essentials including CMOS configuration. However, PC-Technician lacks a flash ROM utility, so you can't use it to upgrade the BIOS on your machine. Fortunately, most motherboard vendors provide this utility for you.

CheckIt

CheckIt Professional Edition (`http://www.smithmicro.com/checkit/`) is the Cadillac of diagnostic programs. Of the three diagnostic programs, this is the most expensive and complex. It does everything the other products will do, only better. (Complete memory testing could be problematic due to the size of this diagnostic program.)

You'll also find that CheckIt tests all of the current bus technologies including PCI, PCMCIA, and AGP. CheckIt analyzes the PCI cards in your system and provides complete information about them. It includes many burn-in and certification tests that the other products don't support. For example, you can run a power cycling test on your system.

Space doesn't allow me to describe the entire feature set of this product, but CheckIt is an example of getting what you pay for. Of course, the price is the major negative of this product. Only those who need the ultimate in diagnostic utilities will need to consider this one.

Serial and Parallel Port Loopback Plugs

Sometimes, a problem with a serial or parallel port is outside the confines of the chips you can test, and yet not within the cable. The problem might exist in the plug or in other connection-related areas of the port. Using a loopback plug enables you to test a serial or parallel port completely.

Loopback plugs pass the signal from the port output back to its input. To create a loopback plug, you use a blank connector without wires and then connect wires between specific pins. Most of the high-end diagnostic programs you buy (such as PC-Technician, AMI Diags, or the Norton Utilities) provide these plugs. Others, such as CheckIt, don't

21

provide them (some packages from Touchstone do include loopback plugs now, but you need to purchase their high-end products to get them).

Loopback plugs eventually break. In addition, many systems today have multiple output ports that you might want to test without switching the port around. This means building loopback plugs of your own. It's not hard; all you need to do is buy the blank connector and add some wires to it. The following tables contain the connections you need to create loopback plugs of various types.

TABLE 21.1. Parallel port (DB25P) loopback plug connections.

First Pin	Connected to Second Pin
11 (Busy +)	17 (Select Input -)
10 (Acknowledge -)	16 (Initialize Printer -)
12 (Paper Out +)	14 (Autofeed -)
13 (Select +)	01 (Strobe -)
02 (Data 0 +)	15 (Error -)

TABLE 21.2. 9-pin serial port (DB9S) loopback plug connections.

First Pin	Connected to Second Pin
02 (RD: Received Data)	03 (TD: Transmitted Data)
07 (RTS: Request to Send)	08 (CTS: Clear to Send)
06 (DSR: Data Set Ready)	01 (CD: Carrier Direct)
01 (CD: Carrier Detect)	04 (DTR: Data Terminal Ready)
04 (DTR: Data Terminal Ready)	09 (RI: Ring Indicator)

TABLE 21.3. 25-pin serial port (DB25S) loopback plug connections.

First Pin	Connected to Second Pin
03 (RD: Received Data)	02 (TD: Transmitted Data)
04 (RTS: Request to Send)	05 (CTS: Clear to Send)
06 (DSR: Data Set Ready)	08 (CD: Carrier Direct)
08 (CD: Carrier Detect)	20 (DTR: Data Terminal Ready)
20 (DTR: Data Terminal Ready)	22 (RI: Ring Indicator)

As you can see, the pin connections are relatively easy to make. Whether you buy pre-made loopback plugs or make your own, this is an essential tool for your toolkit. Without loopback plugs, you'll never know whether the serial or parallel port you tested really works.

Locating Network Problems

Networks are one of the most difficult areas of your system to fix because you have multiple machines, lots of cable, and devices such as routers and hubs to consider. The fact that most vendors make their networking equipment extremely reliable doesn't help much when you're tracking a cable at two in the morning, rather than sleeping.

Some problems occur more often than others do. For example, you'd think that a cable would be extremely reliable since it never has to move. However, cables are one of the nightmares that network administrators face regularly because users always manage to find a way to crush or damage them.

The following sections describe some of the common problems that you'll run into when working with networks. This list isn't complete; some authors use entire books to describe what they consider common problems. This list represents the problems you'll run into most often.

Using the PING Utility

One of the utilities that you'll use more often than you think is the PING utility. This command line tool helps you test TCP/IP connections with another computer. You can actually use it for a number of purposes, but we'll only look at the diagnostic function today. The two command lines you'll commonly use for PING in a diagnostic mode are:

```
PING <Host Name>
PING <IP Address>
```

So, if you wanted to contact a machine named AUX, you'd type **PING AUX** and press Enter. PING will output four messages of 32 bytes and tell you about the response to each one. You can modify the size of the packet sent to the remote computer using the -l <Size> switch. If you wanted to test the computer at 192.168.0.1 with 1024 byte packets, you'd type **PING -l 1024 192.168.0.1**. Using a different packet size often reveals problems that the standard packet size won't show. The maximum packet size is 65,500 bytes.

You can also use the -n <Count> switch to change the number of packets sent to the other computer. You might suspect that an error won't occur until you send the fifth or sixth packet, so you can adjust the count to 5 or 6. If you use a value of -1, PING will continue sending packets until you press Ctrl+C (using Ctrl+Break won't work).

21

Using a Cable Scanner

Finding flaws in the cables that connect your network is a major problem even on smaller networks without the proper tools. Network administrators, especially those managing large networks, can spend a lot of time tracing cables. Standing on a ladder while you trace cables in the ceiling is a lot less fun than it sounds. Tracing cables in other places is even less exciting.

Cable scanners help find cable flaws by sending a signal on the cable and waiting for it to return. The time required for a return signal tells the location of a break or other flaw. Fixing the cable is a matter of tracing the specified distance from the source. This is a lot easier than trying to guess where a cable has a break.

Many people use the term time domain reflectometer (TDR) to refer to a cable scanner, but a cable scanner works just fine for most people. Theoretically, a TDR is a special, high-end version of a cable scanner. An average cable scanner costs about $1,000, although you can find them a little cheaper. Less expensive cable scanners provide fewer features and may not provide much accuracy in finding a cable flaw.

 Tip

You can build your own cable scanner for about $200 by using plans in some electronics magazines. For example, Circuit Cellar INK's October/November 1992 issue contains a set of plans on page 22. You can find this resource online. You can order a reprint of the article at http://www.circuitcellar.com/backissues.html. The source code for the cable scanner appears at http://www.dtweed.com/circuitcellar/caj00029.htm.

Most cable scanners provide both text and graphic output. This is a handy feature for maintaining records on your system. In some cases, the cable scanner also offers the option to send output to a printer through a serial, parallel, or wireless connection. All you need to do is print the results of the cable check and add it to the network documentation.

You should also look for a cable scanner that can detect the noise level of the cable on your system. Using this feature helps you to reduce the number of packet errors by reducing the noise that the packet signal must overcome. Just about everyone can benefit from reducing noise on his network.

Some cable scanners provide an oscilloscope interface. This enables you to monitor the signal that flows across the network. An experienced network administrator can use this information to troubleshoot problem installations. However, this is a feature that most small businesses will never use because their cable setup isn't complex enough.

Summary

Today you've learned about different types of maintenance you should perform on your machine. It may seem like a lot to do at first, but once you've done it a few times and set up a schedule, it won't seem like much time at all. The important consideration is to perform the work regularly. A little bit of maintenance here and there won't do much for your system or for you.

We've also looked at the types of maintenance you should perform. You've learned how to care for your disk and keep your system clean. In addition, you've learned how to run diagnostics so you can find problems when they occur. While we haven't covered every potential problem you'll run into, you should have a better idea of what the technician is talking about the next time you do run into a problem you can't handle alone.

Q&A

Q: Which type of backup system is best?

A: Most people find that a tape backup works best and is extremely economical. However, many home and small office users now rely on alternatives such as DVD-RAM drives. The backup you need depends on the size of your system and your backup strategy. A quarter inch cassette (QIC) tape such as those from Colorado Systems will work fine for a small system. Medium to large systems will use technologies such as digital audio tape (DAT) drives to do the job.

Q: How can I determine when my machine is "clean enough" or too dirty?

A: The first place you'll see dust on your machine is around the air openings in the case. That's because the air concentrates the dust particles in this area. If you're seeing dust around the air intakes, you know that the rest of your machine is too dirty. Most people find that they need to clean their machine once every three months for casual use or once a month for business level use.

Q: Why do I need to buy an expensive third party diagnostic product when Microsoft appears to provide everything I need in Windows?

A: The problem is that Windows doesn't provide everything you need. The diagnostics you receive with Windows will help find problems, but Windows maintains such a tight grip on the hardware that it's difficult at best to diagnose any hardware problem while running it. Windows hides many of the problems that could occur in the hardware so that you can't see them. The reason you need an external diagnostic program is to find hardware faults quickly.

21

Workshop

It's the end of the twenty-first day. You've learned all kinds of troubleshooting information that will hopefully make your PC experience more enjoyable. Now it's time to see how much of this troubleshooting information you learned. You can find answers to the quiz and exercise questions in Appendix A at the back of the book.

Quiz

1. Which utility do you use to remove excess files from your system?
2. How does the System Configuration utility help you restart a stalled system?
3. What are the four kinds of information that the System Information utility can provide?
4. What's a loopback plug?
5. What's a time domain reflectometer?

Exercises

1. Create a backup of your system.
2. Clean and inspect your machine.
3. Perform diagnostics on your system.

Answers to the Quiz Questions

This appendix provides answers to the quiz and exercise sections at the end of each chapter.

Day 1

Quiz

1. The user interface has changed considerably. It uses a new flat appearance, and Microsoft has tried to simplify usage.

2. Windows 2000 provides stability, reliability, and high security, but it doesn't provide flexibility. Windows 9x runs most applications but falls short when it comes to security, stability, and reliability. The main design goal for Windows XP is to provide security, reliability, and stability, yet allow a maximum number of applications to run.

3 No. While the compatibility modes do increase the number of applica-

tions that Windows XP can run over Windows 2000, application support still isn't perfect, especially when it comes to misbehaved applications. (An application is *misbehaved* when the vendor doesn't follow all the rules for creating Windows applications. Such applications cause all kinds of problems, including loss of data and frequent crashes.)

4. The Home Edition artificially prohibits you from using NTFS security. Although the security feature is theoretically available, you can't access it. This is one reason that businesses will probably want to install the Professional Edition, rather than use the Home Edition.

5. The multi-monitor support allows you to drive multiple computer desktops from a single computer. It allows you to extend the display area across multiple computers. DualView allows you to present the same desktop display on two monitors. Anyone who gives presentations or teaches computer courses will find this feature attractive because it allows you to see the screen from your local terminal at the same time the audience is viewing it.

Exercises

1. Look through the list of features in the "What's New in Windows XP?" and "Updated Windows XP Features" sections of the chapter. Prioritize the list according to your needs. Write why you think the feature is important. Assign some goals to learning about the new feature.

   This is one possibility, but there are multiple ways of accomplishing this task.

2. Create a list of the hardware you have in place now. You can usually get this information by looking at the manuals that came with your system. Verify your hardware list by checking the System Properties and the Device Manager dialogs. Match the hardware requirements to the list in the "Hardware Requirements" section of the chapter. Upgrade any hardware that doesn't match the minimum requirements, unless you're willing to live with slower performance or lack of functionality.

   This is one possibility, but there are multiple ways of accomplishing this task.

3. Create a list of Windows XP problem areas for your system using the "Windows XP Problem Areas" section as a starting point. This list can make the difference between installing Windows XP in an hour or two, or wasting several days trying to get your crippled installation to work. Check online sources, such as the Microsoft newsgroups, for information on any problems with product features that you may want to use in your XP setup. The Microsoft Knowledge Base (http://search.support.microsoft.com/kb/c.asp) provides a wealth of infor-

mation about potential bumps in the road for your installation.

This is one possibility, but there are multiple ways of accomplishing this task.

A

Day 2

Quiz

1. You normally use the CD-ROM installation technique when upgrading a machine. The character mode installation works best on a new machine or on a machine where the CD-ROM installation fails. Use a network installation to keep the number of trips to the office down on a network. Unattended installations work best with large organizations because of the time needed to set up the required files.

2. Windows XP and Linux can coexist on the same machine only if you use a third-party partition manager. The Windows Boot Manager doesn't work with non-Microsoft products very well (if at all).

3. You'll use DXDIAG.EXE to locate version-specific information about your DirectX setup. We'll use this utility in other chapters to diagnose problems with your DirectX and gaming setup.

4. The Event Viewer typically contains three logs: Application, Security, and System. The log that you're most interested in viewing is the System log because it contains critical operating system information. You also want to view the Application log because some Windows applications use that log to report errors.

Exercises

1. Make sure that you complete all of the required steps. For example, it's important to plan your installation before you begin it. Set aside enough time and make certain that you have any required drivers. Decide on an installation type. After you complete the installation, make sure that you check for problems. For example, you'll want to verify that all drivers are in place. Checking the installation and the event log are also good ideas.

   This is one possibility, but there are multiple ways of accomplishing this task.

2. Make certain that you install all critical updates for your machine, especially those that concern security. You'll also want to read about any application updates before you install them. Keeping your applications updated is a good idea because otherwise you'll run into bugs that keep you from being productive.

   This is one possibility, but there are multiple ways of accomplishing this task.

3. You need to know that your system is fully functional and stable before you install any applications. A solid operating system setup is essential to a good application

installation. In addition, you'll find that a stable operating system experiences fewer application-related problems. Finally, if you don't ensure that the operating system is stable, you won't know if problems are related to the application or the operating system.

This is one possibility, but there are multiple ways of accomplishing this task.

Day 3

Quiz

1. An Explorer Bar is one of the following panes in Windows Explorer: Search, Favorites, History, Media, Contacts, Folders. Each Explorer Bar allows you to manage or interact with a specific Windows resource, such as the hard drives on your system. The Explorer Bar provides an overview of the selected resource, while the Details pane shows you the content of that resource. For example, selecting a folder in the Folders Explorer Bar will display a list of files found in the folder in the Details pane.

2. The three toolbars are Standard Buttons, Address Bar, and Links. You'll modify the Standard Buttons toolbar by using the Customize Toolbar dialog box accessible with the View | Toolbars | Customize command. Modify the Links toolbar by changing the content of the Links folder in the Favorites folder. Anything you add to the Links folder will appear on the Links toolbar.

3. The changes you make to the Folder Options dialog affect every folder within Windows XP. This means that a single change in the Folder Options dialog can significantly affect your ability to work with Windows XP. Because this feature is so powerful, you need to exercise care when using it.

4. They are the Address, Links, Desktop, and Quick Launch toolbars. Of the four, the Quick Launch toolbar is the only one that Windows XP turns on by default.

Exercises

1. Try each of the Windows Explorer elements to obtain the best presentation for your needs. For example, decide when you want to enable the Task pane or use the Status Bar to learn more about files on your system. Work with the individual Explorer Bars to understand better what they do. Keep Tip of the Day on for a while so that you can learn new tricks about Windows Explorer. Most important of all, have fun!

This is one possibility, but there are multiple ways of accomplishing this task.

A

2. Try both of the Start menu options to see which one you like best. Most novices and some power users will like the simple Windows XP Start menu because it presents less clutter and allows you to work more efficiently. Many power users will prefer the Classic Start Menu because it provides more flexibility and offers more configuration options. After you select a Start menu, try customizing it one feature at a time until you're happy with this important part of the Windows experience.

    This is one possibility, but there are multiple ways of accomplishing this task.

3. The four Taskbar toolbars offer quick access to specific Windows XP features. You should design your setup with speed in mind. Anything that you access daily could go on the Taskbar. Everything else should appear in the Start menu.

    This is one possibility, but there are multiple ways of accomplishing this task.

Day 4

Quiz

1. No, the Internet Connection Wizard simply allows you to continue the configuration process. The connection is live the second that you complete the connection configuration process. You can begin using Internet Explorer immediately. If you decide to complete the e-mail and newsgroup configuration process later, Outlook Express will display the appropriate dialog boxes when you first start it.

2. No. Although Search the Web always uses one search engine and defaults to using MSN Search, you can change this default using registry settings. You can change many Internet Explorer defaults by modifying the right registry values.

3. The Connection field should tell you the particulars of the data encryption used to transfer the data to your machine. You want the Web site to use version 3.0 SSL or above to ensure that all security patches are in place. The site should also use 40-bit or 128-bit encryption. Using 128-bit encryption is better. The Connection field will also tell you which encryption algorithm was used and the size of the encryption key.

4. When you select a page for offline viewing, Internet Explorer downloads just that page. Selecting one level of links will download all of the pages that the first page links to in addition to that first page. When you get to the second level of links, you're also downloading all of the links found on the subordinate pages. In short, it's a geometric progression. Your hard drive can quickly fill with pages of Web content that you'll never use. It's better to download just the pages you need.

5. Internet Explorer makes both SSL 2.0 and SSL 3.0 available for secure communications with third parties. You can also use SSL 1.0. Many security experts feel that

you shouldn't settle for anything less than SSL 3.0 because this level of encryption has been available for a while, and it offers superior protection.

6. One of the more important features is that every piece of the drawing is an object, so you can move the pieces around as needed. The Whiteboard also includes a highlighter you can use to highlight text or other drawing features. A pointer allows you to draw everyone's attention to a specific area of the drawing. You can also create multiple-page drawings to ensure that all of your ideas fit into one file.

Exercises

1. Use one of the three methods we discussed for creating a connection to the Internet. The two automated methods have the advantage of being less work. The automated routes will save you time and could present IPSs that you don't know exist. However, you can save money by checking all of the ISPs in your area first. Most of them will charge the same rates, but you'll find that not all IPS provide the same service. For example, many will provide more Web page space than others do. In other cases, you'll find that the price of admission doesn't include unlimited hours. Some ISPs set limits on your Internet connection time.

   This is one possibility, but there are multiple ways of accomplishing this task.

2. The Internet provides a multitude of search engines. None of these search engines will answer every question. Some search engines are better than others, but none of them are complete. If a search engine were to provide every possible answer, you'd spend more time digging through the answers than using a specialized search engine to find what you need.

   This is one possibility, but there are multiple ways of accomplishing this task.

3. Use the Favorites | Add to Favorites command to add new favorites to the menu. Make sure you select a final location for the link before you create it. Use the Favorites | Organize Favorites command to change the name and location of both links and folders. You can use the Organize Favorites dialog box to delete both links and folders, and well as move them to new locations.

4. NetMeeting allows you to chat, teach, and share ideas with other people over any TCP/IP connection. This means you can share information with someone in the next room, another city, or even another country. You can use NetMeeting with LANs, WANs, MANs, and the Internet. As long as you can create a connection with another Windows user, you can use NetMeeting.

   This is one possibility, but there are multiple ways of accomplishing this task.

Day 5

Quiz

1. Click Reset List in the Newsgroup Subscriptions dialog box. Outlook Express always performs a complete download of the names of the newsgroups that your news server hosts, so the process will take about the same amount of time every time you do it.

2. Click To: on the message dialog box to display the Select Recipients dialog box. Highlight a contact or group in the contacts list and then click Bcc-> to place it in the Bcc list. Using this option will keep the identity of that person secret.

3. Unlike word processing or presentation graphics applications, Outlook Express uses the same generic terms for font sizes that a browser would use. You select one of five sizes from smallest to largest.

Exercises

1. Follow the steps found in the "Creating Newsgroup Accounts" section. You should end up with a display similar to the one in Figure 5.2 when you finish. After you have some newsgroups to look at, use the steps in the "Viewing and Subscribing to Newsgroups" section to add newsgroups to your viewing list. At this point, it's time to enjoy some online conversations.

2. Highlight any e-mail folder within Outlook Express. Click Create Mail. Add recipients to the To:, Cc:, or Bcc: fields. Type a subject. Type your message. Click Send.

3. Highlight the newsgroup in which you want to participate. Click New Post. Type a subject. Type your message. Click Send.

4. Set the View | Current View menu option to Hide Read or Ignored Messages. Toggle the Watch/Ignore column state to match your current preference for the message. You should see a marked reduction in newsgroup traffic. In addition, you should see more messages of interest and be able to find a conversation of special interest with ease.

5. Outlook Express provides many customization features, so it may take awhile for you to find the set of features that work best for you. In most cases, you'll have more success looking through all of the options first, trying them out one at a time, creating a setup that you think you'll like, and then making incremental changes as needed.

This is one possibility, but there are multiple ways of accomplishing this task.

Day 6

Quiz

1. The MouseKeys feature turns your numeric keypad into a mouse cursor-positioning device. It allows precise positioning of the mouse cursor, which means you get precise positioning of graphic elements or text within a document.

2. You can set the Accessibility features using either the Accessibility Wizard or the Accessibility Options dialog box. The Accessibility Options dialog box allows you to set individual features. Use the Accessibility Wizard if you want more help setting the options or if you want to be sure that you don't miss any settings.

3. The two utilities are Notepad and Wordpad. Notepad allows you to create simple text documents that lack any formatting. Use this utility to create batch and script files, as well as edit HTML files. Wordpad does allow you to use formatting. You can create simple documents that contain objects and formatting. While this utility won't replace a word processor, it does work well for simple word processing needs.

Exercises

1. My personal favorites in the Accessibility features arena are MouseKeys and the display modifications. MouseKeys really does make it easy to create precision drawings or move objects around when you're tired. Some people find using them faster than a mouse, but that's a topic for debate. Of course, you can always use MouseKeys in place of a mouse, should yours fail to work. The display features are a welcome relief for tired eyes. The larger characters and lack of distractions keep eye fatigue under control.

   This is one possibility, but there are multiple ways of accomplishing this task.

2. Many people don't realize how many characters they can access with this product. You can find many uses for these characters. For example, they come in handy if you need a special symbol and have poor drawing skills. Some of the fonts, such as Wingdings, consist entirely of special drawings. For example, you can find drawings of computers and mailboxes in this file.

   This is one possibility, but there are multiple ways of accomplishing this task.

3. The Remote Desktop Connection utility allows you to work with another machine as if you were sitting in front of it. This is an important utility for several uses, including training and configuration. You'll want to see how well this utility works for configuration purposes, compared with using the MMC snap-in route. Test it in

A

several different ways to see how well your system holds up to the extra network traffic this product generates.

This is one possibility, but there are multiple ways of accomplishing this task.

Day 7

Quiz

1. Open the Volume Control by double-clicking the Volume icon in the notification area of the Taskbar. Click Mute for each playback device in turn. When the noise or hiss goes away, you've found the likely culprit. If the noise or hiss never goes away, the problem is in the cable going to the speakers or within the speakers themselves.

2. All video and audio media that you place on a CD must use the 44KHz, 16-bit setting. Some applications, such as the Windows Media Player, make these adjustments automatically. In other cases, such as the Sound Recorder, you must make the adjustment manually or convert the sound later. The CD recording process doesn't care if the file is in mono or stereo.

3. The Windows XP CD Writing Wizard only allows you to create data CDs. However, a third party may eventually provide an add-on that enables you to create music CDs as well. All burnable CDs are write-once devices. You can't erase the data they contain once you burn them. Some CD burning programs can create multi-session CDs that allow you to record on different areas of the CD at different times. However, the old data still consumes space, making it a limited use media.

Exercises

1. The Windows Media Player is a lot of fun, besides providing good media management capabilities. You can adjust the Windows Media Player to meet your specific needs. Everything is changeable, including the appearance of the interface. This is one of the few times when learning isn't mutually exclusive with fun.

   This is one possibility, but there are multiple ways of accomplishing this task.

2. Creating an animation is your chance to have a little fun and test your drawing skill. Learning how things move in the real world has many practical benefits because it helps you create practical graphics on screen. The animations I've created have helped in areas such as woodworking and even analyzing problems with my computer (just try figuring out where that strange noise is coming from without knowing how things move).

Slide shows have so many practical uses for both business and pleasure that any attempt to list them all would certainly fail. You can use slide shows to do more than show other people the pictures from your vacation, although that's a good use of the technology. For example, if you're a small business owner, you can use slide shows to help your customers to learn more about your products. The point is that using the Microsoft Movie Maker and a few simple tools can help you create a professional looking presentation for pennies.

This is one possibility, but there are multiple ways of accomplishing this task.

3. Begin by creating some data for your CD. You could do anything from archiving an old project to designing your own content to send to a friend. Use the instructions in the "Recording Your Own CDs" section of the chapter as a guide to creating the CD. Once you finish, enjoy the final product.

This is one possibility, but there are multiple ways of accomplishing this task.

4. Use the settings on the Volume and Audio tabs of the Sounds and Audio Devices dialog box to optimize your sound system. You'll definitely want to use the settings on the Advanced Audio Properties dialog box to adjust your speaker setting and set the level of soundboard performance your system can support.

This is one possibility, but there are multiple ways of accomplishing this task.

Day 8

Quiz

1. Type **MMC** in the Open field of the Run dialog box. Click OK. After MMC starts, you'll see a blank console. Use the File | Add/Remove Snap-in command to display the Add/Remove Snap-in dialog box. Click Add in this dialog box to display a list of snap-ins that you can add to your blank console. Use File | Save to save your console after you add all of the desired snap-ins to it.

2. The three user-controlled elements include memory, processor cycles, and hard drive space. While many other factors contribute to high performance, they usually aren't under user control. For example, the bandwidth of the bus used to transfer data between a display adapter and the processor makes a big difference in graphics performance, but this feature isn't under user control. It pays to buy high performance parts to optimize your setup, but exercising control over memory, processing cycles, and hard drive space can often contribute more than high performance parts alone.

3. Windows XP will add these entries even if you don't have the application installed. For example, you'll often see the Internet Information Services entry even if you don't have Internet Information Server installed. When you click on this entry, it produces an error message because you don't have the service installed. Generally, you can ignore the error message unless you do have the service installed.

4. The ability to set your password hint the same as your password has to be one of the biggest password security holes in Windows XP, at least in the category of user-implemented. The user can set the password and hint the same without thinking about it. In fact, this is one of the truly "accidental" holes in Windows XP because a user could make this mistake without any thought at all. The fact that the network administrator is powerless to prevent this problem makes it even worse. None of the local security policies prevents the user from making the password and the hint the same. In addition, you can't disable the hint feature.

5. The most secure callback is one when the server calls the same number each time. This ensures that the server always calls to the same location and reduces the chance that someone will force the server to call a non-secure location. However, this option also reduces the flexibility of the call-in option. Many users will need to call from other locations, so you'll need to use the Set by Caller option on the Dial-in tab of the User Properties dialog box.

6. You can set the auditing features by using the Advanced Security Settings dialog box that's accessible from the Shares folder. However, you can't set quotas using this snap-in. You must use Quota tab of the Drive Properties dialog box to perform this task.

Exercises

1. MMC is nothing more than a container application designed to hold snap-ins that give it a personality. A console is a combination of MMC and a specific set of snap-ins. Creating your own console allows you to put the tools you use most often together in one place. You can also create custom configurations that answer specific administration needs. Using custom designed consoles can make you more productive and help you see the big picture of your network with greater ease.

   This is one possibility, but there are multiple ways of accomplishing this task.

2. Learning the various ways to perform a task makes network administration easier in the end. In addition, it shows you which tools work better in a particular situation. You should see that the User Accounts applet is easier to use, but limited in scope. While the Local Users and Groups MMC snap-in isn't overly complex, it's

still more difficult, but gives you greater flexibility in determining the user account setup.

This is one possibility, but there are multiple ways of accomplishing this task.

3. Monitor various types of access using the Shares, Session, and Open Files folders. Right-click the entries to see the entries each context menu contains. Open the Properties dialog box to learn what settings you can change from this snap-in. The Shared Folders snap-in contains a lot of hidden functionality that comes in handy when you're monitoring your system.

This is one possibility, but there are multiple ways of accomplishing this task.

4. Part of the performance tuning for your system includes keeping track of hard drive resources and ensuring everyone gets his fair share of this resource. Use auditing to verify the effectiveness of security and drive quotes. Use the quotas to limit the amount of drive space that each user can access.

This is one possibility, but there are multiple ways of accomplishing this task.

Day 9

Quiz

1. You'll modify the SYSOC.INF file found in the \WINDOWS\inf directory of your system. Removing the word HIDE from an entry displays it in the Windows Component Wizard. In some cases, displaying the entry won't allow you to remove it from the system. Windows XP normally prevents you from removing required entries.

2. You'll use the TraceRpt utility to perform the conversion. The output of this file is a SUMMARY.TXT document that shows the number and type of events the log recorded. In addition, you'll see a DUMPFILE.CSV file that you can read into System Monitor or a spreadsheet application such as Excel. In this case, using the spreadsheet application is actually better because you can view the log output easier. A spreadsheet also enables you to manipulate the data for your needs.

3. You need to change the data source from Current Activity to a log or database file on the Source tab of the System Monitor Properties dialog box. You can choose to view a specific interval of time when working with logged data. When working with log files, you'll need to supply a folder and file name. Database files require a data source name (DSN) and a log set.

4. Windows XP will register an error in the application event log if you attempt to send a message to a person or to the current machine. You must ensure that the

recipient is a machine name and that the machine is different from the one on which the Alert resides.

A

Exercises

1. Check both new and old applications on your system. You'll find that new applications generally provide more information than the old ones do. Most new applications tell you when you last used the application, how often you used it, and how much hard drive space the application requires. The drive space indication doesn't tell you about any room required by data files. You should also see a link for obtaining product support. This link opens a dialog box containing a Repair button that will help diagnose problems with your setup. Finally, you should see one or two buttons that allow you to remove or change the application. Use the change option to add or remove application features without changing the entire application.

   This is one possibility, but there are multiple ways of accomplishing this task.

2. Make sure that you spend some time looking at the various counters. Try using counters that will produce a result immediately, such as the counters found in the Processor object. Use different sampling intervals and see how the different views look. Check the properties for each graph and try different configurations. For example, you'll want to see the effects of the horizontal and vertical grids. Finally, try saving your settings to disk and then looking at them with Internet Explorer. You might be surprised at what you find.

   This is one possibility, but there are multiple ways of accomplishing this task.

3. Almost every system has tuning problems. Few applications come out of the box fully tuned to meet your needs and still use resources efficiently. Generally, spending an hour or two to tune a system will net high returns in productivity and system reliability.

   This is one possibility, but there are multiple ways of accomplishing this task.

4. Knowing how to set up a DSN is essential to make some applications work (as we saw for the Counter Logs in this chapter). Unfortunately, many vendor manuals fail to tell you about this requirement or show how to perform it if they do. Creating a DSN isn't difficult, but it can seem difficult until you know what you're doing.

   This is one possibility, but there are multiple ways of accomplishing this task.

Day 10

Quiz

1. No, normally you want Windows to recognize the hardware and tell you that it sees the hardware. The two times you should ignore this rule are when the hardware is old and Windows is unlikely to recognize it, and when the hardware is so new that Windows can't recognize it. Always follow the vendor instructions to the letter when working with hardware because the instructions may differ from those found in this book.

2. The General tab helps you determine the device status. You can also use it to enable or disable the devices as needed. The Driver tab contains driver information. It enables you to add, remove, or roll back device drivers. Use Driver Details to find information on all the drivers used to power the device. Finally, the Resources tab contains a list of all the resources this device uses. You can use this tab to diagnose and fix resource conflicts.

3. You can only use disk compression and file encryption with NTFS formatted disks. FAT and FAT32 formatted disks lack the required features for disk compression. Using compression makes files smaller, which means you can fit more files on a given drive.

4. Open the Regional and Language Options applet and click the Languages tab. Click Details to display the Text Services and Input Languages dialog box. This dialog box shows a hierarchical display of your language choices. Click Add, and you'll see an Add Input Language dialog box. This is where you'll choose Windows language options as well as a keyboard layout.

5. The Pointers tab contains a list of the pointers that Windows XP uses for various needs. For example, you'll see the hourglass used to show Windows XP is busy. The Pointer Options tab contains a list of pointer features. For example, you can select a mouse pointer speed or set up mouse trails to make the mouse easier to see.

Exercises

1. When you start a laptop that contains a NIC but lacks a network connection, Windows XP can register an error saying it can't find the network. The error is minor, but annoying. Removing the NIC from the list of powered devices when you're undocked can circumvent this problem. Removing all unnecessary devices while you're on battery will save power. Many laptop users see a significant power savings, which means extended battery life and longer computing times.

This is one possibility, but there are multiple ways of accomplishing this task.

2. Right-click the floppy drive and choose Format from the context menu. You'll see the Format Disk dialog box. Select the formatting options you want to use and click Start. Windows XP will tell you when it completes the task. You can monitor the progress of the format by watching the progress bar at the bottom of the display.

3. Creating a list of troubleshooting and diagnostic aids can save you a lot of time and headaches when you're in a hurry. This list will become indispensable when your system is down and you need to know ways to fix it quickly. It also pays to become familiar with these utilities. Try them out and see how they work. You need to know an error condition from an anticipated reaction. In short, learn all you can about your machine through Device Manager.

This is one possibility, but there are multiple ways of accomplishing this task.

Day 11

Quiz

1. I seldom place trick questions in the book, but this seemed like a perfect opportunity. The Administrative Tools entry in the Control Panel is actually a folder, not an applet. This folder contains a list of tools used to configure and manage Windows XP. The vast majority of the applets in this folder are MMC snap-ins. The exception to the rule is the Data Sources (ODBC) utility, which allows you to manage your data source connections.

2. Active Directory is a hierarchical database that contains a wealth of information about the network, individual machines, applications, and users. In addition, Active Directory often contains ancillary information required to make the operating system work. Because of the special nature of Active Directory, you need special tools to work with it. This means creating your own MMC consoles under Windows XP. The Active Directory tools provided with Windows 2000 won't work on a Windows XP setup.

3. A service can fail three times before Windows XP will stop trying to start it. You can assign an action to each failure or choose not to do anything at all. Actions include restarting the service, running an application, and restarting the machine.

4. When using standby mode, all of the machine data remains in RAM. In addition, most machine components receive enough power to maintain the content of system memory and the current processing environment. Hibernate mode places all system data on the hard drive. Windows XP shuts the system down so it no longer uses

power. When you restart the machine, the system reads the saved data and settings from the hard drive back into memory.

Exercises

1. Novice users usually find the category view easier to work with. It helps them choose the correct applet and provides the means to use a task-based approach to working with the Control Panel. On the other hand, advanced users normally prefer the classic view because it requires fewer steps to use, and they already know what task each applet performs. Of course, the view you choose depends on how comfortable you feel using the Control Panel and your personal preferences.

   This is one possibility, but there are multiple ways of accomplishing this task.

2. Spending time learning about services now will help you manage your system in a crisis later. Because services form the main connection between many applications and the operating system, you need to know which service to check when an application fails. In addition, you'll want to know how to correct security problems in the service and how to disable it temporarily during maintenance actions.

   This is one possibility, but there are multiple ways of accomplishing this task.

3. Indexing helps you find data quickly. Make sure that you create indexes that actually serve your needs. If you create a massive index of every file on your LAN, you might as well search in real time. It's important to create special purpose indexes for those areas of your network where you only need to search occasionally.

   This is one possibility, but there are multiple ways of accomplishing this task.

4. Some people think that power management is a one-time setting that never changes. However, power use on your system isn't constant. In addition, power conservation needs change as the tasks you perform change. Make sure that you create power schemes for maintenance, normal operation, and special tasks such as long file downloads.

   This is one possibility, but there are multiple ways of accomplishing this task.

Day 12

Quiz

1. Always save the entire registry, or at least the branch you intend to edit, to disk. Use the REG file to create a backup if an edit goes wrong. Also remember that the

REG file is in text format, so you can view it and learn more about registry construction in the interim. You can make every registry edit safe using this simple rule.

2. The (Default) value must appear for every key in the registry. If you highlight this value, you'll notice the Rename option is disabled. While you can select the Delete option, you'll notice that only the value is changed. The (Default) entry remains in place. Microsoft supplied the (Default) value to ensure that developers can query every key for a value and receive a return, even if the return value is empty.

3. Both portions of the file association appear under the HKEY_CLASSES_ROOT key. The first part is the file extension entry. You look for the actual extension used in Windows Explorer. The second part of the file association is the application entry. Look at the (Default) value for the file extension to locate the application type. If you want to change a file association, all you need to do is change the (Default) value for the file extension to the application type you want to use.

4. The number one error is failing to make a backup. If you fail to make a backup before editing the registry, you're betting that the edit will work perfectly the first time. Considering the price of failure, the few seconds required to make a backup is cheap insurance.

Exercises

1. Learning how the registry is constructed is an important part of learning about the registry as a whole. You want to know as much as possible about the registry before you attempt to edit it in any way. When you know enough about the registry, make sure that you learn how to save the registry as a whole and how to save particular branches. The final step is to make small edits as needed to the registry to customize your environment. Working with file associations and application icons is a good place to start because the damage potential is small.

   This is one possibility, but there are multiple ways of accomplishing this task.

2. The only way to become proficient in working with the registry is to perform some safe edits. Using a temporary key allows you to make edits without the fear of "messing something up." Viewing the results of your edits from several perspectives ensures that you completely understand the ramifications of a change. After you work with temporary entries for a while, you can move on to less important edits, such as changes to file associations. Of course, there isn't any "graduation" from registry school. You always have to exercise extreme care in making any

change or face the consequences of an incorrect edit.

This is one possibility, but there are multiple ways of accomplishing this task.

3. Nothing is worse than knowing that the registry contains the data you want but not being able to find it. The search capabilities of the Registry Editor are rudimentary at best, so you need to know how to use the search engine to the best advantage. The recommended way to learn about the search features of the Registry Editor is to try finding values. You might learn something new about the registry in the interim, making it a worthwhile experience from several perspectives.

This is one possibility, but there are multiple ways of accomplishing this task.

4. Save a copy of the registry branch using the instructions in the "Importing and Exporting Registry Data" section. A good backup is your first line of defense against editing errors. Use the directions in the "Modifying File Associations" section to make the changes. Make sure that you choose an application that's compatible with the file extension. If you make a mistake, try to correct it using the backup copy of the registry branch. You can also correct it using the manual method described in the "File Types" section during Day 3.

This is one possibility, but there are multiple ways of accomplishing this task.

Day 13

Quiz

1. Most people use laptops in more than one environment. For example, they might use the laptop as a desktop replacement at work, in which case they may plug the laptop into a docking station. The laptop might see use without a docking station or network connection in a motel room. Plane flights might require use of the laptop on battery power. All of these environments require special profiles to enhance battery life and reduce configuration problems.

2. Failure to follow vendor instructions to the letter is the main problem. Every vendor seems to have a different set of rules for drivers, connections, and connectivity applications. In addition, vendor instructions are often unclear and difficult to follow. Make sure that you call the vendor if you don't understand the instructions provided.

3. Type **"AT"** test commands in the HyperTerminal window. Most commands will respond with an output of OK. If you forget which commands your modem supports, use the AT$H command to display a help screen.

4. The Wireless Link applet helps you configure IrDA communications. The dialog

box contains a minimum of three tabs. The Infrared tab sets the communication properties for the port. You'll use the Image Transfer tab to enable communications with a camera and other alternative input devices. Finally, the Hardware tab lists the wireless hardware on your machine. It contains buttons that help you to troubleshoot or change the properties of your IrDA port.

5. Briefcase maintains a copy of your data. It synchronizes this data with the original on request. The folder contains a Briefcase menu that contains the synchronization options. This menu also contains the Split from Original option that orphans a file you don't want to update on the desktop machine.

Exercises

1. Laptops are the one device that should always have more than one defined profile because users employ laptops in more than one environment. Make sure that you create an "on battery" profile as a minimum to enhance the battery life of your machine while on the road. A good "on battery" profile should get rid of non-essential devices, like the soundboard and NIC. You should also look at eliminating devices such as modems. Most laptops can provide increased battery life if you reduce the number of power-robbing peripherals.

   This is one possibility, but there are multiple ways of accomplishing this task.

2. Admittedly, Windows XP provides a myriad of ways to connect two machines. For example, you could use Remote Desktop to create the connection. However, sometimes the low-tech approach presented by HyperTerminal is best because it allows you to make a connection under adverse conditions. You don't need a high-speed connection to use HyperTerminal—almost any connection will do.

   This is one possibility, but there are multiple ways of accomplishing this task.

3. Briefcase offers features such as file synchronization that make it easier to work on data using two machines. A laptop definitely benefits from having this feature installed. Make sure that you try using both folders and individual files so that you can determine which is easier to use.

   This is one possibility, but there are multiple ways of accomplishing this task.

Day 14

Quiz

1. A client is a user of resources. It's an endpoint on the network. Every network requires a unique client because every network issues and uses resources in a dif-

ferent way. As a result, you need to know the client requirements of your network before you begin a network installation.

2. Biometrics is a technique for identifying an individual user based on the unique characteristics of a body part. The most common scanning methods today include using fingerprints and the iris. However, scanned characteristics can also include voiceprints, hands, and facial features. In the future, it may be possible to use other unique characteristics or to use features in combination.

3. The main reason to use a network-ready device is to eliminate the need for a dedicated file, print, or communication server. Because you're cutting out the server, you'll find that you can share peripherals at a reduced cost and that device configuration is much easier than with a server. However, it's also important to remember the caveats of using a network-ready device that we discussed in the "Working with Network-Ready Devices" section.

4. The RIP Listener enables a satellite machine to build a routing table of remote machine locations. Using the routing tables reduces the time required to locate a remote machine and send it data. The main timesaving occurs because your machine won't waste time sending packets to the wrong router. Your machine knows the best and most efficient route to send the packets.

5. Many organizations are using disconnected applications today. Disconnected applications allow a user to continue working, even if they don't have a network connection. Queued Components represents one of many technologies used to implement disconnected applications. In short, from a user perspective, Queued Components is a productivity aid.

Exercises

1. Unfortunate as it may seem, Windows XP provides little to no help in understanding the features on the Advanced tab of the NIC Properties dialog box. This means you must spend time with the vendor manual. In some cases, it also means spending a little time in research on the Internet. However, optimizing your NIC means increasing potential network throughput. This makes both the workstation and the network as a whole faster. It also means you'll use bandwidth more effectively.

This is one possibility, but there are multiple ways of accomplishing this task.

2. All Universal Plug and Play compatible devices also provide a network-ready device mode of operation because many users don't have access to an operating system that provides the required support. After you install Universal Plug and Play support for a compatible device, you'll notice that you can configure the device with greater ease. In addition, the device provides you with more status

information, and you might find that maintenance is easier as well. In short, Universal Plug and Play is a big win for both network administrator and user—when it works.

This is one possibility, but there are multiple ways of accomplishing this task.

3. Windows XP doesn't install SNMP support by default, so you'll have to install the support. This includes configuring the SNMP Service. Make sure that you include agent information, as well as traps and security entries. The next task is to create an event file. You can create this file entirely by hand, but using the Event to Trap Translator (EVNTWIN.EXE) is much easier. Export your entries from the Event to Trap Translator and use a text editor to add a destination for event messages. Finally, use the EVNTCMD utility to make changes to the SNMP setup and begin generating event messages.

This is one possibility, but there are multiple ways of accomplishing this task.

Day 15

Quiz

1. Use the Network Setup Wizard to create small networks consisting of just a few machines. This wizard won't help you create complex network setups. The novice user who lacks any previous networking experience will gain the most from this utility.

2. Use the Allow Callers to Set the Callback Number option for callers on the road who may call from a different location each night. However, the Always Use the Following Callback Number option is even more secure because it forces the user to call from the same number every time. Avoid using the Do Not Allow Callback option, whenever possible, to avoid the security problems it invites.

3. The NETSH command line utility not only helps you configure RAS, but it also provides options for viewing RAS configuration. Several of the options can save you time and effort configuring other machines. For example, you can use the DUMP command to create a script that contains the local machine settings. If you edit the resulting file to remove machine-specific entries, you can configure other machines with a simple script.

4. A dial-up connection relies on a direct telephone connection. The VPN connection tunnels through the Internet. Both connection types enable communication with a company network.

5. DMI relies on SMS to perform all of the work. SMS reads the contents of the MIF

file for each piece of compatible equipment on your machine. It records this information in a SQL Server database in the server. The database acts as a repository of information you can use for a variety of needs, including checking your network for compatibility concerns before a software upgrade.

Exercises

1. Use the information found in the "Building a Network" section to create a new network or document an existing network. Make sure that you include the network layout, equipment specifications, and workgroup responsibilities in the plan. It's also important to collect the documentation for each computer in a place where you can find it and you won't mix it up with documentation for other computers. Begin creating logs of maintenance actions for your network.

   This is one possibility, but there are multiple ways of accomplishing this task.

2. Creating connections from home is becoming ever more important as people work one or two days a week from a home office. Not only do home offices reduce traffic and environmental problems, but also most employers find employees are more productive when they work from home. Windows XP provides many ways to create a connection between your home and office; RAS is just one of the answers. However, trying the various solutions that Windows XP provides is the only way to determine which connection works best for your situation.

   This is one possibility, but there are multiple ways of accomplishing this task.

3. This is another situation when knowing how to make a connection can save the day. One of the most common connections in the world is the direct machine-to-machine serial port connection. You connect two machines together with a serial cable and NULL modem device. Even machines that can't talk to each other in any form can use this connection type to exchange text data. I've often had to rely on dial-up or infrared connections to exchange data with other machines. In fact, when I first received my PocketPC, the USB port wouldn't work, so I used an infrared connection instead to exchange data.

   This is one possibility, but there are multiple ways of accomplishing this task.

Day 16

Quiz

1. Assigning security by using groups reduces the workload for a network administrator and makes it less likely that you'll have user-oriented security holes. Creating groups forces the people responsible for security to think about the dynamics of

security for their organization. Finally, using groups assigns security evenly. One person doesn't end up with more rights than someone else in the same position within the company. Security, above all else, must manage users equally and fairly.

2. You never have a good reason to use the Password never expires option. Local and group policies should force users to change their password regularly. Changing the password often will help keep crackers at bay. In addition, there's never a good reason for using the User cannot change password option. Doing so removes responsibility for the account from the user's shoulders to those of the network administrator. You must keep the user involved in security efforts if you want the security plan for your company to succeed.

3. Use the Effective Permissions tab of the Advanced Security Settings dialog box. All you need to do is enter the name of the user or group that you want to test and Windows XP will show you its effective permissions to the current resource. This includes any permissions the user or group inherits from a higher level of the resource hierarchy.

4. Open the Encrypting File System folder. You'll see a list of certificates on your system. Right-click the certificate you want to export; then choose All Tasks | Export from the context menu. Follow the Certificate Export Wizard prompts to complete the task.

Exercises

1. One of the biggest problems that many companies face is failing to understand their security needs. However, knowing your security needs is only part of the answer. You also need to spell out security requirements, emergency procedures, and punitive measures for those who fail to follow the rules. Managing your security is essential in an age when crackers seem to break in everywhere and companies demand more security daily.

   This is one possibility, but there are multiple ways of accomplishing this task.

2. Use the information in the "Security Considerations for User Accounts" section to check your user accounts for problems. For example, you want to verify that every account maximizes the use of groups. Make sure that you log every individual setting so you can find them quickly. Finally, make sure that all users have access to resources they need, but avoid giving users access to other resources on the network. Remember, the best way to keep a secret is not to tell anyone.

   This is one possibility, but there are multiple ways of accomplishing this task.

3. Use the content of the "Managing File/Folder Access" and the "Encrypting Data on Your Hard Drive" sections to validate drive security. Make sure that you test user

and group effective rights and perform any required auditing. Try to use group security exclusively. A physical audit of your system can reveal significant flaws in security. You want to plug as many of these security holes as possible.

This is one possibility, but there are multiple ways of accomplishing this task.

4. Use the ideas presented in the "Setting Local Security Policy" section to refine your local security policy. In addition, use the tips in the "Overcoming Windows Security Deficiencies" and the "Tips for Thwarting Crackers Inside and Out" sections to make your system more secure. Of course, the bottom line is that policies, system configuration tricks, and upgrades can only go so far. You also have to have a monitoring and management plan in place.

This is one possibility, but there are multiple ways of accomplishing this task.

Day 17

Quiz

1. Samba is available for the Linux and Unix platforms at a minimum. The entire list is presented at the first of this chapter.

2. SMB stands for Server Message Block, and it is a networking protocol that has been used for many years in various network operating systems.

3. RedHat and Mandrake use the RPM or RedHat Package Manager application to install, upgrade, and verify software packages. RPM is available on other Linux distributions, and it offers a convenient way to install new software on your Linux computer.

4. smbclient is the name of the application that allows you to access Windows servers or computers from your Linux computer. smbclient allows the use of various commands to copy files to and from a Windows computer, as well as directory navigation.

5. Linux uses the Octal numbering system for file and directory permissions. You use the chmod program and the appropriate octal number to set permissions.

Exercises

1. Change to the /etc/rc.d/init.d directory on the Linux computer and issue the commands:

```
./smb stop
./smb start
```

2. Open a Web browser and enter `https://ipaddressofsambaserver:10000`.

Locate the SWAT icon under the Samba configuration options in Servers. Browse to the Passwords page and add a new user.

3. Issue the command, "smbclient '\\computername\sharename' –U username%password." Use dir to get a directory listing and use get to transfer a file from the XP computer to the Linux computer.

Day 18

Quiz

1. Many people will try to subdue banner pages using the Separator Page option on the Advanced tab of the Printer Properties dialog box. Although this feature does control banner pages for Windows XP, it won't affect banner pages for NetWare. You need to clear the Print Banner options of the Client Service for NetWare (CSNW) applet instead.

2. NetWare provides four levels of login script. The container script comes first. It controls the settings for all of the users in an organization or an organizational unit. The profile script comes next. It controls the settings for users of a certain type. For example, you might create a profile for all accountants who work on accounts receivable. The user script comes third. NetWare processes this login script after all of the other login scripts. The user login script contains unique user settings. NetWare also provides a default login script for users who have no script associated with their account.

3. Novell provides two namespaces for long filename support. The first is OS2.NAM. You'll use this support for any server that uses versions of NetWare older than version 5. The second is LONG.NAM. This is the version you'll use for NetWare 5 and above.

4. Every queued setup includes a print server, printer, and queue. The print server is at the top of the hierarchy and manages the printer. The printer comes next. It sends data to the print queue. Using a print queue enables the print setup to work faster and handle more users.

Exercises

1. You'll find that the NetWare client provides robust user environment with access to a number of settings the Microsoft client doesn't provide. This is also your only choice if you're using IP on a NetWare 5.x (or above) server because the Microsoft client only supports IPX. As a minimum, you'll want to install the NetWare client on network administrator machines so that the network administrator has full

server access.

This is one possibility, but there are multiple ways of accomplishing this task.

2. NetWare Administrator is the central tool for working with NetWare versions 4.x and above. You need to know how to create new objects, delete old objects, and configure existing objects. Every object has at least one page of information. However, most, like the user object, have several pages, so you need to know where to find specific information when you're in a hurry. Practicing with temporary objects is one of the best ways to learn NetWare Administrator. Think up test scenarios and figure out the least number of steps for accomplishing the task.

This is one possibility, but there are multiple ways of accomplishing this task.

3. Use the procedure found in the "Installing Long Filename Support" section to add long filename support. Make sure you bring down the server and restart it to ensure that the support loads. In addition, log off NetWare and log back in from your workstation. Finally, test the support by creating new files containing long filenames.

4. Use the procedures found in the NetWare Printer Support to add either queued or NDPS support to your server. Install the printer on your workstation using the procedures found in the "Printer Installation" section of Day 10. Make sure that you configure and test the printer support after you install it on the workstation.

Day 19

Quiz

1. The Files and Settings Transfer Wizard doesn't have a network setting, so it's not something you can select directly from the wizard. However, you can save files to any drive on your system, even a network drive. The easiest way to perform a network transfer is to save the files to a network drive on the old machine and then select that same network drive on the new machine. Of course, you can't perform a simultaneous transfer this way, but it's still faster than using a serial cable.

2. Windows XP provides support for both VBScript and JavaScript. However, you can also add support for languages such as Perl by downloading other packages from the Internet. The extensibility of WSH is an important feature for many users.

3. You can store the information on floppies or on a common drive, such as a network drive. The wizard also provides the means to use a serial cable connection. Unlike the media storage methods, using a serial connection enables a live connection that occurs on both machines simultaneously. This makes the serial method faster than

A

floppies, but the serial method is still slower than using a common network drive.

4. You'll find the Task Scheduler log entries in the SCHEDLGU.TXT file in the \Windows folder. Make sure that you use a program like WordPad to read this file because it's in a Unicode format.

5. The Synchronize utility helps you manage offline content and determines when Windows XP will refresh that content. You have a choice of updating during logon or logoff, during idle time, or at a time you schedule using the Schedule tab of the Synchronization Settings dialog box. Every piece of offline content also has individual settings that you can adjust to meet specific needs.

Exercises

1. Both scripting languages provide features that enable anyone to automate tasks. All you need is access to either WScript or CScript to run your application. Make sure that you provide some type of output command so that you can see the results of running the script.

   This is one possibility, but there are multiple ways of accomplishing this task.

2. Task Scheduler provides several interfaces that help you automate tasks. You can use the AT (character mode) interface at the command prompt. The AT interface is also the best selection when you want to schedule tasks using a script. The GUI interface is easier to use if you want to schedule tasks manually. It pays to know how to use both interfaces so that you have the tools required to work in various administrative and user settings.

   This is one possibility, but there are multiple ways of accomplishing this task.

3. Scripting provides the means to perform tasks that Microsoft didn't program into Windows XP. For example, today we looked at a simple program that displays information about WSH. You can also use scripts to read the registry and perform other low-level tasks. Combining scripting with the Task Scheduler means you can create a form of automation that's both flexible and reliable. Your script will run as needed without your intervention.

   This is one possibility, but there are multiple ways of accomplishing this task.

Day 20

Quiz

1. If you check the Enable Content Expiration option found on the HTTP Headers tab of the Web Site Properties dialog box, IIS will include expiration information with

each Web page it uploads to a client. The next time the client requests the Web page, the browser will compare the current date with the expiration date of the Web page. If the Web page has expired, then the browser downloads a new copy.

2. The NCSA Common Log Format is a Web server logging format developed by the National Center for Supercomputing Applications. The benefit of using this format is that Apache and other servers use it as well. You can use the same analysis tools for all the servers in a particular system, regardless of operating system. The disadvantage is that the NCSA Common Log Format consumes more space than other logging formats.

3. The Virtual Directory tab is actually a renamed form of the Home Directory tab. You'll use this tab to identify the physical location of the directory and set directory security.

4. Windows XP Professional Edition doesn't provide NNTP support, even though you'll find the option for creating an NNTP server in the Internet Information Services snap-in. The only time you could support an NNTP server using Windows XP Professional Edition is if you see a Network News Transport Protocol (NNTP) entry in the Services snap-in.

5. Use Narrator to read the Web page back to you. Hearing the words often helps you find errors in both spelling and grammar. In addition, Narrator will also point out flaws in the tags and other "hidden" features of your Web site.

Exercises

1. You can use IIS to create test Web pages that you can view in your browser, just like you can online. Having a local server to test the pages before you upload them helps you make fewer mistakes in Web page design. It also allows you to test new ideas. Make sure that you check the global and Web site configuration at a minimum.

   This is one possibility, but there are multiple ways of accomplishing this task.

2. Learn to create a Web site setup that makes it easy to find information that will attract people to your site. You want to be certain to use a hierarchical design of folders so you an protect information and keep it well organized. Using just one layer for all of your Web pages will almost certainly result in chaos for both user and you.

   This is one possibility, but there are multiple ways of accomplishing this task.

3. Working with Web pages is equal parts technology and art. A good Web page is both easy to use and aesthetically pleasing. You need to perform all of the little tasks like checking the spelling of your document. Check the size of any images

on the page to ensure they aren't too large t download. You'll also want to try several Web page editors. There are few wrong choices when it comes to editors, but you'll find that you have a preference based on feature set. If you decide to work with many Web pages, you'll want to buy a professional tool to do the job. Many shareware products are a good place to start, but they don't provide the functionality of the commercial products.

This is one possibility, but there are multiple ways of accomplishing this task.

Day 21

Quiz

1. The Disk Cleanup utility helps you remove files that you no longer need from the hard drive. It's important to understand that this tool is a simple aid in optimizing your drive. You can still remove files that you didn't really intend to remove. That's why the Disk Cleanup utility includes so many options for verifying what you'll remove before you actually remove anything.

2. The System Configuration utility controls the way that Windows XP boots. This utility has settings that adjust the boot configuration, determine which services start, and which applications load. Using the System Configuration utility to disable and enable boot options, services, and applications helps you diagnose the problem; or, at least, find the responsible application.

3. The System Information utility provides a detailed view of your system. The first display you'll see is the system summary. Below the system summary are four classifications of information including Hardware, Components, Software Environment, and Internet Settings. Each of these classifications breaks down further to provide you with detailed information in easy-to-understand pieces.

4. A loopback plug works with your diagnostic program to test the ports on your machine fully. A diagnostic program can normally test the internal circuitry of a port, but it can't test the port connection to the outside world. The loopback plug sends a single from an output connector pin back through an input connector pin. By checking the signals, the diagnostic program can detect problems in the connections between the port and the outside world.

5. A time domain reflectometer (TDR) is just another name for a cable scanner. A cable scanner locates breaks or other flaws in network cable by sending a signal on the cable and waiting for it to return. The time required for the two-way trip determines the distance to the flaw. All you need to do is locate that distance from the starting point and you can fix the problem.

Exercises

1. Creating a backup of your system is one of the most important tasks you can perform. Your data is the most valuable commodity on your network, so protecting it
   is important. Make sure that you address the details. For example, clean and
   inspect your tape drive as often as needed to ensure a good backup. Replace tapes
   as they wear and age. Finally, replace your backup system when it shows any sign
   of aging, rather than risk your data.

   This is one possibility, but there are multiple ways of accomplishing this task.

2. Most people don't realize how vulnerable their computer is to dust until the system
   fails. The fact that your system always chooses to fail at the worst possible moment
   is perhaps an indicator that you needed to observe its behavior more closely. A
   clean machine also yields benefits to you. For one thing, a clean machine makes
   less noise. You'll also find that a clean machine is easier to use—the screen is clear
   and the mouse moves freely.

3. Diagnostic programs often find problems with your system long before they
   become apparent through casual use. This is especially true of mechanical parts. A
   hard drive often shows an increase in data errors and an increase in lost sectors
   before it finally fails. Memory displays similar bit errors as it begins to age and
   fail. Display adapters and monitors will begin to have problems passing the various
   color bar tests and will show signs of distorting output. Using a diagnostic program
   regularly helps you listen to your system and make unexpected problems a thing of
   the past.

   This is one possibility, but there are multiple ways of accomplishing this task.

APPENDIX B

52 Productivity Tips that Really Work

Most of us are constantly looking for new and interesting ways to do our work faster. After all, getting the job done quickly leaves more time to enjoy life. However, fast isn't always better. Sometimes, a slower way of doing something nets gains in quality. In addition, getting the task done quickly might cost you more time further down the road. In short, productivity isn't always about getting the job done fast. It's about getting the job done in a way that costs less time and effort overall, without affecting quality.

This appendix contains 52 tips that will make you more productive using Windows XP. There is one tip for each week of the year. Not all of them will make you work faster. In fact, some of them might take more time than what you're doing now.

It's important to realize that some of these tips won't fit your work style. You'll still want to try them, though. Some of the best tips I've ever received changed the way I worked in some way. With this in mind, here are my 52 favorite productivity tips for Windows XP:

> **Note**   I love to hear from readers. If you have a favorite productivity tip that you'd like to share with me, send it my way at JMueller@mwt.net.

1. Try all the interface options that Windows XP has to offer. Use the interface that works best for you. Many people find the simplified interface the best choice if they use the same small set of applications each day.

2. After you complete setting up your system (including applications), create a complete backup, including the registry. Use this backup to restore your applications and settings to reduce the time for getting your system back into a pristine state. This way, you can use the backup to restore your applications after you reformat the drive.

3. Use printer fonts whenever possible. A printer usually prints its internal fonts faster than those it downloads. Using this technique also reduces the memory and processing requirements for the print job. Of course, you do give up some flexibility to use this technique.

4. Visit Paul Thurrott's SuperSite for Windows (http://www.winsupersite.com/) to get news, reviews, FAQs, and other information about Windows XP.

5. TweakXP (http://www.tweakxp.com/) is the latest version of the TweakUI product that first appeared in Windows 95. You can use this utility to make small changes to the display and other areas of your system that would normally require registry edits.

6. If you regularly use some Control Panel applets, such as the Fonts applet, place a shortcut to it on the desktop or within the Quick Launch toolbar on the taskbar. You'll find that you can access the applet more quickly and with less effort. Of course, you don't want to clutter either the desktop or the Quick Launch toolbar with so many shortcuts that they become ineffective.

7. You'll find many of the default images that Windows XP uses in the \WINDOWS\system32\oobe\images folder. To modify these images, you'll need a graphics application that supports modern file format, such as PNG. You'll also find animate GIF and JPG files in this folder, all of which affect the appearance of Windows XP.

8. Double-click on any folder entry in the Start menu, and you can open it as a stand-alone Explorer view. This is handy if you want to perform maintenance on just one section of the Start menu.

9. Windows XP uses the Favorites folder for storing pointers to just about everything. For example, you'll find the Help and Support Center uses this feature. Keep your

Favorites folder uncluttered by creating a special folder for each application that uses Favorites, rather than place the application-specific pointers in the general list of Web locations.

10. Looking for that special site containing more multimedia enhancements for Windows XP? Try out the Ultimate Windows Whistler Resource Site (`http://ultimateresourcesite.com/whistler/main.htm`).

11. Sometimes, you'll make a change to an Explorer folder and won't see the change immediately. Always try refreshing the display by right-clicking anywhere in a clear area of the folder and then choosing Refresh from the context menu. This feature also works in many areas that you might not consider Explorer specific, such as the desktop.

12. Sometimes, you'll want to check your system's performance level after an application or hardware install. If you open the Windows Task Manager, it normally stays on top and makes it difficult to work. However, you can minimize this dialog box to the taskbar. You'll see an icon containing the current CPU usage level in the notification area of the taskbar, giving you a quick indicator of system activity.

13. Save yourself some time and effort learning how to design Web pages and sites. Webmonkey (`http://hotwired.lycos.com/webmonkey/`) provides tutorials on a wealth of Web page design issues. Order their free electronic newsletter (`http://www.hotwired.com/email/signup/webmonkey.html`) and you'll get a weekly dose of great information for the Internet.

14. Windows XP provides a versatile environment for your applications. For example, you can drag an application icon from the Start menu into a WordPad document, and Windows XP will create a link of that type within the WordPad document. Of course, the application you use to hold the icon must be an OLE container application, and the application you place in the document must be an OLE server.

15. Keep the Registry Editor (and other utilities) out of the hands of those who won't know how to use it by assigning it better security. The default Windows XP setup allows users to both read and execute the Registry Editor, making it possible for them to damage their setup. Limiting Registry Editor access to administrators will prevent this from happening.

16. Always right-drag (click and drag using the right mouse button rather than the left) objects you want to copy or move within Windows. This allows you to change your mind or correct movement errors by using the context menu that Windows provides. You can also see the range of actions you can perform with the object. In some situations, you can do more than the usual move, copy, or create a shortcut.

17. Use the accessibility features to reduce fatigue. For example, if you find yourself rubbing your eyes at the end of a long day, try the high-contrast screens provided

for accessibility users. You'll find that they're easier on the eyes. It's also helpful to use features such as MouseKeys to keep your mouse cursor under control, especially when you need to make small adjustments to a drawing or perform other intricate tasks.

18. If you find that you're addicted to themes for your desktop but don't like the interface Microsoft provides for managing them, try Theme Doctor (`http://www.themedoctor.com/cafe_pg.shtml`). This Web site also provides reviews of other third-party products, such as the XrX Animated Logo utility.

19. Many applications provide a command line interface that vendors don't document in their manuals but do document as part of the application itself. In many cases, you can learn about these "secret" features by typing the name of the application at the command prompt and adding a question mark.

20. Windows XP lacks a usable FTP application—one that's functional and includes a graphical interface. You could use either the FTP command line utility or Internet Explorer, but many people want something better. Two good alternatives include FTP Explorer (`http://www.ftpx.com`) and WS_FTP Pro (`http://www.ipswitch.com/Products/WS_FTP/`).

21. Whenever you purchase a new piece of hardware for your machine, look for the Windows XP certification. If you can't find a certification (meaning Microsoft has not checked the hardware for compatibility), check with the vendor to ensure that they provide Windows XP-specific drivers. In many cases, older drivers, even those for Windows 2000, won't work.

22. Perform regular maintenance on your machine to reduce problems later. Small businesses should make daily backups, perform diagnostics and disk defragmentation weekly, and clean the machines monthly. Home users will want to make weekly backups, perform diagnostics and disk defragmentation once a month, and clean the machine quarterly (every three months). Of course, the level of use your machine receives determines the level of support it requires.

23. Most keyboards today have a Windows key (it has a little Windows flag on it) and a context menu key (it shows what looks like a menu). These two keys can really help if you lose your mouse support. Using these keys along with the standard Windows shortcuts will help you shut your machine down or gain access to the Mouse applet. To shut your system down using just the keyboard, press Windows, use the arrow keys to select Shut Down, and press Enter. Use the arrow keys to select a shut-down mode and press Enter to shut the computer down.

24. The Internet Explorer Administration Kit (IEAK) can save you significant time in customizing settings. This is especially helpful for network administrators who

have many systems to configure. Find out more at
`http://www.microsoft.com/windows/ieak/downloads/ieak6/default.asp`.

25. The computer industry uses a lot of jargon. In fact, you'll see a lot of jargon in this book. Make sure that you use the Glossary in the back of the book to answer your jargon questions. You'll also find some Web sites listed in the Glossary that will help you find terms and acronyms the Glossary doesn't list. The point is to ensure that you actually understand what someone is saying to you or what you're reading. Misunderstood jargon often leads to disaster.

26. Many users reduce the screen resolution when they have a hard time seeing print on the display. Unfortunately, that choice is also hard on the eyes because you can see more of the jagged edges of the fonts. Instead of making the resolution lower, make the fonts larger. You can do this using the individual font options in the Advanced Appearance dialog box. You can also use the DPI setting on the Display Adapter Settings dialog box (accessible using the Advanced button on the Settings tab of the Display Properties dialog box).

27. To keep your system secure from internal threats, change your password regularly (at least once a month). Use complex passwords that include uppercase and lowercase letters, numbers, and special characters. Increase external security by using virus checkers and firewalls. You'll also want to apply any patches that the software or hardware vendor supplies. Crackers often make use of the security holes they find the second someone publishes the security hole information.

28. Now that Windows XP has so many multimedia features, you'll want to make use of them. We explored several multimedia options during Day 7. One of the places we didn't look at was MP3.COM (`http://www.mp3.com/`). This site has quite a few tips and provides multimedia news, along with the requisite downloads.

29. Most performance tuning isn't a matter of spending absurd quantities of time studying arcane statistics. The best performance tuning relies on simple premises. If your system has enough memory, you'll see a performance gain over someone using a memory-starved system. Keeping your machine free of extra data and performing disk defragmentation as needed both improve performance. You can learn additional performance tips during Day 3.

30. If you can't find a driver you need for Windows XP and the vendor is being less than helpful, try Web sites that specialize in driver management. The three I normally check include Driverzone.com (`http://www.driverzone.com/`), Totally Drivers (`http://www.totallydrivers.com/`), and WinDrivers (`http://www.windrivers.com/`).

31. Learn to use emoticons in your e-mail and newsgroup messages. Emoticons replace body language that written forms of communication lack. The use of

emoticons is so prevalent on the Internet that some vendors, like AOL, include them as part of their product. If you're using a product that doesn't support emoticons natively, you can still add them manually using standard keys. Two of the better emoticon sites are Smileys for E-mail Communication (`http://www.windweaver.com/emoticon.htm`) and The Original Emoticon Site (`http://www.angelfire.com/hi/hahakiam/emoticon.html`).

32. Many people experiment with their systems. This is actually good because it helps everyone in the end. However, some people experiment without making a proper backup first. Always back up anything you plan to change. It doesn't matter if the change is in a directory or in the registry. Make sure that the unmodified data resides in a separate directory or, better yet, a separate machine.

33. It's always nice to know something about a piece of hardware before you buy it. Tom's Hardware (`http://www.tomshardware.com/`) is the place to go for hardware-specific information. You'll find the latest news, reviews, and tips for making your hardware work. You'll also want to try WinOScentral (http://www.winoscentral.com) if you want the latest news, reviews, and other information about both hardware and software for Windows XP.

34. Start your day right. Let your computer set up your desktop for you by placing items you'll work on in the Startup folder of the Start menu the night before. Windows XP will automatically open the files for you when it starts the next day. All you need to do is begin working.

35. The Internet runs on standards, as do many things in the computer industry. The problem is finding out which standard applies in a given situation. One of the best places to find standards information is the Internet RFC/FYI/STD/BCP Archives (`http://www.faqs.org/rfcs/`).

36. One of the first places to check if you're having problems with dial-up networking is the TCP/IP address of your machine. Right-click on the Local Area Connection in the Network Connections folder and choose Status from the context menu. You'll see a Local Area Connection Status dialog box. Select the Support tab, and you'll see the IP address for your machine. Generally, if you can't get the client and the host machine to link up, you need to reboot the host machine and then reboot the client. The client should accept an IP address from the host after both machines reboot.

37. Never assume anything about the security setup on a Windows machine. Always verify that you have the proper settings for your networking needs. The default settings often leave you wide open for attack, even though Windows provides the functionality to protect your system from a given threat.

38. Windows XP contains a wealth of animated files in the form of GIF and PNG files. The only way to edit these files properly is to use an application that works with such files. The GIF Construction Set and the PNG/MNG Construction Set by Alchemy Mindworks, Inc. (`http://www.mindworkshop.com/ alchemy/alchemy.html`) perform these tasks well. You can download shareware versions from their Web site, and the registration fees are very reasonable. You'll also want to try the shareware version of Paintshop Pro from Jasc, Inc. (`http://www.jasc.com/`), which offers support for a broad range of graphic types.

39. Look for added bonuses on the context menus of objects you work with under Windows XP. Most objects provide standard entries, but you'll find additional entries as well. For example, right-click the Recycle Bin, and you'll see an Empty Recycle Bin option.

40. Lock as many system elements as you can after you're happy with their configuration to avoid accidental changes. For example, you can lock both the taskbar and the desktop to avoid configuration changes.

41. It's important to keep up-to-date on PC developments, especially those that affect your Windows XP setup. You'll find a wealth of free electronic newsletters that will help you learn more about Windows XP while keeping you informed about Windows XP developments. The three electronics newsletters that many people turn to include W2KNews (`http://www.w2knews.com/subscribe.cfm?id=W2K`), InfoWorld (`http://www.iwsubscribe.com/`), and eWeek (`http://enewsletters.ziffdavis.com/pc_subscribe.asp?SubID=44`).

42. Keep all of your graphics for a project in a single folder. Windows XP generally selects the Thumbnail view if it sees all graphics in a folder so that you can glimpse the content of your files without making changes to the interface. Using a single folder for some file types also helps you keep them organized.

43. If you need an update or patch for Windows XP or a related Microsoft product but don't see it on Windows update, try looking at the Microsoft.com Download Center (`http://www.microsoft.com/downloads/search.asp`). This site provides a search engine that you can use to locate downloads by product name or operating system.

44. Never open e-mail attachments directly in Outlook Express. Save the attachment to disk first, conduct a virus check on it, and only open the attachment if you feel it's safe to do so. Clearing the Hide extensions for known file types entry on the View tab of the Folder Options dialog box will further enhance your ability to detect scripts posing as data.

45. Looking for a hard-to-find piece of shareware? Try finding it at C/Net Download.com (`http://download.cnet.com/`). This site caters to everyone. I've even found great software for the Macintosh on this site. This is also a great place to find add-ons for your Linux system. Speaking of places to find shareware, try Dave Central (http://www.davecentral.com) for both Windows and Linux shareware.

46. Sometimes, you'll find that Windows won't recognize a CD or DVD that you place in the drive. You've double-checked to make sure that the CD or DVD is in the drive correctly, but it still refuses to play. More often than not, there's a fingerprint somewhere on the CD or DVD that's interfering with normal operation. Carefully clean the CD or DVD and try it again.

47. Windows application developers go through a certification process as part of getting the Windows logo. The only problem is that the Microsoft logo requirements have changed with each new version of Windows. This means that the only way you can be sure that an application will run on Windows XP is if it has a Windows XP logo. Fortunately, Windows XP does provide a higher level of compatibility than Windows NT or Windows 2000, so you should have a minimum of problems.

48. Do you need to find something you remember seeing on an FTP site long ago? The problem with most search engines is they don't help you with FTP sites. Fortunately, FTP Search (`http://ftpsearch.lycos.com/ ftpsearch?form=medium`) helps you find everything FTP on the Internet.

49. Sometimes, you'll need to capture a screenshot for your Web site or other use. You don't have to have expensive software to do it. Use Ctrl+Print Screen to capture the entire desktop. If you only want the current window, use Alt+Print Screen. Paste the resulting image into a word processor or graphics application. You can also paste the image into applications such as FrontPage Express.

50. When working with a PDA, always read the vendor documentation before you connect it to the PC. In some cases, the vendor wants you to install the PDA first and then install the software. Other vendors require you to install the software first. In most cases, you'll find that a serial port connection is the least worrisome, wireless connections come next, and USB connections are last.

51. During Day 7 we looked at all of the standard media features that Windows XP provides. Most vendors provide additional settings for their hardware. For example, a soundboard vendor might provide settings to adjust the 3D effects that the soundboard can produce. Likewise, graphics vendors often provide settings to adjust the color levels and lighting effects that the video card can provide. Make sure that you learn about these additional features to gain full benefit from your hardware.

52. Use folders on the desktop to hold project items in one place. Even if the files appear in other areas of your network, you'll find what you need quickly and easily. The data view of handling your projects keeps files together.

B

APPENDIX C

Top Ten Windows Web Sites Exposed

You'll literally find hundreds, perhaps thousands, of Windows Web sites. Each site has an orientation, a way in which it can help you use Windows better. Not every site provides high-quality information, though, so sifting through Web sites that don't tell you much to find the one that does can be a frustrating experience.

This appendix contains a list of the ten Web sites that I visit most often. They may not meet every need you have, but you'll find them packed with some of the best Windows material around. In all cases, the Web site owner spends time verifying the facts and updating the information presented. In a few cases, you'll also find some level of peer support that you can use in addition to the newsgroups. The ten Web sites don't appear in any particular order.

1. Paul Thurrott's SuperSite for Windows
(`http://www.winsupersite.com/`)

When you think of Paul Thurrott's site, think of news and in-depth information. This is one of the best places to find out what's actually happening in the world of computers. Figure C.1 shows a typical view of Paul's site.

FIGURE C.1

Paul Thurrott provides a wealth of detailed information on his Web site.

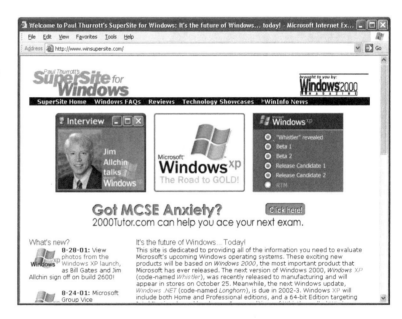

Notice the Windows XP area in Figure C.1. Click any of the entries, and you'll learn more about this product. Paul tracked the beta for everyone involved with Windows XP. You'll also find interviews and a list of news stories on the main page. These stories aren't of the usual sort. They're in-depth, well informed, and extremely useful.

2. W2KNews (`http://www.w2knews.com/`)

Another good place to visit for news is W2Knews, shown in Figure C.2. This site is interesting because Sunbelt has been involved in more than a few surveys about Windows. You'll always find a link to the current survey on the main page. It's also easy to find the results of past surveys so that you can learn more about the human side of Windows computing.

FIGURE C.2

W2KNews provides a wealth of information on how people feel about Windows issues.

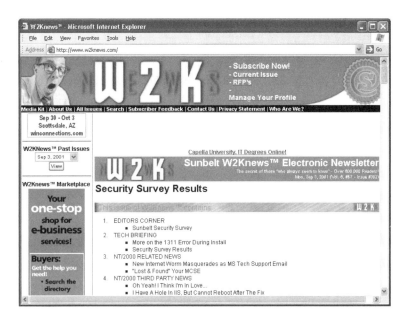

Sunbelt also puts out a newsletter that's full of the latest information about all things Windows. Some of the information is editorial, some comes from other readers, and all of the stories are interesting. You can order a free subscription and receive the latest Windows news in your mailbox.

One service that Sunbelt provides that you won't find in the other offerings in my list are sales on quality products for your server or workstation. Sunbelt tends to focus on administrator utilities and security software. You'll occasionally find other offers as well.

3. Desktop Engineers Junk Drawer
(`http://desktopengineer.com/`)

The Desktop Engineers Junk Drawer, shown in Figure C.3, is the place to go for the unusual and arcane. Over the years I've found more bits and pieces of information on this site than just about any other site I visit. At times, you'll find information on this site that you didn't even know existed. For example, I found a story on a hand-cranked Linux server on this site one day. I knew it was possible, but finding one was completely unexpected.

FIGURE C.3

Look for the arcane bits of information you need at Desktop Engineers Junk Drawer.

Like many of the Web sites in this appendix, the Desktop Engineers Junk Drawer offers an electronic newsletter free for the asking. What you'll get is a newsletter packed with facts both interesting and fun. While you won't receive a fancy presentation from this Web site, the information is carefully and thoughtfully compiled.

4. WinOScentral.com (http://www.winoscentral.com/)

WinOScentral.com, shown in Figure C.4, is an amalgamation of many information sources. The first is the news that you'll see on the home page. Most of these stores provide enough information without getting too technical. The site archives old news stories and categorizes them by operating system. Many of the news stories could also pass for frequently asked question (FAQ) sheets because they contain a lot of information in a terse format.

One of the more interesting links on this site is Top Ten. Click it, and you'll go to a page containing links organized by category. For example, you can find the link that people read most often or the one they commented about most. Viewing the story list this way gives you a different perspective on the information they contain.

This site has a download area. The files appear in categories in a manner reminiscent of C/Net. Need a patch? You'll find it in the Patch category. There are categories for Windows Tweaks and another for Video Drivers. The types of files also prove interesting because I've found a few here that you won't find elsewhere.

FIGURE C.4

WinOScentral.com is a type of Swiss Army knife because it contains a wealth of information in various formats.

If you need a laugh, this site can fix you up. Near the bottom of links on the left side of each page, you'll find a Jokes/Humor button. Click it, and you'll find a short list of jokes in relatively good humor (of course, some people claim that my sense of humor is permanently warped).

5. BrainBuzz.com (http://networking.brainbuzz.com/)

BuzzBrain.com (Figure C.5) is an interesting place to visit because of the news stories you find there. Most of them are opinion pieces by people in the trenches, the ones who really know what's going on in the business world. This is an IT career Web site, so you'll see stories about all kinds of topics. I've found everything from security to the rigors of standing in an unemployment line.

If you look at the left side of the home page, you'll see a wealth of other interesting links. Click Product Reviews, and you'll see a list of reviews on training materials and books. Because many of us need to go back to school so often, knowing what to expect from a particular book or training series comes in handy.

The other links include topics such as scripts. You'll find a modest list of scripts on this site for a few of the more unusual things you might have to do with your machine. The Tips and Tricks link is on par with many of the Web sites I've visited, and the contributors have provided me with at least a few interesting ideas.

FIGURE C.5

For an IT career site, BrainBuzz.com seems to have more than its share of interesting stories to read.

6. Tucows (`http://idirect.tucows.com/`)

One of the main reasons to visit the Tucows Web site, shown in Figure C.6, is to find something to download. The supply of software to download on this site is vast. There are many other sites where you can download software on the Internet but few have the same level of software to choose from as Tucows.

FIGURE C.6

Tucows offers a broad range of downloads for your Windows machine.

What makes this site so interesting is the presentation. All of the software are rated, with five cows being the best. Each piece of software also has a short description (perhaps too short in some cases), an upload date, file size, and operating system version. If the software happens to come in several versions, you can download the best one for your operating system with a single click.

You'll find a few other valuable links hidden on this site. Look at the bottom of the home page for links to news stories and tutorials. Tucows also has an online store for buying the shareware that you can download from their site. (You'll also find some interesting coffee mugs, mouse pads, and other cow-infested merchandise.)

7. ZDNet (`http://www.zdnet.com/`)

It's hard to find a better source of news than ZDNet. This is the home of PC Magazine and eWeek. You'll also find tips, tricks, downloads, product reviews, and a lot more on this site. Figure C.7 shows the main page for this Web site. As you can see, it offers lots of links to just about everywhere.

FIGURE C.7

ZDNet offers news, product tips and reviews, and downloads.

About the only thing you have to watch out for on this site is getting completely lost. It's easy to find yourself buried in a sea of good information that has nothing to do with the topic you had in mind when you first visited the site. Fortunately, ZDNet also has a relatively good search engine to keep you out of trouble.

8. NoNags Software (`http://nonags.com/`)

The NoNags Web site has the advantage of offering software for download in more than one language. In fact, one of the first things you'll do is choose a satellite location near your home. If you live in Europe, you'll find satellite sites for places like Lithuania, Russia, France, Italy, and Poland. There are also a number of sites in the states. Figure C.8 shows a typical example of the page you'll see after you find a satellite location.

FIGURE C.8

NoNags is one of the friendlier Web sites, and it offers multiple language support.

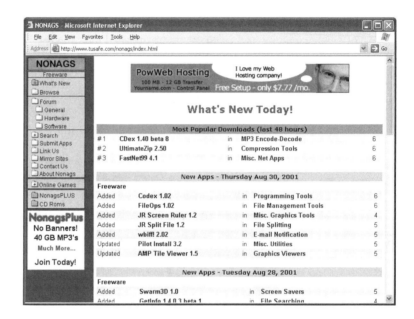

After you reach the download page, you'll understand the name for the Web site. This is a "no nags" Web site because much of the software is freeware and not shareware. This is also a "no frills" site. You won't find any cute reviews, and there's no online store. Generally, this is a download, a "try" site for those occasions when you don't mind spending a little time experimenting with new products.

9. CryptoGram Newsletter
(`http://www.counterpane.com/crypto-gram.html`)

You'll find the CryptoGram Newsletter site shown in Figure C.9 packed with detailed security information. This is the place to go if getting the facts isn't sufficient. If you want to know the practical details of security, CryptoGram can help you out.

FIGURE C.9

The CryptoGram Newsletter Web site tells you about the security needs of your system.

As with most news sites, you'll find a well-stocked archive of previous articles. Current articles appear on the main page, where you'll likely find information you need for a current security threat.

This site also contains links for a few interesting security products. These are high-end security programs for the most part and not the shareware programs you'll find on other sites. Whether you need all of the information this site provides depends on your security needs.

10. WinFiles.com (`http://winfiles.cnet.com/`)

WinFiles.com has always been one of the more interesting offerings on the Internet. At a single site, you can get help on technical questions, learn some new tips and techniques, and download some software. Figure C.10 shows what this site looks like. Notice the icons in the Welcome to WinFiles! window. Click any of these icons, and you'll go to that location.

In some ways, it's unfortunate that WinFiles has merged with C/Net. I used to go to both places for helpful advice and software downloads. I still go to the WinFiles site to select a C/Net location from the list of icons. Although the site does redirect you to the main C/Net site if you wait for a while, clicking one of the icons is actually better. Not all of the C/Net sites are well-organized or easy to access. In a way, this particular entry is as much about C/Net as it is about WinFiles. Both are phenomenal places to learn more about your system.

FIGURE C.10

*Check the WinFiles
Web site for answers to
technical questions,
tips, and techniques.*

Summary

This is my list of favorite Web sites—the ones on my "must visit" list. Hopefully, you'll
find them as useful as I have over the past few years. I'd like to hear about your favorite
Web sites. Make sure that you e-mail me at JMueller@mwt.net with your favorites. If I
find a Web site that's especially appealing, you might see it in my next book or, at least,
posted on my Web site.

Appendix D

Windows XP Command Line Reference

Microsoft has always provided a wealth of tools that you can use at the command line. The only problem is that these tools are often difficult to find. You need to know they exist before you can use them.

I've already told you about many command line utilities throughout this book. You might have thought that we covered them all. This appendix tells you about the command line tools we haven't discussed and documents a couple of them in more detail.

Using Telnet and Telnet Server Administrator

Telnet might seem like an old-fashioned (in computer terms) utility that no one would seriously use anymore. It's command driven and uses an archaic command line interface. Some of the commands verge on the arcane, and their syntax lies buried in ancient UNIX. Yet, for all this, many network administrators still use Telnet because it's reliable and well known.

You won't use Telnet to run modern graphic applications. It only provides a character mode interface. This is one of the reasons that Microsoft continues to support character mode utilities in Windows. You can use Telnet to configure a server and diagnose certain types of low-level problems when utilities such as MMC won't work. It might even appear that the server has locked up, yet Telnet still has a chance of working.

Tip

Many Webmasters use Telnet extensively. A Web server can freeze, leaving the Web site inaccessible to users and the Webmaster alike. However, Telnet uses a different port connection from the Web server. If the Web server freezes, you can always restart it by creating a Telnet connection to the server and manipulating the Web server from the command line. This is one of the reasons why you want to ensure that Telnet access is secure.

Most server operating systems provide Telnet access of some type, so this is an exceptionally useful utility for server management purposes. Because you have access to the command prompt, you can list directories, work with files, and start any character mode application. If you plan to add Telnet to your inventory of administrator tools, it's important to learn the various command line tools that Windows provides.

When using Telnet on a Windows XP machine, you'll need to activate and configure the server. Microsoft assumes that you won't need Telnet services on a workstation. The reason is simple: most workstations don't act as servers. After you have the server set up, you'll want to test the connection locally. The following sections tell you how to work with the client and the server.

Starting and Configuring the Server

Windows XP installs the Telnet server on your system in the \WINDOWS\System32\ folder as TLNTSVR.EXE. To start the server, open the Services MMC snap-in, right-click the Telnet entry, and choose Start from the context menu. (The context menu also contains the usual options for stopping, restarting, and pausing the server.) You'll see a Service Control dialog box as Windows XP starts the Telnet server. After the server starts, you can begin logging into it.

Note

If you want the Telnet server to start automatically each time you start Windows, open the Telnet Properties dialog box. Change the Startup Type field from Manual to Automatic.

The Telnet server doesn't require configuration as such. After you start the server, it will continue to run until you stop it. In addition, you won't find any special configuration options in the Services snap-in beyond those found for a normal service.

However, you do need to consider security configuration for the Telnet server because Microsoft assumes that only the administrator will require access. Given the level of access that the Telnet server provides, you need to configure security carefully.

To add other people to the list of those given access to Telnet, you must add them to the Administrators group, or you must create a TelnetClients group. The TelnetClients group is a predefined group, but it doesn't appear in the Groups folder of the Computer Management snap-in. Again, Microsoft assumes that only members of the Administrators group will use Telnet.

After you add the TelnetClients group, you can add user names or groups to it. Users will have the same level of access to the system that they normally have. In most cases, this means you're granting the user reasonably safe access to the server because you would not grant them access to the dangerous character mode commands.

Using the Simple Telnet Client

This section of the appendix tells you about the simple character mode Telnet application. The advantage of using this form of Telnet client is that it works even under extreme conditions. In addition, the character mode version of Telnet works with any version of Windows (Telnet clients provided with other operating systems work similarly but may have differences to the one discussed in this appendix). We also discussed a friendlier GUI Telnet client in the form of HyperTerminal in the "Using HyperTerminal" section of Chapter 13.

You'll start the Telnet client at a command prompt by typing Telnet and pressing Enter. Telnet will display a Welcome message, the escape character, and a Microsoft Telnet prompt. You can also specify options at the command line. The following list tells you about these options:

- **-a** Performs an automatic logon using the currently logged on username and password. This option works about the same as the -l option except you don't have to specify the username. Windows XP ignores this option if you have NTLM security enabled. It will automatically log on using the currently logged on username and password.

Note

The Windows XP version of Telnet sets Windows NT LAN Manager (NTLM) authentication on by default. This means that it will always attempt to log on using the current logged on username and password. Using this option makes access somewhat automatic. All you need to do is type **TELNET <Host Name>** at the command prompt and Telnet will connect you if you have proper rights. However, this option has two unfortunate drawbacks. The first is that you can't specify another username and password to log onto the system. The second is the NTLM option appears to interfere with operation of some Telnet clients. We'll see how to turn NTLM authentication off in the "Using the Telnet Administrator" section.

- **-e**   Modifies the escape character use to enter the telnet client prompt from a remote session. Telnet defaults to Ctrl+], which is a good choice because it isn't used by anything else.

- **-f <Filename>**   Sets the filename for client side logging. Using this option also turns client side logging on. Client side logging doesn't track the commands you type at the Telnet prompt; it only records what you've done at the remote terminal connection. For example, if you type a DIR command at the remote prompt, you'll see the DIR command and results in the log. However, you won't see the command used to open the connection because that occurs at the Telnet prompt.

- **-l <Username>**   Specifies the user name for logging in on the remote system. You can't specify a password at the command line, so you still have to provide a password before the session will start. Windows XP ignores this option if you have NTLM security enabled. It will automatically log on using the currently logged on username and password.

- **-t <Terminal Type>**   Specifies the terminal type used for command processing and text display. Telnet supports the VT100, VT52, ANSI, and VTNT terminal types. The terminal type determines the characteristics of the session. It dates back to a time when people accessed mainframes using utilities such as Telnet. Using the default ANSI terminal usually works fine. Telnet will remember your preferred terminal type from session to session.

Tip

The default terminal type of ANSI does work fine for most connections, especially those with a mainframe. However, the ANSI terminal type will cause problems when you run certain Windows XP character mode utilities. Any utility that has a display and a functional menu system will likely require you to use the VTNT terminal. For example, if you normally use the EDIT command to work with text files, you'll want to use the VTNT terminal.

- **<Host Name> [<Port Number>]**   Specifies the hostname or IP address of the remote computer. You may optionally specify a service name or port number. The only time you'd need to specify a port number is to access a service other than Telnet or if the Telnet administrator changes the port number, as shown in the "Using the Telnet Administrator" section.

After you reach the Telnet prompt, you can execute a number of commands. For example, O <Host Name> will open a particular host if it's available and you have sufficient rights. All of the server commands work the same as they do from the command line. To see a list of all client commands, type **?** and press Enter.

The client has default settings that it can use for connecting and interacting with the server. The session also relies on settings that the server sets through the administration utility, so you might not always see an effect when using these commands. To see your current client settings, type **D** and press Enter. Figure D.1 shows the default client settings for Telnet.

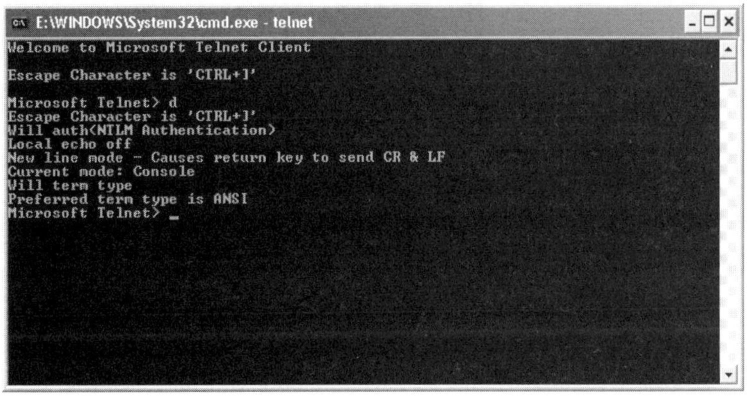

FIGURE D.1

Display the current settings for your terminal session using the D command.

You'll use the SET and UNSET commands to change the default client configuration. The SET command provides access to more settings because you can't turn some settings off. For example, you always have to have a mode set. However, any settings you can turn off, such as local echo, work with the UNSET command. You can display the list of subcommands for either command by typing **SET ?** or **UNSET ?** at the Telnet prompt and pressing Enter.

Most of the client options are easy to understand. However, you might have trouble understanding the need for stream or character mode until you work with Telnet for a while. Generally, you'll want to use character mode because it interprets control characters that you type. For example, if you press enter, character mode will execute a command. Stream mode is useful when you want to send all data to the server in raw form. For example, if you want to embed a carriage return into a document, you'd use stream mode.

Using the Telnet Administrator

The Telnet Administrator utility helps you control Telnet sessions on your machine. You access it by using the TLNTADMN command. If you use TLNTADMN alone, you'll see a display of the current server status as shown in Figure D.2. Adding start, stop, pause, or continue to the command line controls the Telnet service state. Note that these commands only work if you set Telnet to manual or automatic mode—the command fails if you disable the Telnet service.

FIGURE D.2

Use the TLNTADMN command to display the status of your Telnet server.

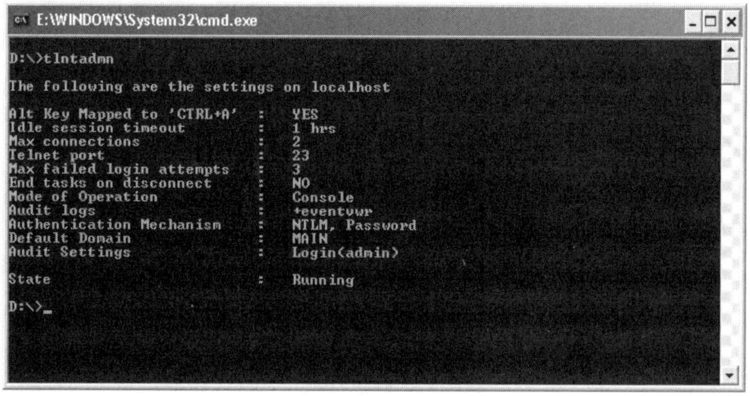

The TLNTADMN utility includes three user-specific commands. Use the -s switch with an optional session identifier to display the user status information. Figure D.3 shows a typical example of this command. As you can see, each user entry includes the user ID, name, remote connection point, and logon time. The idle time column is a good indicator of who has gone to lunch with his Telnet connection intact. Use the -m switch with a session identifier to send the user a message. For example, looking at Figure D.3, if you wanted to send John a message, you would type **TLNTADMN -m 676 Hello John** and press Enter. The third user option is the -k <Session Identifier> switch. Use it to end a user session.

The TLNTADMN utility also includes options for configuring the Telnet server. Simply type **TLNTADMN config <Configuration Option> <Configuration Value>** and press enter to change a setting. The following list tells you about the various options:

FIGURE D.3

The -s switch shows a list of users currently visiting your Telnet server.

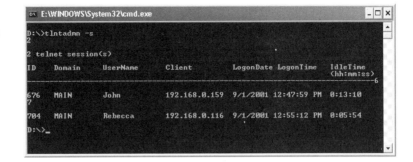

The TLNTADMN utility might not display any information if you enter a bad command, especially a configuration command. The only time you can assume that a command is accepted is if you see a "The settings were successfully updated" reply from the server. It also pays to check the Telnet service configuration again to verify the change.

- **dom = <Domain>**   Sets the default domain for checking user names. If you're using a peer-to-peer configuration, the only domain is your machine. The only time you can set this to another domain is if you have a Windows server set up as a domain controller.

- **ctrlakeymap = <Yes|No>**   Sets the mapping of the ALT key to Ctrl+A when on. This is the default setting. This setting doesn't affect the VTNT terminal but does affect other terminal types.

- **timeout = <hh>:<mm>:<ss>**   Determines how long the Telnet server will wait before it logs a user out automatically. You must include the colons between the hours, minutes, and seconds. In addition, if you want to set a value to 0, include a 0 on the command line. For example, if you want to set the timeout value to 30 minutes, type **TLNTADMN config timeout = 0:30:00** at the command line.

- **timeoutactive = <Yes|No>**   Enables the idle session timeout counter. Whenever a session reaches the timeout value, the Telnet server disables it automatically.

- **maxfail = <Attempts>**   Sets the maximum number of login failure attempts before disabling the user account. Telnet won't allow disabled user accounts to connect.

- **maxconn = <Connections>**   Determines the maximum number of connections that the Telnet server will accept. Note that the Microsoft documentation states that you can accept a maximum of two sessions. This is incorrect. Using this

D

configuration option will allow you to accept the maximum number of connections that your machine can handle.

- **port = <Number>**   Changes the connection port number. It's always a good idea to change this number to something other than the default to help thwart crackers. Of course, if you leave the port open and use poor security, someone will still get in.

- **sec = [+/-]NTLM [+/-]PASSWD**   Determines the acceptable security (authentication) mechanisms. Allowing NTLM enables the user to log in using their default Windows username and password.

- **fname = <Filename>**   Specifies the name of the audit (user access) file. The default Telnet server settings don't use a log file, so you must also use the audit location configuration option to set the Telnet server to use a file or both a file and the event log.

- **fsize = <Size>**   Determines the maximum size of the audit (user access) file. The default Telnet setting is 5MB, but you can use smaller or larger sizes. The minimum value is 1MB; you can't create smaller logs.

- **mode = <Console|Stream>**   Controls how the server reacts to control character input. Always use console mode to ensure that users can use applications such as EDIT.

- **auditlocation = <Eventlog|File|Both>**   Determines where Telnet will place user access (audit) entries. The default setting is the application event log. A Telnet log entry uses the special audit entry shown in Figure D.4. If you open this event log entry, you'll see the username, terminal name, and IP address in the description field. In many cases, the event log organization is harder to use than a log file because you have to open each event individually.

FIGURE D.4

Telnet event log entries use a special symbol that sets them apart from the usual error, warning, and information entries.

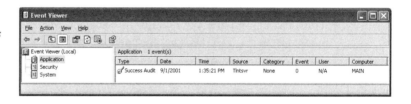

- **audit = [+/-]USER [+/-]FAIL [+/-]ADMIN**   Determines which user events Telnet server will log. The default setting logs everything.

Using Simple TCP/IP Services

Windows XP doesn't install the simple TCP/IP services by default, so you'll need to install them using the Windows Component Wizard. You'll find this optional feature in the Networking Services folder. The simple TCP/IP services include Character Generator, Daytime, Discard, Echo, and Quote of the Day.

 Caution Installing the simple TCP/IP services opens additional ports on your server. Some crackers use these ports to break into servers. In short, install these services only if you need them for diagnostic or other legitimate uses. Fortunately, Windows XP doesn't support some services, such as Active Users (port 11).

You can access all of these services by using Telnet and the optional port number argument. For example, if you wanted to test the current time of day on a remote server, you'd type **TELNET <Host Name or IP Address> 13**. The port number for the Daytime service is 13. Table D.1 contains the port numbers supported by the simple TCP/IP services. You can learn more about the service by looking up its associated RFC number. Remember to use the Ctrl+] (or other) escape key for services such as character generator that don't stop automatically. Note that many of these services will report that the connection to the server is lost.

D

TABLE D.1   Port Number for Simple TCP/IP Services

Service	Port Number	RFC Number
Character Generator	19	864
Daytime	13	867
Discard	9	863
Echo	7	862
Quote of the Day	17	865

Using the Most Popular Command Line Utilities

We've already discussed many command line utilities in the book. You'll want to spend some time looking at these utilities as you learn Windows XP. The following sections contain other utilities that we haven't discussed. All of them will work from Telnet if you use the VTNT terminal. Many will also work with other terminal types.

 Tip

Most of these utilities will work with the standard redirection commands. For example, you could send the output of a command to a file using <Command Name> >> <Filename>. The pipe operator is also available. For example, you could type **<Command Name> | MORE** to display the output of the command one screen at a time.

DEFRAG

Windows XP includes a command line disk defragmenter. All you need to type is **DEFRAG <Drive Letter>** to start the defragmentation process. The command line switches include -a (analyze only), -f (force defragmentation even if space is low), and -v (verbose output). Use the verbose option if you run DEFRAG from a remote location. Note that you can defragment local drives only using a local copy of DEFRAG.

DRIVERQUERY

Use the DRIVERQUERY utility to obtain a list of drivers loaded on your machine. This utility also works with other machines. All you need to do is add the \S <System Name>, \U <Username>, and \P <Password> switches. If you're a member of a domain, make sure that you include the domain name as part of your username like this: Domain\User.

It's handy to place the information you receive from this command in a database, so DRIVERQUERY supports the \FO <Output Format> switch. If you use the CSV option, the output uses command-delimited format. You can also output the driver list in TABLE (the default) or LIST format. The LIST format places all of the information for a single entry together and separates entries by a blank line. If you don't want to display a header, use the /NH switch.

DRIVERQUERY defaults to a simplified driver information output. If you want detailed information, you'll need to use the /V option. You receive Module Name, Display Name, Description, Driver Type, Start Mode, State, Status, Accept Stop, Accept Pause, Paged Pool (bytes), Code (bytes), BSS (bytes), Link Date, Path, and Init (bytes) as additional output.

The /V option doesn't include signed driver information. If you want this additional information, use the /SI switch. Note that adding the /SI switch substantially increases the time required to gather driver information. One of the interesting bits of information you receive when using this option is the name of the INF file used to configure the driver.

EDIT

This actually isn't a Windows XP command. EDIT has been around since the days of DOS. It's a fully functional character mode editor that you can use to edit text files. Figure D.5 shows an example of EDIT in action.

FIGURE D.5

Use the EDIT utility to modify the contents of text files on the remote server.

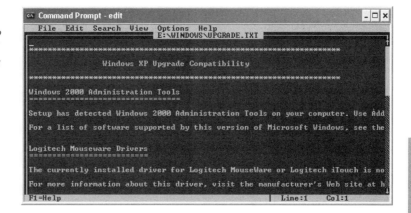

D

Note

An interesting side effect of using the EDIT utility is that you lose long file-name display on the remote server. The long filename support is present, just hidden. To restore long filenames, change directories to the root direc-tory (using CD \ and pressing Enter) and then back to your work directory.

As you can see, EDIT provides full editing features using a menu-driven interface. This includes search and replace, along with the capability to set display options and print output. EDIT provides multiple file support, and you can split the window to facilitate editing large files. The multiple windows also allow viewing of more than one file at a time. However, this editor doesn't include word processing features, such as a spelling checker.

EDIT provides a few interesting command line switches. For example, if you use the /H switch, EDIT will resize the window to accommodate the maximum lines of text your display supports. Use the /R switch to open files in read-only mode (ensuring that you don't modify them accidentally). The /<Width> option sets the word wrap size if you open a binary file using EDIT. Note that EDIT doesn't provide a hex mode view, so it has limited value when viewing binary files.

EVENTCREATE and EVENTQUERY

Working with event logs using Event Viewer is fine if you have enough time to check them manually. Unfortunately, most network administrators don't have that much time. Using EVENTQUERY will help you check the logs faster. Use this utility to output the log entries of interest and then use a script or a custom application to analyze the entries.

 Note

> You may run into a problem using EVENTQUERY in some cases. If so, locate EVENTQUERY.VBS in the \System32 folder and change the VBS extension to a VBE extension. In addition, because EVENTQUERY is a script, you must use either CScript or WScript to run it.

You'll use several switches to work with EVENTQUERY, all of which are options. Use the \FO <Output Format> switch to format the output. If you use the CSV option, the output uses command-delimited format. You can also output the driver list in TABLE (the default) or LIST format. The LIST format places all of the information for a single entry together and separates entries by a blank line. If you don't want to display a header, use the /NH switch. The /R [<n> | -<n> | <n1>-<n2>] switch filters the output by event rage. Use positive numbers for the newest records, negative numbers for the oldest records, and two numbers to show a record range. EVENTQUERY also support an /FI switch that filters the output by such criteria as date, type, ID, user, computer, source, and category.

The EVENTCREATE utility is an essential resource for anyone who writes scripts. If you had an error in the past, you had to rely on using text files to record errors. The EVENTCREATE utility makes it easy to add events to the application or security logs using the /I <SYSTEM | APPLICATION>. Note that EVENTCREATE restricts access to the SECURITY event log. You also have to include the /ID <Event ID>, /D <Description>, and /T <ERROR | WARNING | INFORMATION> switches. The Event ID value has to be within the range of 1 to 1000 (the custom ID range)—you can't use existing IDs even if one fits your needs. Always include your description in quotes like this: /D "My Description." An optional switch is /SO <Source Name>, which is the source of the error.

Both utilities also work with other machines. All you need to do is add the \S <System Name>, \U <Username>, and \P <Password> switches. If you're a member of a domain, make sure that you include the domain name as part of your username like this: Domain\User.

OPENFILES

The OPENFILES utility makes it easy to check for open shared files on a system. It has two modes. You can use the \QUERY switch to determine which files are open, or the \DISCONNECT switch to close open files. Like other utilities discussed in this section, you can use the \S <System Name>, \U <Username>, and \P <Password> switches to connect to other machines.

When used in query mode, you can use the \FO <Output Format> switch to format the output. OPENFILES supports the standard CSV, LIST, and TABLE format. The /NH switch suppresses header output. Use the /V option to create verbose output that includes the number of locks on the file and the mode in which the user opened it. Unlocked files opened for read-only access are always safe to close.

When used in disconnect mode, OPENFILES enables you to close files using several criteria. You can use the specific id of the file (/ID), the username (/A), open mode (/O), session name (/SE), and open filename (/OP).

Summary

Admittedly, this appendix hasn't touched on every character mode command or utility. However, between this appendix and the character mode command references scattered throughout the book, you have a good working knowledge of how to control your server from a remote location by using Telnet. Although Telnet isn't the most user-friendly utility out there, it does provide an essential service for remote connectivity.

D

GLOSSARY

Introduction

This book includes a glossary so that you can easily find terms and acronyms. It has several important features of which you need to be aware. First, every acronym in the entire book is listed here—even if there's a better than even chance you already know what the acronym means. This way there isn't any doubt that you'll always find everything you need to use the book properly.

Second, these definitions are specific to the book. In other words, when you look through this glossary, you're seeing the words defined in the context in which the book uses them. This might or might not always coincide with current industry usage as the computer industry changes the meaning of words so often.

Finally, the definitions here use a conversational tone in most cases. This means they might sacrifice a bit of puritanical accuracy for the sake of better understanding. The purpose of this glossary is to define the terms in such a way that there's less room for misunderstanding the intent of the book as a whole.

While this Glossary is a complete view of the words and acronyms in the book, you'll run into situations when you need to know more. No matter how closely I look at terms throughout the book, there's always a chance I'll miss the one acronym or term that you really need to know. In addition, I've directed your attention to numerous online sources of information, and few of the terms the Web site owners use will appear here unless I also chose to use them in the book. Fortunately, many sites on the Internet provide partial or complete glossaries to fill in the gaps:

- Acronym Finder (   )
- Microsoft Encarta (   )
- University of Texas Acronyms and Abbreviations (   )
- Webopedia (   )
- yourDictionary.com (formerly A Web of Online Dictionaries) (   )

Let's talk about these Web sites a little more. Web sites normally provide acronyms or glossary entries—not both. An acronym site only provides the definition for the acronym that you want to learn about; it doesn't provide an explanation of what the acronym means concerning everyday computer use. The two extremes in this list are Acronym Finder (acronyms only) and Webopedia (full-fledged glossary entries).

The owner of Acronym Finder doesn't update the site as often as the University of Texas, but Acronym Finder does have the advantage of providing an extremely large list of acronyms from which to choose. At the time of this writing, the Acronym Finder sported 164,000 acronyms. The University of Texas site receives updates often and provides only acronyms (another page at the same site includes a glossary).

Most of the Web sites that you'll find for computer terms are free. In some cases, such as Microsoft's Encarta, you have to pay for the support provided. However, these locations are still worth the effort because they ensure that you understand the terms used in the jargon-filled world of computing.

Webopedia has become one of my favorite places to visit because it provides encyclopedic coverage of many computer terms and includes links to other Web sites. I like the fact that if I don't find a word I need, I can submit it to the Webopedia staff for addition to their dictionary, making Webopedia a community-supported dictionary of the highest quality.

One of the interesting features of the yourDictionary.com Web site is that it provides access to more than one dictionary and in more than one language. If English isn't your native tongue, then this is the Web site of choice.

Terms

Active Directory   A method of storing machine, server, and user configuration within Windows 2000 that supports full data replication so that every domain controller has a copy of the data. This is essentially a special purpose database that contains information formatted according to a specific schema. Active Directory is designed to make Windows 2000 more reliable and secure while reducing the work required by both the developer and network administrator for application support and distribution. The user benefits as well because Active Directory fully supports roving users and maintains a full record of user information, which reduces the effects of local workstation downtime.

Active Server Page (ASP)   A special type of scripting language used by Windows servers equipped with Internet Information Server (IIS). This specialized scripting language allows the programmer to create flexible Web server scripts. The use of variables and other features, such as access to server variables, allows a programmer to create scripts that can compensate for user and environmental needs, as well as security concerns. ASP uses HTML to display content to the user.

American Standard Code for Information Interchange (ASCII)   A standard method of equating the numeric representations available in a computer to human-readable form. The number 32 represents a space, for example. The standard ASCII code contains 128 characters (7 bits). The extended ASCII code uses 8 bits for 256 characters. Display adapters from the same machine type usually use the same upper 128 characters. Printers, however, might reserve these upper 128 characters for nonstandard characters. Many Epson printers use them for the italic representations of the lower 128 characters, however.

API   See Application Programming Interface.

Application   The complete program or group of programs. An application is a complete environment for performing one or more related tasks.

Application Programming Interface (API)   A method of defining a standard set of function calls and other interface elements. It usually defines the interface between a high-level language and the lower level elements used by a device driver or operating system. The ultimate goal is to provide some type of service to an application that requires access to the operating system or device feature set.

Argument   A value you pass to a procedure or function. The procedure or function recognizes the value by using the Parameters command to retrieve it.

ASCII   See American Standard Code for Information Interchange.

ASP   See Active Server Page.

Bandwidth   A measure of the amount of data that a device can transfer in a given time.

BBS   See Bulletin Board System.

Binary A method used to store worksheets and graphic files. Although you can use the DOS TYPE command to send these files to the display, the contents of the file remain unreadable. Other binary files include programs with extensions of EXE or COM.

Bindery The set of files used to store network-specific configuration information on a network. These files contain user data, security information, and other network configuration data. You can't start the file server without this information. Corruption of any of these files might prevent the network from starting properly.

Biometrics A statistical method of scanning an individual's unique characteristics, normally body parts, to ensure that they're who they say they are. Some of the scanned elements include voiceprints, irises, fingerprints, hands, and facial features. The two most popular elements are irises and fingerprints because they're the two that most people are familiar with. The advantages of using biometrics are obvious. Not only can't the user lose their identifying information (at least not very easily), but also, with proper scanning techniques, the identifying information can't be compromised either.

BMP Files Standard bitmap graphics data format. This is a raster graphic data format that doesn't include any form of compression. OS/2 can also use this data format to hold graphics of various types.

Browse A special application interface element designed to show the user an overview of a database or other storage media (for example, the thumbnail sketches presented by some graphics applications). Think of the browse as the table of contents for the rest of the storage area. A browse normally contains partial views of several data storage elements (records or picture thumbnails, in most cases) that a user can then zoom in on to see in their entirety. A browse form normally contains scroll bars or other high-speed interface elements to make it easier for the user to move from one section of the overall storage media to the next.

Browser A special application normally used to display data downloaded from the Internet. The most common form of Internet data is the HTML (hypertext markup language) page. However, modern browsers can also directly display various types of graphics and even standard desktop application files, such as Word for Windows documents. The actual capabilities provided by a browser vary widely depending on the software vendor and platform.

Bulletin Board System (BBS) A form of electronic message center that relies on a dial-up connection. BBSs normally provide services for special interest groups or software and hardware vendors. The BBS server allows reading and upload of messages, as well as download of software and text.

Cache Buffers A term that refers to the smallest storage elements in a cache (an area of RAM devoted to storing commonly used pieces of information normally stored on the hard drive). Think of each buffer as a box that can store a single piece of information. The more buffers (boxes) you have, the greater the storage capacity of the cache.

CD-ROM See Compact Disk Read-Only Memory.

CD-RW See Compact Disk-Rewriteable.

Challenge Handshake Authentication Protocol (CHAP) One of several authentication protocols used with Windows.

CHAP See Challenge Handshake Authentication Protocol.

Client The recipient of data, services, or resources from a file or other server. This term can refer to a workstation or an application. The server can be another PC or an application.

Client Services for NetWare (CSNW) A special applet Windows NT adds to the Control Panel when you install NetWare support. The applet allows you to configure the NetWare connection.

COM See Component Object Model.

Common Unix Printing System (CUPS) The default printing system used on a SAMBA server.

Compact Disk Read-Only Memory (CD-ROM) A device used to store up to 650MB of permanent data. You can't use a CD-ROM the same way as a hard or floppy disk because you can't write to it. The disks look much like audio CDs but require a special drive to interface it with a computer.

Compact Disk-Rewriteable (CD-RW) A form of CD-ROM drive that allows both reading and writing. In addition to standard CD-ROM disks, this drive will accept CD-R and CD-RW disks. You can only write to a CD-R disk one time. A CD-RW disk allows multiple rewrites and functions similarly to a hard drive or floppy disk.

Component Object Model (COM) A Microsoft specification for an object-oriented code and data encapsulation method and transference technique. It's the basis for technologies such as OLE (object linking and embedding) and ActiveX (the replacement name for OCXs, an object-oriented code library technology). COM is limited to local connections. DCOM (distributed component object model) is the technology used to allow data transfers and the use of OCXs within the Internet environment.

Compressed Serial Line Internet Protocol (CSLIP)   A type of connection supported by older remote servers. CSLIP works much like a SLIP connection, except it also adds file compression. Windows NT provides support for remote network connections as a client. It doesn't provide this support as a server.

Connectivity   A measure of the interactions between clients and servers. In many cases, connectivity begins with the local machine and the interactions between applications and components. Local area networks (LANs) introduce another level of connectivity with machine-to-machine communications. Finally, wide area networks (WANs), metro area networks (MANs), intranets, and the Internet all introduce further levels of connectivity concerns.

Console   The generic term for a workstation used to monitor server status information. In most cases, the workstation and server are the same device. Most people associate consoles with a character mode interface, but this isn't a requirement.

Cookie   One or more special files used by an Internet browser to store site-specific settings or other information specific to Web pages. The purpose of this file is to store the value of one or more variables so that the Web page can restore them the next time the user visits a site. A Webmaster always saves and restores the cookie as part of some Web page-programming task using a programming language, such as JavaScript, Java, VBScript or CGI. In most cases, this is the only file that a Webmaster can access on the client site's hard drive. The cookie could appear in one or more files anywhere on the hard drive, depending on the browser currently in use. Microsoft Internet Explorer uses one file for each site storing a cookie and places them in the Cookies folder that normally appears under the main Windows directory. Netscape Navigator uses a single file named COOKIE.TXT to store all of the cookies from all sites. This file normally appears in the main Navigator folder.

Cracker   A hacker (computer expert) who uses his skills for misdeeds on computer systems where he has little or no authorized access. A cracker normally possesses specialty software that allows easier access to the target network. In most cases, crackers require extensive amounts of time to break the security for a system before they can enter it.

CSLIP   See Compressed Serial Line Internet Protocol.

CSNW   See Client Services for NetWare.

CUPS   See Common Unix Printing System.

Data Source Name (DSN)   A name assigned to an Open Database Connectivity (ODBC) connection. Applications use the DSN to make the connection to the database and gain access to specific database resources, such as tables. The DSN always contains the name of the database server, the database, and (optionally) a resource, such as a query or table. OLE-DB connections may also use a DSN.

DCOM   See Distributed Component Object Model.

DDE   See Dynamic Data Exchange.

Denial of Service (DoS)   A type of Web-based attack crackers perpetrate against companies. The cracker attempts to flood company routers with useless requests in order to cause the router to crash or make it unavailable for legitimate requests. The attack often depends on servers from other companies (known as *zombies*) that the cracker has entered and taken over. These other servers all generate random messages with improper content in an attempt to overload the target systems. Recent DoS attacks also rely on viruses created by the cracker that install the zombie program on the host computer. For example, the Code Red virus uses this technique in order to commit a DoS attack on the U.S. Government (specifically, the White House).

Device-Independent Bitmap (DIB)   A method of representing graphics information that doesn't reflect a particular device's requirements. This has the advantage of allowing the same graphic to appear on any device in precisely the same way, despite differences in resolution or other factors that normally change the graphic's appearance.

DHCP   See Dynamic Host Configuration Protocol.

DIB   See Device-Independent Bitmap.

Digital Video Disk (DVD)   A high capacity optical storage media with capacities of 4.7GB to 17GB and data transfer rates of 600Kbps to 1.3Gbps. A single DVD can hold the contents of an entire movie or approximate 7.4 CD-ROMs. DVDs come in several formats that allow read-only or read-write access. All DVD drives include a second laser assembly used to read existing CD-ROMs. Some magazines will also use the term *digital versatile disk* for this storage media.

Disk Operating System (DOS)   The underlying software used by many PCs to provide basic system services and to allow the user to run application software. The operating system performs many low-level tasks through the basic input/output system (BIOS). The revision number determines the specifics of the services that DOS offers; check your user manual for details.

Distributed Component Object Model (DCOM)   The advanced form of the component object model (COM) used by the Internet. This particular format enables data transfers across the Internet or other non-local sources. It adds the capability to perform asynchronous, as well as synchronous, data transfers, which prevents the client application from becoming blocked as it waits for the server to respond. See COM for more details.

DLL   See Dynamic Link Library.

DNS   See Domain Name System.

Domain Name System (DNS)   An Internet technology that allows a user to refer to a host computer by name rather than using its unique IP address.

DoS   See Denial of Service.

DOS   See Disk Operating System.

DSN   See Data Source Name.

Dual Boot   Putting more than one operating system on the hard drive so that when you turn on the computer's power, you can select which OS you want to use. Common dual-boot configurations include DOS and Windows NT or Windows 2000 (so that you can more easily recover from problems if Windows NT 2000 won't load), and Windows 95/98 and Windows NT/2000 (so that you can play games in Windows 95/98 that won't work in Windows NT or Windows 2000).

DVD   See Digital Video Disk.

Dynamic Data Exchange (DDE)   The capability to cut data from one application and paste it into another application. You can cut a graphics image created with a paint program, for example, and paste it into a word processing document. After it's pasted, the data doesn't reflect the changes made to it by the originating application. DDE also provides a method for communicating with an application that supports it and requesting data.

Dynamic Host Configuration Protocol (DHCP)   A method for automatically determining the IP address on a TCP/IP connection. A server provides this address to the client as part of the setup communications. Using DHCP means that a server can use fewer addresses to communicate with clients and that clients don't need to provide a hard-coded address to the server. You must configure your server to provide these services.

Dynamic Link Library (DLL)   A specific form of application code loaded into memory by request. It's not executable by itself. A DLL does contain one or more discrete routines that an application may use to provide specific features. For example, a DLL could provide a common set of file dialogs used to access information on the hard drive. More than one application can use the functions provided by a DLL, reducing overall memory requirements when more than one application is running.

EC   See Error Correction.

Encryption   The act of making data unreadable unless the reader provides a password or other key value. Encryption makes data safe for transport in unsecured environments, such as the Internet.

Error Correction (EC)   Normally refers to self-correcting hardware or software. One or more built-in features monitor the system or application for flaws and alerts a correcting feature. The correcting feature usually rebuilds the data or other resource lost as the result of an error.

FAT   See File Allocation Table.

FIFO   See First-In First-Out.

File Allocation Table (FAT)   The method of formatting a hard disk drive used by DOS and other operating systems. This technique is one of the oldest formatting methods available. There have been several different versions of FAT based on the number of bits used to store disk locations. The original form was 12 bits, quickly followed by the 16-bit version used by many computers today. A 32-bit version of FAT, also called FAT32, was introduced with the OSR2 version of Windows 98. This new version of FAT stores data more efficiently on the large hard drives available on today's computers.

File Transfer Protocol (FTP)   One of several common data transfer protocols for the Internet. This particular protocol specializes in data transfer in the form of a file download. The site presents the user with a list of available files in a directory list format. An FTP site may choose DOS or UNIX formatting for the file listing although the DOS format is extremely rare. Unlike HTTP sites, an FTP site provides a definite information hierarchy using directories and subdirectories, much like the file directory structure used on most workstation hard drives.

Firewall   A system designed to prevent unauthorized access to or from a network. Firewalls are normally associated with Web sites connected to the Internet. A network administrator can create a firewall using either hardware or software.

First-In First-Out (FIFO)   A term used for a variety of purposes. It normally refers to a queue or a queue-like structure where the first data that arrives in the queue is also the first data that exits the queue. Both hardware and software developers use this term. For example, you'll find the term FIFO used for both application structures and buffers within modems.

FTP   See File Transfer Protocol.

GIF   See Graphics Interchange Format.

Globally Unique Identifier (GUID) A 128-bit number used to identify a component object model (COM) object within the Windows registry. The GUID is used to find the object definition and allow applications to create instances of that object. GUIDs can include any kind of object, even nonvisual elements. In addition, some types of complex objects are actually aggregates of simple objects. For example, an object that implements a property page will normally have a minimum of two GUIDs: one for the property page and another for the object itself.

Graphical User Interface (GUI) **(1)** A method of displaying information that depends on both hardware capabilities and software instructions. A GUI uses the graphics capability of a display adapter to improve communication between the computer and its user. Using a GUI involves a large investment in both programming and hardware resources. **(2)** A system of icons and graphic images that replaces the character mode menu system used by many machines. The GUI can ride on top of another operating system (like DOS and UNIX) or reside as part of the operating system itself (like OS/2). Advantages of a GUI are ease of use and high-resolution graphics. Disadvantages consist of higher workstation hardware requirements and lower performance over a similar system using a character mode interface.

Graphics Interchange Format (GIF) One of two standard file formats used to transfer graphics over the Internet (JPEG is the other). There are several different standards for this file format, the latest of which is the GIF89a standard that you'll find used on most Internet sites. CompuServe originally introduced the GIF standard as a method for reducing the time required to download a graphic and the impact of any single-bit errors that might occur. A secondary form of the GIF is the animated GIF. It allows the developer to store several images within one file. Between each file are one or more control blocks that determine block boundaries, the display location of the next image in relation to the display area, and other display features. A browser or other specially designed application will display the graphic images one at a time in the order in which they appear within the file to create animation effects.

GUI See Graphical User Interface.

GUID See Globally Unique Identifier.

Hacker An individual who works with computers at a low level, especially in the area of security. A hacker normally possesses specialty software that allows easier access to the target application or network. In most cases, hackers require extensive amounts of time to break the security for a system before they can enter it. The two types of hackers include those who break into systems for ethical purposes and those who do it to damage the system in some way. The proper term for the second group is *crackers*. Some people have started to call the first group "ethical hackers" to prevent confusion. Ethical hackers normally work for security firms that specialize in finding holes in a company's security. However, hackers work in a wide range of computer arenas. For example, a person who writes low-level code (like that found in a device driver) after reverse-engineering an existing driver is technically a hacker.

Hierarchical   A chart or graph in which the elements are arranged in ranks. The ranks usually follow an order of simple to complex or higher to lower.

Hive   The physical storage area on a disk used to hold Windows registry settings. Each hive is associated with a particular set of related keys. For example, all user settings appear in one hive, while application settings reside in another. Some hives contain specific types of data, such as the security access manager (SAM) information used to secure Windows.

Host   A form of server normally associated with communications. A terminal will make data or other requests of the host application through a remote connection. The terminal normally makes the connection using modems and a telephone line, but this isn't a requirement. For example, most people use the term *host* to refer to the servers on a TCP/IP network, most notably the Internet.

HTML   See Hypertext Markup Language.

HTTP   See Hypertext Transfer Protocol.

Hub   A device used to connect two or more nodes on a network. A hub normally provides other features, such as automatic detection of connection loss.

Hypertext Markup Language (HTML)   **(1)** A scripting language for the Internet that depends on the use of *tags* (keywords within angle brackets <>) to display formatted information onscreen in a non[nd]platform-specific manner. The non–platform-specific nature of this scripting language makes it difficult to perform some basic tasks, such as placement of a screen element at a specific location. However, the language does provide for the use of fonts, color, and various other enhancements onscreen. There are also tags for displaying graphic images. Scripting tags for using more complex scripting languages, such as VBScript and JavaScript, were recently added, but not all browsers support this addition. The latest tag addition allows the use of ActiveX controls. **(2)** One method of displaying text, graphics, and sound on the Internet. HTML provides an ASCII-formatted page of information read by a special application called a *browser*. Depending on the browser's capabilities, some keywords are translated into graphics elements, sounds, or text with special characteristics, such as color, font, or other attributes. Most browsers discard any keywords they don't understand, allowing browsers of various capabilities to explore the same page without problem. Obviously, there's a loss of capability if a browser doesn't support a specific keyword.

Hypertext Transfer Protocol (HTTP)   One of several common data transfer protocols for the Internet. This particular protocol specializes in the display of onscreen information, such as data entry forms or information displays. HTTP relies on HTML as a scripting language for describing special screen display elements, although you can also use HTTP to display nonformatted text.

ICMP   See Internet Control Message Protocol.

Icon   A symbol used to graphically represent the purpose and/or function of an application or file. For example, text files might appear as sheets of paper with the name of the file below the icon. Applications designed for the environment or operating system usually appear with a special icon depicting the vendor's or product's logo.

ICS   See Internet Connection Sharing.

IIS   See Internet Information Server.

Infrared Data Association (IrDA)   The association responsible for creating infrared data port standards. These ports are normally used to create a connection between a laptop and a device or network. Devices include printers, PCs, modems, and mice.

Internet Connection Sharing (ICS)   A special type of proxy server that allows more than one workstation on a peer-to-peer network to share a single Internet connection. ICS requires that one workstation act as the server and have a connection to the Internet through dial-up or other means. All other workstations act as clients and access the Internet through the connection provided by the server.

Internet Control Message Protocol (ICMP)   A set of rules that control the types of information that a remote computer can request. IP is notoriously unreliable, so vendors require a method for gathering status information. In short, ICMP doesn't make IP more reliable; it just makes it possible for others to find out if IP failed to do its job.

Internet Information Server (IIS)   Microsoft's full-fledged Web server that normally runs under the Windows Server operating system. IIS includes all the features that you'd normally expect with a Web server: FTP, HTTP, and Gopher protocols, along with both mail and news services. Both Windows NT Workstation and Windows 95 can run Personal Web Server (PWS), which is a scaled-down version of IIS.

Internet Packet Exchange (IPX)   A Novell-specific peer-to-peer communication protocol based on the internet protocol (IP) portion of the TCP/IP pair. Think of this as the language used on the network. If everyone speaks the same language, then all the nodes can understand each other. Messages are exchanged in the form of packets on a network. Think of a packet as one sheet of a letter. There's a letterhead saying who sent the letter, an introduction saying whom the letter is for, and a message that tells the receiving party what the sending party wants to say.

Internet Service Provider (ISP)   A vendor that provides one or more Internet-related services through a dial-up, ISDN, or other outside connection. Normal services include e-mail, newsgroup access, and full Internet Web site access.

Interrupt Request (IRQ)   A device might signal the processor that it requires servicing by sending an interrupt request to the programmable interrupt controller (for example, the serial port does this when it has data for the processor to act on). The controller notifies the processor that a device has requested service. The processor, in turn, interrupts its current processing activity, checks to see which device made the request, takes care of the device's needs, and then resumes its previous processing task. Each device must use a different IRQ to prevent system conflicts. Older PC-class machines provided 8 interrupt lines. The newer AT class machines provide 16. However, only 15 of those are usable because one of them is used for internal purposes.

IPX   See Internet Packet Exchange.

IrDA   See Infrared Data Association.

IRQ   See Interrupt Request.

ISP   See Internet Service Provider.

Joint Photographic Experts Group File Format (JPEG)   One of two graphics file formats used on the Internet. This is a vector file format normally used to render high-resolution images or pictures.

JPEG   See Joint Photographic Experts Group File Format.

LAN   See Local Area Network.

Local Area Network (LAN)   Two or more devices connected together using a combination of hardware and software. The devices, normally computers and peripheral equipment such as printers, are called *nodes*. An NIC (network interface card) provides the hardware communication between nodes through an appropriate medium (cable or microwave transmission.) There are two common types of LANs (also called networks). A *peer-to-peer network* allows each node to connect to any other node on the network with shareable resources. This is a distributed method of files and peripheral devices. A *client-server network* uses one or more servers to share resources. This is a centralized method of sharing files and peripheral devices. A server provides resources to clients (usually workstations). The most common server is the file server, which provides file-sharing resources. Other server types include print servers and communication servers.

MAN   See Metropolitan Area Network.

Management Information File (MIF)   A special file used with Desktop Management Interface (DMI) support that contains all the particulars about a piece of equipment. When the System Management Server looks at a workstation and finds this file, it adds its contents to a SQL database that you can open with any number of products. Besides the hardware information, System Management Server adds the software-auditing information it finds to the database. The combined software and hardware information will give you the data required to know whether a particular workstation can run a piece of software without an upgrade.

Message Queue Information Service (MQIS)   The database used to hold the definitions for Queued Components sites, machines, queues, and users. Queued Components implements the database using SQL Server, which is why Windows Server provides a "limited" version of SQL Server as part of the package. You won't find MQIS on every machine and definitely not on any client. MQIS is a central repository of data and is therefore found on just a few servers (at least one) on the network.

Metropolitan Area Network (MAN)   A partial extension and redefinition of the WAN, a MAN connects two or more LANs together using a variety of methods. A MAN usually encompasses more than one physical location within a limited geographical area, usually within the same city or state. (A WAN can cover a larger geographical area, and sometimes includes country to country communications.) Most MANs rely on microwave communications, fiber optic connections, or leased telephone lines to provide the Internet work connections required to keep all nodes in the network talking with each other.

Microsoft Management Console (MMC)   A special application that acts as an object container for Windows management objects, such as Component Services and Computer Management. The management objects are actually special components that provide interfaces that allow the user to access them within MMC to maintain and control the operation of Windows. A developer can create special versions of these objects for application management or other tasks. Using a single application like MMC helps maintain the same user interface across all management applications.

MIF   See Management Information File.

MMC   See Microsoft Management Console.

Modem   An electronic device used to connect computers and terminals over the telephone lines. A modem can be internal (a card fitting into an expansion slot directly connecting your telephone to a serial port on your PC) or external.

Motion Picture Experts Group (MPEG)   A standards group that provides file formats and other specifications in regard to full-motion video and other types of graphic displays.

MPEG   See Motion Picture Experts Group.

MQIS   See Message Queue Information Service.

MSMQ   See Microsoft Management Queue.

NAS   See Network Attached Storage.

NDPS   See Novell Distributed Print Services.

NDS   See Novell Directory Services.

NetBIOS   See Network Basic Input/Output System.

Network Attached Storage (NAS)   One of several methods for packaging a SAN and then allowing network access to it. A NAS attaches directly to the LAN through an ethernet or other common network connection. The storage array or cluster is installed within a box in a SAN configuration. The box also includes all of the features of a server but in embedded form, in most cases, that's designed to handle disk requests very efficiently. In other words, other servers access the drive array operating system, not the clients. Because the operating system for the NAS is optimized for disk access and there isn't any overhead for application processing or client requests, the NAS gains a very large performance boost over the bus-attached drive configuration.

Network Basic Input/Output System (NetBIOS)   This is an application programming interface (API) originally developed for IBM's PC LAN. It's a network communication protocol that resides at the session and transport layers of the OSI model for applications, which use it.

Network Interface Card (NIC)   The device responsible for allowing a workstation to communicate with the file server and other workstations. It provides the physical means for creating the connection. The card plugs into an expansion slot in the computer. A cable that attaches to the back of the card completes the communication path. Some newer NICs also use a USB, FireWire, or other interface.

Network Loadable Module (NLM)   An NLM usually adds some capability that the entire network shares. Examples of NLMs include tape backup software, virus protection, UPS detection/management, and database servers. Unlike a VAP, you can load and unload an NLM while the file server is active.

NIC   See Network Interface Card.

NLM   See Network Loadable Module.

Novell Directory Services (NDS)   An object-oriented approach to managing network resources. (Novell originally called this technology *NetWare Directory Services*, but subsequently renamed it.) It includes a set of graphical utilities that allow the network administrator to view the entire network at once, even if it includes more than one server or more than one location. There are a variety of object types, including servers, printers, users, and files. NDS not only allows the administrator to manage the resource, but it provides security as well. As with any object-oriented management approach, NDS gives each object a unique set of properties that the administrator can change as needed.

Novell Distributed Print Services (NDPS)   A method of managing printers on a large NetWare installation. NDPS includes a series of client and server additions that make it easier to allocate a large number of printers among multiple clients and ease printer congestion.

NTFS   See Windows NT File System.

Object Linking and Embedding (OLE)   The process of packaging a file name, application name, and any required parameters into an object and then pasting this object into the file created by another application. For example, you could place a graphic object within a word processing document or spreadsheet. When you look at the object, it appears as if you simply pasted the data from the originating application into the current application (similar to DDE). The data provided by the object automatically changes as you change the data in the original object. Often you can start the originating application and automatically load the required data by double clicking on the object.

ODBC   See Open Database Connectivity.

OLE   See Object Linking and Embedding.

Open Database Connectivity (ODBC)   One of several methods for exchanging data between DBMSs. In most cases, this involves three steps: installing an appropriate driver, adding a source to the ODBC applet in the Control Panel, and using SQL statements to access the database.

Path   A drive and/or directory where an expert system stores files on a disk.

PCMCIA   See Personal Computer Memory Card International Association.

PCX   A raster graphic data format originally used by ZSoft Paintbrush. This format has gone through many nonstandard transitions and occasionally presents problems when accessed by applications other than the original. It provides for various levels of color and includes data compression.

PDA   See Personal Digital Assistant.

PDC   See Primary Domain Controller.

Peer-to-Peer Network A group of connected computers where every computer can act as a server and a client. Selected computers normally provide services to others, but unlike a client/server network, the network administrator can distribute the processing load over several machines. In addition, all nodes of a peer-to-peer network also act as workstations.

Personal Computer Memory Card International Association (PCMCIA) A standards group responsible for the credit card-sized devices originally used in laptop PCs. A PCMCIA card could contain devices such as a modem or network card. Some of the more esoteric uses for this card include solid-state hard drives and added system memory. Some people refer to a PCMCIA card as a *PC card*. The typical bus speed of PCMCIA is 8.33MHz.

Personal Digital Assistant (PDA) A very small PC normally used for personal tasks, such as taking notes and maintaining an itinerary during business trips. PDAs normally rely on special operating systems and lack any standard application support.

Personal Identification Number (PIN) A special sequence of numbers that identifies someone as the legitimate user of a security card. A security card can take many forms, the most common of which are ATM and credit cards. In the computer world, security cards are used to grant access to various types of information and to resources such as computers and printers.

PIN See Personal Identification Number.

Point-to-Point Protocol (PPP) A set of communications rules that provide a method for conducting on-line (from one point to another) communications. In most cases, you'll use PPP to connect to a UNIX host or the Internet, or to enhance your Dial-Up Networking capability.

PPP See Point-to-Point Protocol.

Primary Domain Controller (PDC) The Windows NT server responsible for tracking changes made to the domain accounts and storing them in the directory database. A domain has one PDC.

Protocol A set of rules used to define a specific behavior. For example, protocols define how networks transfer data. Think of a protocol as an ambassador who negotiates activities between two countries. Without the ambassador, communication is difficult, if not impossible.

Proxy When used in the COM sense of the word, a proxy is the data structure that takes the place of the application within the server's address space. Any server responses to application requests are passed to the proxy, marshaled by COM, and then passed to the application.

QC   See Queued Components.

Queued Components (QC)   The COM+ version of Microsoft Message Queue (MSMQ). This integrated product offers enhanced support for transferring components from client to server using messages. Because this version of MSMQ is also guaranteed full access to Microsoft Transaction Server (MTS), all message transfers may take place within a transaction.

RAM   See Random Access Memory.

Random Access Memory (RAM)   The basic term used to describe volatile storage within a computer system. RAM comes in a variety of types, each of which has specialized features. These special features make the RAM more acceptable for some storage tasks than others.

RAS   See Remote Access Server.

Real-Time Processing   The ability of an operating system to provide immediate response to client queries. The length of time between client query and server response is defined by the requirements of the application. For example, a computer that controls the braking system in a car has to provide a faster response to input than a computer used to maintain the inventory of a corporation. In both cases, real-time processing is required, but the acceptable response time of real-time processing varies.

REG File   A special file used by the registry to hold a text version of the keys and values it contains. Some applications provide .REG files that you can use to incorporate their file associations and OLE capabilities into some programs.

Registry   A freeform database used to hold settings, configuration, and other information for Windows. The registry is a hierarchy or tree consisting of keys and associated values. The operating system searches the registry tree for keys that it requires and then requests values for those keys to perform tasks, such as configuring an application. The registry is organized into hives. Each hive contains settings for a particular operating system element, such as user information and hardware configuration. Users share common hives, such as those used for hardware, but have separate hives for their information as long as Windows is configured to provide separate desktops for each user.

Remote Access   The ability to use a remote resource as you would a local resource. In some cases, this also means downloading the remote resource to use as a local resource.

Remote Access Server (RAS)   An optional Windows service that allows users to call into the server from a remote location in order to access server resources. There are a variety of ways that this service can be used, including as a call-back mechanism.

Remote Procedure Call (RPC)   One of several methods for accessing data within another application. RPC is designed to look for the application first on the local workstation and then across the network at the applications stored on other workstations. This is an advanced capability that will eventually pave the way for decentralized applications.

RIP   See Routing Information Protocol.

Router   A device used to connect two LANs together. The router moves signals from one LAN to the other.

Routing and Remote Access Service (RRAS)   The Windows service that provides routing and remote access services. Routing is the act of moving data between network segments. Remote access enables users to log into a local system from a remote location.

Routing Information Protocol (RIP)   The method TCP/IP uses to communicate with other routers. It allows all the routers in the Internet to exchange information about the Internet configurations without human intervention.

RPC   See Remote Procedure Call.

RRAS   See Routing and Remote Access Service.

SAM   See Security Access Manager.

SAN   See Storage Area Network.

Scalability   A definition of an object's ability to sustain increases in load. For example, companies often rate networking systems by their capability to scale from one to many users. Software scalability determines the capability of the software to run on more than one machine when needed without making it appear that more than one machine is in use.

Script   Usually associated with an interpreted macro language used to create simple applications, productivity enhancers, or automated data manipulators. Windows currently supports a variety of scripting languages at the operating system level. You'll also find scripting capability in many higher-end applications, such as Web browsers and word processors. Scripts are normally used to write small utility-type applications rather than large-scale applications that require the use of a compiled language. In addition, most script languages are limited in their access of the full set of operating system features.

SCSI   See Small Computer System Interface Adapter Controller.

Secure Socket Layer (SSL)   A digital signature technology used for exchanging information between a client and a server. Essentially an SSL-compliant server will request a digital certificate from the client machine. The client can likewise request a digital certificate from the server. Companies or individuals obtain these digital certificates from a third-party vendor, such as VeriSign, that can vouch for the identity of both parties.

Security Access Manager (SAM)   A database containing information about users and their security settings. Some texts also call this the *Security Accounts Manager*. In either case, the information appears within a special hive of the registry. Windows secures this hive to make it difficult to access using the Registry Editor.

Security Identifier (SID)   The part of a user's access token that identifies the user throughout the network—it's like having an account number. The user token that the SID identifies tells what groups the user belongs to and what privileges the user has. Each group also has a SID, so the user's SID contains references to the various group SIDs that he belongs to, not a complete set of group access rights. You'd normally use the User Manager utility under Windows NT to change the contents of this access token. You'll use the Active Directory Users and Computers console when working with Windows 2000.

Sequential Packet Exchange (SPX)   This is the part of the IPX/SPX protocol pair that guarantees delivery of a message sent from one node to another. Think of SPX as the postal clerk who delivers a certified letter from one place to another. In network terms, each page of the letter is called a *packet*. SPX delivers the letter one page at a time to the intended party.

Serial Line Interface Protocol (SLIP)   An IETF-approved method for transferring data by using a serial port. One of the problems with this method is that it doesn't compress the data and therefore suffers from poor performance. CSLIP is a newer form of this protocol that provides improved performance.

Server   An application or workstation that provides services, resources, or data to a client application or workstation. The client usually makes requests in the form of OLE, DDE, or other command formats.

Server Message Block (SMB)   A network messaging format used on DOS and Windows machines to gain access to resources, such as devices, files, and directories. NetBIOS uses SMB as a basis for communication.

SID   See Security Identifier.

Simple Mail Transfer Protocol (SMTP)   One of the most commonly used protocols to transfer mail messages between clients and servers. This is a stream-based protocol designed to allow query, retrieval, posting, and distribution of mail messages. Normally, this protocol is used in conjunction with other mail retrieval protocols like point of presence (POP).

Simple Network Management Protocol (SNMP)   A network protocol (originally designed for the Internet) to manage devices from different vendors.

Simple Service Discovery Protocol (SSDP)   A multicast protocol that provides two message types: OPTIONS and ANNOUNCE. The client issues the OPTIONS message to ask all the servers on the network if they provide a certain service. The server uses the ANNOUNCE message to tell all the clients that it provides a given service. Between the two message types, your machine will locate a service that it needs. For example, Windows uses this service to locate Universal Plug and Play devices on a network.

SLIP   See Serial Line Interface Protocol.

Small Computer System Interface Adapter Controller (SCSI)   A computer interface card that allows you to connect up to seven devices to the computer system. The current SCSI standard is SCSI-2. Typical SCSI devices include tape drives, hard disk drives, and CD-ROM drives. SCSI devices typically provide high-transfer rates (10-15MB/s) and access times (device-type dependent).

Smart Card   A type of user identification used in place of passwords. The use of a smart card makes it much harder for a third party to break into a computer system using stolen identification. However, a lost or stolen smart card still provides user access. The most secure method of user identification is biometrics.

SMB   See Server Message Block.

SMTP   See Simple Mail Transfer Protocol.

Snap-ins   Component technologies allow one application to serve as a container for multiple subapplications. A snap-in refers to a component that's designed to reside within another application. The snap-in performs one specific task out of all of the tasks that the application as a whole can perform. The Microsoft Management Console (MMC) is an example of a host application. Network administrators perform all Windows 2000 management tasks using snap-ins designed to work with MMC.

SNMP   See Simple Network Management Protocol.

SPX   See Sequential Packet Exchange.

SSDP   See Simple Service Discovery Protocol.

SSL   See Secure Socket Layer.

Storage Area Network (SAN)   One of several methods used for network-specific storage because it offers several distinct advantages over the normal methods of storing data locally within the server. A SAN is a special form of local area network (LAN). It's a high-speed subnetwork that consists exclusively of storage devices. The goal is to take the hard drive out of the individual server, create a new entity out of the existing peripheral device, and make it accessible to multiple servers on the same network. The concept of a SAN has been around in mainframe systems for quite some time. The original mainframe version relies on a bus technology known as *Enterprise System Connection (ESCON)*. ESCON allows the mainframe to connect to many peripheral devices dynamically, including drive arrays and clusters. In fact, the DEC VMS network environment is based on a combination of SANs and clustered servers.

SWAT   See Samba Web Administration Tool.

Tagged Image File Format (TIFF)   A bit-mapped (raster) graphics file format used on the PC and Macintosh. The TIFF file format offers a broad range of color formats, including black and white, gray scale, and color. One of the advantages of using TIF is that it provides a variety of compression methods and offers smaller storage form factor. Files on the PC often use a TIF extension.

TCP/IP   See Transmission Control Protocol/Internet Protocol.

Threshold   A predetermined point within the range of operation for a device or piece of software. The threshold normally indicates the point at which the device is overwhelmed and requires correction. Of course, thresholds can indicate anything that the person setting the threshold desires. For example, it could indicate the point at which the network administrator needs to add another server to a cluster to process user requests.

TIFF   See Tagged Image File Format.

Transmission Control Protocol/Internet Protocol (TCP/IP)   A standard communication line protocol developed by the United States Department of Defense. The protocol defines how two devices talk to each other. Think of the protocol as a type of language used by the two devices.

UDP   See User Datagram Protocol.

UNC   See Universal Naming Convention.

Uniform Resource Locator (URL)   A text representation of a specific location on the Internet. URLs normally include the protocol (http:// for example), the target location (World Wide Web or www), the domain or server name (mycompany), and a domain type (com for commercial). It can also include a hierarchical location within that Web site. The URL usually specifies a particular file on the Web server, although there are some situations when a Web server will use a default filename. For example, asking the browser to find http://www.mycompany.com would probably display the DEFAULT.HTM file at that location.

Uninterruptible Power Source (UPS) Usually a combination of an inverter and a battery used to provide power to one or more electrical devices during a power outage. A UPS normally contains power-sensing circuitry and surge-suppression modules. Some UPSs provide standby power and a direct connection between the power source and the protected equipment. Other UPSs use the power source to constantly charge the battery. The protected equipment always derives its power from the inverter, effectively isolating the equipment from the power source.

Universal Naming Convention (UNC) A method for identifying network resources without using specific locations. In most cases, a user will employ this convention with drives and printers, but the user can also apply it to other types of resources. A UNC normally uses a device name in place of an identifier. For example, a user might refer to a disk drive on a remote machine as "\\AUX\DRIVE-C." The advantage of using UNC is that the resource name won't change even if the user's drive mappings do.

Universal Serial Bus (USB) A form of serial bus that allows multiple external devices to share a single port. This technique reduces the number of interrupts and port addresses required to service the needs of devices, such as mice and modems.

UPS See Uninterruptible Power Source.

URL See Uniform Resource Locator.

USB See Universal Serial Bus.

User Datagram Protocol (UDP) Allows applications to exchange individual packets of information over a TCP/IP network. UDP uses a combination of protocol ports and IP addresses to send a message from one point of the network to another. More than one client can use the same protocol port as long as each client using the port has a unique IP address. There are two types of protocol port: well known and dynamically bound. The well-known port assignments use the ports numbered between 1 and 255. When using dynamically bound port assignments, the requesting applications queries the service first to see which port it can use.

VBA See Visual Basic for Applications.

VBE See Visual Basic Editor.

VBScript See Visual Basic Script.

Virtual Private Network (VPN) A special setup that newer versions of Windows provide to allow someone on the road to use the server at work. The connection is virtual because the user can make or break the connection as needed. The reason that this connection has to be private is to deny access to either the client machine or remote server by outside parties. A user gains initial access to the server through an ISP using Dial-Up Networking. After initiating access to the Internet, the user employs Dial-Up Networking to make a second connection to the server using Point-to-Point Tunneling Protocol (PPTP). The setup is extremely secure because it actually uses two levels of data encryption: digital signing of packets and encrypted passwords.

Visual Basic Editor (VBE)   A development environment normally used to create and edit Visual Basic for Applications (VBA) code. VBE is also the extension used for many modern script files. The VBE extension replaces the Visual Basic Script (VBS) extension used in the past.

Visual Basic for Applications (VBA)   A true subset of the Visual Basic language. This form of Visual Basic is normally used within applications in place of a standard macro language. Normally you can't create stand-alone applications using this language in its native environment; however, you could move a VBA program to Visual Basic and compile it there.

Visual Basic Script (VBScript)   A subset of the full Visual Basic language used for creating small applications and macros. VBScript works well as a stand-alone language. Many developers also use it within Web pages and as part of Internet Information Server (IIS) Active Server Pages (ASP).

VPN   See Virtual Private Network.

Windows NT File System (NTFS)   The method of formatting a hard disk drive used by Windows 2000/NT. Although it provides significant speed advantages over other formatting techniques, only the Windows 2000/NT operating system and applications designed to work with that operating system can access a drive formatted using this technique. Windows 2000 uses NTFS5, a version of this file system designed to provide additional features, such as enhanced security.

Wizard   A specialized application that reduces the complexity of using or configuring your system. For example, the Printer Wizard makes it easier to install a new printer.

INDEX

O

P